ROBERT J. DONOVAN

TUMULTUOUS YEARS

The Presidency of Harry S Truman
1949–1953

———

W · W · NORTON & COMPANY · NEW YORK · LONDON

FRONTISPIECE PHOTOGRAPH: Truman, at a tense press conference on November 30, 1950, at which he caused near panic abroad by saying that the United States was considering using the atomic bomb in the Korean War. *Courtesy of Historical Pictures Service, Chicago.*

The text of this book is composed in photocomposition Times Roman. Typefaces used for display are Garamond and Palatino. Composition and manufacturing are by the Maple-Vail Book Manufacturing Group. Book design is by Marjorie J. Flock.

The maps on pages 252, 274, 304, and 407 are from *The Korean War* by Matthew B. Ridgway. Copyright © 1967 by Matthew B. Ridgway. Reprinted by permission of Doubleday & Company, Inc. The map on page 190 is by Ben Gamit.

FIRST EDITION

Library of Congress Cataloging in Publication Data
Donovan, Robert J.
    Tumultuous years.
    Bibliography: p.
    Includes index.
    1. United States—Politics and government—
1945–1953.   2. United States—Foreign relations—
1945–1953.   3. Truman, Harry S, 1884–1972.   4. Presidents—
United States—Biography.   I. Title.
E813.D63   1982   973.918   82-6304
                                                AACR2

ISBN 0-393-01619-6

W. W. Norton & Company, Inc. 500 Fifth Avenue, New York, N.Y. 10110
W. W. Norton & Company Ltd. 37 Great Russell Street, London WC1B 3NU

1 2 3 4 5 6 7 8 9 0

To Gerry with Love

Contents

IV

MACARTHUR

V

THE END OF 20 YEARS OF
DEMOCRATIC RULE

Photographs follow page 224
Maps on pages 190, 252, 274, 304, and 407

Acknowledgments

THE RECORDS of the Harry S Truman Library at Independence, Missouri, were researched for this book by Dr. Lawrence A. Yates, now supervisory historian at the Combat Studies Institute, Fort Leavenworth, Kansas.

I owe a great debt to Roger W. Tubby, last of President Truman's press secretaries, for access to his unpublished personal journal, a rich new source of material. I am also indebted to W. Averell Harriman and W. Stuart Symington for access to their personal and still-closed papers. Dr. John R. Steelman, the assistant to Mr. Truman, and former Secretary of the Treasury John W. Snyder kindly gave me access to their still-closed oral history transcripts at the Truman Library.

Major parts of this book were written during senior fellowships at the Woodrow Wilson International Center for Scholars, in Washington, and the (no relation) Woodrow Wilson School of Public and International Affairs at Princeton University. Nothing in this book reflects, except by coincidence, the opinion of those institutions. I am very grateful to the Ford Foundation for a research grant.

The idea for this work on the Truman presidency, which evolved into two volumes, of which this is the second, was the inspiration of Evan W. Thomas, of W. W. Norton & Company. He has nurtured, guided, and shaped this undertaking through ten long years. They were years that would have been difficult indeed without the support and skill of a fine editor, who is also a rare friend.

I am indebted beyond words to the work done in the Pentagon by an exceptional group of military historians who have recently turned out volumes on military affairs, including the Korean War, during the Truman administration. These books, based on many hitherto unpublished documents, are complete and definitive and range over material so vast that it would take an individual writer many years to research it. The work was done under the supervision of Dr. Alfred Goldberg, historian of the Office of the Secretary of Defense (and his predecessor, Dr. R. A. Winnacker), and by Dr. Robert J. Watson, chief of the historical division of the Joint Chiefs of Staff. The works in question were written by Dr. Watson, James F. Schnabel, Steven L. Rearden, Kenneth Condit, Larence S. Kaplan, and Walter S. Poole. In addition, I have had the assistance of Mrs. Doris Condit, another of the historians, whose volume is still in preparation.

John H. Ohly, a highly placed Pentagon official under Secretaries of Defense James V. Forrestal and Louis A. Johnson, did me the most valuable service of writing a long critique on parts of this book dealing with national security affairs in the Truman administration. I have had rare help, too, from scholars, including Richard W. Leopold, Walter LaFeber, Martin L. Sherwin, Stephen E. Pelz, and Robert Pollard, who have read and criticized parts of this book. Nothing in it necessarily represents their viewpoints. I am indebted in more ways than I can enumerate to the historian Samuel F. Wells, Jr.

John Snyder and Charles S. Murphy, administrative assistant and later special counsel to President Truman, have generously helped me for years at every turn. I received valuable assistance in interviews with persons formerly in the Truman administration, including Clark M. Clifford, Dr. Steelman, Mr. Harriman, George M. Elsey, David E. Bell, James E. Webb, Robert A. Lovett, Henry J. Nicholson, Paul H. Nitze, General J. Lawton Collins, William McChesney Martin, Donald S. Dawson, Philip C. Jessup, Lucius D. Battle, Leon H. Keyserling, Theodore Tannenwald, Jr., and Mrs. Beth Short.

Finally, a word of deep appreciation is due to the men and women of the Harry S Truman Library. For ten years Dr. Yates and I received the most kind, patient, expert, willing help from Dr. Benedict K. Zobrist, the director, George H. Curtis, assistant director, Philip Lagerquist, research archivist, Mrs. Elizabeth Safly, Erwin J. Mueller, Dennis Bilger, Warren Ohrvall, Harry Clark, John Curry, and Pauline Testerman.

I

THE DARKENING
MOOD

1. *Vindication*

FTER A HAM SANDWICH and a glass of buttermilk, Harry S Truman, the
perennially embattled thirty-third president of the United States, was
already asleep in a hideout in Excelsior Springs, Missouri, when the
polls closed on election night, 1948. Early returns tended to confirm
what everyone from Truman's mother-in-law to George Gallup had believed,
which was that Truman did not have a ghost of a chance against the Republican
candidate, Governor Thomas E. Dewey of New York. After the buffeting Truman had suffered in the political turbulence during the years immediately following the Second World War, a second term seemed completely beyond his reach.

It was not surprising, therefore, when Dewey led off the night by winning
New York, New Jersey, Pennsylvania, Maryland, Connecticut, Delaware, Maine,
Vermont, Indiana, and Michigan. After midnight in New York, Herbert Brow-
nell, Jr., Dewey's campaign manager, announced that the governor would be
the next president. In Chicago, the *Tribune* went to press with the headline
DEWEY DEFEATS TRUMAN

A puzzling phenomenon intruded. From the start Truman had led in the
total popular vote and maintained the lead as the counting moved westward
through the different time zones. Even in California, whose governor, Earl Warren, was the Republican candidate for vice-president, the Democratic vote was
much stronger than had been expected. It was from the traditionally Republican
Middle West, however, that intimations of disaster for Dewey mounted. Returns
showed that farmers had voted for Truman out of fear that economy-minded
Republicans would cut agricultural price supports. After midnight it became clear
that the election was so close that the outcome turned on the votes in Illinois,
Ohio, and California. If Dewey had carried any two of those states, the election
would have been thrown into the House of Representatives.

A few hours before dawn, Secret Service agents guarding the president at
the hotel in Excelsior Springs received word that Truman had won Illinois. They
peered into his room. He had been sleeping with the radio off but was awakened
by the sound of the door. They told him the news.

"That's it," he said, and climbed out of bed, squinting without his glasses.
"Well, boys, we'll have one and then we'll all go to sleep." "I'll pour the first
one," he added, taking a bottle of bourbon from the dresser.[1] Unaware that Ohio
and California also were going for Truman, the three Secret Service men toasted
the victor, of all persons the one least surprised by what had happened.

"I do not feel elated at the victory," Truman said in a speech from his train on the way back to Washington. "I feel overwhelmed with responsibility."[2]

Sturdy at the age of sixty-four, Truman was, as befitted a former Missouri dirt farmer, a buoyant, good-natured, secure individual with a sense of well-being that had carried him through the storms and crises. Signs of the strains of three years and nine months in the presidency were remarkably absent from his smooth-shaven face, which was distinguished by steady, blue eyes strikingly magnified by his thick, steel-rimmed glasses. He carried an air of Middle Western friendliness. He was a neat dresser, favoring double-breasted suits, and always wore a triple-band, gold Masonic ring on his left hand and a First World War discharge button in his left lapel. He was endowed with a gusty laugh and, in other moods, a large capacity for anger and indignation. He enjoyed the deep affection and respect of his subordinates. It was one of his political traits that, in response, he was loyal to them to a degree that boded trouble for him.

Truman was the very model of what was approvingly referred to then as a strict family man, devoted throughout his life to his wife, Bess, a former schoolroom sweetheart, and to their only child, Margaret. Fragments from his occasional diaries in later years suggested that he regretted not having had a son as well. His dedication to his family did not keep him from frequent trips to the poker table, even in the crush of postwar events. He enjoyed bourbon, plenty of it, and cussed like the old farmer he had been, though almost never in public. Because of the precarious family budget when he was growing up, Truman was the last president we have had who did not go to college, although from boyhood he was a prolific reader, preferring history and biography. He was also the last president we have seen, barring Gerald R. Ford, who neither had money nor availed himself of access to the privileges of wealth through rich friends. Except for a two-year hiatus early in his political career, Truman had held public office, in Jackson County, Missouri, as a county commissioner and in Washington as senator and vice-president, since 1922, shortly after his discharge from the army after the First World War and the failure of his Kansas City haberdashery during the inflation of 1920–21.

Truman's first term had revealed him as a tough, decisive, sometimes impulsive president, not immune to occasional erratic streaks yet fortified by common sense. He was more admired for his courage, wit, forthrightness, earthiness, and unpretentiousness than for finesse of leadership. Still, on an initiative as massive and unprecedented as the Marshall Plan, for example, he had been skillful in marshaling public and congressional support. No other president comes to mind who tried harder than he to do what was right. This, of course, did not always rescue him from the eternal presidential dilemma of what *is* right. If anything, he had a weakness for rushing into action without fully weighing the consequences. Truman had come to the presidency well grounded in domestic issues but entirely lacking in experience, not to say expertise, in foreign affairs. Ironically, throughout his entire presidency foreign affairs were the dominant problem before the nation.

He had a faith in the principles and destiny of the Democratic party that is hard to grasp in this day of television dominance of American politics. By temperament and political acumen he stationed himself in the center, or slightly to the left of it. This had been a major reason why he had emerged as the necessary compromise candidate for vice-president under Roosevelt. The ticket was elected, and the two men were sworn in on January 20, 1945, Roosevelt for the fourth time.

Eighty-three days later, on April 12, Roosevelt died suddenly in Warm Springs, Georgia. Truman, unprepared, was thrust into the White House at the climax of the Second World War to serve out the remainder of Roosevelt's fourth term, thereby retaining the Democrats in power for a stretch of sixteen years. It had been widely supposed that the normal swing of the political pendulum would—and perhaps in the best interests of a two-party system—should have finally returned the Republicans to office in the election of 1948. Despite his low fortunes at the start of the campaign, however, Truman's tatters had obscured the underlying strength of the Democratic party. His famous whistle-stop campaign was shrewd, aggressive, and theatrical. With the advantage of incumbency, he pulled out all the stops in playing to New Deal sentiment, still a powerful force in American politics in 1948. The Roosevelt coalition held together to produce one more victory in a presidential election.

Stung by the Taft-Hartley Act, passed by the Republican-controlled Eightieth Congress in 1947, labor made a prodigious effort to elect a Democratic Senate and House, thereby helping Truman at the polls also. Farmers were fearful of cuts in price supports under a Dewey administration. Jews were grateful to Truman for having recognized the new State of Israel on May 14, 1948. Millions of Americans, though apathetic about new reforms promised by Truman, were determined to retain the major Roosevelt reforms, including Social Security; to be on the safe side, they voted for Truman. In several major states the Democrats put up exceptionally strong tickets, and the candidates for lower offices helped pull Truman along. Two third-party movements that, combined, had threatened to defeat him, fell short in the end. The leftist Progressive party, led by the former Democratic vice-president Henry A. Wallace was discredited by the recent Communist seizure of Czechoslovakia and the Berlin blockade. The States' Rights Democrats, or Dixiecrats, formed to fight Truman's civil rights program, proved strong enough to carry only Alabama, Mississippi, Louisiana, and South Carolina, having a total of thirty-eight electoral votes. Finally, Dewey put on a mistakenly cautious performance and was outshone by Truman's "give 'em hell" tactics.

Truman's victory assured that Democratic rule in the White House would be lengthened to twenty years at least. Moreover, while the Democrats had elected him, they also had recaptured a majority of seats in the House of Representatives and the Senate, terminating the Republican control that had prevailed in the Eightieth Congress of 1947 and 1948. In consequence, however, Truman faced a new term with a sullen, resentful Republican minority on Capitol Hill, its bruises the sorer because in the campaign he had concentrated his attack not on Dewey but on the "good-for-nothing, do-nothing Eightieth Congress." His victory was a bitter reminder to Republicans that everything they had tried since President Roosevelt first took office March 4, 1933, had failed to turn the tide in their favor.

After returning, briefly, to Washington and a happy welcome from hundreds of thousands of persons along Pennsylvania Avenue, Truman flew to his customary vacation spot in Key West, Florida, for a two-week rest. Not having a compound at Hyannisport or an elegant cottage at the Augusta National Golf Club or an ocean view at San Clemente, he had looked about early in his first term for a place where he could vacation at little expense and still have all necessary communications at hand. He chose the naval base at Key West and loved the place. It was secluded, yet he could walk out the gates and through the town, wearing loud sport shirts, which scandalized many Americans who still found Herbert Hoover's starched collar and Roosevelt's cape more fitting attire for a president. The postwar boom in resorts and vacation houses had not yet hit the southernmost city in the United States. Despite the lovely seascape, framed by palms, Key West then had a rather foreign, rundown look and a drunken, sexy aura created by cheap bars and strip-tease joints, heavily patronized by sailors. It was not unusual for hotel guests to awake during the night to the sound of brawling in the streets. During one of Truman's visits a man was thrown through the plate glass window of an automobile showroom. Turtleburgers sold for a dime at sidewalk stands. The *pièces de résistance* in the few good restaurants were stone crab and Key lime pie.

Truman settled down, quietly, saying, "I am through giving them hell." Or was he? In the early days of his presidency he did not appear to be a man who would give anyone hell. He talked about the moon and the stars having fallen on him with Roosevelt's death. He bemoaned his own inadequacy. He said that a million other men were better qualified to do the job than he and humbly insisted that he had never wanted to be president in the first place. As the power of the office began to fill his veins, however, he spoke in sterner tones. By 1948 he was one of the hardest-fighting politicians the country had seen in a long time. When he was boarding a train for his first major campaign trip that September, he was told by his running mate, Senator Alben W. Barkley of Kentucky, "Go out there and mow 'em down." "I'll mow 'em down, Alben," Truman promised, "and I'll give 'em hell." As his train rolled across the country, spectators shouted, "Give 'em hell, Harry." The war cry became a great political asset for the underdog. Truman relished it. He perceived that giving his enemies hell was what his audiences expected to hear. It may well have had a psychological effect on him that was, however faintly, to color his dealings not only with his enemies at home but with those abroad as well.

As the reverberations of the 1948 election grew, Truman appeared to feel very much in command and very much in the right. In his postelection press conferences he did not suffer foolish questions gladly. His correspondence reflected bitter hurt over slights in the press during the campaign. When a political friend wrote to him in December to congratulate him, Truman replied:

If you will notice in the analysis of the pollsters and columnists they found every excuse possible for the Republicans having lost the election but the fact that a campaign by the President knocked them into a cocked hat.[3]

A newspaper article concerning the decision early in the 1948 campaign by Elmo Roper to discontinue his well-known poll on the grounds that Dewey already had won the election caused Truman to write—but not mail—a tart letter to Roper. "Candidates make election contests," Truman wrote in longhand, "not pole [sic] takers or press comments by paid column writers." Maintaining that people generally had lost faith in the press, he added:

That is a good thing too. No one segment should be able to control public opinion. Leadership still counts. The publishers press is a very small part of our population. They have debauched the responsibility they owe to the country and the people have shown them just how they like it.[4]

To Claude G. Bowers, United States ambassador to Chile, he observed that the election "certainly was a blow to all the ivory tower columnists and also the gutter snipe columnists."[5]

Truman remarked in a letter to former Representative Maury Maverick of Texas that "the Republicans had the money and we had the votes and that is what it took to win." An article in *U. S. News & World Report* with a quite straightforward analysis of the election returns nettled Truman, who somehow interpreted it to suggest "that I have not yet won the election."[6] He asked William J. Bray of the Democratic National Committee for a compilation of official returns. The figures, Truman ventured, would convince "even the likes of the editor of this magazine . . . that I'll necessarily have to be President for another four years."[7]

The election returns, according to his most intimate friends, gave Truman a feeling of being out from under the shadow of Roosevelt at last, although the domestic program he was to propose in his second term was essentially a continuance of the New Deal. When Representative Sam Rayburn, Democrat, of Texas, who would become the Speaker of the House in the newly elected Congress, visited Truman at Key West after the election, he found the president's mood transformed from the humility of 1945 and 1946. According to one account of the Key West meeting, Truman spoke to Rayburn about purging from the Democratic party all members of the new Congress who had joined the Dixiecrats in the campaign. The taciturn Rayburn, master of his own domain, was said to have squelched the suggestion on the ground that such a reprisal would jeopardize Democratic control on Capitol Hill.[8]

Certainly, victory had filled Truman with a tremendous sense of vindication, welling up through layers of disdain, contempt, and ridicule that had accumulated around him during his first term. Scorned by many people as a little man, condemned by Republican spokesmen and the Republican press as a misfit in the White House, Truman had even witnessed an attempt by a liberal faction in his own party to deny him the nomination because public opinion polls indicated that his chances of winning were all but hopeless. But then, on a dramatic election night, he had sprung forth as the wonder man of American politics. His Democratic detractors looked as foolish as his boastful Republican foes. Never before in American politics had there been such a personal triumph. Only a saint would have disdained the acclaim. Truman's gratification was amplified by the rapture of his staff, few members of which had truly believed he would win and some of whom now went to the other extreme of regarding him as infallible in matters political. In the opinion of some of his associates Truman's assessment of himself as a political leader reflected their judgment.[9]

As his staff gathered with him on various occasions after the election, spirited chatter went round about Democrats and others who had guessed wrong. Major General Harry H. Vaughan, Truman's military aide, reported having overheard Mrs. J. Borden Harriman, minister to Norway in the Roosevelt administration, say at a dinner party that Truman did not have a chance against Dewey.[10] White House Press Secretary Charles G. Ross remembered that in the campaign a supportive letter had come from Rexford G. Tugwell, an original member of Roosevelt's "Brain Trust." "Too late" was the verdict around the room. For the same reason, thumbs were turned down on the eventual offer of good wishes that had been received from Leon Henderson, a founder of Americans for Democratic Action, the liberal organization that had been in the forefront of the move before the 1948 Democratic National Convention to dump Truman for General Dwight D. Eisenhower. On the other hand, Myron C. Taylor, the president's personal representative to the Vatican, was accepted as being no "Tuesday Democrat."

Sternly regarded, of course, were those Democrats who had bolted the party to support either Wallace's Progressives or the Dixiecrats.

"I don't want any fringes in the Democratic party—no Wallaceites or States Righters," Truman told his staff four days after the election.[11]

Woe, too, to James J. Maloney, chief of the United States Secret Service, who, overly ambitious, had turned up at Dewey's headquarters in New York on election night instead of at Excelsior Springs. Within weeks it was announced that he was being replaced as chief of the Secret Service to become coordinator of law enforcement agencies in the Treasury Department. At that, he fared better than Arthur M. Hill, a Republican business executive who was chairman of the National Security Resources Board. The Hills had given an election night party in Washington. On the invitations Mrs. Hill had written a suggestion that wives of administration officials come dressed in black as appropriate to an occasion of mourning. Truman saw to it that Hill's "resignation" was announced on December 6.[12]

While Truman was at Key West, the drafting of his State of the Union message to the new Congress and his subsequent Inaugural Address was begun. The president held some talks on the tasks ahead, although no record of the discussions exists. Two of his most important visitors were Rayburn and Vice-President-elect Barkley, both of whom had entered the House of Representatives on March 4, 1913, the day Woodrow Wilson was inaugurated as president.

Rayburn—"Mr. Sam"—was one of the most powerful Democrats to serve in Washington thus far in the twentieth century. He was speaker of the House longer than any other in history, having been first elected to the post in 1940. He had to step down in 1947 after the Republicans had won control and elected Joseph W. Martin, Jr., of Massachusetts in his place. But the Democratic triumph of 1948 returned Rayburn to the speaker's chair. In the 1930s, as chairman of the House Committee on Interstate and Foreign Commerce, he had played a vital role in the passage of New Deal legislation. In the Truman administration his role was less definable but still important, especially because of the president's respect for his judgment. After Truman became president, leaving the office of vice-president vacant, he persuaded Congress to change the law of succession to make the speaker of the House rather than the secretary of state next in line of succession upon the death of a president.*

Truman never had served in the House, and, therefore, his personal relationship with the speaker was not the same as, for example, the relationship between Rayburn and his fellow Texan, Lyndon Baines Johnson. During Truman's ten years in the Senate, beginning in 1935, he and Rayburn had become increasingly good friends. During Truman's short vice-presidency he and Rayburn were opposite numbers as presiding officers, respectively, of the Senate and the House. Indeed Vice-President Truman was in the speaker's office at the Capitol for a late-afternoon drink when he was summoned to the White House upon the death of Roosevelt. To any president the House is very important if only because of its power to pass tax bills and appropriate funds. Since foreign affairs were the predominant concern of the Truman administration, however, the major legislative actions were in the Senate. Many of Truman's foreign policy initiatives required funding, and Rayburn generally gave strong support to Truman's foreign policy, as was true, on the whole, of domestic policy. There were proposals, civil rights measures among them, that Rayburn knew Truman could not get through the House. Truman sent them up anyhow. Rayburn was no racist, but, as a southern politician, neither was he an enthusiast for civil rights bills.

While he was not a purified liberal such as might be found in Americans for Democratic Action, he was a pragmatic liberal in the context of the Roosevelt and Truman administrations. As one of the "big four" Democratic congressional leaders who, throughout Truman's presidency, went to the White House every Monday during congressional sessions to consult the president, Rayburn was in a position to exert direct influence on Truman on legislative strategy. Truman did not always accept the speaker's advice. When, in 1950, for example, the House was considering the controversial Kerr bill to curb federal regulation of the sale of natural gas, Rayburn in the interest of his Texas constituents took the floor and appealed for passage of the measure. Like the Senate, the House approved the bill. Truman vetoed it "in the public interest."[13] The effect on

---

*Since February 10, 1967, when the Twenty-fifth Amendment was fully ratified, the Constitution has provided that a vacancy in the office of vice-president shall be filled by appointment of the president, subject to congressional confirmation.

Rayburn's formidable temper is not a matter of record, but this conflict did no lasting damage to their friendship. Truman also consulted Rayburn on difficult questions not pertaining to legislation. The president's troubles with General of the Army Douglas A. MacArthur was such a case. Without question, Truman felt more secure in the White House because of the strength of Rayburn's personality and leadership on Capitol Hill.

Barkley had been more the choice of the Democratic National Convention than Truman's personal choice for vice-president, but a warm attachment prevailed between the two men, who had served together in the Senate. At seventy-one—six years Truman's elder—Barkley was much beloved by the Democrats. One of the leading orators in the party, he was the keynote speaker at the Democratic National Convention in Chicago in 1932, which nominated Roosevelt for his first term. When the New Deal blew into Washington, Barkley was one of its stalwarts in the Senate, where, with Roosevelt's blessing, he eventually was chosen majority leader. His name became well known in America's households as a result of certain "Dear Alben" letters that Roosevelt wrote to him, especially one during a row between Congress and the White House in 1944. Over the pleas of Barkley, Rayburn, and the other Democratic congressional leaders, Roosevelt vetoed a tax bill. In protest, Barkley resigned as majority leader. At the prompting of Roosevelt, the Democratic senators reelected Barkley the next day.

After the victory of the Democratic ticket in 1948, Barkley with his rollicking humor and skill as a raconteur, was affectionately known to one and all as the Veep. Soon the courtly seventy-one-year-old widower set Washington agog by marrying the prominent Mrs. Jane Rucker Hadley, thirty-eight, of St. Louis, to whom he had been introduced by Mr. and Mrs. Clark M. Clifford. Clifford was special counsel to Truman.

Truman's own unhappy experience as vice-president caused him to bring about a broadening of the role that now devolved upon Barkley. When Truman was vice-president, Roosevelt largely ignored him and excluded him from the innermost discussions of strategy and diplomacy as the Second World War was nearing a climax. When Roosevelt died, Truman's enforced ignorance of the great problems he then had to deal with multiplied his burdens. He was angry that Roosevelt had left him in such a predicament. While Barkley was to be a less important figure in the second Truman administration than some of his successors were to be in later administrations, Truman quickly brought the Kentuckian much deeper into the councils of high policy than any vice-president had regularly been in the past. Not only did Barkley sit in the cabinet, as had been customary for vice-presidents, but at Truman's request Congress made the vice-president a statutory member of the National Security Council, so that Barkley was kept in continuous touch with diplomacy, national defense, and intelligence.

On a chilly Inauguration Day—January 20, 1949—wind assailed the top hats that Truman and Barkley wore as the two men rode together in an open car to the Capitol. At noon they stepped upon the most monumental and costly inaugural stand ever seen up to that time. In 1948, the otherwise economy-minded Republicans in the Eightieth Congress had voted $80,000 (a fat sum then) in the expectation that Dewey would be the next president. Truman's friend, fellow poker-player, and appointee, Chief Justice Fred M. Vinson, administered the oath of office to the president in the first inaugural ceremony ever televised.

Before a great crowd and under fleets of bombers the inaugural parade was long and lively. In the reviewing stand in front of the White House Truman danced a little jig when a band played *I'm Just Wild About Harry*. He turned aside when the South Carolina float passed, accompanied by that state's governor, J. Strom Thurmond, who had been the Dixiecrat candidate for president.

The reception after the parade was held in the National Gallery of Art because the White House had been closed for complete renovation of the interior. It was a peculiarity of the president's second term that for three years and two months of the four-year term the Trumans lived not in the White House but, rather claustrophobically, in Blair House, a lovely historic mansion, dating to 1824, diagonally across Pennsylvania Avenue in the next block to the west. The president worked as usual in the White House offices, which were unaffected by the renovation of the living quarters.

The inaugural festivities ended with a white-tie ball so large that it had to be held in the National Guard Armory. While the Trumans watched from their box in the balcony, thousands of guests danced to the orchestras of Guy Lombardo, Xavier Cugat, and Benny Goodman. For the first time in history, on orders from the White House, blacks had been invited to all of the main events.[14] The president's face, as his daughter, Margaret, noted afterward, "was shining like a new moon."[15] It was 3 o'clock in the morning when Truman finally got to bed. As customary, he was up at 5 to face his second term. It was destined to be a troubled one.

2. *A Disturbing Beginning*

IN JANUARY OF 1949 the aftershocks of the Second World War were still jarring large parts of the globe, although they had greatly diminished in the United States. In Asia, however, turbulence continued to rise as a result of the collapse of Japan, the tottering of the European empires after the war, and the combustion produced by nationalism mixed with communism. Because a segment of American opinion, generally represented in the more conservative wing of the Republican party, was very sensitive to events in Asia, the tremors in the Far East came as harbingers of disturbing political conflict in the United States.

On the other hand, the country was in a state of good times for most people—an important factor in Truman's election. Although signs of a recession had begun appearing late in 1948, employment was high, prices were relatively steady, interest rates were low, and strikes were at a minimum. In his first term Truman had managed to keep the federal budget balanced, or nearly so. While this course suited the mood of the people and the Congress, it was to a considerable extent accomplished by reducing the military establishment. In an unstable world this policy held risks for Truman. Another general war so soon after the exhaustion abroad in 1945 was considered unlikely, and, in any case, the United States enjoyed the enormous advantage of a monopoly on atomic bombs. Truman, therefore, persisted in his policy of curbing military spending, determined to capitalize on good times to reduce the national debt. In January 1949, it stood at what seemed a shocking total: $252 billion.

Truman came to the second term hoping that with a requested tax increase and a low military budget he could cut the debt and still provide benefits like more low-cost housing, higher Social Security payments, and federal aid to education. He expected to have four years of peace in which to reach his goals. His victory and the Democratic capture of Congress filled liberals with visions of reforms such as repeal of the Taft-Hartley Act and the great strides in civil rights proposed in Truman's first-term program and the Democratic platform. "The President," wrote the liberal columnist Thomas L. Stokes in December 1948, "can get most of his program, and without too much compromise, if he constantly calls upon the great public support manifest for him in the election . . . and uses his political skill to organize the progressive forces."[1]

The reality of the "great public support," as Truman well knew, was that, because of defections to the Progressives and the Dixiecrats, he had been elected by only 49.5 percent of the popular vote. Truman had won partly because many voters did not wish to run the risk that Dewey and the Republicans would undo the, by then, well-established reforms of the New Deal. But it is difficult to read the 1948 election as a cry for extensive new reform. The public had been indifferent toward further reform in Truman's first term, and no sudden new stirring was apparent.

In a friendly letter to Truman in mid-December, Charles E. Wilson, president of the General Electric Company, deplored the Democrats' anti-business rhetoric in the 1948 campaign. He cautioned against new legislation that business would consider unfavorable. In reply, Truman, who liked Wilson, chided him for being biased toward big business. He said:

> I am sure that right down in your heart you know that the ordinary man is the backbone of any country—particularly is that true in a Republic and what I am trying to eliminate is the fringe at each end of the situation. I think small business, the small farmer, the small corporations are the backbone of any free society and when there are too many people on relief and too few people at the top who control the wealth of the country then we must look out.[2]

Truman distrusted concentrations of economic power, whether in business or labor. While he favored a balanced budget and was skeptical of social experimentation, he believed that the government had a responsibility to help solve social and economic problems and to offer security to the poor and the elderly. He rejected the idea of trickle-down prosperity. Without notice to his speechwriters he penciled into a draft of the 1949 State of the Union message, ". . . I expect to try to give every segment of our population a fair deal."[3] The statement was incorporated in slightly different wording in the final draft. And after Truman delivered it to a joint session of the Eighty-first Congress on January 5 the press seized upon "fair deal" as a label, as the press had done in 1932 following Roosevelt's acceptance speech at the Democratic National Convention, in which he had said, "I pledge you, I pledge myself, to a new deal for the American people." Truman did not realize that he was giving his administration the nickname Fair Deal.[4]

The election had not wrought the kind of political transformation that Truman's words seemed to imply. A low turnout of voters and the narrow margin of the president's victory had failed to produce a realignment beyond the break in the traditional Democratic "Solid South" when four states went to the Dixiecrats. Once the excitement of election night was over, the national political landscape looked much as it had before, though darkened on the horizon by the sullen mood of the Republicans.

The Democrats' elation obscured for the moment the continuing difficulty that was bound to face Truman in pressing for the kind of liberal program that he had promised in his campaign. The return of Democrats to control of Congress meant a restoration to committee chairmanships of senior southerners who had little use for the New Deal or the Fair Deal. On the Republican side, other conservative leaders, notably Senator Robert A. Taft of Ohio, became ranking minority members of the major committees. New among the Democratic majority in the Senate, it is true, were promising liberals, like Hubert H. Humphrey of Minnesota, Paul H. Douglas of Illinois, and Estes Kefauver of Tennessee. Nevertheless, the old coalition of southern Democrats and Republican conservatives that had thwarted Roosevelt's domestic legislation in the latter years of the New Deal and had blocked Truman in his first term was back astride the path of legislation dealing with civil rights, health insurance, antitrust legislation, public power, appropriations for social welfare, and the like.

While Truman's victory in 1948 had ended for the time being any chance of rolling back the New Deal, powerful conservatives were thus positioned against its advance under the name of the Fair Deal. In his State of the Union message Truman simply urged Congress to adopt the program long familiar by then through previous legislative proposals by Roosevelt and Truman and through Truman's campaign speeches and the 1948 Democratic platform.[5] Proposed repeal of the Taft-Hartley Act was one of the most controversial issues because of promises Truman had made to labor in the campaign. Enacted over his veto in the Eightieth Congress in a swirl of political emotion, the act had sought to strike a different balance between the rights of business and those of labor than had developed under the pro-labor Wagner Act, passed at the height of the New Deal.

In 1949, as during the Roosevelt administration and Truman's first term, civil rights was a politically explosive question. In his State of the Union message Truman asked Congress to pass the same measures he had proposed in his celebrated "Special Message to Congress on Civil Rights" in 1948.[6] Without directly attacking segregation, that message, not yet acted upon, included recommendations for antilynching legislation, an anti-poll tax law, a commission on civil rights, a permanent fair employment practices commission and reform of voting laws that, particularly in the South, barred blacks from the polls.

The Fair Deal program was condemned by conservatives as perpetuation of Roosevelt's policies. Under Truman, as a matter of fact, the emphasis had shifted somewhat from largely economic measures to government action through social measures such as federal aid to education, federal health insurance, and construction of public housing. Questions like that of civil rights, which was decidedly in the category of social measures, and repeal of the Taft-Hartley Act exacerbated ideological differences that had spread among Democrats since the latter part of the New Deal. Truman, therefore, faced a continuing split in his own party.

At the approach of Inauguration Day he made only one major change in his cabinet. It was forced upon him by the failing health of a man whom Truman—and not only Truman—regarded as one of the greatest America had ever produced: General of the Army George Catlett Marshall, army chief of staff in the Second World War and secretary of state since 1947. Marshall resigned from the State Department after the election, following the removal of a kidney. To be the new secretary of state Truman chose Dean Gooderham Acheson. As will be seen, the repercussions of that appointment were to follow Truman to the end of his term. James E. Webb, director of the budget in the first term, was named under secretary of state, succeeding Robert A. Lovett, who resigned.

Although the composition of the White House staff and the cabinet was to be much the same in the second term as in the first, other changes were coming, notably the easing out of James V. Forrestal, last of the holdovers from Roosevelt's cabinet, as Secretary of Defense, and also the appointment of Senator J. Howard McGrath as attorney general. Furthermore, a year into the new term, Clark Clifford, a major figure in the first term, was to resign to practice law and to be replaced as special counsel by Charles S. Murphy of South Carolina, a graduate of Duke Law School. Murphy was closer to Truman personally than Clifford had been. He was more Truman's type and got along very well with the others around Truman, as was not always the case with Clifford. Clifford had been born to the limelight, Murphy to self-effacing, hard staff work. When Truman was a senator, Murphy was in the Office of Legislative Counsel in the Senate, a school, if there ever was one, for learning the interplay between politics and legislation. Murphy was used as a legislative draftsman by Truman, who enjoyed, Murphy later recalled, the reputation of being "the nicest man in the Senate."[7] Truman brought Murphy into the White House as an administrative assistant in 1947 and, like Clifford, Murphy played an important part in the president's 1948 campaign. Clifford preferred working with only one assistant, the able George M. Elsey. Murphy preferred more assistants, particularly since he retained some of the areas he had been responsible for as an administrative assistant. In the change from Clifford to Murphy, therefore, the office of special counsel was enlarged from two to five or six.

A curse of Truman's first term had been the suffocating spread of anticommunism. The worst was yet to come—and soon. The onset of the Cold War and mistrust of Soviet aims had aroused latent fear and loathing of communism in the United States. The result was an unloosening of anti-liberal, anti-intellectual, and demagogic forces, spraying poison through the political atmosphere.

American society had long been conditioned to popular fear of radicalism. The plague of totalitarianism in Europe and the approach of the Second World War had intensified alarm over subversion in the United States. That was when the House of Representatives established the Committee on un-American Activities under the chairmanship of an anti–New Deal Democrat from Texas, Martin Dies, who pioneered the congressional hunt for Communists in government. That was when agents of foreign governments were required to register with the attorney general. That was when federal employees were forbidden to belong to any party that advocated the overthrow of the government. That was when the War and Navy Departments were authorized summarily to remove any employee considered to be a threat to national security. That was when Congress passed the Smith Act, making it unlawful for anyone to join an organization that taught, advocated, or encouraged the overthrow of government by force. It was then too, when the Civil Service Commission issued a war regulation, disqualifying any applicant for federal employment, if the commission entertained "a reasonable doubt as to his loyalty."

In the Red Scare after the First World War, in which thousands of alleged radicals were arrested, Attorney General A. Mitchell Palmer listed certain organizations as subversive, subjecting their alien members to deportation. During the Second World War Attorney General Francis J. Biddle revived the so-called attorney general's list of subversive organizations. Membership in one of those organizations could have made a government employee liable to questioning as to his loyalty to the United States. In Truman's first term, as the heat of anticommunism rose, the attorney general's list became larger, more publicized, more seriously applied, and potentially more damaging to anyone belonging to one of the organizations on it.

Having failed to defeat New Deal reforms with the cry of socialism, Republicans turned to the smear of communism. Dewey used the issue cautiously against Roosevelt in the 1944 election, when anticommunism was muted in the wartime alliance of convenience with the Soviet Union against Hitler. When the alliance soured at the end of the war and Stalin began imposing his control on Poland and much of Eastern Europe and the Balkans, the restraints dissolved. Truman's initiation to the presidency occurred in a rising tide of anticommunism. By the 1946 congressional elections Republicans—Richard M. Nixon in the vanguard in his campaign against Representative Jerry Voorhis in California—discovered the effectiveness of using the Red issue against Democratic candidates.

Truman had no more use for the Soviet system and communism than had the typical American of the 1940s and 1950s. His quarrel was with Soviet foreign policy, which he viewed as expansionist, imperialistic, and militaristic. He believed that it was the God-given duty of the United States to lead the forces of freedom, democracy, and capitalism to ascendency through a combination of peaceful competition and a balance of power. At the same time he had a quite sensible view of the Communist problem within the United States.

Truman did not believe that Communists menaced the American political system in the postwar period. He recognized that the issue was specious on the whole. He was an old enough hand at politics to discern that the Republicans and some of the conservative press were turning domestic communism, what there was of it, into a phantasm to frighten voters away from the Democratic party and liberal policy. "The Communist bugaboo is being used by a great many people like Hearst to cover up shortcomings of their own," he wrote to a friend.[8] Espionage, of course, was a problem, especially in the nuclear age. Witch hunts, however, were a foolish way to try to cope with it.

Where Truman failed was in not waging a fight to lead the American people to a more enlightened view of communism—in not putting the issue in a public perspective that would have dampened hysteria. To be sure that would have been asking a political leader to risk a great deal, given the postwar mood. Truman might not have been listened to. He might have been driven out of office in 1948. In any case what happened was that he went both ways on the Communist issue. He made known his belief that it was a red herring, yet he whipped up sentiment against international communism to get the Truman Doctrine and the Marshall Plan through Congress. In other words, to obtain authority for what he considered necessary measures against Soviet expansionism, he appealed to anti-Communist feelings at home. To be in a position to take a tough stance against the dangers of communism abroad, he took a tough stance against domestic communism.

To play it safe politically and to keep the Eightieth Congress from possibly legislating a program to get rid of "subversives" in government, he promulgated in 1947 his own Employee Loyalty Program, a vehicle, as it turned out, for imputing guilt by association and an undertaking about which Truman himself later felt regrets. The following year the Department of Justice obtained indictments, under the Smith Act, against twelve members of the national board of the Communist party. They were tried, convicted, and sentenced to the penitentiary. Evidently, the department and Attorney General Tom C. Clark acted on their own initiative in this case under the wide discretion Truman allowed cabinet officers. "I have been accused," Clark said years later, "of filing cases against communists in order to bolster the president's image in that regard, but there is no truth to this. The president never talked to me about it at all."[9] When under heavy attack from red-baiters in the future, however, Truman in self-defense boasted of the prosecutions under the Smith Act.[10]

A reassuring note at the start of 1949 was that the election had strained but not ended the so-called bipartisan foreign policy, dating to the war years. In essence this bipartisanship confirmed agreement between the Democrats and the Republicans on measures affecting the relationship between the United States and its European allies. It also had come to signify agreement on the policy of containment of the Soviet Union and international communism. An aspect that was very significant at the beginning of the second term and in the midst of rising disturbances in the Far East was that bipartisan agreement did not necessarily hold on questions involving policy toward Asia. In fact, sharp differences had developed between the Truman administration and the Republicans over the spreading civil war in China.

Otherwise, under the glow of bipartisanship great measures had been approved. Among them were the postwar British loan, the creation of the International Monetary Fund and the International Bank for Reconstruction and Development, the Truman Doctrine, the Marshall Plan (in mid-passage by January 1949), and the "Vandenberg Resolution" of 1948.[11] Full effects of the adoption of this resolution by the Senate were just being realized at the start of the second term. The Communist seizure of Czechoslovakia in 1948 had frightened Western European leaders into proposing a defense pact with the United States. The Truman administration was agreeable, and the Vandenberg Resolution paved the way for Washington to enter negotiations. By the time of Truman's inauguration diplomats of the North Atlantic powers were nearing agreement on final terms of a military treaty to be submitted to the legislatures of the various members.

After the election the National Security Council had reviewed the situation around the globe. In a paper, NSC 20/4, dated November 23, 1948, and approved by the president the next day, the most worrisome conclusion was this: "Present intelligence estimates attribute to Soviet armed forces the capability of over-running in about six months all of continental Europe and the Near East as far as Cairo. . . ."* By 1955 the Soviets would be capable, according to the estimates, of air attacks on the United States with atomic, biological, and chemical weapons.

"Even though present estimates indicate that the Soviet leaders probably do not intend deliberate armed attack involving the United States at this time," NSC 20/4 said, "the possibility of such a deliberate resort to war cannot be ruled out."

Consistent with Washington's view since the early postwar period, the National Security Council concluded that the "ultimate objective of the leaders of the USSR is the domination of the world."[12]

Three developments in Europe were paramount as the second term opened.

One, of course, was the nascent alliance of the North Atlantic powers.

The second was the birth struggle of an independent West German government, occurring in the face of bitter Soviet opposition. After the breakdown of the 1945 Potsdam agreement on joint control of all Germany by the United States, Great Britain, the Soviet Union, and France and after the Communist seizure of Czechoslovakia, the Western allies decided to sponsor formation of a West German government separate from Soviet-occupied East Germany. In January 1949 Bonn announced that all West German political parties were prepared to cooperate on the writing of a constitution for a new state.

The third development was the continuing Soviet blockade and Allied counter-blockade of Berlin, whose Allied sectors were being kept alive by a massive airlift of supplies from the West.

A new device of American foreign policy—the Point Four Program—was proposed in Truman's inaugural address. It was an idea that had come to the White House out of the blue from former *Atlanta Journal* reporter Benjamin H. Hardy, then a minor official in the office of public affairs in the State Department.

Government agencies, private institutions, and even some corporations had long been carrying on projects for sharing scientific knowledge with and giving technical assistance to certain underdeveloped areas. As a government official stationed in Brazil in 1944, Hardy was impressed by what he saw of this enterprise. Back in the State Department at the height of the Cold War in 1948, he had hatched the idea of unifying and expanding the work within a central government program, making technical assistance an instrument of the United States for combatting the spread of communism in poor countries.

---

* Frequently cited throughout this book, the formerly classified reports prepared by the National Security Council on international problems were designated by numbers. Recommendations in such papers became the policy of the administration when approved by the president, a statutory member of the NSC.

One day a memorandum arrived at the State Department from Clifford, soliciting suggestions for a statement on foreign policy, which was to be the heart of the inaugural address. From his superior Hardy obtained permission to include his idea in the State Department's reply, only to have Acting Secretary of State Lovett eliminate it, largely because of cost. On his own initiative Hardy took his proposal to Clifford's assistant, George Elsey, whom Hardy knew only from some previous telephone conversations.[13] Elsey, Clifford, and Truman were enthusiastic over Hardy's suggestion and decided to present it in the inaugural address.

The plan became known, prosaically, as the Point Four Program because it was listed in the address as the fourth of four proposed courses of action intended to achieve "peace and freedom." The fourth point was that the United States must embark on a "bold new program for making the benefits of our scientific advances and industrial progress available for the improvement and growth of under-developed areas." Truman described America's aim as one of helping "the free peoples of the world, through their own efforts, to produce more food, more clothing, more materials for housing and more mechanical power to lighten their burdens."[14]

Bureaucratic disagreements and Republican unenthusiasm delayed enactment of the program until May 1950, and then it was dwarfed by military and economic aid programs. Reduced largely to symbolic importance, the Point Four Program received an initial appropriation of only $26.9 million. The Foreign Economics Assistance Act, of which Point Four was a part, did for the first time establish the economic development of poorer areas as a national policy.[15]

Circumstances, and they were not happy ones, that were largely to define the nature of Truman's second term began flowing together almost from the time of his election victory.

One circumstance was the smashing gains in the Chinese civil war by the Communists under Mao Tse-tung (Mao Zedong) at the expense of the Nationalists under Chiang Kai-shek.* Another was the continuing threat of hostilities in Korea. The tinder there had been lying about since the end of the war in the Pacific, as United States troops supported a regime in the southern part of the country under challenge from a Soviet-backed Communist regime in the northern half.

A third circumstance was the resentful mood of the Republicans, convinced by Truman's victory that they needed a new and more radical strategy for recapturing the White House in the future. Finally, the circle was closed by the indictment in December 1948 of Alger Hiss, a former State Department official, accused of perjury in denying that he had passed classified government documents to a Communist agent. The Hiss case, when combined with a forthcoming crusade against alleged reds in government by Senator Joseph R. McCarthy, Republican,

---

*In this book Chinese names are spelled as they were during the events of the 1940s and 1950s since that was the spelling used in the official correspondence and records and the public prints of that period.

of Wisconsin, almost shook the nation from its moorings. Mao's victories and the suspicions aroused by the Hiss case and McCarthy's thunder created a perfect atmosphere for charges of a stupendous plot inside the Truman administration—a plot that enabled communism to triumph in the world with the help of conspiracy and treason in Washington.

Crises in Asia were spinning a web in Truman's path. To a degree unsuspected in the flush of victory, his destiny as president bobbed on the tide of events flowing in China and Korea. The tide rose swiftly.

The day before the American election, the forces of Chiang Kai-shek, a wartime ally of the United States rather fervently admired by millions of Americans, yielded Mukden (largest city of Manchuria) to the Communists. Subsequent cables pouring into the State Department from its posts in China chronicled a sweeping advance by the Communists, who were widely regarded by the government and people of the United States as a potential long-term threat to American security in Asia. Shock and dismay were the reaction in the United States.

Republicans glimpsed the vulnerability of the Democrats in the event of a Communist seizure of China. In contrast to their support of European policy in Truman's first term, the Republicans bore no share of responsibility for China policy. Calamity for American policy in Asia, moreover, would create an issue that would prove to be not only rich in emotion and aimed at a weak spot in Truman's armor but also historically congenial to the Republican party.

During the Second World War conservative Republicans believed that Roosevelt had gone too far in giving priority in global strategy to the campaigns in Europe. They looked upon General MacArthur as one of their own and felt that Roosevelt's policy had unnecessarily hampered MacArthur in the war against Japan. Since the United States had become a Far Eastern Power with acquisition of the Philippines in the Spanish-American War, fought under the McKinley administration, Republicans regarded American strength in Asia as their special concern. Enunciating a theme long familiar to them but foreign to the Democrats, Senator Taft had said in 1948, "I believe very strongly that the Far East is ultimately even more important to our future peace than is Europe."[16] For many Republicans Chiang Kai-shek, along with his chic, Wellesley-educated wife, was a hero to be supported stoutly because of his opposition to communism and his show of dedication to Christianity.

Nationalist defeat would have been a threat to Truman's leadership if for no other reason than that it would tighten the bonds among his potential enemies: Republicans, the right-wing press, MacArthur, Henry R. Luce, publisher of *Time, LIFE,* and *Fortune,* and the "China lobby." This last was a loosely organized group of Americans and of Chinese representing Chiang Kai-shek, who were well financed and not above at least the contemplation of bribery in Washington.[17] The China lobby was well connected with military, press, business, religious, patriotic, congressional, anti-liberal, and old isolationist circles and had its own chain of associations and publications, including *The China Monthly: The Truth About China.*

In its rising attack on Truman's policies the China lobby had been shrill, harsh, and vindictive. Its forte was brewing suspicion about supposed conspiracies within the government, particularly by exploiting complex events about which the public knew little, such as the Yalta Conference among Roosevelt, Churchill, and Stalin in 1945. Thus, as if lifting the lid on a dark side of American diplomacy, the China lobby accused Roosevelt, posthumously, of treachery at Yalta—he and British Prime Minister Winston S. Churchill had played "the part of traitors," according to an editorial in *The China Monthly*. "Yalta betrayal" had become the group's epithet for Roosevelt's assent at Yalta to Soviet concessions in Manchuria and Outer Mongolia—regions in which the Soviets doubtless could have taken what they pleased whether or not a conference had been held.

Insuring the most divisive imaginable controversy, the China lobby struck the theme that the Roosevelt and Truman administrations had sold China down the river—down the Amur, according to the title of an article in *The China Monthly*.[18] The cause of the Nationalist retreat, in the rhetoric and propaganda of the China lobby, was to be found not in China but in Washington. And not only because of Washington's "stupidity," as Alfred Kohlberg, importer of Chinese laces and dominant figure in the China lobby, suggested in another article in *The China Monthly,* but because of "treason"[19]—a charge that was to spread, poisonously, in the years after 1948.

The China lobby and its much more powerful friends in Congress—the so-called China bloc—embraced an array of interests that sought an end to Democratic rule, especially of the Roosevelt-Truman variety. They seized upon China as a way of achieving that goal and were to darken Truman's second term. The merest foretaste of what was to come was a headline in *LIFE* magazine of December 20, 1948: MACARTHUR SAYS FALL OF CHINA IMPERILS U.S. The unsigned article beneath it was an editorial, mentioning a purported "urgent message" from MacArthur to the Joint Chiefs of Staff and asking, "In the face of the facts which seem so plain, how could Washington have ever been complacent about the military consequences of a Communist victory in China?"[20]

Truman's 1948 triumph had shocked the Nationalists and their friends, who had hoped to fare better under a Republican administration. After he had been nominated for president, Dewey accused the Truman administration of having been niggardly in financial aid to China. He pledged that one of the cardinal principles of a Dewey administration would be to help China combat Communist influence within its borders. He said that the United States should provide military advisers, the kind of material the Chinese needed, and far greater financial assistance.[21] In his campaign he promised to end the "tragic neglect" of China. In a cable to Secretary of State Marshall from Nanking on August 23, 1948, J. Leighton Stuart, United States ambassador to China, said, "In fact, there is surprisingly frank admission in official circles that the Government's eyes are glued to a sympathetic Republican Congress in January. . . ."[22] Simply by winning the election Truman had incurred the wrath of Chiang Kai-shek's friends.

In August 1948 at the start of the presidential campaign, Whittaker Chambers, former member of a Communist underground in Washington, and Elizabeth T. Bentley, a former courier for Communist agents, had testified before the House Committee on un-American Activities about Communist infiltration of high federal offices before the Second World War. Chambers, a senior editor of *Time,* swore that Alger Hiss, former director of the special political affairs division in the State Department, had been a member of a Communist underground group. Chambers said that the original purpose of the group was infiltration of the goverment, but "espionage was certainly one of its eventual objectives."

At a press conference on August 5, 1948, a reporter asked Truman if he thought the hearings in the Republican-controlled Congress were, to quote the reporter, "a red herring to divert public attention from inflation." Angry at Congress, Truman allowed the reporter to put words in his mouth. "Yes, I do," he replied.[23] Being thus placed in the position of branding the proceedings a red herring was incautious because it left Truman vulnerable in case of future unfavorable developments.

Chambers later declared on radio outside the immunity of congressional hearings that Hiss had been a Communist and might still be one. Hiss sued for slander. During the pretrial proceedings in November 1948, Hiss's lawyer, seemingly confident that his client never had been involved with Chambers in a Communist underground, had asked Chambers to furnish any letters or other communications he might have received from Hiss. Chambers's response led to one of the weird events of the epoch.

Twelve days after the election the senior editor of *Time* delivered to Hiss's lawyer sixty-five typed pages of copied State Department documents, or summaries of documents, and four pieces of paper bearing Hiss's handwriting, all of which, Chambers later said, he had secreted in an abandoned dumbwaiter in Brooklyn in 1938. If genuine, the material indicated that Hiss had lied in testifying before the House Committee on un-American Activities that he had not seen Chambers after January 1, 1937. The material also indicated that Hiss had been engaged in espionage. Chambers, for his own future use, if necessary, had withheld from Hiss's lawyers two strips of developed films of documents and three canisters of undeveloped microfilm.

The pretrial proceedings, of course, had been private, but a lawyer gathering material for Chambers's defense in the slander suit had tipped off the staff of the Committee on un-American Activities to the existence of the Chambers documents. Chambers had then confided to Representative Nixon, a member of the committee, that he possessed documents other than those given to Hiss's lawyers.[24] Nixon signed a *subpoena duces tecum* and ordered it served on Chambers. The melodrama was played out on a farm owned by Chambers near Westminster on the Eastern Shore of Maryland. Complying with the subpoena, Chambers on December 2, 1948, led two investigators from the committee into a pumpkin patch and groped for a particular pumpkin. He lifted its severed top and extracted two strips of developed film and the three canisters of undeveloped microfilm, all of which he had stuffed in the pumpkin earlier that day.

The headlines and radio and television news reports about the "pumpkin papers" fairly ignited the gaseous mass of suspicion about Communist infiltration, intrigue, and spying that had been accumulating in the United States since the 1930s.

At a postelection press conference on December 9, Truman was asked whether he still considered the House investigation a red herring. In anything but a diffident mood in those rosy days he snapped, "I do."[25] Waving aside the political perils lurking in the Communist issue, he indicated a belief that the voters had endorsed his views about the red herring—a dubious assumption.

His attitude was colored by hostility to the majority of the House Committee on un-American Activities, a body he hoped to see terminated by the incoming Democratic Congress. Unfortunately, the pumpkin papers gave the committee a new lease on life. Truman's answer in the press conference simply opened the door to further attacks upon himself, as Nixon promptly demonstrated by asserting that the president's comment was "a flagrant flouting of the national interests. . . ." Nixon increasingly got under Truman's skin. Nixon was a "crook," Truman was to say later in his term.[26]

On December 15, Alger Hiss—once a brilliant student at Johns Hopkins and Harvard Law School, law clerk to Associate Justice Oliver Wendell Holmes of the Supreme Court, rising young New Dealer and State Department official, and now president of the Carnegie Endowment for International Peace—was indicted by a federal grand jury in New York on two counts of perjury for denying the passing of papers to Chambers.

For large numbers of Americans the indictment held a special message. As former President Herbert C. Hoover was to write Nixon at a later stage of the Hiss case, "At last the stream of treason that has existed in our government has been exposed in a fashion all may believe."[27]

The eleven weeks between Truman's victory and his inauguration were a time of darkening mood in the United States and abroad.

3. *Acheson and the Approaching Storm*

THE SELECTION OF Dean Acheson as secretary of state was the most important appointment Truman ever made, not only with respect to the direction of the foreign policy of the United States but also to the tenor of domestic political controversy in the tumultuous years between 1949 and 1953.

Of commanding bearing, Acheson was theatrical in appearance, his features dominated by an aristocratic mustache and brown eyes under intimidating eyebrows. He was a man of extraordinary intelligence and style, reflected in his fluency of speech and pen. An elegantly tailored American of British and Canadian descent, he would have looked as much at home at 10 Downing Street as in Foggy Bottom, as appropriate to his heritage and inbred esteem for the British Empire and its stabilizing influence in the Ninetenth Century. A dominant trait was hauteur, moderated by civility and wit. His imperious demeanor could be deceptive. What were assumed to be notes he took on foreign ministers' speeches in the United Nations sometimes turned out to be limericks inspired by the fatuity of those performances.

At fifty-five Acheson was an eminent Washington lawyer who already had moved in and out of government. In the Roosevelt administration he had served as under secretary of the treasury and later as assistant secretary of state—first for economic affairs and then for congressional relations and international conferences. Carried over into the first Truman administration, he had been under secretary to Secretary of State James F. Byrnes and then to Secretary of State Marshall. Acheson had returned again to private law practice on July 1, 1947.

In 1948 when some other liberals wanted to dump Truman, Acheson stood by him. Acheson already had left a pronounced mark on foreign policy in Truman's first term. Although they were unalike in many respects, Acheson and the president worked well together. Acheson was, therefore, a logical successor to Marshall, although the very gifts of mind and manner that won Acheson favor in London and Paris were to make him vulnerable to vengeful Republicans looking for a target.

Acheson's role with Byrnes and Marshall was inadequately conveyed by the title of under secretary. Much of the time and at critical moments, Acheson had been acting secretary of state, dealing personally with Truman, the cabinet, and Congress, while simultaneously managing the State Department during the prolonged absences of Byrnes and Marshall at postwar conferences. He had chaired the committee that produced the Acheson-Lilienthal report, which became the basis of the Baruch Plan for international control of atomic weapons. He was a leader in developing the policy of economic and military aid to Greece and Turkey—the Truman Doctrine—and was a major force behind the creation of the Marshall Plan. He was an advocate of the restoration of defeated Germany and Japan as strong supporters "of a free-world structure."[1]

At the time of Roosevelt's death, Truman and Acheson knew each other only slightly. It was just before Roosevelt died that Assistant Secretary of State Acheson while talking to Vice-President Truman had his first chance personally to appraise the man who was then forty-eight hours away from the presidency. "It was a very good impression," Acheson later wrote to his son.[2] Truman and Acheson had come to the crossroads of 1949 from different backgrounds, Truman being a product of rural Missouri and a simple upbringing and Acheson a well-bred New Englander with an international outlook, a graduate of Groton, Yale College, and Harvard Law School. He had been a student and protégé of Felix Frankfurter's, law clerk to Associate Justice Louis D. Brandeis, and star of the preeminent Washington law firm then named Covington, Burling, Rublee, Acheson & Shorb.

Marx Leva, another Washington lawyer who also moved in and out of government in those days, later recalled, "You really could never talk with Dean Acheson for long without getting a put-down feeling."[3] This was one typical view of Acheson, namely, that he could be domineering, even overpowering. Truman did not feel in danger of being overpowered, obviously. He would not be the secretary of state, but neither would Acheson be the president. It was a key to their unusual relationship that Acheson understood this very clearly. Truman did not expect important decisions to be made without his knowledge, and Acheson understood that, too.

"Truman was the boss, and Dean played it that way," Charles E. Bohlen, counselor of the State Department in 1949, recalled later. "He never did anything without touching base with Truman."[4]

The office of secretary of state was at a peak of importance then, because the president, having come to the White House with no experience in international affairs, gave his secretary of state wide authority in the conduct of diplomacy. Truman wanted to be kept informed, to be sure. When Byrnes ignored this wish, especially at the foreign ministers' meeting in Moscow in December 1945, he fatally weakened his relationship with Truman.

Even though Truman allowed his secretary of state great latitude, he himself reacted decisively when diplomacy impinged on domestic politics or was contrary to his wishes. Thus when Byrnes's seemingly conciliatory dealings with the Soviets after the war gave rise to Republican charges that the Truman administration was "appeasing" the Soviets, Truman forced a harder American stance, barren of almost any concessions. When Truman wanted to grant quick diplomatic recognition to the new state of Israel in May 1948, he did so against the wishes of Marshall, Lovett, and the division of Near Eastern and African affairs in the State Department.

Inconspicuous at the moment was a flaw in Acheson's otherwise impressive credentials. The field in which he was expert was Europe. He was candidly pro-British, much more of an Anglophile than Truman was. But, unfortunately, Acheson lacked a deep knowledge of and familiarity with Asia. His only intimate experience with the Far East was in 1946 when he served as the "rear echelon," as General George Marshall called it, for the general's mission to China.

The simple truth about the outwardly incongruous Truman-Acheson relationship was that the two men liked each other. Their wives, also of different backgrounds, liked one another. Truman never held Acheson in the kind of awe he felt toward General Marshall, nor did the president seek Acheson's companionship in relaxation. Acheson was too intellectual to appeal to Truman as a companion. But in the first term Truman and Acheson had found it congenial working together. Truman welcomed hardheaded advisers on difficult problems, and Acheson, like Marshall and Lovett, was all that. To a greater extent than Marshall perhaps, Acheson, who was steeped in the ways of Washington and tempered by a trying stint in the Roosevelt administration, understood the political problems that foreign policy often created for Truman.

"Acheson spoke with appreciation and some amazement," former Ambassador at Large Philip C. Jessup recalled, "at Truman's dedication in reading memos at night. Dean could send him very long stuff, and Truman would go through it."[5]

Truman and Acheson were men of gusto, each with his own mischievous streak. They were earthy, thick-skinned, risible, and capable of lacerating sarcasm against a common foe. "Dean likes Truman because he is straightforward and frank," the then Secretary of Interior Harold L. Ickes wrote in his diary February 3, 1946, after a luncheon with Acheson.[6] Acheson had disliked Roosevelt because Roosevelt was devious. Acheson also later wrote that he found Roosevelt patronizing.[7] If any partronizing was to be done, Acheson preferred to do it. Some people who watched the two of them together over the years believed that Acheson patronized Truman. Certainly he dealt with him with immense tact and deference. As one of the ablest advocates of his time, Acheson was undoubtedly a master at persuading Truman. "Acheson respected Truman's judgment," James Webb recalled, "but he studied Truman carefully in terms of how he could meet Truman's political needs and requirements and still preserve his own standard as to what should be done in the international field."[8]

However much all presidents may relish attention and flattery, Truman was no more tolerant of being patronized than Acheson was. His relationship with Acheson was on a sounder footing than condescension. Truman needed a strong secretary of state and usually accepted Acheson's views on foreign affairs without being putty in Acheson's hands. Acheson, having no political following of his own, needed a president who would give him leeway and unquestioned support against his enemies. Each had found the right man.

A foretaste of what lay in store for Truman and Acheson at home came soon after the president had sent the Acheson nomination to the Senate. Coincident with Acheson's public appearance before the Senate Foreign Relations Committee in January the press recalled that his name had been linked with that of Alger Hiss at hearings of a subcommittee of the House Committee on un-American Activities in August 1948. The matter moved to the center of the stage at the January Foreign Relations Committee public hearing on his nomination. Acheson then explained that the relationship between himself and Hiss had been misrepresented. Nevertheless, he said that Hiss, though now under indictment, was his friend. Headlines resulting from the public hearing of the Foreign Relations Committee heralded the Acheson-Hiss friendship.

The troublesome issue had originated in the testimony that former Assistant Secretary of State Adolf A. Berle, Jr., no great friend of Acheson's, had given in 1948 before the subcommittee of the House Committee on un-American Activities.

In 1939 Berle, then in charge of security in the State Department, had been approached by Whittaker Chambers after Chambers had abandoned the Communist underground to become an informer. Chambers gave Berle a list of members of the underground. It included the names of the brothers, Alger and Donald Hiss. "Specifically," Berle testified in 1948, "I checked with Dean Acheson, and later I checked when Acheson became the assistant secretary of state and Alger Hiss became his executive assistant. . . . Acheson said that he had known the family and these two boys from childhood and could vouch for them absolutely."[9] Berle also talked of an Acheson group with a "pro-Russian point of view."[10] Although this statement was without substance, it planted the idea that Acheson had left-wing tendencies.

When, in January, the Foreign Relations Committee publicly questioned Acheson about his relationship with Alger Hiss, Acheson explained that Berle had confused Alger with Donald. It was Donald Hiss who had been Acheson's assistant in the State Department from the time Acheson arrived in 1941 until Donald Hiss departed in March 1944. Acheson testified that never until the spring of 1946 was Alger Hiss in any branch of the State Department for which Acheson was responsible. But that spring Alger Hiss was put in charge of a division dealing with American relations with the United Nations. Between then and the end of 1946, when he left the department for the Carnegie Endowment for International Peace, Alger Hiss did report to Acheson on those occasions when Byrnes was absent and Acheson was acting secretary.

After Berle had talked to him, Acheson testified, he, Acheson, had asked Donald Hiss "to take time to reflect and let me know whether he had any associations which would embarrass me. He did take time to reflect. He told me he had no such associations." Acheson accepted Donald Hiss's word and never had any reason afterward to doubt it.[11]

At the time of Acheson's testimony in 1949 Donald Hiss was one of his law partners at Covington, Burling, Rublee, Acheson & Shorb, a firm in which Donald was to remain for many years. Although less brilliant than his older brother, he had followed in Alger's footsteps to Johns Hopkins and Harvard Law School. Whereas Alger had been clerk to Holmes while the justice was on the Supreme

Court, Donald served in the same position after Holmes had retired. It was through Holmes that Acheson had met the brothers. Until Acheson went to the State Department in 1941, however, he said, his acquaintance with Alger was slight.[12]

Acheson told the senators at the public hearing on his nomination that he and Alger Hiss were friends and remained friends. His friendship, Acheson said, was not easily given nor readily withdrawn.

The day after the hearing, the Foreign Relations Committee met with Acheson in executive session. The record, which was not released until 1976, provides a rare sample of the atmosphere enveloping Truman at the start of his second term.

Senator Arthur H. Vandenberg, Republican, of Michigan, the ranking minority member of the committee and the man on whom the administration relied for Republican support of foreign policy measures applying to Europe, expressed shock over the prominent display in the press of the Acheson–Alger Hiss relationship. In considering whether to recommend confirmation of Acheson, Vandenberg said, the relationship saddled the committee with a serious problem in public relations. Acheson's testimony, he said, would require amplification "lest it be construed as so blind a friendship as to be dangerous to the public interest."

Acheson replied that the puzzling aspects of the Hiss case, as well as Hiss's guilt or innocence, had yet to be resolved in a trial. The very refrain he then sounded in discussing his attitude toward Hiss foreshadowed a public comment of his at a State Department press conference a year later—a comment that was to be a political calamity for President Truman. Acheson told Vandenberg that he had not wished "to associate myself with the people who have been throwing stones" at Hiss when he was in trouble.

"I am not willing to say that he is not my friend," Acheson testified. "He was, and is—not a close friend, but I am not going to abandon him and throw rocks when he is in trouble. If it is proved that this feeling I have about him is quite unfounded, that I have been misled, I shall be glad to say so at that time, but I am not willing to say so now."

Senator Walter F. George, Democrat, of Georgia, spoke up.

"I do want you to see," he told Acheson, "the position we are in, crudely expressed, from the standpoint of critics of the administration and critics of the [State] Department—severe critics. They are ready to believe almost anything— that maybe there is a Communist cell over there that is operating day by day. Of course, I don't think that is true, but nevertheless the state of the public mind is a fact that one just cannot quite overlook."

Senator Alexander Wiley, Republican, of Wisconsin, declared that in the last twenty years a certain "intellectual bankruptcy" had befallen the country— a condition in which "men have acquired great brilliant brains but they have lost some of the ancient landmarks, such as love of country, love of morality, love of honesty—and it is all because of the integration in their thinking of what they call the Marxist concept of communism."

Vandenberg then had an inspiration as to how Acheson and the committee could pick their way through the dilemma posed by Hiss. The committee, he told Acheson, could "ask you for a straight-shooting statement of your estimate of communism *per se.*"

Forthwith Acheson made a speech, calling communism "one of the basically corrupting ideologies, doctrines, movements, which has happened to the human mind over a long period of time." Communism, he continued, was "basically evil" in its assault upon freedom and truth. As a tool of the Soviets' foreign policy, however, Acheson said, communism was effective. "It is," he explained, "a method by which they can penetrate into countries which are not contiguous to them and where the power of their arms does not carry."

The committee was pleased with the commentary, but the chairman, Senator Tom Connally, Democrat, of Texas, found it too long for the newspapers.

"What do you think," he inquired, "of making a short, swift statement of general attitudes regarding communism and totalitarianism for release from this secret meeting to the press?"

Two sentences would do the trick, Vandenberg interposed. On the basis of the Acheson discourse Vandenberg suggested the following statement:

> Communism as a doctrine is economically fatal to a free society and to human rights and fundamental freedoms. Communism as an aggressive factor in world conquest is fatal to independent governments and to free people.

"I agree with it, senator," Acheson said. "I should be perfectly happy to have you say that that is what I said."[13]

A statement by Acheson was issued in substantially Vandenberg's language. This ritual of self-purification having been performed, the Foreign Relations Committee unanimously recommended that Acheson be confirmed as secretary of state. On January 18 the Senate voted for confirmation, 83 to 6. Those opposed, all Republicans, were, in large part, voting in protest against the administration's China policy.

China was too chaotic in January 1949 for Truman and his new secretary of state to attempt to enunciate a new American policy. In any event China was not considered an immediate threat to the security of the United States. As had been true since the end of the Second World War, American policymakers at the start of Truman's second term were most concerned with the threat of Soviet power and the safety of Western Europe, particularly Berlin.

Ostensibly in protest against a new currency introduced in the Allied sectors of the city but largely to prevent establishment of a West German government allied with the United States and Western Europe, the Soviets had blockaded Berlin in July 1948. Allied rail, water, and vehicular routes to Berlin were cut, leaving only an air corridor as a lifeline from the west to the former German capital. The Allies retaliated with a counter-blockade against shipments from their zones of occupation to the Soviet zone. Truman decided that the United States would stand its ground in Berlin, but he rejected proposals for an American military thrust through the blockade lest it cause war with the Soviet Union.

Even so, the dangerous confrontation in Berlin kept fear of war alive through the summer and fall of 1948.

The Western powers submitted the Berlin dispute to the United Nations Security Council. The Soviets maintained, however, that the proper agency to deal with the question not only of the blockade but also of Germany as a whole was the Council of Foreign Ministers, created at Potsdam. The Allies agreed to a meeting of the foreign ministers but on the condition that the Soviet blockade first be lifted. The Soviets demurred. The blockade continued. By the time of the inauguration, therefore, the situation in Berlin was still perilous, but fear of war had subsided. Then, unexpectedly, nine days after Acheson was sworn in January 21, the conflict took a sudden new turn.

Passing through Paris, Lieutenant General Walter Bedell Smith, United States ambassador to Moscow, had had a drink at the Meurice Hotel with Kingsbury Smith, European manager of the old International News Service. The ambassador had remarked to the journalist, as the latter recalled his words, that the Soviets "wanted to get off the hook in Berlin but did not know how to." After mulling this over, Kingsbury Smith resorted to a then familiar journalistic practice of trying to elicit news from Stalin by cable.[14] Smith sent a message inquiring of Stalin whether, if the Americans, British, and French should agree to postpone the establishment of a West German state pending a meeting of the Council of Foreign Ministers, the Soviets would lift their blockade.

On January 30 Stalin replied that should the three Western powers agree to such a delay pending a meeting of the council, the Soviet government would see no obstacle to lifting the blockade, provided the Allies ended the counter-blockade simultaneously.[15]

In truth, the Soviets' blockade had backfired on them. To begin with, it was not effective because of the airlift. On the other hand, the Allied counter-blockade dealt a hardship to the Soviet zone. Instead of thwarting the movement toward a West German state and hampering the Marshall Plan, the Soviet blockade had, if anything, hastened the day of a West German government and of the North Atlantic Treaty.[16] Furthermore the drama and comradery of the airlift had drawn the West Germans and Americans together in the winter of 1948–49. "From then on," wrote the German historian Alfred Grosser, "no foreign policy was acceptable to the West Germans except on the basis of meriting the Americans' confidence so that they would continue to extend their protection over Berlin and West Germany."[17]

The arresting aspect of the reply to Kingsbury Smith was that Stalin did not list among the conditions for ending the blockade the usual Soviet demand for elimination of the new Allied currency in Berlin. Truman agreed to a suggestion by Acheson that Dr. Phillip Jessup, then deputy chief of the United States Mission to the United Nations, sound out Jacob A. Malik, the Soviet permanent representative at the United Nations, as to whether Stalin's omission of the currency question was significant.[18] Jessup put the question to Malik in mid-February in the delegates lounge at the United Nations headquarters, then at Lake Success, Long Island. Malik said he did not know whether the omission was important but would inquire.[19]

A month later his secretary telephoned Jessup and asked him to call at the New York office of the Soviet delegation. Malik had the answer Jessup was hoping for: Stalin's omission of the currency issue was "not accidental"—the matter could be discussed by the foreign ministers as part of the whole Berlin question. In other words, the Soviets were ready to negotiate. Stalin took the position, however, that the creation of a new West German state should be postponed pending a meeting of the foreign ministers.

The United States would not make such a commitment, nor would it agree to abandon plans for formation of a West German government. On the other hand, the United States and its allies agreed that preparations for the new state would not preclude a new four-power agreement on the whole of Germany. The Western powers prevailed. On May 4 the United States, the Soviet Union, Great Britain, and France issued a communiqué announcing the end of the Berlin blockade and counter-blockade as of May 12, 1949. The Council of Foreign Ministers was to meet in Paris on May 23.

At the opening of the conference, Andrei Y. Vishinsky, the new Soviet foreign minister, proposed a return to the status of Potsdam and the agreement on joint control of all Germany by the Americans, British, French, and Soviets through the Allied Control Council.[20] The council had broken down in the 1948 disputes. Vishinsky proposed to revive it and create a subsidiary German state council as a central economic and administrative organ for the whole of Germany. The interallied Kommandatura of Berlin would be re-established to knit the former German capital together after the disruption of the blockades. In addition Vishinsky reasserted the long-standing Soviet demands for increased reparations and a share in control of the Ruhr, rejected by the Allies in 1945.

With the support of British Foreign Secretary Ernest Bevin and French Foreign Secretary Robert Schuman, Acheson spurned Vishinsky's proposals. The conditions envisioned at Potsdam no longer existed, Acheson said. Mistrustful of the Soviets and unwilling to compromise on Germany, the secretary of state was determined to avoid any more Soviet vetoes and any further reparations payments to the Soviet Union that might weaken the West German economy.

Coming to the nub of the American attitude toward Germany, Acheson said that great progress had been made in the Western zones and the West Germans were prepared to institute self-government. The Vishinsky proposals, he concluded, would simply revive procedures and institutions that had failed disastrously.

Because of Germany's place in the heart of Europe, because of Germany's industrial and military potential, and because Germany was the point at which Allied and Soviet interests and power came face to face, German policy was one of the highest responsibilities of Truman as president. As he had entrusted the development of this policy to Byrnes in the fluid aftermath of Potsdam, he now relied on Acheson when the structure of postwar Germany was settling into permanent mold. Acheson's views on Germany, therefore, were crucial. To summarize them he himself dictated a memorandum dated May 10 titled "An Approach to the CFM [Council of Foreign Ministers]."

"Our major premise," he said, "is that our concern is with the future of Europe and not with the German problem by itself." The overriding goal was the integration of Germany into a democratic Europe. What the United States sought was a permanent Western European union or association, where none currently existed, as the embodiment of the collective skills, power, resources, institutions, and traditions of the European peoples outside the Soviet sphere. An alliance between the United States and a Western European union would have a look of invincibility. The Marshall Plan had been designed in part as an economic underpinning of such a union, and the proposed North Atlantic Treaty, it was hoped, would provide the military sinews.

The Western Allies, Acheson noted, had made a good deal of progress toward integrating the western half of Germany with the rest of Western Europe, "and we shall not jeopardize this progress by seeking a unified Germany as in itself good." In other words, the unification of Germany was not the goal unless Germany could be unified on terms satisfactory to the West. The test "is whether the unification can be achieved under conditions which help and do not retard the unification of a free Europe."[21]

The Policy Planning Staff of the State Department under George F. Kennan had recommended to Acheson a solution in which the Soviets and the Western powers would mutually withdraw their occupation forces from the heart of a reunified Germany to its fringes. The purpose would be to lessen tension and give a provisional German government under four-power control a chance to function.[22] As Acheson noted in his memorandum of May 10, he, too, would have wished to see Soviet troops withdrawn from Eastern Germany, unlikely as that development would have been at the time, yet he feared the West might have to yield too much in return. "The net withdrawal of all troops in Germany," he observed, "would do harm to our objectives and to the progress we have made toward them."

He gave his memorandum to Truman to read, and Truman approved it. Five days before the opening of the foreign ministers conference, Acheson had reviewed before the National Security Council the development of West Germany since the war. He emphasized that the United States had no intention of abandoning the gains that had been made—a statement that also won the president's approval. The secretary of state made it plain that the United States and its allies would take a hard stance at Paris.[23] This resolve was reflected in position papers prepared in the State Department, exuding determination to push ahead with the West German republic. According to the position papers, any agreement on a future government of all of Germany would have to be in character with the constitution and laws being drafted for the West German government. This would entail, improbably, Soviet assent to an Eastern half of Germany with a population as politically free as the population in the Western half. On these proposed terms, the permanent division of Germany was a foregone conclusion.

The United States delegation to Paris was embued with the notion that the Soviet objective was to prevent the integration of West Germany into the economic and political structure of Western Europe. Complete domination of Germany was still seen as the ultimate Soviet purpose. As against Vishinsky's "back-to-Potsdam" plan, as Acheson called it, the Western powers recommended free elections leading to unification of Germany under the proposed West German constitution. The recommendation specified freedom of assembly, freedom from arbitrary arrest, freedom of the press, freedom of speech, freedom of elections, and independence of the judiciary in all parts of a unified Germany.[24]

Vishinsky said that the recommendation demonstrated that the West did not want an agreement with the Soviet Union. He rejected it. The Soviets were no more willing to weaken their control over East Germany than the Allies were willing to relinquish any of their gains in West Germany. The Berlin blockades and the airlift were over, but as Truman said in a statement after the Paris conference had ended, "real progress for the unification of Germany and its people was impossible."[25] Both sides continued on their way in a divided Europe, where far-reaching developments were now taking shape.

4. *The North Atlantic Treaty*

T HE NORTH ATLANTIC TREATY (still the cornerstone of United States policy in Europe but an increasingly shaky one of late) was signed by twelve nations in Washington on April 4, 1949. At a state dinner for the assembled diplomats that night in the Carlton Hotel, President Truman offered a toast.* "I think," he said, "we have really passed a milestone in history today. . . ."[1]

For the United States the milestone that had been passed was the policy of no permanent alliances outside the Western Hemisphere, which had been followed pratically since George Washington's Farewell Address on September 17, 1796.† The North Atlantic Treaty, under which the United States, Canada, and ten European signatories resolved "to unite their efforts for collective defense," was the very end of the old American isolationism.

United States membership in the pact was the culmination of America's resolve after the Second World War to participate in the enforcement of peace for the sake of its own security rather than to retire behind the oceans as the United States had done after 1918. In the ensuing years of isolationism, aggression had spread from Manchuria to Ethiopia to the Rhineland and finally to Pearl Harbor. The lesson the American people drew was that henceforth their power and influence must be exerted for the prevention of war. As the lesson was embodied in the North Atlantic Treaty, this meant that an aggressor must be deterred from picking off one nation after another in the manner of Adolf Hitler until the whole of Western civilization was in jeopardy. This time, as provided in article 5, an armed attack on any member of the pact was to be regarded as an attack upon all.

"It is a simple document," Truman said at the ceremony of the signing of the treaty in the Departmental Auditorium that April 4, "but if it had existed in 1914 and 1939, supported by the nations who are represented here today, I believe it would have prevented the acts of aggression which led to two world wars."

Through the treaty, he explained, "we seek to establish freedom from aggression and from the use of force in the North Atlantic community. . . . In

---

*Owing to renovation work at the White House, state dinners were held elsewhere in Truman's second term.

†A supposedly permanent alliance with France, entered into on February 6, 1778, was terminated by the United States on September 30, 1800.

this pact, we hope to create a shield against aggression and the fear of aggression. . . ."[2]

The enthusiasm with which the American people embraced the United Nations in 1945, in contrast to the Senate's refusal to approve the covenant of the League of Nations in 1919 and 1920, had made collective security a virtue at last. Hence as the menace of Stalin took on for many Americans the appearance of the menace of Hitler, the stigma long attached to "entangling alliances" faded.[3] Public acceptance of the North Atlantic Treaty was furthered by the fact that, as in the case of the Inter-American Treaty of Reciprocal Assistance, signed at Rio de Janeiro on September 2, 1947, it conformed with article 51 of the United Nations Charter. In this article the charter recognizes the right of individual and collective self-defense against armed attack until the United Nations Security Council has taken measures to restore peace. The administration, therefore, could—and did—present the North Atlantic Treaty as a legitimate application of regional collective self-defense, buttressing the United Nations, and not as a traditional military alliance, even though the pact was intended to restore the balance of power in Europe, which was then a major goal of United States foreign policy.[4]

Although the North Atlantic Treaty marked a point of departure in American history as well as a major advancement in the foreign policy of the Truman administration, it had evolved slowly out of the disintegration of the Grand Alliance against Hitler. The rift between the Soviet Union, on the one hand, and the Western Allies, on the other, over the status of Poland and Eastern Europe, over the independence of Iran, and over control of the Black Sea Straits had to all intents and purposes brought an end by 1946 to mutual concessions toward a postwar settlement. Still more important, the postwar agreement among the United States, Great Britain, the Soviet Union, and France for joint four-power control of Germany had gradually fallen apart, causing a serious confrontation in the heart of Europe between the Soviet Union and the Allied powers.

In 1947, under the Truman Doctrine, the United States assumed the protective British role in Greece and Turkey and provided military and economic assistance to contain the possible spread of Soviet influence to those two countries. Acheson confided to the European leaders at the time of the signing of the North Atlantic Treaty that the Truman Doctrine was the turning point, in his opinion. When Truman had decided to take a strong stand on Turkey, Acheson said, it was the signal for the administration to go ahead, meaning, presumably, on the defense of Western Europe.[5] The Marshall Plan, which followed, had as one of its purposes the rescue of Western Europe from the dangers of communism through restoration of the economies of Western democracies.

After efforts to revive four-power rule of Germany collapsed at a London foreign ministers' conference in December 1947, Great Britain, France, the United States, and the Benelux countries (Belgium, the Netherlands, and Luxembourg) became convinced that rearmament of Western Europe was needed to achieve security. As Ernest Bevin put it, "progress in the economic field will not in itself suffice to call a halt to the Russian threat.'' Without a military shield Europe was thought vulnerable.

The initiative for the North Atlantic Treaty came from Europe, specifically from Bevin with the support of French Defense Minister Georges Bidault, both of whom were apprehensive about new threats from the Soviet Union. Bevin proposed to Secretary of State Marshall that ''we must devise some Western democratic system comprising the Americans, ourselves, France, Italy etc., and of course the Dominions.'' The essential task, Bevin said, ''was to create confidence in Western Europe that further Communist inroads would be stopped.'' Marshall assented to discussions that might lead to such an arrangement. The Allies, he said, had no choice but to proceed with them.

On January 13, 1948, Lord Inverchapel, the British ambassador in Washington, wrote Marshall to say that Bevin was proposing to the French that Britain and France jointly offer a mutual defense treaty to the Benelux countries as a first step toward a broader defense of the North Atlantic community. Inverchapel enclosed a memorandum from Bevin, who explained that ''we should seek to form with the backing of the Americas and the Dominions a Western Democratic system comprising Scandinavia, the Low Countries, France, Italy, Greece and possibly Portugal. As soon as circumstances permit we should, of course, wish also to include Spain and Germany without whom no Western system can be complete.''

Marshall, who played a major role in bringing the United States into an alliance with Europe, formally notified Bevin of American willingness to support creation of a Western European Union consisting of Britain, France, and the Benelux countries.[6] By the end of January 1948 Bevin was pressing Washington to join London in a general commitment to go to war against an aggressor.

The Communist seizure of power in Czechoslovakia in February ignited fear and outrage in the United States and Western Europe. Bidault urged upon the United States a firm military alliance against the Soviet Union.[7] As time passed, Washington was fairly beseiged by requests from European countries for arms.

Two days after Prague fell to the Communists, a new shock jolted the West when Stalin invited Finland to sign a mutual assistance pact. ''We are actively studying what the US Govt. might do,'' Marshall cabled the United States embassy in Rome March 11, ''to assist in checking further Communist expansion in Europe through steps designed to strengthen confidence of non-Communist elements and deter Soviets from further fifth-column action along Czech model.'' Correctly assessing the mood in America after the Communist seizure of Czechoslovakia, he added, ''We believe US public opinion now prepared support strong measures.''[8]

The same day an *aide-mémoire* arrived from the British embassy in Washington; it notified Marshall that Norway feared a Soviet demand for a mutual assistance pact and, determined to refuse, had inquired as to what help Norway might receive from the Allies if it were attacked. The British *aide-mémoire* urged immediate steps, ''before Norway goes under,'' toward conclusion of an Atlantic pact "in which all the countries directly threatened by a Russian move to the Atlantic could participate. . . ."[9] The next day Marshall asked Lord Inverchapel to notify Bevin that "we are prepared to proceed at once in the joint discussions on the establishment of an Atlantic security system."[10]

On March 17, 1948, Britain, France, Belgium, the Netherlands, and Luxembourg signed in Brussels a fifty-year collective defense treaty. Though of itself a feeble shield against Soviet power, it was, as Marshall told the signatories, "an essential prerequisite to any wider arrangement in which other countries including the United States might play a part."[11] On that same March 17 Truman, reacting to the Communist seizure in Prague, appeared before a joint session of Congress. He asked for the restoration of selective service and declared that the Brussels pact deserved the full support of the United States "by appropriate means."[12]

By the time of the Czechoslovakian crisis, the idea had taken root on both sides of the Atlantic that the United States not only must join in a mutual defense treaty with Western Europe but must help the Western Allies rearm. On March 30, 1948, the National Security Council circulated NSC 7, a study suggesting that the United States should undertake a counter-offensive against "Soviet-directed world communism" by, among other means, strengthening non-Communist nations, priority going to those of Western Europe. Such assistance, the report suggested, should take several forms: supply of military equipment, provision of machine tools to rehabilitate munitions industries abroad, and technical information to facilitate standardization of arms.[13] Throughout that troubled spring of the Czech crisis and the Berlin blockades, the twin concepts of a North Atlantic Treaty and a military assistance program to put steel in it were shaped by the administration. But Congress was still debating the Marshall Plan. It was an election year. The congressional session would be shorter than usual.

The skeleton of a treaty was drawn during Anglo-American-Canadian talks in the spring of 1948. On the strength of the Vandenberg Resolution, these talks, under Lovett's guidance, were expanded to include France and the Benelux countries. Vandenberg cautioned Lovett that the outlines of the clause providing for the contracting parties to take armed action against an aggressor were too broad. The Senate, Vandenberg said, would not consent to a treaty that automatically committed the United States to go to war. Lovett then made it clear to the foreign representatives that the treaty must recognize that in the United States, Congress alone had the power to declare war.

When Acheson took over, he worked with Connally and Vandenberg to satisfy senators through the language of article 5—keystone of the pact. According to the final wording, the parties agreed that "an armed attack against one or more of them in Europe or North America shall be considered an attack against all." If such an attack occurred, it was agreed that each of the parties "in the exercise of the right of individual or collective self-defense recognized by Article 51 of the United Nations Charter, will assist the Party or Parties so attacked by taking forthwith, individually and in concert with the other Parties, such action as it deems necessary, including the use of armed force, to restore and maintain the Security of the North Atlantic area.''

"This does not mean,'' Acheson said in a letter of transmittal to Truman, "that the United States would automatically be at war if we or one of the other parties . . . were attacked. Under our Constitution, the Congress alone has the power to declare war. The United States would be obligated by the treaty to take promptly the action which it deemed necessary to restore and maintain the security of the North Atlantic area. That decision as to what action was necessary would naturally be taken in accordance with our Constitutional processes.''

But Acheson also said that "in the world of today the security of the parties . . . is so interdependent that an armed attack on any one of them would be in effect an attack on all.''[14]

Acheson testified at an executive session of the Senate Foreign Relations Committee on February 18, 1949. Concerning article 5, he said that "what is done here, and all that can be done, is to enter into a commitment about a policy''—the policy of collective self-defense, leaving it to each party to decide whether an attack had occurred and what should be done about it. Aggressors, Acheson noted, would know "that this decision of policy has been made. And I think they can have no question whatever that if an armed attack was made on one of these nations and it was perfectly clear what was happening, that the Congress of the United States would go through with this policy without any difficulty.''

Would the European Allies be left in doubt, the secretary of state was asked, simply because the United States could decide for itself what action to take?

"I think they have every confidence,'' he replied, "that the executive and the legislative branches of the government are serious about action of this sort. . . .

"If the government of the United States, in their solemn way, as set up by the Constitution, says, 'We are agreeing to an agreement here by which we say that when this armed attack occurs we will do what we deem necessary to restore the security, to maintain the security of the North Atlantic area,' everybody in the world knows that the United States will not do something which it knows is not adequate.''[15]

"If these countries are attacked by Russia,'' said Senator Millard E. Tydings, Democrat, of Maryland, at an executive session of the committee on March 8, "I think we will get in on the ground floor and get in our attack right away.''[16]

Senator Theodore Francis Green, Democrat, of Rhode Island, said: "There is a very strong implication there, as it is written, it seems to me, almost unavoidably, that we would have to use armed force. We would still be left, I think, to say how much and at what time, maybe, if it is a situation that you can time at all.''[17]

"Aggression cannot take place in the face of this strengthened [economic] recovery, this strengthened self-defense by some coup, by some simple measure,'' Acheson told the committee on April 21. "An aggressor has got to be prepared, really, to start World War III or to abandon his aggression.''[18]

"Surely,'' Vandenberg observed to his fellow senators at the executive session on June 2, "when we signed this treaty with article 5 in it, something has happened to change the status of our obligations toward our fellow signatories. Now we are not just the free agents that we were before we signed it. . . ."[19]

Without altering the constitutional powers of the president, the treaty did—at least in the State Department's view—introduce new circumstances in which the president might feel required to use the armed forces in furtherance of American policy.

However earnestly the point was argued that the treaty did not commit the United States automatically to go to war, the question was to become moot in the near future when, as had not been foreseen in 1949, American troops were stationed in Europe as part of what was to be the North Atlantic Treaty Organization. The moment those forces were attacked, the United States would be at war.

Before the treaty was signed, the question of Italian membership caused difficulties. Truman was inclined to oppose bringing Italy in as an original signer and doubted whether the Italians should ever be included—a view shared by some of the European Allies. Grounds for opposition were obvious. Italy was not a North Atlantic nation. Because of the arms limitations clauses of the Italian peace treaty, Italy would not be able to make an early important contribution to the defense of Europe. In two world wars the Italians had not been dependable allies, having switched sides in both wars. On the other hand, the Western powers were now intent on keeping Italy from falling within the Soviet sphere through either subversion or aggression. And in land warfare in Europe, Italy would be strategically important.

Because of their common border with Italy, the French insisted on admitting the Italians. Acheson took up the problem with Truman February 28, 1949, and was apprised of the president's reluctance about Italian membership. Truman was under pressure from leading members of the Senate Foreign Relations Committee, who feared public resistance to ratification of the treaty if its scope were to include defense of a Mediterranean nation.

Truman asked Acheson to keep the Italian question open. The French, however, were threatening to pull out if Italy was not included. Acheson had to go back to Truman on March 2, therefore, and tell him that United States' objection would raise havoc. He asked Truman for authority to support Italian membership, and Truman assented.[20]

On April 4, therefore, Italy signed the treaty along with France, Norway, Denmark, Iceland, Portugal, Belgium, the Netherlands, Luxembourg, Britain, Canada, and the United States. To American strategy Denmark was important because of Greenland, a Danish territory, and Portugal was vital because of the Azores, the islands being politically part of Portugal. Eight days after the treaty was signed, Truman sent it to the Senate.

To a large extent the debate there was dominated by doubts about the still-unveiled military assistance program. While its scope was not known to Congress, because Truman delayed submission of the arms program until the Senate had acted on the treaty, critical senators bristled at the thought of a new foreign aid program on top of the multi-billion-dollar Marshall Plan. They used the pro-spective military assistance program as a weapon for trying to defeat the treaty. The treaty, they charged, would obligate the United States at its own expense to rearm Europe under article 3, which was the provision that tied the arms program to the treaty. It provided that the parties "separately and jointly, by means of continuous and effective self-help and mutual aid, will maintain and develop their individual and collective capacity to resist armed attack."

At public hearings of the Senate Foreign Relations Committee before the treaty went to the floor, Acheson first insisted that article 3 did not commit the United States to the military assistance program. But he said that the United States could and should provide military assistance to its allies. Having gone that far, however, he reassured the senators that a vote for the treaty would not bind Congress to reach the same conclusion as the Executive Branch about the arms program. But then there was more to the matter after all.

"Thus," Acheson explained, "if you ratify the pact, it cannot be said that there is no obligation to help. There is an obligation to help, but the extent, the manner and the timing is up to the honest judgment of the parties."[21] Nothing in the treaty determined how a senator must vote on the military assistance act, Acheson maintained. On the other hand, he said: "No member of the Senate, after the treaty is ratified, in exercising his judgment, can properly say to him-self, 'I do not believe in the principle of mutual assistance. I think that principle is silly and I will put it out of my mind.' That should not be done, because by ratifying this treaty, you accept that principle. . . ."[22]

When the treaty came before the Senate in early July 1949, Senator Ralph E. Flanders of Vermont, seconded by his Republican colleague from Missouri, Forrest C. Donnell, argued that article 3 morally and legally committed the United States to implement the treaty with shipments of arms. Taft informed the Senate that he would oppose the treaty in its present form because it was "inextricably involved with the arms program" and hence constituted a threat to the welfare of the American people. Taft said he would vote for the treaty if it carried a reservation denying any moral or legal obligation to provide arms.

Senate critics, however, were up against overwhelming public acceptance of the North Atlantic Treaty. On July 21 the Senate by a vote of 82 to 13 advised ratification. That was eighteen votes more than the required two-thirds majority. Seemingly in good spirits for a man who had just lost six hundred dollars playing poker over the weekend aboard the presidential yacht *Williamsburg*, Truman signed the instrument of ratification on July 25.[23]

The gathering of the European leaders in Washington in early April for the signing of the treaty had achieved another important goal as well. For some time the Allies had been unable to agree among themselves on terms for establishing a West German government. On April 7, three days after the signing, Bevin, Schuman, and Acheson called on Truman and told him they had reached com-plete accord. The agreements mainly concerned organizational changes that would have to be made as military government ended in West Germany, as well as revised sets of supervisory controls to be instituted by the Allies.[24] The occasion was a gratifying one for the president despite his dislike of the blunt and often tactless Bevin. Among other things, Bevin had angered Truman in 1947 by accusing him in the House of Commons of having impeded Palestine negotiations by catering to the Jewish vote in the United States.[25] Time had not soothed the president's feelings. The British foreign secretary was a bull in a china shop, Truman told his staff early in 1949, speaking of events in the Middle East. A week later, again on the same subject, Truman said, according to Eben Ayers, "he didn't like 'the s-- o- b----,' which he has said before."[26]

Still the White House meeting of April 7 came off happily. Truman said that the three-power agreement on a West German government was the best thing that had happened in his presidency because of its bearing on future peace and prosperity.[27] The North Atlantic Treaty itself also constituted a further large step toward integration of West Germany with the rest of Western Europe.

After the accord on Germany had been reached in Washington, the West German Parliamentary Council in Bonn approved the constitution for the future Federal Republic of Germany on May 8, 1949, four years exactly after the surrender of Nazi Germany.

The second act of this drama followed swiftly. In October the Communist-dominated German Democratic Republic was established in East Germany under Soviet auspices. Thus as one of the great consequences of the Second World War, two Germanies existed in the heart of Europe in political, economic, and ideological conflict with each other.

Four days after the Senate had approved the North Atlantic Treaty, Truman submitted to Congress the already controversial military assistance program, unprecedented in peacetime. When Congress saw what Truman wanted, the dispute grew more rampant still, so much so that Tom Connally was to say that the new program was the most difficult foreign policy legislation to enact since the battle over the Lend-Lease Act in 1941.[28]

For a start on rearming the treaty powers in Europe and for continuing military aid for Greece, Turkey, Iran, the Philippines, and Korea, Truman requested an authorization of $1.4000 billion. Of this, $1.161 billion would be for NATO members.

In testifying before the Senate Foreign Relations Committee earlier, Acheson had explained the rationale of the military assistance program. The Western European governments, he said, anticipated that a Soviet invasion would take time gathering momentum. Once the attack began, the Allied governments assumed that the United States would drop atomic bombs on Soviet territory to break up troop concentrations. Since some of the enemy forces might still sweep westward, the Allied countries wanted to have enough troops to deal with them.[29]

From the outset of the debate on arms, the conservatives waged a hard fight against piling up such an expensive new aid program on top of the Marshall Plan. The House of Representatives voted to cut Truman's program practically in half. Truman told his staff that some members had voted in resentment against sending money abroad when they could not get appropriations for new post offices in their own districts.[30]

More complex difficulties arose in the Senate. Taft, Truman's implacable critic, fought to cut the president's request. Taft was joined by such powerful economy-minded Democrats as Senators Richard B. Russell and Walter F. George, both of Georgia, and Harry F. Byrd of Virginia. To make matters more troublesome for the administration, the bipartisan collaboration on European issues that had prevailed in Congress during Truman's first term was being strained because the switch in party control of Congress resulting from the 1948 election had moved Tom Connally back into the chairmanship of the Foreign Relations Committee in place of Vandenberg. As had been true since the war, Washington continued to lionize Vandenberg, and Connally was jealous. On one occasion he caused a row in the White House by threatening to have the chief usher, Howell G. Crim, fired for putting Vandenberg ahead of him in a reception line. Early in 1949 Connally caused a similar scene in Blair House, insisting that since he was now chairman of the Foreign Relations Committee again, he should precede Vandenberg. Regardless, Crim stood on protocol and gave Vandenberg precedence because he had one year's seniority over Connally in the Senate.[31]

And now, in mid-1949, as a new menace to further bipartisan collaboration on European issues, Vandenberg's health was failing. He was in pain from a lesion that had been discovered on his left lung.

Although Vandenberg favored arms for Europe, he rallied strong support in the debate for changes in the Mutual Defense Assistance legislation, objecting mainly to the wide discretion given to the president to furnish military assistance "to any eligible nation." "It would virtually make him the number one war lord of the earth," the senator complained in a letter to his wife, adding, "The old bipartisan business is certainly 'out the window' on this one."[32] Truman readily agreed, according to Acheson, to revise the language of the bill so as to limit his discretion in furnishing military assistance.[33] Ultimately, the administration obtained substantially what it wanted in the way of money.

Closely related from the outset, the North Atlantic Treaty and the Mutual Defense Assistance Program thus were fixtures on the international scene by the close of 1949 but in a state barely beyond embryonic. What became familiar later as NATO—the North Atlantic Treaty Organization—could not have been glimpsed in them as they stood. The dramatic transformation was to be the result of crises unforeseen yet rapidly approaching.

5. *Forrestal, Louis Johnson, and Upheaval over National Security*

OR THREE YEARS OF tense international conditions, Truman governed in the midst of the worst feud among the armed forces that the United States has ever known.

James Forrestal, a distinguished public servant, was mentally, physically, and emotionally torn to pieces while trying as secretary of defense to stop fierce bureaucratic fighting among the three services. Only weeks before Forrestal committed suicide, Truman replaced him with the stormy Louis A. Johnson, who took the Pentagon by the throat and behaved so unmanageably that Truman had to sit him down at a desk and compel him to sign a letter of resignation.

In a personal and frequently abrasive campaign to develop American air power, Secretary of the Air Force W. Stuart Symington was often uncontrollable by his superior, Forrestal. On July 23, 1948, Forrestal went to Truman and threatened to fire Symington for insubordination over a critical speech Symington was reported to have delivered in Los Angeles.[1] Then Forrestal apologetically relented when it developed that the *New York Times* had based its report on an earlier text that Symington had discarded because it was too critical of Forrestal's policies. The Forrestal-Symington relationship, however, was troubled. Once Symington refused to support before Congress a $3.8 billion budget that Forrestal had alloted to the air force.

"Then quit," Forrestal said, as Symington later recalled his words.

"I won't support it," Symington replied, defiantly, "and I won't quit."[2]

The air force waged a relentless campaign of lobbying and propaganda to make strategic air power supreme in the American military system. The blue chip for the air force was a new bomber, the B-36, designed to carry an atomic bomb on intercontinental missions. Although the navy had developed a potent air arm in the Second World War, the air force was determined to take sole charge of strategic air warfare in the future. It fought in public and private for this objective, notwithstanding the fact that the navy was building a supercarrier, the *United States,* designed to launch and land planes capable of carrying an atomic bomb. The navy envisioned this vessel as a vehicle for its own role in strategic air warfare. In the running battle the navy established a special staff organization—Op. 23—to gather and discretely disseminate unfavorable information about the B-36. The navy considered the bomber expensive and unreliable in combat, as well as competitive to its own role.

Without informing Secretary of the Navy John L. Sullivan, Louis Johnson canceled construction of the *United States* after the keel had been laid. Sullivan resigned in a rage. At about the same time, Secretary of the Army Kenneth C. Royall, a southerner, resigned in a dispute with Johnson over racial integration of the armed forces.

In what was dubbed the revolt of the admirals, a navy officer leaked copies of official letters written by some of the country's highest navy commanders. The dramatic publication of these letters left the widespread impression that morale in the navy was sinking as the navy's role was being threatened by the way the recent unification of the armed forces was being carried out under Louis Johnson. Congressional hearings magnified the dispute, as a procession of admirals testified against the B-36 and the strategy of nuclear bombing of cities that the new bomber implied. The incident angered Truman and greatly embarrassed Johnson and Franklin P. Matthews, the new secretary of the navy, who had succeeded Sullivan.

During these same boisterous years, while he was still in office, Forrestal tried time and again to get the Joint Chiefs of Staff to agree upon the functions of the respective services. Time and again the chiefs became so mired in quarrels that they could not reach an agreement. Time and again Forrestal tried to get them to agree upon apportionment of the defense budget among the three services. Time and again agreement proved impossible.

All the while events were sliding toward a precipice in Korea.

The disorder in military policy had its origins in Truman's first term and reached a climax in the second. The causes were numerous, beginning, of course, with apprehension that the Cold War might turn into a shooting war after the United States had cut its forces from nearly 12 million at the close of the war in 1945 to 1,565,000 by the summer of 1947. Then there was the fundamental development of unification of the armed forces, so called, which Truman had edged through Congress in 1947 after monumental bureaucratic struggles.

Since 1798 the War Department and the Navy Department had been separate organizations with no common superior except the president. In the Second World War the army air forces were a part of the army, though a semi-autonomous one. Wartime experiences indicated the importance of re-establishing the army, navy, and air force under some kind of unified command. Under the much-compromised National Security Act of 1947, the Departments of the Army and the Navy and the new Department of the Air Force were designated as executive departments, each with its own secretary and all encamped within a nebulous new entity: the National Military Establishment, which was headed by a secretary of defense. Truman chose Forrestal as the first man to hold this post—a circumstance filled with irony and, ultimately, with horror for Forrestal. For the Navy Department, then headed by Forrestal as secretary of the navy, had opposed unification in the form of merger, fearing that the navy would lose to the air force its cherished role as the nation's first line of defense. The issue, therefore, was broader than the controversy over the B-36. The navy was convinced, as Admiral Arthur W. Radford later wrote, that the air force would challenge the very existence of the navy's carrier-borne air fleet. The navy was also convinced, he said, that the army was determined "to shrink the Marine Corps down to boy's size—a naval police or guard force—if it remained at all."[3]

What was ironical about Forrestal's situation was that as the then secretary of the navy fighting against merger he had thwarted Truman's desire for legislation creating a boss of the Pentagon. Under the 1947 law, which Forrestal did much to shape, the three departments retained all their powers and duties, as the navy had demanded, except for vague responsibilities conferred on the secretary of defense. The act made the secretary a weak coordinator with no deputy or assistant secretaries. Secretary of the Navy Forrestal, in other words, had helped create a situation in which Secretary of Defense Forrestal could not control the military establishment—a task that would have been gigantic under any law, or any secretary, amidst the rivalries of 1947–49.

The maneuvering for power among the three services that had dominated the debates on the National Security Act carried over into operations of the unified National Military Establishment after the legislation went into effect in September 1947. Without adequate authority to manage or to command a consensus, Forrestal was pulled this way and that. What with the demobilization of America's wartime forces, the specter of the Red Army, the destruction of the traditional European balance of power, and the crumbling of the European empires, the United States felt less secure after 1947 than it had at the end of the war. The Selective Service Act had expired on March 31, 1947. To compensate for demobilization, Truman proposed universal military training, a program under which young men would have received a year of basic training as civilians. The idea was to create a reserve "citizen army," which could have been mobilized quickly by act of Congress. Congress, however, refused to adopt such an unpopular program.

The sense of a deteriorating military position and concern over the Soviets' capability of overrunning Europe were agitating Washington. Rising costs and rapidly changing technology of aircraft and weapons and uncertainty about the decisiveness of the still minute arsenal of atomic bombs in the event of hostilities with the Soviet Union made it difficult for the Joint Chiefs of Staff to agree on plans in case of a third world war. That, in turn, made it hard to agree on roles and missions for the three services in wartime and for a proper apportionment of money among them.

Finally, the Pentagon was turned into a pressure cooker when, after the war, Truman embarked upon a course of severely restricting military spending in an effort to restore a normal peacetime economy. As domestic needs took precedence, the sudden reduction from the wartime budgets was staggering. In 1946 Truman adopted the unusual pattern of placing upon military spending a ceiling that was not to exceed one-third of the total government income.[4] Thus it became his practice in the years under consideration here to give the Pentagon every twelve months a hard-and-fast budget total and leave it to Forrestal and the services to thrash out a division of funds among the army, navy, and air force.

The guiding intelligence estimates in the immediate postwar years were that the Soviet Union was not planning war against the West but that the possibility of such aggression could not be excluded. Truman and his advisers were more concerned with the danger that the Communists, through political means, would seize power in Greece, Turkey, Italy, or France, for example. The main emphasis of Truman's policy in his first term, therefore, was on creating political stability and on strengthening with American aid the economies of supposedly vulnerable countries through the Truman Doctrine, the Marshall Plan, and aid to Nationalist China. That, of course, placed heavy burdens on the budget and was compensated for in part by reduction of military spending, since foreign economic assistance as well as armed strength was viewed as contributing to United States security. Incongruously, however, administration leaders continued both to exalt military power as essential to preservation of the peace and to assume obligations abroad that might have to be discharged with military force when that force no longer existed because of demobilization and economies.

In the pressure cooker, interservice rivalries boiled and never more so than in the case of the competition between the navy and the air force. In the general clutching for the largest share of the budgetary pie, navy–air force rivalry focused in public on the relative merits of the navy's projected supercarrier *United States* and the air force's B-36. The dispute went to the heart of critical questions. Should American strategy be built around air power and the atomic bomb in the hands of the air force? Or should the navy with its seaborne air fleets be an integral part of the air-power strategy? Would the air force alone attack an enemy with atomic bombs? Or would navy planes from carriers participate in strategic nuclear strikes? If not, what major role was left for the navy in the nuclear age? While the issue of the land-based bomber versus the supercarrier was drifting toward an explosive climax, new crises abroad brought Truman and the military into protracted conflicts over military budgets.

Despite two years of heavy demobilization, the Truman administration had followed the unprecedented course of maintaining a relatively large military establishment after the war ended. Reduced though it was, the armed force of mid-1947 was nearly five times the size of the one that had existed on the eve of the Second World War. The Communist seizure of Czechoslovakia in 1948, however, alarmed American military leaders. They were struck by the extent to which the global demands of United States foreign policy outran American military power, even with the unprecedented and expensive peacetime establishment.[5] Forrestal and the Joint Chiefs of Staff recommended that selective service be restored and Congress be asked for a supplemental appropriation to bring military strength more into line with the new challenges.

In a special message delivered to Congress personally on March 17, 1948, Truman requested revival of selective service, which Congress later enacted.[6] Instead of asking for a supplemental appropriation, he opened discussions within the Executive Branch and soon found himself at odds with the civilian and uniformed leaders in the Pentagon. Their requests for more money would have put new burdens on the budget at the very time when Truman's priority was to check inflation by cutting spending and reducing the war-swollen national debt.

Truman was disappointed by the fruits of unification. He had supposed that henceforth the secretary of defense would come to him with agreed-upon plans for national security. Instead, the president was dragged into the thicket of bitter fighting among the services. Naïvely, no doubt, Truman had hoped that unification would end all overlapping of functions among the services. That had been a principal purpose of the reform, but the goal was long in being realized. Often requests were frivolous in the eyes of Truman and the Bureau of the Budget. Truman came to suspect that interservice rivalry was partly to blame for the Pentagon's request for more money. The view became prevalent in the White House and the Bureau of the Budget that the brass were heavy spenders and blatant lobbyists for ever-larger appropriations.

President Truman occupies an important place in American history largely because he guided the United States to unprecedented international leadership in peacetime. He understood, for example, the significance of the Marshall Plan to that role. He seemed less clear in grasping the new requirements that international leadership imposed upon the American military structure, especially when it came to translating requirements into specific numbers of divisions, ships, and aircraft.[7] This was not altogether surprising, considering the differences of opinion in the Pentagon itself regarding the nature of future warfare.

After the Czechoslovakian scare, Truman called a meeting on the budget question, attended by, among others, George Marshall, who was still the secretary of state. Doubtless it was an important moment in the debate because of Truman's respect for Marshall's opinion. In a blow to Forrestal and the Joint Chiefs, Marshall said that foreign policy was based on the assumption that war would not occur. Hence, he said, the country should not plunge into military preparations lest they cause war. As usual, the course he favored was universal military training.

Marshall's comments won the president's approval. Reflecting an opinion held by the general after the latter's experience with stingy military appropriations between the two world wars, Truman warned that a large increase in funds voted in 1948 by Congress would only bring compensatory cuts in the future.[8] As he wrote to Forrestal on May 13, 1948, "it is necessary to accelerate our national defense program at a steady rate rather than to attempt an immediate very large increase."[9]

Since a balanced budget was popular, he did not want to sacrifice it for military expenditures that could not, so far as he could see, guarantee national security. If American commitments in Europe and the Far East were outstripping conventional American military power, he chose to live with the problem for the time being, fortified by the monopoly on the atomic bomb. He resisted major new outlays but did agree to a limited expansion. Working closely with the then budget director, the conservative James Webb, he agreed to ask Congress for an additional $1.5 billion only. All Truman wanted to do was strengthen the armed forces sufficiently in the wake of Czechoslovakia to signal American firmness.

With $1.5 billion, he believed, deterioration of the occupation forces could be halted, air power could be increased substantially, and more ships could be made serviceable for the navy.[10]

The moment he lifted the lid on expansion, however, the uniformed leaders descended on Forrestal with a host of requests that would have necessitated a supplemental appropriation of $9 billion, insuring a heavy budget deficit.[11] On its own, moreover, Congress voted $822 million for a start on enlarging the air force from fifty-five to seventy groups.

Without being doctrinaire, Truman had an old-fashioned predilection for accumulating a surplus in prosperous years to reduce the national debt. Population growth and his advocacy of expanded social programs would have made this course difficult enough without higher defense spending. The Republican-controlled Congress in 1948 cut taxes over Truman's veto. Thus proposals for a larger military establishment were caught between his desire for a balanced budget and Congress's unwillingness to increase taxes. Because of continuing appropriations for the Marshall Plan and funds for revived selective service, the prospect in any case was for a deficit. Truman, therefore, dug in his heels against a seventy-group air force and the $9 billion expansion favored by the Joint Chiefs of Staff.

He finally agreed to ask Congress for a supplemental appropriation of $3.1 billion and told the military leaders to their faces on May 13, 1948, that he expected them to support it, publicly and privately.[12] Congress approved the sum. Truman informed the military leaders that in accordance with Webb's advice, the next defense budget—the one for the fiscal year 1950, which would be submitted to Congress in January 1949—was to have a ceiling of $14.4 billion, excluding stockpiling.

In pondering defense spending, Truman was clearly influenced less by the strategic requirements as argued by the military leaders than by fiscal considerations raised by his conservative advisers like Webb, who was a force behind the policy of tight military budgets. Fiscal considerations had definite political consequences in terms of the taxes people would have to pay. In setting a limit on defense spending, Truman seemed rather detached from the hard strategic questions with which the military were grappling. When the military pressed him too forcefully he was apt, in his indignation, to distort their purposes, as when he complained to Edwin G. Nourse, the then chairman of the Council of Economic Advisors, that most of the military officers "would like to go back to a war footing." "We must be very careful," Truman said, "that the military does not overstep the bounds from an economic standpoint domestically."[13]

Concerning air force requests for expansion, he wrote to a friend that "we are having some difficulty with the boys who fly and who evidently think that the whole National Defense budget should be placed in the 'air' and I put air in quotation marks because that is exactly where it would be." "My principal worry," he added, "is the Two Hundred and Forty-seven Billion Dollar national debt. . . . It has always been my ambition to reduce the national debt below Two Hundred Billion Dollars in the next six years. . . ."[14] (In his State of the Union message three months earlier Truman had placed the national debt at $252 billion.)

At that time the opinion was widely held that it would be grievously inflationary to spend more than $15 billion a year on defense. This was conventional wisdom in the White House, as Charles Murphy of Truman's staff was to say.[15] Caught up in the consensus, Truman regarded $14 billion or so a year for defense as a necessary but temporary expedient. At the time it was felt that to breach the $15 billion barrier would be so inflationary as to necessitate wage and price controls, which Congress was unlikely to enact at that point.

The consensus was reinforced by another prevalent theory, espoused by some of the highest military leaders themselves, which was that the Soviet Union was deliberately trying to scare the United States into spending itself into bankruptcy.

Despite Truman's announced $14.4 billion budget ceiling for the fiscal year 1950, the three services in the summer of 1948 submitted requests totaling $30 billion. The Joint Chiefs of Staff ordered a new study, which still recommended a total of $23.6 billion in the new budget. Again Truman was dragged into the bickering but stood his ground. Forrestal appealed to Marshall for help but was disappointed. "Our policy," Marshall cabled him from a meeting in Paris, "should be to build up Western European ground forces. . . . We should not, at this stage, proceed to build up US ground forces for the express purpose of employing them in Western Europe."[16] As a last effort Forrestal proposed to Truman abandoning both the president's ceiling and the Pentagon proposals and substituting a $16.9 billion defense budget. The next morning Truman sent Webb a memorandum stating that "The 14.4 billion budget is the one we will adopt."[17]

Soberly, Forrestal wrote to former Representative Walter G. Andrews of New York:

. . . I am frank to say . . . I have the greatest sympathy with [Truman] because he is determined not to spend more than we take in in taxes. He is a hard-money man if I ever saw one, and believing, as I do that we can't afford to wreck our economy in the process of trying to fight the "cold war," there is much to be said for his thesis of holding down spending to the absolute minimum. . . .[18]

Truman's decision, then, was to reject major expansion of the armed forces in what was to prove the dangerous period beginning in 1949. A number of considerations—belief that war was not imminent, fear of inflation, Marshall's influence, the rising cost of civilian programs, the desire to avoid peaks and valleys in military spending, and uncertainty as to whether an extra billion or so would insure security—molded the decision. Truman knew, of course, that the country could not fight a war on $14.4 billion. His decision involved a calculation that the United States would not be at war in the fiscal year ending June 30, 1950. This judgment was to come within six days of being correct.

After the 1949 election, Truman was asked at a press conference whether Forrestal would remain secretary of defense. The question was prompted by published rumors that Truman would accept Forrestal's formal resignation customarily tendered by cabinet members at the start of a new term. "Mr. Forrestal has been asked to stay," Truman replied.[19]

A taut, immensely complex man, formerly president of the New York investment firm of Dillon, Read and Company, Forrestal had expected to retire from the government in 1949, partly because of the prospect that Dewey would be president. After the election, however, he was simply too much absorbed in his job to leave.

"Do you want to and expect to continue as secretary of defense?" a reporter asked Forrestal when he called on Truman on January 11, 1949.

"Yes," he said. "I am a victim of the Washington scene."[20]

A victim indeed. The 1948 campaign and the advent of the new term had opened the gates to his enemies. Converging on their target were critics of Forrestal's Wall Street background, his conservatism, his hard line against the Soviet Union, and, above all, his well-known opposition, on strategic grounds, to the recognition of Israel in 1948.

On the radio and in print, his policies, his ethics, and—even though he had, as secretary of the navy, landed with the Marines at Iwo Jima—his personal courage were assailed in what *Time* called "one of the biggest head-hunts in the history of Washington politics."[21] The magazine identified the hunters as "Communists, Zionists, Wallaceites, liberals, deserving Democrats who coveted his job and gossip columnists." The list omitted some of the most vocal hunters of them all—certain members of the White House staff, notably Truman's old friend and military aide, Major Harry H. Vaughan, who noisily recommended *his* friend, Louis Johnson, for secretary of defense. Johnson had the qualification of having been assistant secretary of war in the Roosevelt administration. More to the point, as the Democrats' chief fund raiser in the 1948 campaign, he had a special claim on Truman.

The most partisan of Truman's associates resented Forrestal's abstention from the 1948 campaign and let Truman know it.[22] Like Secretary of State Marshall, the secretary of defense believed that an official in his position should refrain from partisan activities. He had contributed to Truman's campaign— more than $2,500, according to Forrestal's biographer, Arnold R. Rogow.[23] Unfriendly Democrats, however, believed that with the right spirit he could have raised more through his Wall Street connections. Ostensibly to discuss defense problems, he had called privately on his acquaintance, Tom Dewey, the Republican nominee, two or three times in the latter half of 1948. Furthermore, according to Arthur Krock of the *New York Times,* Forrestal in anticipation of a Dewey victory had favored preparations for an efficient transition between administrations.[24] From all that it was but a short step to Vaughan's loud aspersions on Forrestal's loyalty to Truman.

For the president the situation with regard to Forrestal had taken on other troubling aspects also. The relationship between the two men had been strained in the struggles over the defense budget. For some time, moreover, the secretary of defense had been manifesting, at least in Truman's opinion, increasing indecisiveness and inability to keep the armed services firmly in line. Once the president was so exasperated that he wrote a curt note to Forrestal about a problem, saying, ''That is your responsibility.''[25]

Then in the weeks after the inauguration, signs of irrational behavior by Forrestal were reported to Truman, who was himself mystified when the secretary of defense would on occasion telephone him several times a day on the same subject. To Secretary of the Treasury John W. Snyder and others, Forrestal, now in a visibly nervous and fatigued state, complained that his telephone was being tapped, even when inspection proved otherwise. He often voiced fears that he was being pursued by Zionist, Communist, and FBI agents. Snyder, a friend and admirer of Forrestal's, felt bound to mention this behavior to the president, who was surely hearing about it from others as well.[26] In any case, therefore, the mental condition of the secretary of defense would have forced his departure from the cabinet soon. On March 3, 1949, Truman announced the resignation of Forrestal and nominated Johnson as Forrestal's successor. He was a man whom Forrestal despised and distrusted. The appointment was made after Truman conveyed to Johnson through Snyder the president's expectation that Johnson would be a ''team player''—a preposterous expectation, as it developed.[27]

Bald and square-shouldered, Louis Johnson, two hundred pounds of power, competence, acerbity, wile, and bumptiousness, hit the Pentagon like a thunderstorm. Workmen obstructed passage of a main corridor on the Potomac River front of the building for days as Johnson—''to show who was boss,'' he said later—evicted army officials from the largest office in the place and had it renovated as his own.[28] As if in celebration of his service as a captain of infantry in France in the First World War, he appropriated the desk of the late General John J. Pershing, commander of the American Expeditionary Force of 1917–18. Across its surface Johnson barked at generals, issued commands, and aggressively set about to show that if James Forrestal could not control the Pentagon and enforce unification of the armed forces, Louis Johnson would.

A natural leader, organizer, and politician, Johnson had begun a career in law in Clarksburg, West Virginia, with the firm of Steptoe & Johnson, which became over the years a large organization with a principal office in Washington. At twenty-six, Johnson was elected majority leader in his first term in the West Virginia House of Delegates—an early venture in politics that was interrupted by the First World War. After the war Johnson fought his way up to the then politically influential position of national commander of the American Legion, a post he held in 1932–33. It was at American Legion gatherings that he and Truman first met. Johnson moved into national Democratic circles in the Roosevelt administration. Using the Legion as a stepping-stone, he became assistant secretary of war in 1937 but resigned in bitterness three years later when Roosevelt, for political reasons, passed him over for appointment as secretary of war.

Eight years later Johnson's dream of rising to the top of the military establishment—and beyond—was revived. After a series of fund-raising meetings at the White House and the Democratic national headquarters in 1948, he emerged as the man who was to chair the Democratic Finance Committee in the campaign when other more prominent Democrats had declined. By all signs he was laboring for a loser. Instead, he played an important part in bringing about one of the most sensational election victories in history. It is not surprising, therefore, that during inauguration week he made the rounds of the Democratic state delegations who were in Washington for the occasion, asking their help in bringing his name before Truman for consideration as secretary of defense.[29]

Again, as in the Roosevelt years, Johnson seemed, when appointed secretary, to be on his way up in Washington—but this time to even greater heights. Speculation was rife that he was aiming for the Democratic presidential nomination in 1952 with a political base consisting of conservatives, the American Legion, and a business community grateful for the economies he was determined to impose in the Pentagon in accordance with Truman's policy. The speculation was not fanciful. When Brigadier General Louis H. Renfrow, one of the several old American Legion colleagues whom Johnson had brought to the Pentagon as assistants, gave instructions on behalf of the new secretary of defense, he would sometimes explain, "We've got to do it the way that helps the boss get to be president."[30] Truman, who was eligible to run again but had not made his intentions known, told his staff dryly in August of 1949 that Johnson was a candidate for president in 1952.[31] "Louis began to show an inordinate egotistical desire to run the whole government," Truman observed later.[32]

In another way, especially trying for Truman, the appointment of Johnson was bad medicine. Almost instantly, animosity flared between the new secretary of defense and Secretary of State Acheson. A more dissimilar pair could not have been placed in the same harness than the urbane, intellectual, lawyerly Acheson and the abrasive, cocksure, hyper-ambitious Johnson. Their relationship grew steadily worse. The time came when the two were hardly on speaking terms. In a period of difficulties abroad, Johnson reduced relations between the Departments of State and Defense to the most formal liaison. The worst of the feud was to center on policy on China and, more particularly, on Formosa.

The two men also differed on the Japanese peace treaty, but their first vociferous clash occurred over contingency plans drawn in case the Soviets reimposed a Berlin blockade after the settlement announced in May. After a National Security Council paper had been completed for Truman's approval, Acheson had a change made in wording. When Johnson discovered it, he thundered at Acheson at a meeting, charging that the secretary of state was trying to usurp control of the NSC. At Johnson's insistence a protesting letter was sent to Truman. The president's decision was a poor clue to what lay ahead: he sided with Johnson. Language that had been suggested by Acheson was eliminated. Truman found another way of satisfying Acheson's wishes.[33]

Johnson did move into a position to become a more powerful secretary of defense than Forrestal had been, because at Truman's request Congress made the office a much stronger one, reformed along lines that still exist. The inadequacy of the National Security Act of 1947 had become so painfully evident that

Forrestal himself had urged that it be strengthened. In 1949 the nebulous National Military Establishment was converted into the Department of Defense, a full-fledged executive department, whose secretary, a true boss and no mere co-ordinator, exercised direction, authority, and control, aided by a deputy secretary and three assistant secretaries. The army, navy, and air force were stripped of their status as independent executive departments and became military departments within the Department of Defense. Created, too, was the post of chairman of the Joint Chiefs of Saff as a nonvoting presiding officer over that body. General Omar N. Bradley, the army chief of staff and the famous commander of American ground forces in Europe in the Second World War, was appointed as the first chairman, a position he was to hold through the remainder of the Truman administration. The military establishment thus was soundly reorganized. Legislation, however, could not produce true unification of the three services. Unification was a state of mind, and, as Johnson soon discovered, the military mind was a long way from being unified.

He landed in the Pentagon in the thick of the navy–air force feud. The National Security Act and Truman's executive order implementing it had assigned the conduct of strategic air warfare to the air force. Because of its powerful air arm, however, the navy persisted in claiming a role in strategic atomic bombing. With its control of the seas, the navy argued, it could move carrier task forces close enough to vital areas of enemy territory to make devastating nuclear attacks. The navy even held that its capability for such attacks was in some ways greater than that of the B-36.

The navy denied that it intended to infringe on the responsibilities of the air force for strategic bombing. According to the navy, planes from carrier task forces would have been valuable partners for land-based bombers. But the air force in turn rejected an independent role for the navy in strategic warfare. Secretary of Defense Forrestal had tried to resolve the conflict, ruling that the navy could retain its air power but could not create its own strategic air force. Casting a cloud over this resolution, however, was a new dispute as to which of the two services would control the atomic bomb in case of war. The air force sought to stake out a claim; the navy objected. The Joint Chiefs of Staff favored the air force yet did not really nail down the issue.

The supercarrier was a major element in the navy's postwar program. So vital did naval officers regard the *United States* to the future of the navy in the age of nuclear warfare that they had voluntarily relinquished millions of dollars for construction of thirteen smaller vessels to assure funds for the great ship. It was with flourish, therefore, that in the last days of Forrestal's secretaryship the keel of the *United States* was laid at Norfolk. In a matter of weeks the new secretary of defense ordered construction permanently canceled. Secretary of the Navy John Sullivan was in Corpus Christi, Texas, to make a speech and had not been notified in advance about Johnson's decision. He returned to Washington in a rage. To the men in blue, Johnson's act was living proof of an anti-navy bias in the administration's strategic and budgetary decisions. By 1949, as the historian Steven L. Rearden has noted, budgetmaking was ''tilted not only in the direction of air power but, more specifically, toward the Air Force and increased reliance on long-range land-based bombers.''

A prominent New England Democrat, Sullivan appealed Johnson's decision to the president. Truman upheld Johnson. Sullivan resigned. The White House staff had to dissuade him from writing an angry letter to Truman. Instead he sent a courteous private one to the president and a vehement public one to Johnson.[34] As will be seen, cancellation of the *United States* caused continuing discontent in the navy. Truman's tight budget policy had forced the navy to discontinue building ships of established design. It concentrated instead on prototypes. The *United States* was categorized as a prototype, but now in this instance the navy was thwarted again.

What was the rationale for Johnson's decision, which was within a few months to have spectacular consequences?

From the beginning, support for the supercarrier among the Joint Chiefs of Staff had been divided, the air force opposing the ship's construction. On the recommendation of Forrestal, Truman proposed funds for the *United States* in the 1949 budget, and Congress appropriated the money. The keel was laid. Having come to office predisposed toward air power and eager to economize, Johnson asked the Joint Chiefs to reconsider the decision. In their re-examination Admiral Louis Denfeld, chief of naval operations, delivered the case for the supercarrier. General Bradley, reversing an earlier stand, took the opposite side of the question. The supercarrier, he now argued, was costly and was intended to carry out a function already assigned to the air force. The air force chief of staff, General Hoyt S. Vandenberg (the senator's nephew), reiterated his service's opposition, leaving the chiefs two to one against proceeding with the carrier. Johnson sided with Bradley and Vandenberg and reported the positions of all three chiefs to Truman. Truman approved cancellation.[35]

In one respect that Johnson was not aware of, his actions backfired. For while Truman, having approved cancellation, was bound to support Johnson upon Sullivan's appeal, the president nevertheless was displeased with the way Johnson had handled the matter. Truman liked Sullivan and urged him not to resign.[36] Truman thought Johnson had been arrogant to the secretary of the navy.[37] According to Assistant White House Press Secretary Ayers, Truman said he did not blame Sullivan for having quit.[38]

Then on April 27, the very day after Sullivan's resignation, Johnson vexed Truman again. Following an appointment with the president, Johnson gossiped to reporters in the White House lobby about an array of pending appointments and personnel changes in the defense establishment. A story went out on the United Press, although Johnson was not identified as the source. On major points the story was inaccurate.

''The president clearly was displeased with what Johnson had done,'' Ayers noted. ''In fact he commented . . . that what 'made me mad' was Johnson's holding a press conference there. He also said to let Johnson 'stew in his own juice.' '' At a staff conference on the twenty-eighth, Truman told Matt Connelly it might be well to cancel the secretary of defense's regular weekly appointment with the president. Truman suggested "letting Johnson think about it for a while," Ayers noted.[39]

The new secretary of defense, therefore, did not have the president's confidence to the degree that he doubtless supposed he had. Meanwhile the secretary of the navy was out, and work on the *United States* was terminated. By fall the navy was to be in a state of public political warfare with the air force, creating scenes quite unprecedented in American history.

6. The China Time Bomb

ALL IN ALL, China was the most momentous, the most explosive, the most damaging issue that Harry Truman confronted as president. Unlike the great questions in Europe, the China problem caused severe political stress in the United States, eroding Truman's leadership. China, for example, was to become a major factor in the rise and devilish success of Joseph McCarthy. Abroad, China caused difficulties among Truman's and America's traditional allies. At home, it provoked bitter quarrels within the administration itself.

The situation in China forced a historic change in the focus of American policy in Asia under Truman, a change in which defeated Japan rather than allied China became the main reliance of the United States in the Far East. The related matter of Taiwan, or Formosa, as it was usually referred to then, grew apace into a perennial American problem also.

American soldiers and marines fought, died, and retreated in the onslaught of Chinese troops in Korea. Over the question of how to deal with China in those circumstances, Truman caused a political crisis in the United States by relieving General MacArthur of his commands in the Far East. China extinguished American hopes for a conclusive victory in the Korean War. Because of fear of Communist China's hegemony over Indochina, Truman intervened in Vietnam with funds for economic and military assistance, the consequences of which could not have been imagined.

The revolution in China was the most profound international event of the late 1940s and early 1950s. Because of its involvement in Asia resulting from the Second World War, the United States felt the heavy impact of the revolution at a time when the political mood of the country was most sensitive to a great new Communist triumph abroad. Without the China problem the history of the Truman administration would have been radically different.

The American involvement with China as inherited by Truman dated from the 1930s, when Japan invaded Manchuria, in effect ushering in the Second World War. Toward the end of the decade, wrote the historian Michael Schaller, "American leaders believed successful Japanese aggression in China was a prelude to a direct assault on other American interests and allies in the Pacific."[1] Simultaneously war was threatening in Europe. Therefore, in the late 1930s, and on a large scale in the 1940s when Lend-Lease went into operation and Pearl Harbor was attacked, the Roosevelt administration sought to block Japanese advances in China by extending assistance to Chiang Kai-shek.

This commitment to Chiang deepened during the war in military, economic, political, and emotional terms. Maintenance of a pro-American regime in China became a fixture of Roosevelt's policy.[2] In the face of long-standing conflict between the Nationalists and Communists, Roosevelt's goal was to keep Chiang in power while persuading him to carry out social reforms. To insure that the United States would play a major role in shaping postwar Asia through alliance with Chiang, Roosevelt persisted in trying to elevate Nationalist China to the status of a great power and to treat Chiang as a world leader.

The flaw in Roosevelt's policy was that Chiang's regime was cruel, corrupt, reactionary, inept, undemocratic, and unpopular. It was a dying order.

Roosevelt constantly feared that the hostility between the Nationalists and Communists would erupt into armed combat between them even while Japanese troops overran coastal China. In hope of averting such strife and at the same time reducing the danger of Soviet intervention in China in support of the Communists, he sent a mission to Mao Tse-tung's headquarters in Yenan in 1944 to assess the possibility of a coalition government under Chiang's leadership. Mao and Chou En-lai (Zhou Enlai) displayed an eagerness for cooperation with the Americans. Mao asked for American assistance and recognition. United States foreign service officers in China recommended that Washington give the Communists military and political support lest they be driven into the arms of the Soviet Union by default. Mao and Chou sent a message to Roosevelt asking if he would receive them for talks in Washington. No invitation came back.

If that were a time when useful and permanent ties might have been forged between the United States and the Chinese Communists, it faded. Roosevelt showed no disposition to support the Communists.[3]

To the advantage of the Nationalists, all United States aid to China continued to flow through Chiang's regime as the legitimate government of China. Influential army and navy officers in China worked clandestinely to keep Washington on Chiang's side.[4] Chiang's severest American critic, Lieutenant General Joseph W. Stilwell, commander of the China-Burma-India theater, was recalled by Roosevelt on Chiang's demand. Stilwell was replaced by Lieutenant General Albert C. Wedemeyer, a strong anti-Communist who deferred to Chiang. Roosevelt late in 1944 named as his ambassador to China Major General Patrick J. Hurley, a narrow, foolish, headstrong man, ignorant of Chinese affairs and opposed to direct American dealings with the Communists. By this time Roosevelt's basic policy was to effect political unification of China through a coalition of the Nationalists and the Communists, and Hurley took charge of the negotiations between the rivals. Without interference from Roosevelt, Hurley banished foreign service officers in China who were critical of Chiang and favored assistance to the Communists.

That, in sum, was the situation in China that confronted Truman when he took office in mid-April 1945. The China policy he inherited was a time bomb ticking at the end of a labyrinth.

The swearing in of a new president provided an opportunity for the scuttling of Roosevelt's China policy, which was, as may be seen in hindsight, headed for grief. Given the character of the man and the circumstances he faced, however, the probability that the new president would have changed course was near zero. Truman had no experience in dealing with Chinese affairs. He had never visited Asia. Swamped with great problems foreign and domestic, he probably never saw the past reports written by the dissenting foreign service officers about the strength and promise of the Chinese Communists. Truman certainly knew little about Mao and his followers and obviously not too much about what was going on among the Nationalists. As Truman was to say, "I thought Chiang Kai-shek's Government was on the road to real reform. . . ."[5]

Until recently Truman had been a member of the Senate, where he was exposed to sentiment favoring Chiang Kai-shek. When he moved to the White House, the sentiment was the same. Hurley was still ambassador to China. Wedemeyer was still commander of American forces there. Fleet Admiral William D. Leahy, chief of staff to the commander in chief under Roosevelt was still in the White House in the same role at the new president's elbow. "Pinkies" was Leahy's word for any State Department officials who might favor aid to the Chinese Communists.[6] Roosevelt had seen to it that Nationalist China had become one of the five permanent members of the United Nations Security Council. Although disillusionment with the Nationalist regime swelled in the United States late in the war, a long and manifold commitment to Chiang Kai-shek lay on the new president's desk.

Truman became president when the wartime alliance with the Soviet Union was disintegrating, partly over Stalin's insistence on establishing pro-Communist governments in Eastern Europe. Mao Tse-tung's regime thus caught the reflection of Washington's fear of Communist aggrandizement.

Truman had been thrust into office without preparation and without a mandate for fundamental change in foreign policy. In the tradition of vice-presidents succeeding dead presidents, he pledged to carry on Roosevelt's policies. At the time no pressure was felt, no agitation heard for abandoning Chiang Kai-shek. Chiang had a considerable constituency in the United States. Mao had none to speak of. Chiang was almost universally regarded in America as the leader of the Chinese people and the most powerful figure in China. Around the time Truman took office, Hurley and Wedemeyer made the rounds in Washington, giving assurance that Chiang could defeat the Communists in a civil war.[7]

Upon entering the White House, Truman's primary concern was winning the support of the people and the Congress. He had no national following. Indeed his name was barely familiar to millions of Americans. The country was aghast at the loss of Roosevelt. The war in Europe was entering its final phase. But in those days, before the atomic bomb was even ready for testing, long and bloody fighting in the Pacific was being forecast. The American people were restless over wartime economic controls and dismayed by daily casualty figures. Truman understood the power and influence of Roosevelt in maintaining equilibrium. He worried about the effect of Roosevelt's death on the conduct of the war and retention of controls.

A challenge immediately ahead of Truman was to get the Senate to approve

United States membership in the United Nations. His years in politics had taught him the need for political harmony and compromise. It was simply not in his nature to do something like stunning the nation at a critical moment with a radical change in foreign policy, especially one aimed at shifting American support from Chiang Kai-shek to the Chinese Communists. Truman probably never gave a thought to such a step, which surely would have had a powerfully divisive effect just when he needed harmony.

A time of trouble and failure of American policy was coming when Truman was to regret the quality of advice on China that he had received in the beginning. He was to rue having gone along so solidly with Chiang Kai-shek. In a memorandum August 12, 1950, for example, he lamented how difficult it is for a president to obtain facts. "I had no way of finding out the facts," he wrote, "except through General Stilwell, General Wedemeyer and General Marshall. It was not possible for me to make a personal investigation after I became President and that is the only way in the world factual information could be obtained. We did bet on a bad horse but no use shedding tears over that now."[8]

That view, of course, was just the opposite of what it had been in the Washington of 1945. In the normal course of things then, Roosevelt's policy on China was carried forward by Truman, thereby starting the new president on his way supporting the losing side in the Chinese civil war.

Complications soon set in with the approach of the Japanese surrender. From Washington's viewpoint the problem had several main elements.

Having entered the war against Japan in accordance with an agreement with the Americans and British at the Yalta Conference, Soviet forces were spread across Manchuria, strategically placed to help the Chinese Communists, if they chose to. In certain areas in northern China, Mao's troops, upon the collapse of Japan in August, tried to take the surrender of Japanese forces and to seize their arms. The ending of the war had stranded millions of Japanese soldiers and civilians in China, and Chiang Kai-shek lacked the facilities to repatriate them. Furthermore, an outbreak of war between the Nationalists and the Communists seemed imminent.

In this stew the Truman administration took a number of actions. The general intent of them was to discourage Soviet forces in Manchuria from meddling in China; to avert civil war; to strengthen and preserve Chiang's regime and maintain American influence in China; and to repatriate the Japanese as quickly as possible lest they become pawns in the struggle between Chiang and Mao. A consequence of these actions was that they led to intermittent clashes between American units and Chinese Communist forces and rendered such important assistance to Chiang as to incur Mao's enmity and poison relations between the United States and the Chinese Communists.

General Wedemeyer's basic directive upon Japan's collapse stated that he was not to support Chiang's regime in a civil war. Military assistance to Chiang was to be continued for the time being in support of Nationalist operations to reoccupy areas held by the Japanese. American forces from the Pacific theater were to "secure control of key ports and communication points" in China. The positions liberated by these forces were to be restored to the Nationalist government. Also Wedemeyer was to assist Chiang in the rapid transport of his forces "to key areas in China."[9] While wishing to prevent a Chinese civil war, the Truman administration was so intent on maintaining Chiang in power that it transported Nationalist troops to places where they were bound to come into conflict with the Communists.

American officials also were worried that Mao would move Communist forces into Manchuria to occupy areas expected to be evacuated by Soviet troops. Under pressure from Leahy and Wedemeyer particularly, the Joint Chiefs of Staff directed that American shipping be made available as quickly as possible to transport Chiang's troops to Manchuria so that the Nationalists could seize the evacuated areas.[10] The United States was committed by wartime pledges to help China regain territory lost to Japan since 1905 and to give China postwar military and economic assistance.

Although Mao's troops as well as Chiang's had fought the Japanese, Truman through MacArthur instructed Japanese units in China to surrender to the Nationalists, not the Communists.[11]

Confronted by the chaos of postwar China and the danger of Communist gains, Truman solicited the collective advice of then Secretary of State James F. Byrnes, then Secretary of the Army Henry L. Stimson, and then Secretary of the Navy Forrestal. Acting upon their recommendations, he received T. V. Soong, Chiang Kai-shek's emissary, and took the United States deeper into China affairs on the side of the Nationalists. Consistent with wartime commitments, Truman said that the United States was prepared to assist China in building armed forces of moderate size for the maintenance of internal security and the exercise of adequate control over liberated areas of China, including Manchuria.[12]

In furtherance of the earlier directive to Wedemeyer on securing control of key ports and communication points, more than fifty thousand United States marines were landed at Tientsin and Tsingtao in the fall of 1945. During a visit to Washington in mid-October, Wedemeyer called on Truman. According to the general, the president took a hard line, telling him he had determined to continue full support of Chiang and to stiffen American policy toward the Soviets in the Far East.[13]

Despite disillusionment with Chiang, the Roosevelt administration had propped up the Nationalists as Japan crumbled. Roosevelt's intention was that China should fill the impending power vacuum in Asia. The idea carried over. In November 1945 Truman remarked to his cabinet that unless the United States made a strong stand in China, the Soviet Union would take Japan's place in the Far East.[14] By the time of the Wedemeyer visit to Washington, the Truman administration had agreed to transport four Nationalist armies to the north of China by air and five armies by sea.[15] Chiang's main strength was in the south; the north was Mao's stronghold. The angry Communists protested American intervention and at one point attacked a convoy, wounding several marines. Against Wedemeyer's advice, Chiang moved troops into Manchuria. The marines were drawn into skirmishes with Communist guerrillas.

At that point, a messy situation dropped into Truman's lap in Washington.

Home on leave in that November of 1945, General Hurley released to the press without warning to the president a sensational letter, which announced his resignation as ambassador to China. In words that caught Republican ears, he charged that "a considerable section of our State Department is endeavoring to support Communism generally as well as specifically in China."[16] His motives remain obscure. One of them may have been his suspicion that some officials in the State Department were conniving to make him a scapegoat for the worsening situation in China.[17]

To neutralize unfavorable publicity sure to flow from Hurley's allegations, Truman immediately named General of the Army George Marshall, recently retired as army chief of staff, as his personal representative to China.

No basic change was made in China policy at the time. Marshall was to continue the efforts Hurley had begun under Roosevelt to mediate between the Nationalists and the Communists in quest of a unified government under Chiang.

At a White House meeting before he departed, Marshall alluded to the possibility that Chinese unification might prove impossible. If the United States were to abandon Chiang, however, he said, the effect might be a divided China and Soviet control of Manchuria, nullifying American war aims in the Far East. One of these aims was the return of Manchuria to Chinese control. Marshall asked, therefore, if he would not have to support Chiang in any event by continuing to move Nationalist troops north. Truman and Byrnes replied that the United States would have to continue supporting Chiang to that extent.[18] At a final meeting to clarify his mission, Marshall said that if he failed to obtain reasonable but unspecified concessions from Chiang, it would still be necessary for the United States to go on backing the Nationalists. Truman and Dean Acheson, then under secretary of state, confirmed this.[19]

In a public statement on December 15, 1945, Truman declared that Chiang's regime was "the only legal government in China"—the "proper instrument through which a more representative government could be developed."[20] From that point on through the remainder of his first term, Truman in effect entrusted the conduct of China policy to Marshall. The hallmark of Marshall's stewardship was the refusal of the United States even to consider military intervention in China in an effort to save the Nationalist regime.

In China, Marshall's labors at trying to harness in one government Chiang's dying order and Mao's new order were practically hopeless. Despite the pervasive mistrust between the two sides, Marshall succeeded in arranging a truce. But the American policy of transporting Nationalist troops to the north and giving Chiang Kai-shek military and economic assistance had only encouraged Chiang to fight the Communists rather than negotiate. Soon the truce foundered on the outbreak of civil war in Manchuria. After a year Marshall called it quits and returned to Washington with a low opinion of Chiang's regime and a belief that both sides were determined to fight to the end. Early in 1947 Truman named Marshall secretary of state, succeeding Byrnes.

As Chiang continued to falter, the old Roosevelt and early Truman policy of strong support began to fade. The commitment to the Nationalists continued but on a declining scale. In line with the wartime policies of the Roosevelt administration, the Truman administration gave priority to the reconstruction and defense of Europe.

Strengthened by the acquisition of surrendered Japanese arms conveniently left behind them in Manchuria by evacuating Soviet troops, Mao's forces turned the tide of the war. By the end of 1947 all major Nationalist garrisons in Manchuria had been isolated.

In the United States a reassessment of China policy was inevitable. It was bound to have domestic political repercussions, for which Truman had failed to prepare his defenses. As Chiang's position deteriorated, Truman had not educated the American people about the reality in China or prepared them for the shock and consequences of Chiang's likely defeat. Truman's reluctance had been due in part to the administration's preoccupation with urgent situations in Europe after the war. Seeking Republican support for such measures as the Truman Doctrine and the Marshall Plan, Truman had tried to avoid premature controversy over the ultimate fate of China. He also had deliberately refrained from calling public attention to the extremity of China lest his words be regarded as the final act of pushing Chiang over the brink.[21] It was a course concurred in even by Senator Vandenberg, chief Republican spokesman on foreign affairs in Congress.[22]

After the 1948 election, the predicament became painfully clear as Chiang's regime unraveled spectacularly. In Washington the Chinese ambassador, V. K. Wellington Koo, declared that the "whole of Asia" might fall to communism if the United States did not rush greater amounts of arms and cash to China. Generalissimo Chiang Kai-shek played what had once been an ace, sending his wife to the United States to plead for a large new aid program and for appointment of some American general to be the "spark plug" of the Nationalists' military effort.[23]

On a wartime visit in 1943, the "Missimo" had drawn throngs of American admirers into the streets. This time her arrival attracted relatively little attention. Truman, who had met Madame Chiang on her previous visit but disliked her, now gave a White House tea for her.[24] But he and Marshall spurned her requests. They believed that past assistance to Chiang had proved useless or worse, with much of it falling into the hands of the Communists or the bank accounts of Chiang's friends and all of it failing utterly to stem the Communist advance. They also suspected that Chiang's appeal for an American military leader was a device for drawing the United States into the war on his side.

Truman and Marshall had acquiesced in moderate appropriations for assistance to China in 1947 and 1948. They wished to quiet domestic critics of China policy and obtain support of pro-Chiang Republicans in Congress for Marshall Plan appropriations. The administration wished to demonstrate to friend and foe that the United States was standing by its interests in a "free and independent" China. Finally, Truman did not want to jerk the rug out from under Chiang while any small hope of averting disaster remained.[25] Nevertheless, since the end of the Marshall mission, the administration had been edging back from Chiang to avoid being trapped in the wreckage. As for developments on the other side, Mao Tse-tung listed in a Communist journal in November 1948 the task facing his party, "To unite all revolutionary forces within [the] whole country to drive out aggressive forces of American imperialism . . . and establish a unified democratic people's republic."[26]

Coming to the fore meanwhile was a related question that was soon to be the focus of intense controversy involving the president, General MacArthur, the Department of State and the Department of Defense, the Joint Chiefs of Staff, and the China bloc. The question was to be a problem for United States diplomacy for more than a generation. It was the question of policy respecting Formosa.*

A large island off the mainland of China, of which it had long been a province, Formosa had been seized by Japan in the Sino-Japanese War of 1894–95 and held by the Japanese until their defeat in the Second World War. In keeping with the decision of the Cairo conference of 1943 that Formosa should be returned to China, the Allies after the war recognized Nationalist Chinese control of the island on a *de facto* basis pending a peace treaty with Japan. Retreating before the Communists in 1948, the Nationalists asked Washington that such aid as was still being furnished be rerouted to Formosa, destined to be the last bastion of Chiang Kai-shek. On November 24, 1948, the Joint Chiefs of Staff declared that it would be "seriously unfavorable" to the security of the United States if Formosa should come under some rule that "would be susceptible to exploitation by Kremlin-dominated Communists." In such circumstances, the chiefs held, the Soviet Union would be capable of dominating sea routes between Japan and Southeast Asia and might threaten the Philippine and Ryukyu Islands.

The Joint Chiefs of Staff recommended—and this was the policy of the Truman administration—that the United States endeavor not by military means but by diplomatic and economic measures "to insure a Formosan administration friendly to the United States."[27]

Thus matters stood with regard to China at the end of Truman's first term.

---

* In the Truman period the island was usually referred to as Formosa in everyday usage as well as in official discussions and government documents. For that reason it is referred to as Formosa in this book. Taiwan is Chinese; Formosa is Portuguese. In 1590 the Portuguese discovered the island and made several unsuccessful attempts at settlement.

7. Debacle: "The Loss of China"

T HE START OF Truman's second term coincided with a crucial phase in China. Ten days after his inauguration on January 20, 1949, all of China north of the Yangtze (Chang Jiang) was in Communist hands. Mao's forces were poised along the river for the final battles that soon were to bring all of mainland China under his rule.

In the last months of Chiang's regime on the mainland, China was in such turmoil and the future was so murky that, as a paper of the Policy Planning Staff in the State Department declared on September 7, 1948, "It would . . . be misleading at this stage to attempt any detailed charting of a course to be followed for the next several years." Hence "our policy for the immediate future must be defined in the most flexible and elementary terms."[1]

The administration entered this critical period, therefore, in a state of waiting for events to clarify. The expectation of Truman's advisers was that when it finally became evident that diplomatic relations with Mao's forthcoming government were in the interests of the United States, Washington would recognize the new Communist government and enter into a period of initially cool dealings with it. Time seemed to be on the side of the United States.

Among large numbers of Americans the idea of recognition of a Chinese Communist government was unpopular but not intolerable. Among a vehement minority, including certain members of Congress, the idea was anathema. Everything considered, therefore, the question of granting diplomatic recognition when Mao's government was proclaimed loomed as troublesome for Truman. It was obvious that he would not rush into recognition. The move not only must appear to America's advantage but also must come at a moment when it would cause the minimum damage to the administration. It was the kind of decision that Truman would have been comfortable deferring until after the off-year elections in November 1950.

What no one knew in January 1949 was that there were not to be the "several years" of leeway for temporizing that had been anticipated by the State Department planners. In eighteen months East Asia was to explode—not in China but in Korea. As a result, what had not been settled in Sino-American relations by the first few months of the Korean War was not to be settled for nearly a quarter of a century. Meanwhile, unaware of how short a span of opportunity lay before them, Truman and Acheson, not to mention Mao and Chou En-lai, struggled for direction in a sea of fiercely conflicting international and domestic political currents.

While Acheson probed for diplomatic solutions, Truman was more preoccupied with, and more influenced by, the political tide around him. It rose as the growing rout in China sharpened Republican instincts about the Democrats' vulnerability to a final Communist victory. Events in China pushed Truman on the defensive. "We can't be in a position of making any deal with a Communist regime," he remarked at one of the first cabinet meetings of 1949.[2]

The postelection attack on his China policy was begun in earnest in mid-January by the principal spokesman for Chiang Kai-shek's cause in the House of Representatives, Walter H. Judd. The Minnesota Republican was a former medical missionary in China and a member of American China Policy Association, an organ of the China lobby. Popularly regarded as an expert on China, he was convinced that American "leftwingers" were at the root of Chiang's troubles.[3]

In his speech in the House, Judd said that the administration had been "making every possible effort to help the . . . governments of Western Europe resist the further expansion of Communist control and no real effort . . . to help the Chinese government resist Communist expansion. . . . [S]ince December, 1945, our policy in Asia, in fact if not in words, has been one of abandonment of the Chinese government."[4]

The contrast between granting massive aid to Western Europe but not to Nationalist China did indeed give Truman's partisan critics an opening. American intelligence, as noted in the previously cited NSC 20/4, assessed the objectives of Soviet leaders as being the domination of the world. In the same assessment it was held that the Soviet Union was the "base of the world Communist movement." If true, how much more effective would that base have been for world domination if Mao's Communist forces were to seize control of all China.

As Judd and his friends pressed the question, it was a difficult one for Truman to answer satisfactorily. That was all the more so because of the administration's policy of containment of the Soviet Union and of communism and because of the president's own pronounced anti-Communist rhetoric, notably in the Truman Doctrine of 1947.[5] The containment policy provided useful political leverage for Chiang, the China lobby, and the China bloc. For if communism was to be contained in Greece and Turkey and in Western Europe, why not in China, too? And who was in the field against the Chinese Communists but Chiang Kai-shek?

The primary reason for granting massive economic assistance to Europe, and an essential element in military priority for Europe as well, was that Europe was viewed as the core of the civilization of which the United States was a part. To revive the strength and vitality of Europe, to restore its culture, polity, economy, finances, trade, cities, and farms was considered essential to the continuing health, strength, and prosperity of the United States itself. As their votes for the Marshall Plan had revealed, Republicans accepted this argument as far as it went.

Many of them believed, however, that a larger share of the help should have gone to China. They were more outspoken about the importance of Asia and the need for containing communism there. When it came to that problem, however, the United States was in a stronger position in Europe than in Asia.

American occupation forces were stationed in Europe. Americans had a monopoly on the atomic bomb to deter attack on those troops. In Europe, the United States had major allies, soon to include West Germany. These allies were industrial states with a potential for supporting modern military power. No such situation existed in the then still relatively primitive Asia, where the old order had been demolished by war and where nationalist revolutions were creating turmoil. Sophisticated programs of economic assistance on the pattern of the Marshall Plan would not work in underdeveloped Asia as they did in industrial Europe. Furthermore in China the scale of things was vast in comparison with Europe. No responsible official in the Truman administration could think of anything practical that could be done in the circumstances to save Chiang Kai-shek.

Judd and his colleagues were in no mood to grant the limitations in America's capability of influencing events in China through material assistance to Chiang. The partisan critics played down the fact that the United States had—futilely—extended a great dal of military and economic aid to Chiang during and after the Second World War, although now on a much diminished scale.

They were careful not to advocate American military intervention in China. They expounded proposals far more acceptable to the voters than that. Thus the critics clamored for dispatch of American military advisers, extension of loans, and supply of weapons to Chiang. But, mainly, their stock in trade was denunciation and even villification of the Truman administration for the undeniable failure of its policy in China. "The loss of China," they called it. Without question, the critics had by early 1949 convinced many Americans that Truman was, shockingly, "abandoning" China, China being equated with Chiang's dying order. Truman's ambiguous policy of recognizing the Nationalist regime as the legitimate government of China and helping it, yet not helping it enough to survive, caused raw dissatisfaction among those who would not acknowledge what the cost of attempting Chiang's rescue might have been to the United States. A glimpse of the cost was to be provided later in the American experience in Vietnam.

Fifty-one Republican members of the House, including Representative Nixon, wrote to the president inquiring about future support of Chiang.[6] On February 24, 1949, Acheson met with thirty-five of them, with sorry results. Reiterating in his own language what former Secretary Marshall and other leading State Department officials had been saying for months, he explained that a new policy could not be outlined until some of the dust and smoke of the Chinese civil war had cleared.[7] This amounted to a restatement of the aforementioned Policy Planning Staff assertion that the situation was so chaotic that "any definite prescription for action would be bogus."

After the closed session some congressman leaked to the press a report that Acheson had defined American policy in China as waiting "till the dust settles."

The phrase became a veritable Republican slogan, alleging that the administration had no policy other than to await a Communist victory. But such a victory was almost at hand. The policy was not that negative. Truman and Acheson were groping toward the best course to follow when the Chinese Communists took over all of China. Early in 1949 Truman considered ending military aid to the Nationalists but retreated under congressional pressure.

Nevertheless, the wait for the "dust" to settle did leave a seeming vacuum at an overheated time. As the historian Lewis McCarroll Purifoy observed, "frenzied men rushed in to fill it with their reckless charges and their angry recriminations. . . ."[8] In the fullness of the China debacle the State Department—increasingly a target for Republican critics since the Communist issue had taken hold after the war—was bombarded with allegations of sheltering pro-Communist officials. Offering no evidence, Representative Robert Hale, Republican, of Maine, said on the House floor that the department was "permeated with Reds and leftists"—a phrase endlessly parroted in those years by Republican speakers.[9] William C. Bullitt, former United States ambassador to the Soviet Union and a prophesier of Soviet hegemony over all of Asia, told a joint session of the Texas legislature that the State Department was "rancid" with men who believed that the Chinese Communists were "agrarian reformers."[10] Senator Kenneth S. Wherry, of Nebraska, the Republican floor leader, had said during the Senate debate on the confirmation of Acheson that "If the senators will talk to the people in various sections of the country, they will find it to be a matter of common knowledge that Mr. Acheson has . . . been considered as one who had gone along in an appeasement policy toward Russia."[11] Acheson, an agent of containment, an architect of the Truman Doctrine, the Marshall Plan, and integration of West Germany into Western Europe!

More of the rancor of the administration's foes spilled after Acheson succeeded, in the winter of 1949, in getting the Senate Foreign Relations Committee to stifle a bill for a $1.5 billion loan to Nationalist China for economic and military assistance. Senator Styles Bridges, Republican, of New Hampshire, accused Acheson of having sabotaged "the valiant efforts of the Chinese Nationalists to keep at least part of China free."[12] Patrick Hurley said that "America's failure in China today is the result of America's surrender of principles in the secret Yalta agreements." Senator William F. Knowland, Republican, of California, an intense moose of a man, who was becoming increasingly fervent in the cause of Chiang Kai-shek, introduced a resolution calling for an investigation of Truman's policies in the Far East.[13]

Speaking in Sacramento, Senator Owen D. Brewster, Republican, of Maine, injected a new and, initially, cautious tactic among the partisan critics. It was to chip away at the renowned figure of General Marshall, whose great prestige as the "true organizer of victory" in the Second World War, as Winston S. Churchill called him, buttressed Truman's China policy. Brewster recalled that on Marshall's mission to China in 1946 the general had brought about temporary suspension of portions of a United States program of military aid to the Nationalists, ostensibly to demonstrate his impartiality as a mediator between Chiang and the Communists. Attempts to discredit Chiang went on, full tilt, Brewster said, "with apparently the full sympathy of the responsible authorities in our State Department."[14]

Meanwhile in a development of great moment, the break-up of Nationalist China caused a major shift in American focus toward Japan. By the spring of 1949 Japan had a new constitution and a popularly elected government. The major war crime trials were out of the way. The rigors of the American occupation were being relaxed. United States policy now called for the Japanese to assume an ever greater responsibility for their own affairs. On May 6 the National Security Council promulgated, and Truman later approved, NSC 13/3, a policy paper reflecting the administration's desire for a strong Japan. All restrictions on Japanese plants were to be terminated and the use of former war industries for nonmilitary production authorized.

NSC 13/3 not only called for American retention of military facilities at Okinawa, from which Japan could be defended, but cautiously anticipated permanent American bases in Japan, notably the naval base at Yokosuka.[15] Increasingly, therefore, a friendly Japan rather than China loomed as a likely partner for the United States in the maintenance of stability—and containment—in Asia. Although unremarked at the time, the drift toward partnership with Japan was bound to affect the potential importance of Korea. For if the North Koreans were to seize all of Korea, not only would international communism be seen as posing a menace to Japan but such a Communist conquest in Korea would give the Japanese pause about the value of the United States as a protector.

In the spring of 1949 Communist armies swarmed across the Yangtze, capturing Nanking in a major step toward final victory. The American public was dowsed in gloom. *Time* reported that the "Red tide has risen mightily in Asia and now threatens to engulf half the world's people."[16] Almost echoing the China lobby, the *New York Times* lamented in an editorial that the United States had entered "a period of moral retreat," having failed to help "free peoples," presumably meaning those Chinese who lived under Chiang's regime, "to remain free."[17] Read into the Senate record was a column by Joseph Alsop, saying: "If the Soviet Union can extend its sphere beyond China into Indochina, a chain reaction will become highly probable. All of Southeast Asia will be threatened. If Southeast Asia goes, Japan and India will be immediately menaced."[18]

The faultfinding failed to shake the conviction of Truman and Acheson that they were doing the right thing. In a handwritten note the president jotted, "A currupt [sic] inefficient government has caused us an upset in China, but we, eventually, will have a stabilized far east with India, Australia, the Phillipines and Japan living in peace and harmony."[19]

The dawn of a new age in China inevitably forced reassessments in the foreign offices in Peking and Washington. Below the surface of mutual animosities between the Truman administration and Mao's movement, the issue of diplomatic relations reawakened.

In talking with Ernest Bevin in Washington in mid-April of 1949, Acheson said that the United States had abandoned the idea of supporting Chiang and would extend for only a limited time the last $58 million available under the China Aid Act of 1948. He remarked that the Chinese Communists would have to deal with the West to some extent because the Soviets had no resources to offer them. Despite the political difficulty in withdrawing support from the Nationalists, the secretary concluded, the administration henceforth would pursue a more realistic policy.[20] Afterward, W. Walton Butterworth, director of the Office of Far Eastern Affairs until March 1950, said that what had been contemplated in the State Department was "[F]ormal, regularized relations . . . not intimate but proper."[21]

For months the administration explored alternative policies, ranging from aid to anti-Communist elements in China to influencing Mao Tse-tung to follow the path of Marshall Tito of Yugoslavia, a Communist leader who stayed independent of Moscow. In China certain inconclusive events occurred that seemed to hint at a desire by the Communists, or a faction of them, for diplomatic relations with the United States.

After the fall of Nanking, Leighton Stuart, United States ambassador to Nationalist China, remained in the city. A former president of Yenching University in Peking, he lingered in Nanking to hear what the Communists might have to say about relations with the United States. He was acting with the authorization and encouragement of Acheson.[22] Through a former student, Stuart got in touch with Huang Hua. Later China's foreign minister, Huang was then chief of the aliens' affairs office in Nanking. He and Stuart met cordially in May. "Huang expressed much interest in recognition of Communist China by USA on terms of equality and mutual benefit," Stuart reported to Acheson. Stuart had explained to Huang that with the civil war still in progress no Chinese Communist government yet existed to be recognized.[23]

The central committee of the Chinese Communist party already had erected a particularly difficult barrier for the Truman administration in contemplating recognition. The committee had declared February 1, 1947, that when the Communists came into power, they would disavow foreign loans, treaties, and agreements negotiated by the Nationalist government.[24] This was unacceptable to Washington. Respect for treaty obligations was basic to diplomatic relations, Acheson informed O. Edmund Clubb, United States consul general in Peking.[25]

Stuart, however, again reported to Acheson that "Chinese Communists have lost no opportunities in emphasizing lack of recognition and official relations between USA and themselves." That was the Communists' "excuse," according to Stuart, for certain ill treatment of Americans in consular offices in north China and Manchuria.[26]

Events in Mukden had dismayed Americans. That city was the point of first contact between the United States officials and the advancing Communists. The Communists discovered that a group attached to the United States Naval Forces in the Western Pacific had been using Mukden as a base for gathering intelligence on Communist operations—for spying. Angus I. Ward, the United States consul general, and his staff were placed under close confinement.[27] The incident festered and soon was to take a turn for the worse.

While the Stuart-Huang affair coasted along in Nanking, an engrossing incident occurred in Peking. According to diplomatic cables to the State Department, Michael Keon, an Australian correspondent for the United Press in the Communist capital, delivered to Colonel David D. Barrett, the assistant American military attaché and an old China hand, what purported to be a secret verbal message from Chou En-lai, a member of the central committee. As roughly paraphrased in a cable from Clubb to the State Department, the purported message was that a moderate faction of the Chinese Communist party, headed by Chou, favored relations with the United States. China would need economic help, and Chou felt that no ideological bar to relations existed.[28]

The reported approach by Chou never has been confirmed by the Chinese Communist government. The historian Steven M. Goldstein has raised doubts about the validity of the message and the likelihood of Keon as an intermediary.[29] A number of other scholars take the incident at face value, as did the Truman administration at the time. Although Chou ostensibly had not solicited a reply, Acting Secretary of State James Webb authorized one—and by no means a negative one at that.

The gist of it was that, while disturbed by unfriendly actions like the detention of Angus Ward, the United States desired relations with China and welcomed "expressions [of] friendly sentiments." Diplomatic relations, however, would have to be based on mutual respect and understanding and would have to be beneficial to both nations. Webb read the pertinent parts of his communication to Truman and noted that "He approved this course of action and directs us to be most careful not to indicate any softening toward the Communists but to insist on judging their intentions by their actions."[30]

Meanwhile there was a new development involving Ambassador Stuart and Huang Hua. Huang intimated to Stuart that Mao Tse-tung was willing to recognize any nation on terms of equality, mutual benefits, and mutual respect for sovereignty. The ambassador inquired what he might do to further good relations between China and America. Huang replied that China needed freedom to work out its destiny without interference. All China wanted from the United States, he added, was cessation of aid to Chiang Kai-shek and severance of American relations with the Nationalists.[31] Then, in an interesting turn of events, Huang learned that in the past it had been Stuart's pleasure to visit Yenching University at commencement and that he might like to do so for the 1949 commencement. On June 28 Huang told the ambassador he had received a message from Mao Tse-tung and Chou En-lai saying that they would welcome the ambassador in Peking for a visit to the university.

Stuart interpreted this, as he promptly reported to Acheson, as a veiled invitation by the Chinese Communist leaders to talk with them while on his visit. He cited possible favorable aspects of such a meeting. It would give him a chance to explain American policies and anxieties to Mao and Chou. It would be a step toward understanding and should strengthen the hand of moderate elements in

China. It would offer the State Department insights into Communist attitudes. On the other hand, pitfalls lay along the way. Stuart acknowledged that a visit by him to Peking would start embarrassing rumors. While he did not go into particulars, it was obvious that a visit to Mao and Chou—mortal enemies of Chiang Kai-shek—by the United States ambassador to Chiang's government would send Knowland, Bridges, Wherry, Judd, and the rest of the China policy critics into an uproar.[32]

At the State Department, Butterworth and John Paton Davies, Jr., of the Policy Planning Staff read Stuart's cable. In a memorandum to his superior, George Kennan, Davies said that the invitation "strikes me as being extremely significant." But what most worried Butterworth, Davies continued, was the domestic reaction to such a visit. Butterworth's position, he concluded, was that "the ultimate decision turns on an estimate of American . . . reaction and that that is a factor which he is not competent to judge. It must be weighed by the secretary and a decision made by him."[33]

The new development chanced to come at a time when a good deal of heat was being generated at home against recognition. To be sure, the American people were not unanimous in opposing relations with Mao. Some scholars, missionaries, and other groups favored recognition, and a number of corporations were interested in doing business in Mao's China. These individuals and interests, however, were not setting the mood in Washington in the embittered days of 1949 and 1950.

Both Tom Connally, chairman, and his Republican counterpart on the Senate Foreign Relations Committee, Vandenberg, had bade the administration go slow in recognizing Peking. As recently as June 24, 1949, Knowland had released a letter to Truman from sixteen Republican and five Democratic senators. It asked for reassurance that the United States would not grant recognition. Rather impressed by the character of some of the signers, Truman remarked that they included some "forward looking" senators.* That counted with him. Understanding Truman as president begins with the recollection that he came to the White House from ten years in the Senate and carried with him senatorial attitudes. In the Senate in which he had served in the prewar and wartime years, the prevailing spirit was that the United States was magnanimous, powerful, and right and ought to have its way. Certainly, it ought not to be manipulated by a Communist power. As later presidents were to be attentive to public opinion polls, Truman was sensitive to congressional opinion. He was understanding, too, of the feelings of Democrats who were to be up for reelection in 1950 and were troubled about China.

The China bloc, much less the China lobby, did not dictate American diplomacy. Nevertheless, the congressional critics exerted pronounced influence in a number of ways. They perpetuated appropriations for the Nationalists, at times forcing minor concessions from the administration. They stirred public doubts about the soundness of Truman's policies. Most significantly, they helped inhibit

*Among the signers were such senators, highly respected by Truman, as Russell of Georgia and Wayne Morse, Republican, of Oregon. (*Congressional Record*, vol. 95, pt. 6, pp. 8406–7)

Truman from recognizing Communist China and giving it a seat in the United Nations. Similarly, their influence militated against Truman's allowing Formosa to pass under the control of Peking. It is also true that these were issues on which Truman had no great enthusiasm himself. Just before the arrival of Stuart's cable about the invitation to Peking, Truman told his staff that Communist China would not be recognized.[34] In fact, however, nonrecognition was not necessarily a permanent policy.

The Stuart cable could not have reached Truman at a worse time. On July 1 his copy of the *New York Times* carried a frontpage story under the headline: MAO EXPECTS NO HELP FROM WEST; HAILS SOVIET AS CHINA'S TRUE ALLY.

On the face of it this seemed to bear out advice Truman had received about the subservience of the Chinese Communists to the Kremlin. The story quoted a statement by Mao saying, "We belong to the anti-imperialist front headed by the U.S.S.R. and we can only look for genuine friendly aid to that front. . . ." Attacking "reactionaries" at home and abroad, Mao said that his regime "leans" to the side of the socialists.

At 5:05 P.M. on July 1 Truman telephoned Acheson. Whatever it was the president said, Acheson cabled Stuart at 6 P.M., saying that "Following highest level consideration . . . you are instructed under no circumstances to make visit Peiping." The principal reasons for rejecting the invitation, Acheson explained, were those set forth in Stuart's own cable.[35]

The secrecy of Communist records frustrates a satisfactory judgment as to whether Truman's rejection of a Stuart visit to Peking made any real difference. Historians are of two minds. "Few American decisions toward China in the postwar period," wrote William Whitney Stueck, Jr., "were as unfortunate as the . . . rejection of the Huang overture."[36] John K. Fairbank, on the other hand, is skeptical. "Recent speculation that we could somehow have been friends with Mao when he came to power," Fairbank wrote, "overlook[s] the larger forces at work. How could a movement bent on expunging the century-long humiliations of the unequal treaties affect a compromise with the vested interests that the unequal treaties had produced?"[37]

Any judgment of Truman that rests too heavily on the premise that he failed to pursue negotiations with the Communist powers must presuppose that fruitful negotiations consistent with American interests and acceptable to Congress could have been concluded with Stalin and Mao Tse-tung between 1945 and the end of 1952.

On August 5, 1949, the State Department published a 1054-page volume entitled *United States Relation With China, with Special Reference to the Period 1944–1949.*[38] Popularly known as the China white paper, it was a compendium of official statements, documents, testimony, and theretofore unpublished diplomatic cables involving American relations with the Nationalist regime.

Sponsored by Acheson, the volume was intended to answer the criticism that was deluging the administration over the defeat of the Nationalists. Along with Acheson, Truman had high hopes for the document's mollifying effect on critics. He had assured his staff that when the complete record was made public the people would perceive that the administration had from the start followed the only course in China open to it in the circumstances.[39] One high official, Secretary of Defense Johnson, warned that the white paper might do more harm than good because of the injury it would inflict on Chiang at a critical moment. Ten days before publication he wrote to Acheson urging reconsideration. In conflict with the secretary of state, Johnson favored the Chiang regime. Acheson took up Johnson's warning with Truman, but Truman sided with Acheson and approved publication.[40]

The white paper began with a letter from Acheson to the president stating with no apology the case for the administration's policy. Nationalist China, Acheson said, could not be revived by military, technical, and economic assistance. Only China could save itself, he argued. Yet, he observed, the Chiang Kai-shek regime lost its spirit, sank into corruption, and sacrificed the confidence of the Chinese people. After the Second World War, Acheson continued, the United States had been faced with three possible alternatives in China.

First, it could have withdrawn completely, but public opinion would have regarded this as "an abandonment of our traditional policy of friendship for China before we had made a determined effort to be of assistance."

Second, the United States could have committed large military forces to help the Nationalists destroy the Communists. In view of the Nationalists' disintegration, however, this would have been impractical and would not have been acceptable to the American people, Acheson maintained.

Third, while assisting the Nationalists to take control of as much of China as possible, the United States could have tried to work out a *modus vivendi* between the two sides in China to avert a civil war but at the same time to preserve and even increase the influence of the Nationalists. That course, favored by Chiang himself as recently as 1943, was the alternative the United States finally chose, Acheson said.

He declared that the Nationalist armies had not lost a battle during 1948 because of lack of arms or ammunition. He said that the United States had extended $2 billion in aid to Chiang since V-J Day (September 2, 1945), but that large amounts of weapons and material had fallen into Communist hands through Nationalist defections and ineptitude.

Flexing the prevailing administration policy, he tried to drive a wedge between China and the Soviet Union. The Chinese Communist leaders were subservient to the Kremlin, he said. But in time the Chinese people would resent exploitation by "a foreign yoke." He urged that "we should encourage all developments" that would divide the Chinese and the Soviets.

Acheson's conclusion was that "the ominous result of civil war in China was beyond the control of the . . . United States. . . . It was the product of internal Chinese forces, forces which this country tried to influence but could not."

With this indictment of Chiang's regime, the administration sought to wash its hands of the Chinese civil war yet without indicating where American policy was headed in the short run.

Any hopes Truman may have entertained for general acceptance of the white paper went up in the smoke of fresh controversy. Partisan critics tried to put the administration in a worse mess than ever over China by turning the document into an indictment of Truman and Acheson for having failed to help Chiang stem the Communist tide.

John Foster Dulles, a Republican spokesman on foreign policy, who was then serving as a United States senator from New York, called the paper an attempt to "explain and excuse past failures."[41] Vandenberg deplored "our well intentioned but impractical insistence upon a Nationalist-Communist coalition."[42] Voices as different as those of Walter Judd and the *New York Times* called the white paper an alibi for, as the *Times* said in an editorial, "a sorry record of well-meaning mistakes."[43] "[T]hose who are resisting Communist forces in China are on our side," Judd said, "and to the extent that we refuse to help effectively those who are on our side we are intervening in favor of those who are mortally opposed to us."[44]

Without offering any evidence, Knowland suggested on the Senate floor that Hiss may have helped shape China policy.[45] Knowland, Bridges, and Senator Patrick A. McCarran, Democrat, of Nevada, produced a white paper of their own, criticizing Marshall and accusing Acheson of having made Chiang a scapegoat for Washington's "blunders." The senators' memorandum said that the administration's white paper was mainly a "whitewash of a wishful do-nothing policy which has succeeded only in placing Asia in danger of Soviet conquest. . . ." They demanded that Truman initiate a program of assistance to areas of China still in Nationalist hands.[46]

On October 1, 1949, Mao Tse-tung proclaimed the People's Democratic Republic of China. Chou En-lai formally asked the United States and other countries to establish normal diplomatic relations with it.[47] Truman was in no hurry. Asked, off the record, on October 19, under what circumstances he would recognize Peking, Truman replied, "I hope we will not have to recognize it."[48] He did not rule out recognition. By then Communist conduct was further darkening the prospect of good relations. While the Communists did not carry out wholesale offenses against Americans and American interests, they committed grievances enough to militate against Truman's softening his position. At the time of Mao's proclamation of the Communist state, Truman privately emphasized that he wanted the Nationalists' recently established blockade of mainland ports to succeed.[49]

Then the Chinese Communists escalated the case against Angus Ward, the American consul general in Mukden, who was being held practically incommunicado along with his staff. In the fall of 1949 Ward was arrested and accused of espionage and assault upon a servant, charges he denied. The episode finally produced a situation that was to be recalled thirty years later when President Jimmy Carter sought the freedom of American hostages held by Iran.

As indignation over the Mukden prisoners soared in the United States and the American Legion demanded an ultimatum to Communist China, Truman became frustrated and incensed. Taking a harder line, he told Acting Secretary of State Webb on October 31, 1949, that he was, as Webb noted, "prepared to take the strongest possible measures, including some utilization of force, if necessary.'' Truman's first thought was to send in a plane on a rescue mission.[50]

Later he asked the State Department to study the possibility of an American blockade of the Chinese coast. His suggestion again was made to Webb, who recorded that Truman had in mind "blockading the movements of coal down the coast of China to Shanghai. He said he felt that if we prevented the movement of coal from Tientsin and another coal port, and prevented the entry of coal to Shanghai, the Communists would understand that we meant business, and release Ward.'' If need be, Truman said, according to Webb, ''we should be prepared to sink any vessels which refused to heed our warning.''

The proposal was submitted to the Joint Chiefs of Staff, who recommended against any form of direct military action on the grounds that it would not insure the safe release of the prisoners and might lead to war.[51] That ended talk of a blockade, but Acheson insisted that United States recognition of Communist China was out of the question as long as Ward was detained. Then Ward was tried, convicted, and freed. His personal account of his ''hellish treatment'' at the hands of the Chinese Communists became a top story in the American press.

The administration may have tried to wash its hands of the Chinese civil war, but in December 1949 Chiang Kai-shek effectively squelched that hope. Two months after the proclamation of Mao's regime, Chiang fled from a still remaining Nationalist foothold on the mainland to Formosa to be reunited with his previously sequestered gold supply and some three hundred thousand Nationalist troops. Presently, he announced that his forces would attack across the Strait of Formosa and reconquer the mainland. Thereupon the administration's standing policy of endeavoring not by military means but by diplomatic and economic measures to save Formosa from the Communists came under a pounding attack. Defense solely by economic and political means did not begin to satisfy Nationalist sympathizers in the United States.

Conversion of Formosa into a bastion for Chiang and the Nationalist remnants made the island a higher concern than ever of the Republicans, the China lobby, General MacArthur, Henry Luce, and miscellaneous critics of the administration's China policy. They had bemoaned the fall of one China—mainland China. Mao's proclamation of the People's Republic of China had been a bloodless but serious defeat for the United States, recognized as such by the administration and its critics alike. Now the Tafts, Wherrys, Knowlands, Judds, Bridges, and their friends were determined that the Communist seizure of a second China— Chiang's Formosa—would not be tolerated. Senator H. Alexander Smith, of New Jersey, a Republican member of the Senate Foreign Relations Committee, urged that Truman draw a line against communism in Asia by occupying Formosa—a move that might have led to war with Communist China. Taft and Herbert Hoover both publicly proposed that the United States Navy be ordered to defend Formosa against a possible Communist invasion. Partisan critics insisted that Chiang's position could still be salvaged with strong American help.

This pressure caused fresh turmoil in the administration. Acheson stood his ground; he thought it futile to give further support to Chiang Kai-shek on Formosa or anywhere else. By the time of Mao's proclamation of the People's Republic in October, Acheson had conceded that it was no longer possible to guarantee that diplomatic and economic measures alone could keep Formosa out of the hands of the Chinese Communists.[52] And under pressure from him, the Joint Chiefs of Staff again declared that the island, however important, was not vital enough to American security to justify military action even if diplomatic and political steps failed. Considering its global obligations, the chiefs said, the United States, as a result of the reduced defense budgets, did not have the forces available to safeguard Formosa.[53]

The strength of the Communist armies on the mainland and diplomatic reports to Washington describing the demoralization, disorganization, and corruption on Formosa led Acheson and his associates to conclude that the Communists would take control of the island, probably during 1950.[54]

Meanwhile Washington continued to accord diplomatic recognition to Chiang Kai-shek's regime on the island, thus continuing to provoke Mao. One of Acheson's purposes in rejecting American military defense of Formosa was to keep the door open to détente with the Chinese Communists.[55] Normalization of relations had to wait until Communist conquest of Formosa had eliminated Chiang's regime from Chinese territory.[56]

Acheson's position on Formosa was challenged by Louis Johnson, who considered the secretary of state's Far Eastern policies weak. Johnson was much closer to the Chinese Nationalist leaders than any but his most intimate advisers knew. Truman never would have tolerated what was happening if he had been aware of it. The story did not come out until years later upon the opening of the papers of Chiang's ambassador, Wellington Koo. These revealed that Johnson had promised Madame Chiang that he would fight for a change in Acheson's policy of barring military measures to safeguard Formosa. The Wellington Koo papers disclosed also that Truman had instructed Johnson to stay out of the China problem because it was Acheson's responsibility. Yet the Chinese ambassador not only saw Johnson with some frequency and showed him copies of diplomatic messages, but also conferred with Assistant Secretary of Defense Paul Griffith, another American Legion friend whom Johnson had brought to the Pentagon. Occasionally Griffith advised Wellington Koo on ways in which the Nationalists could exert pressure on Acheson to change his policy. Indeed, Griffith encouraged the Chinese to believe that Acheson might be forced out of office by public opinion.[57]

Early in December 1949 Johnson talked with the Joint Chiefs of Staff about the feasibility of American protection of Formosa. While the chiefs began a new study, Johnson sent a memorandum to Truman in Key West urging military assistance to Chiang. He included a statement by MacArthur that the United States was bound by the Potsdam agreement of 1945 to protect Formosa pending a determination of its legal status and conclusion of a Japanese peace treaty.[58] Earlier MacArthur had told Max W. Bishop, chief of the State Department's division of Northeast Asian affairs, that, in Bishop's words, "if Formosa went to Chinese Communists our whole defensive position in the Far East was definitely lost; that it could only result eventually in putting our defensive line back to the west coast of the continental United States."[59]

Acheson persisted in opposing any foot-in-the-door approach, such as a military mission or military aid. The conflict between him and Johnson was submitted to Truman. The president decided in favor of Acheson. Freezing Formosa policy along the lines that had been established in 1948 and rejecting the demands of Hoover, Senators Smith, Taft, Knowland, and others, the president made the following statement at his press conference January 5, 1950:

The United States has no desire to obtain special rights or privileges, or to establish military bases on Formosa at this time. Nor does it have any intention of utilizing its armed forces to interfere in the present situation. The United States Government will not pursue a course which will lead to involvement in the civil conflict in China.

Similarly, the United States Government will not provide military aid or advice to Chinese forces on Formosa. In the view of the United States Government, the resources on Formosa are adequate to enable them to obtain the items which they might consider necessary for the defense of the island.[60]

The United States, he concluded, would go on supplying economic assistance to Formosa, which, of course, kept alive the tie with Chiang. The island continued to be regarded as strategically important, though not vital to the security of the United States. Reporters were curious about the phrase "at this time" in the sentence "The United States has no desire to obtain special rights or privileges, or to establish military bases on Formosa at this time." The phrase had been inserted at the last moment at the suggestion of General Bradley, chairman of the Joint Chiefs of Staff, because of the possibility that, in the event of war with the Soviets, the United States would wish to seize Formosa as a military base. Acheson explained at a press conference that the phrase was "a recognition of the fact that, in the unlikely and unhappy event that our forces might be attacked in the Far East, the United States must be completely free to take whatever action in whatever area is necessary for its own security."[61] Truman's statement then was something less than an open-and-shut case. In a hostile situation, a change of policy on Formosa was not precluded.

The United States tried to persuade the North Atlantic Treaty powers to concert their policies regarding diplomatic recognition of Peking but encountered disappointment. Various national interests proved too divergent. With a number of other countries soon to fall in line, Great Britain granted *de jure* recognition to Mao's regime the first week of January 1950. "There are," Bevin explained in a personal message to Acheson, "some factors which affect us specially, not only our interests in China but the position in Hongkong, and also in Malaya and Singapore where there are vast Chinese communities. . . . [W]e have to be careful not to lose our grip of the situation in Asia. . . ."[62]

Early in 1950, Chinese military authorities caused fresh bitterness in Washington by seizing a building in the compound of the United States consulate in

Peking that was to have been used some day as a chancellery. Edmund Clubb wrote to Chou En-lai asking to see him about it. Clubb's letter was returned to him. On January 14, the State Department began withdrawing all its official personnel from mainland China.[63] It was to be more than twenty years before American officials returned during the Nixon administration.

Still, despite his earlier disclaimers about recognition of Communist China, Truman had presided at a meeting of the National Security Council on December 30, 1949, when NSC 48/2 was approved. It declared that the administration would not recognize Mao's regime "until it is clearly in the interest of the United States to do so."[64] That qualification was the key. Time was required, of course, but time was running out.

8. *Korea: A Malignancy. American Occupation Troops Withdraw*

I N THE SHADOW OF China lay Korea.

While Washington, New York, San Francisco, Paris, London, and Moscow celebrated the great victory of 1945, the merest tumor, all but unseen and almost totally ignored, grew in a remote corner of the globe.

Unsung in the battles, ignored in public debates, little known to millions of people, Korea was once again, as often throughout its history, degenerating into a pawn of great powers, caught this time in the rivalry between the Soviet Union and the United States. In the past Americans had paid little attention to Korea. In 1910, after victorious wars against China and Russia, Japan had annexed it. The defeat of Japan in 1945, therefore, turned Korea into a political vacuum. The informal interallied agreement that had evolved as victory in the Second World War neared contemplated a trusteeship by the United States, the Soviet Union, Great Britain, and China, through which the Koreans would be granted independence "in due course." This arrangement did not expunge Soviet and American interests in Korea, a peninsula encircled by China, the Soviet Union, and Japan.

From the Soviet viewpoint a friendly Korea or even a divided Korea with the northern half in friendly hands would have provided a buffer against attack from the Korean peninsula on bordering Soviet territory. The United States also wanted a friendly Korea and not one dominated by the Soviets. Pending trusteeship, the State Department favored American participation in the administration of the country.[1] Furthermore, both the United States and the Soviet Union, which had entered the war against Japan, had a legitimate interest in the surrender of Japanese troops in Korea.

Hence in pursuit of their respective interests and in order to repatriate Japanese soldiers, the United States and the Soviet Union moved troops into Korea after Japan's surrender, sowing seeds of trouble. At the suggestion of the United States, the 38th parallel was designated as an arbitrary and supposedly temporary dividing line between Soviet and American forces.[2] The Soviets occupied the northern half of the country and the United States the southern half, including the capital city of Seoul and its seaport, Inchon.

Without the slightest aura of being an event that was to have calamitous consequences for the peace of the world and the fate of the Truman administration, a small advance party from the United States Twenty-fourth Corps landed at Kimpo Airfield, near Seoul, on September 4, 1945. Four days later, sped by American anxiety over whether the Soviets really would stop at the 38th parallel, the bulk of the corps under the command of Lieutenant General John R. Hodge went ashore at Inchon. An entry in the "XXIV Corps Journal" of August 25 had noted, "Pres. Truman anxious to have Korea occupied promptly."[3]

From the outset the American experience in the strange, bleak, ancient Korean land was miserable and costly. From month to month the United States was dragged deeper and deeper into a commitment that it could not completely sever.

The atomic bombs ended the war with Japan so suddenly that MacArthur had no troops in the vicinity to dispatch to Korea, certainly none with adequate training for especially difficult occupation problems. The Twenty-fourth Corps had to be moved up quickly from Okinawa. General Hodge, a blunt infantry officer, not only had received no specific training for the new assignment but had had no experience with Asian people. The divided nation in which he established his headquarters was ravaged by political and social revolution and economic ruin. His venture began as a babel, in which practically no American present could speak nor understand Korean. Unsuspecting, United States troops had stumbled into a population bursting with determination to govern itself. To impatient Koreans the idea of a prolonged, indefinite trusteeship was intolerable. After thirty-five years of Japanese rule the Koreans considered themselves a liberated people and did not expect to be occupied as if theirs were a defeated enemy country. MacArthur sent a message to Washington on September 18, 1945, calling Korea a powder keg. "Hundreds of thousands are unemployed by collapse of war industries," he reported, "and strikes are threatened in railways and public utilities."[4] The Korean economy was further choked by Soviet refusal to allow commerce to cross the 38th parallel.

Ill-suited for his role in any case, Hodge's approach was dictatorial. He infuriated the people of a supposedly friendly country by imposing a curfew to maintain order. He was quoted in the Seoul press as having said, although he denied it, that "Koreans are the same breed of cats as Japanese." In the brief interval since the Japanese surrender, Korean political organizations sprang to life, but Hodge had no instructions for dealing with any of them. As time passed, he favored those on the right. In part, this was due to the fact that from that quarter came necessary technical skills, competence in management, and some command of English. For this same reason, initially, Japanese officials were kept in government posts. The Korean reaction was explosive, and Hodge was forced to fire the Japanese and fill thousands of jobs with native workers of unknown skill.

Communism was endlessly feared and abhorred by American occupation officials, who tended to relate left-wing activity in the south with the Soviet presence in the north. Conservative Koreans dominated an advisory council to the occupation authorities, and important posts, including those in the police and the courts, were filled not only with conservatives but often with conservatives who had collaborated with the Japanese.

As Korean dissatisfactions grew and signs of left-wing opposition multiplied, the American occupation became increasingly repressive and independent of Washington. Hodge established a reserve organization, or constabulary, to supplement the Korean national civil police, one of whose functions was to watch and restrain left-wing, or "subversive," political organizations. The constabulary consisted of twenty-five thousand men, who were given infantry training by American advisers and equipped with captured Japanese weapons.

Into the South Korean morass came a man who was long to be both the ally and despair of the United States: seventy-year-old Syngman Rhee. Intensely patriotic, canny, mercurial, unpredictable, and periodically given to outrageous acts and utterances, Rhee had lived in the United States as an exile since 1910, a solitary crusader for independence of his native Korea from Japan. He was a Methodist, who had graduated from the George Washington University and then earned an M.A. at Harvard and a Ph.D. at Princeton.

The beleaguered Hodge suggested that the United States sponsor the return of Korean Nationalist leaders to Seoul to offset Communist influence and act as "figureheads" until an election could be held. With MacArthur's support, Rhee arrived in Korea on October 16 and soon engaged in bitter attacks against Soviet policies.[5] Under his leadership a coalition of rightist groups was formed. Spurning the plan for trusteeship, Rhee advocated establishment of an independent government south of the 38th parallel to replace the occupation.

What was thought to be a constructive new approach was agreed to at a meeting in Moscow of the Soviet, British, and American foreign ministers in December 1945. A joint Soviet-American commission was established to consult with Korean political parties and social organizations and to recommend formation of a provisional democratic government for all of Korea. Once the provisional government began to function, the joint commission was to discuss with it a program looking toward a possible trusteeship of up to five years. Korea would become in due course an independent nation again, and the occupying powers would withdraw. The agreement, however, could not survive the postwar sickness, partly because of the opposition of General Hodge and the South Koreans to the idea of trusteeship.

When the joint commission met in Korea early in 1946, an ideological split developed between the American and the Soviet members as to which groups of Koreans should be consulted about the proposed provisional government. Underlying the dispute was the fundamental fact that neither the United States nor the Soviet Union would tolerate a unified Korea dominated by the other.

In the American zone in the fall of 1946, rioting mobs, reportedly inspired by Communists, seized police stations and supplies of arms. Hodge was forced to declare martial law. Then Secretary of War Robert P. Patterson wanted to withdraw from the quagmire. The State Department, on the other hand, held that American withdrawal must be linked with larger considerations of United States objectives in Asia. In particular, the department feared that a Korea dominated by the Communists might suck Japan into the Communist orbit. And the manifest strength of Mao Tse-tung's forces in China intensified anxiety that all of Korea soon would pass under Communist control once the United States withdrew. "Our commitments for the establishment of an independent Korea require that we stay in Korea long enough to see the job through . . . ," Truman in the summer of 1946 wrote to Edwin W. Pauley, a California oil man, who was in the Far East on a government reparations mission.[6]

Thus the American occupation continued, and Korea became a salient in the Cold War. By 1947, the occupation was proving burdensome to the Truman administration because of demobilization, reduced military spending, and plans for heavy foreign aid outlays. Dangerous situations in Europe towered over back-alley squabbles in Korea. Still, Korea was viewed in Washington as a test of strength between the United States and the Soviet Union. Rather than scuttle and run, the administration tried again to reach a Korean settlement with the Soviets in mid-1947. Again deadlock was the result. That summer Secretary of State Marshall sent General Wedemeyer to assess the situation in the Far East. In a report to Truman on September 19, Wedemeyer said that an American withdrawal from Korea would result in occupation of the southern part of the country by Soviet troops or by Korean military units trained by the Soviets. In either event, according to the report, the whole of Korea would be turned into a satellite of the Soviet Union. Withdrawal of all American assistance from Korea, Wedemeyer said, would undermine the prestige of the United States and inflate Soviet influence.[7] Ten days later Secretary of Defense Forrestal wrote to Marshall: "A precipitate withdrawal of our forces . . . would lower the military prestige of the United States, quite possibly to the extent of adversely affecting cooperation in other areas more vital to the security of the United States."[8]

With talks with the Soviets at an impasse, the administration decided to take the case to the United Nations. At the same time, in September 1947, the Joint Chiefs of Staff were asked for their opinion. They replied that in the event of Far Eastern hostilities "our present forces in Korea would be a military liability. . . . [A]ny offensive operation the United States might wish to conduct on the Asiatic continent most probably would bypass" Korea. Because of the current military manpower shortage, the chiefs said, occupation forces could be used better elsewhere, although hasty withdrawal would damage American prestige.[9]

Involving the United Nations appeared to be a way to facilitate early, but not hasty, withdrawal of United States forces while still not abandoning all of Korea to the Communists.

Over Soviet opposition the General Assembly adopted an American resolution calling for the election throughout Korea in the spring of 1948 of a national assembly. The election was to be held under the observation of a United Nations Temporary Commission on Korea. The newly elected national assembly was to establish a national government for Korea, after which the United States and the Soviet Union were to withdraw their troops. The stalemate in the Soviet-American joint commission did make it doubtful whether an election would be permitted in the Soviet zone. Still, it was possible that a Korean government could be established in the American zone under the aegis of the United Nations.

That is roughly the way things worked out. The United Nations Temporary Commission on Korea took up its duties early in 1948. It was barred from entering the Soviet zone and limited its preliminary work to South Korea.

In the circumstances the Temporary Commission questioned whether national elections should be attempted. With the General Assembly in recess, the Temporary Commission sought the counsel of the Interim Committee of the General Assembly (the "Little Assembly"). The United States, the predominant influence in the United Nations then, introduced a resolution in the Interim Committee affirming that it was incumbent on the Temporary Commission to adhere to the General Assembly's decision and to observe elections "in such parts of Korea as are accessible to the Commission." The resolution was adopted. Elections were held in South Korea on May 10, 1948. The Temporary Commission declared that "the results of the ballot . . . were a valid expression of the free will of the electorate in those parts of Korea which were accessible to the Commission and in which the inhabitants constituted approximately two-thirds of the people of all Korea." With the United States fairly well calling the shots in the United Nations and with American soldiers and Syngman Rhee dominating the scene in South Korea, the whole process moved rather smoothly along the path of American interests.

The new national assembly convened on May 31, 1948. A constitution was drafted. Rhee was elected president of the Republic of Korea and established a rightist regime, which had been taking shape since Rhee arrived in Korea in 1945. The republic was proclaimed by MacArthur in Seoul on August 15, 1948. The United States terminated its military government and recognized the new government. John J. Muccio was appointed President Truman's special representative in Seoul with the rank of ambassador.

Within weeks a Communist government came into existence in the northern half of Korea, the capital of which was Pyongyang. This government's origins dated to a meeting of a "People's Assembly" in 1947. In February 1948 the assembly announced the formation of a "People's Army" and two months later adopted a constitution on the Soviet model. Elections to a new assembly were held in August 1948. The assembly ratified the constitution and on September 9 proclaimed the Democratic People's Republic of Korea. It was headed by a former anti-Japanese guerrilla leader, Kim Il-sung. Thus two hostile governments, one leftist, the other rightist, each determined to achieve control of all of Korea and each supported by a superpower, faced one another across the 38th parallel, now a permanent dividing line.

In Washington, in April 1948, the National Security Council promulgated, and Truman presently approved, NSC-8, establishing United States policy on Korea. The policy paper declared that everything possible should be done to create conditions for withdrawal of American occupation forces by December 31, 1948. For the security of South Korea, the United States would expedite plans for expanding, training, and equipping the constabulary, which was in the process of being enlarged from twenty-five thousand men to around fifty thousand. The United States also would continue to furnish economic aid to Rhee's government.

NSC-8 contained a warning: "The United States should not become so irrevocably involved in the Korean situation that any action taken by any faction in Korea or by any power in Korea could be considered a *casus belli* for the U.S."

United States objectives in Korea remained the same, however. As described in NSC-8, these aims were the establishment of a united, self-governing, independent Korean nation. The paper declared: "The extension of Soviet control over all of Korea would enhance the political and strategic position of the Soviet Union with respect to both China and Japan, and adversely affect the position of the U.S. in those areas and throughout the Far East."[10]

Reduction of American forces in Korea began on September 15, 1948. World conditions, especially in blockaded Berlin and in China, were disturbing. The United Nations General Assembly was scheduled to convene in a new session in September and take up Korean problems. In October, rebellions, evidently instigated by Communists, broke out in South Korean constabulary units. Though brief, the riots dramatized the dangerous unrest in the fledgling republic. Rhee appealed to Truman to keep American troops in South Korea until the loyalty of his own forces had been proved.[11] For all these reasons, therefore, American troops were still stationed in South Korea at the end of 1948. By then the Kremlin had pulled out all its occupation troops. Meanwhile, in November, the South Korean national assembly passed a law converting the constabulary into the army of the Republic of Korea.

The final weeks of 1948 witnessed one further major development. At the instigation of the United States, the United Nations General Assembly adopted a resolution declaring the Republic of Korea to be the lawful government of Korea. The action, taken over the opposition of the Soviet bloc, was significant, as it turned out, because the resolution was to provide the basis of United Nations support of South Korea in very difficult days ahead.

In time the Rhee government became harsh, authoritarian, and unpopular. At the start of 1949 such was the sense of insecurity in Seoul that Ambassador Muccio recommended that some American troops remain until June 30, by which time it was expected that the South Korean security forces would be well enough trained to cope with a possible attack by North Korea.[12] Rhee pleaded for more American arms than he was getting, but American officials were worried because Rhee was candidly eager to seize North Korea and incorporate it in the Republic of Korea. "He said he would like to increase the army, provide equipment and arms for it, and then in a short time move into North Korea," Secretary of the Army Kenneth Royall, who had succeeded Patterson, noted after talking with Rhee in Seoul on February 8. "He said that the United Nations' recognition of South Korea made it legal to cover all Korea and that he saw nothing could be gained by waiting."[13] South Korean aggression against the Soviet Union's ally, North Korea, was hardly the manner in which the United States wished to see

Korea unified, especially with American troops on hand. Rhee's motives, there-fore, became one consideration in the decision as to the kinds of weapons the United States would furnish him, which, of course, affected the future power of Rhee's forces. The United States was willing to help Rhee defend his govern-ment but not to help him launch any attacks of his own north of the 38th parallel.

In quest of a practical plan for final withdrawal of troops, Washington asked the advice of General MacArthur, whose title then was commander in chief, Far East. On January 19, 1949, he replied that the long-range prospects of the Republic of Korea were poor. He said that it was ''not within the capabilities of the US to establish Korean security forces capable of meeting successfully a full-scale invasion from North Korea supported by Communist-inspired internal disorder.'' He saw no military reason for prolonging the occupation beyond spring.[14]

In March Truman approved plans for withdrawal of American occupation forces by the end of the fiscal year, June 30. Before the deadline arrived, how-ever, General Bradley, concerned about a possible North Korean invasion of South Korea on the heels of the American withdrawal, had his staff prepare for the National Security Council a study of what the United States ought to do in such a situation.

The study examined—but then rejected—the contingencies that the United States extend the Truman Doctrine to South Korea, providing large-scale mili-tary aid, or intervene unilaterally with its own forces. Instead the study recom-mended that, upon a North Korean invasion, the United States appeal to the United Nations Security Council. Depending upon the council's decision, the United States might participate in a ''police action.'' The term, arresting because of the controversy it caused later, was a familiar one in diplomatic parlance then, as in ''the Second Dutch Police Action of 1948,'' in Indonesia. As contemplated in the study ordered by Bradley, a police action would have been conducted under United Nations sanction and would have involved United States units as part of an international force. The study alluded to the possibility that joint action against aggression by North Korea would be vetoed in the Security Council by the Soviet Union. But in a remarkable bit of prophecy—of what happened, not how it happened—the study said it was also possible that the Soviets would abstain from voting on United Nations action in Korea. At the last minute it was decided not to send the report to the National Security Council.[15]

On schedule, the last American occupation forces were withdrawn from Korea on June 29, 1949. They left behind small arms and ammunition, light artillery, mortars, and some vehicles, all sufficient for a force of fifty thousand men. Subsequently, equipment for an additional fifteen thousand was furnished from United States stocks in Japan.

Left behind also was the United States Military Advisory Group to the Republic of Korea, the responsibilities of which included the training of South Korean forces. Formed from an earlier military mission, it consisted of nearly five hundred officers and men and was assigned to the American Mission in Korea, headed by Ambassador Muccio. With the departure of the occupation troops, MacArthur was relieved of all responsibility for Korea, except for logistical support for the military advisory group and for emergency evacuation of Americans, if necessary. Although United States troops were gone, in reality the United States remained the protector of the Republic of Korea. American objectives in Korea were unchanged, and American economic and military assistance programs continued.

The Truman administration's current assessment of the Korean situation, set forth in NSC 8/2, was that "the predominant aim of Soviet policy in Korea is to achieve eventual domination of the entire country."[16] The Kim Il-sung "puppet" regime, according to the policy paper, could be used "as a vehicle for the eventual extension of Soviet control. . . ." Moreover,

> The extension of Soviet-backed Communist control throughout all of Korea would enhance the political and strategic position of the USSR with respect to both China and Japan and adversely affect the position of the U.S. in those areas and throughout the Far East. . . . The overthrow by Soviet-dominated forces of a government established in south Korea under the aegis of the UN would, moreover, constitute a severe blow to the prestige and influence of the latter; in this respect the interests of the U.S. must be regarded as parallel to, if not identical with, those of the UN.

On the strength of this statement as approved by President Truman a major attack by North Korea across the 38th parallel would have been regarded in Washington as a profound challenge to American interests. When American troops were removed, however, the public generally forgot about Korea.

If the Truman administration had foreseen a North Korean invasion within a year, it is questionable whether American troops would have been withdrawn. A week before the final withdrawal the Joint Chiefs of Staff again declared that "Korea is of little strategic value to the United States." Hence "any commitment to United States use of force in Korea would be ill advised and impracticable in view of the potentialities of the over-all world situation and our heavy international obligations as compared with our current military strength."[17] It is generally understood that the chiefs meant that Korea would not have been of strategic importance to the United States in a general war.

Nearly four wretched years in Korea had brought the United States to a situation where its policymakers perceived that American interests were locked in dispute with Soviet interests on a mountainous peninsula the size of Tennessee and Kentucky combined, which the Joint Chiefs of Staff did not consider to be of strategic value to the United States in a world war.

On August 20, 1949, Rhee sent a personal letter to Truman, appealing for more arms and promising that South Korea would not attack North Korea. He said:

> Mr. President, I beg that you will consider again the very great danger of Communist assault in the immediate future. American officers tell me we have sufficient ammunition for two months of combat; my own officers tell me it is only sufficient for two days. . . . I am convinced that the American advisers are thinking in terms of piecemeal warfare, whereas we Koreans believe that when war comes it will be full scale and total.[18]

Before Truman had a chance to reply, he was overtaken by an event that shook the foundations of the balance of power in the world. It was a surprising and jolting occurrence that made all the old problems seem worse—one that caused shock and muted dread among millions of Americans, instilled a sense of insecurity such as had never before been felt in the United States, and affected both American politics and American strategy.

9. *Stunning News from Siberia: The Soviet Atomic Bomb*

O N SEPTEMBER 3, 1949, the Washington headquarters of the air force's long-range detection system received an arresting, yet not necessarily alarming, teletype message from the field in Alaska; it concerned radioactivity over the North Pacific.

One of the filter papers exposed for three hours at an altitude of eighteen thousand feet aboard a WB-29 weather reconnaissance plane commanded by First Lieutenant Robert C. Johnson on a routine patrol from Japan to Alaska had a radioactivity measurement of eighty-five counts a minute. Any measurement exceeding fifty counts a minute called for an alert.

The system was operating under new procedures that had been established as recently as August 1. Under the old procedures there had been 111 alerts, so the first word from Johnson's flight was not altogether startling. All alerts were treated as possible evidence of a Soviet nuclear explosion. The detection system had been established to discover whether any other nation was testing an atomic weapon. Theretofore, however, each of the alerts had been proved beyond reasonable doubt to have been caused by such natural occurrences as volcanic explosions, earthquakes, or normal variations in background radioactivity. The first alert following the Johnson flight, therefore, was taken in stride at the Washington headquarters.

Then a second filter on Johnson's plane was checked. It showed a measurement of 153 counts a minute.

Other reconnaissance flights were dispatched. As successive measurements were plotted, scientists leaned to the opinion that the radioactivity had been caused by fresh fission products in the atmosphere. But whether these were debris from an atomic bomb the scientists were not sure.

Any sense of calm that remained was completely shattered late on September 5 when a weather flight from Guam to Japan reported that a filter paper exposed at an altitude of ten thousand feet had a radioactivity measurement of more than one thousand counts a minute. By now a massive investigation was in progress from Guam to the North Pole and from Japan to the British Isles.

At 3:30 A.M. on September 7 came electrifying news to the scientists involved. Dr. Lloyd R. Zumwalt of Tracerlab, Inc., in California, notified Dr. William D. Urry, a scientist at the Washington headquarters, that fission isotopes of barium and cerium had been identified in the samples. Five hours later the fission isotope of molybdenum was found to be present in the first Johnson filter. These discoveries indicated that nuclear fission was the source of radioactivity caused by either a test weapon or possibly a reactor accident.

Every resource was thrown into the task of getting at the truth. The air mass containing the heavy radioactivity had passed over North America and was headed for the British Isles. British authorities were notified, and British planes took off to sample the air. Meanwhile American scientists had established that large amounts of uranium had been present in the fissionable material. Early in the week of September 11 the air force asked Dr. Vannevar Bush, president of the Carnegie Institution and wartime head of the Office of Scientific Research and Development, to convene a panel to evaluate the evidence. The panel included Dr. J. Robert Oppenheimer, wartime director of the Los Alamos Scientific Laboratory in New Mexico, where the first atomic bomb—the one exploded at the test at Alamogordo in 1945—had been assembled.

After intense study the panel concluded that the phenomena "are consistent with the view that the origin of the fission products was the explosion of an atomic bomb whose nuclear composition was similar to the Alamogordo bomb and that the explosion occurred between the 26th and 29th of August at some point between the east 35th meridian and the 170th meridian over the Asiatic land mass."[1]

After four years and one month, the American monopoly on nuclear weapons was ended, at least a year or two earlier than had been expected in the United States.

On September 19 the findings of the panel were reported to Truman, who had known of the alert. "I don't recall that President Truman felt any sense of alarm," Clark Clifford, a witness to events in the White House, said afterward.[2] As word trickled down through the highest reaches of the government, however, it spread surprise and shock. Senator Vandenberg captured the feeling when he wrote, "[T]his is now a different world."[3]

As yet the public knew nothing of what had happened.

Theretofore, with the United States short of conventional military power, the saving factor was seen to be the American monopoly on the atomic bomb. That assumed, of course, that, as in 1945, the use of the bomb would again be authorized by the president, who had, under the law, sole discretion in the matter.

In the summer of 1948 after the Soviets had blockaded Berlin, Secretary of Defense Forrestal worried whether Truman would authorize the dropping of the bomb if war broke out. The question arose at a White House meeting on September 13, 1948, attended by Forrestal and other defense officials. As Forrestal recorded Truman's statement in his own diary that day, "the President said that he prayed that he would never have to make such a decision, but that if it became necessary, no one need have a misgiving but that he would do so. . . ."[4] Yet the more that conventional strength was restricted under the budget ceilings, the more the country drifted into reliance on the very bombs that Truman prayed he would not have to use.

At another meeting, on October 10, 1948, Forrestal tried to enlist Secretary of State Marshall's help on behalf of building up conventional military strength. Marshall countered by saying that he thought ''the Soviets are beginning to realize for the first time that the United States would really use the atomic bomb against them in the event of war.''[5] If so, the need for spending on conventional weapons seemingly was less compelling, because fear of the American atomic bomb would deter war.

Truman broached the subject himself in a talk on February 5, 1949, with David E. Lilienthal, chairman of the Atomic Energy Commission. "He began by saying," Lilienthal recalled, "that the atomic bomb was the mainstay and all he had; that the Russians would have probably taken over Europe a long time ago if it were not for that."[6] Evidently, Truman did not carry this comment further and ask whether such heavy reliance on the atomic bomb was wise and whether a larger effort should be made to strengthen conventional military power. Scholars conversant with the subject believe that Truman seldom was briefed on developing nuclear strategy and had only a cursory knowledge of it.

Since 1947 tentative emergency war plans, beginning with one nicely named BROILER, had assumed that the United States would use atomic weapons and would launch a strategic air offensive against the Soviet Union in case hostilities were forced upon the United States by Soviet aggression. A later short-range war plan called TROJAN designated industrial facilities in seventy Soviet cities, including Moscow and Leningrad, as targets of an American atomic air offensive. This plan was replaced by a war plan designated OFFTACKLE and approved by the Joint Chiefs of Staff on December 8, 1949. It called for the nuclear destruction of vital elements of the Soviet war-making capacity in the event the Soviets forced the United States into hostilities.[7]

On February 10, 1949, Truman had appointed a special committee of the National Security Council, consisting of the secretaries of state and defense and the chairman of the Atomic Energy Commission, to advise him on atomic energy problems. Originally the committee was to make recommendations on negotiations then in progress with the British and Canadians for a new agreement to replace the wartime arrangement for exchange of scientific information and allocation of uranium from the Congo. Then, in July, under considerable military pressure for an increase in the stockpile of nuclear weapons, Truman asked the committee to advise him on this question also.[8]

The drift toward greater reliance on atomic bombs was continuing, although in the discussions about the size of the military establishment, the issue did not come before the president in the precise form of a choice between conventional and nuclear weapons. On April 5, 1949, Frank Pace, Jr., the new budget director, had asked Truman whether the course of events was not committing him without his specific consent to unrestricted atomic warfare if hostilities were to break out.[9] Pace was referring to developments like new bomber procurement, pressure from the Pentagon for a larger nuclear weapons stockpile, and the war plans for atomic strikes against seventy Soviet cities. Truman made no direct reply. But in July the stage was set for a major presidential decision on national security policy by a request of the Joint Chiefs of Staff for a substantial increase in the production of atomic bombs.

Several considerations lay behind this proposal. The 1948 nuclear tests at Eniwetok Atoll in the Pacific had pointed the way toward new designs and new uses for atomic weapons. The tests showed that atomic bombs could be made smaller and lighter and used economically instead of conventional bombs against relatively small targets. While no particular emergency prompted the request of the Joint Chiefs, they were moved by the continuing international tension and by economic aspects of nuclear weaponry to be celebrated in the 1950s as "more bang for the buck." The Joint Chiefs wanted more atomic bombs, too, because Truman's budget limitations deprived them of the conventional forces they thought necessary to cope with Soviet military power.

In a top-secret talk to administration and congressional leaders at Blair House on July 14, Truman said that because of Soviet "contrariness," an international agreement on control of nuclear weapons "never" would be reached. "Since we can't obtain international control," he added, "we must be strongest in atomic weapons."[10]

During the summer of 1949 new pressure came from a source that was to prove a veritable powerhouse in generating heat on Truman to build an array of nuclear and thermonuclear weapons. It was the Joint Congressional Committee on Atomic Energy, created by the Atomic Energy Act of 1946 to maintain legislative supervision over the Atomic Energy Commission. Under the chairmanship of Senator Brien McMahon, Democrat, of Connecticut, it consisted of some of the most powerful Democrats and Republicans in the House and the Senate. In a letter to Secretary of Defense Johnson on July 14, Senator McMahon observed that "we are committing ourselves to the concept of strategic bombardment with atomic weapons in case of war. Here is the keystone of our military policy and a foundation pillar of our foreign policy as well."[11] Louis Johnson agreed.[12]

A quiet sense of dismay and dread spread across the country when Truman announced on September 23: "We have evidence that within recent weeks an atomic explosion occurred in the U.S.S.R."[13] At a stroke the American people, who had fought two ravaging wars on other people's lands, could peer into the future and imagine themselves and their country vulnerable to devastation beyond anything they had ever experienced. Suddenly it was no longer preposterous to visualize the end of American civilization. Still, though lasting and deep, the sense of dread was controlled.

Over the protest of David Lilienthal, chairman of the Atomic Energy Commission, Truman had allowed four days to elapse between the report to him on the findings of the Vannevar Bush panel and his public announcement. He chose to delay so as not to make current news seem any worse than it was at a moment when the headlines already were heralding the devaluation of the pound sterling in England and threats of coal and steel strikes in the United States.[14]

Despite his announcement, Truman perversely insisted from time to time over the years that the Soviets did not have a real atomic bomb. He was obstinate about not crediting the Soviets with the technological skills to produce an atomic bomb as soon as they did. Clark Clifford judged that Truman believed that the Soviets had exploded some kind of crude device but had not really developed a usable nuclear weapon. With the military then pressing him to increase America's nuclear arsenal, Truman suspected, as Clifford recalled, that the generals and the scientists were exaggerating the revelations of the detection system. "He had his doubts that they knew what they were talking about," Clifford said.[15]

As Truman had said at an impromptu press conference in Tiptonville, Tennessee, on October 8, 1945, he believed that only Americans had the "know-how" to apply technological principles. When a reporter asked if the United States would share that information with others, Truman replied, "Well, I don't think it would do any good to let them in on the know-how, because I don't think they could do it anyhow."[16]

Even so, Truman's personal doubts about the capability of Soviet technology did not, so far as the record shows, affect his future decisions involving national security. As will be seen, these decisions plainly assumed that the Soviet Union was, or soon would be, in a position to threaten the United States with nuclear and thermonuclear weapons.

In announcing the discovery by the detection system Truman referred to a Soviet "atomic explosion" rather than to the test of an atomic weapon. According to Rear Admiral Lewis L. Strauss (retired) of the Atomic Energy Commission, that was "a concession to a body of opinion which, holding to the fallacy of Soviet scientific inferiority, persisted in regarding the incident as more probably the result of an accident in a Russian atomic experiment than a bomb."[17] Louis Johnson was reportedly one of those holding such an opinion. Truman's otherwise sensibly worded statement said that the eventual development of atomic energy by other nations had been anticipated since 1945: "the probability has always been taken into account by us." "This recent development emphasizes once again, if indeed such emphasis were needed," Truman concluded, "the necessity for that truly effective enforceable international control of atomic energy which this Government and the large majority of the members of the United Nations support."

Through Bernard M. Baruch, its representative on the United Nations Atomic Energy Commission, the United States had proposed a plan for international control of atomic energy on June 14, 1946. Under the plan a United Nations Atomic Development Authority would have assumed ownership or lease of raw materials needed for atomic energy, operated plants that processed materials for weapons, directed research, and licensed nuclear activity. All dangerous work would have been carried on by the authority. Hence, no individual nation, including the Soviet Union, could legally have made atomic bombs. The bedrock of the American plan was international inspection to check on possible violations. Stalin, however, was unwilling to open the Soviet Union to such scrutiny. Pending full operation of international control, according to the Baruch plan, the United States would have retained its then small stockpile of atomic bombs.

Finding that unacceptable, the Soviets introduced their own plan, calling for destruction of all atomic bombs and general reduction of conventional arms. The United States rejected those proposals. The United Nations Atomic Energy Commission overwhelmingly approved a control program conforming almost exactly with Baruch's and sent it to the United Nations Security Council for action. There it died in an unending Soviet-American impasse.

The Soviet atomic bomb set off a wave of reappraisal in the Truman administration. The joint intelligence committee, an arm of the Joint Chiefs of Staff, sent the chiefs a review of the military implications, saying: "A tremendous military advantage would be gained by the power that struck first. . . . Such an attack against the United States might well be decisive by reducing the atomic offensive capability, possibly to a critical degree, and destroying the capability for mobilizing and carrying on an offensive warfare."[18]

At the United Nations Acheson told reporters that foreign policy would not be altered fundamentally. In fact the Siberian explosion filled Acheson with profound misgivings as to whether the military strength of the United States was commensurate with the country's security and its goals. Drastic changes were in the offing, largely because of the Soviet bomb.

One of the earliest political effects was manifested in the final action on the Mutual Defense Assistance Act—the corollary to the North Atlantic Treaty. In a vote taken before the news of the Soviet bomb, the House had sharply reduced the amount of money Truman had requested for the program. The Senate authorized roughly twice as much as the House. To resolve the difference, a Senate-House conference committee met shortly after Truman announced the Soviet blast. Tom Connally warned the conferees, "Russia has shown her teeth."[19] The House conferees readily agreed to the larger authorization. The House itself followed suit.

The public reaction to Truman's announcement was steadied by awareness of the American headstart in nuclear science and technology. Nevertheless, anxiety about Soviet motives grew. Bubbling up under the crust of calm was a hot feeling that the United States must act smartly to outstrip the Soviet Union in the number and power of weapons. It was a demand the president could not ignore. Pressure on him to accelerate the American nuclear weapons program came quickly from the Joint Congressional Committee on Atomic Energy and the Joint Chiefs of Staff. The special NSC committee—Acheson, Johnson, and Lilienthal—reacted to the news from Siberia by recommending to the president on October 10 that "the proposed acceleration of the atomic energy program is necessary in the interests of national security."[20]

Nine days later in a major decision bound to influence American strategy, Truman approved the prompt enlargement of the atomic energy program. He authorized the Atomic Energy Commission to start expanding plants necessary for increased output of bombs. In a letter to Secretary Johnson dated October 19, Truman said that the Joint Chiefs of Staff believed that the greater production "will result in significant gains from the military standpoint in terms of lower unit cost of weapons, probable shortening of a war, increased military effectiveness, decreased logistical and manpower requirements for the prosecution of certain tasks in war, and increasing flexibility in the conduct of the war.''[21]

Accelerated production, wrote Kenneth W. Condit, a historian of the Joint Chiefs of Staff, was "fully in line with the well-known adage, 'the best defense is a good offense,' to which the Joint Chiefs of Staff subscribed. Indeed, budgetary austerity had virtually dictated a strategy built around that principle.''[22]

Important as was the stride toward a large arsenal of atomic weapons, it was already but part of a still more momentous decision being posed for Truman. For on October 5 Admiral Strauss, a very hardheaded member of the Atomic Energy Commission, had written a memorandum to his fellow commissioners, arguing that it would not do simply to go on piling up atomic bombs. Strauss (pronounced "'straws''') said:

It seems to me that the time has now come for a quantum jump in our planning. . . . that is to say, that we should now make an intensive effort to get ahead with the super.[23]

"Super" was the term used in the government for a superbomb—a thermonuclear, or fusion, bomb, generally called the hydrogen bomb, a prospective weapon of far greater power and terror than the atomic bomb. The theoretical possibility of a weapon based upon the fusion of very light elements, including hydrogen isotopes, had been discovered in 1942 by a group of physicists headed by Oppenheimer. Following the news of the Soviet atomic bomb, the question quickly arose in Washington about a response with a superbomb. The matter was discussed September 29 at a meeting of the Atomic Energy Commission and the joint committee. It was against this background that Strauss made his proposal for a hydrogen bomb.[24] In his memorandum he said that he was thinking in terms "of a commitment in talent and money comparable, if necessary, to that which produced the first atomic weapon. That is the way to stay ahead."

Strauss had a potent ally, ready at hand, in the joint committee. The executive director of the committee was William Liscum Borden, a member of a B-24 bomber crew in the Second World War and a graduate of Yale Law School, who was consumed by problems of modern warfare and national defense and who became obsessed with the need to build a hydrogen bomb. With Borden in the background and Senator McMahon, the chairman, out in front, the joint committee began to apply relentless pressure upon the administration.

The question of building a superbomb was bound to come before the president for decision. It was encumbered with a grave dispute within the government as to whether such a decision would open the door to genocide. As events developed, the hydrogen bomb issue was part of a particularly disagreeable period that was brewing for Truman. Charges of influence peddling in the administration were bursting into the headlines. The political climate was riled by the China debate and the start of a second trial of Alger Hiss, the first having ended in a hung jury in July. And now the long-festering fight between the navy and the air force had erupted on Capitol Hill, producing one of the really astounding spectacles in Washington in the postwar years.

10. *The Revolt of the Admirals*

CAPTAIN JOHN G. CROMMELIN, JR., was the kind of man in whom the navy took pride. A graduate of the Naval Academy, he was one of six brothers who were navy officers. Two of them had been killed in the Second World War. John himself, a navy flier, had become an officer on an aircraft carrier and had had an incredible escape from death. He was blown off a deck but pulled from the Pacific seriously wounded. He recovered and after the war took command of the new carrier *Saipan*. In September 1949, at the age of forty-six, he was on the staff of the Joint Chiefs of Staff.

Captain Crommelin was worried about what was happening to the navy, particularly to its air arm. It had been five months since Louis Johnson had canceled construction of the supercarrier *United States*. In the meantime the feud between the navy and the air force over the merits of the air force's B-36 bomber had become so flammable that the House armed services committee had proposed a "duel" between the intercontinental bomber and navy fighter planes to resolve the issue. The Joint Chiefs of Staff vetoed the suggestion, and bitter charges of one sort and another continued. One case in particular, involving unfounded allegations against Secretary of Defense Johnson and Secretary of the Air Force Symington, had landed the author of the charges—a navy civilian employee—before a navy court of inquiry.

Crommelin followed the case avidly. He had expected to be called as a witness before the court and prepared a statement. The court, however, recessed without hearing him. Incensed, Crommelin without the permission of his superiors, summoned reporters on September 10, 1949, and handed them his statement. The next day the front pages of the newspapers resounded to his charges that the navy's offensive power was being "nibbled to death." He attacked unification of the armed forces as a woeful mistake and held that the navy was being gradually but intentionally eliminated by the Joint Chiefs of Staff and Louis Johnson. He told reporters that in speaking out he was throwing away a thirty-three-year navy career but was doing so anyhow because the navy's fighting spirit was "going to pot." The situation was unbearable to him. "I hope," he said, "this will blow the whole thing open and bring on another congressional investigation."[1]

Navy officers rallied behind Crommelin. The breadth of the sentiment he had touched was evident when Fleet Admiral William F. Halsey, Jr. (retired), the colorful wartime commander of navy forces in the South Pacific, lunched with him and issued a statement saying: "I feel very strongly that he is attempting to do something for the good of the country and that he has shown wonderful courage in jeopardizing his career by doing this. I feel that he deserves the help and respect of all naval officers."[2]

Generally speaking, dissenters were or had been connected with naval aviation. Hanson W. Baldwin, the military correspondent of the *New York Times* and a graduate of the Naval Academy himself, reported that many of the navy's best aviators "are bitter, discouraged and resentful over what they consider a deliberate plan to emasculate naval aviation." With some of them, Baldwin wrote, the fear that naval aviation was about to be absorbed by the air force had become a phobia.[3] There were other considerations, too. Like the army, the navy had been sharply cut in size after the war. Some aircraft carriers were inactivated and a number of air squadrons reduced. Also Truman's budget ceiling diminished funds for new aircraft. The navy learned with fresh alarm in September that Louis Johnson was at work on a program to cut naval aviation—the ascendant branch of the navy—in half. The pressure of Truman's budget policy, combined with fear that the navy's future was being stunted by attrition of its air arm, was the fountainhead of Crommelin's rebellion.[4]

On the morning of September 15 admirals in the Pentagon elevated Crommelin to deputy chief of naval personnel, a post previously held by a rear admiral and thus one that put Crommelin in line for promotion. Seven hours later the newly appointed Secretary of the Navy Franklin P. Matthews, criticized Crommelin's judgment in issuing his statement. Matthews reversed the admirals and limited Crommelin to a captain's billet to serve under a rear admiral in the office of deputy chief of naval operations.[5] At a press conference Truman supported Matthews's decision.[6]

Eighteen days after Crommelin had been checkmated by Secretary Matthews, the headstrong navy captain set Washington agog.

On October 3 in civilian tweeds he embarked on a secret mission with copies of three sets of confidential letters from the highest-ranking navy officers to the secretary of the navy. By prearrangement Crommelin went first to the United Press office in the National Press Building and delivered one set of the letters. Then he met an Associated Press reporter by the elevator on the fifth floor of the same building and gave him a set. Then Crommelin went upstairs and left a copy for the old International News Service at the desk of the National Press Club.[7] He distributed the letters with the understanding that he not be identified as the source of the news.

The original letter, expressing "hearty and complete agreement" with Crommelin's published statement, was addressed to Secretary Matthews by Vice Admiral Gerald F. Bogan, commander of the First Task Fleet in the Pacific. The nub of the problem, he said, was the genuine fear in the navy that unification of the armed forces was imperiling national security. "The morale of the Navy is lower today," he added, "than at any time since I entered the commissioned ranks in 1916."

To Bogan's letter were appended procedural endorsements by Admiral Arthur

Radford, commander in chief, Pacific Fleet, and Admiral Louis Denfeld, chief of naval operations.

Radford wrote, "Rightly or wrongly, the majority of officers in the Pacific fleet concur with Captain Crommelin and with the ideas expressed by Vice Admiral Bogan above."

Denfeld wrote, "Naval officers . . . are convinced that a Navy stripped of its offensive power means a nation stripped of its offensive power."[8]

The fact that Radford's and Denfeld's letters were simply procedural did nothing to lessen the impact of the publication of the three documents simultaneously. Collectively, the Associated Press lead said, the confidential letters by the three flag officers "pictured the navy's morale as shot to pieces and the country's security imperiled under the present unified defense setup." The resulting headlines around the country mocked Louis Johnson's show of controlling the armed forces where Forrestal had failed to do so.

Greatly embarrassed by the spectacle, Matthews ordered an inquiry. The path led all too easily to Crommelin's door, and the captain confessed. He proclaimed publicly that he had released the letters "in the interests of national security." Matthews suspended him and ordered him confined to Washington pending a court-martial.

The House Armed Services Committee promptly resumed hearings it had been conducting earlier on the B-36 program. This time the hearings were a national sensation. Crommelin had acted to compel an airing of navy grievances, seeking to go to the public over the heads of the president, the secretary of defense, the secretary of the navy, and the Joint Chiefs of Staff. So stunningly had he succeeded that the proudest names in the navy, practically the entire uniformed high command, found themselves on battle station on Capitol Hill, full spirited and articulate. Admiral Radford later sought to epitomize their grievance. "The army, as a whole," he wrote, "resented the marine corps, and the air force was still determined to be the *only* air force."[9]

Representative Carl Vinson, Democrat, of Georgia, chairman of the Armed Services Committee, opened the hearings with a statement that set the stage for a later controversy. "We are going to the bottom of this unrest and concern in the navy," he said, adding that the committee wanted witnesses to speak frankly and freely and without "reprisals" in the Department of Defense. "We want these witnesses to speak what is in their minds, to put their cards on the table and to do so without hesitation or personal concern." Vinson said he had asked Denfeld, Radford, Bogan, and Matthews to be present.[10]

Little inkling of what was in store came from the first witness, Secretary of the Navy Franklin Patrick Matthews, a Nebraska lawyer and insurance executive. Matthews and the admirals did not talk the same language. To begin with, Matthews had come to office the previous May as the resigned John Sullivan's successor with no experience in Washington, and his Pentagon career was destined for disaster. His only venture afloat, he said, had been in a rowboat in Nebraska. Secondly, Matthews was a Johnson man who had promised Truman to uphold unification, and by that time the navy distrusted and feared Johnson.

Johnson and Matthews had become friends after Matthews had swung a divided Nebraska delegation to Truman at the 1948 Democratic convention. Matthews was one of the leading Catholic laymen in the United States and an outspoken anti-Communist. And since John Sullivan was a Catholic, Johnson, according to Truman's naval aide, Admiral Robert L. Dennison, "had the bright idea that politically it would be just great to get as [the new] secretary a super Catholic . . . in spite of the fact that he knew absolutely nothing about the navy and never found out."[11]

Taking the witness stand, Matthews said that "the general morale of the navy is good." Without mentioning names, he denounced Crommelin as disloyal and said that most of the dissent came from navy aviators. When he said he knew of no "block" against naval officers' voicing their opinions, the audience, generously sprinkled with blue uniforms, jeered.[12]

Then the navy officer corps had its day and went straight for the air force jugular. Admiral Radford, who was to be a power in Washington as chairman of the Joint Chiefs of Staff in the Eisenhower administration, testified that the B-36 was "a billion-dollar blunder . . . a bad gamble with national security." He warned the country against "bomber generals" fighting to save the "obsolete" heavy bomber—"the battleship of the air." "Like its surface counterpart," he said, "its day is largely passed."[13]

Commander in chief of the Pacific Fleet and a navy flier for nearly thirty years, Radford denounced the B-36 as "a symbol of a theory of warfare—the atomic blitz—which promises . . . a cheap and easy victory."[14] Actually, the air force had never made such a claim, although many air force officers were increasingly confident that the Soviet Union could be defeated by an atomic air offensive.

The navy was fighting the air force as well as the administration because it believed that the money being spent for the B-36 was not only unwise in terms of strategy, but was also causing curtailment of navy programs.[15] By the end of 1949, certainly, the air force was preeminent among the services, receiving the largest appropriation of the three. What had brought matters to a head between the navy and air force in 1949 was the air force reaction to Truman's budget limitations. Forced to cut back, the air force decided to attain maximum striking power by canceling orders for other types of planes and using the savings to buy more B-36s, as had been announced on January 17, 1949. In April thirty-six more of the big bombers were ordered. To the navy, this smacked of air force aggrandizement. Thus Radford on the witness stand not only accused the air force of over-emphasis on heavy bombers but also charged that in disregard of unification Symington had hoodwinked the rest of the defense establishment with surprise orders for B-36s.[16]

Supported by a panel of expert witnesses, Radford declared that the "unescorted B-36 is unacceptably vulnerable" and that the plane could not "hit precision targets from very high altitudes under battle conditions."[17]

Without mentioning him by name, Radford also turned on Symington for having testified in the previous hearing on the B-36 bombers that the atomic bomb and the plane to deliver it constituted the surest deterrent to war. If war occurred, Symington had added, the bomb and the intercontinental bomber "represent the one means of unloosing prompt, crippling destruction upon the enemy. . . ."[18]

"In my opinion," Radford countered, "the American people, if they were well informed on all factors involved, would consider such a war morally reprehensible."

Having predicated the navy's case in part on a moral issue, he went on to explain: "This basic difference of military opinion concerning the bombing blitz has been at the root of our principal troubles in unification. . . . These differences have grown to malignant proportions."

What Radford was arguing for was greater flexibility through more fighters and small fast bombers designed, as he drew the picture, for conventional war and accurate tactical nuclear bombing and not just for "atomic annihilation." "I don't believe in mass killing of noncombatants."[19]

Navy officers had raised the moral question about a strategy of annihilation in previous debates in the Pentagon. On the purely practical side their case had received some support from an interservice study made under the chairmanship of Lieutenant General Hubert R. Harmon of the air force. The study questioned the effectiveness of an atomic air offensive without simultaneous application of conventional military power. In line with what Radford was saying, navy planners had sought an alternative to mass bombing, in which atomic weapons would be used primarily against tactical military targets, including armies, airfields, submarine pens, and oil fields and pipelines.[20]

Radford called the cancellation of the supercarrier "a grave mistake," halting "the logical development of a valuable weapons system."[21] In language that could have hurt his career, he said that Johnson's decision was arbitrary and that navy men did not feel they had been given a "fair deal." Radford insisted that in a war the navy could get carriers close enough to the Soviet Union for shorter-range bombers to be effective. He said, "I feel that we should continue to be prepared to use the atomic bomb with precision on military objectives." He explained that "what I am against is the mass bombing of cities, and I am convinced that the B-36, if it can reach its target, could only be used for that type of bombing."

Radford was asked if the highest naval officers felt a lack of confidence in or closeness to Louis Johnson's office. "I think so," he replied.

"Does the navy feel, that is, do ranking officers in the navy feel," a committee member inquired, "that other services are making their decisions for them?"

"I think they do," Radford replied. "I do."

He testified to concern throughout the navy that the navy "is being reduced to an ineffective fighting force. . . ."

"Do you have a belief that the air force is trying to take over the navy air arm?" he was asked.

"I don't think they are trying to take it over," he answered. "I think they are trying to eliminate it."[22]

Three days later Secretary Johnson, addressing the national convention of the American Federation of Labor, accused the navy of waging a "campaign of terror" against unification.

The reaction of members of the Armed Services Committee made it evident that Radford had not clinched the navy's case. "Atomic annihilation" was not a prospect that the members relished. Obviously, however, they believed that a situation might arise in which the United States would find it necessary to launch a maximum attack on the Soviet Union. There was no enthusiasm among them for eliminating the weapon that seemingly offered the surest way for delivering such a blow.

While Truman kept his silence, a parade of the most illustrious naval figures of the war and the postwar period moved across Capitol Hill, publicly criticizing administration policies.

Radford was followed shortly by the commander in chief of the Atlantic Fleet, Admiral William H. P. Blandy, whose testimony was critical of the secretary of defense. Louis Johnson had promised at an earlier hearing that under unification he would save a billion dollars a year while still giving the country "a little better security." Blandy said that the budget cuts would render the navy inadequate as a fighting force. Admiral Halsey testified that the B-36 was essentially a siege weapon that could not be decisive. Fleet Admiral Ernest J. King (retired), the wartime commander in chief of the Pacific Fleet and former chief of naval operations, sent a statement to be read. It suggested that under Johnson political and economic considerations were more important than military considerations in the administration of the defense program. Captain Arleigh A. Burke, a renowned wartime destroyer commander and a future chief of naval operations, testified that Johnson's decision to cancel the supercarrier had been made "without adequate understanding of what was needed for the navy's control of the sea."[23]

Fleet Admiral Chester W. Nimitz (retired), a former commander in chief of the Pacific Fleet, sent a statement challenging claims on behalf of the B-36. Admiral Thomas C. Kinkaid, wartime commander of the Seventh Fleet and commander of the Eastern Sea Frontier; Admiral Richard L. Conolly, commander in chief of United States naval forces in the Mediterranean; Vice-Admiral Robert B. Carney, deputy chief of naval operations for logistics; and Admiral Raymond A. Spruance (retired), wartime commander of the Fifth Fleet and victor in the Battle of Midway; all marched to the witness stand, one after another, to help build the navy's case.

Then came Admiral Denfeld, who, as chief of naval operations, was the navy's highest uniformed officer. It was a dramatic moment when he took the stand, because Denfeld had been a conciliator in the unification disputes. The audience waited to see whether he would play that role in the present showdown. He had it in his power to take the sting out of the other admirals' criticism of Johnson and Matthews. Louis Johnson apparently hoped that Denfeld would repudiate his colleagues and support the budget policies of the secretary of defense. "Denfeld hasn't been disloyal—yet," Johnson was reported to have said.[24] The chief of naval operations calmly took the witness chair and in his first sentence threw a bucket of cold water in the faces of Johnson and Matthews.

"As the senior military spokesman for the navy," Denfeld said, "I want to state forthwith that I fully support the broad conclusions presented to this committee by the naval and marine officers who . . . preceded me."

Denfeld was torn between his roles as a member of the Joint Chiefs of Staff and as the highest uniformed officer in the navy. Reflecting the sentiment of admirals who had testified earlier that the navy was being outvoted by the two other services, he endorsed unification but said that it "will not be achieved unless the navy is admitted to full partnership. . . . The fact that the navy is not accepted in full partnership in the national defense structure is the fundamental reason for these apprehensions you have heard expressed here.

"The navy," he continued, "is gravely concerned whether it will have modern weapons, in quality and quantity, to do the job expected of [it] at the outbreak of a future war. We have real misgivings over the reductions that are taking place in the navy today. . . . Our concern is with arbitrary reductions that impair or even eliminate essential naval functions. It is not so much a question of too little appropriated money, but how we are allowed to invest that money."

Denfeld declared that "naval officers cannot understand reductions in the fleet and its functions that are being imposed by arbitrary decisions" and without consultation.[25]

In his harping on arbitrary action in the Pentagon, he was unmistakably and publicly criticizing the secretary of defense, who had the president's support. As a matter of fact Denfeld as a member of the Joint Chiefs of Staff had approved war plans providing for air operations employing the atomic bomb and carried out by the air force as the only major offensive action feasible in the early stage of a war. He also had approved the purchase of the additional B-36s.[26] In elaborating before the committee, he staunchly maintained that "the initial air offensive is not solely a function of the United States Air Force. This country's total military air power is the combined air strength of the air force, the navy and the marine corps."

The admiral said that it was "illogical, damaging and dangerous" to have gone, without sufficient evaluation, directly into mass procurement of the B-36 "to the extent that the army and navy may be starved for funds and our strategic concept of war frozen about an uncertain weapon." He charged that "there is a steady campaign to relegate the navy to a convoy and antisubmarine service." In so many words he accused the Truman administration of having adopted an "unsound concept of war." He said that the way in which the *United States* was canceled was in accord with neither the spirit nor the concept of unification. In effect, he declared that General Bradley had reneged on supporting the supercarrier by reversing his earlier approval after construction had begun.

When Denfeld had finished testifying, the chairman and various members of the committee praised him, and navy officers in the room crowded around their chief to shake his hand. Secretary Matthews abruptly rose and strode from the room, red-faced.

In subsequent days Symington and General Hoyt Vandenberg, the air force chief of staff, joined in the spectacle to fight back at the navy from the witness stand. They denied everything, as it were, and Symington implied that the admirals were trying to wrest military control from civilians.[27]

Disgusted with the whole show, Truman was increasingly worried by the amount of testimony that declared the best way to put the Soviet Union out of commission would be with atomic bombs. On October 20 he expressed to Acheson his fear that the world would get the impression that the United States was preparing for what it regarded as an inevitable war and that the issue being aired before the committee was simply which service would be the spearhead. He asked that the State Department work out a way to correct this impression abroad.[28]

The biggest headlines of all were left for the highly respected Omar Bradley, who took the stand and denounced the admirals as " 'fancy dans' who won't hit the line with all they have on every play unless they can call the signals."

Openly resentful of navy testimony about the alleged mistakes of Louis Johnson and the Joint Chiefs of Staff, the popular commander of American ground forces in Europe in the Second World War said: "Senior officers decrying the low morale of their forces evidently do not realize that the esprit of the men is but a mirror of their confidence in their leadership. . . . In an objective campaign for public attention, over-zealous enthusiasts stepped to the forefront as self-appointed martyrs, impugning the integrity of senior officers in other branches of the service."

Bradley went on to charge that "many in the navy are completely against unity of command and planning as established in the laws passed by the Congress of the United States. . . . This entire investigation, emphasizing the navy's demand for more autonomy of decision and action than demanded by the army or the air force is witness to this conclusion."[29]

The hearings ended on October 21. Congress adjourned. A moment of peace settled over Washington. The president's next regular press conference was scheduled for October 27. When the reporters had filed in, Truman said he had only one announcement to make.

"I have received a request from the secretary of the navy," he said, "to transfer Admiral Denfeld to another post, and I have given him permission to do it."[30]

The firing of the chief of naval operations shocked the navy. Denfeld had just returned to his office from a meeting of the Joint Chiefs of Staff when he learned of Truman's statement. "For thirty-odd years," the admiral said, "I've been sticking to my guns, and if they want to kick me out, I'm still sticking to my guns." High navy officers drifted in to see him, some of them bitter.[31] The next day three hundred navy enlisted men crowded in to say good-by. Speaking for the group, Chief Petty Officer Carl C. Ley, said, "I want you to know that we feel the navy is shot, that our morale is shot, that we feel very low." "Don't worry," Denfeld replied, "the navy has survived worse situations than this."[32]

Only two months earlier Truman had appointed him to a new term as chief of naval operations on Matthews's recommendation. After the Crommelin affair and Denfeld's testimony, the secretary of the navy saw things rather differently. He wrote to Truman, "The existence of the present situation prevailing between the highest civilian and the highest military officer of the Navy makes it utterly impossible for me to administer the Department of the Navy. . . ."[33]

Rather than accept transfer to another post, Denfeld retired.

"There is only one way to handle insubordination and that is to put a stop to it," Truman later wrote to former Secretary of the Interior Harold L. Ickes.[34]

In fact, the relief of Denfeld aroused severe criticism in Congress and brought condemnation by the House Armed Services Committee. In the final report on the hearings, a heavy majority of the committee voted in favor of a finding that the "removal of Admiral Denfeld was a reprisal against him for giving testimony. . . . This act is a blow against effective representative government in that it tends to intimidate witnesses and hence discourages the rendering of free and honest testimony to the Congress; it violated promises made to the witnesses by the committee. . . ."[35]

Crommelin was furloughed and ordered to his home in Alabama. Matthews continued as secretary of the navy—a much damaged one—until a reckless utterance shortened his days in office.[36] Louis Johnson pushed on with economies in the defense budget to the tune of big talk that boded ill for him. In its final report, the House Armed Services Committee deplored the manner in which the *United States* had been canceled but took no action to get the work started again.

Change was on the way, however. For all its unhappy effects, the so-called revolt of the admirals did serve to clear the air in Washington. All services were shown to have borne some of the blame. Furthermore, an outstanding officer with a fine mind and a constructive spirit became the new chief of naval operations. He was Admiral Forrest P. Sherman, who, after long service with the naval air arm, was commander of the United States Sixth Fleet in the Mediterranean and had not appeared at the hearings. Above all, however, the troublesome military budget ceiling, though momentarily made even lower, was soon to disappear in the heat of a new war. When American officials had weighed the meaning of the Soviet atomic bomb and when American troops were fighting on the mainland of Asia, money was no longer to be an insuperable problem for the Pentagon. The navy got the aircraft carriers it wanted and soon moved into an important role in nuclear strategy with the Polaris submarine.

11. *An Aura of Scandal:*
"Five Percenters" and "Deep Freezers"

———

B
Y THE END OF 1949 Truman was greatly annoyed and more damaged than
he admitted by public hearings and headlines about "five percenters"
and "deep freezers"—terms that suddenly became symbols of official
corruption in Washington.

Although relatively petty affairs, the incidents that led to the headlines proved
to be forerunners of more serious misconduct soon to be exposed. Truman never
was implicated personally, but a president is responsible for scotching illegal or
unethical conduct in the government. The effect of months of publicity about
scandals was insidious, marring Truman's administration and sapping his leadership.

The scandals, those that came to light in 1949 and others uncovered in the
ensuing three years, also revealed an imprudent side of Truman, bred of his code
of loyalty between himself and his political friends and subordinates. Former
Secretary of the Interior Harold Ickes had sensed the problem coming. "One
trouble with President Truman," Ickes noted in his diary in 1945, "is that he
becomes defiant when his friends are criticized."[1] Truman angrily regarded attacks
on any of his subordinates as attacks upon himself, which may have been true as
far as it went, yet such a response was not a satisfactory one to allegations raised
against individual officials.

The tale of the five percenters and deep freezers, which spread the notion
that Truman's Washington was crawling with "influence peddlers," burst into
the headlines in the summer of 1949 as a result of a chance meeting of two old
friends at lunch in the National Press Club. They were Paul D. Grindle and
Robert L. Moora. A former reporter in New York for the *New York Herald
Tribune,* Grindle was then the young owner of the Charles W. Laing Woodworking Corporation in Framingham, Massachusetts. Moora was news editor of
the *Herald Tribune* Washington bureau.

In conversation, Grindle asked Moora's advice about an experience he had
just had with a man named Colonel James V. Hunt, to whom Grindle had been
referred by a friend in Massachusetts. Grindle had been intrigued by the idea of
getting a woodworking contract in the current renovation of the White House but
did not know how to proceed. His Massachusetts friend told him that Colonel
Hunt was reputed to be able to negotiate such contracts.[2] By appointment, Grin-

dle called on Hunt on the morning of the luncheon in question and was impressed by the photographs of generals, senators, and high administration officials covering Hunt's walls.

Hunt regaled Grindle with accounts of close relationships with these officials and was effusive about his connections with Major General Harry Hawkins Vaughan, military aide to President Truman. As Grindle recalled the conversation, Hunt said, "General Vaughan is Harry Truman's closest friend, and I am one of Vaughan's closest friends."

Grindle explained that he would like to get a share of the White House renovation work. "No problem at all," Hunt replied.[3]

He told Grindle how often he called at the White House and how regularly he supplied Vaughan with the general's favorite brandy (not mentioning that the general was practically a teetotaler). Then Hunt got down to terms. His fee, he said, was five percent of the contract. He wanted an advance payment of $1,000 for certain expenses that would have to be incurred. Wishing to think the proposition over, Grindle departed, wandered to the Press Club, encountered Moora, and asked Moora's advice.

To Moora the whole business had the makings of a great news story, and he persuaded Grindle, who was having his own misgivings about Hunt, to relate his experience to Moora's boss, Bert Andrews, chief of the *Herald Tribune* Washington bureau. Enthralled with Grindle's tale, Andrews immediately hit upon the term "five percenter" to characterize Hunt. In pursuit of the story, Andrews got the *Herald Tribune* to give Grindle $1,000. Grindle returned to Hunt's office, signed a contract, and handed Hunt a check.

Andrews put his assistant, Jack Steele, to work on the story. Andrews also called his friend, William P. Rogers, later secretary of state in the Nixon administration, who was then counsel to the investigations subcommittee of the Senate Committee on Expenditures in the Executive Departments. Andrews and Rogers correlated the publication of the *Herald Tribune*'s exposé with the launching of public hearings into Hunt's dealings.

Publication of photostats of Grindle's check to Hunt and Hunt's contract with Grindle created the impression of a sorry scandal in the Truman administration and blew Hunt's operations into splinters. Lost in the blizzard of headlines was a line in Steele's story to the effect that the fees charged by five percenters, while out of line with public policy, were not illegal.[4]

The hearings discharged a great fallout, and most of it landed on the Falstaffian figure of Truman's military aide, General Vaughan. Already Vaughan had been in and out of the news for assorted gaffes. Coming on top of these, the testimony at the Senate hearings made him the most notorious member of the White House staff during the entire Truman administration, so much so, in fact, that the teetotaling general, who taught Sunday school, gave a slightly disreputable flavor to the Truman entourage.

As young lieutenants in the First World War, Truman and Vaughan had first met at Camp Doniphan, Oklahoma, in 1918. Vaughan suffered minor wounds overseas and received the Silver Star and the Croix de Guerre for bravery. Then

in the twenties and thirties Truman and Vaughan were colonels at reserve officers' summer camp at Fort Riley, Kansas. By this time a warm friendship had
developed between them. In 1940 Vaughan labored for Truman in the latter's
desperately hard and successful fight for reelection as United States senator in
Missouri. Afterward Truman gave Vaughan a job in Washington with the Senate
Special Committee to Investigate the National Defense Program. Following Pearl
Harbor, Vaughan voluntarily went on active duty, was injured in a plane crash
in Australia, and turned up again in Washington on the then Vice-President Truman's staff.

There, doing small favors for people was a way of life—a way of life,
needless to say, that became full of pitfalls once Vaughan moved into the White
House with his good friend. Vaughan was insensitive to the hazards. Outside his
new office he hung a scroll: ENJOY YOURSELF—IT'S LATER THAN YOU THINK.
Vaughan's associates stated the problem best. Dr. John R. Steelman, the assistant to the president, recalled: "He'd let people come into the White House to
see him. His door was wide open. Vaughan didn't realize the over-all significance of allowing people even to get into the White House."[5] In his diary, Eben
Ayers noted that Vaughan was "completely loyal to the President and would do
nothing intentionally to injure him. But he is entirely lacking in tact and any
sense of propriety or realization of the injury done to the President personally
and to the office he holds by permitting the exploitation of both the President
and the office by commercial enterprises."[6]

Still, unless one happened to be the adversary in one of his periodic feuds,
Vaughan was friendly, likeable, funny, and accommodating. He wore a general's uniform the way people nowadays wear Levi's and shirts. While the archi-
tecture of his political and social views was American Legion baroque, he was
shrewd, and Truman's insights into the reaction of the man in the street must
have been sharpened by listening to Vaughan. Sarcastic and at times vitriolic,
Vaughan had a spontaneous wit and made Truman laugh when he needed to—a
service not without its value to the state. Truman especially relished barnyard
stories Vaughan told that brought back memories of old days on the farm in
Missouri. The price for such *divertissement* turned out to be rather steep for
Truman in the end, however.

One day in 1945 Vaughan was visited in the White House by a former
business acquaintance, an advertising man named Harry Hoffman, who happened to overhear the general talking on the telephone about some problems Mrs.
Truman was having with refrigeration in her home in Independence. Neighbors
insisted on bringing her gifts of food. Because of shortages in the Second World
War, then in its closing stages, she did not have enough refrigeration space and
worried about spoilage.[7]

Eager to please, Hoffman telephoned a client, David Bennett, president of
the Albert Verley Company, a Chicago perfume firm. After Hoffman had related
Mrs. Truman's problem, Bennett authorized him to purchase, at the expense of
the Verley Company, some freezers as gifts for Mrs. Truman, Vaughan, the
White House "mess," or staff lunchroom, and several high administration offi-

cials. Hoffman later testified that Bennett was so wealthy and free-spending that passing out deep freezers was of no more consequence to him than sending boxes of Wisconsin cheese. Indeed, Hoffman said, Bennett "got quite a kick out of the fact that he was pretty close to some very important people, so that he could send a gift of this nature."[8]

What never became known at the time was that one morning after Mrs. Truman quite innocently had received her freezer as arranged by Vaughan, she awoke to an overpowering stench of rotting food. She ordered a Secret Service agent, Henry J. Nicholson, to call a refuse truck, and the $390 gift was carted off, presumably to be flung upon the town dump.[9]

Five years later, when the Senate subcommittee investigated the five percenters, trails led in many directions. The senators discovered the gift of the freezers in 1945 and a good deal more about the activities of the donor and about the cheerful helpfulness of General Vaughan, all to the high embarrassment of the White House.

Thus a flight sergeant with the Air Transport Command disclosed that David Bennett, president of the perfume company, had obtained priority to fly to Europe on business in May 1945, just after the war with Germany had ended. Bennett returned in June with perfume essence valued at $53,405. The sergeant angrily said that Bennett's priority had displaced a wounded soldier waiting for airplane space for a flight home.[10] Bennett had obtained the priority under a State Department program designed to encourage a resumption of business between the United States and Western Europe. Before Bennett had departed the United States, Vaughan had put his foot in it by writing on White House stationery a note "To Whom It May Concern," saying that "Mr. Bennett is a prominent businessman of Chicago and is entitled to the courtesies of American officials abroad."[11]

Disclosure of these incidents in 1949 enabled Republicans to intimate that expensive gifts for Mrs. Truman and White House advisers had been made in return for a favor to a businessman by the president's military aide. On the witness stand Vaughan indignantly denied this, protesting, "This gift was an expression of friendship and nothing more." In a related context he explained, "My duty, as I see it and as the president has seen it for the many years I have worked for him, I do these people the courtesy of putting them in contact with the person with whom they can tell their story to."[12] What was wrong with this, said the final report of the subcommittee, was that government officials seemed to assume that when Vaughan telephoned, he was representing the president."[13]

Vaughan's name came up time and again in the hearings concerning instances when he had telephoned government departments for favors to friends. In one case a former Department of Agriculture employee testified that the general had got "a little rough" on the telephone and stated that as the president's friend he could make or break careers in government. "Fantasy," Vaughan later testified. This particular case involved alleged violation of government controls by the Allied Molasses Company. In its troubles the company paid $1,000 in fees to a friend of Vaughan's named John Maragon, a White House hanger-on.[14] Truman once had ordered Maragon barred from the White House, but Maragon got in anyhow and, on occasion, hid when he heard that the president was coming his way.[15] It brought a splash of bad publicity when, as a result of the subcommittee hearings, Maragon was indicted for perjury and sent to jail. "There is no doubt," the subcommittee report said, "that Maragon's friendship with . . . Vaughan made his activities in his dealing with the Federal Government [on behalf of a client] possible."[16]

The subcommittee also unearthed information that two generals, both friends of James Hunt, had indulged in favoritism toward certain of Hunt's clients. One of the generals, Alden H. Waitt, was suspended by the secretary of the army and retired. The other, Herman Feldman, also was suspended by the secretary but later reinstated with a reprimand. Reporters naturally wondered if such precedents might apply to Harry Vaughan also.

"Mr. President," a reporter asked at a press conference, "if the secretary of the army decides in the case of General Vaughan, as he did in the cases of Generals Feldman and Waitt, that there was indicated indiscretion, will he be free to relieve him from active ——"

"He will not," Truman snapped.[17]

The unfavorable publicity about scandal had come on top of a disappointing legislative record in the first year of the Fair Deal. Although the new session had begun on a high note, the hopes for domestic reforms proposed in Truman's 1949 State of the Union message had been progressively eroded in the Eighty-first Congress.

Since the late 1930s the House Rules Committee had been dominated by the conservative coalition. Because the committee controlled the flow of bills to the House floor and, among its other powers, specified the rules under which bills could be considered there, it was in a position to obstruct liberal legislation. After years of trying to circumvent this roadblock the liberal Democrats pushed through in January, 1949, the "21-day rule." It provided that the chairman of a legislative committee that had reported a bill favorably and had requested a resolution from the rules committee could bring the legislation directly to the House floor if the committee failed to grant a rule within twenty-one days. Acclaimed by one excited liberal writer as "the worst Confederate defeat since Appomattox," the change opened the way for bringing progressive administration bills to a vote in the House.[18]

In the Senate meanwhile an assault was mounted on a rule that had often been used to block civil rights legislation. This time, sadly for the liberals, the outcome provided a different gauge of the way the wind was blowing on Capitol Hill.

Rule 22 of the Standing Rules of the Senate provided that on a pending measure two-thirds of the senators present and voting could invoke cloture to end a filibuster and permit the measure to be brought to a vote. When a motion was made in 1948 to bring up an anti-poll tax bill, Senator Russell made a point of order that a procedural motion was not a pending measure and, therefore, not subject to Rule 22. In the chair as president *pro tempore*, Senator Vandenberg

sustained Russell's point. In effect, the decision nullified Rule 22, giving southerners the opportunity for filibuster on civil rights legislation, because a motion
to bring up a bill had to precede a vote on the bill. But since the motion could
be filibustered, the bill could not be considered.

At the start of the 1949 session a resolution was introduced to circumvent
the Vandenberg ruling.[19] It provided that two-thirds of the senators present and
voting could invoke cloture in a debate on a motion as well as on a pending
measure. Southerners threatened a fight and warned that the Fair Deal program
might be a casualty of it. In league with labor and religious groups, black organizations put pressure on the White House to force a rules change. Generally
speaking, the Senate Democratic leaders were paper tigers on civil rights issues.
The floor leader was Senator Scott W. Lucas from downstate Illinois. Son of a
tenant farmer, he had a liberal veneer over conservative instincts. It was a measure of his softness on civil rights that he had become the Democratic leader with
the assent of Russell, probably the most powerful man in the Senate and the
recognized leader of the coalition of southern Democrats and conservative
Republicans. The resolution was scheduled to come up in the Senate on February
28. On that morning, according to Assistant White House Press Secretary Eben
A. Ayers, Truman complained to his staff that Lucas was not a fighter. Opposed
to a compromise, the president said that he intended to lay down the law to Lucas
and the others when they came in at 10 o'clock for the usual weekly legislative
leaders' meeting.[20]

Hence in the Senate that afternoon Lucas moved to have the rule change the
next item of business. That touched off one of the bitterest filibusters in modern
times, creating a dismal climate for Truman's legislative program. As part of the
southern attack Lyndon Johnson, elected to the Senate in November 1948, made
his maiden speech, denouncing cloture as "the deadliest weapon in the arsenal
of parliamentary procedure," leaving a minority defenseless.

In the face of the southern onslaught northern Democrats hit upon an alternate strategy of obtaining a new rule from Vice-President Barkley as president
of the Senate. To overturn the Vandenberg ruling a petition was submitted to
Barkley that called for application of cloture to a motion as well as to a pending
measure. On March 11 Barkley ruled in favor of the petition. Russell again made
the point of order he had raised in 1948. Barkley overruled him, declaring that
"a motion to proceed to the consideration of a bill is an absolutely indispensable
process in the enactment of legislation."

Russell appealed the chair's ruling to the entire Senate. In a blow to the
civil rights cause that was to be felt for years, the Senate rejected Barkley's
ruling by a vote of 46 to 41. Twenty-three Republicans, half of them from the
Middle West, joined twenty southern and three western Democrats to perpetuate
the barrier to civil rights legislation in the Senate. The defeat of Barkley's ruling,
proof of the continuing power of the conservative coalition, mocked hopes inspired
by the civil rights plank in the 1948 Democratic platform and by Truman's victory. It obliterated the prospect of any major civil rights legislation in his second
term.

Even before the conservatives had won the rule fight it was apparent that Truman's Fair Deal was in trouble despite Democratic control of Congress.

"We are meeting determined opposition," Truman told a Jefferson-Jackson Day dinner at the Statler in Washington on February 24. "The special interests are fighting us just as if they had never heard of November the second."[21]

One of the battlegrounds he cited was his proposal to repeal the Taft-Hartley Act, the ultimate goal of the Democrats' then powerful labor wing. Union leaders did not fear the act as it functioned in the circumstances of nearly full employment prevailing early in 1949. They did fear that in an economic downturn management might be able to take advantage of certain provisions in the act to break the unions.[22] Truman's victory, therefore, had stirred celebrations in the American Federation of Labor and the Congress of Industrial Organizations.* Secretary of Labor Maurice J. Tobin told a cheering AFL convention in Cincinnati two weeks after election day that the returns had been "a clear mandate to wipe out the Taft-Hartley law."[23]

Congressional Digest, however, cast a more sobering light on the situation. Of the 331 representatives who had voted to override Truman's veto of the Taft-Hartley bill in 1947, it reported, 222 retained their seats in 1949. In the Senate sat 54 of the 68 senators who had voted to override. Thus a majority of the members of the Eighty-first Congress had favored enactment of the Taft-Hartley bill in the first instance.[24] Beyond labor circles, furthermore, a pronounced feeling prevailed in the country that the Taft-Hartley Act was working well enough and was not the menace to labor that Truman and the union leaders had alleged. Although the president had said in his 1949 State of the Union message that the act "unfairly discriminated against" workers, he already had invoked it in several labor-management disputes, without unfortunate consequences.

The Wagner Act had guaranteed workers the right to join unions, to bargain collectively, and to strike. It established the National Labor Relations Board with power to conduct elections to determine whether a union should be certified as representing employees in a plant or office. Employers were forbidden to interfere with, restrain, or coerce employees in the rights to organize and bargain. Employers were forbidden to discourage union membership through discrimination in hiring or promoting. They were forbidden also to refuse to bargain collectively.

Replacing the Wagner Act in 1947, the Taft-Hartley Act retained the same framework but contained new provisions designed to strengthen the rights of management. Union hiring halls and the closed shop—a shop in which membership in a particular union was a prerequisite for being hired—were prohibited. Unions were made liable for suits in federal courts for violation of contract. Most significant and controversial was the authority for injunctions. When, in the president's opinion, a national emergency was threatened by a strike or lockout, he was empowered to appoint a fact-finding board. Upon receiving its report, he could ask the attorney general to seek a federal court injunction to prevent the

*The AFL and CIO did not merge until 1955.

disruption. Once the court had granted an injunction, a cooling-off period total-ing eighty days would come into effect to delay a shutdown.

Truman proposed a re-enactment of the Wagner Act that embodied new procedures for preventing strikes that could cause a national emergency.[25] On the critical question of method, however, he was vague and remained so. He did not specify that the procedures should include injunctions, which were anathema to labor. In this respect, however, he was out of step with popular opinion and the prevailing attitude in Congress. The multitudinous strikes during the period of reconversion following the Second World War had strained public tolerance. There was strong support for the powers of injunction contained in the Taft-Hartley Act.

The new administration bill substituted for injunction a thirty-day cooling-off period in national emergency strikes. Under this provision the president would ask both sides of a labor dispute to refrain from a work stoppage, or to resume work, if the stoppage already had occurred, while an emergency board attempted to arrange a settlement.

Administration officials were challenged in the hearings by senators who wanted to know how the administration proposed to prevent national emergency strikes. Truman straddled the question. He said at a press conference on February 3 that he saw no objection to including injunctive powers in the bill, yet he had not asked for them in the first place nor was the bill altered in the face of criticism to provide for injunctions. To be for injunctions was considered an anti-labor position, and Truman shied away. On the other hand, at a press conference he told reporters on the advice of Attorney General Tom Clark that the implied powers of the president under the Constitution gave him broad authority to act in an emergency.[26]

"If you closely read the history of the country," Truman said, "you will find that Washington used them and Jackson used them. They have been used by several presidents. Lincoln used them all the time while he was president. Whenever there is an emergency, the president has immense powers to do what is right for the country.

Q. "Does it require injunctive process?"

A. "I will answer that question if we ever have to cross that bridge."[27]

Truman seemed to be saying that he would not ask Congress to provide the power of injunction in the labor bill but would use comparable power notwith-standing in case of strikes causing national emergencies. Clearly, this approach, with its vague constitutional interpretation, was not strong enough medicine for Congress.

Rayburn had no doubt about the congressional mood. He took the lead in producing a substitute measure—the Sims bill—which was similar to the admin-istration bill except that it authorized injunctions. The Sims bill, however, was defeated. Labor's unwillingness to compromise jeopardized at least substantial revision of the Taft-Hartley Act.[28] For the House then turned to another substi-tute, this one introduced by Representative John S. Wood, Democrat, of Geor-gia, with the support of conservatives of both parties. Though sweetened with certain changes favorable to labor, it preserved the Taft-Hartley Act. While the administration and labor fought the Wood amendment, there was little zeal in Congress or in the country for Fair Deal reform. With ample help from the Democrats the bill passed. One of the Republicans who voted for the bill and against the president was a new member from Michigan, Representative Gerald Ford, who would one day claim Harry Truman as his model for a president.

Truman received the news of his defeat laconically. He commented, Eben Ayers noted in his diary, "that we'd lick them in the end." Ayers further recorded Truman's reaction of the next morning: " 'I don't think that it ever pays to compromise on principle.' He said he felt it would have been better to have stood pat on the administration plan and go down fighting, if necessary."[29] After some further parliamentary maneuvers, all action on labor reform in the House of Representatives in 1949 came to an end.

"I want the Democrats in Congress to carry out the promises made in the Democratic platform," Truman said publicly. "That's all I am asking—just as I am trying to carry out mine."[30]

He then reiterated his support for the administration bill, which was about to come up for action in the Senate. Once again, however, the opposition's strategy was to offer amendments, handiwork of Senator Taft. Admitting certain deficiencies in the Taft-Hartley Act, the Ohioan, one of its sponsors, proposed twenty-nine changes. While these offered concessions to labor, however, they insured that the act would remain basically intact. No more eager for reform than the House, the Senate approved Taft's amendments to the administration bill and then passed it. When the bill was sent to the House, it was routed to a dead end in the Labor and Education Committee. After all the fire and brimstone of Truman's 1948 campaign, the Taft-Hartley Act was not repealed.

"The fight is going to continue just as hard as I can make it to carry out the Democratic platform," Truman said at a press conference on June 30.[31] No great change was ever to be made in the Taft-Hartley Act in the remainder of his term, however. Truman doubtless believed he had a mandate for repeal of the alleged "slave labor act," but Congress, answering to different constituencies, felt no such obligation.

The Truman administration had no better luck with its drastic new farm legislation, a body of proposals known as the Brannan plan. Named after Secretary of Agriculture Charles F. Brannan, a militant liberal and partisan Democrat from Colorado, the plan became one of the political catchwords of Truman's second term. Supported by liberals, the Brannan plan was a complex proposal that generated more passion than comprehension, rubbed the Democrats raw with internal quarrels, and united the Republicans in opposition.

The Brannan plan would have continued high price supports, as demanded by farm interests that had given Truman crucial help in the 1948 campaign.[32] The striking feature was, however, that the subsidy would be applied to farmers' incomes rather than to the price of farm products. The plan would have established a free market for perishable products, with the consumer getting the benefit of lower prices and the farmer receiving direct payments from the government without the process of the government's buying his crop at a high support price.[33] Under the New Deal higher prices for the farmer had been achieved artificially by restricting production and marketing. The Brannan plan would have freed the productive capacity of the farms by paying the farmers directly for producing food in plentiful supply.[34]

Illustrative of his aims, Brannan held out to consumers the prospect of milk for fifteen cents a quart while still maintaining a high income for dairy farmers. "The Brannan plan," wrote Allen J. Matusow, an authority on farm policy in the 1940s, "was an ingenious effort to wed the concept of abundance to the demands of the Administration's farm constituency—an attempt to give consumers more food and farmers higher income."[35]

To the liberals the notion of high prices for farmers and low costs for consumers inspired visions—futilely entertained by liberals in those years—of a new political alliance of farmers and city workers in a revived Democratic party. What was a vision to the Democratic liberals, of course, was a nightmare to conservative Republicans, and they turned on the Brannan plan ferociously, charging that it would cost taxpayers billions of dollars and saddle many farmers with stringent government controls. Since the plan was specially designed to help the family farm, larger farm interests opposed it. Also some economists condemned it for ignoring the plight of poor rural families, thereby aggravating the inequality of income within agriculture. A number of southern Democrats joined the opposition in the belief that large cotton producers would suffer loss of subsidies.

Truman supported Brannan on the submission of the plan, but did not put up a fight for it in Congress. The Brannan plan was finally killed in the House in July 1949 and never reached the Senate floor that year.

Nearly a quarter of a century later, while Brannan was serving as general counsel to the National Farmers Union in Denver, the story had something of a happy ending at last, and one with an odd twist. One of the Republicans who voted to defeat the Brannan plan was Representative Nixon. On August 10, 1973, President Nixon signed a major farm bill embodying as one of its provisions the Brannan approach: in the case of main crops the government would support farm income rather than farm prices. Nixon's secretary of agriculture, Earl L. Butz, said the new bill represented "a historic turning point in the philosophy of our farm programs." He observed that the philosophy was "geared to expanding output" after years of a philosophy of "curtailment and shrinking of our agricultural plant." Commented the happy former secretary of agriculture in Denver: "Back then it was called the 'infamous Brannan plan'."[36]

In his 1949 State of the Union message Truman had asked for a tax increase of $4 billion—a request he finally abandoned under pressure in mid-year when the recession drove unemployment up to 6.7 percent.

He also had recommended federal aid to education and lamented that "millions of our children are not receiving a good education."[37]

For years controversy had swirled around the question of Washington's role in education. The military drafts in both world wars had revealed high illiteracy rates. Serious inequalities of educational opportunity existed between rich and poor states. By 1943 the disparity had worsened as thousands of low-paid teachers switched to jobs in war industries for higher salaries. Construction of schools had lagged during the Great Depression and the war. With a growing population the country was unable to provide adequate classrooms for the new generation of children. "Millions of them," Truman said in his message, "are in overcrowded, obsolete buildings." The problems would multiply in the postwar baby boom, he warned.[38] Traditionally, education had been the responsibility of the states, but the states were faltering under the burden. In his economic report to Congress on January 7, 1949, Truman said that only the federal government had the resources to deal with the plight of the schools.[39]

In 1948 the Senate had passed a bill authorizing, permanently, $300 million a year in grants to states for schools, including private schools, but the measure died in committee in the House. In May, 1949, the Senate again passed a similar measure, but a flaming battle erupted at the other end of the Capitol, especially around the issue of federal aid to Roman Catholic schools. The nub of the question was whether such assistance was permissible under the constitutional doctrine of separation of church and state.

Representative Graham A. Barden, Democrat, of North Carolina, was chairman of a subcommittee of the House Committee on Education and Labor appointed to consider the problem. He set the stage for a free-for-all when he introduced his own bill authorizing $300 million a year for aid to education but restricting it to public schools. The bill made no mention, either, of aid to schools for racial minorities, then segregated under the prevailing separate-but-equal doctrine. The chairman of the parent committee, Representative John Lesinski, Democrat, of Michigan, a Catholic, accused Barden of sponsoring an "anti-Negro" and "anti-Catholic" bill, dripping "with bigotry and racial prejudice." The Barden bill, Lesinski said, would never be reported out by the House Committee on Education and Labor. Lesinski's statement was only the first shot.

In a speech at Fordham University on June 19 Francis Cardinal Spellman, archbishop of New York, criticized the Barden bill for limiting federal funds to public schools. He denounced Barden as a "new apostle of bigotry." G. Bromley Oxnam, the Methodist bishop of New York, joined the issue by assailing Spellman for "bearing false witness" against Barden. The Central Conference of American (Reform) Rabbis came forward with a statement opposing federal or state assistance to religious schools. Next the issue was blown into the stratosphere in a public row between Cardinal Spellman and Mrs. Eleanor Roosevelt.

Mrs. Roosevelt had been grating on the conservative Catholic hierarchy in New York of late by taking such liberal positions as opposing renewal by United Nations members of full diplomatic relations with Franco Spain—a friend of the Axis Powers during the war—and discreetly supporting birth control. Then in her newspaper column "My Day" she snapped Cardinal Spellman's tolerance by disagreeing with him on federal aid to religious schools, relying on constitutional grounds. In an open letter that splashed headlines around the world Spellman told the late president's wife and current chairman of the Commission on Human Rights in the United Nations: "For whatever you may say, your record of anti-Catholicism stands for all to see—a record which you yourself wrote in the pages of history which cannot be recalled—documents of discrimination unworthy of an American mother!"

In a reply goading the cardinal about Catholic political activity, Mrs. Roosevelt said: "I assure you that I had no sense of being 'an unworthy American mother.' The final judgment, my dear Cardinal Spellman, of the worthiness of all human beings is in the hands of God."[40]

Privately, Truman blamed Spellman's criticism of the Barden bill for starting this crippling controversy.[41] Publicly, practical politician that he was, Truman stayed clear of the donneybrook and in the process watched another Fair Deal measure die in committee in the House.

As in 1948, Truman appealed to the new Congress in 1949 to make sweeping changes in the Social Security Act of 1935. A major feature of the act was the familiar old-age and survivors' insurance (OASI), based on a federal payroll tax on employers and employees. As originally provided, the tax was levied on the first three thousand dollars of a person's annual income. This contributory pension system, under which benefits were received as a matter of right and not on the basis of a means test, had been intended by Congress in 1935 as the chief vehicle for guaranteeing income to elderly persons. The 1935 act, however, also contained a separate old-age assistance program (OAA), in effect a charity, under which the federal government offered matching grants to states to help them make monthly payments to old persons who lived in poverty. The recipients, whose eligibility depended on a means test, did not have to have earned their benefits through prior contributions, as was the case of beneficiaries of OASI.

War, postwar reconversion, and conservative power in Congress had delayed significant changes in Social Security since 1939. Thus in 1949 OASI was still operating under the basic coverage and benefits of ten years earlier. By 1949, however, living costs had risen so much that a large proportion of the elderly, even though they had paid Social Security taxes through OASI and were receiving OASI pensions, had to depend also on charitable contributions under OAA because the pensions were inadequate to their needs. Those in need who were not covered by OASI were dependent entirely on OAA charity.

The question facing the country, therefore, was whether OASI should be enlarged to fulfill the role originally intended for it or abolished in favor of greater emphasis on the charitable approach. In his 1949 State of the Union message Truman pleaded for expansion of the Social Security system as it had originally been conceived. He asked for higher benefits and for coverage extended to more persons. "One-third of our workers are not covered," he said. "Those who receive old-age and survivors' insurance benefits receive an average payment of only $25 a month. Many others who cannot work because they are physically disabled are left to the mercy of charity."[42] In his budget message Truman said OASI should be extended to nearly all the 25 million workers not then covered. Benefits for women should be provided at an earlier age than sixty-five, he said. He suggested a slight increase in social security taxes to defray the added costs.[43]

Then on April 22 he sent up a special message renewing his first-term proposal for a compulsory national prepaid program of health insurance within the Social Security system. "I am trying to fix it," he wrote to a friend, "so the people in the middle income bracket can live as long as the very rich and very poor."[44] The new program, as he had said in his State of the Union message, also would have required some additions to the payroll tax rates "in order that the whole social insurance system will continue to be substantially self-supporting." The deep problems of Social Security financing that were to trouble the next generation did not weigh so heavily on policymakers in 1949.

In the face of a massive campaign of opposition to "socialized medicine" by the medical profession, Congress simply sat on the recommendation for health insurance. Eventually the House Ways and Means Committee reported out a bill granting some of the president's other requests and providing for the most important revision of OASI since Social Security began. The bill would have extended coverage to 11 million more workers instead of 25 million more, as requested by Truman. It would have increased benefits substantially but also increased the tax rate in stages and raised to $3,600 the annual wage base on which the taxes were levied. While several other assistance programs under the Social Security Act would have been liberalized, the bill would not have carried out Truman's request that the OASI eligibility age for women be lowered to sixty.

The conservative House Rules Committee refused to send the bill to the floor until after Rayburn had threatened to free it under the new "21-day rule." The House finally passed the bill. The Senate, however, took no action on social security in 1949, and retired persons went on receiving $25 a month. No hundred days of glory bathed the Fair Deal.

Truman privately blamed the Republicans and the "Byrdites"—followers of Senator Harry Byrd of Virginia—for combining to try to sabotage the administration's program in the interests of economy. Boss of the powerful Byrd Democratic machine in Virginia, brother of a renowned Antarctic explorer, and himself a wealthy apple grower, Byrd was, because of his conservatism, a frequent target of Truman's. Earlier Truman had remarked to his staff that Byrd "belongs to that class that wants to pay his apple growers [pickers?] fifteen cents an hour for a ten-hour day."[45]

"It is plain not only that Congress and the President aren't in harmony but that they never were," wrote Richard H. Rovere in the *New Yorker*.[46]

By the time the first session of the new Congress adjourned in the fall, however, enough important foreign affairs legislation had been passed to give Truman at least a mixed feeling about the results. In his occasional diary he wrote approvingly about "one hell of a session," but in a later entry he complained:

Trying to make the 81st Congress perform is and has been worse than cussing the 80th. A President never loses prestige fighting Congress. And I can't fight my own Congress. There are some terrible chairmen in the 81st. But so far things have come out *fairly* well.

I've kissed and petted more consarned S.O.B. so called Democrats and left wing Republicans that [than?] all the Presidents put together. I have very few people fighting my battles in Congress as I [when a senator] fought F.D.R.'s.[47]

Congress did grant the president's request for raising the minimum wage from 40 cents an hour to 75 cents but only after the conservative coalition had defeated an administration proposal for extending the coverage to millions of exempt workers. Actually Congress reduced the number covered by 500,000.

The only significant victory Truman won in the domestic field in the first session of the Eighty-first Congress—and the only major piece of new domestic legislation he was ever to see enacted in his second term—was the National Housing Act of 1949, similar to the Taft-Ellender-Wagner bill, which had been before Congress since the end of the war and which had been twice passed by the Senate and twice blocked in the House. In compromise form it again passed the Senate in 1949.

The issue remained a fierce one in the House, however. Representative Adolph Sabath, Democrat, of Illinois, eighty-three years old, began the debate by denouncing the "unholy alliance and coalition" of Republicans and southern Democrats that had blocked public housing legislation in the past. Representative Eugene E. Cox, Democrat, of Georgia, sixty-nine years old, called Sabath a liar and punched him in the mouth. Sabath's glasses flew off, and he swung blindly at Cox until the two men were pulled apart. Meanwhile the real estate lobby, proclaiming the dangers of "socialism," applied heavy pressure against the bill. This "selfish propaganda" was the most "deliberate campaign of misrepresentation and distortion" he had ever seen, said Truman, who was, however, no terror to the real estate lobby. Richard O. Davis, an authority on the housing problems of that time, wrote later that "Truman gave every appearance of staunch liberalism in his housing policies, but in the day-to-day conduct of his housing agency he closely adhered to the real estate lobby's position."[48]

This time the House passed the bill under increasing political heat from the overcrowded cities. Truman signed it on July 15, saying, too optimistically, that it "opens up the prospect of decent homes in wholesome surroundings for low-income families now living in the squalor of the slums."[49]

Pathetically, in light of future conditions, the act declared a national goal of "a decent home and a suitable living environment for every American family." From the perspective of later years the law was a failure, certainly, partly because of the refusal of Congress to appropriate sufficient funds to build the number of dwellings authorized. The act provided that over a six-year period 810,000 housing units were to be built for low-income families. In time, however, early enthusiasm over federal housing gave way to disenchantment. By July 1, 1964, more than fifteen years after the passage of Truman's bill, only 356,203 units had been built.[50]

In the Washington of 1949, questions of housing, the Taft-Hartley Act, Social Security reform, and the Brannan Plan were overshadowed by ominous events occurring around the world.

II

THE SOUND OF
THUNDER

12. 1950: A Savage Year Begins

T HOME, the prologue to the new year was written at a joint session of Congress at which Republicans heckled the president of the United States during his delivery of the State of the Union message.

Abroad, if Nikita S. Khrushchev is to be believed, the prologue had just been written secretly in Moscow at a meeting between Joseph Stalin and Kim Il-sung, premier of the Democratic People's Republic of Korea. Kim and a North Korean delegation had visited Stalin at the end of 1949.

"The North Koreans," recalled Khrushchev, a future Soviet premier, "wanted to prod South Korea with the point of a bayonet. Kim Il-sung said that the first poke would touch off an internal explosion in South Korea and that the power of the people would prevail—that is, the power which ruled in North Korea."

Stalin could not oppose the idea, Khrushchev continued in his memoirs. A North Korean "prod" appealed to Stalin's convictions as a Communist, all the more so "because the struggle would be an internal matter which the Koreans would be settling among themselves." Stalin told Kim to think it over and return with a plan, according to Khrushchev. Kim did so and came back full of confidence. Stalin remained dubious, however.

"He was worried, "Khrushchev wrote, "that the Americans would jump in, but we were inclined to think that if the war were fought swiftly—and Kim Il-sung was sure that it could be won swiftly—then intervention by the USA could be avoided."

Khrushchev emphasized that the "prod" was not Stalin's idea, that Kim was the "initiator." Stalin did not try to dissuade the North Koreans yet decided to ask Mao Tse-tung's opinion. Mao, according to Khrushchev, "approved Kim Il-sung's suggestion. . . ."[1]

Despite the bitter divisions at home over foreign and military policies, uncertainties in Asia, and the Communist issue, Truman stood before a joint session of Congress on January 4 and declared his happiness at being able "to report to you . . . that the state of the Union continues to be good."[2] "While great problems still confront us," he said, "the greatest danger has receded—the possibility which faced us three years ago that most of Europe and the Mediterranean area might collapse under totalitarian pressure."

Since the 1950 State of the Union message ushered in a year of congressional and gubernatorial elections, political sensitivity on Capitol Hill was keen.

The message was essentially a reiteration of the proposals made in the message of 1949. Truman did ask for a revision of the tax system to yield a moderate increase in revenue.

"At present," he said, "largely because of the ill considered tax reduction of the Eightieth Congress, the government is not receiving enough revenue to meet its necessary expenditures."

Republicans began to laugh and jeer. Truman grinned and tried to continue: "To meet this situation I am proposing that Federal expenditures be held to the lowest levels consistent with——"

His words were drowned out by laughter and hooting. Some Republican members booed, mildly. After first smiling, Truman flushed.

"I think I had better read that over," he said. "You interrupted me in the middle. To meet this situation I am proposing that Federal expenditures be held to the lowest levels consistent with our international requirements and the essential needs of economic growth, and the well being of our people."

He paused. "Don't forget that last phrase," he said.[3]

A more important document, the annual presidential budget message, was sent to Congress on January 9. It was a time, incidentally, when the South Koreans were complaining about Communist forays along the 38th parallel. Still in progress was the fiscal year 1950, for which Truman had imposed a budget ceiling of $14.4 billion for the armed services. The struggles of the services under this ceiling are by now a familiar story. What, then, did Truman propose for the fiscal year 1951, which would run from July 1, 1950, to June 30, 1951? Relying heavily on recommendations of the Bureau of the Budget and Louis Johnson, the president asked for a new total for national defense purposes of $13.5 billion. If the figure were to be approved, it would further reduce the number of military personnel then on active duty by 44,456.[4] Truman's budget simply continued what a subsequent Bureau of the Budget memorandum called "the trend towards economy at the expense of national security programs."[5]

Large sums were still going into the Marshall Plan and the Mutual Defense Assistance Program, of course. Partly as a result of those aid programs, the Truman budgets were now running in the red after years of surplus in the president's first term. He projected a deficit of $5.1 billion for the fiscal year 1951 on top of the $5.5 billion deficit estimated for 1950. A way of overcoming the shortfall in revenue would have been to increase taxes. The laughter, jeers, and boos that greeted Truman's statement that he intended to keep federal expenditures to the lowest possible levels was an indication of the mood in Congress toward raising taxes. Conservatives of both parties regarded federal expenditures as too high as it was. Although Truman asked for an increase in taxes to help balance the spending, he put up no great fight to change the congressional mood.

The news about the new military budget already had been passed to dismayed admirals and generals. A new breeze was stirring, however. On January 5 the National Security Council ordered the preparation of a report taking a new look at the balance of power.[6] Two developments in 1949 had undermined assumptions on which national security policies had been based. One was the Communist seizure of China. The other was the Soviet atomic bomb.

As January advanced, the second Hiss trial in New York approached a climax. So far as is known, Truman had met Alger Hiss only twice, both times casually. The first time was on June 17, 1945, when the president spoke at the closing session of the United Nations Conference on International Organization in San Francisco. As secretary-general of the conference, Hiss explained the procedures of the day to Truman and sat on the podium during Truman's speech. The second occasion, a ceremonial one, was when Hiss delivered a signed copy of the United Nations Charter to the president in the White House on July 1, 1945.

The approaching end of the second Hiss trial was given prominent display in the newspapers. On one of his daily early-morning walks, Truman alluded to it in chatting with Henry Nicholson, his favorite Secret Service agent and the agent always at the president's side in those years. Nicholson had indeed become something of a confidant of Truman's. The unspoken rule was that to pass the time Nicholson was free to bring up subjects that were in the press. When the two men turned to the trial that morning, Nicholson later recalled, Truman said: "Dean Acheson tells me Alger Hiss is innocent. After reading the evidence in the papers, I think the s.o.b. is guilty, and I hope they hang him."[7]

Acheson testified in 1949 that while Alger Hiss was not a close friend, he had been his friend and remained one, even though Hiss had by then been indicted for perjury. Years later, in 1978, the historian Allen Weinstein published *Perjury. The Hiss-Chambers Case,* a book containing massive new documentation and raising some provocative questions about the Acheson-Hiss relationship. The book revealed that after Hiss had got into trouble over Whittaker Chambers's testimony, Acheson helped Hiss prepare a statement. Read by Hiss before the House Committee on un-American Activities on August 5, 1948, the statement denied that Hiss had ever been a member of the Communist party or had ever "laid eyes" on Chambers. "I had the benefit of Dean Acheson's advice last night," Hiss wrote to John Foster Dulles, then a New York lawyer, "as I was trying to compose my own thoughts." On the morning of August 5, Weinstein disclosed, Alger Hiss, his brother, Donald, William L. Marbury, Alger's attorney, and Acheson met for a final discussion at Acheson's law office before Alger's appearance at the Capitol.[8]

Acheson was at the time a private attorney, a friend, a wise counselor. It was not wrong for him, assuming the accuracy of Weinstein's account, to have advised Hiss, a target then of unproved charges. The politics of the case was another matter.

If the members of the Senate had known that Acheson had advised Hiss on the latter's congressional testimony, they might have rejected Acheson's nomination, thereby altering the face of the second Truman administration. Even if Acheson had survived the Senate vote, the knowledge that he had counseled Hiss in Hiss's reply to Chambers would have been seized by Nixon, McCarthy, Bridges, Wherry, Mundt, Knowland, Jenner, and their friends to pillory the secretary of state even more than he was to be pilloried. However innocent it may have been, the disclosure of an authentic Acheson-Hiss connection would have been another calamity for President Truman. Fortunately for him and for Acheson, the fact did not become known at the time. Whether Acheson ever told Truman about his counseling of Hiss or whether, if he did, Truman shrugged it off is not known.

According to Acheson, Truman invited him to Blair House late in November 1948, after the election, and offered him the post of secretary of state. The next day Acheson accepted. On December 3, 1948, another of Hiss's lawyers, Edward C. McLean, sent to his legal colleague, Marbury, a couple of sets of photostats of the "pumpkin papers," saying, "one for you and one for Mr. Acheson." Obviously, the lawyers believed Acheson was still taking a personal interest in the case. Another line in the letter was more arresting. McLean wanted to read the copy of an interview a State Department security officer had had with Chambers in 1945. "Do you suppose," McLean inquired, "that Mr. Acheson would have any way of getting a look at it?"[9] Whether Acheson was asked to and, if so, what he did about the matter is not known.

It was mid-afternoon Saturday, January 22, 1950. A hush fell over the courtroom on the thirteenth floor of the United States District Court on Foley Square in Manhattan when the jury filed in in the case of *U.S.* v. *Hiss*. The eight women and four men had been out for almost twenty-four hours. Hiss and his wife, Priscilla, sat quietly together as Mrs. Ada Condell, the forewoman, stood to give the verdict. No other American jury thus far in the twentieth century has held in its hands a decision that was so long and so powerfully to permeate the political life of the nation. Technically, the charge was perjury—allegedly, Hiss had lied in testifying before the grand jury that he had not given State Department documents to Chambers, then a member of the Communist underground. In reality the charge was more than that. If, without authorization, Hiss had passed classified documents to a Communist agent, it would have been espionage. Possible prosecution for espionage had been excluded, however, because of expiration of the statute of limitations. Quietly, Mrs. Condell announced the verdict: Guilty on the two counts. Hiss *had* lied in denying that he had passed the documents.

Mrs. Condell's words were a bonanza for the Republicans. On radio that night Richard Nixon said that "high officials" of the Roosevelt and Truman administration had made a "definite, determined and deliberate" effort to cover up the Hiss "conspiracy." Representative Harold H. Velde, Republican, of Illinois, said that the conviction of Hiss cooked Truman's red herring—"I hope he enjoys eating it." Senator Homer E. Capehart, Republican, of Indiana, demanded that Truman apologize for calling the investigation of Hiss a red herring. Truman now had to pay the price for his carelessness and defiance in allowing reporters on two occasions in 1948 to lead him into saying yes to questions concerning whether or not he considered the investigation of the Committee on un-American Activities, featuring the Hiss case, a red herring. Even though he himself had not spoken the words, he was stuck with them, and before the week was out he had a dead cat hung around his neck also.

By the worst stroke of luck Acheson had a press conference scheduled for

January 25th in a matter of hours after Hiss was to be sentenced to five years in prison. The secretary of state felt certain in advance that he would be asked to comment on Hiss, and the previous night was filled with anxiety for him. He was appalled by the tragedy that had overtaken the Hiss family and seethed with contempt for Hiss's accusers. At Acheson's staff conference on the morning of the twenty-fifth his associates were openly concerned lest he make some damaging comment. James Webb, the under secretary, bade him be cautious and inquired what he expected to say. Acheson indicated he would refer to the twenty-fifth chapter of the Gospel according to St. Matthew, beginning with the thirty-fourth verse.[10] Carlisle H. Hummelsine, director of the executive secretariat of the State Department, observed that the words might mean different things to different people, but, generally, it appears, the anxiety abated.[11]

When the press conference opened, Homer Bigart, of the *New York Herald Tribune,* one of the best reporters of his time, asked Acheson if he had a comment on the Hiss case. Acheson replied that, with an appeal pending, the case was still before the courts "and I think that it would be highly improper for me to discuss the legal aspects of the case or the evidence or anything to do with the case." Never was a sentence more appropriate or more sufficient unto itself. But Acheson edged forward a bit. To the consternation of Hummelsine, who had accompanied him to the press conference, Acheson said, "I take it the purpose of your question was to bring something other than that out of me." He was committed now.

"I should like to make it clear to you," Acheson said, "that whatever the outcome of any appeal which Mr. Hiss or his lawyers may take in this case I do not intend to turn my back on Alger Hiss."[12]

It was the uniquely wrong phraseology by the uniquely wrong man at the uniquely wrong moment. Acheson doubtless intended a simple act of compassion for a fallen friend. His choice of words, however, smacked to critics of condonation of a man just sentenced for a grave crime, thus playing into the hands of Republicans, who maintained that the State Department "coddled" Communists.

Acheson, finally, conveyed the spirit in which he approached the subject by quoting words that Jesus had spoken on the Mount of Olives, according to Matthew, ". . . I was hungry and you gave me food, I was thirsty and you gave me drink, I was a stranger and you welcomed me, I was naked and you clothed me, I was sick and you visited me, I was in prison and you came to me."

By coincidence, the Republicans had managed at that moment to get the floor of the Senate to discuss the conviction of Hiss. Karl Mundt, who had been a member of the House Committee on un-American Activities during the 1948 investigation but had later been elected a senator, referred to Hiss's activities as espionage. It was wholly probable, Mundt said, that Hiss, with his "effective Harvard accent," had influenced the policy "which has helped bring about the entire subjugation of China by Communist forces directed from Moscow." Senator Bourke B. Hickenlooper, of Iowa, accused the Truman administration of "taking us down the road in shaping policies favorable to the Communist party."

Senator Homer Ferguson, of Michigan, charged that the administration had thrown an iron curtain around information about espionage in the government. Knowland picked this thread up quickly. As a member of the Senate Appropriations Committee he offered to collaborate with other senators in serving notice on the State Department that its appropriations would be withheld "until the information to which the Congress . . . is entitled is received from them."

Wherry had begun to expound upon "the secret agreement of Yalta" when he was interrupted by Joe McCarthy of Wisconsin.

"I wonder," McCarthy asked, "if the senator is aware of a most fantastic statement the secretary of state has made in the last few minutes? At a press conference he was asked to comment on the conviction of Hiss. I should like to have the senator's comment on the secretary of state's statement. This is what Dean Acheson said: 'Regardless of the outcome of the appeal, I shall never turn my back on Alger Hiss.' "

Mundt responded, "I am not greatly concerned about what influence Alger Hiss has on the position of Dean Acheson's back, but a great many Americans are concerned about the degree of influence Hiss may have had upon the position of Dean Acheson's mind."

Capehart said, "I am now more proud than ever that I voted against Acheson's confirmation."

McCarthy then asked, rhetorically, "Would the senator think that the statement I have read might be an indication that the secretary of state is also telling the world that he will not turn his back on any of the other Communists in the State Department—in other words—that the statement may go beyond Alger Hiss?"[13]

That same afternoon Acheson telephoned for an immediate appointment with the president, who had news ticker copy about the State Department press conference on his desk when Acheson arrived at the White House. Truman received him with a smile. Acheson offered to resign. Truman demurred. Later Acheson wrote his daughter, Mary Bundy that "He has been, as usual, wonderful about it and said that one who had gone to the funeral of a friendless old man just out of the penitentiary had no trouble in knowing what I meant and in approving it."[14] Truman was referring to the criticism heaped upon him when, as vice-president in 1945, he had flown to Kansas City for the funeral of Thomas J. Pendergast, former boss of the corrupt Kansas City Democratic machine.

Acheson, of course, remained secretary of state. It was advantageous for Republican purposes that he did. He was now a better target than ever for merciless partisan attack.

In the midst of such stress Acheson appeared before a National Press Club luncheon in Washington on January 12 and delivered what was probably the most controversial speech ever given by a secretary of state, certainly in modern times.[15] It was made controversial, however, only by future events. At the time reporters who covered it complained that the speech contained nothing new at all.

Behind it lay the serious strategic situation that confronted the United States in Asia. The defeat of Japan had ended a balance of power that had restrained the Russians in the Far East. Since the Second World War the Soviet Union had become an Asian power of the first magnitude. China, instead of being an ally of the United States, was in Communist hands. Having withdrawn its occupation forces from Korea, the United States had no military footing on the Asian mainland. A major objective of United States policy was to prevent the Soviet Union from dominating Asia.

On December 30, 1949, the National Security Council adopted the previously mentioned NSC 48/2, which based American defenses in the Far East on a chain of islands off the Asian mainland. The policy paper called for developing bases on Okinawa in the Ryukyu Islands and strengthening the American military position in the Philippines and Japan. The policy had been evolving for some time. Ten months earlier MacArthur, tracing the American defense line, had said, publicly that "It starts from the Philippines and continues through the Ryukyu Archipelago. . . . Then it bends back through Japan and the Aleutian Island chain to Alaska."

Two weeks after the NSC action Acheson made his speech to acquaint the American people with the administration's policy of security for the Pacific area. In the course of it he described the American "defensive perimeter"—the same as that defined by MacArthur.

Five months later, when Communist forces struck, Republicans and others remembered that Acheson's speech had excluded South Korea and Formosa from the defense perimeter. Then, and for years afterward, they charged that Acheson had given the Communists the green light to attack across the 38th parallel in Korea. According to Khrushchev, Kim Il-sung already had broached his plans for military action before Acheson's speech. Conceivably, the speech made Kim and Stalin and Mao more confident that the venture could succeed. Thus it was the timing of Acheson's speech that made it so controversial. The content was a restatemement of established administration policy. Furthermore, Acheson did not ignore the problem of areas of Asia, like South Korea, lying outside the defense perimeter. While no one could guarantee them against attack, he said, a guarantee was not necessary "within the realm of practical relationship." He explained:

> Should such an attack occur . . . the initial reliance must be on the people attacked to resist it and then upon the commitments of the entire civilized world under the Charter of the United Nations. . . .

When John M. Chang, the worried Korean ambassador in Washington, called at the State Department later to inquire where Acheson's speech left his country, W. Walton Butterworth, the assistant secretary of state for Far Eastern affairs, interpreted the secretary's statement to him. The United States had associated itself with other members of the United Nations in support of South Korea, Butterworth said, and, therefore, Korea's position transcended a definition of interest by a line drawn in any direction.[16]

At a press conference after Acheson's speech Truman said that the Formosa question had been settled by his own statement of January 5.[17] When it came to Asia nothing was settled. The turmoil went on and on. Senator Bridges suggested that Congress vote to censure the administration and withhold appropriations until China policy was changed. Knowland called for Acheson's resignation. Even a number of Democrats in Congress backed away from supporting the secretary of state.

Twelve months after Truman had been inaugurated for a second term he had suffered a serious setback over China, from which he never was fully to recover. Sensing it, his emboldened critics held him in their sights. After years of being on the defensive and experiencing humiliations at the polls, the Republicans had found in the momentous events in the Far East and in the Communist issue at home powerful weapons against Truman and the Democratic party. Acheson, Hiss, China, Formosa, and the State Department were bricks and mortar out of which a strong opposition to the Truman administration was being built.

13. *Vietnam: The First Grave Step*

ARGELY IN CONSEQUENCE OF the Communist victory in China, Harry Truman early in 1950 made the first of a series of fateful presidential decisions to be reached over a period of more than twenty years, which were to result in calamity for the American people. On the unanimous advice of his cabinet and on the recommendations of an array of advisers, Truman granted diplomatic recognition and later military assistance to a French-sponsored, anti-Communist regime in Vietnam, dedicated to the defeat of Ho Chi Minh and his Vietminh, or League for the Independence of Vietnam.

The arguments, considerations, and assumptions that went into Truman's decision were hauntingly similar to those that in the 1960s and 1970s were debated with a passion that threw the United States into political, cultural, and social convulsion.

Historically, the United States had had but slight interest in the whole of Southeast Asia, of which Indochina, with its common border with China, was a part. Before the Japanese overran Indochina in the Second World War, the land had been under French rule for more than half a century. After the war and the ejection of the Japanese, the French protectorates of Tonkin, Annam and Cochin China were combined to form Vietnam, so that Indochina then consisted of Vietnam and the kingdoms of Laos and Cambodia. A foe of colonialism, Roosevelt had talked during the war about a future international trusteeship for Indochina instead of restoration of French rule. Consistent with his course of deferring postwar settlements until after hostilities, he left no clear and ringing policy objective in Indochina for his successor to follow. The Roosevelt administration exerted no pressure on France to grant immediate independence to Indochina. Rather, in the latter days of the war Roosevelt's concern for trusteeship had seemed to wane under Allied pressures and the shifting course of the fighting. By the time of his death, French forces were infiltrating Indochina without objection from Washington, which had minimum influence then in the region.[1]

New in office, Truman was so swamped with greater events that he had little time to think about remote Indochina. The State Department was opposed to trusteeship and favored restoration of French sovereignty. Truman assented in a routine decision that turned out to be a momentous one. In 1945 the United States formally recognized French rule, while favoring eventual independence for the Indochinese. Hoping that the French would come to terms with Ho Chi

Minh, a Communist and a Vietnamese nationalist, the United States for the time being stood aloof.

By the end of 1946 the American attitude had changed. The Marshall mission had failed to pacify China. The Chinese Communists were beginning to turn the tide against Chiang Kai-shek. At the very moment in the Cold War when the United States was moving toward containment of communism, Ho Chi Minh and his guerrilla forces went to war against their French rulers. The least desirable outcome in Indochina, Acheson, then under secretary of state, said in a diplomatic cable, would be the establishment of a "Communist-dominated, Moscow-oriented state."[2] No longer aloof from events in Indochina, Acheson informed Henri Bonnet, the French ambassador in Washington, that while the United States was not then prepared to intervene, it was "ready and willing to do anything which it might consider helpful in the circumstances."[3]

France planned to form an Indochinese federation in which Vietnam, Laos, and Cambodia would be associated states within the French Union. Laos and Cambodia accepted the proposal, but it went awry with a revolt under Ho Chi Minh, a Communist and a Vietnamese nationalist, the United States for the time in 1946 as Ho Chi Minh withdrew his forces to the jungles and hills and harrassed the French, who held the cities. A professed admirer of the United States and its political ideals, Ho had sought American assistance and support after the war and even telegraphed appeals to Truman in the fall of 1945. The messages probably never reached the president's desk, for by that time the United States had recognized the sovereignty of the French, who nevertheless were stumbling in their efforts to re-establish their rule. So the question was posed, Who would govern Vietnam?

Unable to put down the Vietminh guerrillas, the French turned to the strategy of working through a collaborator and hit upon Bao Dai, an ineffectual figure, as a non-Communist nationalist to head a rival regime in Vietnam, which the French and their allies might support against Ho Chi Minh. The Paris-educated son of a royal Annamese family, Bao Dai in 1932, at the age of nineteen, had become, in name at least, the thirteenth emperor of Annam, later merged into Vietnam. After having occupied the throne under both French and Japanese rule, he abdicated after the war, owing to the rise of Ho. In 1947 the French began negotiations with Bao Dai as an instrument for ending the Vietminh revolution. As the negotiations continued into 1949, the United States became interested. Robert Lovett, the outgoing under secretary of state, cabled the United States embassy in Paris early in 1949 that the State Department hoped that the French might come to terms with Bao Dai "or any truly nationalist group which has a reasonable chance" of winning the Vietnamese over from Ho Chi Minh.[4] By this time the United States was very much alert to developments in Southeast Asia. For not only were the Communists fighting the French in Vietnam, but indigenous Communist forces also were engaged in armed struggles against newly independent governments in Burma, the Philippines, and India and against the struggling new republic of Indonesia as well as against the British in Malaya.

As Mao Tse-tung's armies swept south in China, the situation in Indochina became an emergency in the eyes of American policymakers, who dreaded the effect at home and abroad of a new Communist state in Asia. On June 10, 1949, Louis Johnson wrote to Admiral Sidney W. Souers, the executive secretary of the National Security Council: "I am becoming increasingly concerned at the course of events in Asia. The advance of communism in large areas of the world and particularly the successes of communism in China seriously affect the future security of the United States. . . . A major objective of United States policy, as I understand it, is to contain communism in order to reduce its threat to our security. Our actions in Asia should be part of a carefully considered and comprehensive plan to further that objective." Johnson asked the National Security Council to re-examine the situation in Asia.[5]

While this study was in progress Acheson ordered a State Department review of Far Eastern policy under the direction of Philip Jessup around the time of the issuance of the China White Paper in the summer of 1949. "You will please take as your assumption," Acheson instructed him, "that it is a fundamental decision of American policy that the United States does not intend to permit further extension of Communist domination on the continent of Asia or in the southeast Asia area." This was indeed the language of containment, now applied to the Far East. Ambassador Jessup later said, however, that in Acheson's words he did not discern "any thought of embroiling American manpower on the Asian continent."[6]

The strategic study requested by Louis Johnson resulted first in NSC 48/1, a report that said, among other things, that for the foreseeable future "our immediate objective must be to contain and where feasible to reduce the power and influence of the USSR in Asia." The report was refined into the previously mentioned policy paper, NSC 48/2, which went before the National Security Council's fifthtieth meeting on December 30, 1949. Entitled "The Position of the United States with Respect to Asia," the subsequently approved NSC 48/2 called for the gradual reduction and eventual elimination by nonmilitary means "of the preponderant power and influence of the USSR in Asia to such a degree that the Soviet Union will not be capable of threatening from that area the security of the United States or its friends. . . ." The paper favored "development of sufficient military power in selected non-communist nations to maintain internal security and to prevent further encroachment by communism." It advocated "prevention of power relationships in Asia which would enable any other nation or alliance to threaten the security of the United States from that area, or the peace, national independence and stability of the Asiatic nations."[7]

As was to be the case with its successors, the Truman administration was in a dilemma over Vietnam. It had recognized French sovereignty yet saw no end of deep trouble in Vietnam so long as France's colonialism continued. Clearly, the French had not been able to turn the tide of the fighting. On the other hand, the Truman administration did not want France to withdraw and leave Vietnam in Communist hands. Rich in food and other natural resources, Southeast Asia was viewed in Washington as a strategic area within the great crescent curving from India through Australia and northward to Japan. Very urgently, the United

States wanted a stable France as a keystone of the security system being organized to save Western Europe from communism. Hence, France must retain access to Indochinese resources. A cooperative government must be kept in power in Paris. "Failure to support French policy in Indochina would have the effect of contributing toward defeat of our aims in Europe," said a report by a working group in the State Department.[8] Finally, the Truman administration had no solution of its own to offer for the problem in Vietnam.

During the negotiations with Bao Dai in France the State Department marked time, fretting that the French were not offering him enough concessions on self-government for Vietnam to enable him to win over a majority of the Vietnamese people. But as Jefferson Caffery, the United States ambassador in Paris, cabled Acheson—in words that were to be repeated over and over again in the State Department—the "Bao Dai experiment" was the "only non-Communist solution in sight."[9] Finally, on March 8, 1949, the so-called Elysée Agreement was signed by Bao Dai and French President Vincent Auriol. Subject to ratification by the French Assembly, a process that was to take months, the agreement recognized the independence of Vietnam, with the catch that France retained responsibility for foreign affairs and defense and enjoyed various special privileges. Vietnam and the other associated states of Laos and Cambodia were obliged to become members of the French Union.

A week after the signing, Ambassador Caffery recommended to Acheson that the United States extend economic aid when Bao Dai had established a government in Vietnam. The ambassador also passed on information that Bao Dai hoped that the United States would help him obtain arms.[10]

Bao Dai arrived in Dalat, a city northeast of Saigon, on April 28, 1949. On May 10 Acheson cabled the consulate general in Saigon:

At proper time and under proper circumstances Dept will be prepared [to] do its part by extending recognition Baodai Govt and by exploring possibility of complying with any request by such Govt for US arms and econ assistance.

There appeared, Acheson said, to be no other alternative to the establishment of a "Commie pattern" in Vietnam. Bao Dai, he added, "must certainly be fully warned of danger [of] yielding to any temptation [to] include Commies [in] his govt. . . ." On the other hand, the secretary admonished, the Bao Dai government must avoid the coloration of a puppet regime.[11]

State Department cables continued to deplore the unwillingness of the French to grant Vietnam sufficient autonomy to win popular loyalty, or, in the parlance of a later period, "the hearts and minds of the people." Differences had existed in the department as to the terms on which the United States should agree to grant recognition. Some officials maintained that the French should first be required to liberalize their concessions to the Vietnamese, or to pledge that new reforms were on the way, or even to establish a "timetable" specifiying what steps toward full independence of Vietnam would be taken and when. Otherwise, it was said, the United States would be recognizing a futile regime. The counter-argument was that the French government could not survive such a departure, politically, that the Assembly would balk at ratifying the Elysée Agreement, and that, in any case, the United States had no choice but to recognize Bao Dai in a desperate effort to forestall a Communist Vietnam.

Emperor Bao Dai assumed power in a ceremony in Saigon June 14, 1949. The Vietnamese flag was raised to the booming of a twenty-one-gun salute. The emperor reviewed troops. The guard of honor included Caodaists and members of the Hoa Hao, Ben Nguyen, and the local Catholic defense corps. Security arrangements prevented spectators from getting close to the new chief of state. But he and Leon Pignon, French high commissioner for Indochina, made speeches. In his talk Bao Dai promised a new popular constitution but said that the international situation was too grave for the holding of elections at the moment. Enthusiasm, according to the official report to the State Department, was limited but "apparently spontaneous."[12]

Two and a half months later, addressing Truman as "Great and Good Friend," His Majesty Bao Dai wrote to the president, requesting that the United States establish relations with Vietnam.[13] Since the French assembly had not yet ratified the Elysée Agreement, Truman delayed replying.

Events "beyond our control are marching on the mainland of Asia," Acheson said later in a cable to the United States embassy in Paris. He feared that, because of the circumscribed grant of independence to Vietnam, the Elysée Agreement might be "another instance of too little and too late." Still he viewed a non-Communist Vietnam as crucial. A military solution or the political containment of communism, he said, "is indeed beyond the capacity of France and of Western Democracies unless, at very minimum, the Bao Dai regime obtains the support of a substantial proportion of the Vietnamese." He allowed himself to believe that "Bao Dai has made relatively more progress than had been anticipated."[14]

In reply, the new American ambassador in Paris, David K. E. Bruce, son of a distinguished Maryland family, former son-in-law of Andrew Mellon, and a Democrat whose opinion counted in Washington, said that the United States had a vital interest in a non-Communist Vietnam. The term "blood bath" was not to emerge until a later phase of the American debate over Vietnam, but Bruce predicted a "massacre" of tens of thousands of French civilians and anti-Communist Vietnamese if French troops were withdrawn from the country. Furthermore, if Communist expansion were not checked, he said, Burma and Thailand would fall "like overripe apples"—dominoes became the accepted metaphor in the Eisenhower administration—and Britain's hold on Malaya would be doubtful. Ambassador Bruce was no nervous Nellie, as Lyndon Johnson might have said later. "A view that Ho Chi Minh will inevitably take over Indochina is dangerous and defeatist," Bruce declared. "We should act courageously and speedily within the limits of the possible."[15]

American officials were worried that Mao Tse-tung might order his forces to invade Indochina, or else that Chinese Communist troops might pour into

Vietnam in pursuit of retreating Chinese Nationalist remnants. In any case it was believed that Mao would send Ho arms and technicians. George M. Abbott, the American consul general in Saigon, had cabled Acheson late in December 1949 that failure of the United States to recognize Bao Dai would appear throughout Indochina as "evidence that US Government indifferent and irresolute in opposing spread of Communism. . . ."[16] Loy W. Henderson, United States ambassador to India, added his advice that Washington should act to avoid giving the impression "of lack of convictions."[17] Visiting Washington in the fall of 1949, however, India's Prime Minister Jawaharlal Nehru warned Acheson that, with the French holding only the cities and not the countryside, the Bao Dai venture was hopeless.[18]

The final triumph of the Communists in China that fall put tremendous momentum behind the American move toward recognition of Bao Dai. Because the administration had been embarrassed by events in China, it wanted to be seen as taking a strong stand in Indochina. Furthermore, it rather unexpectedly had the money to finance an activist policy in Indochina, because Congress had appropriated $75 million for use in the general area of China. Curiously, as the historian Robert Marshall Blum has noted, the funds had originated in demands of the China bloc for more assistance to Chiang Kai-shek. In opposing this course, the administration accepted a proposal for funds to be placed at Truman's disposal in the area of China. Interestingly, in retrospect, Congress at the time gave little thought to the consequences of aid to the anti-Communist elements in Vietnam.

By the start of 1950 Acheson had decided, subject to Truman's approval, to recognize Bao Dai's regime when the French Assembly ratified the Elysée Agreement. From the start Washington and London had been reluctant to take the lead in granting recognition lest it seem a move by Western powers to strengthen French colonialism and hence prove a kiss of death for Bao Dai. Acheson and Bevin preferred that Asian states lead the way. But detestation of colonialism in India, Indonesia, Burma, Thailand, and the Philippines caused those nations to recoil from Bao Dai. Acheson was exasperated at what struck him as their apathy toward the new danger of Communist imperialism. "This general indifference or lack of understanding," he cabled the United States embassy in Thailand, "may prove to be disastrous for those nations as Communism relentlessly advances. It is impossible for the United States to help them resist Communism if they are not prepared to help themselves."[19]

Acheson was disturbed by an increase in Vietminh military activity as well as by signs that Bao Dai was having trouble not only in forming a cabinet but also in winning broad support from the people. Acheson clung to the hope that recognition by the United States and other countries would increase Bao Dai's following by giving him stature in the eyes of non-Communists in Vietnam.[20]

The second half of January 1950 was a jarring one for the Truman administration. On January 19, twelve days after the Chinese Communists had seized part of the United States consulate general in Peking, Mao recognized the government of Ho Chi Minh. On January 31 the Soviet Union granted recognition, strengthening the notion among the Western powers that revolutionary international communism was on the march in Indochina. The Soviet action, Acheson declared in a public statement on February 1, "should remove any illusions as to the 'nationalist' nature of Ho Chi Minh's aims and reveals Ho in his true colors as the mortal enemy of native independence in Indochina." The same day the previously mentioned working group in the State Department submitted to Acheson its secret report, saying that already Ho controlled in varying degrees two-thirds of Vietnam. "The choice confronting the United States," according to the report, "is to support the French in Indochina or face the extension of Communism over the remainder of the continental area of Southeast Asia and, possibly, farther westward." The report recommended that the United States furnish military aid, but not troops, to the anti-Communist governments of Indochina.

The French Assembly ratified the Elysée Agreement.

On February 2 Acheson recommended to Truman in a memorandum that the United States recognize Vietnam, Laos, and Cambodia. Acheson's reasons: ". . . encouragement to national aspirations under non-Communist governments in areas adjacent to Communist China; support to a friendly country which is also a signatory to the North Atlantic Treaty; and . . . demonstration of displeasure with Communist tactics which are obviously aimed at eventual domination of Asia, working under the guise of indigenous nationalism."

Through Vietminh propaganda and interviews with journalists Ho Chi Minh, an admirer of the United States during the Second World War, had pictured himself as a true nationalist, not a Communist pawn. He declared his neutrality in the Cold War. Acheson and others had long been suspicious of him, however, and Soviet recognition settled matters. The secretary told Truman in the memorandum that under various aliases, Ho had been a Communist agent in various part of the world since 1925.[21]

At a cabinet meeting on February 3, 1950, according to Acheson, he outlined the case for recognition at Truman's request. Truman then solicited the opinion of each member of the cabinet, Acheson wrote. "All members present," as he later recorded the event, "believed that the only possible course was to proceed with recognition although they fully realized the hazards involved." The last was unlikely. Matthew J. Connelly's regular notes on cabinet meetings, while characteristically sketchy, portray less fulsome participation by the cabinet than Acheson's record suggests. Connelly, the appointments secretary to the president, summarized Acheson's presentation as follows: "The communists are indicating further inroads in Indo-China. Feels that we should block further advances of the Russians in Indonesia." Then, according to the Connelly notes, Vice-President Barkley, Secretary of the Interior Oscar L. Chapman, Secretary of Commerce Charles Sawyer, and Secretary of Labor Maurice Tobin "Feel we should take a stand."

"After considering the advice of the cabinet," Acheson noted, "the President directed me to proceed in accordance with our recommendation to him."[22]

Almost immediately the Truman administration found itself being pulled toward a deeper commitment. In Paris, Maurice Couve de Murville of the French

Ministry of Foreign Affairs told Charles E. Bohlen, minister at the United States embassy, that France would find it difficult going it alone in Indochina. Because of the Communist threat, intensified by Moscow's recognition of Ho, Couve de Murville suggested that Indochina was as much an American and British as a French concern.[23] In Saigon, Bao Dai expressed to Abbott, the American consul general, his hopes for assistance. The emperor said that the first new equipment should go to the troops. As if anticipating the Popular Forces militia of a later day, Bao Dai stressed the wisdom of equipping "village readiness contingents," or home guards.[24] Pignon reminded Abbott that the problem of equipment was "pretty much up to US."[25] In Washington, Ambassador Bonnet called on Acheson and requested not only military assistance for Indochina but also joint military staff talks.[26]

The National Security Council assayed the American position in respect to Indochina and on February 27 promulgated NSC 64, later approved by Truman. The policy paper concluded that it was important to American security "that all practicable measures be taken to prevent further Communist expansion in Southeast Asia." The domino theory was then propounded in everything but name: "Indochina is a key area of Southeast Asia and is under immediate threat. The neighboring countries of Thailand and Burma could be expected to fall under Communist domination if Indochina were controlled by a Communist-dominated government." The Department of State and the Department of Defense "should prepare as a matter of priority a program of all practicable measures designed to protect United States security interests in Indochina."[27]

"The President stated this is one of the most important problems we face," Under Secretary of State Webb noted after conferring with Truman in Key West on March 26. As to whether the United States might intervene in Indochina as it had in Greece and Turkey under the Truman Doctrine, the president said "absolutely not." A different approach must be found, he explained, because of the instability of the French government. He instructed Webb, in the latter's words, "to be most careful in the handling of this situation."[28]

On May 1 Truman allocated $10 million for military assistance to Indochina. After a meeting in Paris with Schuman on May 8, Acheson made the public announcement that the United States would give economic aid and military equipment to Laos, Cambodia, and Vietnam and to France "in order to assist them in restoring stability and permitting these states to pursue their peaceful and democratic development."[29] An American economic mission was established.

Thus in the spring of 1950 the prestige and resources of the United States were committed to the defeat of Ho Chi Minh's guerrillas in Vietnam. At first the resources were small, but the next step in escalation, occasioned by dramatic events, was only weeks away. As the Pentagon Papers later asserted, the United States had become "directly involved in the developing tragedy in Vietnam."[30]

The capstone of containment in the Far East was put in place a year later with the signing of the enlightened, nonpunitive Japanese Peace Treaty and related pacts at San Francisco in September 1951. Negotiated by Dulles, these treaties were the last flowering of "bipartisan foreign policy" in the Truman administration. Truman told the fifty-two-nation conference in San Francisco: "At the present time the Pacific area is gravely affected by outright aggression and by the threat of further armed attack. One of our primary concerns in making peace with Japan, therefore, is to make Japan secure against aggression and to provide that Japan . . . will so conduct itself as not to endanger the security of other nations."[31] Separate security treaties were signed with the Philippines, with Australia and New Zealand (the ANZUS Pact), and with the Japanese, authorizing the stationing of American forces in Japan. Together, these treaties consolidated American power in the Western Pacific.

14. *The Hydrogen Bomb Decision*

B

Y THE START OF 1950 the time was approaching for Truman to decide whether to initiate a program to build a hydrogen bomb. In the previous October he had approved a major acceleration in the production of atomic bombs. Even before "Operation Joe," the American code name for the Soviet atomic explosion in September, the military had been seeking a larger stockpile of American atomic bombs. The Soviet success had made that seem more urgent than ever not only to the military but also to the president's civilian advisers, and pressure for a reassuring response to the Soviet bomb was rising in Congress through the powerful Joint Committee on Atomic Energy.

While Truman was still deliberating the expansion of atomic bomb production, Lewis Strauss made his proposal to fellow members of the Atomic Energy Commission to meet the new Soviet challenge with a crash program to manufacture a hydrogen bomb. Strauss doubted, however, whether David Lilienthal, the chairman, and a majority of the commissioners would agree to it. A wartime acquaintance of Admiral Strauss's was Admiral Souers, consultant to the president on national security affairs and a man who thoroughly enjoyed Truman's confidence. Through Souers, Strauss had his proposal brought to Truman's attention in October 1949. According to Richard G. Hewlett and Francis Duncan, official historians of the Atomic Energy Commission, Truman apparently had never heard of the theoretical hydrogen bomb but showed an immediate interest, which was not surprising in a president at a time when Congress and the country demanded action in the wake of the Soviet blast. "Truman wanted Strauss to force the issue up to the White House and to do it quickly," Hewlett and Duncan reported.[1] The public, of course, knew nothing of any of this, Strauss's proposal having been made in the secrecy of the Atomic Energy Commission.

Dr. Wendell M. Latimer, dean of the department of chemistry at the University of California at Berkeley, was worried about the possibility that the Soviets might move directly into development of a hydrogen bomb as a means of offsetting America's lead in atomic bombs. He mentioned his concern to Dr. Ernest O. Lawrence, winner of the Nobel Prize in physics, one of the developers of the atomic bomb, and then director of the Atomic Energy Commission's radiation laboratory at Berkeley. In turn Lawrence discussed Latimer's concern with a scientific colleague there, Dr. Luis W. Alvarez. Together they agreed, according to Hewlett and Duncan, that a hydrogen bomb "would be an effective response to the Soviet threat." Scheduled to go to Washington in any case, Lawrence decided to take Alvarez with him to stir up interest for such a bomb. On the way, the two stopped at the Los Alamos Scientific Laboratory in New Mexico to consult Dr. Edward Teller, an early advocate of building the atomic bomb and a believer in the feasibility of a thermonuclear weapon, whose principal developer he was to be.

Encouraged by Teller, Lawrence and Alvarez arrived in Washington on October 8, 1949, and talked with the Atomic Energy Commission staff and lunched with McMahon, the chairman, and another member of the Joint Congressional Committee on Atomic Energy. "The outcome," reported Hewlett and Duncan, "was predictable: The legislators and the scientists were more than ever convinced that the superweapon might well save the nation from the Soviet threat."[2] McMahon dispatched a subcommittee to Los Alamos and Berkeley to explore the prospects of a hydrogen bomb.

From Capitol Hill Lawrence and Alvarez went to speak individually with members of the Atomic Energy Commission. With Lilienthal they ran into trouble. The chairman was already apprehensive about the push for more and better atomic weapons. On October 10 he wrote in his journal: "We keep saying, 'We have no other course'; what we should be saying is 'We are not bright enough to see any other course.' The day has been filled, too, with talk about supers, single weapons capable of desolating a vast area. Ernest Lawrence and Luis Alvarez in here drooling over the same. Is this all we have to offer?"[3]

The Atomic Energy Commission had a statutory general advisory committee of distinguished scientists, chaired by Robert Oppenheimer. Principal developer of the atomic bomb, Oppenheimer was one of the nation's most brilliant physicists and cultivated citizens, an enigmatic man with a personality that fluctuated between charm and arrogance. Two years after his wartime work as director of the atomic bomb project at Los Alamos he became director of the Institute for Advanced Study at Princeton. In 1946 he was the chief author of the Acheson-Lilienthal report, the basis of the United States' plan for international control of atomic energy. Oppenheimer also was head of a scientific group that had discovered the theoretical possibility of a hydrogen bomb in 1942.

After talking with Lawrence and Alvarez, Lilienthal asked Oppenheimer to call a special meeting of the advisory committee to recommend whether the Atomic Energy Commission should undertake a crash program to build a hydrogen bomb. Meanwhile Teller, greatly disturbed by the Soviet explosion, set out on something of a personal crusade to enlist support for the hydrogen bomb.

Matching his efforts were those of his friends, Lewis Strauss, who worked tirelessly to fan the enthusiasm of McMahon, Lawrence, and others and who found ready allies in the Pentagon for a hydrogen bomb program. Son of a Virginia shoe wholesaler, Strauss as a young man had walked in off the street, unannounced, to get a job as secretary to Herbert Hoover on the Belgian Relief Commission in 1917. From there Strauss went on to make a fortune in the Wall Street investment firm of Kuhn, Loeb & Company, eventually marrying a daughter of one of the partners. During the Second World War he rose to rear admiral, assigned to the navy's bureau of ordnance. He became close to Secretary of the Navy Forrestal, who appointed him the navy's representative on the old interdepartmental committee on atomic energy, a role that led to Strauss's appointment by Truman to the Atomic Energy Commission. Oppenheimer caught the essence of Strauss: "Very smart and very vain."[4] Behind Strauss's courtly manner lay one of the most steely, determined, uncompromising characters in the Washington of his day. He characterized himself as "a black Hoover Republican."[5] On nothing did Strauss's steel and determination bear so forcefully as on his hostility to communism and his belief in a strong national defense.

Before the scheduled meeting of the general advisory committee, Oppenheimer on October 21, 1949, wrote to his friend and fellow member of the committee, Dr. James Bryant Conant, president of Harvard University, who was dead set against the hydrogen bomb. Technically, Oppenheimer said, the problem of the hydrogen bomb was not much different from what it had been in 1942: ". . . a weapon of unknown design, cost, deliverability and military value."

"But a very great change has taken place in the climate of opinion," he continued. "On the one hand, two experienced promoters have been at work, i.e., Ernest Lawrence and Edward Teller. The project has long been dear to Teller's heart; and Ernest has convinced himself that we must learn from Operation Joe that the Russians will soon do the super, and that we had better beat them to it.

"But the real development has not been of a technical nature. Ernest spoke to Knowland and McMahon and to some at least of the joint chiefs. The joint congressional committee, having tried to find something tangible to chew on ever since [Operation Joe], has at least found its answer. We must have a super, and we must have it fast. . . . The joint chiefs appear informally to have decided to give the development . . . overriding priority. . . . The climate of opinion among the competent physicists also shows signs of shifting."

Pinpointing of a situation that was certain to bring great pressure on Truman, Oppenheimer concluded: "What does worry me is that this thing appears to have caught the imagination, both of the congressional and of military people, as the answer to the problem posed by the Russian advance. It would be folly to oppose the exploration of this weapon. We have always known it had to be done; and it does have to be done, though it appears to be singularly proof against any form of experimental approach. But that we become committed to it as the way to save the country and the peace appears to me full of danger."[6]

The general advisory committee met without public notice and on October 30, 1949, unanimously recommended against a crash program to build a hydrogen bomb—a weapon, they said, whose energy release would be from one hundred to one thousand times greater and whose destructive power in terms of area damage would be from twenty to one hundred times greater than those of the existing atomic bombs. The members objected on both technical and moral grounds.

As to the former, they held that construction of a hydrogen bomb probably would require large amounts of tritium, necessitating immense reactor capacity.

Research on such a weapon was in so early a stage that theoretical design studies had not yet been completed or tested.[7]

On the moral side, a statement signed by six members—Oppenheimer; Conant; Dr. Lee A. DuBridge, president of the California Institute of Technology; Hartley Rowe, vice-president and chief engineer of the United Fruit Company; Oliver E. Buckley, president of Bell Telephone Laboratories; and Dr. Cyril S. Smith, director of the Institute for Study of Metals at the University of Chicago—held that "the extreme dangers to mankind inherent in the proposal outweigh any military advantage that could come from this development."[8] Two other members—Dr. Enrico Fermi of the Unversity of Chicago Institute for Nuclear Studies and Dr. Isidor I. Rabi of Columbia University, a Nobel laureate in physics—appended an opinion. They asserted that a hydrogen bomb would go "far beyond any military objective and [enter] the range of very great natural catastrophes. By its very nature it cannot be confined to a military objective but becomes a weapon which in practical effect is almost one of genocide."[9]

The statement of the six members, written by Conant, noted that a hydrogen bomb would be "in a totally different category from an atomic bomb," because of the vast range of destruction. "Its use," the statement said, "would involve a decision to slaughter a vast number of civilians. . . . Therefore, a superbomb might become a weapon of genocide."

In recommending against production of a bomb the six members said:

> To the argument that the Russians may succeed in developing this weapon, we would reply that our undertaking it will not prove a deterrent to them. Should they use the weapon against us, reprisals by our large stock of atomic bombs would be comparably effective to the use of a super.
>
> In determining not to proceed to develop the super bomb, we see a unique opportunity of providing by example some limitations on the totality of war and thus of limiting the fear and arousing the hope of mankind.

Four and a half years later Oppenheimer was to testify that "I think what was not clear to us then and what is clearer to me now is that it probably lay wholly beyond our power to prevent the Russians somehow from getting ahead with it [the hydrogen bomb]."[10]

Fermi and Rabi said in their separate opinion:

> It is clear that the use of such a weapon cannot be justified on any ethical ground which gives a human being a certain individuality and dignity even if he happens to be a resident of an enemy country. . . . Its use would put the United States in a bad moral position relative to the peoples of the world. . . . A desirable peace cannot come from such an inhuman application of force. The postwar problems would dwarf the problems which confront us at present. . . . [The bomb] is necessarily an evil thing considered in any light.

The two scientists suggested that instead of building a hydrogen bomb, the United States "invite the nations of the world to join us in a solemn pledge not to proceed in the development or construction of weapons in this category."

What was to be done in the event that the Soviet Union refused to make such a pledge the scientists did not say.

These statements were classified top secret and remained unknown to the public for many years.

For Truman, who saw the general advisory committee report within a matter of days, the advice about the hydrogen bomb was dramatically different from that which he had received from an advisory committee he had appointed when he was pondering using the atomic bomb against Japan. In 1945 the Interim Committee, whose members included Conant, had recommended that the atomic bomb should be used as soon as possible.[11] The Interim Committee itself had had a scientific advisory panel, including Oppenheimer and Fermi, which reported to the committee at one point that "we see no acceptable alternate to direct military use."[12] A number of the scientists giving advice regarding the hydrogen bomb in 1949 had been involved in the development of the atomic bomb and had come to feel guilty about it. Indeed, Truman had complained to Acheson in 1946 that Oppenheimer was a "cry baby" because the scientist had called at the White House "and spent most of his time wringing his hands and telling me they had blood on them because of the discovery of atomic energy."[13] Having faced the ordeal of the atomic bomb decision and made a choice, Truman was at peace with himself about his act and did not relish having scientists take up his time with their laments.

Among the relatively small number of officials who knew about the general advisory committee report recommending against a crash program reactions were keen. McMahon, according to Webb, was "almost in tears." The report made him sick, the senator said.[14] Strauss was deeply disturbed.[15] Teller was baffled by the moral distinction between more and better atomic bombs and a hydrogen bomb.[16] Acheson, too, was uncomprehending. "How can you persuade a paranoid adversary to disarm 'by example'?" he asked R. Gordon Arneson, the State Department expert on atomic energy policy. Acheson said rejection of a hydrogen bomb program would sweep the administration into a congressional "buzz-saw."[17] Lilienthal, of course, was pleased by the report. The Joint Chiefs of Staff reported to Louis Johnson on November 23, 1949, that possession of a hydrogen bomb by the Soviet Union while the United States was armed only with atomic weapons would be intolerable. For reasons of military and foreign policy, they maintained, it was imperative to determine the feasibility of a thermonuclear explosion. They said that moral objections to the bomb were outweighed by its potential military value and the danger that the Soviets would acquire it.[18]

In the end, Truman was confronted with a narrowly divided Atomic Energy Commission: three to two against building a hydrogen bomb. On November 9 Lilienthal presented him not a recommendation by the commission but a memorandum containing views of the members and a technical summary. The principal premise of this was that chances were better than even that the bomb could be built and that the Soviets "probably can develop a bomb in a period comparable to that which we would need." The issue, Lilienthal said in his memorandum, could not "be finally resolved within the Commission." "The destructive possibilities of a single 'Super,' " he explained, "are . . . so great and the implications involved in any decision to embark . . . upon the development of it so far reaching, that we have considered it our duty to lay the problem before you." Lilienthal deplored the "misconception and illusion about the value to us of weapons of mass destruction as the chief means of protecting ourselves and of furthering our national policy."[19]

Meanwhile one of the most eminent of American scientists, Dr. Karl T. Compton, who had recently retired as president of the Massachusetts Institute of Technology, wrote to Truman, saying that in the absence of an international agreement on control of atomic energy the country had no choice but to proceed with a hydrogen bomb program.[20] Truman was now getting strong doses of the case for the bomb. From Los Angeles McMahon wrote to him saying that "if we let Russia get the super first, catastrophe becomes all but certain—whereas, if we get it first, there exists a chance of saving ourselves."[21]

Strauss, encouraged by the three-to-two split in the Atomic Energy Commission, also wrote to the president: "I believe that the United States must be as completely armed as any possible enemy. From this, it follows that I believe it unwise to renounce, unilaterally, any weapon which an enemy can reasonably be expected to possess." Referring to the likely reaction of the Soviet Union, Strauss said that a "government of atheists is not likely to be dissuaded from producing the weapon on 'moral' grounds."[22]

Thus, despite the report of the general advisory committee, heavy pressure was being brought to bear on Truman to order a hydrogen bomb program. A most telling form of the pressure was a revelation in Lilienthal's memorandum of November 9 to the president that the Joint Congressional Committee was preparing to take early action on the issue of proceeding with a hydrogen bomb program. That distinctly raised the question of whether, if Truman were to decide against the bomb, he could make the decision stick. In the prevailing mood it was quite possible—and so commentators noted at the time—that Congress might take the lead and appropriate funds for a hydrogen bomb. Under public pressure the president, with serious consequences for his leadership, might not be able to prevail. And by now the public knew what was going on. In a New York television program on November 1, Senator Edwin C. Johnson, Democrat, of Colorado, a member of the joint committee, revealed that consideration was being given to building a superbomb. Alfred Friendly of the *Washington Post* developed the remarks into a major story, published on November 18. The hydrogen bomb became a public issue and one bound to make it very difficult for the president to reject the weapon in view of the Soviet success with an atomic device.

Along with the pressures, there was developing behind the hydrogen bomb proposal a momentum similar to that which had carried along the atomic bomb program. Scientists were aroused by the challenge of mastering a hydrogen bomb. As Oppenheimer was to testify in 1954 in connection with the decision to build it, "when you see something that is technically sweet, you go ahead and do it and you argue about what to do about it only after you have had your technical success. That is the way it was with the atomic bomb. I do not think anybody opposed making it: there were some debates about what to do with it after it was made."[23] "If there is a new possibility," Teller said afterward, regarding the hydrogen bomb, "I would like to see it explored and developed. . . . I did believe in science and in progress and in finding out what can be done. And I did have the confidence that there was at least a good possibility what we developed would be properly used rather than misused."[24]

Because of the magnitude of the decision before him, Truman on November 19 revived the special committee of the National Security Council—Acheson, Louis Johnson, and Lilienthal—which he had appointed in 1949 to advise him on the atomic energy program. He directed that the committee secretly analyze the technical, military, and political aspects of the hydrogen bomb question and submit a recommendation to him.[25] The outcome was hardly in doubt. On the basis of their known attitudes, Acheson and Johnson were almost certain to favor moving ahead on a hydrogen bomb program. Lilienthal later observed, "Our policy was to get rid of atomic bombs through international control on the one hand, and yet our military was relying on these weapons as virtually our only means of defense."[26]

Before the special committee had decided on its recommendation, Johnson, impatient to get on with the hydrogen bomb and acting on his own initiative, forwarded to Truman a new memorandum he had received from General Bradley, which essentially restated the Joint Chiefs' views of November 23. In the new memorandum the chiefs said that it was not necessary to institute a crash program. But the feasibility of a thermonuclear explosion should be determined and studies made of the necessary delivery vehicle and ordnance problems. A decision on whether or not to produce thermonuclear weapons in quantity should be deferred until such studies had been completed.[27] Truman told Admiral Souers, as Acheson noted, that in Truman's opinion this advice "made a lot of sense and he was inclined to think that is what we should do." Acheson had about reached the conclusion that the special committee should advise Truman to proceed to determine the feasibility of the bomb, but he added that "we [the committee] should be quite honest and say that in advising this action, we are going quite a long way to committing ourselves to continue down that road."[28] In reality, determining the feasibility meant proceeding with a hydrogen bomb program.

By then the newspapers were playing up speculation about the superbomb and whether it would be approved by the president. Within the special committee differences had arisen, and these were rumored in the press. Lilienthal maintained that a decision to proceed with the bomb might close the door to international control. Louis Johnson held the point to be irrelevant to the committee's terms of reference.[29] Meanwhile pressures for a decision grew. Bernard Baruch, popularly considered a wise owl in such matters because of the Baruch plan for international control—Truman called him a "phony"—publicly declared himself in favor of building the bomb.[30] On January 27 Dr. Harold C. Urey of the University of Chicago, a Nobel laureate and one of the developers of the atomic bomb, said in a speech: "The hydrogen bomb should be . . . built. I do not think we should intentionally lose the armaments race; to do this will be to lose our liberties."

At noon on January 31 Truman was in his office with Gordon Arneson, the State Department expert on atomic energy policy, waiting for a visit from the special committee, which had been holding its final session across the street in what was then known as Old State and is now called the Executive Office Building. Truman happened to glance at a small sign on his desk: THE BUCK STOPS HERE, which had been given to him early in his presidency by one of his old political handymen, Fred A. Canfil, United States marshal for the Western District of Missouri. With Arneson listening, Truman began to soliloquize.

"He mused," Arneson later wrote, "about how many 'bucks' he had stopped: the abrupt termination of Lend-Lease after the war: bad advice, a blooper; the Truman Doctrine re. Greece and Turkey: good; the Berlin airlift: right again; and the Marshall Plan: a 'ten strike.' Over-all, the batting average was pretty good, he thought."

Then the soliloquy took an interesting turn.

"He wondered, though, whether the decision to reduce drastically the defense budget might have been unwise. True it had been enthusiastically welcomed by the public and the Congress. But, considering the unsettled state of world affairs and especially the uncooperativeness of the Russians, was it prudent? He sighed."[31]

The members of the special committee arrived.

Actually, the two-hour session in Old State had been superfluous. Ten days earlier Truman had indicated to his staff that he had made up his mind.[32] He did not disclose his decision then, but in retrospect it is obvious. The basic recommendation agreed upon by the triumvirate at Old State was that the president approve a program to determine the technical feasibility of a thermonuclear weapon. This was a compromise between a crash program and outright rejection of the hydrogen bomb. At the same time the committee, significantly, recommended that Truman direct the secretaries of state and defense "to undertake a reexamination of our objectives in peace and war and of the effect of these objectives on our strategic plans, in light of the probable fission [atomic] bomb capability and possible thermonuclear bomb capability of the Soviet Union."

In committee Lilienthal had urged that any start on the hydrogen bomb be deferred until after the review had been completed. Otherwise, he argued, the hydrogen bomb program and an arms race with the Soviets would surely go forward. Acheson said that the public pressure for a decision was so great and the feeling in Congress so high that he could not recommend delay to the president.[33]

At the White House Acheson told the president that Lilienthal would like to make some comments of his own.[34] Knowing Lilienthal's feelings, Truman turned to him and said he did not believe a hydrogen bomb would ever be used but that because of the way the Russians were behaving, no other course was open but to proceed with a program. Lilienthal replied that another course was open. For the president to announce a hydrogen bomb program, he continued, would be interpreted as confirmation of the course of relying on nuclear weapons instead of conventional power and in that respect would weaken the country.

Before Lilienthal could go on, Truman interrupted to say that military policy could have been quietly re-examined before a decision was made on the hydrogen bomb if Senator Johnson had not revealed the secret debate over a superbomb. Since then, he said, Congress had talked so much and the people had become so excited that he really had no alternative.[35] That was, to keep things in perspective, nine days after Hiss had been convicted. In the atmosphere created by Communist gains in Asia and rising anti-communism in the United States, it was, as the historian Samuel F. Wells, Jr., has written, "difficult for political leaders to resist steps which increased American strength to deter Communist aggression."[36] The direct pressure on the president not to build the hydrogen bomb was negligible.

Truman asked the special committee, "Can the Russians do it?" All members nodded. "We don't have much time," Admiral Souers said. "In that case," Truman asserted, "We have no choice. We'll go ahead."[37]

He recalled that at some long-past meeting of the National Security Council regarding a decision about Greece, he had been told that the world would come to an end if he went ahead. He noted that he had gone ahead and that the world did not end. He guessed that the same would prove true about the hydrogen bomb decision. In thus accepting the recommendations of the special committee, he took two main steps. One was to launch a program to ascertain the feasibility of a hydrogen bomb. The other was to direct the secretaries of state and defense to undertake a major study of America's military position.

The White House issued a public statement that same January 31, declaring, laconically, that the president had ordered the Atomic Energy Commission "to continue its work on all forms of atomic weapons, including the so-called hydrogen or superbomb."[38] Public and congressional approval was overwhelming. A *Washington Post* editorial said: "The bomb will be constructed because we dare not afford not to build it. It would be a shirking of responsibility to leave the American people one fine day to face a stand-and-deliver ultimatum from a Soviet Union armed with an H-bomb."[39]

In forty-eight hours Truman's compromise solution simply to "investigate the feasibility" of a hydrogen bomb was blown to pieces. On February 2 Dr. Klaus Emil Julius Fuchs, chief of the theoretical physics division of the British Atomic Energy Research Establishment, who had worked on the American atomic bomb, was arrested in London, charged with engaging in nuclear espionage for the Soviet Union. The news undercut those who had argued that the United States should seek a control agreement with Moscow before building a hydrogen bomb. Only by creating strategic areas of strength around the world could the allied powers stop the expansion of communism, Acheson told a press conference. The Joint Chiefs of Staff took a new look at the situation. "They are of the opinion, with which I fully concur," Louis Johnson wrote to Truman, "that it is incumbent upon the United States to proceed forthwith on an all-out program of hydrogen-bomb development. . . ."[40] Around November 1, 1949, the Soviets had begun actual work on a thermonuclear bomb.[41] Truman accepted the advice of his advisers and on March 10, 1950, approved an urgent program to build a hydrogen bomb.[42] At the critical juncture in the winter of 1949–50, neither the United States nor the Soviet Union approached the other to discuss banning thermonuclear weapons.

15. *NSC 68*

O NE OF THE LANDMARKS OF the Truman administration was a top-secret
government document that was drawn up in the spring of 1950 and
designated NSC 68. It proposed a course of action on an international scale that was to be approved by Truman in a moment of
crisis. While, strictly speaking, it was not a basic change in direction for the
United States, it brought about such a change in degree as to seem a change in
substance. In a word, it heralded the end of $13 billion defense budgets in favor
of a huge and costly rearmament program for the United States and its allies.

The immediate step toward NSC 68 was taken by Truman on January 31
when he formally approved the recommendations of his special committee to
advise him on the hydrogen bomb. One of these recommendations was for a
reassessment of the country's military posture. When the committee had first
considered an increase in the production of atomic bombs in mid-1949, Acheson
had argued that Truman's restrictions on the defense budget were unrealistic and
that military spending should be increased.[1] The secretary of state's conviction
was later strengthened by the Soviet atomic bomb, and he pressed for a review
of military policy. In his decision of January 31 Truman turned the undertaking
over to Acheson and Johnson. Without doubt, however, Johnson was cold-shouldered out of the preparation of the report.[2]

At the onset of the review Acheson made the judgment that the danger of
war in the winter of 1950 was considerably greater than it had been in the previous fall, partly because of new signs of toughness in the Kremlin and partly
because of increased Soviet capability for starting a major attack.[3] The review
was heavily influenced by Acheson working with the like-minded Paul H. Nitze,
new director of the State Department's Policy Planning Staff. A handsome and
brilliant Harvard graduate, Nitze had started his career as an investment banker,
rising to vice-president of Dillon, Read & Company, where he met Forrestal.
When Forrestal went to Washington, Nitze joined him as an assistant. In 1945
Nitze was a director, and later vice-chairman, of the United States Strategic
Bombing Survey. Afterward he moved to the State Department as an economic
adviser, working on the Marshall Plan, among other things. In 1949 he was
appointed assistant secretary of state for economic affairs and then succeeded
George Kennan as director of the Policy Planning Staff. In the winter of 1950
Nitze played a leading role in the State-Defense policy review group, which
conducted the re-examination of national security policy.

The work was done under the difficult circumstances of deepening animosity between Acheson and Johnson. Intrigue was rife in Washington, as Johnson maneuvered to outstrip Acheson as the strongman of the administration and as Acheson's friends and their allies in the White House schemed to deflate Johnson's influence. From the start Johnson believed that the State Department had been meddling in Pentagon affairs. He himself became notorious for meddling in other departments, particularly the Department of Commerce, where he knew his way around because his old law firm had represented business clients there. Secretary of Commerce Charles Sawyer complained to his friend, Secretary of the Treasury John W. Snyder, and Snyder, who also disliked Johnson's meddling, told Truman what was going on. Truman warned Johnson to stop it.[4] Truman was doubtless aware, too, that Johnson was slighting Acheson behind the latter's back in conference rooms all over Washington. Once during the fall of 1949 Truman invited Webb to a cruise on the *Williamsburg,* during the course of which he took the under secretary of state aside for some advice.

"Acheson is a gentleman," Truman said, as Webb later recalled. "He won't descend to a row. Johnson is a rough customer, gets his way by rowing. When he takes out after you, give it right back to him."[5]

Webb regarded this as an admonition by the president to protect Acheson against Johnson.[6] Webb, Carlisle Hummelsine, and Lucius D. Battle, personal assistant to the secretary of state, formed their own coterie in the State Department to get rid of Johnson and soon were to have a formidable ally in the White House in the person of W. Averell Harriman.[7]

As the review of national security policy was nearing completion, Acheson invited Johnson and General Bradley to a meeting at the State Department on the afternoon of March 22, 1950, to look at the current draft of the report. According to the official account of the meeting, Acheson started to explain the purpose of the session when Johnson interrupted the secretary of state to ask whether he, Acheson, had read the draft. Acheson replied that he had read most of it the day before. Johnson said he had had the draft called to his attention only that morning before the meeting. He declared that he had not read it nor had Bradley and that neither of them intended to agree to anything he had not read. "He said, further," the official account continued, "that he did not like being called to conferences without having had the opportunity to read the appropriate material, that this was the fourth time the Department of State had done this to him, and that he did not want any more of it."

An effort by Acheson to pacify Johnson by suggesting a brief adjournment to give the secretary of defense a chance to read the draft fizzled. Acheson explained that the purpose of the meeting had not been to reach a decision then. Suspecting that the State Department may have dealt with someone else beside himself in arranging the meeting, Johnson told Nitze that such arrangements should be made only through him and that Nitze was to remember that in the future. At Acheson's request, Nitze began to outline the policy review group's work, but Johnson interrupted Nitze to say that he did not wish to hear what the conclusions were. He said he had some ideas of his own that he would present later.[8]

With the session rapidly unraveling, Johnson said that Bradley was going to Europe on Pentagon business and did not have to consult with anyone outside the Pentagon to do so. Johnson tilted his chair back and gazed at the ceiling.

"Suddenly," Acheson later recalled, "he lunged forward with a crash of chair legs on the floor and fist on the table, scaring me out of my shoes. No one, he shouted, was going to make arrangements for him to meet with another Cabinet officer and a roomful of people and be told what he was going to report to the President."[9]

Acheson suggested adjournment; Johnson agreed. The meeting had lasted fourteen minutes.

Acheson at once reported the episode to Admiral Souers, and Souers informed Truman. Within an hour, according to Acheson's account, Truman telephoned to express his outrage and told Acheson to carry on as he had been. Furthermore, Truman instructed Acheson to report to him any sign of obstructionism in the Pentagon.[10] Acheson pushed the work of the policy review group. No further meetings were held with Johnson. When the final draft was completed, Acheson sent it to Johnson and, to Acheson's surprise, Johnson signed it, and it went to the president, dated April 7, 1950.

"The purpose of NSC 68," Acheson wrote afterward, "was to so bludgeon the mass mind of 'top government' that not only could the President make a decision but that the decision could be carried out."[11]

Rejecting the policy of low defense budgets, NSC 68 asserted that the American people stood "in their deepest peril" because of new weapons of annihilation and because the Soviet Union might become so powerful that no coalition of other powers could confront it with superior strength.[12] Clearly, "our military strength is becoming dangerously inadequate," having declined in relation to that of the Soviets. Moscow was "developing the military capacity to support its design for world domination." As Forrestal and the Joint Chiefs of Staff had pleaded in vain throughout the postwar budget conferences, NSC 68 said that a sharp disparity existed "between our actual military strength and our commitments." The "integrity and vitality of our system is in greater jeopardy than ever before in our history." Continuance of current trends "would result in a serious decline in the strength of the free world relative to the Soviet Union and its satellites. . . . It is imperative that this trend be reversed by a much more rapid and concerted build-up of the actual strength of both the United States and . . . the free world." The task "will be costly and will involve significant domestic financial and economic adjustments."

Despite the outward calm at the time of the announcement, the news of the Soviet atomic bomb had in reality spread fear among American policymakers. NSC 68 said that the Soviet Union, armed with the bomb, had great coercive power and, in war, could launch devastating attacks on the United States. Thus mere continuation of the "dangerously inadequate" current American programs could lead the United States into a "disastrous situation" by 1954.

No longer was it sufficient for the United States simply to try to checkmate the designs of the Kremlin, NSC 68 said. The time had come for action that would foster "a fundamental change" in the nature of the "inescapably militant" Soviet system. Containment, in other words, was not necessarily enough.

NSC 68 envisioned a plan for negotiation with the Soviet Union but not in the existing situation. What the report referred to as a current "diplomatic freeze" must continue until the United States and its allies could, in Acheson's concept, negotiate from areas of strength. After a start had been made on rebuilding American and allied power, "it might then be desirable for the United States to take the initiative in seeking negotiations in the hope that it might facilitate the process of accommodation by the Kremlin to the new situation." If negotiations failed, the United States must rapidly build up its economic and military strength to seize the initiative.

"The whole success of the proposed program," NSC 68 concluded, "hangs ultimately on recognition by this Government, the American people, and all peoples, that the cold war is in fact a real war in which the survival of the free world is at stake."

In sum, NSC 68 was in line with long-existing policy but envisioned a dramatic increase in military, economic, and political means for carrying it out.

Truman forthwith turned the report over to the National Security Council for study, particularly as to the cost of the contemplated program. Thereupon an NSC ad hoc committee set about weighing all the implications. They were serious indeed. They involved a major expansion of American military power and rearmament of America's allies—all to the tune of more billions of dollars. No total was specified, but members of the State-Defense group that had worked on the report had agreed informally that the defense budget should rise from $13 billion a year to perhaps $40 billion. This would have meant a gigantic turnabout in the direction of the Truman administration. Barring a dramatic and dangerous international crisis, the president would have faced a tremendous task in swinging public opinion and Congress behind such a drastic change of program. Unperceived, the dramatic international crisis drew closer, day by day, to be preceded, however, by fierce new blasts at home.

16. *The McCarthy Onslaught*

ON FEBRUARY 11, 1950, Truman received a telegram of that blatantly demogogic type that is familiar to the White House communications room in all administrations and seldom attracts enough lasting attention to be rated as even an annoyance. Because this particular telegram was signed by a senator, it was routinely shown to the president, and the president dictated a draft of a cutting reply, which evidently, was never mailed.[1]

As events soon were to demonstrate, there was nothing transitory at all about this telegram, although Truman mistakenly thought there was. On the contrary, the message signaled a pathological deterioration in the climate in which Truman governed—a miasma that was to erode public trust, envenom political discourse, cause an epidemic of suspicion, and torment numerous individuals. The telegram heralded a storm, in which the Truman administration and the Democratic party were to be soundly battered.

Signed "Joe McCarthy, U.S.S. Wis.," it began:

> In a Lincoln Day speech in Wheeling Thursday night I stated that the State Department harbors a nest of communists and communist sympathizers who are helping to shape our foreign policy. I further stated that I have in my possession the names of 57 communists who are in the State Department at present.*

McCarthy said in the telegram that the department's Loyalty Review Board had certified as " 'dangerous to the security of the nation', because of communistic connections" one group of about three hundred employees. Although the board recommended that these be discharged by the secretary of state, only about eighty were, according to McCarthy, who added, twisting the knife, "I understand that this was done after lengthy consultation with Alger Hiss." Hiss had left the government in 1946.

McCarthy then threw down a challenge to Truman. It was a challenge that the senator was to pursue relentlessly and as a result of which the president in the midst of great clamor and under intense congressional pressure was soon forced to yield on a point of high principle. The challenge was to a presidential directive of March 13, 1948, issued by Truman to block unwarranted intrusions by the House Committee on un-American Activities and other Communist-hunting congressional bodies. The directive required that reports, records, and files com-

---

* Some of those who heard the West Virginia speech remembered that McCarthy had spoken of two hundred and five communists or spies in the State Department.

piled under the Employee Loyalty Program, instituted by Truman in 1947, ''be preserved in strict confidence.'' The purpose of this confidentiality was ''to protect Government personnel against dissemination of unfounded or disproved allegations.''[2]

In his telegram McCarthy demanded that Truman hand over to Congress complete reports on all those still working in the State Department who, the senator said, were listed by the Loyalty Security Board as poor risks ''because of . . . communistic connections.'' ''Failure on your part,'' McCarthy warned, ''will label the Democratic party of being the bedfellow of inter-national communism.''

However beseiged they were by the Communist issue, Truman and his administration had grown hardened to stock off-the-cuff charges and managed to shrug off the usual Lincoln Day outpourings of more prominent Republicans than McCarthy was at that time. Only a week earlier, for example, the administration had taken in stride the ranting of Senator Homer E. Capehart of Indiana, who declared that there were other spies beside Klaus Fuchs ''and there will continue to be as long as we have a president who refers to such matters as 'red herrings' and a secretary of state who refuses to turn his back on the Alger Hisses.'' McCarthy's device of mentioning specific numbers of ''communists'' in the State Department, however, caught the public eye. It caused the administration to retort, whereas treating the senator as an insignificant upstart not worth bothering about might have proved a better tactic—if the administration could have gotten away with it.

Instead, almost as soon as news of McCarthy's speech appeared, the State Department refuted the senator. Then in answer to a question at a press conference on February 16, Truman, in effect, invited McCarthy back into the ring by endorsing the department's comment, saying that ''there was not a word of truth in what the senator said.''[3] Speaking over television that same night at a Jefferson-Jackson Day dinner at the National Guard Armory, Truman declared that the Republicans were trying to find ''some new scare words.'' ''That's what they've been trying to do ever since 1933,'' he said. ''For the last seventeen years they have called every new Democratic measure 'socialism' or 'communism'. . . .''[4]

All that was true. There was blame enough for everyone, including Truman, for the soil that brought forth McCarthy and enabled him to flourish well into the Eisenhower years.

Obviously, the tone and actions of Truman and his administration in responding to Soviet challenge contributed materially to American hostility to communism after the war. To that extent the skyrocketing of McCarthy caught Truman in a trap partly of his own making. In a much larger sense, however, the critical phase of the anti-Communist disease had set in as a result of Dewey's loss to Truman and the almost simultaneous crumbling of Chiang Kai-shek's regime under the blows of Mao Tse-tung. Those events, colored by the Hiss case, stripped the Republican right wing and its friends of decent restraint in political conduct, opened the doors of demagoguery, and generally strengthened the orientation of the Republican party toward the anti-Communist issue as a means of returning to power. It was in that part of the garden that McCarthy's roots sank at a time when the senator was seeking an issue on which to win reelection himself in 1952. The issue was not exactly a novelty to him. A few years previously, as the historian Richard M. Fried has noted, McCarthy "had dabbled in anticommunism."[5]

Within a week of Truman's Jefferson–Jackson Day speech, McCarthy got the Senate floor and held it into the night for six hours of give-and-take, during which he made an erratic presentation of eighty-one alleged but anonymous cases of "communists" in the State Department.[6] In a preview of months and years of exasperatingly successful tactics, he yanked one dossier after another from a bulging briefcase in a confusing barrage of charges. Some records duplicated others. Various records were passed over altogether. Still others concerned neither communism nor even government employees but rather applicants for federal jobs.

McCarthy said that the secretary of state knew, or should have known, of all the cases. Indeed, they were an assortment of old cases that had been investigated. He presented them, however, in the context of a State Department "infested" with Communists—"vast numbers" of them—and harboring an "espionage ring." He said that Truman was a "prisoner of a bunch of twisted intellectuals who tell him what they want him to know." In fact, he said, under the Democrats the executive branch had lost control of the State Department to those intellectuals.

"I am giving the Senate information about persons whom I consider to be communists in the State Department," he said, denouncing Truman's confidential treatment of the loyalty files as an "iron curtain of secrecy."

In the widespread bewilderment in the Senate that night Senator Henry Cabot Lodge, Jr., Republican, of Massachusetts, said that he would move for an investigation of McCarthy's charges by the Senate Foreign Relations Committee, of which Lodge was a member. McCarthy was pleased. He added his own pressure for an investigation by refusing requests of other senators on the floor for names of the "communists" he had cited anonymously. He said he would be willing to give the names to an appropriate Senate committee.

In the circumstances, the Senate Democratic leadership would have had to be willing to take a good deal of heat to reject an investigation. On the other hand, McCarthy's allegations were so reckless, stale, and absurd that it was tempting for the Democrats to seize an opportunity to expose him in hearings and cut the anti-Communist issue down to size with the congressional elections approaching in the fall. The Democrats made the mistake of underestimating demagogic histrionics because the performance was preposterous. Truman among them, Democratic leaders overlooked the fact that a powerful demagogue resonates with a great many people. What McCarthy said may have been haywire; on the other hand, he was panting (for such was the manner of his speech) about matters, such as communism and turmoil in Asia, that millions of Americans had been led to take seriously. Whether or not the Democratic leaders could have avoided doing so, they set out, on their own initiative, upon a road to spectacular disaster by proposing an investigation by the Senate Foreign Relations Committee, or a subcommittee of it.

The investigation produced one of the greatest backfires Washington has ever heard.

With perseverence, with brazenness, with pugnacity, with lies and deception, with cynicism, with irresponsibility, with zeal for a handy issue—any handy issue—with a rascality that he relished with unrestrained good humor, and with mastery in using press, radio, and television to trumpet his charges, McCarthy made himself the talk of America—and soon of the world. Turning the tables on Democrats out to squelch him and his anti-Communist excesses, he used the hearings to bring the Red issue to its highest and most effective pitch and turn himself into its kingpin. With a scowl he cast fresh doubts on Truman's ability to keep Communists out of high places in Washington, though McCarthy never found any new ones there himself. He made Acheson all but an outcast in Acheson's own party. McCarthy became the principal force in terminating the long career in the Senate of one of the most powerful, secure, and respected Democrats, Millard Tydings, who was chairman of the investigating subcommittee.

On the very eve of the hearings the country was freshly disturbed by the conviction of Judith Coplon, a Barnard College graduate employed by the Justice Department. In a case broken not by a congressional committee but by the FBI, she was convicted in United States District Court for the District of Columbia of having passed FBI records to an attaché of the Soviet delegation to the United Nations named Valentin Gubichev.*

As the Tydings investigation proceeded, and in the months that followed, McCarthy won the backing of the Hearst, McCormick, and Scripps-Howard newspapers and the support of right-wing reporters, columnists, and radio commentators. Anti-liberals and anti-intellectuals found in him a new hero. His badgering tactics in the name of exposing Communists in Washington won the plaudits of the old Roosevelt haters, loathers of big government, and despisers of Harvard, Wall Street, and the eastern establishment in general.

From the ranks of manual workers, from midwestern farmers and small businessmen, especially those of German descent, from many Catholics, especially Irish Catholics, from the American Legion, the Veterans of Foreign Wars of the United States, the Marine Corps League, and quite separately, from all manner of hate groups and fringe organizations came the makings of a national following, Democrats as well as Republicans. Anti-Communist zealots of all stripe, including Alfred Kohlberg, mainstay of the China lobby, plied him with speech material. For assistance in exposing "communist spies," contributions of money, many in the amount of one dollar, flowed into the senator's office. On the Republican side of the Senate came support over the months from Nixon,

---

*Miss Coplon was reprieved by the Court of Appeals on the grounds both that she had been arrested without a warrant, and that the prosecution had depended on inadmissible evidence obtained by wiretapping.

Mundt, Wherry, Jenner, Bridges, Brewster, Ferguson, Capehart, George W. Malone, William Langer, and even Taft. So far gone in his determination to discredit Truman and the Democrats was the respected senator from Ohio that he was quoted by several reporters as having said in March that McCarthy should "keep talking and if one case doesn't work out he should proceed with another."[7] The political opposition was in the hands of the Republican party at its worst.

The animating spirit of McCarthyism, as Michael Paul Rogin the political scientist wrote, reflected "the specific traumas of conservative Republican activists—internal Communist subversion, the New Deal, centralized government, left-wing intellectuals, and the corrupting influence of a cosmopolitan society. The resentments of these Republicans and the Senator's own talents were the driving forces behind the McCarthy movement."[8]

The cases McCarthy was dramatizing may have been old hat to federal officials and loyalty boards, but they were new and startling to millions of Americans. "McCarthy has so far proved nothing," Richard Rovere wrote in the *New Yorker* in mid-April, "but he has put his charges on the record and planted them in the public consciousness."[9] A potent new force had entered the political arena, yet at first Truman failed to sense its durability.

"He thought time would take care of McCarthy sooner than it did," recalled the president's assistant, Dr. Steelman.[10] Following McCarthy's speech in the Senate, Truman privately revealed his assessment of the man in a memorandum to David D. Lloyd, a presidential assistant. McCarthy had cited Lloyd for questionable left-wing associations in the past. The matter had long before been investigated in the executive branch and Lloyd cleared. In the memorandum Truman told him: "McCarthy is just a ballyhoo artist who has to cover up his shortcomings by wild charges. I don't think you need pay any particular attention to him."[11]

Truman tended to regard the McCarthy tremor as a kind of aberration that occurred in cycles in American history. For his own use he had his staff prepare a study of such reactionary episodes, beginning with the Alien and Sedition Acts and extending through the anti-Masonic movement, the Ku Klux Klan, and the Red Scare.[12]

"We are just going through one of those hysterical stages and we may be better off when we come out of it," he wrote later to Harold Ickes. "The Republicans have usually profited by these waves of hysteria at the time but have lost in the long run. . . . This stage we are in now is of Republican manufacture and it will burn them surely."[13]

"The people understand the Republican approach to the election and they are not going to be fooled," he wrote to Senator McMahon.[14]

In a subsequent letter to Julius Ochs Adler, general manager of the *New York Times,* Truman said that "hysteria strikes this country about once in a generation." He added: "I am not alarmed at the recent anti-communist hysteria. It will pass just as all these other hysterical programs have passed in days gone by, but we must keep our heads and jealously protect those rights which are guaranteed under our Constitution."[15]

"This McCarthy business is going to be put in the place where it belongs," Truman wrote to Governor Chester Bowles, of Connecticut, adding, in reference to McCarthy, "everybody knows that he is crooked."[16] Truman may have been alluding to publicized relations between the senator and Pepsi-Cola lobbyists, to McCarthy's income tax problems in Wisconsin, and to his acceptance, while a member of the Joint Congressional Committee on Housing, of $10,000 from the Lustron Corporation. Manufacturer of prefabricated housing, the corporation paid the sum to McCarthy for his authorship of an essay on housing.

McCarthy seemed to get off to a hollow start in the Tydings hearings. Truman was encouraged. "I think we have these 'animals' on the run," he wrote to Acheson.[17]

By the time of the McCarthy visitation the Truman administration already was in rough water, lashed by gusts from China, Formosa, and the Senate hearings into scandal. Rather typical of an administration already in power for five years, the ship was leaking. Dissatisfactions accumulated. Recently Truman's protection of General Vaughan and his appointment of some old and undistinguished political friends to government posts struck liberals as examples of cronyism. Of course, liberals were unhappy, too, over a continuing inability of the president to get major Fair Deal reforms through an uninterested Congress. To tune up the Democrats for the forthcoming congressional elections Truman planned a transcontinental trip in May on the pattern of his 1948 whistle-stop campaign.

The administration's problems with domestic issues washed over into foreign affairs, too. "I have been very much disturbed," Truman wrote to Senator Vandenberg in March, "about the situation as it has been developing in the Congress with regard to whole bipartisan foreign policy."[18]

"Bipartisan foreign policy" was in such disarray indeed that Truman and Acheson felt themselves forced into a decision made with great distaste in April. This was the appointment of John Foster Dulles as a Republican consultant to Acheson. As a prominent New York lawyer, Dulles had long been close to Thomas Dewey. When Dewey ran for president against Roosevelt at the height of the war in 1944 Dulles, was his liaison with the Roosevelt administration on what were in a sense ground rules for political discussion of the forthcoming organization of the United Nations. When Dewey ran against Truman in 1948, the State Department again kept Dulles in touch with current diplomatic developments, this time in the expectation that he would be the new secretary of state in a Republican administration. Truman's victory was a sickening blow to Dulles. Dewey sustained his friend's chances for a future great role by appointing him a United States senator from New York in mid-1949 upon the resignation of the ailing Senator Robert F. Wagner, a Democrat. Under the circumstances a special election had to be held that November. Senator Dulles ran against Herbert H. Lehman—and lost—in a nasty campaign. Truman infuriated Dulles by intervening on behalf of Lehman, the Democratic candidate, and Dulles enraged Truman by attacking the Fair Deal as a welfare state.

As 1950 progressed, Republican broadsides against the administration's record on China and Formosa, now reinforced by McCarthy's onslaught against the State Department, so threatened such future major foreign policy issues as Senate approval of a Japanese peace treaty that Acheson's own advisers favored bringing a Republican into the department to assuage congressional critics. A first effort was made early in March with the appointment of former Senator John Sherman Cooper, a Kentucky Republican, as consultant to the secretary of state. Cooper had no background in foreign policy. His selection was considered an ineffective one, as Senator Vandenberg, the ranking minority member of the Foreign Relations Committee, who was by then dying of cancer, let the administration know.

In further discussions at the State Department several Republicans, including Earl Warren, then governor of California, were mentioned for appointment as ambassador-at-large.[19] Vandenberg, however, favored Dulles, with whom he had worked since the war years in marshaling Republican support for Democratic foreign policy, and Vandenberg's advice counted in the administration—especially at a time of so much trouble in the Senate over foreign affairs. Dulles himself had let it be known to the State Department that he was available. He came close to threatening that he would run again for senator in New York if he were not taken into the department.[20] When Under Secretary of State Webb talked with Truman on March 26, however, the president said that under no circumstances would he appoint Dulles—a "stuffed shirt," he had once called him—to any position.[21] Yet that same day he wrote to his cousin, Ralph Truman:

I am in the midst of the most terrible struggle any President ever had. A pathological liar from Wisconsin and a blockheaded undertaker from Nebraska [Wherry was a licensed embalmer] are trying to ruin the bipartisan foreign policy. Stalin never had two better allies in this country.[22]

Five days later Vandenberg wrote to Acheson, exerting new pressure on behalf of Dulles.[23] Truman was having second thoughts. Talking to Acheson on the telephone, he expressed his unwillingness to nominate Dulles for ambassador-at-large but agreed that it might be expedient to appoint him as a consultant to the secretary of state.[24]

When Dulles received the news from Acheson, he evidently was disappointed at not being named ambassador-at-large. He told Acheson, pointedly, that Dewey and Vandenberg felt, in the words of an official memorandum on the telephone conversation, that "the Republican Party was selling out awfully cheap." Dulles wanted the department to make it clear to the public that nobody else, presumably meaning Cooper, "was above me."[25] Thereupon Dulles moved into the State Department and proceeded to distribute among his new highly placed colleagues excerpts of Stalin's writings lest the danger of Soviet communism be underestimated in Foggy Bottom.

In appointing Dulles a consultant to the secretary of state Truman was to a certain extent making the State Department a hostage to the Republicans. Dulles was now in a position to make things even worse for the administration by resigning dramatically if he disagreed with a policy. Henceforth his views had to be listened to, seriously. In fact he made all this rather plain to Acheson. After a talk with Truman, Dulles sent the secretary a memorandum on the conversation, in which Dulles had emphasized to Truman that merely having installed him in the State Department did not turn the weeds into roses as far as the Republicans were concerned. Much would depend, Dulles told Truman, "on whether I [Dulles] was in a position to help work out policies that I could genuinely endorse." Dulles let Acheson know that Truman "said he fully understood that this would be the course events would have to take."[26] Presently, Dulles was put in charge of negotiations for a Japanese peace treaty, a task in which he could be helpful in getting the treaty through the Senate.

Contrary to Democratic expectations, McCarthy's free-swinging performance became more and more of a national spectacle. Newspapers were filled with his charges, as he loudly challenged the loyalty of such prominent Americans as Ambassador Jessup, Dr. Harlow Shapley, a Harvard astronomer, Professor Owen J. Lattimore, director of the Walter Hines Page School of International Relations at Johns Hopkins University, and John Stuart Service, former foreign servicer officer in China, who was than assigned to India.

McCarthy also managed to keep at a boil his original demand upon Truman for access to files on the loyalty cases the senator cited. From the start Tydings, who was coming up for reelection in Maryland in the fall, found McCarthy unmanageably tough. Also, therefore, he found himself under increasing pressure to get Truman to release the loyalty files. Although Truman previously had indicated that he would not do so, Tydings formally asked for them by letter on March 22.[27] McCarthy followed this up with a telegram to the president at Key West, where Truman was vacationing. Calling him "arrogant," McCarthy warned Truman that his refusal of the files "is inexcusable and is endangering the security of this nation."

In a reply to Tydings on March 28 Truman declined the subcommittee's request on the recommendation, he said, of Attorney General J. Howard McGrath, J. Edgar Hoover, and Seth Richardson, chairman of the Loyalty Review Board. "They have unanimously advised me," Truman said, "that disclosure of loyalty files would be contrary to the public interest, and would do much more harm than good."[28] Thereupon, Tydings felt that he had no other alternative under the terms of the investigation but to subpoena the files. Truman ordered that the subpoenas be ignored by government departments, informing Tydings:

No President has ever complied with an order of the Legislative Branch directing the Executive Branch to produce confidential documents, the disclosure of which was considered by the President to be contrary to the public interest.[29]

The heat only grew worse, however, as Washington sank into sheer bitterness over McCarthy's continuing broadsides. They reached sensational proportions in late March when the senator said that the Soviet Union's "top espionage agent" in America was connected with the State Department. McCarthy did not name the person at first, leaving that morsel for Drew Pearson, who revealed in a radio broadcast that the alleged agent was Professor Lattimore, an Asian scholar, whom Roosevelt had chosen during the war to serve as Chiang Kai-shek's political adviser. Proving nothing about Lattimore as an espionage agent, McCarthy played the case for all it was worth before angry sessions of the Senate and of the subcommittee. In the presence of Attorney General McGrath and J. Edgar Hoover, four members of the subcommittee had the FBI file on Lattimore read to them. The senators concluded that there was nothing to indicate that Lattimore, whose connection with the State Department had been peripheral and sporadic, had been a Communist or had engaged in spying.[30] McCarthy and some other Republicans kept the case going. Unquestionably, it strengthened McCarthy when he needed to be strengthened.

In perturbation Lattimore's sister, Mrs. Eleanor Lattimore Andrews, wrote to Truman, who assured her in reply that McCarthy "will eventually get all that is coming to him."

"You can understand now, I imagine," Truman said, "what the President has to stand—every day in the week he is under a constant barrage of people who have no respect for the truth and whose objective is to belittle and discredit him."[31]

He was angry at the Associated Press and United Press for their wide-open play of McCarthy's unsubstantiated charges. Almost daily, the capital reverberated to bitter exchanges between the two ends of Pennsylvania Avenue. Relations between the president and the Republican right wing were ripped to shreds. Truman only made matters worse by giving in to his wrath during a press conference at Key West.

"Do you think that Senator McCarthy can show any disloyalty exists in the State Department?" a reporter inquired.

"I think the greatest asset that the Kremlin has is Senator McCarthy," Truman replied.

He went on to say that "the Republicans have been trying vainly to find an issue on which to make a bid for the control of the Congress for next year." Confessing that he was "fed up with what is going on," he said that "To try to sabotage the foreign policy of the United States is just as bad in this cold war as it would be to shoot our soldiers in the back in a hot war." The Republican right wing, he declared, was trying "to torpedo the bipartisan foreign policy." Asked which others beside McCarthy were engaged in this effort, he named Bridges and Wherry. As to the charge against Lattimore he said, "It's silly on the face of it."[32]

Taft accused the president of having libeled McCarthy. "Do you think that is possible?" Truman asked a reporter who brought the matter up at his next press conference.[33]

17. *Interlude: A Quiet Decision*

APRIL 16, 1950, was a beautiful Sunday in Washington, happily free of crisis and clamor. The *Washington Post* estimated that a hundred thousand visitors were in the capital to see the cherry blossoms and other sights. At some point Truman sat down in a philosophic mood and put his thoughts on paper. There is no evidence that his private note was prompted by any particular event, criticism, or strain, or by discouragement, disillusion, or general unhappiness over the drift of affairs.

"I am not a candidate for nomination by the Democratic Convention [in 1952]," he wrote.

"My first election to public office took place in November 1922. I served two years in the armed forces in World War I, ten years in the Senate, two months and 20 days as Vice President and President of the Senate. I have been in public service well over thirty years, having been President of the United States almost two complete terms.

"Washington, Jefferson, Monroe, Madison, Andrew Jackson and Woodrow Wilson as well as Calvin Coolidge stood by the precedent of two terms. Only Grant, Theodore Roosevelt and F.D.R. made the attempt to break that precedent. F.D.R. succeeded.

"In my opinion eight years as President is enough and sometimes too much for any man to serve in that capacity.

"There is a lure in power. It can get into a man's blood just as gambling and lust for money have been known to do.

"This is a Republic. The greatest in the history of the world. I want this country to continue as a Republic. Cincinnatus and Washington pointed the way. When Rome forgot Cincinnatus, its down fall began. When we forget the examples of such men as Washington, Jefferson and Andrew Jackson, all of whom could have had continuation in the office, then will we start down the road to dictatorship and ruin. I know I could be elected again and continue to break the old precedent as it was broken by F.D.R. It should not be done. That precedent should continue—not by a Constitutional amendment but by custom based on the honor of the man in the office.

"Therefore to reestablish that custom, although by a quibble I could say I've only had one term, I am not a candidate and will not accept the nomination for another term."[1]

Although he did not mention it, Mrs. Truman was totally opposed to his running again.

In a posthumous settling of accounts with Roosevelt, the Republican-controlled Eightieth Congress passed in 1947 the 22nd amendment to the Constitution, providing that no one could be elected president more than twice. The amendment, which became effective February 27, 1951, after ratification by three-fourths of the states, was specifically worded so as not to apply to Truman as the incumbent president at the time of its introduction. He was eligible to run in 1952.

Truman later said that he had made up his mind in 1949 not to seek another term. Had his note in mid-April of 1950 been known, it would have flung the Democratic party into a scramble for a presidential nominee. Truman kept his intentions secret, presumably, to avert loss of political power as a lame duck.

If his decision freed him from the necessity of expedients in the interest of renomination and reelection, it did not, being secret, change the political atmosphere. When Monday arrived, the Tydings subcommittee prepared for the next hearings on McCarthy's charges. While Truman's political future beyond 1952 was no longer at stake, his reputation and the fate of the Democratic party in 1952 were, and both appeared to be much involved in McCarthy's depredations.

The administration groped for a strategy for dealing with McCarthy, but with little success. The task was bewildering. If a senator could get away with depicting Professor Lattimore as the leading Soviet espionage agent in the United States, there was no limit to the mischief he could do. Cornering McCarthy was extremely difficult. When the Democrats exposed the emptiness of one of his cases, he immediately wheeled about and filled the press and the Senate chamber with scattershot details of some other cases to the glee of the Republican right.

"No one had any experience in dealing with the likes of McCarthy," George Elsey recalled. "He could out-yell everyone and evade being pinned down to the facts. The State Department was worried because they had picked up a lot of employees during the postwar reorganization, and they were not sure exactly what they had."[2]

McCarthy was aware of the possibility of striking gold with some Communist who might have entered the department by transfer. "There were thousands of unusual characters in some of those war agencies," he said.[3]

He skilfully adopted the tactics of the House Committee on un-American Activities under the chairmanship of Dies and his successor, Representative J. Parnell Thomas, Republican, of New Jersey. For one thing, the tactics were designed to trap an administration by the making of unsupported charges of disloyalty against certain federal employees, followed by the pilloring of the administration for not dismissing those persons. For another, the tactics were to equate an administration itself with disloyalty, as exemplified in Parnell Thomas's remark about an alleged "fifth column" under Roosevelt. "In some respects," Thomas said, "it is synonymous to the New Deal, so the surest way of removing the fifth column from our shores is to remove the New Deal from the seat of government."[4] On McCarthy's terms, the way to get rid of the alleged subversives in Washington was to get rid of the Truman administration.

Basically, however, the problem for Truman was not so much the extravaganza that McCarthy made of particular cases. Rather, it was the pervasive suspicions that his performance aroused at a moment when Americans were fearful that, having won the war, they were "losing the peace."

"In a sense," recalled David E. Bell, an administrative assistant to President Truman, "there was nothing the Executive Branch could do that would successfully respond to the feeling of fear and frustration which was being played upon by McCarthy. In other words, the specific charges being made were less important to his impact than the general difficulties the United States was having in the world."[5]

Acheson's own usefulness in the predicament had been badly impaired by his indiscreet remark about not turning his back on Alger Hiss. Mounting a counterattack against McCarthy was complicated by the shellshock of the Hiss case among Democrats in general. Even an outstanding liberal like Senator Paul Douglas was fearful that taking on McCarthy would lead into a trap. "[Douglas] said, too, as we know," Clair Wilcox, of Swarthmore College, wrote to Roger W. Tubby, then a State Department press officer, "that many Democrats have feared that there may be something on some of the people McCarthy has attacked and they don't want to get out on a limb in another Hiss case. . . . It would take but a single case to give [McCarthy] a victory."[6]

Tubby, who was soon to move to an important role on the White House staff, lamented in his journal: "The screaming headlines show up all over the country—200 Reds in the State Department; 87 Reds; Four Named. The rebuttals seldom make the front pages and practically never the headlines."[7]

Another nasty turn was the device of McCarthy and his cohorts in picturing the State Department as crawling with security risks in the form of homosexuals liable to blackmail. Under pressure the department announced in February that in the preceding three years it had dismissed ninety-one persons, most of them homosexuals, on moral grounds. The State Department hierarchy was appalled in the spring of 1950 by what proved to be a false rumor that McCarthy would name a distinguished American diplomat, then in a high post, as a homosexual. "We sit abashed and confounded and sick at heart," Tubby noted, adding in another entry in his journal, "This business is likely to be more damaging around the country than the commie charges."[8]

Truman chose the occasion of a Federal Bar Association dinner in Washington on April 24 to defend the administration against McCarthy's attack. He enumerated steps taken—the Greek-Turkish aid program, the Marshall Plan, the North Atlantic Treaty, the Mutual Defense Assistance Program—to counter "Communist imperialism." Although communism was not a "major force" at home, he said, the administration was striving to keep it in check through wholesome living standards and such direct actions as the Employee Loyalty Program and the prosecution of the Communist party leaders. He continued:

174 The Sound of Thunder

No known instance of Communist subversion—or any other kind of subversion—has gone uninvestigated.

No case where the facts warranted has gone unprosecuted. . . .

There is no area of American life in which the Communist Party is making headway, except maybe in the deluded minds of some people. . . .

Not a single person who has been adjudged to be a Communist or otherwise disloyal remains on the Government payroll today.

Turning on McCarthy without naming him, Truman assailed those who publicly denounced persons as Communists "without having evidence to support such a charge, or by blackening the character of persons because their views are different from those of the accuser, or by hurling sensational accusations based on gossip, hearsay or maybe just a hunch." Forcefully, Truman restated the high principles upon which he refused to turn the security files over to Tydings. "Disclosure of the files," he said, "would result in serious injustice to the reputation of many innocent persons."[9]

Exactly ten days later Tydings announced that Truman had agreed to open to the subcommittee the files on eighty-one persons accused by McCarthy. The subcommittee had established, Tydings said, that McCarthy's eighty-one cases were identical to those that had previously been investigated and the dossiers on which had been shown to four congressional committees before Truman's 1948 order closing the files. Because these files had been shown to other congressional committees, Tydings said, Truman was not setting a new precedent by releasing them.[10] That was not the whole truth. In a confidential White House memorandum, Charles Murphy, the influential special counsel to the president, said that Truman had agreed that the subcommittee should see new material added to the files since the previous congressional inspection.[11]

Truman offered no public explanation of his turnabout. Doubtless he concluded that Tydings had taken almost all the heat he could stand from Republicans, who charged that the Democrats were "covering up" by withholding the files. From the outset Murphy, for one, had felt that Truman ought to be more accommodating in the circumstances, and possibly Truman would have yielded earlier had not McGrath and Hoover objected.[12] After his lofty public refusals to release the files, however, the president's capitulation made McCarthy look all the more formidable. For Truman's pains McCarthy sneeringly accused the administration of having first "raped and rifled" the files, thus preserving his own option of denouncing the investigation as a whitewash.

"I hope you . . . come back to Washington 'full of whistle stop beezum,' " Vandenberg wrote to Truman, wishing him good luck on his transcontinental "nonpartisan" speaking tour, which began May 7.[13] Nostalgic for 1948, Truman contemplated the ten days aboard his special train with zest, vainly hoping for a turn in the political tide. "I think by the time I arrive at Grand Coullee [sic]," he had confided to Secretary of Commerce Charles Sawyer, "evidence will have been presented which will put Mr. McCarthy in the 'doghouse' and we won't have to mention him any more even politically."[14]

Whatever evidence it was that Truman referred to had surely been drowned in the McCarthy din. The president's own trip, ostensibly for the dedication of Grand Coulee Dam in the state of Washington, took place against background noises of the hearings on Lattimore.

Truman delivered fifty-seven speeches in twelve states. All along the way he had friendly, good-sized crowds—the largest in Chicago, where the fanfare included a torchlight parade. While the style of the trip was 1948, the meaning was not at all up to that of the famous campaign. Clearly, Truman's homey efforts to get people behind public power, the Brannan farm plan, repeal of the Taft-Hartley law, and other Fair Deal goals were not going to bear fruit. People's minds were on other troubles and so, really, was Truman's.

McCarthy rumbled on, but the president made no attempt on the trip to deal with him. What was interesting was Truman's warning against a return to isolationism. It reflected his concern about support for foreign policy in Congress at a time when events abroad were sobering.

18. *The Gathering Clouds Abroad*

BENEATH THE CLAMOR at home in the spring of 1950 dwelt great uneasiness about peace in the world. It was not a feeling of emergency about any one boundary in Europe, the Middle East, or Asia but, rather, a gloomy doubt as to how far tensions could stretch before something snapped somewhere. In the shadows of the Siberian bomb test and the Communist seizure of China, this vague sense of trouble was freighted with worry that the Soviet Union was getting the upper hand.

Although no signs of hostilities involving major powers were apparent in any particular spot and even though Truman himself publicly predicted a period of international economic progress, talk of war was commonplace. General George C. Kenney, an air force commander, said in a speech in Wichita, Kansas, that the Soviets had probably decided to start the third world war in 1950. General Bradley said Cold War pressures were growing worse. After a Soviet fighter had shot down an unarmed United States navy plane and its crew engaged in reconnaissance in the Baltic area, Acheson accused the Kremlin of "saber-rattling." Trygve Lie, secretary-general of the United Nations, traveled, fruitlessly, to see Truman in Washington and to see Stalin in Moscow to propose a meeting of heads of state with the United Nations Security Council. Herbert Hoover recommended that the United Nations be reorganized to exclude Communist states.

Nearly five years after the end of the Second World War no peace treaties had been signed with Germany, Japan, or Austria. The United States and the Soviet Union were unwilling to come to grips with the question of controlling or outlawing nuclear weapons. As stated in NSC 68, the Americans and the Soviets were locked in a "diplomatic freeze."

During the spring Acheson told an executive session of the Senate Foreign Relations Committee: "I think we have to start out with the realization that the main center of our activity at the present time has got to be in Europe. We cannot scatter our shots equally all over the world. We just haven't got enough shots to do that."[1]

At that point the newly established North Atlantic Treaty and Mutual Defense Assistance Program had had little more than psychological impact on militarily weak Western Europe. Nothing had yet come into being to compare with the elaborate international defense system later familiar as NATO. Under the treaty there had been created a North Atlantic Council, supported by a loosely knit grouping of supply, finance, and regional planning committees. At the start of

1950 the North Atlantic Treaty countries had only twelve divisions, randomly deployed, four hundred airplanes, and a small number of naval vessels. The ground forces included two American units, approximately the strength of divisions, spread through the United States zone of Germany. Confronting these allied forces, according to an official study by the historian Lawrence S. Kaplan, were probably twenty-five well-trained and well-equipped Soviet divisions, reinforced by thousands of planes.

The task of getting the Mutual Defense Assistance Program into operation was a ponderous one. By April 1950 shipments of military supplies had been little more than tokens. The total sum appropriated for the arms program was pitifully small when matched against Europe's needs. As for the European members of the pact, they simply did not bring themselves to make the sacrifices necessary for substantially reviving their own military power. Under the stimulus of the Marshall Plan their standard of living had been inching upward, and they did not intend to jeopardize it by putting guns ahead of butter. The immediate future did not worry them enough to move them to greater austerity. From the start it had been the policy agreed to on both sides of the Atlantic that the best way to strengthen Western Europe was to invigorate its economy. The Europeans did not wish to undermine this goal with heavy military budgets. After all, the United States had decided to send military equipment and had pledged to respond with its own power if the Western Europeans were attacked. Behind the shield of the treaty they proceeded on the assumption, apparently, that they could strengthen themselves in their own good time.[2]

During the spring of 1950 concern was growing in Washington over continuing Soviet pressure on Germany. Anxiety about the Kremlin's perceived efforts to dominate the Germans had been heightened by the establishment of a heavily armed "people's police" in East Germany. On June 8 Louis Johnson caused Truman something of a jolt by raising in the National Security Council the question of whether the postwar policy of demilitarization of Germany should be changed and West Germany rearmed. Barely five years after the death of Adolf Hitler, whose war machine had been completely and deliberately obliterated by the victors of the Second World War, Johnson sent a memorandum to the NSC, reporting a new position by the Joint Chiefs of Staff in favor of West German rearmament. The chiefs held that the change was "of fundamental importance to the defense of Western Europe against the USSR."[3]

The report reached Truman on the heels of another memorandum by the chairman of the Joint Chiefs of Staff, General Bradley. "In the light of the worsening world situation and the likelihood that the North Atlantic Treaty countries could not, now or during the next several years, defend France and the Low Countries successfully in event of a Soviet attack," he said, "the Joint Chiefs of Staff consider it is of paramount importance that the United States and its allies take proper steps to assure that Spain will be an ally in event of war." Specifically, the general sought action "to assure to the United States and its allies military accessibility to and military cooperation with Spain."[4]

In a taut memorandum to Acheson on June 16 Truman said that the two papers were "decidedly militaristic" and "not realistic with present conditions."[5]

Francisco Franco's Spain repelled Truman, who often said that Franco was as bad as Hitler or Mussolini. Although the United States early in 1950 had decided to support a United Nations resolution to allow member nations to send envoys back to Madrid after the wartime gap in relations, Truman remained testy. "He feels very strongly on . . . the absence of religious freedom in Spain," Acheson had noted on May 9, 1949.[6]

That was a subject on which Truman heard strong personal complaints from fellow Masons. Even after he had reluctantly nominated Stanton Griffis as ambassador to Madrid in 1951, he talked threateningly about recalling him if Franco did not reform. In a memorandum of August 2, 1951, the president told Acheson:

> I had a conversation with Ambassador Griffis before he left here and informed him that Franco's attitude in these matters is exceedingly obnoxious to me. There was a time, and I think it still exists, when Protestants couldn't have public funerals. They are forced to be buried at night and are allowed no markers for their graves. They are buried in plowed fields like potter's fields. . . .
>
> I've never been happy about sending an Ambassador to Spain, and I am not happy about it now, and unless Franco changes in his treatment of citizens who do not agree with him religiously I'll be sorely tempted to break off all communication with him in spite of the defense of Europe."[7]

Truman also had deep misgivings in mid-June of 1950 about rearming West Germany. On the same day that he got Louis Johnson's report, raising the issue, he also received a copy of a message from John J. McCloy, United States high commissioner for Germany, revealing secret British–West German talks on German rearmament. In a second memorandum to Acheson on June 16, 1950, Truman said, in part:

> France would immediately get a severe case of jitters if the subject is ever seriously considered.
>
> We certainly don't want to make the same mistake that was made after World War I when Germany was authorized to train one hundred thousand soldiers, principally for maintaining order locally. . . . As you know, that hundred thousand was used for the basis of training the greatest war machine that ever came forth in European history.[8]

Partly as a result of the president's attitude no doubt, the issue of German rearmament was treated as premature. It was not to remain premature for long.

While Europe was the area of primary concern to the Truman administration, the situation in the Far East in the spring of 1950 appeared "complex, dynamic and dangerous," Acheson testified.[9]

On February 14, 1950, Stalin and Mao Tse-tung had joined in a thirty-year Treaty of Friendship, Alliance, and Mutual Assistance. A provision in Article I that was soon to cause Washington great apprehension stated that "In the event of one of the High Contracting Parties being attacked by Japan or states allied with it, and thus being involved in a state of war, the other High Contracting Party will immediately render military and other assistance with all the means at its disposal.''[10] The significance of this to Washington was that the United States was to all intents and purposes allied with Japan. If, therefore, the United States were to attack China, the treaty appeared to obligate the Soviet Union to take military action against the United States on a maximum scale. At the time of the signing of the treaty, the Soviets gave China a five-year $300 million loan. And during the spring shipments of Soviet planes and amphibious vessels arrived in China.

Chinese Communist forces were being reinforced along the south and south-eastern coast, facing the large Nationalist-held islands of Hainan and Formosa. In April Mao's troops captured Hainan, causing new fears for the security of Formosa. In May the Joint Chiefs of Staff informed Louis Johnson that conditions in the Far East were taking a turn for the worse, with heightened Communist activities in the Philippines and Indochina.[11]

Formosa and Indochina received the most attention in Washington as danger points in Asia in the spring of 1950, even though Korea, as usual, was caught up in its chronic conflicts. The rival governments of North and South Korea had been in existence for nearly two years by that June. Each side was committed to the eventual defeat of the other. At least since 1948 periodic rumors had been heard about an impending invasion of South Korea by the more powerful military forces of North Korea. In continuance of the north-south conflict that had embroiled the country since 1946, repeated clashes had occurred along the 38th parallel since the spring of 1949, some resulting in heavy casualties on both sides. Communist guerrillas operated behind South Korean lines, although the State Department was more preoccupied at that point with severe inflation in South Korea than with guerrilla raids and chronic border skirmishes.[12] Policymakers feared that inflation might destroy the Rhee government the way it had helped destroy Chiang Kai-shek's regime in China.

In light of American interest in the preservation of the Republic of Korea, the military alignment in Korea by June of 1950 was dangerously unbalanced. As has been noted, the United States deliberately had not equipped the South Korean army with heavy weapons, partly out of concern that Syngman Rhee might start a war. Rather, the purpose of the military assistance program as stated in the previously cited NSC 8/2 was to provide an army for maintaining internal order and border security. The reasoning was that such an army would at least deter a major North Korean attack.

The South Koreans had eight infantry divisions—all below strength—totaling sixty-five thousand men plus thirty-three thousand service troops. Neither in number of pieces nor in range could the artillery match that possessed by North Korea. Supplies of ammunition and spare parts were inadequate. Training had not progressed beyond the level of battalion. South Korea had no tanks. When the Rhee government had asked for tanks the previous October, the American military advisory group had rejected the request on the grounds of inadequate funds and supposed ineffectuality of tanks in Korea's rugged terrain and poor roads. The South Korean air force of nearly nineteen hundred men had twelve liaison aircraft and ten training planes. Fighters recommended by the American military advisory group had not been provided.[13]

As was learned later, the North Koreans that June had a total force of 135,000 men. The People's Army fielded seven infantry divisions at their full combat strength of 11,000 men each, a tank brigade of 6,000 men, a separate infantry regiment of 3,000 men, and a motorcycle regiment of 2,000 men. The border constabulary consisted of more than 18,000 men. In addition to training many of these forces, the Soviet Union had supplied 150 tanks of Second World War vintage and some 180 aircraft, two-thirds of them combat planes. North Korean artillery, most of it from Soviet forces, including 122-millimeter howitzers and 76-millimeter guns.[14]

Early in May John Muccio, the American ambassador to Seoul, returned to Washington for consultations. At a meeting of diplomatic and military officials he said it was necessary to plug certain gaps in the Republic of Korea defense so that, in the words of the official account, "our stake in south Korea could be more adequately protected." Muccio particularly cited lack of air defense.

Major General Lyman L. Lemnitzer, then director of the office of military assistance in the Department of Defense, replied that the question was a political one for the State Department to deal with, since South Korea was not held to be strategically important to the United States. Muccio said he was in an awkward situation with Rhee because certain American fighter planes in Japan were being junked as surplus when the South Koreans felt an urgent need of them. If the planes were to be transferred to Korea, Lemnitzer said, the United States Air Force would have to be reimbursed for transportation costs. It would be necessary, he continued, for the State Department to take the initiative if it wished to bring about the establishment of a South Korea air force fighter group. The Pentagon would support such a policy, he added, if necessary amendments were made in NSC 8/2. But since the question was political, Lemnitzer did not feel that the Pentagon should sponsor such a revision.[15]

Behind this matter-of-fact attitude lay not only Korea's declared lack of strategic importance to the United States in a general war but the circumstance that no American official and no American intelligence organ anticipated an early invasion of South Korea.

MacArthur had been relieved of responsibility for the security of the Republic of Korea when the American occupation ended June 29, 1949. The chief of his intelligence section in Tokyo, Major General Charles A. Willoughby, had taken it upon himself to maintain a so-called surveillance detachment in Korea. On December 30, 1949, Willoughby forwarded to Washington several reports indicating that North Korea would invade the south the following March or April. By his own evaluation, however, such military action was "unlikely." In late March Willoughby noted, "It is believed that there will be no civil war in Korea this spring or summer. . . ." In March also the chief of army intelligence, Major General Alexander R. Bolling, predicted that "Communist military measures in

Korea will be held in abeyance pending the outcome of their program in other areas, particularly Southeast Asia.'' In May the United States embassy in Seoul reported little likelihood of an early North Korean invasion.

As summer neared, however, army intelligence grew more thought-provoking, if not more convincing. A routine summary dated May 23 reported that ''The outbreak of hostilities may occur at any time in Korea and the fall of Indochina is possible this year.'' Then on June 19 another summary, forwarded routinely, reported: extensive Communist troop movements along the 38th Parallel, evacuation of civilians, suspension of certain civilian freight service, concentration of armored units near the border, and arrival of large shipments of weapons and ammunition.

The flaw in this suggestive report, or so it seems, was that no conclusion was drawn from the observations. ''Some information sent to Washington from the Far East,'' wrote the historian James F. Schnabel in an official study, ''reflected a strong possibility of action toward the end of June, but faulty evaluation and dissemination prevented it from reaching the right people in the proper form.'' This failure of intelligence was compounded by inertia induced by months of menacing news from North Korea and by uncertainty as to what area of the globe might catch the brunt of a Communist attack. On the same day as the report of the North Korean troop and armored movements, Willoughby warned of an early Communist attempt to subjugate the South Korean government ''by political means.''[16]

The Central Committee of the United Democratic Patriotic Front in North Korea adopted a resolution on June 7 that called for the election in early August of a parliament of representatives of North and South Korea. As if to suggest that all of Korea would have been united by then, the resolution proposed that the parliament meet in Seoul on August 15.[17]

Muccio cabled Acheson on June 14 that the South Korean army was thought to be superior to the North Korean army in ''training, leadership, morale, marksmanship and better small arms equipment. . . .'' But, he continued, ''North Korean air power, tanks and heavier artillery, but especially air power, give preponderance [of] strength to the North despite estimated inferiority North Korean ground forces compared to South Korean ground forces.'' Muccio asked Acheson to consider the psychological affect on South Korean officials and civilians of knowing of ''northern capacity [to] control air at will, including capacity [of] uninterrupted bombing [of] Seoul, as well as general knowledge [that] northern artillery outranges southern artillery while northern army has tanks but none here.''[18]

In a statement submitted to the House Foreign Affairs Committee that month Muccio said flatly that ''the undeniable material superiority of the North Korean forces would provide North Korea with the margin of victory in the event of a full-scale invasion of the Republic.''[19]

According to General Bolling, the army intelligence chief, no intelligence agency reported a definite date for a start of hostilities or even that an invasion was imminent.[20]

"The view was generally held," Acheson testified later, "that since the Communists had far from exhausted the potentialities for obtaining their objectives through guerrilla and psychological warfare, political pressure and intimidation, such means would probably continue to be used rather than overt military aggression."[21]

As late as June 19 the Central Intelligence Agency reported that North Korean military forces were still being expanded. Trained and equipped units were being deployed "southward in the area of the 38th Parallel." Said the report, concurred in by the intelligence organizations of the Departments of State, Army, Navy, and Air Force: "Despite the apparent military superiority of northern over southern Korea, it is not certain that the northern regime, lacking the active participation of Soviet and Chinese Communist military units, would be able to gain effective control over all of southern Korea."[22]

If it was forcefully brought to Truman's attention in the early summer of 1950 that a dangerous situation might be developing in Korea, the record does not show it. Confident that war was not imminent anywhere, he told a press conference on May 4, "I think the situation now is not nearly so bad as it was in the first half of 1946. I think it is improving."[23]

Dean Rusk, then assistant secretary of state for Far Eastern affairs, told an executive session of the House Foreign Affairs Committee on June 20: "Our goal . . . is to assist the South Koreans to establish a security force which can deal with domestic disorders, armed bands coming across the 38th parallel, and force the opposition to make the choice to fight a major war as the price for taking over southern Korea. We see no present indication that the people across the border have any intention of fighting a major war for that purpose."[24]

In sum, the Truman administration realized that the Communists had the capability to attack. The situation was rather reminiscent of Pearl Harbor before the Japanese struck. Too little attention was paid to what the enemy *might* do. American officials hoped and believed that the enemy was *unlikely* to do at the time that which he had the power to do.[25]

Yet the potential political damage to Truman of a successful North Korean invasion was startling. Already China had fallen to the Communists. Indochina and Formosa seemed threatened. Imagine the effect, then, of a Communist seizure of American-armed and American supported South Korea! Political restraint in Washington had been sundered by the McCarthy rampage. Anti-Communism was virulent. The Republicans would have had the ingredients for brewing a scandal out of Truman's handling of the Communist threat to American interests in Asia.

The Truman administration had pulled American troops out of South Korea. It had refused Rhee's appeals for tanks and planes to destroy Communist armor in case of an attack, even though the Soviets had been supplying heavy weapons to the North Koreans. As with some other contingencies, the Pentagon had no war plans for dealing with a Communist assault on the Republic of Korea. Instead, Acheson had publicly excluded the area from the American defensive perimeter in the Far East. MacArthur, a Republican favorite, had been left in Japan with a command in which army strength had been reduced below half of what had been authorized. The general had warned of irreparable damage to United States interests in Asia unless his command were strengthened.[26]

Against the advice of the Joint Chiefs of Staff and high civilian officials in the Pentagon, Truman had insisted on tight military budgets that, it would have been argued, had strangled expansion of the armed forces. General Eisenhower, another figure to whom Republicans looked with interest, had testified at a Senate appropriations subcommittee hearing on March 29 that several hundred millions probably should have been added to the defense budget.[27] Already the United States was in a tight corner on ground forces. It had neither plans nor sufficient troops for fighting a limited war anywhere. For ultimate security the Truman administration had come to rely on the atomic bomb, but it was questionable whether enough bombs and bombers were available to knock out the Soviet Union. In any case, the bomb was useless in Korea since it would have destroyed friend and foe.

For weeks the United States had been reverberating to McCarthy's allegations of Communist treachery in the government. How these charges could have been kited by the senator if South Korea had gone under! A Communist military victory in Korea would have fashioned the very capstone for charges that the Truman administration was soft on communism. As it was, Democrats were worried about the effect of the Communist issue in the off-year congressional and gubernatorial elections scheduled for the following November. How much more there would have been to worry about if North Korea had triumphed!

Rival armies tensely faced each other across the 38th parallel. It remained a most serious matter for Truman that the one in the north not strike a blow fatal to the Republic of Korea.

III

WAR IN KOREA

19. *A Summer Day in Independence, Missouri*

O N THE AFTERNOON OF Saturday, June 24, 1950, Truman arrived at his home at 219 North Delaware Street in Independence, Missouri, for a planned forty-eight-hour visit. He wanted to see his wife and daughter, who were on a sojourn at home, and to order a new roof for the family farmhouse at nearby Grandview.

Harry Truman used to say that Independence was to him what Hannibal, Missouri, had been to Mark Twain.[1] It was the scene of his boyhood and schooling, the place where his roots had taken hold. Although he had been born in the village of Lamar, in southwestern Missouri, and had spent a couple of early childhood years at the Grandview farm, the historic town of Independence had been his home since 1890, when he was six years old. A whiff of the Civil War and frontier days was still in the air he had breathed, and the Democratic party was already in his blood when he watched a torchlight parade celebrating Grover Cleveland's election in 1892.

On May 8, 1950, Truman had turned sixty-six. He had been president for more than five grueling years. When he stepped off the plane at Municipal Airport in Kansas City in sweltering weather on June 24, he looked crisp and jaunty in a tan suit and Panama hat and carrying a cane, as he often did on walks. The years in the White House had drastically changed his life but not his manner. He was still at home with old friends in Kansas City and nearby Independence, and they were at home with him. One of those on hand to greet him at the airport was Ted Marks, a fellow artillery officer in the First World War, who had been best man at Truman's wedding. When the president reached the North Delaware Street house, perhaps a hundred persons stood outside the new iron picket fence, waving.

"You should have been at the Eagles meeting last night," one man called.

"There are lots of places I'd like to go that I can't get to," Truman replied, heading inside to see Mrs. Truman.[2]

The dignified white frame house had been built in the 1860s by Mrs. Truman's grandfather, the late George P. Gates. Bess and Harry Truman had made their home there with her widowed mother, Madge Gates Wallace, ever since they were married in 1919. With its modest gingerbread and arches, its ample verandas, high-ceilinged rooms, and tall windows, the house stood in a pleasant, shaded yard, planted with lilac bushes and adorned with a sundial, inscribed: "My Face Marks the Sunny Hours. What Can You Say of Yours?"

Truman had awakened in Blair House that Saturday and read the morning newspapers before most of his fellow Washingtonians were out of bed. The news was routine and quite typical of the times. Richard Rodgers and Oscar Hammerstein, II, were working on a new musical called *Anna and the King of Siam*. Broadway already was having a good year with *Death of a Salesman, Kiss Me Kate, South Pacific,* and *The Cocktail Party*. At the motion picture houses in New York, *Tarzan and the Slave Girl* had opened the day before. Other marquees were alight with the names of Joan Crawford, Jimmy Durante, Humphrey Bogart, Claudette Colbert, Betty Grable, Lauren Bacall, and Maureen O'Hara.

Typically, the news featured events reflecting fear of the Soviet Union abroad and communism at home. The Senate had opened debate on a second-year authorization of $1,222,500,000 for the Mutual Defense Assistance Program. Charging that the Soviets were threatening the peace, Senator Connally said that the only way the United States could head off a third world war was to arm its allies. He strove to justify the size of the authorization in the minds of conservative senators, not knowing that in a very short time $1,222,500,000 for foreign military assistance would look quaint.

Saturday's newspapers also carried the latest accounts of the torment of various organizations in dealing with the Communist issue.

The board of regents of the University of California had voted unanimously to discharge 157 members of the university staff for failure to declare that they were not members of the Communist party. The National Association for the Advancement of Colored People had adopted a resolution providing for the expulsion of any of its branches found to be dominated by Communists. John Stewart Service, the career State Department official accused by McCarthy of "Communist affiliations," had made his second appearance before a Senate investigating subcommittee. David Greenglass, a former army sergeant at the Los Alamos Scientific Laboratory, also had another day in court in connection with charges that he had given secrets about the atomic bomb to a Soviet spy ring. A federal judge had denied pleas for acquittal of three Hollywood film writers who had been cited for contempt for having refused to tell the House Committee on un-American Activities whether they were Communists. In the United States Court of Appeals in New York the government had asked that the convictions of eleven Communist party leaders in October for violation of the Smith Act be upheld. Government lawyers had argued that abridgment of free speech under the act was constitutional because of the Cold War and of recent Supreme Court decisions. And at a press conference at his United Nations headquarters at Lake Success, New York, Trygve Lie, of Norway, the secretary-general, had burst into anger when a *Chicago Tribune* reporter asked him whether he was then or ever had been a Communist.

With a respite at hand from the burdens of Washington, Truman had taken off from National Airport the morning of June 24 in a relaxed mood, to all appearances. Other high officials also had left their Washington posts for vacation spots in the country or by the shore. Acheson was at Harewood Farm, his retreat in Montgomery County, Maryland. Because he had received menacing letters, inspired by McCarthy's attacks, the farm was guarded night and day. Ambassador Warren R. Austin, United States permanent representative to the United Nations, was at his home in Burlington, Vermont. Thomas K. Finletter, the new secretary of the air force, who had succeeded Stuart Symington, now chairman of the National Security Resources Board, was vacationing in New England. General J. Lawton Collins, the new army chief of staff, was relaxing at his cottage at Scientists' Cliff on the Chesapeake Bay.

Truman's flight was in two stages. First he made a short hop to Baltimore to dedicate Friendship International Airport. It was not a time, seemingly, to be looking for war clouds. "I dedicate this great airport," he said, "to the cause of peace in the world."[3] By noon he was airborne again, heading west. Over luncheon aloft with some of his staff he predicted that McCarthy eventually would be expelled from the Senate as a liar.[4]

Independence was enjoying a lazy summer afternoon. In those days, before the urban sprawl from Kansas City, it was more of a small town than it is today. People sat on their porches or did errands, and Millicent Somerset and Thomas C. Twyman were married. The service was in Trinity Episcopal Church, the same small, red brick church in which Bess and Harry Truman had been wed. Since the Twymans were old friends of the Trumans, Mrs. Truman and Margaret went to the wedding, leaving the president at home to rest. It was probably the last moment of its kind he was to enjoy during his remaining thirty-two months in office. Although Truman did not know it yet, he was caught in a frightful predicament.

While he had been traveling from Baltimore to his home, the time on the other side of the international date line in Korea was just before dawn on Sunday, June 25. At about 4 A.M. in Korea, or as Truman was beginning to savor his holiday, Communist artillery and mortars suddenly shattered the rainy darkness along the 38th parallel. The roar signaled a coordinated attack at key points across the width of the Korean peninsula, the first thrust of which struck the Onjin Peninsula below the 38th parallel on the west coast. Soon after daybreak five American military advisers with the 17th Republic of Korea Regiment* on the peninsula radioed their headquarters in Seoul that the regiment was about to be overrun.[5] On the east coast enemy amphibious landings were made inside South Korean territory.

The South Koreans and the American military advisory group were taken completely by surprise when, supported by tanks and aircraft, seven Communist infantry divisions and smaller units, some ninety thousand men, smashed forward against elements of five Republic of Korea divisions in thin defensive positions along the parallel. Within hours the Communist troops in the west broke through the border and captured Kaesong, an ancient Korean capital thirty-five miles northwest of Seoul.

---

*The five were safely evacuated by air.

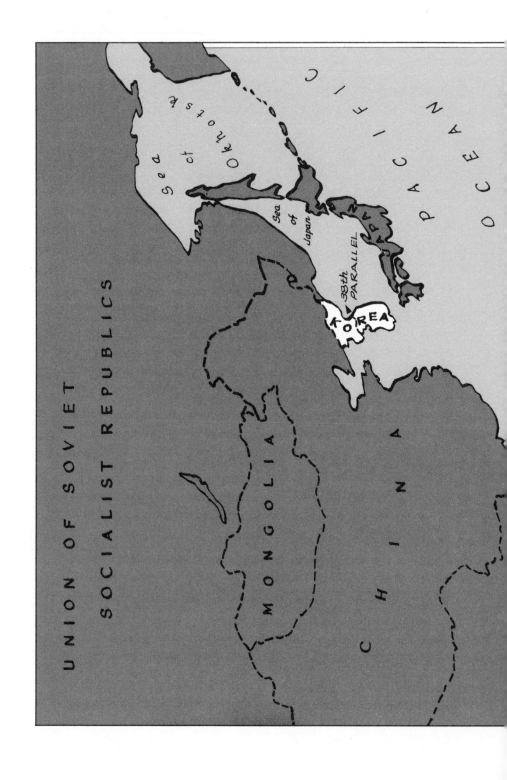

In the confusion it was several hours before Ambassador Muccio cabled Acheson about the invasion, saying, "It would appear from nature of attack and manner in which it was launched that it constitutes all out offensive against ROK [Republic of Korea]."[6]

After Mrs. Truman and Margaret returned from the wedding, the unsuspecting family settled down for a pleasant Saturday evening around the dinner table. When they had finished eating, the telephone rang. It was 9:20 P.M., and Acheson was calling Mr. Truman.

"Mr. President, I have very serious news," the secretary of state said. "The North Koreans have invaded South Korea."[7]

This was the great crisis, the ultimate turning point in the presidency of Harry S Truman.

20. *Sunday Night at Blair House*

O N SUNDAY MORNING, JUNE 25, Truman left home by car to visit the farm in Grandview, his first decision in the Korean crisis behind him.

On the telephone the night before, Acheson had recommended that the United States ask for a meeting of the United Nations Security Council. Acheson's own advisers had just urged such a course, and, subject to Truman's approval, he had directed them to proceed with preliminary arrangements. Since the withdrawal of American troops from the Republic of Korea, no plans had been prepared for action in case of a North Korean attack. In the past when speculation in the government had turned to the possibility of such an emergency, the thought was advanced that the United States should respond by taking the case to the United Nations. To the particular officials who had gathered at the State Department that night, this seemed a logical course because, among other considerations, South Korea had been established under the aegis of the United Nations.

Acheson's proposal Saturday night seemed logical to Truman, too, and he approved it.

Assistant Secretary of State Rusk recalled later that it was considered "of utmost importance that the decision to present the case . . . should appear in the morning papers simultaneously with the news of the North Korean attack." Hence Acheson acted "shortly in advance of the press deadline."[1] Newspaper readers were to know that the Truman administration was not soft on communism in the face of the march across the 38th parallel.

In talking with Acheson on the telephone, Truman had suggested that he make a sudden nighttime flight back to the capital. It was already 11:20 P.M. in Washington, however. What the president could have done upon a middle-of-the-night arrival was unclear. Furthermore, the extent of the danger in Korea was still uncertain. Acheson persuaded Truman to turn in for the night and see how the land lay on Sunday. On Sunday morning, therefore, rather than unnecessarily arouse public anxiety by rushing back to Washington, Truman marked time by going to Grandview, as planned, pending the next call from Acheson.

Great decisions impended, yet on June 25, 1950, the Office of the President was still a small and simple organization, compared with what it was to become under Presidents Kennedy, Johnson, Nixon, Ford, Carter, and Ronald Reagan. Truman had barely a dozen White House assistants of one kind and another. All were generalists. In the White House he had no separate staff or individuals, like McGeorge Bundy, Walt W. Rostow, Henry A. Kissinger, or Zbigniew Brzezinski, who specialized in advising the president on foreign policy and national security affairs. On such matters Truman dealt, essentially, with Acheson and Louis Johnson. The Central Intelligence Agency and the National Security Council were less than three years old, and the Policy Planning Staff of the State Department was only a few months older. These agencies were not nearly so elaborate nor sophisticated then as they were to become. The decisions that lay ahead were to be made by Truman in consultation with Acheson, Louis Johnson, members of the Joint Chiefs of Staff, and—over the wires—MacArthur. The information on which the decisions were made came essentially from the State Department, the CIA, various diplomats, especially Muccio, and the military services.

Since Acheson's first call to Truman on Sunday night, much already had happened. Several hours after its opening barrages, North Korea declared war on South Korea, claiming that the north had been invaded by the south.

At 2:05 A.M. on Sunday a message arrived at the State Department from Muccio, saying that American military advisers in Seoul had asked MacArthur to ship a ten-day supply of ammunition for use by the Republic of Korea army. Appealing for State Department concurrence, the ambassador said, "Without early receipt [of] such ammunition and assuming hostilities continue at present level, [it] is feared modest stocks in Korean hands will be exhausted within ten days time."[2]

MacArthur's first report on hostilities arrived. It said that all territory west of the Imjin River was considered lost to the enemy. This extreme northwestern part of South Korea included the Onjin Peninsula and the cities of Yonan and Panmunjom as well as Kaesong.[3] At 6:46 A.M., in Washington, Muccio reported that four North Korean fighter planes had strafed Kimpo Airfield, near Seoul. Recalling his previous warnings about South Korea's lack of military aircraft, he hoped that "some positive and speedy action can be taken at this late date to remedy this deficiency which is [an] exceedingly serious threat and handicap. . . . Rhee and other Korean officials will look to US for air assistance above all else. Future course of hostilities may depend largely on whether US will or will not give adequate air assistance."[4] The idea of the use of American air power had entered the picture almost at the outset.

Two hours later General J. Lawton Collins and other high-ranking army officers in Washington held a teletype conference with General Willoughby, MacArthur's intelligence chief, and other officers in Tokyo. The Tokyo group reported that because of the proximity of North Korean tanks to the United States embassy in Seoul, evacuation of American personnel would begin the next day. When MacArthur had been relieved of responsibility for the security of South Korea in 1949, he retained responsibility for any emergency evacuation of Americans. The Tokyo group said that for the evacuation currently planned MacArthur would provide naval and air protection.[5]

At 9:59 A.M. a cable arrived from Walworth Barbour, counselor of the

American embassy in Moscow, which struck a note that was to take on increasing credibility in the administration with every hour that passed. Barbour said that if North Korea had indeed launched an all-out offensive, the attack represented a "clear-cut Soviet challenge which in our considered opinion US should answer firmly and swiftly as it constitutes direct threat [to] our leadership of free world against Soviet Communist imperialism. ROK is creation of US policy and of US-led UN action. Its destruction would have calculably grave unfavorable repercussions for US in Japan, SEA [Southeast Asia] and in other areas as well." Barbour stressed the importance of making it immediately clear that the United States was ready upon request "to assist ROK maintain its independence by all means at our disposal, including military help. . . ."[6]

In Tokyo on a visit, meanwhile, John Foster Dulles and John Allison, State Department Asian expert, had the following message sent to Acheson:

> It is possible that South Koreans may themselves contain and repulse attack and, if so, this is best way. If, however, it appears they cannot do so then we believe that US force should be used even though this risks Russian counter moves. To sit by while Korea is overrun by unprovoked armed attack would start disastrous chain of events leading most probably to world war. . . .[7]

This message not only advanced the idea that a Communist victory in Korea would be a prelude to other Communist thrusts elsewhere. In proposing American military intervention, if necessary, it also was more explicit than Barbour's message and constituted the strongest recommendation yet before the Truman administration that morning for possible employment of United States forces in Korea.

In mid-morning MacArthur said that he was expediting shipment of ammunition to Korea and suggested that the United States Seventh Fleet be moved toward Korean waters as a precaution.[8] The bulk of the messages described a crumbling situation, thus underscoring the shortage of time and exerting pressure on policymakers in Washington. Muccio reported a meeting with Rhee. Distraught, the Korean president said that the approaching enemy tanks could not be halted and that the government would move south within hours to Taejon—a shift he later postponed.

At 11:30 A.M. in Washington high-ranking officials of the Departments of State and Defense met to weigh the course to be followed if, as was expected, the North Koreans were to refuse to accede to any request from the United Nations Security Council, soon to meet in emergency session.

Repeating a theme that was already coloring the thinking in Washington, John Paton Davies, of the State Department, interpreted the hostilities as meaning that the Soviets considered the Far East their "oyster." If the Soviet Union could get away with aggression in Korea, it would probably strike in other areas as well, Davies said. The discussion revealed a consensus that, since American reaction would be extremely important, Washington must not be content with half measures. "It either had to take a stand and stick to it or take no stand at all," in the words of the official account of the meeting.[9]

The State Department suggested a tentative course—and the military tentatively assented—as follows:[10]

1. MacArthur should be authorized to send to Korea any military equipment recommended by Muccio's mission, unrestricted by current aid programs.

2. MacArthur's area of responsibility should be extended to include operational control of all United States military activities in Korea.

3. Forces from his command, principally navy and air, should be employed to establish a protective zone around Kimpo Airfield, Seoul, and its port city, Inchon, to safeguard the evacuation of Americans and to gain time for international response to the action pending before the Security Council.

4. In the event that the Security Council should call on members to take direct action in Korea, MacArthur should be directed to use forces of his command as well as units from the Seventh Fleet to stabilize the front and, if feasible, restore the original boundaries at the 38th parallel.

The State Department concurred in a suggestion that a group from MacArthur's command be dispatched to Korea to determine how much aid, possibly including military forces, would be needed to hold the Seoul-Kimpo-Inchon area.

While the president was still down on the farm, therefore, his subordinates in Washington, Acheson the senior, had in the legitimate discharge of their responsibilities set in motion tentative planning for American intervention in Korea.

When the tentative program was transmitted to Tokyo later on Sunday, it was explicitly stated that its execution hinged on the president's approval. The trend of the thinking in Washington, however, so elated MacArthur's staff that a message came back on the teletype: "Come over and join the fight. We are delighted with your lines of action and this should turn the trick. Thank you."[11]

While Truman was temporarily absent from the conferences, his mood by that time seems to have been such that no differences would have arisen between his highest advisers and himself.

He ended his visit to Grandview and was back in Independence when Acheson called around 12:30 P.M. Acheson later said that he had on his mind Dulles's message recommending military intervention in Korea, if necessary, and warning that a Communist victory might start a chain reaction leading to a third world war. Although he was not certain, Acheson said he probably mentioned the message to Truman.[12] In any case, Truman and Acheson agreed that the president should return to Washington promptly. According to Truman's recollection, Acheson said that the United Nations Security Council shortly would call for a cease-fire but North Korea was likely to ignore it. A decision would have to be made, therefore, on what the United States was to do.[13]

Truman had lunch with his wife and daughter and put Margaret to work helping with preparations for the flight to Washington. She was, therefore, exposed to her father's mood and wrote in her diary for that day that "Northern or Communist Korea is marching in on Southern Korea and we are going to fight.''[14]

Having finally made up his mind that it was necessary to return to Washington, Truman moved with such celerity it seemed as if he could not wait to make decisions and act. In the haste to get to the Kansas City airport two members of the White House staff were left behind. On the scamper to the plane Brigadier General Wallace H. Graham, the president's personal physician, said to Anthony H. Leviero, of the *New York Times,* and Edwin W. Darby, of *Time,* "The boss is going to hit those fellows hard.''[15] But Truman paused to tell a group of reporters, "Don't make it alarmist. It could be a dangerous situation, but I hope it isn't.''[16] Then he boarded the *Independence* as the pilot Colonel F. W. (Frenchy) Williams, was about to warm the engines. Truman said he wanted to leave at once. The plane did not move. Truman asked Henry Nicholson, the secret service agent, what was causing the delay. Nicholson inquired and reported that the navigator, Captain E. P. Christiansen, had not yet arrived. Truman insisted on taking off without a navigator. The boarding ramp was removed and the door closed. As the plane was about to taxi to the runway, Christiansen sped alongside in a car and climbed into the nose of the *Independence* on a rope ladder.[17]

While Truman was flying east, the rush of activity continued in Washington and the United Nations. When the Security Council met at 2 o'clock to consider an American resolution calling for a halt in the fighting, the Soviet move was of critical importance. On the previous January 10 Jacob Malik, the Soviet representative, had walked out of a meeting of the Security Council when the council refused to unseat Nationalist China for Communist China. He had continued to boycott the council ever since, and the question of the moment was whether he would return for the Korean crisis. If Malik took his seat, he could have vetoed the American resolution and thus changed the nature of the events of the next several days. Malik did not appear. Shortly before 6 o'clock, therefore, the resolution was adopted, 9 to 0, Yugoslavia abstaining. The salient points were these:

1. The Security Council determined that the North Korean armed attack "constitutes a breach of peace."
2. The council called for "the immediate cessation of hostilities" and for North Korean forces to withdraw to the 38th parallel.
3. The council called upon all members "to render every assistance to the United Nations in the execution of this resolution and to refrain from giving assistance to the North Korean authorities.''[18]

Late in the afternoon the office of intelligence research in the State Department circulated a report that "US withdrawal would signify the end of organized resistance in South Korea."

The opinion was already growing in Washington that afternoon, supported by the intelligence report, that, as the report said, there was "no possibility that the North Koreans acted without prior instruction from Moscow. The move against South Korea must therefore be considered a Soviet move." According to the report, the "liquidation of the South Korean Government would fit into the Soviet global strategy," dealing a "severe blow" to United States prestige in Asia. "Soviet military domination of all Korea would give Moscow an important weapon for the intimidation of the Japanese in connection with Japan's future alignment with the US." That alignment continued to loom ever more important in American thinking. "Rapid and unhesitating US support for the ROK, on the other hand, would reassure the Japanese . . . ," the report said. But success of "the current Soviet-sponsored invasion of South Korea" would cause Europeans, particularly Germans, to question the capacity and the will of the United States to face the supposed challenge of the Soviet Union.[19] That theme weighed heavily in Washington.

Truman was met at National Airport in Washington by Acheson, Webb, and Louis Johnson. Johnson, accompanied by General Bradley, had returned only the day before from a trip to Japan, where they had talked with MacArthur. Truman seemed grim. "That's enough," he snapped at photographers pressing for one more shot. "We've got a job to do."[20] He had already arranged for a dinner and meeting in Blair House that night with his highest military and diplomatic advisers. On the ride into the city he and Acheson sat together in the back seat, with Johnson and Webb directly in front of them on jump seats. Truman said he did not believe the Trans-Siberian Railroad had sufficient capacity to support Communist forces in a war in Korea. "By God," he exclaimed, as Webb recalled his words, "I am going to let them have it!" Louis Johnson swung around and shook his hand.[21] With Truman's determination to resist, the course of the ensuing deliberations was basically set.

As officials gathered at Blair House, he sat in a window seat. Ambassador Jessup recalled: ". . . I heard him repeating, half to himself, 'We can't let the U.N. down! We can't let the U.N. down!' "[22] Then the president joined the others for a drink.

Bradley read aloud from a memorandum given to him and Johnson in Tokyo by MacArthur, saying that the strategic interests of the United States would be "in serious jeopardy" if Formosa should become dominated by a power hostile to the United States.

"Unless the United States' political-military strategic position in the Far East is to be abandoned," MacArthur wrote, "it is obvious that the time must come in the foreseeable future when a line must be drawn beyond which Communist expansion will be stopped."

Thus was introduced in the dialogue another facet of the conviction that was taking hold—the drawing of a line at which the United States and its allies would say to the Communist countries: thus far and no farther.

To prevent "a disaster of utmost importance to the United States," MacArthur suggested that he be authorized immediately to make a survey of the military, economic, and political measures required to prevent Communist seizure of Formosa.[23]

After the reading of the memorandum, the group dined and then when the table had been cleared, Truman opened the meeting by calling on Acheson, who was unmistakably the chief architect of the unfolding American policy. The secretary made several recommendations.[24]

In line with the course tentatively approved earlier by officials of the Departments of State and Defense he recommended that MacArthur be empowered to supply South Korea with arms, ammunition, and equipment beyond those items previously authorized.

He recommended that United States planes provide cover for the evacuation of Americans and that the air force be authorized to attack North Korean tanks and aircraft interfering with the evacuation.

He recommended that the president order the Seventh Fleet to the Formosa Strait to prevent an attack from the island against the mainland or from the mainland against the island. In other words, in a reversal of his past opposition to military assistance to Formosa, Acheson proposed that the fleet seal off the island. On the other hand, he opposed having MacArthur go to Formosa until American policy was clarified.

Finally, Acheson recommended increasing aid to Indochina over and above the $10,000,000 Truman had allotted only several weeks earlier.

When it came Bradley's turn to speak, the chairman of the Joint Chiefs of Staff supported Acheson's proposal for interposing the Seventh Fleet between Formosa and the mainland. Referring to the Far Eastern situation, Bradley said that the United States must draw the line somewhere.

Truman said he agreed with that.

Bradley said that because the Soviets were not yet ready for war, the situation in Korea offered a good occasion for drawing a line. Yet he questioned the advisability of committing American ground forces in Korea, particularly if large numbers were to be involved.

General Collins, army chief of staff, then reported on a teletype conference with Tokyo. He disclosed that MacArthur had elected to ship mortars and artillery along with the supply of ammunition requested by Muccio. Collins said that F-51 fighter planes were available in Japan and that South Korean pilots would be flown from Kimpo to get them. Collins asked that MacArthur be authorized to send a survey group to Korea.

Inquiring about Soviet air strength in the Far East, Truman introduced an especially dramatic note by asking General Vandenberg if the United States could knock out Soviet air bases in the area. Vandenberg replied that this might take time but could be done with atomic bombs.

Frank C. Pace Jr., who had replaced Kenneth Royall as secretary of the army, joined Bradley in expressing doubts about the wisdom of sending American ground forces into Korea. Louis Johnson said he, too, was opposed to such a commitment.

Secretary of the Air Force Finletter drew an analogy between the existing situation and the situations preceding the two world wars and said that the United States should take calculated risks in hope that American action would help keep peace.

Johnson seconded Acheson's recommendation for authorizing MacArthur to send arms to Korea. Adding a noteworthy reservation, however, the secretary of defense said the instructions to the general should be precise so as not to allow him too much discretion. Johnson warned against delegating presidential authority to MacArthur.

Truman then announced his decisions up to that point:

1. MacArthur was to send military supplies to Korea.

2. MacArthur was to send a survey group to Korea.

3. The Seventh Fleet was to steam north from the Philippines, but its actual mission would be decided when it reached the area of the Formosa Strait.[25]

4. The Air Force was to prepare plans—but take no action—to destroy all Soviet air bases in the Far East.

5. The Departments of State and Defense were to calculate "the next probable place in which Soviet action might take place."

"Next" denoted that Truman and his advisers believed that the North Korean attack was a "Soviet action."

Finally, the president authorized the air force and navy to take necessary action to prevent the Seoul-Kimpo-Inchon area from being overrun during the evacuation of American dependents. Thus United States forces were being committed to combat conditions for the first time since August 1945. Unknown to Congress and to the public, the president's principal decisions were dispatched to MacArthur in the form of orders. As yet Truman had taken no irrevocable step. But MacArthur was admonished in the dispatch that "further high level decisions may be expected as military and political situations develop."[26]

As the orders were going out from the Pentagon, General Bradley was asked by Lieutenant General Matthew B. Ridgway, deputy chief of staff for the army for operations and administration, whether the commitment of naval and air forces to cover evacuation was deliberately intended to exclude the use of ground forces in Korea. "Yes," Bradley replied.[27] Later Bradley was to testify, ". . . I don't think you can say that any of us knew, to start, when we went into this thing, what would be involved." "No one believed," he said, "that the North Koreans were as strong as they turned out to be."[28]

When the Blair House meeting ended, Truman said: "Let's all have a drink. It's been a hard day." As the group relaxed, he added: "I have hoped and prayed that I would never have to make a decision like the one I have just made today. Now, with this drink, that's out of my mind." He turned to John D. Hickerson, assistant secretary of state for United Nations affairs, and said: "Jack, in the final analysis I did this for the United Nations. I believed in the League of Nations. It failed. Lots of people thought it failed because we weren't in it to back it up. Okay, now we started the United Nations. It was our idea, and in this first big test we just couldn't let them down. If a collective system under the U.N. can work, it must be made to work, and *now* is the time to call their bluff."[29]

During the meeting Truman had stressed, in the words of the official notes, "that we are working entirely for the United Nations." Obviously, his meaning was that the United States and the United Nations were bound in a common purpose in Korea. Fifteen months before, the previously cited NSC 8/2 had called attention to the parallel of interests that would exist if war should erupt in Korea. The policy paper also had stated that the overthrow of South Korea by Soviet-backed forces in the north would constitute a severe blow to the prestige of the United Nations. To be sure, Truman had bypassed the United Nations when he felt it necessary in extending aid to Greece and Turkey under the Truman Doctrine. On the other hand, he and his administration were deeply committed to the principle of collective security in a world in which atomic war was possible. They believed that through collective action, aggression had to be stopped before it spread.

Unquestionably, Truman was apprehensive that the crushing of South Korea might wreck the United Nations and with it the hope for collective security. He entertained probably exaggerated visions of the help other members of the United Nations could or would provide in repelling the North Korean attack. Acting under the banner of the United Nations had the advantage of sanctioning whatever military measures the United States might decide to take in Korea. Truman's course, however, was by no means exclusively dependent on the United Nations. He later told Acheson that if the secretary had not acted promptly in arranging for a special session of the Security Council, "we would have had to go into Korea alone."[30]

From the first word of the North Korean attack, the reaction of practically every American official involved, so far as the historical record shows, was to move to force the invaders back to the 38th parallel.

Without a second thought, Truman and his advisers elected to appeal immediately to the Security Council. It was Rusk "who from the first pressed for American intervention . . .," Roger Tubby, then a State Department press officer, noted in his private journal.[31] Quickly, high officials of the Departments of State and Defense made tentative plans for possible use of American forces to repel the North Korean attack. State Department intelligence perceived a severe blow to American prestige, with potentially serious consequences in Japan, if North Korea were to defeat South Korea, and in Europe, if the United States did not respond to Communist aggression.

The entire record of events in the first twenty-four hours was as if the National Security Council and the Joint Chiefs of Staff had never found South Korea to be without strategic value to the United States in a general war. It was as if the United States had never pulled its troops out of South Korea to make better use of them elsewhere. It was as if Acheson and MacArthur had never excluded South Korea from the American defense perimeter in Asia. Instead, Acheson now wanted American planes to attack North Korean tanks and aircraft interfering with the evacuation of American civilians and recommended that MacArthur speed to South Korea arms and ammunition beyond any already authorized.

In the glare of Soviet-supplied artillery the menace of North Korea was magnified. Suddenly, at a troubled time in the Cold War, American prestige was put in jeopardy. At the very least a great political embarrassment to American interests was threatened. Moreover, with the Communists in control of mainland China and with Communist forces pressing in Indochina and Indonesia, the loss of South Korea might disturb the balance of power in the Far East.

The reaction of Truman and his advisers was heightened by the judgment, or misjudgment, that the Kremlin had instigated the attack to challenge American interests in Asia, expand Communist power, and possibly divert attention from the danger of a more serious assault elsewhere.

This judgment reinforced the conviction expressed by Truman and Bradley—and echoed across the land in ensuing days—that the United States must draw a line somewhere. It was a reflection of the lesson that Truman and the men around him had absorbed from having witnessed in the 1930s the appeasement of Hitler at Munich and the failure of other countries to halt German and Japanese aggression before it was too late, before the strength the aggressors gathered in one conquest helped them to succeed in larger conquests. Truman had recited this lesson fourteen months earlier at the signing of the North Atlantic Treaty, when he said that if the Allies had joined in such a defensive pact in 1914 and 1939, the two world wars would not have occurred. In a message to Congress on the American response in Korea, Truman was to say: "The fateful events of the Nineteen-thirties, when aggression unopposed bred more aggression and eventually war, were fresh in our memory."[32] To "draw the line" was another way of saying containment, and if there was one word that epitomized Truman's policy as president, up to that point, it was containment, or containment combined with deterrence.

In his contemplation of the Soviet problem early in the Cold War Truman had been exposed to George Kennan's famous "long telegram" from Moscow in 1946.[33] Kennan painted a dark picture of Soviet ambitions but said Moscow usually backed off "when strong resistance is encountered at any point." Soon afterward Truman had approved in advance a speech by the then Secretary of State Byrnes, declaring that the United States could not overlook "a unilateral gnawing away at the status quo." When, through the vehicle of a proposed Soviet-Turkish defense pact, the Kremlin sought a foothold in the Black Sea Straits, Truman not only stood fast against it but sent a naval task force led by the aircraft carrier *Franklin D. Roosevelt* to the Mediterranean to underscore his resolve. To avert a threatened Soviet encroachment in Iran in 1946 he insisted on precipitating a minor crisis in the United Nations Security Council, even though Moscow already had indicated an intention to desist.

In the Truman Doctrine the president had captured the quintessence of containment when he said, "I believe that it must be the policy of the United States to support free peoples who are resisting attempted subjugation by armed minorities or by outside pressures." The Marshall Plan, the Berlin airlift, the North Atlantic Treaty, and the Mutual Defense Assistance Program were instruments to contain the Soviet Union in Europe. For more than two years the National

Security Council had been promulgating top-secret documents emphasizing containment, though not calling it that, as a foundation stone of United States foreign policy. The previously mentioned NSC 20/4 stated as an objective of this policy the encouragement and promotion of "the gradual retraction of undue Russian power and influence from the present perimeter areas around traditional Russian boundaries." The aforementioned NSC 8/2 said that "The extension of Soviet-backed Communist control throughout all of Korea would enhance the political and strategic position of the USSR with respect to both China and Japan and adversely affect the position of the U.S. . . . throughout the Far East." After the fall of China the Truman administration extended the concept of containment from Europe and the Middle East to Asia. Containment was the purpose of Truman's support of the Bao Dai regime in Vietnam. So, in part, was the prospective Japanese peace treaty a measure of containment.

In the understanding of the men gathered in Blair House the extension of Communist domination in Asia was the very thing that was happening, blatantly. Truman, Acheson, and the rest of them had been conditioned by experience and doctrine to try to contain it before it led to worse trouble. The lesson that their generation had drawn from the origins of the Second World War was epitomized by Truman in his statement of China policy on December 15, 1945. "Events of this century . . . would indicate," he said, "that a breach of peace anywhere in the world threatens the peace of the entire world."[34] In accordance with decisions being made at Blair House, containment was about to be applied by military force rather than by the primarily economic and political means of the past.

The United States was not legally committed by treaty to defend South Korea. The Americans had played roles as occupiers, suppliers, and protectors and, currently, were military advisers and armorers to the Rhee government. Through American initiative in the United Nations, the Republic of Korea had been established. Against this background the Truman administration could not easily have escaped the fact of a practical commitment to the Republic of Korea and to the United Nations.

The shocking way the war began galvanized Truman. The smashing, unexpected attack was a blow he felt personally, if only because of its implications for his effectiveness as president. In the atmosphere in Washington vicious domestic political repercussions damaging to the president would have been inevitable if the "loss" of China were to be followed by the "loss" of Korea. Characteristically, Truman was not a belligerent man, yet his back went up when he was attacked or put on the defensive. In the 1948 campaign he had effectively cast himself in the pose of a man who was out to "give 'em hell." On election night he learned that the American people liked that kind of grit. His own heroes were men of bold action, like Andrew Jackson. It was Truman's nature to respond to challenge. An affront to his country and to himself, especially one that struck him as wrong, uncapped his ample reserves of anger and righteous indignation. Furthermore, he had an appetite, too much of a one, really, for unhesitating decision. In the crisis of the sort that had exploded in Asia, subtleties were not his strong suit.

The record of June 25 makes it obvious that before he conferred with his advisers at Blair House he had made up his mind to fight, if necessary, to hit back at the North Koreans and thwart their attack by measures still to be determined.

The character of the North Korean attack and the American perception of it as a move inspired by the Soviet Union created a consensus that the time had come to draw the line one way or another. Republicans soon were to find openings to attack Truman on Korea. Disagreements were to arise on actions to be taken. But on the question of drawing a line no fundamental difference existed in the last week of June 1950 among Truman, Acheson, Louis Johnson, Taft, Eisenhower, Knowland, Bridges, Kenneth Wherry, George F. Kennan, the Democrats, the Republicans, MacArthur, the Joint Chiefs of Staff, the *New York Times*, and leading commentators. Walter Lippmann foresaw international anarchy "if a wretched little satellite government in northern Korea can thumb its nose at the United Nations."[35] Even Henry Wallace came round to support American intervention.

21. *The Commitment of U.S. Air and Naval Forces*

EARLY ON MONDAY, JUNE 26, reports of the fighting raised hopes that the South Koreans were holding their own. Then the picture turned grim. At 9:31 A.M. a cable arrived from Muccio reporting "rapid deterioration and disintegration."[1] Rhee and his cabinet fled Seoul by rail for a naval base near Pusan.

In late morning Truman issued his first formal statement in the crisis. In the nature of a report on the Blair House meeting the night before, the statement commended the United Nations Security Council's action and, without amplification, said that the United States "will vigorously support the effort of the Council to terminate this serious breach of the peace." If Truman and his advisers had been caught napping by the North Korean attack, Kim Il-sung had been in a slumber about Truman's psychology and the sensitivity of the administration to Communist challenge.

Those responsible for this act of aggression [Truman's statement said] must realize how seriously the Government of the United States views such threats to the peace of the world. Willful disregard of the obligation to keep the peace cannot be tolerated by nations that support the United Nations Charter.[2]

While the statement was still on the mimeograph machine, Truman discussed the crisis with George Elsey, then an administrative assistant. Elsey said he feared that the Communists next would take the logical course of invading Formosa. Truman beckoned him to a large globe in front of the fireplace in the Oval Office. What worried him, the president said, was not so much Formosa as the Middle East. His concern had been aroused by hearing of a remark that Stalin had made during the Second World War to Edwin Pauley. In a conversation, which Pauley later recounted to Truman, the Soviet dictator said that unless the United States supplied oil under Lend-Lease, he could not maintain a large army east of the Urals.[3] In the summer of 1950 Truman surmised that Stalin was under the same constraints and might, therefore, move against Persian Gulf states. Bending over the globe, the president put his forefinger on Iran and told George Elsey, "Here is where they will start trouble if we aren't careful."

"Korea is the Greece of the Far East," he continued. "If we are tough enough now, if we stand up to them like we did in Greece three years ago, they won't take any next steps. But if we just stand by, they'll move into Iran and they'll take over the whole Middle East. There is no telling what they'll do, if we don't put up a fight now."[4]

Pressure was building on Truman to act. In an editorial that morning the *New York Times*, which he was in the habit of reading, called the North Korean attack "obviously Soviet-authorized" and a menace not only to Japan but to Alaska. The fighting, the editorial said, "will, in the immediate future, force upon the United States the necessity for a decisive and unequivocal policy. . . . Thus far we have temporized and improvised. Our time for that ran out when the North Korean tanks crossed the border. We can lose half a world at this point, if we lose heart."[5]

After the Senate had convened at noon Styles Bridges, a wellspring of relentless right-wing assault on Truman's Asia policy, arose.

"Will we," he asked, "continue appeasement? Will we wait for the dust to settle? . . . Now is the time to draw the line."

When Knowland got the floor he said: "Korea today stands in the same position as did Manchuria, Ethiopia, Austria and Czechoslovakia at an earlier date. In each of those instances a firm stand by the law-abiding nations of the world might have saved the peace. . . . The destruction of the Republic of Korea would be catastrophic. . . . If this nation is allowed to succumb to an overt invasion of this kind, there is little chance of stopping communism anywhere on the continent of Asia."

Senator George W. Malone, Republican, of Nevada, dragged in the name of Alger Hiss and said that "it is fairly clear that what happened in China and what is now happening in Korea were brought about deliberately by the advisers of the president [Roosevelt] at Yalta and by the advisers of the State Department since then." McCarthy observed the occasion by introducing in the record a copy of a speech denouncing Acheson.[6]

The Republican right wing was ready to make trouble if, through "appeasement," to quote Bridges, the North Korean Communists were to be allowed to carry the day. The issue was outdated now. At a stroke Kim Il-sung had ended "appeasement" in Washington.

As the hours passed, the worst news from the field was that the North Koreans had seized Uijongbu, a town so situated that its capture opened the door to a drive on Seoul. MacArthur cabled:

> South Korean units unable to resist determined Northern offensive. Contributory factor [is] exclusive enemy possession of tanks and fighter planes. South Korean casualties as an index to fighting have not shown adequate resistance capabilities or the will to fight and our est[imate] is that complete collapse is imminent.[7]

At 7:29 P.M. Acheson telephoned Truman to suggest a second Blair House conference. Thus, the group that had met the night before resumed deliberations at 9 P.M.[8]

General Vandenberg reported that the first Soviet YAK plane had been shot down.

Truman said he hoped it would not be the last. In the first clash of North

Korean and United States forces, two American pilots had shot down the YAK-3 over Kimpo Airfield during an evacuation.

Again the architect, Acheson proposed the commitment of United States air and naval forces to the fighting in South Korea. He advocated that, without restriction, these forces be ordered to give the fullest support to South Korean troops by attacking North Korean planes, tanks, guns, and troop columns. The immediate purpose was to allow the South Koreans a chance to regroup.

In a seemingly routine manner Truman approved the full commitment of United States planes and ships to the fighting below the 38th parallel. Turning back in Korea thereafter was practically out of the question.

No action, Truman said, should be taken north of the 38th parallel. He added, "Not yet."

The risks and costs of intervention were taken in stride.

In a move of great importance Acheson recommended that the Seventh Fleet, nearing Formosa, be stationed in the Formosa Strait. Its mission would be to prevent the Chinese Communists from invading the island and to bar an attack by Chiang's forces upon mainland China.

Truman approved. After having refused for months to undertake the military defense of Formosa, he chose to do precisely that. The action was not based upon the United Nations' cease-fire resolution. It was purely an American initiative, taken in the interest of the security of the Pacific area and of United States forces there.

As Elsey's discussion with Truman had revealed, even members of the White House staff feared an attack on Formosa in the wake of the North Korean invasion. On the prevailing assumption of possible coordinated Communist moves, anxiety about an attack on Formosa was understandable.

Domestic political considerations also weighed heavily on Truman and Acheson. It would have been next to impossible for them to justify to Republican critics the commitment of American air and naval power to South Korea while leaving Formosa undefended. Defending Formosa would help win support for Korean policy in Congress.

Despite the heat on the Formosa issue, the administration and the Republicans never had been as far apart as it seemed. While Truman and Acheson had been unwilling to mount a military defense of the island against Mao's forces in earlier circumstances, they had never been ready to allow the island to fall under Soviet domination, as suddenly appeared conceivable after the North Korean attack. Truman had stated in January that the United States had no intention of establishing bases on Formosa "at this time." The phrase had been recommended by General Bradley against the possibility of war with the Soviets. Acheson had explained that the United States must be free to take whatever action might be necessary for its own security if its forces were to be attacked in the Far East.

The decision Truman made about Formosa on June 26, 1950, was a momentous one, however. It put the United States back in the middle of the Chinese civil war, from which Truman and Acheson had striven for months to disentangle themselves. With MacArthur already pushing to survey Formosa's military needs, the way was opened for renewal of American support of Chiang Kai-shek and, therefore, creation of a greater abyss than ever between the United States and Mao Tse-tung. Mao and his government regarded Formosa as part of China, which historically it was. To the consternation of the Chinese Communists, however, Truman's public statement about the interposition of the fleet left the future status of the island in some question. Determination of that status, Truman said, "must await the restoration of security in the Pacific, a peace settlement with Japan, or consideration by the United Nations."[9]

Together with terrible events in Korea barely four months off, Truman's decision on Formosa started the United States on a tortured course, leading, in the Eisenhower administration, to an alliance and mutual defense pact with Formosa. Truman's decision was one of the events also that led to postponement for a generation of formal relations between the United States and mainland China and to complications over Taiwan, as it was then called, even after such relations had been established under President Carter in 1979.

After the Formosa decision had been agreed to at the Blair House meeting, Acheson next proposed the strengthening of the United States base in the Philippines. He recommended enlargement of American military forces in the islands and accelerated aid to the troubled government in Manila. Truman approved. Since the death in 1948 of Manuel Acuña Roxas, first president of the Philippine Republic, the government had been plagued with corruption and was shaken by civil unrest, stirred by the outlawed, pro-Communist Hukbalahap peasant guerrillas in central Luzon.

Acheson, as a fourth proposal, recommended increasing aid to French Indochina and sending a military mission there. Truman approved. This decision meant an escalation of the United States role in Vietnam.

Acheson reverted to Formosa to say that it would be undesirable for the United States to get involved in the question of which Chinese should administer the island. Ironically, in view of the large future programs for Taiwan, Truman said he was not going to give the Chinese "a nickel" for any purpose. All the money the United States had already given the Nationalists was now invested in American real estate, he said.

Acheson observed that the United Nations Security Council would meet again the next day, and he had an assistant read a draft of a new American resolution. Broader than the first one, it called upon members to render such assistance as was needed in Korea to repel the attack.

Truman approved that, emphatically. He said he wanted everyone in on the action in Korea, including Hong Kong.

The discussion turned to the military situation in Korea and its possible consequences. General Bradley reported that the predicament of the South Koreans was bad, and he did not know to what extent American planes could make a difference. It was important for the United States to do something, Acheson declared, even if the effort was unavailing.

Truman said that for five years he had done all he could do to prevent a situation like the one in Korea. But since it had come about, the United States must strive to meet it. The United States must do everything it could for the United Nations, he said.

If ground forces were to be committed in Korea, Bradley advised, the United States could not carry out its other obligations as well without mobilization.

"I don't want to go to war," Truman said.

General Collins asserted that if the United States committed ground forces, mobilization would be imperative. Nothing in the official record shows that anyone had advocated sending ground forces up to that point. Johnson expressed hope that the measures already authorized would save the situation.

Again unbeknown to Congress and the people, orders were dispatched for unrestricted use of American air and sea power in South Korea and for sealing off Formosa by the Seventh Fleet.

"I don't want to take a course which will involve the United States in war until all aspects . . . have been considered," Truman told Tom Connally, as the senator recalled the president's words. "But don't worry, I'm not going to tremble like a psychopath before the Russians, and I am not going to surrender our rights or the rights of the South Koreans."[10]

On Tuesday morning, June 27, Truman met with senior Democratic and Republican members of Congress, told them of his decisions, and read a statement that would be issued at noon.[11]

Acheson gave a general review and said that two considerations made it clear that the United States should have taken a firm stand. One was that the South Korean forces had seemed to wilt under indecisive leadership. The other was that the governments of Western Europe appeared in near panic while waiting to see what the United States would do. Truman then read the statement announcing his decision, reached, he said, pursuant to the Security Council's first resolution.

> The attack upon Korea makes it plain beyond all doubt [the statement said] that Communism has passed beyond the use of subversion to conquer independent nations and will now use armed invasion and war. It has defied the orders of the Security Council. . . . In these circumstances the occupation of Formosa by Communist forces would be a direct threat to the security of the Pacific area and to United States forces performing their lawful and necessary functions in that area.[12]

Addressing the meeting, Truman said that the United States could not have let the invasion pass unnoticed. Obviously, he said, the attack was inspired by the Soviets. If the United States were to let Korea down, the Soviets would swallow up one piece of Asia after another.

In answer to a question, Acheson said that diplomatic reports indicated that most of the Western European nations would offer what little military assistance in Korea they could. Military help could not be expected from the French, whose hands already were full in Indochina, he said.

Later in the day, after the issuance of Truman's statement committing air and naval forces, Representative John W. McCormack, Democrat, of Massachusetts, the majority leader, interrupted the proceedings in the House of Representatives to read the text. Members rose and cheered. In the Senate the statement was read by Senator Lucas, the Democratic leader there. Knowland applauded it, saying that Truman "has drawn the line in the Far East . . ." and should receive "the overwhelming support of all Americans, regardless of their partisan affiliation."[13] From Albany Governor Dewey, titular head of the Republican party, telegraphed the president to voice his complete approval and support. Truman's action, Dewey said, "was necessary to the security of our country and the free world."[14]

Unmistakably, Truman's action was in harmony at that moment with a large segment of public opinion. The distinguished radio commentator Elmer Davis, former director of the Office of War Information, praised him on the air that night. The president had learned the lesson, Davis said, that the right time to halt aggression is the first time. The next morning the *New York Herald Tribune,* a preeminent Republican newspaper, carried a rare frontpage editorial, saying: "The President has acted—and spoken—with a magnificent courage and terse decision. . . . It was time to draw a line somewhere, somehow." In the spirit of the moment a bill to extend selective service for one year was passed by the House of Representatives, 315 to 4, and by the Senate, 76 to 0. Eisenhower considered Truman's decision in the circumstances "wise and necessary."[15]

The acclaim for Truman's move to halt the Communist drive with air and naval forces was bound, of course, to have the effect of pushing him toward another solution if air and sea power failed.

Some sixteen hours after the president had committed such power, Ambassador Austin introduced in the Security Council on June 27 a resolution declaring that "urgent military measures are required," because the North Koreans were continuing to attack. Proposing sanctions for the first time in the history of the United Nations, the resolution contained two recommendations. The first was that "the Members . . . furnish such assistance to the Republic of Korea as may be necessary to repel the armed attack. . . ." The second, which, though unsuspected at the moment, was to provide a basis for a change in American objectives in the fall, called for the restoration of "international peace and security in the area."[16] Again Malik was absent. The resolution was adopted, 7 to 1, Yugoslavia opposing. India and Egypt abstained, although India later expressed its support of the resolution.

Finally, on that same day Senator Joseph C. O'Mahony, an influential Wyoming Democrat, wrote to Truman to warn about the president's political vulnerability over the Communists' advance in Korea. Testifying before the Senate Appropriations Committee, Rear Admiral Roscoe H. Hillenkoetter, director of central intelligence, had said that the United States had not known when the North Koreans would attack but that intelligence had indicated for months that they intended to overthrow South Korea. Yet despite signs of threatened aggression, the administration had not provided Syngman Rhee the weapons needed for a successful defense. O'Mahony said that the testimony "will undoubtedly be used to support a charge that our policy was soft toward the Communists in Korea.'' To counter the critics he suggested that Truman announce that the United States would veto admission of Communist China to the United Nations.

By the time Truman replied on June 28, of course, he had committed air and naval forces in the defense of South Korea. He explained to the senator that American assistance before the invasion had been limited to helping South Korea maintain internal security and prevent border raids. ''I think,'' he said, ''we have now covered the situation to a point where we will either get results or we will have to go all-out to maintain our position.''[17] If air and naval support failed, that was not to be the end of the road for the United States, obviously.

Wednesday, June 28, dawned in Washington with the news that Seoul had fallen to the North Korean invaders.

Upon receiving Truman's last order MacArthur had sent every available aircraft into an attack below the 38th parallel on North Korean troops, tanks, planes, artillery, convoys, and railroads. First came night attacks by B-26 bombers, but their effectiveness was limited by poor weather. At daylight more B-26s and F-80 fighter planes carried on the attacks, joined by B-29 heavy bombers from Guam. The survey group that had been authorized by Truman on June 26 was sent by MacArthur to Korea under the command of Brigadier General John H. Church. After studying the situation, Church radioed a message to MacArthur, saying that United States ground forces would have to be committed in order to drive the invaders back to the 38th parallel.[18]

During the morning Truman received an ovation when he appeared before a meeting of the Reserve Officers Association at the Mayflower Hotel.

The National Security Council met early in the afternoon, and Truman, who presided, said he was doing his best to prevent the spread of fear among the people over the Korean involvement. Acheson warned of a serious situation ahead if the involvement did not meet quick success. Even so, Truman said, he did not intend to back out unless it were necessary to meet a graver threat elsewhere.

As was to be a continuing concern of his, Truman said he wanted all the help in Korea that could be obtained from other members of the United Nations. He alluded to the fact that congressional leaders had pressed him on this matter, and he wanted all offers of help reported to Congress. The first had just come from Great Britain. Prime Minister Clement R. Attlee had placed British naval vessels in Japanese waters at the disposal of the United States.

Secretary of the Air Force Finletter showed Truman a map of enemy air bases in North Korea. He said that in its present combat role in South Korea the United States air force could not be fully effective unless it could attack these North Korean bases and the fuel supply. Thus Truman came under pressure to take another step escalating the American involvement. He said that such attacks might have to be authorized but he did not wish to do so then. Acheson said he hoped American forces would not cross the 38th parallel. Truman said they were not to do it. Secretary of Defense Johnson reminded General Vandenberg, of the air force, that those were his orders. That was correct, Truman confirmed.[19]

Evidencing the serious pass to which things had come, Acheson said that the president might wish the military to review what forces were available in the Far East in case Truman should decide later that they were needed. Truman approved.[20]

The situation in Korea had worsened after the fall of Seoul. North Korean infantry captured Kimpo Airfield. The South Korean central front collapsed when the Republic of Korea 6th Division, its position untenable, withdrew southward. Speculation began appearing in American newspapers that American ground forces would have to be committed. The Joint Chiefs of Staff ordered its joint strategic survey committee to study what military measures should be taken if air and sea power failed to halt the attack. The committee was instructed to weigh air operations north of the 38th parallel as well as other actions that might be tried "in lieu of committing ground troops." Rear Admiral Arthur C. Davis, director of the Joint Staff, noted, "[the chiefs] do *not* want to commit troops."[21] Relentlessly, however, the North Korean advance pushed Truman, Acheson, Johnson, and the Joint Chiefs of Staff closer to the edge of the cliff.

Thursday, June 29, was a day of ceaseless activity. Determined to make his own assessment of the battle, MacArthur, then seventy, undertook a hazardous inspection of the front in Korea. Even before he arrived aboard his plane *Bataan,* he issued orders on his own initiative to air force headquarters in Japan to launch strikes against airfields north of the 38th parallel.[22] This was directly contrary to Truman's order to General Vandenberg, word of which may not yet have reached MacArthur at that time.

The Joint Chiefs of Staff tentatively approved a new directive to MacArthur, which had been prepared by their staff to consolidate all previous instructions. In fact, the order went beyond previous instructions by authorizing MacArthur to extend his operations into North Korea when he believed "serious risk of loss of South Korea might be obviated thereby." If possible, he was to consult the Joint Chiefs before taking such action. The Departments of State and Defense approved, and in talks between the Joint Chiefs and Louis Johnson the trend toward greater commitment in Korea moved up another notch. Having been ordered into action, the air force needed runways for its planes, and the runways needed to be guarded and serviced by troops. Hence Johnson undertook to get Truman's assent to use of service troops for communications and transport and sufficient combat troops to protect the port and airfield at Pusan. Subject to Truman's approval, all this was incorporated in the draft of the new directive to MacArthur.[23]

Johnson asked for another meeting of the National Security Council to consider this draft, and Truman called it that same evening.[24] When the session began and Johnson started to read the draft, Truman interrupted.

"I do not want any implication in the [directive]," he said, "that we are going to war with Russia at this time."

He was referring to a paragraph regarding what should be done if Soviet troops were to intervene in Korea. The directive said that in such circumstances

American air and naval forces were to defend themselves but to take no action to aggravate the situation pending new orders from Washington.

"We must be damned careful," Truman admonished, momentarily under the misapprehension that the directive was to be published. "We must not say that we are anticipating a war with the Soviet Union. We want to take any steps we have to to push the North Koreans behind the line, but I don't want to get us overcommitted to a whole lot of other things that could mean war."

Defending the directive, Secretary of the Army Pace said it was important to employ ground forces in establishing a beachhead at Pusan, on the southeastern coast. He said it was doubtful whether limitations should be placed on air and sea actions north of the 38th parallel, although these should be conducted carefully.

Some limitations were necessary, Truman said. He specified that north of the parallel he wanted American planes to destroy only such targets as air bases, fuel supplies, and ammunition dumps. His goal, Truman said, was to restore peace in South Korea—he did not want to do anything north of the parallel except to "keep the North Koreans from killing the people we are trying to save. You can give the commander in chief [MacArthur] all the authority he needs to do that, but he is not to go north of the 38th degree parallel."

Truman asked Acheson if he had had a reply from the Soviets to a United States request of June 27 that Moscow use its influence to persuade North Korean forces to withdraw. The reply had just been received: the Kremlin declined to interfere in the internal affairs of North Korea.[25] Acheson interpreted this to mean that the Soviets did not intend to commit their own forces in Korea at the moment.

The secretary of state also spoke about the new directive to MacArthur. He said he had no objections to the air force's attacking enemy airfields and army units. And if, for example, an American pilot espied Communist tanks coming down a road, he should attack them regardless of which side of the parallel they happened to be on. But he insisted that American planes not go beyond North Korea, since no one could foresee the consequences of an invasion of Manchurian air space.

Acheson supported defense of a Pusan beachhead. He said he was willing for American ground troops to enter Korea. For the anti-Communist forces to lose at that point, he said, would be a great disaster. Thus, as Elsey's notes recorded Acheson's comments, "it was essential to give [MacArthur] whatever he needs to stop a disaster."

Acheson called attention to a statement just issued in Peking by Premier Chou En-lai, branding the decision to interpose the Seventh Fleet in the Formosa Strait an act of "armed aggression against Chinese territory."[26] Indirectly, Acheson suggested that the Chinese might be seeking a pretext for involvement in Korea.

The discussion turned to offers of facilities made by Australia, New Zealand, Canada, and the Netherlands for use by ships and planes. Truman told his associates to "take everything. We may need them."

Acheson asked Johnson if it would be possible to get MacArthur to report on what was going on. Truman interposed to instruct Johnson to order MacArthur in the name of the president to submit complete daily reports. In the closing days of the Second World War, Truman said, he practically had to put in a personal telephone call to MacArthur to get information from him. He ended the meeting, however, by saying that he had no quarrel with anybody and did not intend to have—he just wished to know what the facts were.

The battle for South Korea had been going for nearly a week, therefore, when new orders, approved by Truman, went out that evening to MacArthur. Authority was given him to use army troops for communications and other essential military services and for guarding the Pusan port and airfield. He was authorized, if necessary, to extend his air and naval operations north of the parallel against air bases, depots, tank farms, troop columns, and other "purely military targets," taking care that operations stayed "well clear of the frontiers of Manchuria or the Soviet Union. . . ."[27] Airstrikes were launched against the north.

During the day a further development occurred, which, months later, was to evolve into an abrasive issue between Truman and MacArthur. Chiang Kai-shek's minister, Shao-hwa Tan, offered at the State Department to make available for use in South Korea approximately thirty-three thousand seasoned troops with the best equipment available in Formosa.[28] When informed by Acheson, Truman was inclined to accept the offer because he wished to see as many members of the United Nations as possible in a kind of legion against the North Korean aggressors. Acheson demurred, holding that it would be inconsistent to spend the money to protect Formosa with the Seventh Fleet while redeploying the very troops who should be the island's defenders. He also thought that Chiang's troops would need a great deal of then scarce American equipment. Truman put the subject in abeyance until the next day.[29]

Meanwhile MacArthur had returned to Tokyo from Korea, despairing of the effectiveness of South Korean units and convinced that the Republic of Korea would fall unless American ground forces were committed. He wrote a strong message to this effect, but for some reason did not send it to Washington for nearly twelve hours.[30] In any case Truman retired that night, knowing that little margin of military action remained for him except, if necessary, to do what had long been opposed in American military doctrine, namely, to commit ground forces to battle on the continent of Asia. As things turned out he had but a short sleep.

22. *Truman's Fateful Decision: Ground Forces in Asia*

SOON AFTER 1:30 A.M., JUNE 30, the army chief of staff, General Collins, who had been nicknamed "Lightning Joe" for his exploits as a division commander in Guadalcanal in 1942 and who later commanded the 7th Corps in Normandy, was handed a stark message from MacArthur. The message was the one MacArthur had delayed sending after returning from his reconnaissance of Korea. It put squarely up to Washington the question Truman and his advisers had been holding at an arm's length—one that had been pressing upon them ever more relentlessly each day.

Unprepared for attacks by aircraft and armor, MacArthur reported, South Korean forces had been reduced to not more than twenty-five thousand effectives and were incapable of counterattack. A dangerous new enemy breakthrough threatened. "If the enemy advance continues much further," he said, "it will seriously threaten the fall of the Republic." He declared:

The only assurance for the holding of the present line, and the ability to regain later the lost ground, is through the introduction of US ground combat forces into the Korean battle area. . . .

If authorized, it is my intention to immediately move a US regimental combat team to the reinforcement of [a] vital area . . .* and to provide for a possible build-up to a two division strength from the troops in Japan for an early counter-offensive.[1]

Collins asked for a teleconference with MacArthur, which began at 3:40 A.M., Washington time on June 30. "There was an eerie quality about this telecon that makes it stand out in my memory," the army chief of staff was to recall. "The air was fraught with tension as we assembled in the middle of the night in the Army's darkened telecon room in the Pentagon. All of the men present, though outwardly calm, realized the critical importance of the impending discussions between the conferees on opposite sides of the world. We instinctively spoke with hushed voices as the questions . . . were flashed on the screen, and we pictured in our minds the gathering in Tokyo where answers were being framed that would vitally affect our participation in this strange new war."[2]

Collins began by telling MacArthur that his request to commit ground forces

---

* Since the end of the Second World War the United States had maintained tactical forces in Japan, at least pending a Japanese peace treaty.

to battle necessitated a presidential decision. Hence a delay of several hours was inevitable. Meanwhile, however, the army chief of staff authorized MacArthur to move a regimental combat team to Pusan under the previous order to defend the beachhead at that Korean port. Collins explained that at the National Security Council meeting the day before Truman had made it clear that he would wish to weigh the matter with his top advisers before committing American troops to the battle area. Collins noted that his own authorization for the movement of a regimental combat team to Pusan would at least get things started for MacArthur.

"Prior to completion of this movement," Collins said, "we should be able to obtain definite decision on your proposal. Does this meet your requirement for the present?"

MacArthur replied: "Your authorization, while establishing basic principle that US ground combat forces may be used in Korea, does not give sufficient latitude for efficient operation in present situation." "Time is of the essence," he added, "and a clear cut decision without delay is imperative."

"I will proceed immediately through Secretary of Army," Collins said, "to request Presidential approval your proposal to move RCT (regimental combat team) into forward combat area. Will advise you as soon as possible, perhaps within half hour."

Collins and his associates in the darkened room scanned the screen for a response from Tokyo. MacArthur did not reply.[3]

Since the military situation seemed so critical, Collins did not take time to consult the rest of the Joint Chiefs, who, like himself, according to Admiral Davis, had not, as recently as two days earlier, wanted to commit ground forces to Korea. Instead, Collins telephoned Secretary of the Army Pace at home, reported MacArthur's request, and, having changed his own mind, supported the request. At 4:57 A.M. on June 30 Pace telephoned Truman, who was already out of bed, and relayed MacArthur's message.

Because of the rapid deterioration of the South Korean position, Truman could not have been surprised by MacArthur's recommendation for the commitment of American ground forces to combat. Beginning with recourse to the United Nations, Truman had increased his stake from diplomatic approach up through military action on a rising scale, and all the efforts had failed to stop the invasion. Acheson had said the day before that a North Korean triumph after the United States had moved in to try to block the enemy with airpower would be a disaster. Truman could not have felt differently. With acclaim from the American people and their allies, he already had gone too far to pull back without high embarrassment to himself, to the United States, and to the United Nations—and without creating a political riptide in Washington. By 5 A.M. June 30, it is doubtful whether the thought of accepting defeat and abandoning South Korea ever crossed Truman's mind.

Without hesitation he passed the point of no return.

"I told Pace," he recounted afterward, "to inform General MacArthur immediately that the use of one regimental combat team was approved."[4]

Truman reserved decision on the commitment of additional troops.

The line between the Pentagon and Tokyo was still open. Collins informed MacArthur: "Your recommendation to move one RCT to combat area is approved. You will be advised later as to further build up." "Acknowledged . . . ," MacArthur replied.[5]

Thus Dean Acheson, secretary of state; Louis Johnson, secretary of defense; Secretary of the Air Force Finletter; Secretary of the Navy Matthews; other members of the cabinet; members of the White House staff; members of the Senate and House of Representatives; and the American people as a whole all awoke that morning to learn that the United States troops were about to go into action in Korea. "The request from the front and the President's response came as no surprise to me," Acheson wrote later.[6]

After the decision had been communicated to MacArthur, Collins notified his colleagues on the Joint Chiefs of Staff. Admiral Sherman later recalled: "I had some apprehensions about it, and in the following days I felt that the decision was a sound one, it was unavoidable, but I was fully aware of the hazards involved in fighting Asiatics on the Asiatic mainland, which is something that, as a naval officer, I have grown up to believe should be avoided if possible."[7]

Sherman and his colleagues knew, of course, that the number of ground forces available to North Korea, China, and the Soviet Union exceeded anything that the United States conceivably could commit to Korea. Undoubtedly, Truman was aware of it, but one reason he committed forces to Korea was to deter another Communist invasion elsewhere.

Truman had called a meeting of his advisers at 9:30 A.M. MacArthur's appeal for ground forces seems to have had a most stimulating effect on the president. Sometime after 7 A.M. he had telephone conversations with Pace and Johnson and asked them to consider not only MacArthur's request for two American divisions but Chiang Kai-shek's offer of thirty-three thousand troops.[8] As reflected in one of Elsey's notes, Truman's comments ran along these lines: The Chinese Nationalist government was a member of the United Nations. Since Great Britain, Australia, Canada, and the Netherlands had made offers of ships and planes for the United Nations' effort, Nationalist ground troops probably should be used also. What Mao Tse-tung's response would be Truman did not know. Great care must be taken not to cause "a general Asiatic war." Elsey's note, quoting or reflecting Truman, concluded: "Russia is figuring on an attack in the Black Sea and toward the Persian Gulf. Both are prizes Moscow has wanted since Ivan the Terrible, who is now their hero along with Stalin and Lenin."[9] Once the day's business sessions began, Truman let the air out of his rhetoric.

He opened the 9:30 meeting in the White House by announcing that he had authorized commitment of a regimental combat team. He also brought up Chiang's offer of troops, saying that he was inclined to accept it, whereas Acheson was opposed, lest such an action provoke intervention by Communist China. The Joint Chiefs of Staff then stated their opposition, too, largely on grounds of logistics and supply.[10] As it developed, MacArthur at that point, for much the same reasons, also thought it inadvisable to use Nationalist troops. Later he underwent a change of heart, thereupon falling into serious conflict with Washington.[11] After having listened to the advice of Acheson and the chiefs, Truman decided to decline Chiang's offer.

Turning to the larger problem, he solicited advice on the deployment of forces over and above the regimental combat team. After his approval earlier that morning of the commitment of the limited force, the Joint Chiefs had drafted a tentative order further to authorize the dispatch of two divisions, as suggested by MacArthur. Now, suddenly, and apparently without explanation, Truman waded in all the way and announced to the meeting that he would give MacArthur authority to deploy, as needed, ground forces under his command, which then totaled four divisions. The president also approved a proposal by Admiral Sherman to establish a naval blockade of North Korea. No objections were raised against these decisions. The meeting lasted about half an hour.[12]

Later in the morning Truman invited congressional leaders of both parties to the White House and, after a review of the military situation by Bradley, read them a statement that was released to the press even as the meeting was in progress. It said, in part:

In keeping with the United Nations Security Council's request for support to the Republic of Korea . . . the President announced that he had authorized the United States Air Force to conduct missions on specific military targets in northern Korea wherever militarily necessary, and had ordered a naval blockade of the entire Korean coast. General MacArthur has been authorized to use certain supporting ground units.[13]

The last sentence was grossly obscure and did not convey the scope of Truman's decision on the commitment of ground forces. Furthermore Elsey's notes on the meeting reported, "The President pointed out that we had not yet committed any troops to actual combat"—obviously not, since the order had not yet been transmitted to MacArthur—"and that our present plan was just to send base troops to Pusan to keep communication and supply lines open."[14]

Presumably Truman chose his words out of concern for military security. Later Acheson told the political scientist Glenn D. Paige that the congressional leaders "could not have been told the exact nature, timing and extent of troop movements for reasons of the safety of the troops and of Japan. General MacArthur had a tricky operation to perform and required protection."[15] Comments of legislators as reported in Elsey's notes make it clear that some of them at least understood that Americans soon would be fighting in the front lines and that casualty lists would be appearing. Although Senator Smith later recalled with puzzlement Truman's reference to the use of troops at Pusan, no complaints about deceit were voiced by those who had attended the conference.[16] The press was not misled as to what was happening. Within an hour or so the *Evening Star* appeared on the streets of Washington, carrying the banner headline U.S. SENDS GROUND TROOPS INTO KOREA. The lead sentence said that the troops were bound for the battlefield.

Senator Chan Gurney, Republican, of South Dakota, declared that having made the military commitment, the United States could not back down from complete support of the South Koreans. He said he hoped the president understood that.

"I certainly do understand that," Truman replied.

The record discloses no opposition at the meeting to Truman's decision to commit ground forces—a decision that the *Washington Post* said in an editorial was "as wise as it was inevitable" and about which the *New York Times* commented: "To stop short of the necessary measures now would be folly. The United Nations cannot lose this first great battle in defense of peace . . . nor can the United States, which is now so deeply committed, contemplate a failure."[17] For reasons that will be related in the next chapter, however, Senator Wherry objected strongly to the manner in which the decision was reached.

One hour and 37 minutes after the meeting with the congressional leaders— at 1:22 P.M. in Washington June 30, 1950—an order of the Joint Chiefs of Staff was dispatched to MacArthur:

> Restrictions on use of Army Forces . . . are hereby removed and authority granted to utilize Army Forces available to you as [you] proposed . . . subject only to requirements for safety of Japan in the present situation which is a matter for your judgment.[18]

In Japan on the evening of June 30 Lieutenant Colonel Charles B. Smith, West Point '39, commanding officer of the 1st Battalion, 21st Infantry, 24th Division, had retired at 9 o'clock in his quarters at Camp Wood, near Kumamoto on the island of Kyushu. He had been asleep for about an hour and a half when he was awakened by his wife to take a telephone call from his regimental commander, Colonel Richard W. Stephens.

"The lid has blown off," Stephens exclaimed. "Get on your clothes and report to the CP!"

The experience was not unique for Smith. He had been at Schofield Barracks in Hawaii when the Japanese attacked Pearl Harbor December 7, 1941. By 3 A.M. on July 1, 1950, he and his battalion, less A and D companies, were on trucks lurching through a downpour to Itazuke Air Base, seventy-five miles from Camp Wood. When the battalion, now designated Task Force Smith, arrived at the waiting planes, Major General William F. Dean, commanding general of the 24th Division, was on hand to tell Smith that his small force was bound for Korea.

"When you get to Pusan," Dean ordered, "head for Taejon. We want to stop the North Koreans as far from Pusan as we can. Block the main road as far north as possible. Contact General Church. If you can't locate him, go to Taejon and beyond, if you can. Sorry I can't give you more information. That's all I've got. Good luck to you, and God bless you and your men."[19]

23. *A Costly Mistake: War without Congressional Approval*

AFTER SCOTT LUCAS had read to the Senate on June 27 Truman's initial statement, committing air and naval forces and ordering the fleet to neutralize Formosa, Senator James P. Kem, Republican, of Missouri, rose.

"I notice," he remarked, "that in the president's statement he says, 'I have ordered the fleet to prevent any attack on Formosa.' Does that mean he has arrogated to himself the authority of declaring war?"

In the nearly seventy-two hours since the North Korean invasion began, Truman had responded with executive action independently of Congress.

Kem asked Lucas, "Can the senator tell me under what authority the president of the United States has authorized the fleet to make an armed attack?"

Without admitting that an attack had been authorized, Lucas replied that "history will show that on more than a hundred occasions in the life of this republic the president as commander in chief has ordered the fleet or the troops to do certain things which involved the risk of war." The majority leader said he did not consider giving armed support to South Korea an act of war.

From the Republican side, Arthur Watkins spoke up, asking: "Should it not have been called to the attention of the Congress before ordering our fleet and our air force to support the government of South Korea?" If he were president, Watkins said, he ". . . would have sent a message to the Congress . . . setting forth the situation and asking for authority to go ahead and do whatever was necessary to protect the situation."

"A state of emergency exists," Lucas said, ignoring the fact that Truman had not legally declared one.

"But," Watkins persisted, "does the senator consider the action taken justified by the fact that we have ratified the United Nations [Charter] and have become a member . . . and if a request is made by the United Nations through the Security Council to send support, whether the president would be justified by that alone in sending support which might result in war?"

Lucas quoted the line in the president's statement noting that the Security Council, in its initial resolution, had called upon all members "to render every assistance" in bringing about a cease-fire and a withdrawal of North Korean troops. The resolution had not specified military assistance—that was provided for in the second resolution of June 27.

"Based upon the action of the United Nations Security Council," Lucas explained, "the president of the United States has ordered action. It is a demonstration of our keeping the faith."

Senator John W. Bricker, Republican, of Ohio, interposed, "Am I correct in saying that the president's action was taken as a result of the cease-fire order issued by the Security Council . . . ?"

Lucas said that Bricker was correct as far as action in Korea was concerned.

Watkins declared that Truman had taken a step leading toward war.

"The Congress is now in session," the senator said, "and unless there is power in the United Nations to order our forces into action of this kind which may result in a major world clash, then I think we should have been informed by the president in a message to the Congress today. As I recall, we were told time and time again when we were considering the [North Atlantic Treaty] that nothing would take us into war under that pact without action by Congress. The president could not do it. . . . Now, according to the action taken, by the mere order and request of the United Nations our own troops can be sent into a fighting war without the Congress saying 'yes' or 'no.' "

Article 1, section 8 of the Constitution provides that Congress shall have the power to declare war.

Defending Truman, Senator Hubert Humphrey said: "I think every senator should be mindful of what happened in Ethiopia when there was delay, when there was indecision and when there was ineffective action. I think we should be mindful of what happened in the Ruhr and the Rhineland when Hitler marched in . . . and took over and when no effort was made by the democracies to prevent that kind of aggression. . . . The president's action indicates that he is exercising the leadership and the statesmanship which the people require of the president."[1]

Certainly, the action was taken at a time when, historically, presidential authority was on the rise, relative to that of Congress, in matters affecting national security. The rise had received its impetus from Roosevelt's exercise of power during the Second World War and its approach.

The big gun went off in the Senate on June 28. In a crackling speech Taft— an "old time isolationist" to Truman—alleged "a complete usurpation by the president of authority to use the armed forces of the country."

"His action," Taft said, "unquestionably has brought about a *de facto* war with the government of northern Korea. He has brought that war about without consulting Congress and without congressional approval. We have a situation in which in a far-distant part of the world one nation has attacked another, and if the president can intervene in Korea without congressional approval, he can go to war in Malaya or Indonesia or Iran or South America."

With but the slightest detour on a map Taft might have included Vietnam.

When the administration withdrew the occupation forces from South Korea in 1949, Taft said, it should have deterred North Korea by making it clear that the United States would resist an invasion. "With such a policy," he added, "there never would have been such an attack by the North Koreans." The argument about a commitment that might have deterred the Communists was to be reiterated by subsequent critics. In fact such a commitment had been considered, but rejected, in the aforementioned guiding policy paper NSC 8/2 before the American withdrawal. For the United States to have guaranteed indefinitely the territorial integrity of South Korea, the National Security Council stated, would have tied down American forces in Korea and risked involvement in a major war "in which virtually all of the natural advantages would accrue to the USSR." In opting instead for military and economic assistance to South Korea the United States took what was viewed in NSC 8/2 as the middle course between leaving the Rhee government defenseless and indefinitely guaranteeing South Korea's territorial integrity.

In connection with the lack of deterrent Taft zeroed in on Acheson's speech of January 12 excluding South Korea and Formosa from the American defense perimeter. The senator called on Acheson to resign because the president had now repudiated his policies, notably by neutralizing Formosa.

Taft noted claims that Truman's action in Korea was in a special category because of American obligations under the United Nations Charter. "I think it is true," he said, "but I do not think it justifies the president's present action without approval by Congress." The Ohioan argued that "there is no authority to use armed forces in support of the United Nations in the absence of some previous action by Congress dealing with the subject and outlining the general circumstances and the amount of force that can be used."[2]

The point was questionable. The charter, approved by the Senate in 1945, says in Article 39 that the Security Council "shall determine the existence of any threat to the peace, breach of peace or act of aggression and shall make recommendations, or decide what measures shall be taken. . . ." Article 41 says that the council may decide on the need for measures, such as economic sanctions, not involving the use of armed force. But Article 42 says that, should the council consider such measures inadaquate, "it may take such action by air, sea or land forces as may be necessary to maintain or restore international peace and security." It was under these provisions that Truman had acted.[3]

Taft emphasized that Republicans had not been consulted before Truman made his decision to commit air and naval power to the support of South Korea and to interpose the fleet in the Formosa Strait. The senator correctly noted that on the morning of June 27 Truman had simply called in senior members of Congress from both parties. Twelve hours after his decision he read to them the same statement that Lucas later read in the Senate and answered questions about the Korean situation. No pretense of bipartisanship on the decision had been offered, as Taft said.

With the military situation in Korea in the last week of June crumbling toward a point of no return, Truman did have to act swiftly if the Republic of Korea was to be saved. Moreover events continued to erupt so rapidly that, as time passed, composing a coherent message became a problem. Still Truman might have gone to Congress for approval of his action as soon as he could have managed to do so and on the simplest terms. In their meeting on Monday, June

26, he inquired of the chairman of the Senate Foreign Relations Committee, Tom Connally, whether Congress would have to be asked for a declaration of war if the president were to decide to send American forces into Korea.

"If a burglar breaks into your house," the senator replied, "you can shoot him without going down to the police station and getting permission. You might run into a long debate by Congress, which would tie your hands completely. You have the right to do it as commander in chief and under the U.N. Charter."[4]

Especially because of the United Nations commitment, Truman undoubtedly was apprehensive of a possible delay in Congress. How easily his problem might have evaporated if only he had paused to communicate with Congress was demonstrated by Taft's assertion in his speech that "I should be willing to vote to approve the president's new policy" of assisting South Korea. With Taft's support a resolution introduced by the Democrats upholding the president's actions would have had no opposition of consequence. In general the critics of the administration's Asian policy were so enthusiastic that Truman had drawn the line against Communist expansion that not even Knowland disapproved of the way in which the president had proceeded. "They are all with me," Truman said to Secretary of the Army Pace in explaining why he did not rush to Congress for a resolution.[5]

Taft's speech was a warning, but Truman failed to take advantage of the consensus that existed. On June 29 he independently authorized the use of ground forces to protect Pusan and approved the use of air and sea power to attack targets north of the parallel. And on June 30 he committed American land forces to combat with the North Koreans. In his meeting that day with congressional leaders to inform them of his fateful decision, it will be recalled, only Wherry had raised a sharp objection—not to the commitment of these forces but to the manner of it.

Wherry told Truman he thought that Congress should have been consulted before the president took such actions. Elsey's notes of the meeting record the following exchange:

> The President said this had been an emergency. There was no time for lots of talk. There had been a weekend crisis and he had to act.
> Senator Wherry said "I understand the action all right. But I do feel the Congress ought to be consulted before any large-scale actions are taken again."
> The President responded [Elsey recorded] that . . . "If there is any necessity for Congressional action, . . . I will come to you. But I hope we can get those bandits in Korea suppressed without that."[6]

The comment points to one of the likely reasons why Truman wandered off the wise path in relations with Congress in the crisis. While, by his own account,[7] he knew that his decisions might lead, ultimately, to a general war, the supposition that he and others soon reached was that a world war did not then impend.

From the beginning, when he admonished reporters at the airport in Kansas City not to write alarmingly, he had tried to give a relatively small dimension to the affair. Even after he had approved on June 26 the commitment of air and naval power to the defense of South Korean forces below the parallel, he had told his advisers, "I don't want to go to war." The lesser dimension in which he saw the developing conflict had been particularly evident at a regularly scheduled press conference on June 29—one that produced a comment that was to keep his critics in ammunition for a long time.

"Mr. President," a reporter asked, "everybody is asking in this country, are we or are we not at war?"

"We are not at war," Truman replied and later added that "the members of the United Nations are going to the relief of the Korean Republic to suppress a bandit raid. . . ."

"Mr. President, would it be correct, against your explanation, to call this a police action under the United Nations?"

"Yes. That is exactly what it amounts to."[8]

Again, Truman had let a reporter put in his mouth words that were later to be held against him. He did not initiate, nor volunteer, the phrase "police action" any more than he had "red herring," but the result was to be the same as if he had.

He seems not to have had a sense of a major war's blossoming in Korea, although he was ready to go "all out," if necessary, to squelch the Communist invasion—as he told Senator O'Mahony in his letter of June 28. Once American forces were fully involved in what obviously was a major and difficult war, it was probably too late for Truman, as George Elsey noted in a historical memorandum a year later, "to get a resolution through by anything like a unanimous vote."[9]

The Elsey notes continue, "the subject of a congressional resolution was discussed half-heartedly from time to time, but the issue was never clearly threshed out."[10] Actually, his papers contain the draft of a joint resolution, dated July 3, 1950, prepared by Acheson for use if required. In the resolution Congress would have commended the American response in Korea. There was also the proviso that "It is the sense of Congress that the United States continue to take all appropriate action with reference to the Korean situation to restore and maintain international peace and security in support of the Charter of the United Nations and of the resolutions of the Security Council. . . ."[11]

Congress took an Independence Day recess and was not scheduled to reconvene until July 10. On July 3 Truman held a large conference at Blair House to consider an approach to Congress, a matter on which he and his advisers displayed considerable uncertainty.[12] Acheson recommended that Truman go before a joint session and review all that had happened with respect to Korea, not asking for a resolution of approval but standing on his constitutional authority as commander in chief. Acheson granted that it might be helpful in the future if Congress did pass such a resolution, but on the initiative of its members rather than on the initiative of the administration.

Senator Lucas ventured that Congress would pass a resolution but questioned the wisdom of a presidential appearance since Congress already was supporting Truman. For the president to appear before a joint session, Lucas suggested, might convey the impression that he was asking for a declaration of war.

That was exactly the point, Truman broke in to say. Truman concluded the conference on the third by saying he would mark time on a message pending a discussion with the legislative leaders when Congress returned.

By then, however, a sudden wave of panic-buying and hoarding had sent prices up. Truman drew back out of concern that a message at that moment would arouse fear of economic controls and make the panic worse.[13] In the period between July 10 and 15 Acheson exerted such daily pressure for a statement to Congress by Truman that Elsey, who was part of a group trying frantically to draft a message in the confusion, considered the secretary's pressure "highly offensive." It was, Elsey noted, "ridiculous to force the President to make a speech prior to the time that he could announce decisions on (a) necessary legislation and (b) necessary supplemental appropriations."[14]

Whatever thought there may have been, if any, about a simple resolution of support had yielded to time-consuming plans for a message embodying program and appropriations. It was to be July 19—twenty-five days after the North Korean attack—before he sent a message to Congress on the war.

Meanwhile Acheson had had the State Department prepare a memorandum on the legal and historical precedents. Constitutionally, the president as commander in chief had full control over the use of the armed forces, according to the memorandum, and had the authority to conduct foreign relations. Throughout history, the memorandum said, presidents had upon numerous occasions utilized these powers in sending armed forces aboard. Thus the memorandum noted that without express congressional authority President William McKinely sent some five thousand troops to China during the Boxer Rebellion to join with soldiers of other countries in relieving the siege of foreign quarters in Peking. Noted also was President Franklin Roosevelt's order, without congressional authorization, for American troops to occupy Iceland in 1941.

Eighty-five instances were listed in which land and naval forces were used abroad by presidential order to suppress piracy, punish offenses, or protect American lives and property. Most of these affairs took place in the Western Hemisphere and were of short duration.

Whatever applicability the legal precedents of these cases may have borne to the new crisis, it was the political considerations that counted in what was rapidly developing into a major undeclared war in Korea. The political rather than the legal aspect of war without congressional approval was to hurt Truman, to make the prosecution of the war more difficult for him, and to cause future public concern about what was to be called the "imperial presidency."

When Congress in 1973 passed a war-powers resolution intended to strengthen its own authority over commitment of American troops abroad, Truman's dispatch of forces to Korea without congressional approval was a secondary cause. Overwhelmingly, of course, Congress was reacting to Lyndon Johnson's and Richard Nixon's escalations in Vietnam.

Truman being sworn in for his second term on January 20, 1949, by Chief Justice Fred M. Vinson.

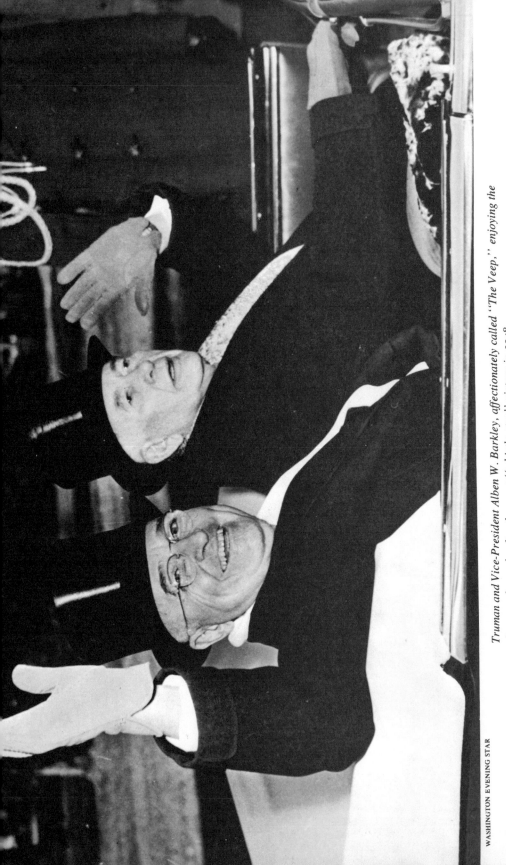

Truman and Vice-President Alben W. Barkley, affectionately called "The Veep," enjoying the 1949 Inaugural parade after the great "whistle-stop" victory in 1948.

Above: Truman delivering the 1949 State of the Union message.

Below: On Veterans Day, 1949, Truman with (left to right) Admiral Louis Denfeld, chief of naval operations; General Omar N. Bradley, chairman of the Joint Chiefs of Staff; and Secretary of Defense Louis A. Johnson.

Truman with his assistant, Dr. John R. Steelman.

James V. Forrestal, removed by Truman as secretary of defense to make way for Louis A. Johnson.

Truman at the swearing-in of his special counsel, Charles S. Murphy, while West-brook Murphy, Mrs. Murphy, and Associate Justice Tom C. Clark look on.

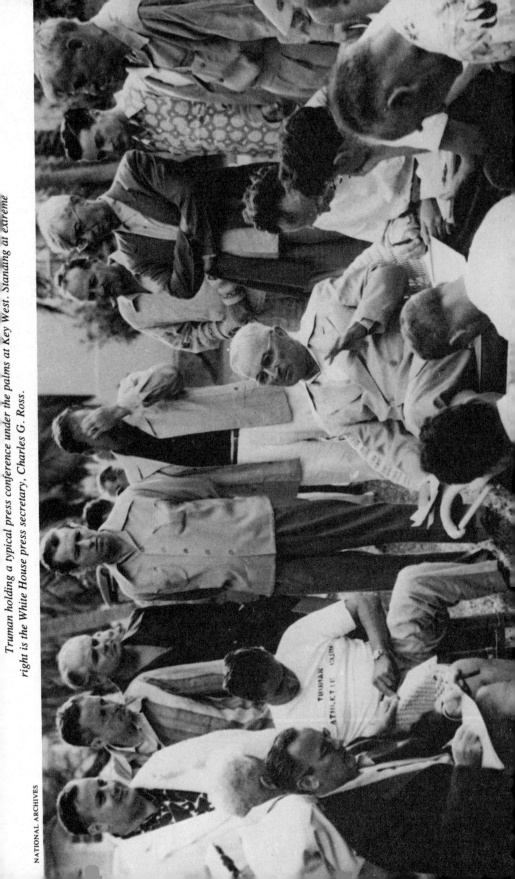

Truman holding a typical press conference under the palms at Key West. Standing at extreme right is the White House press secretary, Charles G. Ross.

Oscar Collazo of the Puerto Rican Nationalist party lies wounded at the foot of the stairs leading to Blair House on November 1, 1950. Collazo tried to storm Blair House to assassinate Truman with the aid of an accomplice, Griselio Torresola, who was slain, beyond the reach of the camera, to the left.

Truman and MacArthur meet on Wake Island on October 15, 1950, at the high point of their relationship. It was all downhill from there.

Above, left: Truman at Kansas City airport on June 25, 1950, hastening back to Washington after hearing news of the invasion of South Korea. "It could be a dangerous situation," he said, "but I hope it isn't."

Above, right: The president signing a proclamation of national emergency on December 16, 1950, at the height of the Korean War.

ON OPPOSITE PAGE

Above: Truman welcomes British Prime Minister Clement R. Attlee to Washington in December 1950 for an emergency conference on Korea and the atomic bomb.

Below: A lighthearted moment at the darkest time of the Korean War. Truman at Washington National Airport with the two men on whom he most depended in international crises: Secretary of State Dean Acheson (left) and Secretary of Defense George C. Marshall.

STARS & STRIPES

One famous general's reaction to another famous general's downfall. In Germany, Dwight D. Eisenhower grimaces at news of Truman's relieving Douglas MacArthur of his command in Korea.

ON OPPOSITE PAGE

The author, as White House correspondent for the old New York Herald Tribune, *taking notes on Truman at an impromptu curbstone interview in Washington on May 17, 1951.*

Top: Task Force Smith arrives at Taejon, South Korea, on July 2, 1950. These officers and men of the 24th Infantry Division were the first American ground forces committed to combat in the Korean War.

Bottom: Officers and men of the 17th Regimental Combat Team, 7th Infantry Division, enter Hyesanjin, North Korea, on November 21, 1950. The village was on the Yalu River, separating Korea from Manchuria. ARMY SIGNAL CORPS PHOTOS

ON OPPOSITE PAGE

Truman and then Assistant White House Press Secretary Roger W. Tubby, bound from the White House to a press conference in the Executive Office Building. Tubby kept a massive journal of his experience in government.

A happy handshake between Truman and Attorney General J. Howard McGrath before a sad ending.

ON OPPOSITE PAGE

Above: Senator Joe McCarthy. A White House aide said, "Truman thought time would take care of McCarthy sooner than it did."

Below: A great moment in a bittersweet relationship. At the 1952 Democratic National Convention in Chicago, Truman introduces the new Democratic nominee, Governor Adlai E. Stevenson of Illinois.

As the crowd sang "Auld Lang Syne," Harry and Bess headed for home in Independence after the inauguration of President Eisenhower. Said the former president, "I'm just Mr. Truman, private citizen, now."

THANKS PRES. TRUMAN
STOPPED RUSSIA
SAVED OUR OIL
SAVED OUR COUNTRY
LEFT US RICH
FAMILY LIFE GRAND
CHURCHILL SAYS GREAT
YOU'RE HISTORY

NATIONAL LIMITED

B&O

24. *Korea: Springboard for a U.S. Global Build-up*

THE KOREAN WAR was not yet a week old when high State Department officials were told that Acheson believed they were paying too much attention to Korea and not enough to the effects of the war in other parts of the world.[1] The North Korean attack had increased Washington's apprehensions about Soviet intentions. It had stimulated such fears as expressed in Truman's recent comment to Elsey that "if we just stand by, they'll move into Iran and they'll take over the whole Middle East."

Actually by the end of June administration officials were more worried about Chinese intervention in Korea than direct Soviet intervention. But they were most apprehensive about a Soviet move somewhere else. At a meeting in the State Department on June 30, at which Acheson's views had been conveyed by Deputy Under Secretary Matthews, Charles Bohlen, one of the department's leading Soviet experts, warned that it would be dangerous for the United States to increase its troops commitment in Korea without replacing any units that might be deployed to Korea from other areas. The Soviets, he ventured, might blockade Berlin again, offering a challenge that would have been impracticable for the United States to counter with another full-scale airlift because of the heavy concentration of its planes in the Far East. To maintain American military strength in other areas, Bohlen added, Truman probably would have to order partial mobilization.

Believing that the Soviets had shown their hand in Korea, Pentagon officials pressed the administration for a decision on future global military posture. The shape of the decision soon began coming into focus.

On July 13, while the first ill-prepared American units sent to Korea were falling back before the momentum of the Communist attack, Bohlen wrote a memorandum, noting that in the Departments of State and Defense there was "unanimous agreement . . . that the present world situation is one of extreme danger and tension. . . ." The memorandum, which was given to Acheson, reported that the feeling among Washington military and diplomatic officials was that the Korean fighting could lead to "new outbreaks of aggression possibly up to and including general hostilities." It was urgent, therefore, Bohlen said, "to initiate measures necessary to bring about a rapid build-up of the United States military position both in manpower and production in order to place us as speedily as possible in a military situation commensurate with the present state of international affairs.'' It was also necessary, he said, to strengthen the European allies, who had suddenly been confronted with the realization that a Communist attack on West Germany would find the North Atlantic Treaty signatories no better prepared than the South Koreans.[2]

Bohlen's words matched the prescription of NSC 68. NSC 68 was the dramatic proposal for reviving the military power of the United States and its allies, which Truman had kept under secret study since April. Its implementation would have entailed a radical and politically daring shift in administration policy that would have involved unspecified billions in new military spending at home and abroad.

The South Korean attack seemed fully to justify the warnings of NSC 68. Changing direction, the administration thrust forward with money, manpower, industrial production, and weapons in a great effort that was to continue long after Truman's tenure. The aim of this endeavor went far beyond the necessities of the Korean War. As more aptly stated in NSC 68, the goal was one of eventually ''gaining the initiative in the 'cold' war and . . . materially delaying if not stopping the Soviet offensives in war itself.''

It was the Korean War, incidentally, that brought the National Security Council to maturity. Although the council had been created by the National Security Act of 1947, largely at Forrestal's instigation, Truman had made little use of the NSC until the country was suddenly at war.

Fortified by Bohlen's memorandum on the gravity of the crisis and the need for a rapid build-up of American and allied military power, Acheson made a vigorous appeal to the cabinet on July 14 for what amounted to a start on implementing NSC 68.

Europeans, he said, were questioning the value of the North Atlantic Treaty ''since it means only what we are able to do.'' Turning to what he described as fears in Asia caused by the Communist advance, he warned: ''In Japan the Socialist Party has adopted officially the principle that there must be a treaty with the Soviet Union as well as with the other belligerents [of the Second World War]; that Japan should be neutralized and that American troops should be withdrawn. This is evidence that they believe association with the U.S. is dangerous to them.''

What then must the United States do? According to his own account prepared after the meeting, Acheson answered that obviously the United States must do all possible to deal with the Korean situation and other present dangers, but it must do more than that now. Acheson's memorandum on the meeting continued:

The Secretary listed the actions and announcements which must be made:

The President's actions regarding increased forces must be announced. He must ask for money, and if it is a question of asking for too little or too much, he should ask for too much.

He should stress production and ask for powers of allocation and limitation. This last the Secretary thought most important; for what we announce as to military steps will be of some reassurance to our friends, but will not deter our enemies; whereas what we do in the line of stepping up production will strike fear into our enemies, since it is in this field that our great capabilities and effectiveness lie. . . .''

Truman, according to the memorandum, said he agreed.[3]

As with intervention in Korea, the historic turn in the making toward American rearmament and transformation of the North Atlantic Treaty into NATO—the integrated, militarized, defensive North Atlantic Treaty Organization—was not the inspiration of chauvinistic generals. The Pentagon followed the State Department. The charge of the heavy brigade, as it were, was led by Dean Acheson.

The message that Truman was to send to Congress on July 19 went through seven drafts by assistants to the president and to Acheson and Johnson. As chairman of the National Security Resources Board, Stuart Symington recommended that Truman ask Congress for sweeping mobilization powers. That was opposed by Leon H. Keyserling, the new chairman of the Council of Economic Advisers, and others. Keyserling argued that the country was not yet ready for mobilization. His viewpoint prevailed.[4]

In the message Truman asked, more moderately, for legislation empowering the government to establish priorities, allocate materials, and control consumer credit.[5] He said that if it became necessary later, he would recommend the more drastic measures of price control and rationing.

It was in the military field that Truman's message made the great break with past policy. "The attack on the Republic of Korea," he said, "gives added urgency to the efforts of the free nations to increase and to unify their common strength in order to deter a potential aggressor.'' The increased strength that was needed, Truman said, fell into three categories. First, more men, equipment, and supplies must be sent to MacArthur, quickly. Next, "the world situation requires that we increase substantially the size and material support of our armed forces over and above the increases which are needed in Korea.'' Finally, "we must assist the free nations associated with us in common defense to augment their military strength.''

He asked Congress to remove the statutory limit of two million persons in the armed forces. By about July 12 the Joint Chiefs of Staff had recommended that Truman request a maximum of some $6 billion in new military outlays for the Korean fighting and for military expansion generally. On July 17, as gloom deepened over the relentless North Korean advance, the chiefs proposed that the sum be increasee to about $10 billion.[6] This is the figure Truman finally cited in his message. When his specific requests went up later they totaled $11,642,906,000 in supplemental military appropriations in the budget for the remainder of the fiscal year 1951. This was almost as much as the $13,546,000,000 he had estimated for defense for the entire fiscal year in his budget message the preceding January.

Congress was still deliberating the administration's earlier request for

$1,222,500,000, for the second year of the Mutual Defense Assistance Program, the one to help rearm the North Atlantic Treaty powers and other friendly countries. Truman said in his message he soon would ask for additional funds for that program, too. In urgent language ten days later he pressed Congress for $4 billion on top of the original $1.2 billion, and Congress in time came up with the money, as it did with the additional $11.6 billion for defense. And more was soon to come. Meanwhile, of course, economic aid continued flowing under the Marshall Plan, although a trend was developing toward more military assistance to other countries and less economic assistance.

The spirit of resurgence swelled. At a meeting of the National Security Council on July 27 Truman cautioned against allowing immediate events in Korea to divert attention from long-range strategy outlined in NSC 68. "Recommendations based on that report have, in my opinion," he said, "become more rather than less urgent since the Korean development. In view of this situation, as well as the need to be developing our 1952 budget plans . . . I would like the council to submit to me its response to NSC 68 not later than September 1st."[7]

By the end of summer Truman announced in a televised speech that he planned to expand the armed forces from one and a half million "to close to three million." "We shall have to maintain larger forces for a long time to come," he said.[8] Negotiations were begun with Denmark for more extensive use of American military bases in Greenland. Washington sought from Australia the right for American ships and aircraft to use Australian bases "when and as the occasion rises." King Ibn Saud, of Saudi Arabia, was asked to extend American rights to the air base at Dhahran and assented.[9] Money was soon to pour into enlargement of the air force and research and development programs. A dramatic growth in the Central Intelligence Agency impended.

Large appropriations went to restore not only lagging conventional strength but nuclear power as well. The historian Samuel Wells noted in a recent study that the administration "poured money at a furious rate into the improvement of American strategic nuclear forces and into the program for the creation of tactical atomic weapons." Meanwhile, wrote the official military historian Walter S. Poole, the administration concentrated on the growth of air power, foreshadowing the policy of "massive retaliation" in the Eisenhower administration. As Wells stated it, "the Eisenhower administration inherited from the Democrats the nuclear weapons and the strategic strikeforce on which its rhetoric was based."[10]

On the last day of July 1950 Truman and Acheson had a talk about grand strategy. The eyes of the American people were glued to Korea where Lieutenant General Walton H. Walker, commander of the United States Eighth Army, had just issued a reported "stand-or-die" order to his troops in the fighting north of the Naktong River above Pusan. The president and the secretary of state fixed their gaze on the Rhine and the Elbe. "The most important single event affecting the future of Germany," wrote the German historian Hans W. Gatzke, "occurred not in Europe but on the other side of the globe—the invasion of South Korea.

. . .''[11] To Truman and Acheson the Korean War was a treacherous ordeal, but the greater danger it signaled was the vulnerability of West Germany and hence of Europe to a Communist invasion of German soil similar to the attack across the 38th parallel.

With great urgency, therefore, Truman and Acheson contemplated the strengthening of NATO in two exceptional ways, primarily. One, without precedent in American history, was the deployment of more United States troops in Europe as part of a collective force at a time of peace in the continent. The other was the rearmament of West Germany, an idea that had matured very quickly with the Communist invasion of South Korea.

At least by mid-1949 inclusion of the new West German government in NATO was envisioned in most of the Western European capitals and in Washington as being desirable at some vague point in the future.[12] As far as the United States was concerned, the Korean War ended the vagueness. In American eyes, certainly, defending German territory without the help of West German soldiers appeared not only unrealistic but also an unconscionable burden on American soldiers.

In his discussion with Truman on July 31 Acheson said that the question was not whether West Germany should be enlisted. Rather, he declared, the problem was how West German participation might be arranged without disrupting the alliance and without permitting the Germans to dominate the balance of power in Europe. To create a West German army with a general staff and to turn the Ruhr into a West German arsenal would be the worst possible policy, Acheson said.[13]

Obviously, after three wars with Germany in eighty years France would not tolerate revival of unrestricted West German military power. To allay old fears of German militarism a plan was discussed among the allies for enlarging American forces in Europe and appointing a supreme commander of NATO forces— an American if so requested by the European members. France and the other European members insisted upon assurances in the form of more troops that the United States would participate in the defense of Europe on the ground as well as from the air.

In a cable to Acheson dated July 12, 1950, Lewis W. Douglas, United States ambassador to the Court of St. James's, had offered the following advice about West German participation: "If we can persuade the French to put their military house in order—and they do—we then will have got the framework in which real Western European military strength can be developed. And when that has been substantially achieved and actual strength has been developed—and not until then—we will be in a position to consider the rearming of Western Germany."[14] In his memoirs Acheson recalled his agreement with this viewpoint.[15] The Pentagon, however, did not see the problem that way.

The Joint Chiefs of Staff were simply not persuaded that the French needed time and reassurances to prepare themselves for German rearmament. The chiefs did not accept the premise that Paris first required a new American commitment of troops and the development of effective safeguards against revival of the German military before it would agree on a West German role. Harassed by the difficulties besetting American soldiers in Korea, the chiefs were haunted by the dangers that would confront limited American forces in Europe if NATO should have to meet a Soviet onslaught without the help of the West Germans. The chiefs, therefore, insisted that an American offer to send new forces to Europe be linked with West German participation.[16]

Truman directed the Departments of State and Defense to agree on a set of recommendations. Acheson and Johnson replied to him on September 8. They recommended that additional American forces be sent to Europe to strengthen the will of the Allies to resist any aggression. "We agree," the two secretaries said, "that the overall strength of the United States forces in Europe should be about 4 infantry divisions and the equivalent of 1½ armored divisions, 8 tactical air groups, and appropriate naval forces; and that these forces should be in place and combat ready as expeditiously as possible."

On the issue of West German participation in the defense of Europe Acheson was forced to yield to military insistence that this step accompany dispatch of additional American troops and appointment of a supreme commander. In other words, all three measures—more American troops, a supreme commander, and West German rearmament—were to be presented to the NATO allies as one indivisible program. Acheson and Johnson envisioned the creation of a European defense force within the framework of the North Atlantic Treaty. The field forces, though operating within NATO control, would be composed of national contingents under immediate commanders of their particular nationality. This did not involve creating a German national army. German contingents would have had no existence apart from the NATO forces. The units would be raised, uniformed, and paid by the West German government. Their arms and equipment, however, would come from outside Germany. In that sense West Germany would not be rearmed.[17]

Truman announced on September 9 his approval of "substantial increases" in American forces in Europe, subject to a greater European contribution to "our collective defense."[18] Acheson testified that strengthening NATO was the crux of American policy. Thereupon he went to the Waldorf-Astoria in New York and presented the comprehensive administration program to British Foreign Secretary Bevin and French Foreign Minister Schuman. The result was deadlock between the United States and France. Schuman would not hear of early formation of West German units under West German field commanders for assignment to NATO forces. He said the subject caused "a serious psychological problem" in France. Puncturing the Pentagon's case for linking three measures in one, Schuman said it would take time for France to adjust to West German participation. Furthermore, he insisted, NATO first would have to be strengthened under a supreme commander before France would consider the question of recreating West German military forces.[19]

Talks on German military participation ensued with scant progress. Undertakings for building NATO forces were set afoot and eventually were to produce deep changes in Europe and in Europe's relations with the United States, even though West German rearmament did not come about until the Eisenhower administration.

Meanwhile plans for a great American military expansion went forward in mid-1950. With Truman presiding, the National Security Council adopted the conclusions of NSC 68 ''as a statement of policy to be followed over the next four or five years. . . . ''[20] That was one of the major consequences of the Korean War, marking a turning point in American history in the period since 1945. The total budget for defense and international affairs was to rise from $17.7 billion for the fiscal year 1950 to $53.4 billion in fiscal 1951.

25. Bitter Summer: First Troubles with MacArthur, Last with Johnson

TASK FORCE SMITH, the modified battalion of the 24th Division that had been ordered to Korea following Truman's decision to commit troops, landed at an airstrip near Pusan on July 1.[1] Numbering 406 officers and men, perhaps five-sixths of whom had not had combat experience, this vanguard of what presently would be designated United Nations forces was trucked to the railroad station in Pusan through cheering crowds of Koreans.

Colonel Smith's hasty orders in Japan from General Dean, the division commander, were to head for Taejon, some 135 miles northwest of Pusan in order to stop the North Korean advance as far from Pusan as possible. With its airstrip and harbor at the southeast tip of the peninsula, Pusan was the American gateway to Korea now that Seoul and Inchon were in enemy hands. Pusan had to be held at all costs if American units being committed to action were not to be driven off the peninsula.

The North Korean People's Army was advancing in the west below Seoul and in the central mountains and along the east coast, an area defended by ROK divisions, whose positions crumbled alarmingly. In the west Taejon was a key point. Task Force Smith arrived there by train on July 2.

General Church, who had been flown from Tokyo with a headquarters detachment, welcomed Smith. "We have a little action up here," the general said. "All we need is some men up here who won't run when they see tanks." "Up here" referred to an area around Osan, some eighty miles farther north. It was one in a line of towns—Osan, Pyongtaek, Chonan, Kongju, Taejon—strung south from Seoul on a railroad and highway axis, along which the western wing of the North Koreans' front was striking toward Pusan.

Task Force Smith, its experience typical of the trials that lay ahead of thousands of other American soldiers that summer, moved up, first by train and then by truck over roads cluttered with fleeing South Korean civilians and fully armed South Korean soldiers and national policemen. Smith was joined by the 52nd Field Artillery Battalion, also just rushed from Japan, where supplies of ammunition were so inadequate that the battalion had been able to draw only eighteen rounds of high-explosive antitank shells. Americans, now numbering 540, dug in on high ground north of Osan, astride the main road.

In the rain on the morning of July 5 Smith saw a formidable column of Soviet-built T 34 tanks approaching from the north. His task force had no anti-tank mines.

At 8:16 A.M. the first American artillery fire of the war whistled up the road. The tanks rumbled on, not even breaking formation. When the column came abreast of Task Force Smith, infantrymen fired bazookas, inflicting no great damage. Direct hits by the artillery disabled two tanks. From the turret of one of them a North Korean soldier fatally shot an American machine gunner, who was probably the first American soldier killed in action in the Korean War. The artillery battalion quickly used up its supply of high-explosive antitank shells. The rest of its ammunition was feeble against the tanks, which rolled through to Osan, having killed twenty of Smith's men in the engagement.

A new dread filled the survivors. In the distance appeared a column of enemy troops and vehicles led by three tanks. As it moved south, Smith estimated that the line was six miles long. Grossly outnumbered, his men stayed at their posts. At least the advantage of surprise was theirs; the enemy evidently was unaware that American forces were in the field. It took an hour for the head of the column to reach a point a thousand yards from the American positions. Smith ordered his mortars and .50-caliber machine guns to fire. North Koreans were blown into the air. Trucks burst into flame. The enemy soldiers tumbled into the fields and began to advance. For more than two hours Task Force Smith held its main position until the danger of encirclement became acute.

While withdrawing, the task force suffered its heaviest casualties. Twenty-five or more seriously wounded men had to be left behind. A medical sergeant voluntarily remained with them. The rest of the task force, including Smith, escaped the closing trap through hills and rice paddies. When the ordeal was over, the number of dead, wounded, and missing in Task Force Smith ran into the scores. Osan was taken by the enemy.

Fresh units of the 24th Division disembarked at Pusan. They were rushed, piecemeal, to engage in delaying actions at Pyongtaek, then Chonan, then Kongju, then Taejon to allow time for American reinforcements to arrive in Korea and fight the North Koreans on even terms.

One by one the division's defenses were crushed or scattered. On July 9 MacArthur telegraphed the Joint Chiefs of Staff: "The situation in Korea is critical. . . . to date our efforts against [enemy] armor and mechanized forces have been ineffective. . . . Our own troops are . . . fighting with valor against overwhelming odds of more than ten to one. To build up, under these circumstances, sufficiently to hold the southern tip of Korea is becoming increasingly problematical."[2]

Out-gunned, lacking in heavy antitank weapons, unfamiliar with the terrain, ill-prepared for combat after the soft life of occupation duty in Japan, the 24th Division soldiers were disorganized and confused, hampered by early-morning fog, exhausted by midday heat, and frustrated by faulty communications. Misdirected mortar fire from one unit caused injuries and death in another. Chronically, supplies of ammunition ran low. Men were ambushed or were completely cut off in strange villages and were never seen again. Mortars and machine guns were abandoned in the bedlam of battle. Some men fled; others refused to advance. Wounded were abandoned. After a fight at Chonui six captured American soldiers, their hands tied behind them, were found dead with bullet holes in the backs of their heads. Order was hard to maintain as battalion and regimental commanders were killed or wounded. Colonel Robert R. Martin, commander of the 34th Regiment of the 24th Division, was cut in two by a shell from an enemy tank, at which he had aimed a rocket launcher. In the first week in action fifteen hundred men of the 24th Division were missing.

At the start of the second week General Dean deployed more than seven thousand of his men behind the Kum River to impede the drive of the North Korean 3rd and 4th Divisions toward Taejon. For Dean's 24th Division each day's experience was overwhelming, and the unit was still the only American ground force in Korea. In Washington the joint intelligence committee of the Joint Chiefs of Staff estimated that nine North Korean divisions numbering eighty thousand men were in the field. The committee concluded that the North Koreans were capable of threatening Pusan within two weeks.[3]

The fighting along the Kum River began in familiar circumstances for the beleaguered 24th Division. One company had to be sent to the rear because the mental and physical condition of its men was thought to make the company a liability in combat. YAK fighters drove off American observation planes. Among the gaps in the undermanned American line enemy tanks and soldiers crossed the river on sandbars and barges, creating havoc among the defenders, even among the artillery units. One battery seeing troops approach assumed they were Americans and held its fire. In fact, they were North Koreans, who overran the machine gun outpost, turned the captured gun around, and pulled the trigger.

American casualties and loss of guns and vehicles under punishing mortar and artillery fire were heavy. At 3 A.M. on July 16 an enemy plane dropped a flare above the Kum River. On this signal a wave of enemy troops started crossing. An American artillery battery failed to respond to an infantry call for illuminating flares. In the darkness the North Koreans made deep penetrations of the American positions, again disrupting artillery and temporarily blocking the road to Taejon. Its defense of the Kum River crushed, the battered and outflanked 24th Division pulled back in a desperate effort to hold Taejon, the next town, for a day. The plan was changed to two days by General Walton Walker, who had been named by MacArthur on July 13 as commander of all United States ground forces in Korea.

American army forces in Japan during the occupation (the 7th, 24th, and 25th Infantry Divisions and the 1st Cavalry Division—entirely infantry by then) constituted the United States Eighth Army, of which Walker was commander. With the war expanding, the Eighth Army's jurisdiction was extended to Korea, and Walker flew to Taejon on July 18 to confer with Dean. The 25th Division had already begun arriving in Korea, and the 1st Cavalry was disembarking that same morning of the eighteenth, bringing promise of help for the 24th Division at last. The enemy attack had to be slowed, however, to allow time for the 1st Cavalry to be deployed in support of the 24th. Walker told Dean that two days' delay would be needed at Taejon.

With two fresh American divisions already converging on the fighting fronts and with the renowned 2nd Infantry Division under orders to sail from the United States, MacArthur and Walker could begin to think of longer-range strategy. They visualized the area north of Pusan and east of the Naktong River as the place for an ultimate defensive stand. It was a sector bordered on two sides by the sea that was to become celebrated in American military history as the Pusan Perimeter.

The enemy assault on Taejon began on the morning of July 19. Throughout the day the 24th Division held up well despite intense artillery fire. After dark, however, damaging blows fell. Somehow the North Koreans had managed to encircle Dean's troops on the east and dig in at his rear. Meanwhile under bursting flares tanks and infantry launched a frontal attack, loosening the American's grip on the city. Heavy fighting continued into daylight on July 20, badly scattering the 24th Division's defensive formations. American movements became increasingly chaotic. T 34 tanks rumbled into the heart of Taejon. Firing by both sides turned a large part of the city into flames. Dean himself led a group of soldiers on a hunt for tanks, and the group destroyed one with rockets.

With the second day of the defense of the city approaching its close, Dean decided to withdraw before nightfall. Fresh North Korean forces were descending on the city unimpeded by the scattered 24th Division units, and the whole American operation dissolved into confusion. A convoy in which Dean rode rumbled out of the flaming city at 8 o'clock. In the confusion vehicles became separated; some were never seen again. The group Dean was with was attacked. Along with the general, the men crawled to the Taejon River, crossed it during the night of July 20, and climbed a mountain in search of another road. One soldier was wounded. In the darkness Dean went to get him water, fell down a slope and was knocked unconscious. His shoulder was broken, and he was cut and bruised. When he came to, he tried without success to find his way back to the 24th Division. For thirty-six days he wandered in mountains, dodging North Koreans, who had, of course, overrun the area. On August 25, nearly starved, his weight down by sixty pounds, he was captured thirty-five miles south of Taejon. He was held prisoner until September 4, 1953.

By July 26, 1950, the American predicament was so serious Walker asked MacArthur for permission to move Eighth Army headquarters from Taegu in the central mountains to Pusan. Along with the rout of the 24th Division at Taejon, collapse, demoralization, even panic, had beset the 1st Cavalry and 25th Divisions when they went into action in the central mountains and along the east coast. ROK forces there already were retreating. Everywhere the enemy continued to advance. Ignoring Walker's request to move Eighth Army headquarters, MacArthur flew to Taegu on July 27 to tell Walker that retreats must cease. Two days later the Eighth Army commander went to the 25th Division headquarters at Sangju and verbally issued an order to the highest officers to hold the line, a

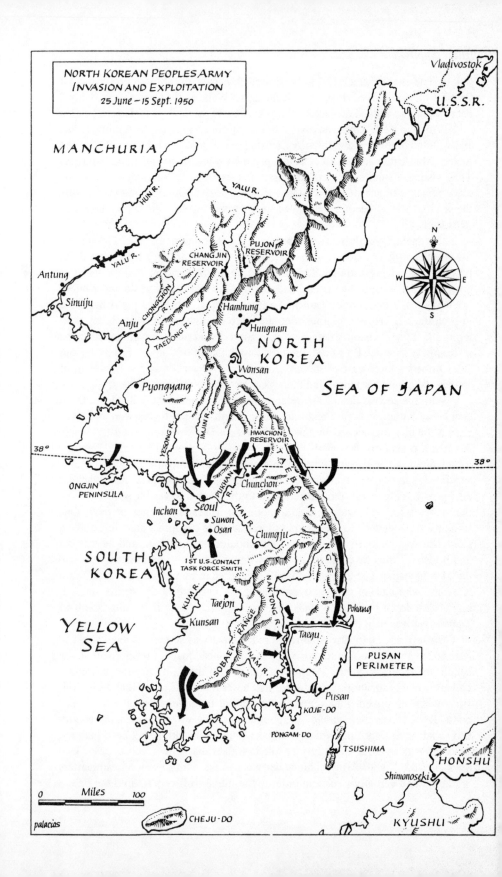

NORTH KOREAN PEOPLES ARMY
INVASION AND EXPLOITATION
25 June – 15 Sept. 1950

MANCHURIA

Vladivostok

U.S.S.R.

HUN R.

YALU R.

YALU R.

Antung

Sinuiju

CHANGJIN
RESERVOIR

PUJON
RESERVOIR

Anju

CHONGCHON R.

Hamhung

TAEDONG R.

Hungnam

NORTH
KOREA

SEA OF JAPAN

Pyongyang

Wonsan

YESONG R.

IMJIN R.

HWACHON
RESERVOIR

38°

38°

ONGJIN
PENINSULA

PUKHAN R.

Chunchon

T
A
E
B
A
E
K

R
A
N
G
E

Inchon

Seoul

HAN R.

Suwon
Osan

Chungju

1ST U.S. CONTACT
TASK FORCE SMITH

SOUTH
KOREA

KUM R.

Taejon

NAKTONG R.

Pohang

YELLOW
SEA

Kunsan

SOBAEK RANGE

NAM R.

Taegu

PUSAN
PERIMETER

Pusan

KOJE-DO

PONGAM-DO

TSUSHIMA

HONSHU

Shimonoseki

0   Miles   100

palacias

CHEJU-DO

KYUSHU

command referred to in the press as "stand or die." According to a paraphrase of his comments in official notes, he said in part: "There will be no more retreating, withdrawal, or readjustments of the lines or any other term you choose. . . . There will be no Dunkirk, there will be no Bataan, a retreat to Pusan would be one of the greatest butcheries in history. We must fight until the end.''[4]

In the latter part of July the United Nations troops, in spite of brave fighting, were forced to fall back everywhere in the worst crisis thus far in the Korean War. For while the fighting had been raging in the central and eastern areas of Korea, fresh enemy forces had slipped down the western fringe of the peninsula, unopposed. Soon they swept all the way to the southwestern coast, flanking the Eighth Army on the left.

Having accomplished this maneuver, the North Koreans made what appears to have been the extravagant mistake of pausing to occupy strategically unimportant towns along the southwestern coast. If, instead, they had raced straight to Pusan, the Eighth Army would not have been able to stop them, Walker said afterward. In that case the Eighth Army would have been completely flanked, and victory for the North Koreans would have been within grasp. As it was, units of the 24th and 25th Divisions were rushed to the area of greatest danger and succeeded in halting the enemy advance thirty miles west of Pusan.[5]

On August 1, Eighth Army headquarters ordered all United Nations ground forces to withdraw behind the Naktong River and, with their backs to the sea, to defend the Pusan Perimeter.[6] Thus a month after Truman had committed American troops to battle they and their allies were penned, in the southeastern corner of Korea, into a rectangle that was at the optimum a hundred miles long and fifty miles wide. For the rest of the summer they were to wage a frantic fight to keep the enemy from crushing it. The other side of the coin was that the painful, grudging United Nations retreat and final defensive stand had sucked the cream of the North Korean army to the southern limits of the peninsula. The North Koreans' supply line had grown long and vulnerable to American air attacks. With each passing day the chances that the United Nations forces would be driven out of Korea by the Communists faded. Furthermore, an American amphibious landing to the north would threaten the North Korean army with entrapment. No one knew it better than MacArthur. He had had an eye on such strategy practically from the start of the war.

Americans at home were shocked at the spectacle in the Far East. Still living with recent memories of Normandy, the Bulge, the Rhine, Guadalcanal, Midway, the Coral Sea, the Philippines, Iwo Jima, and Okinawa, they were unprepared for the mauling of United States troops in Korea. Recriminations were soon heard. Weekly magazines assailed a military policy of too little and too late. The columnists Joseph and Stewart Alsop blamed Truman and Louis Johnson for the low pre-Korean military budgets. Senator Wiley said that the State Department was to blame for "having made us withdraw from Korea" in 1949 in order, he alleged, to appease the Soviet Union.

From the beginning the Korean War was enmeshed in domestic politics.

The overtones were to grow louder and bitterer. When some Senate Republicans early in August attempted to pin the responsibility for the North Korean attack on Truman and Acheson, the president snapped at a White House staff meeting that the statement was "demagogic." Eben Ayers noted in his diary afterward that it was "understood that the Republicans have been planning to make the Korean situation their leading issue in [the 1950] congressional elections."[7]

The optimistic assumptions of June had been shattered. MacArthur weeks earlier had realized that the United States and the Republic of Korea could not drive the enemy back with the help of the two American divisions he had originally requested on June 30. Truman no longer supposed he was up against "bandits." People began to sneer at "police action." The United States was in a major war. It was unprepared for war, as democracies usually are. The emergency threw the administration into a great scramble to repair the weaknesses created by Truman's pre-Korean budgets. 'The outbreak of the Korean War, coming without warning at a time when major emphasis in defense planning had been on the reduction of expenditures," wrote the official military historians James F. Schnabel and Robert J. Watson, "severely strained the resources of the US Military Services, and particularly the meager, ten-division army."[8] "Our armed forces had been economized almost into ineffectiveness . . . ," General Ridgway was to recall.[9]

Still, it is debatable whether the rapid advance of the North Koreans would have been very much different if Truman had approved a couple of billion dollars more in the 1949 and the 1950 budgets. It is unlikely that the money would have been spent on Far Eastern ground forces, which had to meet the attack. Even with larger defense budgets, weeks would have been required to get adequate forces into Korea. That American military strength as a whole would have been greater in mid-1950 without the Truman ceilings is evident.

Of the ten divisions in the army at the start of the war, five were in general reserve in the United States, one was on occupation duty in Germany, and four were under MacArthur's control in the Far East. In 1947 after the helter-skelter demobilization following the Second World War the army had set a goal of expansion to twenty-five divisions, but the plans had to be scuttled under Truman's defense budget ceilings. For the same reason all of the services were below the manpower strength that had been authorized by Congress. In discussing American air power, General Vandenberg, the air force chief of staff, spoke of his "shoe-string air force."[10] At the outbreak of the Korean War all four divisions in the Far East were below strength. After all, with Europe viewed as the principal theater of action if the Cold War were to explode, it had not been anticipated that American forces in the Pacific would take a major part in the conflict.

"The effects of budgetary austerity," wrote Schnabel and Watson, "were most readily apparent in the Army. . . . Fund restrictions were reflected in worn-out or obsolete equipment, inadequate stocks of supplies, shortened training periods, and other serious deficiencies. Although the number of divisions remained constant, the figures masked a serious decline in effectiveness. In the Eighth

Army, for example, most combat units were short one-third of their combat strength. . . ."[11]

The implications were wide. "It is a bruising and shocking fact," General Bradley was to say, "that when we Americans were committed in Korea we were left without an adequate margin of military strength with which to face an enemy at any other specific point. Certainly we were left without the strength to meet a general attack . . . except for the atomic bomb."[12]

Three days after Truman had authorized the commitment of ground forces MacArthur first asked for reinforcements: a marine regimental combat team with its own tactical air support and 700 other aircraft to bring air force units in the Far East to war strength. The Joint Chiefs of Staff promptly approved the sending of the marine regimental combat team, with air support, plus 2 groups of B-29 bombers, 22 B-26 bombers, 150 F-51 fighters, all the aircraft that could be made available at that time, according to the records of the Joint Chiefs of Staff. Truman approved these movements.

Then on July 5, the day Task Force Smith went into action, MacArthur asked specifically for three units in the United States: an engineer brigade, 1 regiment of the 82nd Airborne Division, and the entire 2nd Division. Together these represented a sizable proportion of the army's general reserve. The harassed Joint Chiefs granted his request, essentially, again with Truman's approval. On July 7 the chiefs received another message from MacArthur, assessing the strength of the North Korean attackers and requesting more reinforcements: "To halt and then hurl back this powerful aggression will, in my estimation," he said, "require the . . . equivalent of not less than 4 to 4½ full strength infantry divisions, an airborne RCT [regimental combat team] complete with lift and an armored group. . . ."

Then came the rout of the 24th Division and MacArthur's previously cited message calling the Korean situation critical. In that same message dated July 9 he said, "I strongly urge that in addition to those forces already requisitioned, an army of at least four divisions with all its component services, be dispatched to this area without delay and by every means of transportation available."

The very next day another message arrived, in which MacArthur changed his initial request, namely, for one marine regimental combat team to a full marine division. "Thus within the space of two days," Schnabel and Watson noted, "General MacArthur had approximately doubled his estimates of the ultimate force required (eight divisions instead of four)." The Joint Chiefs were overwhelmed. The departure of the 2nd Division would leave only four divisions in the general reserve. Admiral Sherman asked how far the United States should go in committing troops to Korea in light of potential dangers elsewhere. Truman and Acheson were facing up to the necessity for enlarging American forces in Europe at about the time General Collins was compelled to tell MacArthur that the 82nd Airborne was "the only effective infantry unit left in the United States." It was to be some months before any substantial reinforcements were sent to Europe.

Worried about the growing demands of global strategy, Collins flew to Tokyo in mid-July to discuss reinforcements. MacArthur argued that the United States must win in Korea or lose everywhere. A victory in Korea, he said, would do more than anything to retard communism. In his view, therefore, the outcome of the Cold War would be decided in the Far East. In addition to the four American divisions already in the Far East Collins assured MacArthur he could count on the 2nd Division, the 1st Marine Division, and three regimental combat teams. MacArthur agreed to make his plans on that basis. Three weeks later he requested—and received with presidential approval—the 3rd Infantry Division.

Illustrative of the frenzied shuffle required to put American forces in the field, the 3rd Division, shipping out of Fort Benning, Georgia, had to be brought to strength with the 65th Regiment, stationed in Puerto Rico and ordered directly from there to the Far East. Since the regiment, too, was below strength, however, it had to be augmented by a battalion in Panama. The battalion also moved on its own across the Pacific to join the 3rd Division, and in the meantime a regiment of the Puerto Rican national guard was called into federal service to replace the departed 65th.

In sum, the ground forces MacArthur had under his command by the fall of 1950 consisted of eight American divisions plus the regimental combat teams, along with ROK units and the relatively small contingents of United Nations allies. This was, essentially, the force that was to fight the main battles of the Korean War.[13]

"We have met the challenge of the pagan wolves—we shall continue to meet it," Truman wrote in drafting a speech.[14]

The Korean War was a landmark in one respect. As recently as the Second World War the armed services had been racially segregated. On July 26, 1948, Truman issued an executive order requiring equality of treatment for all military personnel. The order did not mention desegregation, but Truman said that such a goal was envisioned. By the time of the Korean War, racial segregation had been eliminated in the navy and air force. Demands for manpower after the fighting began led to dramatic progress in integration of the army, although the last all-black army units were not abolished until 1954.

Early in the war a step was taken that was without parallel in American history. At the instigation of the United States, the United Nations Security Council adopted a resolution on July 7 welcoming support in Korea from all members and recommending that those members providing military forces make them available to a unified command under the United States. The command was to fly the blue-and-white United Nations flag. The resolution also asked the United States to designate a commander. American forces were to carry much the heaviest burden of the fighting. On the recommendation of the Joint Chiefs, Truman made the only imaginable choice: MacArthur.

MacArthur then established the United Nations Command with headquarters in Tokyo. Basic control of military operations was in American hands. The United States government was the executive agent of the United Nations. MacArthur was responsible solely to the United States government, that is, to

Truman as commander in chief of the armed forces. In practice MacArthur dealt with the Joint Chiefs of Staff through General Collins, the army chief of staff, and the chiefs reported to the secretary of defense and ultimately to the president. The United Nations might provide general guidance in the war, but it exercised no control over events on the battlefields.

The struggle against North Korea took on the character of a cooperative international effort in which the United States led a coalition of non-Communist nations under the aegis of the United Nations, the decrees of which provided the political sanction for the operation. In time, fifteen nations, beside the United States, contributed forces to the battle. They were Australia, Belgium, Canada, Colombia, Ethiopia, France, Greece, Luxembourg, the Netherlands, New Zealand, the Philippines, South Africa, Thailand, Turkey, and the United Kingdom. All sent ground forces in at least battalion strength, except Luxembourg, which sent a single company, and South Africa, an air unit. The Belgian, Luxembourg, Ethiopian, and Colombian troops did not arrive until 1951. The only one of the units mentioned above to arrive before mid-September 1950 was the British 27th Infantry Brigade from Hong Kong, which helped defend the Pusan Perimeter.

"Ultimately," wrote Schnabel and Watson, "these UN contingents gave a good account of themselves, and several of them compiled outstanding combat records, notably the British, French, Turkish, Ethiopian, and Greek contingents. However, aside from the British Commonwealth Division, their aggregate strength was insufficient to have a significant effect on the overall course of the war."[15]

A number of United Nations members that did not send troops did contribute medical supplies, food, and other nonmilitary items.

ROK troops were placed under the command of the Eighth Army. Because of a Soviet veto, the Republic of Korea had not been admitted to the United Nations.

This unique cooperative effort came as close as anything ever has to fulfillment of the old dream of collective security to halt aggression and punish an aggressor. Fighting a war under the aegis of the United Nations, however, was to cause some heavy stress for Truman and his advisers. The times of greatest complexity for the president were to be those in which sentiment among United Nations allies collided with sentiment in the Congress of the United States.

Except for tension over Formosa and some differences about the timing and terms of the Japanese peace treaty, neither Truman nor Acheson nor the Joint Chiefs had had any serious difficulties with MacArthur before the Korean War. Nor did they have trouble with him during the searing month of July 1950, until the very end when he suddenly turned up in Formosa. His trip rattled the administration, which was concerned lest he try to usurp the conduct of foreign relations.

The relative harmony prevailing before the war, however, was anything but robust. As has been noted, for example, the Truman administration continued Roosevelt's policy, so thoroughly at odds with MacArthur's views, of giving priority to Europe over the Far East in matters pertaining to American security.

Then, too, MacArthur was, as he had been for several years, a potential Republican candidate for president; he had allowed his name to be entered in the Republican presidential primary election in Wisconsin in 1944, the year Roosevelt and Truman ran on the Democratic ticket. The general still had influential Republican supporters. Finally, the lofty MacArthur was a totally different kind of man from the earthy Truman, and neither looked up to the other. As the Korean War progressed, certainly, MacArthur came to be contemptuous of Truman. Truman, for his part, had entered the White House in 1945 with a grumpy dislike of the five-star general.

From the outset, and for most of his years in the White House, Truman liked General Eisenhower and trusted him politically. As Truman saw it, Eisenhower had risen to fame under the Roosevelt administration. At first, therefore, Truman tended to suppose that Eisenhower finally would come down on the side of the Democrats. In an extraordinary chapter in American politics President Truman let Eisenhower know in 1948 that he, Truman, would be willing to step aside and support the general for the Democratic presidential nomination that year. Eisenhower declined.

In the case of MacArthur, Truman distrusted him politically and judged him personally to be a "stuffed shirt." As early as April 29, 1945, two weeks after Truman had taken office, the then Secretary of the Interior Ickes noted in his diary: "Truman apparently has definite reservations about MacArthur. As a matter of fact, he has, I think, his reservations about brass hats in general." Again, on May 6 of that year, Ickes jotted, "The President made it very clear that he did not care for MacArthur." And on June 9, "He [Truman] indulged in some pretty vigorous Missouri expletives in expressing his opinion of MacArthur."[16]

In a memorandum of his own dated June 17, 1945, Truman referred to the general as "Mr. Prima Donna, Brass Hat, Five Star MacArthur. He's worse than the Cabots and the Lodges—they at least talked with one another before they told God what to do. Mac tells God right off. It is a very great pity we have to have stuffed Shirts like that in key positions. I don't see why in Hell Roosevelt didn't order Wainwright home"* and let MacArthur—a "bunco man," Truman called him—be a martyr.

"Don't see how a country can produce such men as Robert E. Lee, John J. Pershing, Eisenhower & Bradley and at the same time produce Custers, Pattons and MacArthurs."[17]

At the end of the Second World War MacArthur had been absent from the United States for eight years. As a new president, Truman wanted to have a look at him. The two had never met. In September 1945 Truman asked General Marshall, then army chief of staff, to invite MacArthur to visit the United States to be acclaimed by Congress and the people. MacArthur replied that he could not

---

*The Japanese attack on the Philippines in 1941 had trapped MacArthur and General Jonathan M. Wainwright with American forces on Corregidor. On Roosevelt's order MacArthur was rescued by PT boat and submarine to command American troops in the Pacific. Wainwright remained in command at Corregidor and was captured.

leave Japan until conditions stabilized. The following month Truman directed Marshall to send a second message which read, ''The President has asked me to inform you that he wishes you to understand that he would like you to make a trip home at such time as you feel that you can safely leave your duties.'' Probably no military officer ever rejected such a request by a president. MacArthur did. The situation in Japan, he explained, was "extraordinarily dangerous.''[18]

Margaret Truman said her father suspected that MacArthur was awaiting ''a political summons from the Republican party, so he could combine a triumphal return with a nomination for the presidency.'' Even after the Korean War began Truman disparaged MacArthur before the White House staff. ''He feels, as do most others,'' Ayers noted, ''that MacArthur is a supreme egotist, who regarded himself as something of a god.''[19]

Once war broke out MacArthur, with his fame, forensic skills, and influence with the opposition party in Washington, became a potential problem for Truman, as Truman himself mentioned to Dulles at the end of June. Having been in Japan at the start of Korean hostilities, Dulles was offended by MacArthur's seemingly relaxed attitude and sometimes erratic behavior at the first news.[20] On his return to Washington, Dulles evidently suggested to Truman that MacArthur be recalled. Truman related the story to Eben Ayers. As Ayers recounted it in his diary, the president pointed out to Dulles ''that the General is involved politically in this country—where he has from time to time been mentioned as a possible Republican Presidential candidate—and that he could not recall MacArthur without causing a tremendous reaction in this country where he has been built up, to heroic stature.''[21] For Truman at any time to have recalled MacArthur would have caused the kind of political earthquake that no president would needlessly bring upon himself.

In the beginning, Truman had no reason to do so. As the summer and early fall wore on, no fundamental conflict over Korean strategy and Korean policy developed between Truman and MacArthur.

In mid-summer some squalls did indeed arise and cause serious irritation, but these concerned the collateral issue of Formosa, not Korean strategy. Even these differences over Formosa grew out of questions of diplomatic considerations and presidential prerogative. MacArthur and the administration did not differ basically on the strategic importance of Formosa once the Communists had attacked in Korea and Truman had stationed the Seventh Fleet in the Formosa Strait.

Almost since the start of the war Acheson and MacArthur had been at odds as to whether the general should visit Formosa. In the memorandum that MacArthur had given to Bradley and Johnson and Bradley had read to the first Blair House conference, MacArthur suggested that he be authorized to make a survey of Formosa to determine what measures were necessary to prevent a Communist seizure. When the conference began, Acheson recommended that MacArthur not go to Formosa, pending further developments. Acheson said he did not want the United States to ''tie up'' with Chiang Kai-shek. The vision of

MacArthur and Chiang hatching plans chilled Acheson, as he knew it would some of the United Nations allies.

While these allies had approved Truman's response to the attack in Korea, they were uneasy about the unilateral American action in Formosa. Their concern was that Formosa somehow might provide the spark to reignite the Chinese civil war and thus trigger a general war. After Truman had interposed the fleet between the island and the mainland Chou En-lai protested to United Nations Secretary General Lie that the United States had committed aggression against the People's Republic of China, which regarded Formosa as part of its territory. The Nationalists and Communists both talked, threateningly, of attacking each other. Among the United Nations members, Britain and India had recognized the People's Republic. It would have been a nightmare for them if somehow the United States were to wind up backing a Nationalist assault upon the mainland, which was Chiang's undying ambition. Truman's policy did not countenance such a venture, and MacArthur had not yet advocated it. Nevertheless, because of his ardor for Chiang's cause, he was not the person Acheson and the allies preferred to see in Taipei at that point.

Acheson continued to try to delay a meeting between Chiang and MacArthur. MacArthur, however, was responsible for the defense of Formosa and informed members of the Joint Chiefs of Staff that he would visit the island. Meanwhile in the National Security Council on July 27 Truman again revised Formosan policy. Prefiguring renewal of closer ties with Chiang Kai-shek, he approved in principle a military assistance program for Formosa and dispatch of an American military mission.[22] As Acheson acknowledged, MacArthur had the discretion to go to Formosa.[23] And he went, although the timing of his trip took Truman and Acheson by surprise. "President Truman's comments," Acheson recalled, "evoked the admiration and envy of us all."[24]

The two-day meeting of Chiang and MacArthur exasperated Acheson. State Department representatives on the island were cold-shouldered by MacArthur and could learn nothing of what was happening. Because Truman and Acheson were thus left in the dark, news reports and statements from Formosa fanned suspicion, as when K. C. Wu, governor of the island, told reporters, "I think you may safely say that General MacArthur's arrival . . . is a demonstration to the world that the forces fighting communism in Asia today are united."[25] Such rhetoric smacked of the very thing Acheson wanted to avoid, namely a "tie-up" with Chiang. Chiang issued a statement hailing MacArthur's "deep understanding of the menace of communism." In words that might seem to hint at some newly arranged cooperation between the United States and Formosa Chiang said, "now that we can again work closely together . . . I am sure not only will our determination in the struggle for this common cause be strengthened but the peoples of all Asia will be aroused to fight communist aggression."[26]

MacArthur maintained that his talks with Chiang were purely of a military nature, concerned with the defense of the island. Nothing has come to light to refute that. Afterward the general said he was astonished at the "furor" caused by the meeting. "This visit," he declared in a statement, "has been maliciously misrepresented to the public by those who invariably in the past have propagandized a policy of defeatism and appeasement in the Pacific.''[27]

After the meeting with Truman on August 3, Acheson recorded that he ''reported to the President the very difficult situation which was arising on Formosa as a result of General MacArthur's visit.''[28] Forthwith MacArthur received a message from Truman: ''At my direction, my assistant, W. Averell Harriman, will leave here Friday 4 August . . . to confer with you in Tokyo on political aspects of Far Eastern situation.''

When the North Korean invasion began, Harriman called Truman from his European post as ambassador at large to the Marshall Plan countries and offered to return home to be helpful. Truman agreed and appointed him special assistant to the president, whereupon Harriman became a major adviser and troubleshooter not only on Korea but on a range of foreign affairs. In that sense he was predecessor to the now familiar line of presidential assistants on national security. On receiving Harriman, Truman alluded to the attacks on Acheson and said, ''Help Dean—he's in trouble.''[29]

While Harriman was en route to Japan a story hit the American press quoting a ''reliable source'' in Tokyo about what MacArthur intended to tell Truman's envoy. According to the story, the general was going to say that the Korean War would prove useless unless the United States fought communism wherever it arose in Asia, which meant, among other things, the story reported, supporting Chiang Kai-shek.[30] Coming almost at the moment when Truman and Acheson had settled on the overriding importance of strengthening NATO, this intelligence ran counter to the administration's policy of limiting the war to Korea.

The meeting between MacArthur and Harriman—duck-hunting companions in the days when the general was the superintendent at West Point—was cordial, but, as reflected in Harriman's subsequent report to Truman, faintly ominous.

Harriman conveyed to MacArthur Truman's determination to support the general as fully as possible. The president wanted the Far Eastern commander to know, however, that he must not permit Chiang to be the catalyst for a war with the Chinese Communists. MacArthur replied that, as a soldier, he would obey any orders from the president.

''For reasons which are rather difficult to explain,'' Harriman reported to Truman, ''I did not feel that we came to a full agreement on the way we believed things should be handled on Formosa and with the Generalissimo. He accepted the President's position and will act accordingly, but without full conviction. He has a strange idea that we should back anybody who will fight communism, even though he could not give an argument why the Generalissimo's fighting communists would be a contribution towards the effective dealing with the communists in China.''

Harriman said that he himself ''explained in great detail why Chiang was a liability, and the great danger of a split in the unity of the United Nations on the Chinese-Communist-Formosa policies. . . .''

Harriman listened to what he described as MacArthur's views that the United States never should recognize the Chinese Communist government and should, if necessary, cast a veto to bar it from membership in the United Nations. Harriman later quoted MacArthur as having said: "We should fight the communists every place—fight them like hell!"[31]

While the MacArthur visit annoyed Truman, it did not affect his confidence in MacArthur's military leadership. With the army's knowledge, Truman had a personal observer in MacArthur's headquarters, Major General Frank E. Lowe, an admirer of MacArthur's, incidentally. Truman and Lowe had been friends since the time the general was the War Department's liaison with the Senate Special Committee to Investigate the National Defense Program—the Truman Committee.[32] In the Korean War Truman had him assigned to MacArthur's headquarters, and communications between Truman and Lowe were secret and candid. Writing to Lowe on August 11, Truman said, "Please say to General MacArthur I have never had anything but the utmost confidence in his ability to do the Far Eastern job and I think I've shown that by action, as well as by words."[33]

The Formosa incident proved to be but a prologue to an episode that shook the administration, disturbed the allies, and caused Truman to ponder the immediate relief of MacArthur of his command in Korea.

During August and the heavy fighting around the Pusan Perimeter the Truman administration had been striving to counter Peking's charges of American aggression on Formosa, an allegation the Soviets eagerly exploited in the United Nations. Ambassador Warren R. Austin, United States permanent representative to the United Nations, circulated a letter among member nations on August 25. It said, "As President Truman has solemnly declared, we have no designs on Formosa and our action is not inspired by any desire to acquire a special position for the United States."[34]

That very evening Michael J. McDermott, special assistant to the secretary of state for press relations, telephoned Acheson at home to report some suprising news. The Associated Press was moving an advance story on a quite dramatic statement by MacArthur on the question of Formosa. The statement was in the form of a message to be read on August 28 to the annual convention of the Veterans of Foreign Wars in Chicago in lieu of a speech that the VFW had invited the general to deliver.

"In view of misconceptions currently being voiced concerning the relationship of Formosa to our strategic potential in the Pacific," the message began, "I believe it in the public interest to avail myself of this opportunity to state my views thereon. . . ."[35]

Thus at a time of international tension over Formosa the world was to receive the views of General MacArthur on the subject instead of those of the president of the United States.

MacArthur declared that from an island chain off the coast of Asia the United States "can dominate with air power every Asiatic port from Vladivostock to Singapore and prevent any hostile movement into the Pacific."

This particular passage in the statement mentioned only—without naming them—the islands strung from the Aleutians to the Marianas. Since the entire message was a veritable celebration of the strategic importance of Formosa, a close reading was required to discern that MacArthur had not specified Formosa as one of the islands from which the United States could attack Asian ports. As two members of the Joint Chiefs of Staff, General Collins and Admiral Sherman, were to testify, the tone of the message created an impression that the United States wished to use Formosa as a military base.[36] This was precisely the point that the Chinese Communists and the Soviets were making in the United Nations and that Ambassador Austin was attempting to refute.

In an aspersion, intended or not, on Acheson's views, MacArthur also said that "Nothing could be more fallacious than the threadbare argument by those who advocate appeasement and defeatism in the Pacific that if we defend Formosa we alienate continental Asia." Before the Korean War and the neutralization of Formosa Acheson had wanted the United States to keep its hands off the island. If encroachments were to be made on Chinese territory, he preferred that they be Soviet encroachments so as to direct Chinese ire at Moscow rather than at Washington. "Those who speak thus do not understand the Orient," MacArthur said in his message. "They do not grant that it is in the pattern of Oriental psychology to respect and follow aggressive, resolute and dynamic leadership. . . ."

On fundamentals MacArthur had stayed within the bounds of administration policy in that this policy recognized Formosa's strategic importance and provided that the island should be denied to the Chinese Communists. The message ignored some fine points of American policy. Among these were (1) that the Seventh Fleet had been ordered to prevent Chiang from attacking the mainland as well as preventing the Chinese Communists from invading Formosa, (2) that the neutralization of Formosa was without prejudice to political questions affecting the island's future, and (3) that the United States had no territorial ambitions on Formosa nor sought any special position or privilege, which, therefore, excluded American bases from which bombers might attack Asian ports. Finally, the timing of the message, news of which came right on top of Austin's letter, was atrocious. It was too late to expunge MacArthur's words. Not only had copies already been distributed to the press in Chicago by the VFW but MacArthur's headquarters in Tokyo had sent copies earlier to certain publications, and *U. S. News & World Report* was already off the presses carrying the full text.

On August 26 Harriman showed a copy of the message to Truman, who read it in rising anger. For another purpose he had already called a meeting of his highest advisers later in the morning. When the group assembled he read MacArthur's comments to them. Then he turned to Louis Johnson and repudiated MacArthur's statement and said he wanted it recalled. Johnson replied that he did not know in advance about the statement but would call MacArthur and ask him to withdraw it. Truman inquired of General Collins whether he had known of the statement. The army chief of staff said that he had not. Harriman declared that the release of the statement in the circumstances would be a diplomatic catastrophe. Truman agreed. Acheson seconded the view, and the meeting ended. Thirty minutes later Charles Ross and George Elsey returned to see Truman to advise him that Johnson should not telephone MacArthur, as he had suggested, but should order the general in writing to withdraw the statement. This procedure proved anything but simple of execution.

Johnson had cold feet about sending MacArthur such a message. He telephoned Acheson and said that he and the Joint Chiefs thought the order would cause embarrassment. They preferred to cable MacArthur to say that they would have to issue a statement to the effect that the message was just one man's opinion and not government policy.

Acheson replied that such a statement would lead to confusion as to precisely what parts of the MacArthur message were not government policy. The issue had been raised, the secretary of state said, as to who was president of the United States. Nothing was left to do, he added, but for Truman to assert his authority and insure that his position on Formosa stood.

Johnson asked point-blank whether they dared send a message ordering MacArthur on the president's authority to withdraw the message. Acheson replied that there was nothing else to do.

Johnson said it was not clear to him that Truman had directed him to order MacArthur to withdraw the message.

Acheson said it was clear to him. To make sure, he agreed to call Harriman, who said that the matter was so serious it could be straightened out only by drastic measures, even if they should cause MacArthur to resign.

Acheson called Johnson back and said Harriman clearly understood that Truman wanted MacArthur's message withdrawn. Johnson then decided to call Harriman himself and request that the president reopen the question. Obviously the secretary of defense and the military had no stomach for disciplining MacArthur.

Before Johnson could reach Harriman, Truman telephoned Johnson and dictated to him the order he wanted sent to MacArthur by Johnson. It read:

> The President of the United States directs that you withdraw your message . . . because various features with respect to Formosa are in conflict with the policy of the United States and its position in the United Nations.

Astonishingly, this did not settle the matter then and there. Deputy Secretary of Defense Stephen T. Early urged Johnson not to issue an order to MacArthur. By then, Early said, MacArthur's message had been distributed around the world by press wires and could not be withdrawn. To attempt to do so, he thought, would only make matters worse. It struck Early that the thing to do was to have William Sebald, the State Department's man in Tokyo, call on MacArthur and explain the difficulty as a way of getting the general to withdraw the message on his own. Johnson broached this idea to Acheson on the phone. Acheson said that Sebald was subordinate to the general and the general might not receive him without a directive from the president.

Early then suggested that Truman himself might telephone MacArthur.

Acheson was disdainful. Such a call, he said, would put the president in the position of a suppliant.

The next in the round of telephone conversations was between Acheson and Harriman. Acheson said he did not agree with Johnson or Early. Neither did Harriman, but he felt Truman should be acquainted with all the opinions that had been aired on the telephone. Acheson was displeased at the thought of reopening the issue but did not oppose it. Since it was Johnson who wanted reconsideration, Harriman said he would ask the secretary of defense to approach Truman about it. But before Harriman had a chance to call Johnson he, Harriman, had occasion to talk with Truman. According to Harriman, Truman knew exactly what he was doing and wanted the order as dictated by him to the secretary of defense sent to MacArthur.[37]

Johnson sent it. MacArthur cabled VFW officials: "I regret to inform you that I have been directed to withdraw my message. . . ."

"I was utterly astonished," he said in his memoirs.[38]

Republicans accused Truman of silencing MacArthur. Inserting the general's message in the *Congressional Record*, Joe Martin, the House Republican leader, called Truman's order another example of bungling—"bungling which delivered Manchuria and most of China to the communists and which culminated in the Korean conflict."[39]

Reflecting the views of some of the White House staff at least, Eben Ayers noted in his diary, "MacArthur is regarded as a Republican and seemingly playing the Republican line in Far Eastern . . . policy."[40] Truman said in his memoirs that he had considered replacing MacArthur with Bradley as commander in Korea, while retaining MacArthur for the Japanese occupation. "But after weighing it carefully," he wrote, "I decided against such a step. It would have been difficult to avoid the appearance of a demotion, and I had no desire to hurt General MacArthur personally. My only concern was to let the world know that his statement was not official policy."[41] Firing MacArthur would have caused a Republican explosion, and Truman knew it.

The situation with respect to Louis Johnson "has become almost impossible," Ayers noted in his diary.[42]

When Stuart Symington resigned as secretary of the air force in the spring, Truman decided to appoint Thomas Finletter, a New York lawyer, as his successor. In Truman's first term Finletter had chaired the President's Air Policy Commission. If such a thing as the Eastern Establishment existed, Finletter was part of it and hardly, therefore, a Johnson man. Johnson let the White House staff know that he would not assent to Finletter's appointment. If the president insisted on nominating Finletter, Johnson said, he would resign. Truman told Charles Murphy that he was going to nominate Finletter and that Johnson could resign if he wished.[43] Johnson backed down.

Harriman had had an occasion to call on Johnson one day shortly after Taft had delivered his speech in the Senate criticizing Truman for not having sought congressional approval for intervention in Korea and demanding that Acheson resign. Harriman heard Johnson talking to Taft on the telephone. Harriman heard the secretary of defense congratulate the senator on the speech and remark that Taft's points needed to be made. After hanging up, Johnson told Harriman that if they could force Acheson out, he, Johnson, would see to it that Harriman would be the next secretary of state. Indignantly, Harriman reported the incident to Truman.[44]

In his newspaper column on August 25 Marquis Childs reported that Johnson was feeding Republicans information damaging to Acheson. In return, Childs wrote, Johnson had received assurances that the Republicans would spare him in their attacks on the administration and thus preserve his own political prospects. Some members of the White House staff believed that the column was probably correct. Johnson had grown reckless in his denunciation of Acheson, even to virtual strangers.[45]

Contemporaries surmised that Johnson resented Truman's esteem for the secretary of state. Korea did not help Johnson's mood, either, because many people thought the war proved that he had been wrong in his theatrics over cutting the defense budget. The full responsibility for the low budget ceilings, to be sure, was Truman's. In general, Johnson had been carrying out the president's policy. But because he had been more Catholic than the pope in doing it, he had become a political burden for the administration. American reverses in Korea had convinced many Americans that Johnson had cut more than the "fat" out of the budget.

On September 9 the Associated Press carried a story by its White House correspondent, Ernest B. Vaccaro—the unidentified source was the new Democratic national chairman, William M. Boyle, Jr.—that Johnson was on his way out as secretary of defense.[46] Johnson refused to believe it.

His deputy, Steve Early, made inquiries and told his boss, candidly, "You're fired." "I'll find out," Johnson retorted.[47] He telephoned Truman and inquired about the story. Truman asked him to come to the White House at 4 P.M.

"Well he came," Truman later recalled in a memorandum, "and I opened the conversation by telling him he'd have to quit. He was unable to talk. I've never felt quite so uncomfortable. But he finally said he'd like a couple of days to think about it. I said all right."[48]

By noon the next day, September 12, according to the Truman memorandum, Johnson still had not submitted his resignation. The president, therefore, telephoned Early and said that Johnson should bring in a letter of resignation before the end of the day. Truman wanted Johnson to recommend in his letter that General Marshall be named as his successor. Truman already had talked to Marshall and won his consent. As the president well knew, that would be a dramatic appointment because of Marshall's unique standing in America. Early and Ross drafted a letter of resignation in the form the president wished.

"Johnson came to the 4 o'clock Cabinet meeting . . . ," Truman's memorandum continued. "He looked like he'd been beaten. He followed me into my office after the Cabinet adjourned and begged me not to fire him. Then he handed me the [prepared] letter—unsigned. I said 'Louis you haven't signed this—sign it.' He wept and said, he didn't think I'd make him do it." "You are ruining me," Johnson said.[49]

Senator Tydings called Ross and suggested that MacArthur be asked to send a message commending the appointment of Marshall. "The President commented that MacArthur would never do that," Ayers recorded.[50] MacArthur knew very well he would not have the kind of ally on Asia in the new secretary of defense that he had had in Johnson. More than a year before, MacArthur had told the American diplomat, Max Bishop, according to the latter's notes, that Marshall "had always held that the Far East and Asia were vastly inferior to Europe in relative importance to the United States." MacArthur linked Marshall to what he called "the policy of the military to 'scuttle the Pacific.' "[51]

Truman had to ask Congress for special legislation to clear the way for the Marshall nomination because the law prohibited a military man from serving as secretary of defense until he had been out of active service for ten years. Against the votes of right-wing Republican senators the bill passed, but not until after Senator William E. Jenner of Indiana had made a speech that fairly well delineated the limits that the McCarthy style had reached. Jenner linked Marshall with many of the things Jenner and his conservative, isolationist colleagues hated, from Lend-Lease aid to the Soviet Union in the Second World War to the advancement of Hiss to the "sellout" of Nationalist China.

"General Marshall," Jenner said, "is not only willing, he is eager to play the role of a front man for traitors. . . . The truth is . . . that no one has been as much a part of the tragic betrayal of America that has taken place during these recent years. . . ."[52]

Jenner scorned Marshall for "joining hands once more with this criminal crowd of traitors and Communist appeasers who, under the continuing influence and direction of Mr. Truman and Mr. Acheson, are still selling America down the river." "I think," Truman wrote to Senator Lyndon Johnson, "Jenner's statement on Marshall set an all-time low for attacks in the Senate."[53]

26. *Prelude to Disaster: The Decision to Cross the Parallel*

VEN AS THE BATTLE for the Pusan Perimeter raged, American reinforcements flowed into Korea as the summer advanced. At the same time MacArthur's plans materialized for a counteroffensive designed to propel United Nations forces northward to the 38th parallel, trapping large numbers of enemy troops in the process. These developments forged a harsh dilemma for Truman.

Should United Nations forces halt permanently at the parallel, leaving the North Koreans free to resume the war when they were ready again? Or should Truman, risking hostilities with China or the Soviet Union, authorize MacArthur to cross the parallel to destroy the North Korean army completely and thus dispose of the Korean problem?

To halt was to insure loud dissatisfaction at home with an inglorious outcome that left Kim Il-sung in power in North Korea and American troops stationed indefinitely in South Korea, securing the parallel. To proceed was to seize a rare opportunity victoriously to roll back the Communist orbit in Asia to the borders of China and the Soviet Union, realizing the grandest dream of containment.

The war aim of the United States when it committed its forces in Korea was to compel the Communists to withdraw to the 38th parallel. This aim, in the administration's view, was not so categorical as to prohibit some tactical movement across the parallel by United Nations troops in forcing the enemy to retreat or even in completely defeating the North Korean army. The basis cited for this discretion was the clause in the Security Council's resolution of June 27, calling on members not only to furnish assistance to repel the North Koreans but also "to restore international peace and security in the area." Essentially, however, the war aim contemplated restoration of the five-year-old dividing line in Korea. As far as it went, a repulse of the enemy to that line would have been a notable achievement for the United States and for the ideal of collective security through the United Nations.

The issue was not simple, however. For the war aim, stated in the frantic days of late June and early July, was not the same as the long-standing objective of the United States and the United Nations, which was to promote the establishment of a free, independent, and united Korea. The North Korean attack had acutely thrust to the fore the question of how to end the division of Korea and give its people the opportunity to elect a united government free of foreign domination yet friendly to the United States.

Behind the scenes in Washington the issue was already stirring by July 1. An unfounded rumor that Truman's message of July 19 to Congress would state that the United Nations intended to drive the enemy only to the 38th parallel drew a protest from John Allison, director of the office of Northeast Asian affairs. In a memorandum to Assistant Secretary Rusk, he advocated a military solution to the problem of North Korea. "I personally feel," he said, "that if we can . . . we should continue right on up to the Manchurian and Siberian border, and, having done so, call for a UN-supervised election for all of Korea."[1]

Syngman Rhee blew the issue into the open on July 13 when he declared that the North Korean attack had obliterated the dividing line. A week later he pressed the point in a letter to Truman, saying that it "would be utter folly to attempt to restore the *status quo ante,* and then to await the enemy's pleasure for further attack when he had had time to regroup, retrain and reequip." To make his position unmistakable, Rhee declared that the Republic of Korea would not be bound by any settlement that left his country divided.[2] In a secret memorandum Acheson called the question of crossing into the Democratic People's Republic of Korea, a satellite of the Soviet Union, "explosive."[3]

One of the first officials in the State Department to express a strong position was Dulles. In a memorandum to Nitze as director of the Policy Planning Staff, which was studying the question, Dulles agreed with Rhee that it would be foolish to allow the North Koreans to retire behind the parallel and regroup. "To permit that would mean," Dulles said, "either the exposure of the Republic of Korea to greater peril . . . or the maintenance by the United States of a large military establishment to contain the North Korean army at the 38th parallel."[4]

In another memorandum Allison said, "If any one thing seems certain as a result of our experience in Korea over the past five years it is that a perpetuation of the division of that country at the 38th parallel will make it impossible 'to restore international peace and security in the area'." He also made the point, to which Washington was receptive, that the North Koreans should not go unpunished lest their deed encourage other potential aggressors.[5]

As the problem was studied, the risks of invading North Korea loomed. A draft report of the Policy Planning Staff on July 22 concluded:

> If U.N. forces were to continue military ground action north of the 38th parallel except to the extent essential for tactical requirements as fighting approaches that line, the danger of conflict with Chinese communist or Soviet forces would be greatly increased.
>
> From the point of view of U.S. military commitments and strength, we should make every effort to restrict military ground action to the area south of the 38th parallel. . . .[6]

Allison, an increasingly staunch advocate of crossing the parallel, promptly wrote to Nitze, labeling this conclusion a "policy of appeasement." The tone of the draft report, Allison complained, "implies that the North Korean regime has a legal status and that the area north of the 38th parallel is, in fact, a separate nation." The North Korean regime, he argued, was a creature of the Soviet Union, established in defiance of United Nations resolutions.

The "real prize in Asia," said Allison, was Japan. Hence "we cannot afford to allow a regime hostile to American interests in Japan to dominate Korea." He conceded that crossing the parallel might lead to general war and said, laconically, that "the American people should be told and told why and what it will mean to them."[7]

The next day the Policy Planning Staff modified its position in a new draft memorandum, declaring, "It is U.S. policy to help bring about the complete independence and unity of Korea." Whether to halt at the parallel was a decision that should be deferred for the time being, the memorandum said.[8]

From that point on, the record shows, talk about stopping at the parallel dwindled. United Nations air and sea actions were being conducted north of the parallel. On July 17 Truman asked the National Security Council to consider what should be done about ground action after the enemy had been driven back into North Korea.

The decision that was jelling in Washington paralleled MacArthur's attitude in Tokyo. In a meeting with Generals Collins and Vandenberg in mid-July MacArthur said, as Collins later recalled: "I intend to destroy and not [merely] to drive back the North Korean forces. . . . I may have to occupy all of North Korea." In August, Collins, accompanied by Admiral Sherman, conferred with MacArthur again. "We agreed with the General," Collins wrote afterward, "that he should be authorized to continue the attack across the 38th Parallel to destroy the North Korean forces, which otherwise would be a recurrent threat to the independence of South Korea."[9]

A tempting thought appeared in a Defense Department draft memorandum July 31. Had the North Koreans succeeded in conquering the south, the memorandum noted, the whole Korean peninsula would have been absorbed into the Soviet orbit. "Furthermore, the building of a 'cordon sovietaire' from the Soviet borders of Sinkiang to the southern shores of Korea would have neared completion. Only Japan, at the edge of the orbit, and Southeast Asia . . . would have still remained outside." But, hold! North Korean aggression was stalling. The war might yet bring about an opposite result: failure of the Soviets to complete a cordon. Thus the developing situation "provides the United States . . . with the first opportunity to displace part of the Soviet orbit." The consequences were viewed by the memorandum as being enormous:

Penetration of the Soviet orbit, short of all-out war, would disturb the strategic complex which the USSR is organizing between its own Far Eastern territories and the contiguous areas. Manchuria, the pivot of this complex outside the USSR, would lose its captive status. . . .

Nor was that all:

The significance in Asia of the unification of Korea under UN auspices would be incalculable. The Japanese would see demonstrated a check on Soviet expansion. Elements of the Chinese Communist regime, and particularly important segments of the Chinese population, might be inclined to question their exclusive dependence on the Kremlin. Skillfully manipulated, the Chinese Communists might prefer different arrangements and a new orientation. Throughout Asia those who foresee only inevitable Soviet conquest would take new hope.

MacArthur, the Defense Department memorandum concluded, "should seek to occupy Korea and to defeat North Korean armed forces wherever located north or south of the 38th parallel."[10]

Acheson's view at the time was that, within certain unspecified limits, MacArthur should be allowed to go wherever necessary to destroy the North Korean army and restore security. Under prodding by Rusk, Acheson opposed an arbitrary prohibition against crossing the parallel.[11]

In a guarded reply to Rhee's letter Truman wrote to the president of the Republic of Korea on August 10, "It has always been the expressed policy of the US to support the independence and unity of Korea."[12] Neither the United States nor the United Nations, however, was committed to unify Korea by force.

Kennan opposed crossing the parallel.[13] And on August 18 a CIA memorandum declared that "grave risks" would be involved in such a move. Not only might the Soviets view it as a dangerous challenge and respond, but the Chinese Communists "might well take up defensive positions north of the 38th parallel."[14] Other and stronger forces were at work on policy in Washington, however.

By mid-August the Truman administration obviously was tending toward a decision to cross the parallel, at least for tactical operations, barring major Soviet or Chinese intervention. After the anguish of recent weeks any outcome other than Korean unification seemed unexciting, unsatisfactory, and politically unappealing at home. The American people yearned to be rid of the Korean problem. "It would have taken a superhuman effort to say no," recalled Harriman, reflecting on his experiences in the White House that summer. "Psychologically, it was almost impossible not to go ahead and complete the job."[15]

"There is," said a mid-August memorandum by Allison and his colleague John K. Emmerson, "a growing sentiment in the United States favoring a 'final' settlement of the Korean problem as opposed to any settlement which smacks of a compromise or a 'deal'. . . ."[16] Influential Republicans were opposing a halt at the parallel.

One of the first publicly to suggest that United Nations forces might have to cross it to destroy the North Korean army was General Eisenhower, still at that time president of Columbia University.[17]

As MacArthur approached a great counteroffensive at Inchon, Truman was so encouraged by the outlook that he wrote to a friend, "I think we are over the hump, as far as Korea is concerned, and if the Russians do not decide to come in and make it a total effort that situation ought to be cleaned up before many months."[18]

Increasingly, the strategic advantage to the United States that would have been gained by unifying Korea, beckoned the Truman administration. Such a policy, which, incidentally, would have shown Truman dealing with the Communists with a strong hand, dovetailed with the political realities in the United States. A final victory over Kim Il-sung's army, ending Communist rule in North Korea and rolling back the Soviet orbit, would have been regarded as a great achievement of the Truman administration.

By the end of August the trend of thought in the Departments of State and Defense and in the NSC senior staff was reflected in the top-secret policy papers.

A memorandum that the State Department drafted for the National Security Council staff asserted that it "would not make political or military sense" for United Nations forces to halt at the parallel unless the risks of hostilities with the Soviets or Chinese "were so great as to override all other considerations." In so many words the memorandum advocated a change in war aim from the repulse of the North Korean invasion to the unification of Korea under one freely elected government.[19] By September the United States and its major allies were in agreement that MacArthur might cross the parallel in tactical operations against the North Korean forces. For other purposes, such as formal occupation or reunification of the country through elections, he could not proceed except at the direction of the United Nations.[20]

On September 9 the National Security Council sent to the president the study—NSC 81/1—he had requested in July on the course that should be followed when United Nations forces reached the parallel.[21] The primary conclusion was a hedge. Final decisions could not be made, the study said, until it became clear what the Soviets and Chinese would do and what the attitude of the United Nations was.

NSC 81/1 advocated unification of Korea if that could be achieved without risk of general war. Decidedly, the National Security Council did not contemplate a stabilization of the line at the parallel. Barring major Soviet or Chinese intervention, the report said, it "would be expected that [MacArthur] would receive authorization to conduct military operations . . . in pursuance of a rollback in Korea north of the 38th parallel, for the purpose of destroying the North Korean forces. . . ." Since, however, United Nations operations in North Korea might involve a risk of wider war, MacArthur was not to cross the parallel until the president gave his approval.

One provision, apparently included at the instigation of the Joint Chiefs of Staff in order to grant MacArthur flexibility, was to cause trouble soon enough. In a preliminary draft the National Security Council had recommended that "U.N. operations should not be permitted to extend into areas close to the Manchurian and U.S.S.R. borders of Korea." In NSC 81/1 this was changed to read "U.N. operations should not be permitted to extend across the Manchurian or U.S.S.R. borders of Korea." In other words, barring prior Soviet or Chinese intervention, MacArthur was to be permitted to advance all the way north to the Yalu, which formed the boundary between Korea and China, and the Tumen River, dividing Korea from Soviet territory. The undertone of NSC 81/1, however, was unmistakable: to cross the parallel was to gamble on armed conflict with the Soviet Union or Communist China.

Truman promptly approved the document, which became the basis of future directives to MacArthur.

The president had not committed the United States to the occupation of North Korea or to its unification by force. These questions remained in abeyance pending decision by the United Nations. NSC 81/1 did hold that "there is a clear legal basis for taking such military actions north of the 38th parallel as are necessary" to the accomplishment of the mission, authorized by the United Nations in June, to compel the withdrawal of the enemy to the 38th parallel and restore peace to the area.

All told, the recommendations endorsed by Truman added momentum to the gathering thrust toward a concerted United Nations advance into North Korea.

At dawn on September 15 MacArthur's daring counterattack, a blend of skill, power, and good luck, staggered the enemy in a great turning point of the Korean War. In an engagement considered by some military historians as one of the classic battles of history MacArthur's forces assaulted Inchon, which was two hundred miles behind the main enemy line, by means of a hazardous amphibious operation.[22] The United States Tenth Corps was put ashore, positioned to cut off North Korea's main force, still assaulting the Pusan Perimeter. Overpowering a weak detachment of defenders at Inchon, who were caught by surprise, the Tenth Corps, under Major General Edward M. Almond, fought its way inland toward Seoul, eighteen miles to the east.

Meanwhile the Eighth Army, penned throughout the summer in the Pusan Perimeter, finally broke out through heavy resistance. The tables were then completely turned. North Korean troops encircling the perimeter fled north before the Eighth Army in an effort to escape through the trap being closed by the Tenth Corps a short distance below the 38th parallel. On September 26 the vanguard of the Eighth Army—Task Force Lynch—linked up with elements of the Tenth Corps at Osan, where, eighty-three days earlier, Task Force Smith had made the first brave stand.

By the time of the link-up, Seoul was falling into American hands and soon was to be turned back to Rhee. Meanwhile, caught between the hammer of the Eighth Army and the anvil of the Tenth Corps, the North Korean army was being knocked to pieces. Even so, an estimated twenty-five thousand enemy soldiers contrived by one means or another to straggle across the 38th parallel to keep alive a threat from the north.

As United Nations forces moved into positions close to the parallel a time of crucial decision descended on the administration. In fact, the drift of policy toward crossing the parallel was sucked into a rapids by the Inchon triumph.

Notwithstanding, at the State Department there were still a few anxieties and random thoughts about an alternative course. At one meeting Ambassador Ernest Gross of the American delegation to the United Nations inquired why the United States did not put a straightforward question to the Soviets as to how they

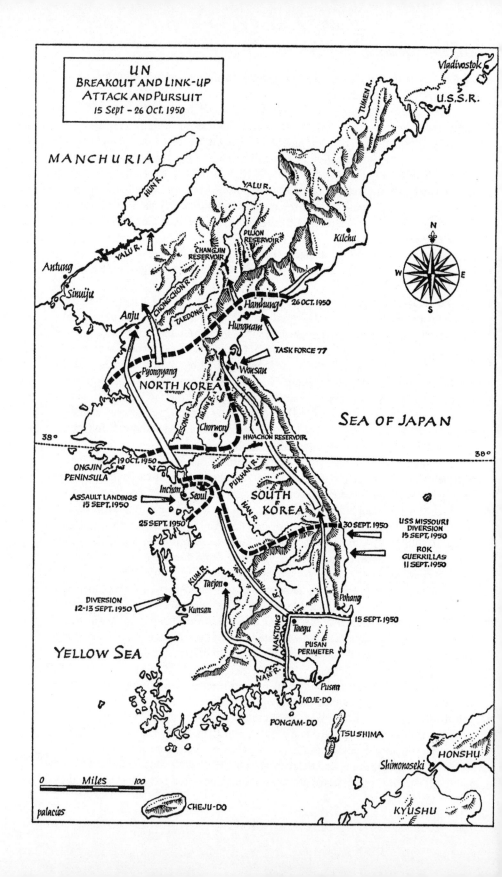

UN
BREAKOUT AND LINK-UP
ATTACK AND PURSUIT
15 Sept – 26 Oct. 1950

MANCHURIA

Vladivostok

U.S.S.R.

TUMEN R.

HUN R.

YALU R.

YALU R.

Antung

Sinuiju

Anju

CHANGJIN
RESERVOIR

PUJON
RESERVOIR

Kilchu

CHONGCHON R.

TAEDONG R.

Hamhung

26 OCT. 1950

Hungnam

TASK FORCE 77

Pyongyang

NORTH KOREA

Wonsan

YESONG R.

IMJIN R.

Chorwon

SEA OF JAPAN

HWACHON RESERVOIR

38°

38°

ONGJIN
PENINSULA

19 OCT. 1950

Inchon

PUKHAN R.

ASSAULT LANDINGS
15 SEPT. 1950

Seoul

HAN R.

SOUTH
KOREA

25 SEPT. 1950

30 SEPT. 1950

USS MISSOURI
DIVERSION
15 SEPT. 1950

ROK
GUERRILLAS
11 SEPT. 1950

KUM R.

Taejon

DIVERSION
12-13 SEPT. 1950

Kunsan

Pohang

15 SEPT. 1950

NAKTONG R.

Taegu

PUSAN
PERIMETER

YELLOW SEA

NAM R.

Pusan

KOJE-DO

PONGAM-DO

TSUSHIMA

HONSHU

Shimonoseki

0   Miles   100

KYUSHU

palacios

CHEJU-DO

N
W   E
S

would like to see the Korean problem resolved. Rusk, a formidable influence as one of Acheson's chief advisers, explained the problem. The Soviet reply, he said, probably "would be to stick to the 38th parallel and with the military situation moving as rapidly as it is, we don't want to have to negotiate with them on that point."[23]

Thus the enticement of victory, the thrust of public opinion, the pressure of domestic politics, the drama of Inchon, and the advice of his highest advisers all bore upon Truman as he resolved his hard dilemma. The memorable directive went to MacArthur on September 27, approved by the president, Acheson, and Marshall.[24] Drawn by the Joint Chiefs of Staff in what was a routine action following the approval of NSC 81/1, the instructions to MacArthur stated, "Your military objective is the destruction of the North Korean Armed Forces."

He was authorized to conduct military operations north of the 38th parallel, provided that at the time "there has been no entry into North Korea by major Soviet or Chinese Forces, no announcement of intended entry, nor a threat to counter our operations militarily in North Korea." MacArthur was not to cross the Chinese or Soviet borders. Furthermore, "support of your operations . . . will not include Air or Naval actions against Manchuria or against USSR territory." Though authorized to plan for an occupation, he was cautioned not to get involved in the political future of North Korea.[25]

The choice of tactics was left to MacArthur. He promptly sent back an outline of his plan. It embodied a most striking arrangement: the Eighth Army and the Tenth Corps were to be separated from one another, operating on opposite sides of the Korean peninsula. Between them, creating a gap on the order of fifty miles, would run the Taebaek Mountains. Both the Eighth Army and the Tenth Corps, therefore, would have exposed flanks in the center of the peninsula, and in a pinch one would not be able to support the other. In the west the Eighth Army under General Walker was to attack northward from Seoul across the parallel to seize Pyongyang, the Communist capital. In the east the Tenth Corps under General Almond was to make an amphibious landing at the North Korean port of Wonsan and strike out from there.

The Joint Chiefs of Staff did not challenge the plan, although Collins later recalled some skepticism of his own. He acknowledged that he and his colleagues were "perhaps somewhat overawed" by the success of Inchon. They had reason to be. They had tried mightily, before giving their consent, to dissuade MacArthur from a hazardous landing at that location in Korea with its dangerous tides, its shoals, rocks, mudflats. Having accomplished the remarkable feat that others doubted, MacArthur was riding so high that it would have been difficult for the president himself to cross him, by deciding, for example, that under no circumstances could the general have pursued the enemy across the 38th parallel.

The Joint Chiefs on September 29 notified General Marshall, now secretary of defense—a man who was tired and past his prime—that they approved MacArthur's plan of attack but felt it should be cleared at higher levels. They asked that Marshall obtain such approval as quickly as possible because "certain

ROK Army forces may even now be crossing the 38th parallel.'' Marshall immediately cleared the plan with Truman and Acheson. The Joint Chiefs so notified MacArthur.[26] A cabinet meeting was held on the twenty-ninth. A comment by Acheson was summarized by Matthew Connelly as follows: ''Plans are being developed to set up a commission to go into Korea and start rehabilitation. The 38th Parallel will be ignored. Korea will be used as a stage to prove what Western Democracy can do to help the underprivileged countries of the world.''[27]

In the United Nations considerable support was developing for the unification of Korea. Bevin urged an end to the artificial division of the country. In a report to Trygve Lie, Colonel Alfred G. Katzin, of the Union of South Africa, Lie's personal representative in Korea, said that a halt by United Nations forces at the parallel would only give the North Koreans a chance to regroup and strike back. Lie himself later wrote that the United Nations had ''no alternative to an advance north of the thirty-eighth parallel.''[28] The United Nations did not manage to come to grips with the question of unification by force. Unification by negotiation on American terms was clearly not in the cards, as Kim Il-sung disdained a demand by MacArthur for surrender.

In the circumstances many United Nations delegates simply chose to act as though the parallel was of no consequence whatever. Preferring not to talk too much about it, they seemed quite willing to let MacArthur be guided by tactical considerations when he reached it. Washington shared this attitude and was eager to avoid making an issue of the parallel until after the North Korean army had been defeated. Hence annoyance was felt over incidents calling attention to the parallel, as in the case of an apparently false report from Eighth Army headquarters that ROK divisions would halt at the line for regrouping. With this report in mind Marshall, with Truman's approval, sent a message to MacArthur on September 30. The purport was that MacArthur should proceed with his planned operation without further explanation or announcement and, as the Joint Chiefs were to say, ''let action determine the matter.'' Marshall told MacArthur:

We want you to feel unhampered tactically and strategically to proceed north of the 38th parallel.

The report from the Eighth Army, the secretary of defense added, ''may precipitate embarrassment in UN where evident desire is not to be confronted with necessity of a vote on passage [crossing] of 38th parallel, rather to find you have found it militarily necessary to do so.''[29] ''As far as I know,'' MacArthur testified later, ''the crossing of that parallel had the most complete agreement by everybody that was concerned with it, except the enemy.''[30]

Marshall's counsel to MacArthur to feel unhampered pertained, of course, to the particular situation of crossing the parallel. How ready MacArthur was to put the broadest possible interpretation on instructions was demonstrated when he replied that ''Unless and until the enemy capitulates, I regard all of Korea open for our military operations.''[31]

The government's decisions were not yet known to the public. On September 30 the *New York Times*, typifying a widespread attitude in the press in favor of Korean unification, carried an editorial advocating the crossing of the parallel. The same day Senator O'Mahoney, reflecting broad sentiment in Congress, wrote to Truman:

> Let the United States, which has given so much of its blood and manhood in the defense of Korean freedom, not be a party to the tragic error of permitting the Communists to retire in defeat beyond the 38th parallel and there, re-establishing the iron curtain which has now been destroyed, prepare anew for future aggression.
>
> Let us wrest the weapon of aggression from their hands. Let us occupy every military air field in North Korea and every military stronghold. When that is done, let us release all North Korean prisoners and send them back across the 38th parallel as proof that the United Nations do not seek vengeance but only peace and freedom.[32]

With congressional elections only weeks away, a good deal of political current flowed around this issue, with Republicans demanding an aggressive policy. Certainly, a politician of Truman's experience would have known that complete victory in Korea would have been a tonic for the Democrats in the elections. Incredibly, Representative Hugh D. Scott, Jr., of Pennsylvania, former Republican national chairman, accused the State Department (the "Hiss Survivors Association") of planning "to subvert our military victory by calling a halt at the 38th parallel. The scheme is to cringe behind this line. . . ."[33] Knowland said that failure to cross the parallel would amount to appeasement of the Soviet Union. The conservative columnist, David Lawrence, wrote that if United Nations forces "are not permitted to go beyond the 38th parallel to disarm the government which has committed the aggression, the Republicans will certainly make capital out of that policy. . . ."[34] Had Truman ordered MacArthur to halt at the parallel, the Republicans undoubtedly would have raised a tempest, as they would have in the improbable event that Truman had yielded Formosa and a United Nations seat to the Chinese Communists.

It was hard to find many persons in or out of the government who, like Kennan, opposed crossing the parallel, at least to achieve the break-up of the North Korean army. And that was all Truman committed himself to, although he hoped that this would lead to the promised land. He had reminded the National Security Council that, as he put it, the German army in the Second World War had disintegrated after being driven back across the Rhine. He said that he was counting on a similar disintegration of the North Korean army.[35] He and his advisers hoped that the destruction of Kim Il-sung's remaining forces would result in the unification of Korea and the withdrawal of American troops.[36]

On September 27 India's minister of external affairs, Girja S. Bajpai, received the American ambassador in New Delhi, Loy Henderson. Bajpai said that the government of India had reason to believe that there was a danger that the Chinese Communists would intervene if United Nations forces crossed the parallel.[37]

As the critical moment dawned near the parallel following the landing at Inchon, ominous words began to flow out of China. A week after the amphibious landing the Chinese Foreign Office said that China always would stand with the Korean people.[38] The same day as Henderson's talk with Bajpai, the British showed the State Department copies of two messages to Prime Minister Nehru from his ambassador in Peking, K. M. Panikkar, who had been having a series of talks with Chou En-lai. The essence of Panikkar's messages was that the ambassador now believed China would react to a crossing of the parallel.[39]

The same day, too, Edmund Clubb, then director of the office of Chinese affairs in the State Department, sent a memorandum to Rusk, noting reports "indicating that important elements of Lin Piao's (Lin Biao's) 4th Field Army have moved into Manchuria. . . ." "That those Chinese troops will participate in the Korean fighting is the most interesting possible explanation of their movement," Clubb said. "Peiping has belatedly admitted that certain Korean personnel have returned to Korea 'to defend it and take part in building up their country.' "[40]

Henderson cabled Acheson the next day, reporting that Nehru had told a British diplomat that it would be unwise for United Nations forces to enter North Korea.[41]

In Panikkar's talks with Chinese officials the latter had displayed outrage over a recent incident in which two United States fighter planes, evidently having strayed across the Yalu River, strafed an airstrip in Manchuria. Acheson and Rusk seemed to feel, upon learning of this anger, that the incident had much to do with the menacing talk in Peking. With Truman's approval, therefore, they had Bevin send a message to Nehru for Chinese ears, stating that the United States regretted the attack as an accident and offered to make restitution.[42]

The view was also held in the State Department that China was subjecting India to a "war of nerves" because of Peking's ire at being excluded from the United Nations seat still held by Chiang Kai-shek. As of September 28, as a message from Webb to the embassy in New Delhi indicated, it was believed in the department that China was not likely to intervene in Korea because it was not in China's interest to do so. This coincided with the British view.[43] On the heels of the Webb message, however, came a cable from Ambassador Kirk in Moscow, citing reports from British and Dutch diplomats of a hardening of Chinese determination to intervene if MacArthur crossed the parallel.[44] Later, Henderson notified Washington that Nehru thought it was dangerous to assume that Peking was bluffing.[45] In the absence of diplomatic relations the opportunities for mutual misunderstanding between the United States and China were unlimited.

The next day Chou En-lai warned publicly that "The Chinese people absolutely will not tolerate foreign aggression, nor will they supinely tolerate seeing their neighbors being savagely invaded by the imperialists."[46] He paid no attention to the distinction being made in the Truman administration between invasion for the tactical purpose of mopping up Kim Il-sung's army and invasion for the strategic purpose of unifying Korea.

Two days later, on October 2, MacArthur reported to the Joint Chiefs of Staff that "Probings by elements of the ROK Army are now well across the 38th parallel. Advances on the extreme right are between ten and thirty miles in the coast sector with practically no resistance."[47]

At 5:35 A.M. on October 3, a cable arrived at the State Department from Julius C. Holmes, chargé in the American embassy in London, so coded that the message was to be brought to Acheson's attention at any hour of the day or night. It reported that the British had just shown the embassy a telegram received from Peking. The telegram stated, according to Holmes, "that on October 3 Foreign Minister Chou En-lai called in Indian Ambassador Panikkar and informed him that if UN Armed Forces crossed 38th parallel China would send troops across frontier [to] participate in defense North Korea. He said this action would not take place if only South Koreans crossed parallel."[48]

Some State Department officials took Chou's warning very seriously; others thought it was a bluff.[49] Acheson, declining to regard the message as an authoritative statement of Chinese policy, although not a matter to be disregarded either, sent the dispatch to Truman at noon.[50] Like many another official in Washington, the president was inclined to discount it because of distrust of Panikkar. He recalled that the Indian ambassador "had in the past played the game of the Chinese Communists fairly regularly, so that his statement could not be taken as that of an impartial observer." Truman surmised that Chou's warning might have been propaganda intended to divert the United Nations General Assembly from a strong stand on Korean unification.[51] "It was not considered very solid information at the time," Harriman recalled.[52] Policy was not changed.

Completely forgotten or ignored was the provision in the order of September 27 to MacArthur that he was not to send forces above the parallel if there were any Chinese or Soviet threat "to counter our military operations in North Korea."

"Among the reasons for believing that [the Chinese] would not come in," Acheson later testified, "were the amount of well trained troops which they would have to commit, the possible weakening of the government in China itself, the lack of real advantage to China itself in coming in . . . [and the assumption that] its position internationally . . . would probably lose ground. . . ."[53]

This last doubtless referred to the fact that, by combatting United Nations forces, Communist China would hurt its chances of replacing Chiang Kai-shek in the United Nations.

The momentum for crossing the parallel grew, unchecked by any effort at negotiation with China and the Soviet Union, taking into account their interests also in the future of North Korea. The General Assembly adopted on October 7 a resolution that the United States had helped to draft, which was worded with deliberate vagueness and was intended to offer guidance and sanction for military operations. The wording recalled that the "essential objective" of previous resolutions of that body had been the establishment of a unified, democratic, and independent Korean government. The new resolution recommended, therefore, that all "appropriate steps be taken to ensure conditions of stability throughout Korea." The resolution looked toward elections under United Nations auspices for the establishment of such a unified government.[54]

On that same October 7 MacArthur's patrols began crossing the 38th parallel in furtherance of the plan to wipe out the army of a Soviet satellite, something that had never been attempted before. The full invasion of North Korea began on October 9 with the advance of the 1st Cavalry and 24th Infantry Divisions in concert with the ROK 1st Division and the 27th British Brigade.[55] The next day the Chinese Ministry of Foreign Affairs issued the statement that ''The American war of invasion in Korea has been a serious menace to the security of China from its very start.''[56]

IV

MACARTHUR

27. *The Wake Island Conference*

IN THE CRYSTAL SUNRISE OVER the Pacific on October 15, 1950,* the presidential plane *Independence* circled Wake Island and landed on the lone runway there, carrying President Truman to a meeting with General MacArthur. "Have to talk to God's righthand man. . . ."[1] the president had written to his cousin. The general had arrived from Tokyo the night before.

When the *Independence* stopped, Truman, with Henry Nicholson of the Secret Service at his side, glanced out the open cabin door, scanning the small gathering of government officials, reporters, photographers, and military officers on hand to welcome him. Instead of descending the ramp, however, Truman beckoned Nicholson back to the cabin.

Truman said that MacArthur was still sitting in a jeep behind the crowd. Settling down in his own seat with an air of finality, the president said that MacArthur was not going to upstage him the way the general had upstaged Roosevelt in Honolulu on July 26, 1944. Aboard the *Independence*, therefore, no one budged.[2]

The incident referred to by Truman was the general's performance at a wartime conference to which Roosevelt had summoned MacArthur and Admiral Nimitz. Roosevelt had made the trip on the cruiser *Baltimore,* and when the vessel docked in Honolulu, he sent word to the two officers as well as to other admirals and generals in the area, inviting them aboard for a reception. Before cheering crowds on the dock, Nimitz and some fifty officers boarded the cruiser to greet the president on the quarterdeck. Roosevelt pointedly asked Nimitz where MacArthur was. The absent MacArthur had flown in an hour earlier from Australia, grousing about having been hauled half-way across the Pacific for a meeting he believed to have been arranged to further Roosevelt's chances for reelection in November.

The president's query to Nimitz drew an embarrassed silence. After the reception Roosevelt was preparing to go to the quarters assigned him ashore when a siren pierced the air and MacArthur came screeching onto the dock in a huge open car with a motorcycle escort. Dashing gallantly up the gangplank, he suddenly turned around and acknowledged an ovation from the spectators. Then he proceeded to the deck to greet the president.

"Hello, Doug," Roosevelt purred, taking notice that the general was wear-

*October 14 in the United States.

ing a casual jacket. "What are you doing with that leather jacket on? It's darn hot today."[3]

The plane flying in from Australia had been cold, MacArthur replied.

During the pause on Wake Island, while Truman sat resolutely in his seat, MacArthur suddenly materialized in the forefront of the gathering at the foot of the landing ramp. Not even the reporters who had been looking for him quite knew how he had got there.[4] Truman then came briskly down the steps, noting, like Roosevelt, MacArthur's attire. "General MacArthur was at the Airport," Truman commented later, "with his shirt unbuttoned, wearing a greasy ham and eggs cap that evidently had been in use for twenty years."[5] Reporters at the scene noticed that MacArthur did not follow a common practice among military officers of saluting the president on such occasions. Yet this first meeting between two men whose relationship was to create a singular episode in American history was most cordial. "I've been a long time meeting you, general," Truman said. "I hope it won't be so long next time, Mr. President," MacArthur replied.

The idea for the conference had originated with Truman's staff before the Inchon landing, according to contemporary notes by George Elsey. Who came up with the notion first is not remembered. From the start, however, Elsey played the major role in nurturing and advancing it, enlisting the support of Harriman over luncheon in the Metropolitan Club after Inchon and then persuading Harriman and Charles Murphy to broach it to Truman around September 28. Evidently the proposal first passed in and out of Truman's head, because when it was raised again early in October while he was cruising on the Chesapeake Bay with some of his staff for a few days aboard the *Williamsburg,* he appeared to have forgotten the earlier mention of it.[6]

At a time when Truman's popularity had been further drained by a summer of reverses in Korea, the motivation of the White House staff in proposing a meeting with MacArthur was largely political. "The thought was that it was good election-year stuff," Murphy recalled. Truman's first reaction was negative, Murphy said, because he "thought it was too political, too much showmanship. He did not know how much of a real need there was for him to confer with MacArthur. . . . Maybe we took unfair advantage of the president in pressing it." Despite the colorful antics of the 1948 campaign, Truman was not a president given to stunts. In this case Murphy had to work hard to persuade him. Murphy felt afterward that what finally clinched the argument with Truman was the precedent of Roosevelt's meeting with MacArthur in Honolulu in 1944.[7]

As in most such decisions, of course, various motives come into play. After Inchon and the threats out of China Truman doubtless saw some good reasons, beside favorable headlines, for talking with MacArthur. In any event he agreed to the trip while aboard the *Williamsburg* and asked Secretary of Defense Marshall to invite MacArthur to meet the president in Hawaii. Because of the delicate situation in Korea, Marshall thought that MacArthur might not wish to travel that far. At Marshall's suggestion MacArthur was given the option of naming Wake as the site, and he did.

Furthermore, he was as grouchy about going to Wake Island to give Truman a political shot in the arm as he had been about going to Honolulu to drum up votes for Roosevelt.[8] When Truman came off the plane, however, the general adopted his most engaging manner, and the cordial hours on Wake Island were the high watermark of the Truman-MacArthur relationship.

Before holding a general conference to be attended by other officials from Washington and Tokyo, Truman wished to talk with MacArthur alone in a quonset hut a short drive away. He escorted him to an old Chevrolet sedan, and the two of them climbed into the back seat, with Nicholson and the driver in front. With the four of them crowded into such a small car, Nicholson could not help but overhear the conversation in the rear during the drive.

After an exchange of inquiries about one another's family Truman went straight to the question that seems to have been troubling him at that time more than anything else. He asked MacArthur whether he thought the Chinese would enter the Korean War. As Nicholson recalled the conversation, MacArthur replied that his intelligence reports indicated that the Chinese would not intervene. In any case, he said, as Nicholson remembered, it would not make any difference because the United Nations forces could defeat them. Truman said he was glad to hear it and added, as Nicholson recalled his words, "I have been worried about that."[9]

Six weeks earlier, in his televised speech from the White House on September 1, Truman had made the point of appealing to the Chinese people not to be "misled or forced into fighting against the United Nations and against the American people, who have always been and still are their friends."[10]

He was sufficiently uneasy about Chinese intentions that before departing for Wake Island he asked the CIA for a new assessment. Particularly since Inchon, reports had been trickling into Washington about a rise in the number of Chinese troops in Manchuria. There had even been reports that Chinese soldiers had moved into North Korea. The view persisted in the government, however, that substantial Chinese participation in the war was improbable. On the eve of the Truman-MacArthur meeting the CIA submitted the report requested by the president. Concurred in by the intelligence organizations of the military services, the report reaffirmed earlier CIA assessments. It said:

> While full-scale Chinese Communist intervention . . . must be regarded as a continuing possibility, a consideration of all known factors leads to the conclusion that barring a Soviet decision for global war, such action is not probable in 1950. During this period, intervention will probably be confined to continued covert assistance to the North Koreans.[11]

Though worried, Truman accepted the improbability of China's entry into the war, according to Acheson.[12]

It was all a rerun of the story of the intelligence reports in June that the North Koreans would not attack. Washington did not wish to believe that the Chinese Communists would intervene. Washington did not believe it.

Little is known of the private talk between Truman and MacArthur in the quonset hut. After his return to Washington Truman recounted some of the conversation to his staff.

"He said," Eben Ayers noted in his diary, "that . . . MacArthur spent some time apologizing for the Veterans of Foreign Wars statement.''

Obviously, this pleased Truman. "It seemed clear to me," Ayers said, "that the President's feeling toward MacArthur had changed from what it may have been before the meeting and that he now looked upon him far more favorably and in a far more friendly spirit."[13]

After their private meeting the president and the general repaired to a one-story concrete-and-frame building for what was later to become a celebrated and controversial session. The participants included General Bradley, Rusk, Jessup, Harriman, Ambassador Muccio, Secretary of the Army Pace, Admiral Radford, commander of American forces in the Pacific, and members of the White House staff and MacArthur's staff. In the building also was Miss Vernice Anderson, the only woman on Wake Island that day and later a subject of much dispute.

A former secretary in the White House and the Pentagon, she was then administrative assistant to Ambassador Jessup, in whose official party she had previously traveled extensively, visiting, among other places, Tokyo, where she had stayed in the MacArthur compound and met a number of the general's staff. At the last minute Jessup and Bradley had decided to include her on the Wake Island trip to type the conference communiqué and drafts of a speech that Truman was to deliver in San Francisco on the way home. Before the general meeting began on Wake that morning, Miss Anderson spoke to some of the MacArthur aides she had met in Tokyo, including Major General Courtney Whitney, Colonel C. C. Canada, MacArthur's physician, and Colonel Tony Story, MacArthur's pilot. She was standing in the conference room when Truman and MacArthur approached but thereupon withdrew to a small side room, separated from the conference room by a slatted swinging door. She already had set up her typewriter there for later work on the communiqué. She sat at the desk. She could not be seen by at least most of those at the conference table, but she could hear all of them.

When the meeting commenced, she took her pencil and pad and started making shorthand notes, though not a complete verbatim transcript. "I had nothing else to do," she said afterward. "No one told me to or not to."[14] In accordance with common practice six of those at the table from Washington—Bradley, Harriman, Jessup, and Rusk among them—also openly made notes of the discussion.[15] At Bradley's request after the Wake Island meeting all of the notes, including Miss Anderson's, were compiled in a document as the substance of statements made at the conference.

Truman opened the discussion by asking MacArthur about the rehabilitation of Korea after the fighting.[16] In the course of his reply MacArthur said, according to Miss Anderson's shorthand record:

"It is my belief that organized resistance throughout Korea will be ended by Thanksgiving. . . .

"In North Korea unfortunately the government is pursuing a forlorn hope."

Then, according to Bradley's composite document, MacArthur recounted his plan of the twin advance in the west and east by Walker and Almond, aimed at entrapping the enemy again as had been done after Inchon.

"At that time," he continued, as Miss Anderson recorded his words, "it is my hope that we will be able to withdraw the Eighth Army and get them back into Japan by Christmas."

After a discussion about postwar conditions in Korea Truman repeated the question he had asked in the car earlier about the chance of Soviet or Chinese interference.

"I should say in my opinion there is very little," MacArthur answered, as Miss Anderson recorded his words. "Had either country intervened, their intervention would have been decisive. I do not believe at this time they will endeavor to throw good money after bad."

Saying that he no longer feared intervention, he continued:

"In the case of the Chinese Communists, they have in Manchuria scattered around three hundred thousand troops. Of these probably not more than a hundred thousand or a hundred and twenty-five thousand are distributed along the Yalu River. Of those, they would have the greatest difficulty getting more than fifty thousand or sixty thousand across the river into North Korea. They have no air."

Against the United States Air Force in Korea, MacArthur was quoted in the composite document as having said, the Chinese would be slaughtered if they tried to drive to Pyongyang.

In their respective memoirs, the general and Admiral Radford interpreted MacArthur's reply as having meant that MacArthur would crush an invasion by bombing bases, supplies, and troops in Manchuria. No known record exists, however, of Truman's agreeing to lift the ban on bombing north of the Yalu in any circumstance.[17]

Bradley referred to the problem of finding additional American troops for Europe. He inquired whether the 2nd or 3rd Infantry Division would be available for redeployment from Korea to Europe by January. According to the composite document, MacArthur's answer was Yes. He would make one of them available by January.

Rusk alluded again to the return of some troops to Japan from Korea. "Hope to get them back by Christmas," MacArthur reiterated, according to the Anderson record.

Possibly referring to MacArthur's apology for the message to the Veterans of Foreign Wars, Truman told the conference that he and the general already had talked about Formosa and were in complete agreement. If this statement were wrong or distorted, MacArthur made no effort to rectify it. The session wound down after some more talk about Korean elections. "This has been a most satisfactory conference," Truman concluded.

When the meeting adjourned, Rusk took MacArthur aside to sound out his opinion on the Chinese threat to intervene if United Nations forces crossed the parallel. Rusk noted MacArthur's reply, "He said he did not fully understand why they [the Chinese] had gone out on such a limb and that they must be greatly embarrassed by the predicament in which they now find themselves."[18]

While a communiqué was being penciled, Miss Anderson stepped into the conference room.

"Where did this lovely lady come from?" MacArthur asked.[19]

General Whitney introduced her, and she thanked MacArthur for the hospitality shown her at his headquarters compound in Tokyo.[20]

No inkling there of the storm that would break around Miss Anderson six months later. The Wake Island conference came and went without dispute from anyone.

Truman and MacArthur had traveled thousands of miles for a couple of hours of rather insignificant talk. No new issue had burdened the agenda. Indeed, there was no agenda. No new decision was taken. Policy that had been made in Washington previously remained intact. Directives already sent to MacArthur by the Joint Chiefs of Staff to cover current operations were left unchanged. "There had been no discussion of basic US and UN policy objectives in Korea," wrote the historians Schnabel and Watson, "and thus no opportunity to reach a real meeting of the minds between the President and the General—or, alternatively, to bring into the open their disagreement. Such discussion did not take place because there seemed no need for it."[21] The war appeared to be in its final stage. MacArthur did not believe the Chinese would enter the war, but then neither did Washington. The CIA had already reached essentially the same conclusion as Truman heard from MacArthur.

Everyone seemed to be in good spirits and probably happy to be taking off for his particular destination. Before departure Truman pinned on MacArthur's breast a fourth oak leaf cluster to his Distinguished Service Medal. In words that were soon to sound ironic Truman said in his citation that MacArthur had "so inspired his command by his vision, his judgment, his indomitable will and his unshakeable faith, that it has set a shining example of gallantry and tenacity in defense and of audacity in attack matched by few operations in military history."

The two men never met again.

28. The Depths

WHEN TRUMAN RETURNED to Washington, MacArthur's forces were rolling toward the Yalu, and peace plans were being made. A sense of relief permeated the White House. "We came back from Wake feeling pretty good because the war was over," Charles Murphy recalled.[1]

Truman's speech in San Francisco on the way home from the Pacific rang with optimism. He referred to the expected victory of United Nations forces as a "tremendous step forward in the age-old struggle to establish the rule of law in the world." He said, "We know now that the United Nations can create a system of international order with the authority to maintain peace."[2]

The dewy mood drowned the old sarcasm about "Mr. Prima Donna, Brass Hat Five Star MacArthur." "It is fortunate for the world," Truman told the San Francisco audience, "that we had the right man [to command United Nations forces]—a man who is a great soldier—General Douglas MacArthur." At a press conference in Washington after the return from San Francisco, Edward A. Harris, of the *St. Louis Post-Dispatch,* almost had his head taken off by Truman for asking whether the president and General MacArthur were finally in agreement over Formosa.

"Let me tell you something that will be good for your soul," Truman snapped. "It's a pity that you columnists and reporters . . . can't understand the ideas of two intellectually honest men when they meet . . .

"General MacArthur is the commander in chief of the Far East. He is a member of the government of the United States. He is loyal to the government. He is loyal to the president. He is loyal to the president in his foreign policy, which I hope a lot of your papers were—*wish* a lot of your papers were.

"There is no disagreement between General MacArthur and myself."[3]

"The President told us," Eben Ayers noted, "that the reason he stopped any discussion of Formosa was because of MacArthur's apology to him in their discussion and his desire to avoid any possibility of humiliating MacArthur before others."[4]

A great moment in the war had arrived. Having already captured Pyongyang, sending Kim Il-sung's government fleeing, Walker's Eighth Army drove across the Chongchon River toward the lower Yalu, sixty-five miles away. In the east Almond's Tenth Corps made an amphibious landing at Wonsan and moved toward the upper Yalu. On October 26, 1950, the reconnaissance platoon of the 7th Regiment of the ROK 6th Division, operating under Walker's command, reached the Yalu at Chosan. By that time American commanders thought the war was all but over. The 1st Cavalry Division was buoyed by visions of a Thanksgiving Day parade in Tokyo.[5] The *New York Times* said in an editorial that "except for unexpected developments along the frontiers . . . we can now be easy in our minds as to the military outcome."[6]

South of Chosan, however, an ominous action had taken place. Even as the aforementioned reconnaissance platoon had headed for the Yalu, the movement of another unit of the ROK 6th Division had come under enemy fire eight miles west of the village of Onjong. When the unit deployed to disperse what was thought to be a small force of North Koreans, it was blasted by fire from Chinese and put to rout. Heavy fighting spread. In the east on that same October 25, while moving toward the Changjin Reservoir, a ROK regiment under Almond's command encountered a Chinese roadblock and took prisoners in the skirmish. One of the prisoners said that nearly five thousand Chinese stood deployed in the vicinity.[7]

Word spread that Chinese "volunteers" had joined the fight. News of the Chinese prisoners hit the press. To many American readers the reports were almost too disturbing, too preposterous to be believed. On October 29 Everett Drumright, chargé in the recently reopened United States embassy in Seoul, cabled Acheson that some of the reports were "extravagant." Drumright said: "Eighth Army Headquarters states its field units have not reported coming into contact with any sizable number of Chinese troops. On basis current information Eighth Army is not inclined to accept reports of substantial Chinese participation in North Korean fighting."[8]

The alarm bell rang in the American intelligence system, but none of the firemen donned boots. The information as well as the sources of it were thought to warrant a low appraisal. "As with the North Korean invasion four months earlier," wrote Schnabel and Watson, "there had been abundant warnings of what was possible, but no clear and specific evidence of precise Chinese intentions. The belief prevailed that Communist China would have little to gain by intervening in Korea at that time."[9] Especially around MacArthur, the view was held that if the Chinese had intended to intervene, they would have done so at the time of the Inchon landing. Another theme, which had recurred in recent policy papers, was that Chinese intervention was unlikely because the Soviets regarded South Korea as being in their own sphere of interest. No one in Washington, CIA analysts included, comprehended the threatened feelings aroused in China by the stationing of the Seventh Fleet in the Formosa Strait, the spectacular victory at Inchon, and MacArthur's attack on North Korea. No one wanted to believe that the Chinese would really upset the applecart at the last moment.

Newly captured Chinese said, however, that their forces had entered Korea in large numbers. Drumright sent Acheson a more pessimistic message on October 30, enlarging estimates of Chinese strength in battle and suggesting that Chinese forces might be "instrumental in checking advance to the Yalu."[10] In fact, the Chinese had so disastrously mauled some ROK troops in the west that

General Walker had to delay the offensive by withdrawing the Eighth Army back across the Chongchon River, leaving only a bridgehead on the far side. By the end of October the position of the Eighth Army was precarious.

After the Wake Island illusions and the misleading promise of the first phase of the United Nations offensive in North Korea, therefore, October was ending on a worrisome note for Truman. Victory had appeared almost in reach. In weeks or even days his resoluteness in entering the Korean War and his boldness in crossing the parallel in the face of Chinese warnings might have been vindicated, handsomely. Ultimate triumph by the United Nations in halting aggression through collective action and terminating Communist rule in North Korea would have been widely viewed as the crowning achievement of the Truman presidency, a cause for tribute to the courage and foresight of the man of Independence. Instead, by October 31 a dark cloud hovered over the battlefields, threatening to wash out the great prospect.

The president went about his business with characteristic verve that last day of October, his calendar filled with appointments. At 3:30 P.M. he was winding up the last of them before presiding at a cabinet meeting.

In Pennsylvania Station in New York at that same hour two men, Oscar Collazo and Griselio Torresola, boarded a train for Washington. For the occasion they were dressed in new suits and new snap-brim hats. Collazo had purchased two one-way coach tickets for himself and Torresola. With good reason the passengers did not expect to return. They were going to Washington to assassinate President Truman.[11]

Natives of Puerto Rico and residents of the Bronx, the two slightly built travelers were members of the Puerto Rican Nationalist party, which advocated Puerto Rican independence. In that fall of 1950 the Nationalists were staging a full-scale but futile revolt on the island against local government forces. Collazo, at least, according to his own subsequent testimony, bore no grudge against Truman personally. But he and Torresola were fanatical in the cause of Puerto Rican independence of the United States. Either they did not know or else were unimpressed by the fact that in a speech in San Juan February 21, 1948, Truman had declared, "I have said to the Congress several times—and I repeat it here—that the Puerto Rican people should have the right to determine for themselves Puerto Rico's political relationship to the continental United States."[12]

Ironically, Truman probably did more for Puerto Rico than any president before him. He appointed the first native to serve as governor of the island. He succeeded in getting Social Security extended to its population. Also he lent his support to an improved form of government and a new constitution, which was approved by Congress and gave Puerto Rico a so-called commonwealth status, making it partially independent of American law and almost entirely in control of its domestic affairs.

This was not enough for Collazo. As he fretted over what he considered American colonialism in Puerto Rico, it occurred to him that if the president of the United States were to be assassinated, revolution might erupt in America. In the throes of it Puerto Rico might gain complete independence. Such at least was the purport of his subsequent testimony and statements. The Secret Service came to doubt that Collazo and Torresola acted entirely on their own. Particularly because of recent contacts between Torresola and leaders of the Nationalist uprising in progress in Puerto Rico, the Secret Service believed that Collazo and Torresola were part of a larger conspiracy in the Nationalist party against the life of the president. The party had had a long record of violence. Evidence was lacking, however, to prove such a conspiracy, and Collazo denied it.

In any event, Collazo and Torresola arrived in Washington, a city neither had visited before, at 7:30 P.M., by which time the cabinet meeting had ended and Truman had returned to Blair House for the night. The two visitors headed for one of the first hotels they saw—the Harris, an establishment since demolished, which was a block and a half from Union Station. Pretending not to know each other, they entered separately, Collazo going first. His manner was so benign that the clerk guessed he was a divinity student and assigned him to Room 434 at $3.50 a day. By chance Torresola was then assigned to a connecting room. After dinner and a stroll through Union Station Plaza, the two returned to Collazo's room and made plans for the next day with the aid of a map of Washington in a hotel directory.

November 1 dawned unseasonably warm. Truman was driven across Pennsylvania Avenue to the White House for a staff meeting and a visit from his first caller that morning, Rudolph Friml, the composer. Friml asked the president why he was not playing golf on such a beautiful day. Truman did not play golf but he loved music, and he and Friml talked about Beethoven, Chopin, and Jose Iturbi, the conductor. Truman said he did not like "noisy" music.[13]

It soon became evident that these pleasantries were out of keeping with the kind of day that was in store for Truman. That morning he received a memorandum from General Walter Bedell Smith, director of central intelligence, beginning, "Fresh, newly equipped North Korean troops have appeared in the North Korean fighting, and it has been clearly established that Chinese Communist troops are also opposing UN forces." According to the CIA chief, the Chinese "probably genuinely fear an invasion of Manchuria despite the clear-cut definition of UN objectives." The memorandum cited reports of Soviet-type aircraft in action, indicating "that the USSR may be providing at least logistic air defense for the Manchurian border." Throughout the administration it was to be accepted that the Soviet Union was behind the Chinese intervention.

Smith informed the president that in addition to Chinese troops massed in Manchuria, estimates from the field were that between fifteen thousand and twenty thousand Chinese soldiers organized in task forces were opposing United Nations forces in North Korea.[14]

In fact, as later became known, during October, while MacArthur was saying that the Chinese would not intervene and Truman was hailing the feat of United Nations forces and Washington was making postwar plans, six Chinese armies totaling eighteen divisions had infiltrated North Korea, crossing the Yalu, unseen, at night and then hiding amid trees and mountains by day. The nominal strength of these divisions was one hundred and eighty thousand men. Behind them in reserve in Manchuria stood the Chinese 50th and 66th armies.[15]

After his final appointment of the morning Truman returned to Blair House for lunch and a rest before an afternoon engagement, which might have been his last act, if Collazo and Torresola had but known his schedule. At 2:50 P.M. Truman was to leave Blair House for Arlington National Cemetery to speak at the unveiling of a statue to Field Marshall Sir John Dill, a British member of the Combined Chiefs of Staff during the Second World War. At this small outdoor gathering security would have been minimal, and the president would have been vulnerable to two determined gunmen.

The two Puerto Ricans had other plans. After breakfast and a stroll through the Capitol grounds they hailed a cab for Blair House, a four-story Georgian building of yellow brick and stucco, with green shutters. It stands on the north side of Pennsylvania Avenue between Jackson Place and Seventeenth Street. The front steps descend directly to the sidewalk. Hundreds of pedestrians passed the president's door every day. From the cab Collazo and Torresola scanned the scene, noting that guards were on duty in white booths resembling sentry boxes placed on the sidewalk at the east and west ends of the house.

After paying their fare, the two men took another walk to familiarize themselves with the neighborhood. They had a bite to eat and returned to Collazo's room, where Torresola, no novice, showed Collazo how to fire a German Walther P-38 pistol. As a youth Collazo had fired a .22 rifle but had had no experience with automatic weapons. For nearly two hours Torresola taught him how to draw his pistol, insert a clip, and cock the weapon. Then they oiled the pistols, and Torresola gave Collazo three clips, each loaded with eight cartridges.

He also gave Collazo ten extra rounds, which Collazo put in a paper bag and stuffed in his pocket. In another pocket he had three colored postcards that he had bought—views of the Washington Monument, the White House, and Pennsylvania Avenue. He had no holster, so he thrust the P-38 into the waistband of his trousers. Carrying sixty-nine rounds of ammunition between them, Collazo and Torresola departed the hotel just before 2 o'clock. Curiously, considering their destination, Collazo asked the clerk whether, if he did not check out at exactly 3 o'clock, he would be charged for another day, as a notice in his room said he would. An extra hour or two might be overlooked, the clerk assured him, so Collazo and Torresola left without paying their bills and took a cab to the corner of Fifteenth Street and Pennsylvania Avenue, two and a half blocks east of Blair House. They walked the distance to take a closer look at its canopied entrance and the guard booths and then returned to the corner to settle on their tactics.

Their plan was to storm Blair House, hoping, as Collazo said later, to find Truman somewhere in a hall and shoot him. In order not to attract attention they set out on separate routes so they would approach Blair House from opposite directions and meet at the front steps for the assault.

Seated in the west guard booth, in the line of Torresola's approach, was Private Leslie Coffelt, of the White House police. In the east booth, along Collazo's route, Private Joseph O. Davidson, also of the White House police, was sitting and talking to Secret Service Agent Floyd M. Boring. Standing under the canopy on the first step of the stairs leading to the front door and facing away from the sidewalk was another policeman, Donald T. Birdzell.

At two-twenty, Collazo, inconspicuous among other pedestrians, sauntered to a point on the walk about eight feet behind Birdzell and stopped. As was his habit, Truman was taking a nap in his second-floor bedroom facing the sidewalk. The window was open, but the temperature had risen to 84 degrees and the president was stretched out on the bed in his underwear. Mrs. Truman and her mother, Mrs. David W. Wallace, were in another part of the house. Margaret Truman, who had become a professional singer, had gone to Portland, Maine, to give a concert. In the heat the wooden front door of Blair House was open, but the screen door was latched.

Unnoticed, Collazo drew his P-38, pointed it at Birdzell and pulled the trigger. In his unfamiliarity with the weapon Collazo may have engaged the safety lock while intending to disengage it, for all that happened was a sharp click. At the sound Birdzell swung around and saw Collazo holding the pistol against his chest and pounding it with his left fist. This may have released the safety lock. The gun fired, and a bullet struck Birdzell's leg.

Drawing a Luger, Torresola fired three shots at Officer Coffelt, who collapsed, mortally wounded. Torresola then fired at another policeman, Joseph H. Downs, and hit him three times, not fatally. Meanwhile Collazo started up the ten steps to the front door but was pinned down on the second step by bullets from Boring, Davidson, and Secret Service Agent Vincent P. Mroz, who had joined the fight. Collazo's initial misfire had doomed his chances of reaching the door. After hitting the already wounded Birdzell with another bullet, Torresola leaped over a low boxwood hedge in front of Blair House to go to Collazo's assistance when the dying Coffelt pulled himself together and put a bullet through Torresola's brain. As Torresola fell dead behind the hedge, Collazo was hit, not mortally, in the chest, the nostril and right ear and toppled back on the sidewalk, out of action.

Pennsylvania Avenue was in an uproar. The din of the twenty-seven shots that were fired awoke Truman with a start, and he rushed to the window and saw the bleeding Collazo lying below. "Get back, get back!" yelled a guard, who feared that the president would be an easy target, if there were a third assassin still unapprehended. Truman got back.*

After order had been restored, Truman calmly appeared at Arlington and paid homage to Dill without mentioning his own ordeal. In talking with reporters he indulged in a bit of the braggadocio he knew they would relish from him. But in a soberer mood he said, "A president has to expect those things." At a time when events already were becoming grim, the attempted assassination cast a damper, for Mrs. Truman particularly, that never quite vanished while the family remained in Washington.

---

*Collazo was convicted on four counts, including the murder of Coffelt, and sentenced to death. Largely for the sake of good relations with Latin America Truman commuted the sentence to life imprisonment. President Carter set Collazo free in 1979 for much the same reason.

Election day was November 7. Truman needed a Democratic victory in the congressional races to discredit the harsh Republican assault on himself and Acheson particularly and to bolster the administration in its handling of the international crisis.

As usual in such elections, local sentiment and personalities heavily affected the voting in the different states. Reinforcing these in 1950 were such larger concerns as the Fair Deal, federal spending, the power of labor, and, above all, the Korean War. Republican National Chairman Guy G. Gabrielson publicly called attention to the fact that "Chinese communist divisions are pouring into North Korea, inflicting heavy casualties on our troops."[16] "The Korean death-trap," Joe McCarthy said, "we can lay to the doors of the Kremlin and those who sabotaged rearming, including Acheson and the president, if you please."[17] Running for reelection in Ohio, Senator Taft said in a broadcast that the demands of the war "may well require the drafting of every American boy of nineteen. . . . They will certainly involve taxes higher than we have levied on our people before. These sacrifices result directly from the fact that this administration has lost the peace after the American people won the war."[18]

Shrillest of all issues in some places, however, was that of Communist influence in Washington. In parts of the country the campaign was overshadowed by McCarthy, McCarthy's tactics, McCarthy's charges, and McCarthy's emulators. McCarthy himself spoke in at least fifteen states, not all of which, to be sure, were to be scenes of Republican victories.

It might be supposed that when Truman, upon the strong advice of Acheson, committed the United States to the Korean War to draw the line against further Communist gains in Asia, the Communist issue would have subsided in the United States. The very opposite occurred, as new suspicions were aroused by events like the arrest in mid-summer of Julius and Ethel Rosenberg, who were indicted on charges of having tried to transmit atomic secrets to the Soviet Union. Communist military aggression in Korea served to make McCarthy's charges all the more ominous.

Even in the most precarious days of the Pusan perimeter the Senate exploded with rancor when the Tydings subcommittee finally submitted its report, calling McCarthy's performance "a fraud and a hoax . . . perhaps the most nefarious campaign of half-truths and untruth in the history of this republic." Declaring that McCarthy had failed to prove a single charge, the report cleared Lattimore, Jessup, Service, and others. A "green light to the Red fifth column in the U.S.," McCarthy retorted, leading an angry Republican chorus and pushing on with new charges.

In the fall political campaign indiscriminate Republican charges of disloyalty were mixed with such savage attacks on the State Department as to cause some serious minds to fear for the health of the government. Probably there was not a Democratic candidate who did not wish, secretly or openly, that Truman would lower the heat by removing Acheson. Wherry particularly angered Truman by asserting in the Senate that "the blood of our boys in Korea is on [Acheson's] shoulders." "Contemptible," Truman said.[19]

It had long been a right-wing goal to require the registration of Communist-front organizations as well as Communist political organizations and their members. In 1948 these provisions had been embodied in the Mundt-Nixon bill. The bill passed the House but not the Senate. The mood of the first summer of the Korean War was made to order for a new effort, and the task was undertaken by Senator McCarran, whose strategy was to link the danger of Communist subversion at home with that of Communist aggression in Korea. His bill not only would have required registration of Communists with the attorney general but would have authorized emergency detention of persons thought likely to commit espionage or sabotage.

Seeking to sidetrack the bill, Truman sent Congress a special message recalling the disgrace of the Alien and Sedition Laws. The danger of communism, he said, lay in its use of armed force and political alliance to gain power abroad. While effective internal security measures were needed, he argued, these "must not be so broad as to restrict our liberties unnecessarily."

To try to coax votes away from McCarran he recommended that Congress instead remedy certain defects in existing laws dealing with espionage and sabotage. He won no high marks from liberal critics by advocating that persons who had received instruction in espionage or subversive tactics from a foreign government or political party be required to register under the Foreign Agents Registration Act.[20] This diversionary tactic, however, did not work. With the help of jittery Democratic liberals, both houses passed an amended McCarran bill. Six weeks before the election Truman vetoed it, saying, "It would put the Government of the United States in the thought control business."[21] Frightened by the Communist issue, Democrats embarrassed Truman by deserting him in droves and voting with McCarthy, Nixon, and other Republicans to pass the Internal Security Act of 1950 over his veto.

As the election campaign progressed, Representative Nixon, running for United States senator in California, baited his Democratic opponent, Representative Helen Gahagan Douglas, on the red issue. He said in a speech that she was "pink right down to her underwear."[22] Before civic clubs, according to David Halberstam, Nixon implied "that there was something sexual going on between Mrs. Douglas and Harry Truman"![23]

Utah was flooded with campaign literature accusing the veteran Senator Elbert D. Thomas, staunch supporter of the Fair Deal and a friend of Truman's, of being a Communist sympathizer. The issue became so damaging that Thomas included a loyalty statement in his speeches. " 'McCarthyism' is the issue in Wisconsin," *Newsweek* reported on the eve of the election.[24]

It was in Illinois, Connecticut, and especially Maryland, where McCarthy most conspicuously and personally thrust his knife in a vendetta against three Democratic senators up for reelection—Tydings and Lucas and McMahon. The latter two were members of the Tydings subcommittee. On one of three campaign trips into Maryland to attack Tydings, McCarthy said: "Lucas provided the whitewash when I charged there were communists in high places in government; McMahon brought the bucket; Tydings the brush. This trio . . . in my opinion have done more than any others in this nation to shield the traitors, protect the disloyal and confuse Americans in their desperate fight to clean out the communists."[25] Tydings's opponent, John Marshall Butler, a Baltimore lawyer running for office for the first time, was a McCarthy understudy. From all points of the compass the Republican right wing took the cue from McCarthy and sent into Maryland money, speakers, research assistance, campaign literature, and even a fraudulent photograph showing Tydings and the American Communist leader, Earl Browder, together. The confluence of McCarthyism and Korea placed an enormous strain on Truman and the Democratic party.

Preoccupied with Korea, Truman made only one campaign speech. In a televised rally in St. Louis three days before the election, he stressed the pocketbook issues that had sparked his 1948 campaign yet somehow seemed overshadowed in the mean atmosphere of 1950. Without mentioning names he did assail Republican politicians who had "maliciously" exploited the loyalty issue and in doing so had "lost all proportion, all sense of restraint, all sense of patriotic decency."[26]

Truman voted in Independence and then flew back to Washington and cruised down the Potomac for the night to hear the returns on radio. It was a hard time for him. Lucas, the Senate Democratic leader, was defeated in Illinois by the sonorous Republican Everett McKinley Dirksen. McCarthy had played only a part in Lucas's downfall. Dirksen bombarded Truman on the war. "All the piety of the administration," he said, "will not put any life into the bodies of the young men coming back in wooden boxes."[27] Illinois Democrats also had been hurt by reports of police corruption in Chicago. Francis J. Myers, the Senate Democratic whip, lost in Pennsylvania. Recently, in complaining about the failure of bills to grant statehood to Hawaii and Alaska, Truman had grumbled that Lucas and Myers lacked "the guts of a gnat."[28] But aboard the *Williamsburg* on election night the president seemed to his staff almost morose over the news of Lucas's defeat. As returns came in from around the country, he appeared overcome at the thought that he had let his friends down.

In Maryland a wave of McCarthyism on top of other issues swamped Tydings. Of McCarthy's three prime targets, only McMahon had survived. In Utah, Senator Thomas's efforts against red-baiting had failed. He was defeated. In California, Nixon decisively defeated Mrs. Douglas—much to Truman's chagrin, although he had recently complained that she was a nuisance.[29] Taft won by a landslide in Ohio, despite the best efforts of the Democrats and the labor unions to defeat him and thus head off a possible Taft candidacy in the 1952 presidential election.

"One of the sad things about the whole business," Truman was to write to a friend, concerning the election in general, "is that McCarthyism seemed to have an effect on the voter. One of the reasons for this was that the candidates in the States where it did have an effect did not have the nerve to fight it with fire. In the States where the [Democratic] majority was increased in the off year, the candidates supported the Democratic Program and called McCarthy what he is—a liar and a crook."[30]

In all, the Republicans, strengthened as a party, had gained five seats in the

Senate and twenty-eight in the House. The Democrats retained control of both houses, although their margins of control in the Senate had been reduced to two votes. The returns were bad news for the Fair Deal and, over a too steady round of bourbon highballs on election night, Truman showed it. The defeat of Lucas and Myers had wiped out the top Democratic leadership in the Senate, and no other powerful Democratic senators stood in line to succeed them. McCarthy's showy success in Maryland particularly had created an image of power, which, though much exaggerated, enhanced his influence by making him seem a menace to anyone who might oppose him. Finally, the shifts in the composition of the Senate and House dimmed hope for enactment of Truman's liberal reforms in his two remaining years in office. As the bleak night on the *Williamsburg* came to a close he had, as was uncommon for him in his presidential years, certainly, drunk more than he could handle. Members of his staff had never seen him more dejected then he was when, with difficulty, he made his way to bed.

In a speech years later George Elsey asked, rhetorically, "Did Truman drink?" Elsey answered the question: "Yes, bourbon and lots of it. But did he drink to excess? Only once did I see him show the effects and that was the night of the mid-term elections in November, 1950."[31]

Even before the election, difficulties had begun cropping up between MacArthur and Washington, not causing any confrontation between the general and the president at first but spreading increasing unhappiness and concern in the Pentagon and the State Department. Despite the broad administration consensus on crossing the parallel to defeat the North Korea army, it was not an action that rested lightly on the minds of Acheson and the Joint Chiefs of Staff, who had supported the decision. While they did not seek to undo it, they were constantly haunted by the danger of Chinese or Soviet attack and worried about how fast and how far MacArthur should proceed. MacArthur, on the other hand, had few doubts at first and no intention of braking the sweep toward a victory that shone before him.

He felt no constraints in the wording of the General Assembly resolution of October 7 favoring steps to insure stability throughout Korea. "My mission," he insisted in subsequent testimony, "was to clear out all North Korea, to unify it. . . ."[32] Years later Acheson accused MacArthur of having deliberately misinterpreted the resolution as authorizing a military sweep to the north.[33] Yet, as the historians Schnabel and Watson have since noted, the resolution was susceptible to such a reading. The reason for this, they pointed out, was that the preamble cited previous United Nations resolutions that called for unification of Korea. The resolution of October 7 also drew attention to the fact that this goal had not been attained. The Joint Chiefs of Staff informed MacArthur that the resolution, in supporting operations above the parallel, reinforced the United Nations resolution of June 27 that recommended restoration of international peace and security in Korea.[34]

Having been authorized in Washington, the movement across the parallel took on a momentum of its own under a headstrong commander. Whatever the concerns of MacArthur's nominal superiors in the Pentagon, their various orders and messages to him only tended to broaden his discretion, as in the case of Marshall's urging him to feel unhampered, tactically and strategically, in crossing the parallel. Less than two weeks later the Joint Chiefs of Staff with Truman's approval sent MacArthur supplemental instructions on what to do if major Chinese units entered the war. The general was directed to continue his own military action as long as, "in your judgment," such action offered a reasonable chance of success.[35]

Because of the zeal and eminence of General of the Army Douglas MacArthur, it was hard for the Pentagon to influence events in the field. Thirsting for victory and long isolated from opinion in Washington and other leading capitals, MacArthur was a theater commander of unique prestige. His seniority towered over that of the Joint Chiefs, to whom he reported. Furthermore, they, as well as Marshall, who was senior to MacArthur, were wrapped in the tradition of giving a theater commander great latitude.

In mid-October MacArthur succeeded in brushing aside, on grounds of military necessity, a provision in the Joint Chief's order of September 27, stating that as a matter of policy South Korean rather than American troops should be used in areas near the Chinese and Soviet borders to lessen provocation.[36] Regardless, MacArthur sent American troops north. No issue was made of the breach in the Pentagon. It was not brought before the president for judgment.

Unexpectedly and without consulting the Joint Chiefs, MacArthur ordered Lieutenant General George E. Stratemeyer, commanding general of the Far East air forces, to launch at 3 A.M. on November 7, Korean time, a great bombing attack on practically all enemy installations, factories, and communications facilities in North Korea. Most dramatically, however, all bridges across the Yalu River were to be bombed on the Korean side of the river in an attack that was to be sustained for two weeks. "Combat crews," MacArthur ordered, "are to be flown to exhaustion if necessary."[37]

On his own initiative General Stratemeyer reported the planned bombing attack to his superior in Washington, General Vandenberg. Vandenberg thought it necessary to notify Secretary of the Air Force Finletter. The upshot was an emergency meeting in Acheson's office shortly after 10 A.M. on November 6, Washington time, only hours before the B-29 bombers were scheduled to take off for the Yalu. In London that day the British cabinet was to meet to review policy toward China, with which Britain by then had diplomatic relations. The United States had promised the British to consult them before taking any action that might affect Manchuria. In New York, American delegates were striving to line up votes in the Security Council for a resolution to be introduced calling on China to withdraw from Korea. Chinese intervention in the war had caused enormous strains in the United Nations, which made it difficult to maintain concerted policy.

When notified by Acheson of MacArthur's order, Truman agreed that because of the delicate diplomatic situation, MacArthur should be required to justify the bombing attack before it began.[38] The Joint Chiefs thereupon cabled

MacArthur, "Until further orders postpone all bombing of targets within five miles of Manchurian border."[39]

Within hours a bristling reply came from MacArthur, declaring that Chinese troops and equipment were "pouring" across the Yalu bridges, threatening the destruction of United Nations forces. The bridges had to be destroyed, he said. Every hour destruction was postponed would "be paid for dearly in American and other United Nations blood." MacArthur was canceling the bombing under "the gravest protest that I can make." In effect, he demanded that the chiefs immediately bring his message to Truman's attention "as I believe your instructions may well result in a calamity of major proportion for which I cannot accept the responsibility without his permission and direct understanding of the situation."[40]

Truman was worried about a Manchurian incident, but such an appeal by a theater commander to a president was strong medicine indeed. Truman authorized the bombing, but the affair left a bad taste. "There is little question," wrote the historians Schnabel and Watson, "that General MacArthur's actions in this case, in which it appeared he had intended to present the President with a *fait accompli,* reinforced the growing view among Washington officials that he was not to be entirely trusted."[41]

In transmitting the president's approval to MacArthur the Joint Chiefs warned him of the risks involved. If the Soviets were to view the bombing as an attack on Manchuria, they said, the consequences "would not only endanger your forces but would enlarge the area of conflict and U.S. involvement to a most dangerous degree." The chiefs concluded that "it is vital in the national interest of the United States to localize the fighting in Korea."[42] More than ever, upon the entry of Chinese troops, limiting the war to Korea became the bedrock of the Truman administration's policy.

By early November MacArthur was aroused by the threat of Soviet-built Mig-15 aircraft that streaked across the Yalu to attack United Nations troops and planes and then flew back into what was the sanctuary of Manchuria, created by the administration's policy of not violating the border. MacArthur wanted to send his planes in pursuit of these enemy aircraft as they returned to their Manchurian bases. He asked the Joint Chiefs for instructions.[43] They shared MacArthur's view that policy should be changed to permit United Nations pilots to engage in "hot pursuit" of enemy planes to a distance of several miles into Manchuria. Truman, Marshall, and Acheson assented.[44] Hot pursuit was a sufficiently hazardous proposal that the administration felt obliged to query other members of the United Nations with troops in Korea. The allies rejected hot pursuit. To lessen the risk that they might otherwise abandon the war the administration refused to authorize pursuit, much to MacArthur's resentment.

For Truman and his advisers the land war in Asia turned into a nightmare, even though suddenly, mysteriously the Chinese troops broke off engagements on November 7 and vanished.

Decisions, to begin with, were bedeviled by uncertainty about China's aims.

No one in Washington was clear as to whether the Chinese intended simply to help the North Koreans out in the crisis or protect power plants along the Yalu or establish a *cordon sanitaire* below the Manchurian border or crush the United Nations forces and drive them from Korea.

Equally complicating was the ignorance of the number of Chinese troops in Korea. The administration was groping in the midst of an utter breakdown of battlefield intelligence, probably due in part to the administration's prudence in not sending reconnaissance planes over Manchuria. Since the Chinese had been able to seize the initiative on the Eighth Army front in late October, they obviously were present in considerable force. In mid-November, however, a State Department intelligence estimate said, "The military activity of Chinese troops in Korea so far is not sufficiently extensive to indicate a plan for major operations."[45]

No one in Washington understood why the Chinese had disengaged or knew how long the disengagement might last.

At a press conference on November 16 Truman sought to assuage the Chinese by pledging that he would "take every honorable step to prevent any extension of the hostilities in the Far East."[46] China's response was contemptuous. Peking radio said, "America has lied and smashed her way across the world to Chinese territory and into it, has seized Chinese Taiwan and is threatening another neighbor, Vietnam."[47] *Time* sneered at Truman and Acheson over the rebuff. The administration had ignored Henry Luce's past demands for greater aid to Chiang Kai-shek; now it was Luce's turn for revenge. "The U.S. leaders got their answer and it was coming to them," *Time* said.[48]

When the Chinese entered the war in force, the Joint Chiefs suggested to MacArthur that the whole question of his objectives ought to be reexamined. The implication was that MacArthur perhaps might better go on the defensive.[49]

Mistakenly confident that his air power could interdict Chinese reinforcements and believing that no more than thirty thousand Chinese soldiers were in Korea, MacArthur would not hear of the suggestion. It would be fatal, he said, "to weaken the fundamental and basic policy of the United Nations to destroy all resisting armed forces in Korea and bring that country into a united and free nation." Anything less "would completely destroy the morale of my forces and its psychological consequences would be inestimable." "I recommend with all the earnestness that I possess," he cabled the chiefs "that there be no weakening at this crucial moment and that we press on to complete victory which I believe can be achieved if our determination and indomitable will do not desert us."[50]

Pressure on the administration from its allies increased as they came to feel a need for revision of MacArthur's strategy. The British proposed that his advance be limited so as to create a demilitarized zone south of the Yalu to alleviate Chinese fears of invasion.

Whether it would have altered China's course, it seemed the most tangible and sensible proposal that anyone on either side of the Atlantic, or Pacific, was able to suggest. Yet while Acheson sympathized with it, it went on the shoals in Washington and in MacArthur's command. Acheson himself discouraged the British from pressing it in the United Nations for several reasons, notably that

MacArthur's forces already were north of the line suggested by the British and were about to launch an offensive from there. To abandon the positions then, Acheson told Bevin, would have "disastrous" effects on the morale of the troops and the Koreans and on public opinion in the United States. Hoping that the forthcoming offensive would succeed, Marshall resisted the proposal because he doubted that the Chinese would agree to extend the demilitarized zone to their side of the Yalu, too, so as to make the zone acceptable to the American people.[51] Because the zone would have required United Nations forces to come to a halt well short of the Yalu, the whole idea was, of course, an abomination to MacArthur. He told the Joint Chiefs in a message that creation of a demilitarized zone would be tantamount to the cessation of the Sudeten region of Czechoslovakia to Hitler in 1938. All Asia, MacArthur declared, would view such an action as appeasement of Communist China and the Soviet Union. He could see nothing but disaster in altering the aim of destroying the remaining North Korean forces as a means of unifying Korea.[52]

"I think a lot of people were worried," Bradley was to testify, "about the fact that the Tenth Corps was isolated from the rest of the Eighth Army and that the right flank of the Eighth Army was exposed."[53] That was a reference to MacArthur's tactic of separating the Eighth Army and the Tenth Corps. As early as November 9 Marshall had commented on an unusual dispersion and vulnerability of the Tenth Corps. Bradley explained that MacArthur had approved the dispersion because he had to occupy the whole of North Korea and prepare for elections—an extreme interpretation of MacArthur's orders. Acheson later told the National Security Council that the general seemed to have misunderstood them. He had never been required to occupy the northeastern portion of Korea and prepare for elections, Acheson said.[54]

MacArthur nevertheless plunged ahead with plans for a late November offensive to crush whatever enemy resistance remained anywhere in North Korea. He maintained that the separation of the Tenth Corps from the Eighth Army made the corps a threat to the main supply lines of enemy forces facing the Eighth Army. Bradley doubted it. MacArthur held that the Tenth Corps occupied the attention of six to eight enemy divisions that otherwise would have been free to attack the Eighth Army. Bradley doubted it. MacArthur maintained that the Taebaek range made it impractical to form a continuous line of the Eighth Army and the Tenth Corps entirely across the peninsula. Bradley doubted that, too.[55]

General Collins shared Bradley's concern about the exposed position of the separated Tenth Corps, but neither the army chief of staff nor the chairman of the Joint Chiefs of staff sought to interfere with the traditional authority of the theater commander. Upon informing the chiefs beforehand that the Eighth Army advance would be directed at enemy concentrations in northwestern Korea, MacArthur assured them that the recent great air attack had substantially cut the flow of enemy supplies and reinforcements.

None of the authorities in Washington sought to forestall the late November offensive, even though not all of them shared MacArthur's optimism. Acheson told the National Security Council on November 10 that the State Department had been trying to find some way of reaching authorities in Peking but without success. Since the administration had sought to keep the conquest of all of Korea from being a stated war aim, he said, it could settle for something short of that if terms were otherwise satisfactory.[56] That was rather in line with a recommendation by the Joint Chiefs the day before that every effort should be made, urgently, to settle the problem of Chinese intervention by political means.[57] Policy, however, drifted in the direction of negotiation *after* MacArthur's offensive. The lure of Korean unification and rollback of the Soviet orbit still beckoned. Acheson said at the National Security Council meeting that the Departments of State and Defense were agreed that MacArthur's directive should remain unchanged and that, in the words of the official notes, "General MacArthur is free to do what he militarily can . . . without bombing Manchuria."

On the eve of the offensive Marshall proceeded on the assumption that MacArthur would succeed—a sentiment that could be entertained by one who had no idea how many Chinese troops had crossed the Yalu into North Korea. Ultimately, this ignorance was a consideration in support of the offensive. Marshall and Acheson wanted MacArthur to advance if for no other reason than to ascertain the strength and positions of the vanished Chinese.

In disregard of his own recent worry about Chinese troops and equipment pouring across the Yalu MacArthur scorned such doubts as existed in Washington about pushing north. "He seems very disdainful of our concern over the major conflict with the Chinese," Admiral Sherman noted in a memorandum.[58] MacArthur even disdained his own past concerns, such as those he had voiced to the Joint Chiefs in two messages on November 7. In one he had said that the introduction of Chinese troops had "completely changed the overall situation." In the other he acknowledged that continued Chinese reinforcement could compel a United Nations retreat.[59]

In spite of disquieting thoughts in Washington, MacArthur gave the order for the supposedly final United Nations offensive—an ill-planned, reckless venture. The "massive compression envelopment of North Korea," he called it. "If successful," he said in a ringing communiqué, "this should for all practical purposes end the war. . . ."[60] Whatever control the president of the United States may have had over military developments in Korea was gone now.

A snappy, checkered muffler reflecting his own high spirits, MacArthur flew to Eighth Army headquarters to see the troops jump off in snowy weather on November 24 into the seemingly deserted mountains. That very day a new intelligence estimate had been made available to MacArthur, according to Truman. It stated that the Chinese had the capability of forcing United Nations troops to withdraw to defensive positions "for prolonged and inconclusive operations."[61] MacArthur's view was just the opposite. Within earshot of several war correspondents he said, "If this operation is successful, I hope we can get the boys home by Christmas." As William Manchester was to remark, the correspondents "were divided over whether to christen it the 'End-the-War Offensive' or the 'Home-for-Christmas Drive.' Some called it both."[62]

In a matter of a few days, the offensive, the decision of the Truman admin-

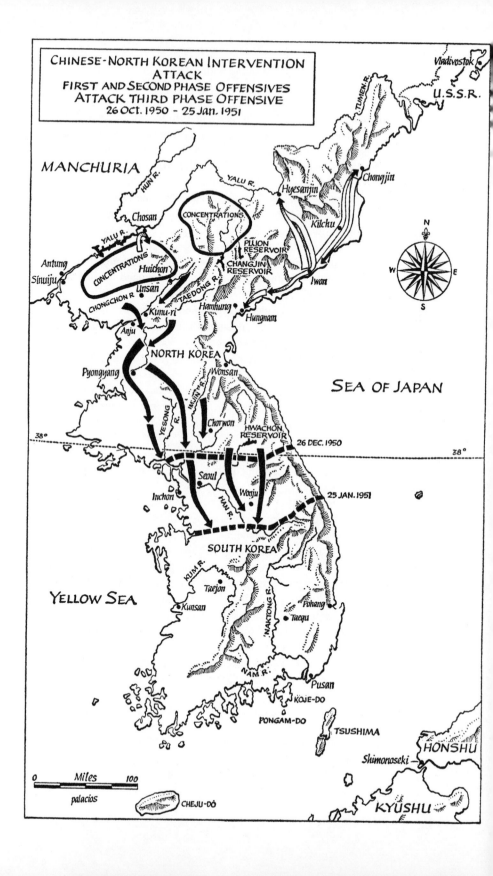

CHINESE-NORTH KOREAN INTERVENTION
ATTACK
FIRST AND SECOND PHASE OFFENSIVES
ATTACK THIRD PHASE OFFENSIVE
26 OCT. 1950 - 25 Jan. 1951

Vladivostok

U.S.S.R.

MANCHURIA

HUN R.

YALU R.

Chongjin

Hyesanjin

Chosan

Kilchu

CONCENTRATIONS

PUJON
RESERVOIR

YALU R.

CONCENTRATIONS

Huichon

CHANGJIN
RESERVOIR

Antung

Unsan

Iwon

Sinuiju

CHONGCHON R.

Kunu-ri

Hamhung

Anju

Hungnam

NORTH KOREA

Pyongyang

Wonsan

SEA OF JAPAN

YESONG R.

IMJIN R.

Chorwon

TAEDONG R.

HWACHON
RESERVOIR

26 DEC. 1950

38°

38°

Seoul

Wonju

25 JAN. 1951

Inchon

HAN R.

SOUTH KOREA

KUM R.

Taejon

NAKTONG R.

Pohang

YELLOW SEA

Kunsan

Taegu

NAM R.

Pusan

KOJE-DO

PONGAM-DO

TSUSHIMA

HONSHU

Shimonoseki

N

W   E

S

0   Miles   100

palacios

CHEJU-DO

KYUSHU

istration to cross the 38th parallel, the posturing of MacArthur, the murmurings of the Joint Chiefs of Staff, the bravery of the soldiers, the dreams of Communist banishment from Korea all toppled into disaster.

Three hundred thousand enemy soldiers, after moving by night and hiding in ravines and forest by day, waited in icy silence across the paths of the Eighth Army and the Tenth Corps.[63] After dark on November 25 a massive counterattack, accompanied by weird bugle calls and whistles, fairly exploded around the Eighth Army. In frigid and harrowing nights and days the western front under Walker buckled as the Eighth Army again retreated to the Chongchon River, unable to call for help from the Tenth Corps across the Taebaek range. The Tenth Corps, itself isolated, was staggering under its own deep troubles, as Almond's 5th and 7th marine regiments were cut off near the Changjin Reservoir. By November 28 the entire United Nations offensive had collapsed.

At 6:15 A.M. on the twenty-eighth Bradley telephoned Truman to read him a message from MacArthur. Grimly, the Korean commander reported that the United Nations did not have sufficient forces in the field to contain the Chinese attack.

"We face an entirely new war," he said.[64]

Harriman saw Truman before 9 o'clock and urged him to take the lead in clarifying people's thoughts and restoring unity in the United Nations. Truman replied that he, too, felt that a firm reaction was the right course. He ventured that the Chinese had been emboldened to attack because of what he called the efforts in the recent political campaign to discredit the administration's foreign policy. Later in the day he specifically blamed the McCormick newspapers [the *Chicago Tribune* and the *Washington Times-Herald*], the Hearst newspapers, and Roy Howard, head of Scripps-Howard Newspapers, as well as McCarthy and others who had been attacking Acheson.[65]

After talking with Harriman, Truman held his usual morning meeting with his staff, the members of which knew nothing as yet of MacArthur's message. Truman began without mentioning it and went through the run of daily business as if nothing out of the ordinary were happening. When the routine matters were out of the way he seemed to brace himself, as was noted by John Hersey, the author, who was permitted to attend the conference while working on a profile of Truman for the *New Yorker*.

"For a few moments," Hersey wrote, "he shifted papers back and forth and straightened a pair of scissors and two paper cutters. . . . He had suddenly drooped a little; it appeared that something he would have liked to forget was back in his mind, close behind his hugely magnified eyes.

" 'We've got a terrific situation on our hands,' Truman said in a very quiet, solemn voice. 'General Bradley called me at six-fifteen this morning. He told me a terrible message had come from General MacArthur.' "

In the hush Truman summarized the message and some of the things that would have to be done in Washington.

"In outlining his concrete plans and acts," Hersey wrote, "the President had hidden, as indeed he had all through the staff meeting up to this point, his feelings about this new development, with which he had lived for only about four hours. Now he paused for a few seconds, and suddenly all his driven-down emotions seemed to pour into his face. His mouth drew tight, his cheeks flushed. For a moment, it almost seemed as if he would sob. Then, in a voice that was incredibly calm and quiet, considering what could be read on his face—a voice of absolute personal courage—he said, 'This is the worst situation we have had yet. We'll just have to meet it as we've met all the rest. I've talked already this morning with Bradley, Marshall, Acheson, Harriman and Snyder, and they all agree with me that we're capable of meeting this thing. I know you fellows will work with us on it, and that we'll meet it.' ''[66]

This time, however, the damage was irreparable.

Acheson appeared before an executive session of the Senate Foreign Relations Committee. He said, ''I think it is impossible to over estimate the seriousness of this whole matter, not merely the immediate military situation in Korea but what this means.'' The Chinese counterattack, he warned, brought the danger of world war ''very close.'' We have got to face the possibility now that anything can happen anywhere at any time.''[67]

Truman convened the National Security Council.[68] The emphasis of the proceedings was on avoiding a general war with China and on intensifying American mobilization. Bradley said that two hundred enemy bombers in Manchuria posed a dangerous threat to the crowded, vulnerable American airfields in Korea and Japan. These were essential to the delivery of supplies to troops in the field.

Vice-President Barkley alluded to MacArthur's ''home by Christmas'' remark. Truman said that care must be taken lest MacArthur lose face. Someone ventured that the general may not have made such a statement. He made it, Truman said.[69]

Marshall declared that the United States must not get ''sewed up'' in Korea but must find a way out without loss of honor. General Collins was confident that MacArthur could hold a line at the narrowest point of the Korean peninsula, north of the 38th parallel. Truman shared his belief.

Acheson said that the United States must extricate itself from the Korean involvement. He reasoned that the Chinese could not be defeated in Korea because they could always commit more forces than the United States. He thought it imperative to find a defense line and turn it over to ROK troops as soon as possible. He said, however, that it would be ''disastrous'' for the United States to pull its troops out at the moment.

Admiral Sherman said that if Chinese bombers attacked from Manchuria, the United States would have to strike back or it could not maintain its position in Korea. Truman agreed but said he would meet that problem when it arose. He met with the Cabinet also that day. Matthew Connelly recorded a summary of his statement: ''We can't take any action in new crisis until the U. N. has a chance to take political action. The situation is very serious and can develop into complete involvement in total war.''[70]

The Korean disaster unloosed political and diplomatic turmoil. Europe and the United States were knocked into the worst war scare since the eve of Munich in 1938. "I think the next three days," Senator A. Willis Robertson, of Virginia, said on the twenty-eighth, "will determine whether we are to be at war with China and Soviet Russia." To his colleagues Acheson described the mood at the United Nations as being one of "a virtual state of panic." James Reston reported that "there is no doubt that United States leadership in the Western world has been damaged by President Truman's acceptance of the bold MacArthur offensive. . . ."[71] Truman himself turned the pressure up to the bursting point on November 30 by answering questions at a press conference in a way that allowed frightened people fed by excited news stories to believe that the atomic bomb might be used in Korea and at MacArthur's discretion.

The press conference was held at a time of enormous stress. The Pentagon was alarmed over the safety of the Tenth Corps. MacArthur poked a hole in what was becoming a hornets' nest by requesting authority to negotiate with Chiang Kai-shek for the use of Nationalist troops in Korea, a policy that MacArthur and the administration had previously rejected. The Joint Chiefs replied that calling for Chiang's help might disrupt the alliance of United Nations members in Korea. The chiefs said:

> It might extend hostilities to Formosa and other areas. Incidentally, our position of leadership in the Far East is being most seriously compromised in the United Nations. The utmost care will be necessary to avoid the disruption of the essential Allied lineup. . . .[72]

MacArthur had stated in his message of the twenty-eighth that the Chinese objective was "the complete destruction of all United Nations forces in Korea." Bradley later told the National Security Council meeting that the United States had no more ground forces available for Korea. A large proportion of the effective American army was in jeopardy in Korea, and, with rising apprehension, the American people came to realize this. Early on the morning of the thirtieth a message was received from MacArthur that massive Chinese reinforcements would compel the Eighth Army to continue "to replace to the rear."[73]

It was in this atmosphere then that Truman opened his memorable press conference later that morning. Two and a half years earlier he had decided to make a stand in the American zone of Berlin, even though it was not yet clear whether the airlift could sustain the zone indefinitely against the Soviet blockade of the German capital. That decision affected the modern history of Germany and hence of Europe. When Truman entered his press conference on November 30, his military advisers had not yet resolved the question of whether United Nations troops could hang on in Korea against the Chinese onslaught. But Truman announced that the struggle would not be abandoned—a decision that was to affect the modern history of Asia.

He said that the United States would rapidly increase its total military strength, for which he would ask Congress for more money—about $18 billion, as it turned out. "The request," he said, "will include a substantial amount for the Atomic Energy Commission, in addition to large amounts for the army, the navy and the air force."[74]

A reporter asked if it was up to the United Nations whether Manchuria would be attacked.

"Yes, entirely," Truman replied.

The reporter began another question, "In other words, if the United Nations resolution should authorize General MacArthur to go further than he has, he will ——"

Truman interrupted, "We will take whatever steps are necessary to meet the military situation, just as we always have."

"Will that include the atomic bomb?" asked Jack Doherty, of the New York *Daily News.*

During precarious days of the Pusan perimeter Truman had been asked by a reporter whether he was considering using the atomic bomb and he answered, "No."[75] This time, in reply to Doherty, he said, "That includes every weapon we have."

Paul R. Leach, of the Chicago *Daily News,* then asked, "Does that mean that there is active consideration of the use of the atomic bomb?"

Truman might have ended the discussion there if he had replied that at his level of the government no new consideration was being given to using the bomb, which would have been, on all evidence, true. Instead, he answered: "There has always been consideration of its use. I don't want to see it used. It is a terrible weapon, and it should not be used on innocent men, women and children who have nothing whatever to do with this military aggression. That happens when it is used."

Civilian and military officials had on numerous occasions speculated about whether the United States might have to use the atomic bomb in Korea. At least three instances are on record where, around the time of the press conference, formal consideration was given, at a lower level of the government, to using the bomb.

At the request of Paul Nitze, General Herbert B. Loper, who was the assistant for atomic energy in the army, had gone to the State Department on November 4 to discuss the question of dropping atomic bombs on Chinese troops and artillery in North Korea. Nitze speculated that a few bombs so aimed would not inflict heavy civilian casualties but might deter further Chinese intervention. After the conference, however, he noted in a memorandum: "It does not appear that in present circumstances the atomic bomb would be militarily decisive in Korea, and there is a serious possibility that its use might bring the Soviet Union into the war. Furthermore its use would help arouse the peoples of Asia against us."[76]

After a study suggested by General Collins, the joint strategic survey committee submitted a report on November 29, the day before the press conference. The report, whether Truman yet knew of it or not, held that a situation might develop in which nuclear weapons would be necessary to save American troops in Korea from being overrun. Another arm of the Joint Chiefs of Staff—the joint strategic plans committee—also submitted a report, on December 3. It said that in case of evacuation of American troops, nuclear weapons should be used against targets of opportunity if necessary to avert a major disaster. The committee recommended that immediate preparations should be made for employing nuclear weapons in the Far East.

The Joint Chiefs did not act on either of these studies, and both were withdrawn from circulation a few weeks later when the situation in Korea seemed less desperate.[77] Still they are a reminder that if the Korean War had taken a worse turn, Truman might have had to face all over again the decision he had made at the time of Hiroshima, except that now the Soviet Union was armed with the atomic bomb, too.

At the press conference, just when the question of the atomic bomb seemed to have been disposed of, Merriman Smith, of the United Press, asked for a recapitulation. Although this led to mischief, it was a fair enough request for a reporter who wanted to be certain that out of the rapid discussion he was clear as to just what the president had meant on a sensitive subject. In effect giving Truman an opportunity to restate the case unmistakably, Smith asked, "Did we understand you clearly that the use of the atomic bomb is under active consideration?"

"Always has been," Truman replied. "It is one of our weapons."

"Does that mean, Mr. President," asked Robert G. Nixon, of the old International News Service, "use against military objectives, or civilian——"

Whether or not he was aware that the reporters were now developing a big story, Truman responded:

"It's a matter that the military people will have to decide. I'm not a military authority that passes on those things."

Then:

Mr. President [began the next questioner], you said this depends on United Nations action. Does that mean that we wouldn't use the atomic bomb except on a United Nations authorization?

No [answered the president], it doesn't mean that at all. The action against Communist China depends on the action of the United Nations. The military commander in the field will have charge of the use of weapons, as he always has.

Truman failed to note that the Atomic Energy Act of 1946 provides that only the president may order the use of atomic weapons. Reporters who knew, or should have known, of the provision bolted for telephones at the end of the conference with the uppermost impression that Truman had indicated that MacArthur might give the order. Truman's language had been a perfect prescription for causing confusion among overexcited reporters working in a hasty, competitive situation.

Given the mindless competition for headline news then prevailing among the three wire services at the White House, the consequences were inevitable. Within minutes the United Press bulletined:

PRESIDENT TRUMAN SAID TODAY THAT THE UNITED STATES HAS UNDER CONSIDERATION USE OF THE ATOMIC BOMB IN CONNECTION WITH THE WAR IN KOREA.

A similar Associated Press lead reported further down in the story that Truman had said that the decision on whether to drop atomic bombs was one for the commander in the field. Shortly, the White House issued a statement saying that Truman's words had not changed the strategic situation in any way and that the president had not authorized the use of nuclear weapons.[78] The news from the press conference had traveled so fast, however, that huge headlines based on wire service stories blossomed across the country.

The news shocked delegates at the United Nations, especially those from Asia and the Middle East. A Saudi Arabian diplomat told Mrs. Roosevelt, a member of the American delegation to the General Assembly, as she reported it to Washington: "The people of the whole Asiatic continent would never understand why the American people had decided to use the atomic bomb against them. They would regard it as an action of the white race against the colored races. They would never forget that the atomic bomb was used first against the Japanese and later against the Chinese, but never against any white peoples. This fact would have a disastrous effect upon the relations of the United States with the rest of the world for years to come."[79]

From Paris to New Delhi headlines blazed. In Finland they conveyed the notion that Truman had already given MacArthur the fateful order. In Rome *Il Momento* reported that bombers were ready to take off on one hour's notice. The headline in the *Kurier Codzienny* in Poland was ATOMIC BOMB PLANS OF TRUMAN, ACHESON & CO. A Socialist newspaper in Italy, *Avanti,* carried the headline WASHINGTON WILL DISREGARD UNITED NATIONS. The *Times of India* ran an editorial under the heading NO! NO! NO![80]

The sharpest reaction occurred in London. At the very moment the news arrived, the Labour government headed by Prime Minister Clement Attlee was embroiled in a debate in the House of Commons in the midst of pervasive fear over a drift to general war in Asia.

Parliament throbbed with anxiety lest MacArthur drag the United Nations into war with China, diverting American assistance from NATO and leaving Western Europe vulnerable to Soviet aggression. Shortly after the presidential press conference, therefore, Attlee felt himself under so much pressure that he sent a message to Truman asking if he could come to the White House at once for talks. The president agreed, and the cheerless-looking prime minister descended on Washington in the midst of Truman's bleakest moment in office. Not since before Pearl Harbor had Americans been so deeply divided over foreign policy. Many newspapers were advocating a retreat from Korea to conserve United States power for a showdown with the Soviet Union on more favorable terrain. Republicans in Congress continued to demand the dismissal of Acheson, and McCarthy said that the president should be impeached if he did not accept Chiang Kai-shek's offer of troops for Korea.

On December 5 the Truman-Attlee talks ran late into the afternoon, and since the evening was to be taken up with an occasion very special for Truman— Margaret Truman's first big Washington concert as a soprano—he and Ross had time to confer only briefly about the news the press secretary was to give out. The relationship between Truman and Ross was an affecting one. They had been youthful friends, graduating together from Independence High School in 1901 when Ross was valedictorian. Since Mrs. Truman had been in the class, too, Charlie Ross was very close to the Truman family. When Truman suddenly became president, he asked Ross, then chief of the Washington Bureau of the *St. Louis Post-Dispatch* and a recent winner of a Pulitzer Prize, to be his press secretary, a job Ross took reluctantly. In the White House the two had gone through many an ordeal together. A wise and kind counselor to the president, Ross was a lovable man, melancholy, tired, and bent. The recent weeks, especially the trip to Wake Island, had been exhausting for him. After conferring together, Truman returned to Blair House to dress for the evening, and Ross went to his office to brief reporters before joining the Trumans after dinner.

Following the briefing he agreed to repeat some of his comments for television. While portable equipment was being assembled at his desk, his secretary admonished him good-naturedly not to mumble. "I don't mumble," Ross said. "I speak very distinctly." The next instant he slumped sideways in his high leather chair, a cigarette falling from his lips. Frantically, the White House physician, General Graham, was summoned from his office on a floor below, but all efforts at resuscitation failed. General Graham telephoned Truman at Blair House that his friend was dead of a coronary occlusion.[81] "Dad was shattered by the news," Margaret Truman wrote.[82]

He and Mrs. Truman were getting ready to escort Prime Minister Attlee to Constitution Hall for Margaret's concert. It had loomed as the first warm moment for the president in a long time, although the crushing news from the White House left him and his wife in a sad dilemma. Before Margaret went on the stage should they tell her about Charlie Ross? They decided not to lest the news prove too upsetting. Constitution Hall was packed with a friendly audience, which applauded Miss Truman enthusiastically. It was a thrilling experience for the Truman family. The president used to tell his friends that Margaret was the apple of his eye. She was never more so than in the glow that night. He was overjoyed by the performance.

The next morning he arose in Blair House at his usual hour of five-thirty and turned to the review of the concert in the *Washington Post,* written by that newspaper's respected music critic, Paul Hume. Hume commented that Miss Truman was extremely attractive on the stage and had a pleasant voice. The rest of what he wrote was more, obviously, than Truman was willing to bear at that time of unceasing frustrations.

On Miss Truman's performance, Hume commented, "She is flat a good deal of the time. . . . she cannot sing with anything approaching professional finish. . . ." Although he regretted having to say so, he concluded that the soprano "cannot sing very well."

The soprano's father went straight to the White House before any of his staff had arrived. Pen in hand, the sixty-six-year-old president slashed off a note to the thirty-four-year-old critic, put a three-cent stamp on the envelope and summoned Samuel Mitchell, an attendant. A delightful man, Mitchell— "Mitch"—had been a porter on the Roosevelt trains and had so charmed the late president and his staff that he was hired by the White House. When Mitch answered the summons that morning, Truman observed that it was a pleasant day. Mitch agreed that it was. It was the kind of morning, Truman suggested, on which Mitch might like to take a walk. Mitch was not averse. Truman handed him the letter and asked that during his walk Mitch post it in a mailbox on the street. In this way the correspondence circumvented the White House staff, which had a responsibility for protecting the president from himself in such moods.[83] It took only two days for the substance of the letter to leak to a shocked public. The text was as follows:

Mr. Hume: I've just read your lousy review of Margarets concert. I've come to the conclusion that you are an 'eight ulcer man on four ulcer pay.'[84]

It seems to me that you are a frustrated old man who wishes he could have been successful. When you write such poppy-cock as was in the back section of the paper you work for it shows conclusively that you're off the beam and at least four of your ulcers are at work.

Some day I hope to meet you. When that happens you'll need a new nose, a lot of beefsteak for black eyes, and perhaps a supporter below!

Pegler [Westbrook Pegler was a columnist antagonistic to Truman], a gutter snipe is a gentleman along side you. I hope you'll accept that statement as a worse insult than a reflection on your ancestry.[85]

29. *National Emergency*

DECEMBER WAS a grim time of holding on in Korea amid doubts in the United Nations and suffering and death in the frozen mountains and valleys below the Yalu. The crisis was made more ominous by tough opposition by MacArthur to Truman's policy of limited war. In conferences with General Collins in Tokyo, MacArthur set the stage for a serious split with the president by urging that the United States use its full power against China. To do less, he declared, would amount to "surrender." Unless reinforcements were sent, and Collins promised none, MacArthur maintained that the United Nations should evacuate Korea.[1]

As the Chinese offensive swept on, many Americans were in dread over the possibility of war with China and perhaps with the Soviet Union. Although no football fan, Truman kept his annual engagement to attend the Army-Navy game on December 2 out of anxiety that cancellation of the trip would cause public fright.[2] On his return from Philadelphia that night he called a meeting in the White House, at which General Bradley said that within forty-eight to seventy-two hours the worsening military situation would reach what he called a crash state.[3]

On the battlefield, MacArthur was "in very serious trouble," Truman jotted afterward. "We must get him out of it, if we can. The conference was the most solemn one I've had since the Atomic Bomb conference in Berlin.* . . . *It looks very bad.*"[4]

Its right flank smashed, the Eighth Army was carrying out a fighting retreat after having fallen back across the Chongchon River. By the time of Truman's journey to Philadelphia the decimated 2nd Division was no longer fit for combat. During the retreat the gap between the Eighth Army and the Tenth Corps widened, to the danger of Almond's troops, as the Joint Chiefs had feared. Units of the Tenth Corps were trying to fight their way back to Hungnam on the east coast to be evacuated by ship.

The day before Truman went to Philadelphia a meeting at the Pentagon wrestled with the crisis. Acheson hoped that a firm defense line could be thrown across the Korean peninsula. That would not be possible if losses in the current retreats were heavy, Bradley said. Marshall, on the other hand, believed that it might prove feasible to dig in somewhere on the east and the west coasts of

---

*Truman was referring to his last-minute talks with his advisers during the Potsdam Conference before the first atomic bomb was dropped on Hiroshima on August 6, 1945.

Korea, if forming a line were out of the question. The dark cloud over the meeting, however, was the danger of Chinese or even Soviet air assault, which would have required the United States to strike back by air, risking a broadening of the war. Were that to happen, Collins warned, the only hope of saving American forces might lie in using the atomic bomb, or threatening to use it.

Bedell Smith, director of central intelligence, said flatly that the United States should get out of Korea because the Soviets could drain American resources in Asia and thereby make it impossible for the United States to rearm Europe. Lovett cautioned that the loss of Korea might jeopardize Japan.[5]

By the time of the meeting the next evening, after the Army-Navy game, the military situation was viewed so pessimistically that high presidential advisers were considering the necessity of obtaining a cease-fire agreement with the Chinese.

"General Bradley thought that the troops from the Tenth Corps could be evacuated in five days at least," Ambassador Jessup noted in a record of the session, "but he wondered about the manner of the evacuation unless the cease-fire were secured."

"General Marshall," according to Jessup, "said that even a Dunkirk type of evacuation might be prejudiced if the Chinese brought in their air."

A discussion ensued as to the price the Chinese might ask for a settlement. One demand, Acheson said, might be United Nations abandonment of Korea; another, a seat in the United Nations; a third, American abandonment of Formosa; a fourth, Chinese participation in negotiation of the Japanese peace treaty. The last would foreshadow an effort to get the United States out of Japan, Acheson said.

More bad news came the next day. MacArthur reported that the retreating Eighth Army would not be able to hold Pyongyang and would have to fall back to the area of Seoul, reviving horrid memories of the previous June. In despairing tones MacArthur told of the exhaustion of his outnumbered forces and the danger of their ultimate destruction unless heavy reinforcements were sent. His directives were utterly outmoded by the new circumstances, he observed. In words that foreshadowed calamitous conflict between himself and his superiors he added, "This calls for political decisions and strategic plans . . . adequate fully to meet the realities involved."[6]

The arrival of MacArthur's message did not find the administration in a mood for new political decisions and strategic plans. The Joint Chiefs of Staff wanted the general to regroup the scattered forces at his disposal, and Truman approved the following directive to him: "We consider that the preservation of your forces is now the primary consideration. Consolidation of forces into beachheads is concurred in."[7] At that moment one army division was left in the United States. No other army or national guard divisions would be ready before spring.[8]

In the wake of MacArthur's message Acheson, Marshall, and their staffs held a gloomy meeting in the Pentagon. Beset by fresh doubts about the safety of American forces, Acheson asked if the time had come when a cease-fire was imperative, perhaps with restoration of a dividing line at the 38th parallel. He said that the United States faced a bitter choice, encompassing the possibility of its being expelled from the Far East.[9] From small beginnings Korea had become a great crisis that might conceivably have resulted in the realignment of power in Asia if American forces were overrun and Washington had to sue for terms.

General Lawton Collins, the army chief of staff, flew to the Far East for conferences with MacArthur and an assessment of the situation on the battlefields. Collins sent back reports of MacArthur's opposition to limiting the war to Korea as well as MacArthur's views about imminent evacuation of Korea unless reinforcements were sent. At almost precisely that moment opinion in the highest councils in Washington was beginning to shift in the opposite direction from MacArthur's.

At a meeting in the State Department on December 4 Dean Rusk made what the newspapers, if they had but known of it, would have called a "fighting speech." He berated the dejected mood among the military. Many a time, he said, the British had had their backs to the wall and had held on against overwhelming odds. American forces, he continued, should be regrouped to compel the Chinese to make a major effort at great cost to themselves in casualties if they were to drive the United Nations out of Korea. The United States would pay a dear price in Asia and in Europe for surrendering Korea, he warned. Having said that, Rusk made a proposal that would have taken the public's breath away, if the public could have heard it. The future secretary of state suggested that MacArthur be relieved of his command in Korea and assigned to spend full time on the Japanese peace treaty and Collins be given command of United Nations forces in the field.[10] The record does not note any comments on this statement.

After the meeting Acheson telephoned Marshall and said that, as he recalled his own words, "what we needed was dogged determination to find a place to hold and fight the Chinese to a standstill. This was a far better stance for the United States than to talk about withdrawing from Korea or going off on a policy of our own of bombing and blockading China." Marshall agreed, but on two conditions. One was that the Tenth Corps could be successfully evacuated. The other was that, as Acheson remembered it, "we must not dig ourselves into a hole without an exit."[11]

Meanwhile Truman by his own later account had been put in a dudgeon by self-serving, controversial statements given to the press by MacArthur.[12] In any case Truman could not have been pleased with MacArthur for the predicament in which the disastrous offensive had left the administration. At least the president was resolved that the general would make no further public remarks without clearance from Washington.

Two examples of such remarks that particularly rankled the administration occurred on December 1 when MacArthur answered questions by editors of *U. S. News & World Report* and gave a statement to Hugh Baillie, president of the United Press. Taken together these commentaries contained public criticism of United States policy by a military officer and intimation that European allies were "selfish" and "shortsighted" for resisting stronger measures in the Far

East. This at a moment when Washington was having some difficulty holding the British in line because of London's fear that MacArthur would enlarge the war.

The magazine's editors had asked MacArthur whether his operations were handicapped by the ban on hot pursuit over Manchuria, imposed by the administration because of objections by allies. MacArthur replied, "An enormous handicap, without precedent in military history." In his statement to Baillie, MacArthur characterized criticism in the European press as due to a somewhat selfish and myopic view resulting from Europe's preoccupation with its own immediate security. Thus, he noted, Europeans regarded the use of resources to stabilize conditions in Asia as resources diverted from their own security.

"This is, of course, fallacious reasoning," MacArthur said. "Any breach of freedom in the East carries with it a sinister threat to freedom in the West. . . . If the fight is not waged . . . here, it will indeed be fought, and possibly lost, on the battlefields of Europe." [13]

On December 5 Truman issued instructions that speeches, press releases, or other public statements dealing with foreign or military policy were to be cleared by the responsible departments in Washington. MacArthur was not mentioned by name. Nevertheless, the instructions applied specifically to "officials in the field as well as to those in Washington." Military commanders were directed to exercise "extreme caution in public statements." The Joint Chiefs of Staff immediately forwarded a copy of the instructions to MacArthur. [14]

From these events emerged legal grounds for a change of command in Korea.

The Truman-Attlee talks covered a five-day period, starting on December 4. At the outset Truman, who came to admire his guest, reminded Attlee that the United States had obligations in the Far East equal to those in Europe, even though, as he drew the distinction, the European obligations were primary. He said, in the words of the minutes, that "we are not going to run out on our obligations" wherever they were. [15]

Attlee was fearful above all that the United States would get into a war with China, indeed that the American people would demand it if their forces were pinned down indefinitely in Korea with heavy losses. "The President said," according to the minutes, "that such demands are now being made. We need a united effort at home. Huge appropriations are being made. He hoped that the line could be held in Korea until the situation was better for negotiation. All of his military advisers tell him there is no chance to do this, but he still wanted to try." [16]

He and Acheson and Marshall were agreed that if allied troops had to evacuate Korea, the Chinese would have to drive them out as the British had been driven off the beaches at Dunkirk. While this would be a disaster, as they recognized, it would not be the disgrace of deliberately sailing off and leaving the South Koreans to their fate. Truman discussed the subject at the Anglo-American talks:

He thought that if we abandoned Korea the South Koreans would all be murdered and that we could not face that in view of the fact that they have fought bravely on our side and we have put in so much to help them. We may be subjected to bombing from Manchuria by the Russians and Chinese Communists which might destroy everything we have. He was worried about the situation. He did not like to go into a situation such as this and then to admit that we were licked. He would rather fight it to a finish. That was the way he had felt from the beginning. . . . He wanted to make it perfectly plain here that we do not desert our friends when the going is rough."[17]

Eventually, he decided that if withdrawal should become necessary, the ROK army and the Rhee government should be evacuated with the rest of the United Nations forces.[18]

At an informal gathering after a dinner during the talks Truman said that the United States was going to remain in Korea and fight. A memorandum on the occasion quoted him, "If we have support from the others, fine; but if not . . . we would stay on anyway."[19]

In his eagerness to avoid war with China, Attlee's objective was to bring about cease-fire negotiations between the United Nations and China. He assumed that as part of the bargain the Chinese would want a seat in the United Nations and a Formosan settlement. He soon found, however, that Truman and his advisers were in no mood to link Formosa and a United Nations seat with a cease-fire arrangement. The administration disapproved of the seating of the Chinese Communists both on principle and on practical grounds of domestic politics.[20]

The China lobby and its friends had seized upon the Korean War as the ultimate reason why Peking should be barred from membership in the United Nations. The war cry was that the Communists should not be allowed to shoot their way in. To Attlee's arguments about the wisdom of bringing the Peking government into the United Nations, Truman replied that the issue was "political dynamite in the United States"—so much so, he added subsequently, that "we could hardly talk about negotiating the question. . . ."[21]

Acheson wanted cease-fire negotiations to be limited to the question of Korea.[22] He had told Bevin earlier "that if the UN should permit the aggressor to inject other issues and extort concessions for desisting from unlawful conduct, the ability of the UN and the free world to prevent aggression would be totally lost."[23] Attlee lamented that the Formosan issue was complicated by Chiang Kai-shek's occupancy of the island. Truman interposed to say that, like Communist Chinese membership in the United Nations, Formosa was a difficult problem for the administration because "Chiang has so many converts here."[24] Yielding on either of these issues would also, of course, have brought Truman into conflict with MacArthur.

In words that could have been spoken by MacArthur, Marshall declared that the United States would be weakened greatly if Formosa were turned over to Communist China. In unfriendly hands, he argued, the island would be a wedge between Japan to the north and the Philippines and Indonesia to the south, which he described as island defenses for the United States. He said, according to the minutes: "We would be taking a step to liquidate our position in the Pacific if we surrendered [Formosa]. It is hard enough anyway to settle the Japanese question. From the military point of view it [would be] very dangerous to give up Formosa."[25]

In strong support Truman said he could not agree to give Formosa to the Chinese Communists lest the flank of the United Nations position in Korea be exposed. Furthermore, he "had to consider the political situation here."[26]

Disturbed by Truman's press conference of November 30, Attlee had come to Washington seeking an arrangement under which the atomic bomb would not be used without prior Anglo-American consultation and perhaps formal agreement. Under Acheson's attentive eye Truman declined to go that far.[27] The president simply assured Attlee that he would not consider using the bomb without consulting the British government. Attlee asked if this understanding should be put in writing, whereupon, as Jessup's notes on the conversation record, "the President replied no that it would not be in writing, that if a man's word wasn't any good it wasn't made any better by writing it down."[28] As Acheson reminded Truman, a formal agreement would have exceeded the president's authority and would have been unacceptable to Congress. When the understanding was finally reduced to the language of the communiqué, it boiled down to an expression of the president's "desire" to keep the prime minister "at all times informed" of any developments that might alter the president's disinclination to use the atomic bomb. On his return to London Attlee confided to his cabinet that he was "entirely satisfied."[29]

Attlee also reported, in the words of the British cabinet minutes, that at the outset of the talks the Truman administration "had been considering the idea of a limited war against China by way of an economic blockade and stirring up internal trouble in China." According to the American minutes, what Truman told Attlee at their first meeting was that if China rejected a cease-fire and moved major forces south of the 38th parallel, the United Nations should mobilize against China "such political and economic measures as are available. . . ." He also spoke of the possibility "of some military action which would harass the Chinese Communists and of efforts which could be made to stimulate anti-communist resistance within China itself, including the exploitation of Nationalist capabilities."[30] When the conference ended, according to Attlee, "the President's advisers had developed doubts about the value of a limited war. . . ." By that time, Collins had returned from Korea convinced that United Nations forces could hold a line somewhere south of Seoul, at least for a considerable time.

In the Truman-Attlee talks the British did not ask the United States to yield on Formosa. The two sides agreed to disagree on membership for Peking in the United Nations. Most significant, however, were signs that a new turn was in the making. It was clear that the United States had lost hope of unifying Korea by force and would be willing to settle on a line at or near the 38th parallel.[31] Truman and Attlee were in full accord against widening the war in Asia—a decision unacceptable to MacArthur and some of his Republican allies in Congress.

Fortified by their party's successes in November, these Republicans planted dynamite in the form of demands that the Nationalist forces on Formosa be unleashed against the Chinese mainland. Some Republicans fell in line with their House leader, Joe Martin, when he proposed that the Truman administration support Chiang in opening a "second front" on the mainland. Before long an effort to enlist support for this Republican position was to trigger the greatest explosion of its kind in the history of the United States.

On December 15, 1950, Truman announced on national television, "I will issue a proclamation tomorrow morning declaring that a national emergency exists." He said: "Our homes, our nation, all the things we believe in are in great danger. This danger has been created by the rulers of the Soviet Union."[32] Partly, the motive for the proclamation was psychological. In a memorandum to Acheson and Webb, Edward W. Barrett, assistant secretary of state for public affairs, said: "The American people are getting the impression that their Washington leadership is utterly confused and sterile. They are saying, in effect: 'Don't just sit there; do something.' "[33]

The proclamation also was considered useful, legally, in facilitating the letting of contracts, as the administration moved to attain by 1952 the goals for military manpower and procurement that previously had been set for 1954.[34]

In his televised speech the president broached plans for what was to be a new chapter in the history of the Truman administration. This was a program of controls aimed at making the economy accelerate without overheating.

In his first formal message to Congress on the war, on July 19, Truman had made a modest request for powers to allocate materials, grant production loans, establish priorities, and control consumer credit. He refrained from asking for stricter controls. For one thing, he did not wish to create an impression that the country was preparing for general war. For another, he did not believe stronger controls were necessary yet. "If a sharp rise in prices should make it necessary," he said, "I shall not hesitate to recommend the more drastic measures of price control and rationing." With the public already protesting the surge in prices since the start of the war, Congress took no chances. In addition to voting Truman the powers he sought, Congress also gave him discretionary authority to impose wage and price controls.

At first Truman resisted using them and appealed instead for voluntary restraints by business, labor, and consumers. This effort fell short. Even before the Korean War the economy had been rebounding from the recession of 1949–50, so that the sudden new spending for defense added great pressure on prices. On September 26 the Council of Economic Advisers warned that "the price-wage spiral is already under way, and it will accelerate."[35] When the Chinese intervened in Korea and the administration planned to increase mobilization, prices shot up again under the certainty of greater demand.

The first attempt at selective controls was made in mid-December when the government ordered a rollback in automobile prices to levels of December 1. Then wages in the automobile industry were frozen until March 1, 1951. Earlier the Federal Reserve Board had squeezed consumers by requiring higher down-payments and a shorter repayment period on loans for the purchase of automobiles, appliances, and furniture. The Federal Reserve also had raised rediscount rates from 1.5 to 1.75 percent. Easy credit for new houses was restricted. Upon announcing that he would proclaim the existence of a national emergency, Truman said that a new series of control orders would be announced shortly.

In retrospect, the whole business of economic controls contributed a great deal to making Truman's presidency a stormy one. For almost his first two years in office he went through a nerve-wracking time of trying to end some of the controls and extend others that had been imposed by Roosevelt during the Second World War. Washington fairly seethed with confusion and quarrels as Truman struggled to balance the interests of agriculture, labor, consumers, and business, big and small, during the upheaval of military demobilization and reconversion of the economy from wartime to peacetime production in 1945 and 1946. Ulitmately, what was left of wartime controls was blown apart by political pressures, public demand for goods that had been scarce during the war, and the intransigence of business, labor, and agriculture. In the process Truman's popularity was all but trampled into the ground. Finally a shortage of beef brought about by conflict over price controls led to Democratic defeat in the 1946 congressional elections.

Now, at the close of 1950, Truman was plunging back into the political hurly burly of controls. Not in a period of patriotism and willing sacrifice, such as attends a world war, but in that of the hugely unpopular limited war, he was taking upon himself the thankless burden of moving toward control of wages, prices, rent, production, and credit.

A bad year was ending with scarcely a rift in the clouds. American troops were back on South Korean soil. Mail was pouring into Congress asking, "Why does my son have to stay in Korea?" Truman's popularity continued to decline. The president and MacArthur were veering into a collision course as the administration asserted stricter control over strategy and tactics in Korea. And against the perceived dangers of Soviet aggression in Europe, a major effort was developing to reinforce NATO.

30. *1951: A Year of War, Mobilization, and the "Great Debate"*

THE YEAR 1951 DAWNED to the thunder of a new enemy offensive in Korea. After retaking the North Korean capital of Pyongyang, advancing Chinese forces drove across the 38th parallel in yet another invasion of South Korea. With little opposition they quickly captured Seoul as well as Inchon, stealing forever much of the luster of MacArthur's famous landing four months earlier. The CIA reported that "it is infeasible under existing conditions . . . to hold for a protracted period a position in Korea."[1]

In the midst of grave uncertainties came the making of a partisan rupture over foreign policy, such as Truman had feared at the time of the McCarthy onslaught. The fabric, in fact, had commenced to rip before the old year was out under the stress of shock over the Chinese intervention in Korea and opposition to Truman's decision to send American ground forces to Europe to strengthen NATO—a decision that he had announced in September 1950.

Doubtful that Europe could be defended now that the Soviets had atomic bombs, Taft had emerged from his victory in November urging a reexamination of United States foreign policy. A familiar isolationist voice was heard in December 1950 when, speaking at the University of Virginia, Joseph P. Kennedy, former ambassador to the Court of St. James's, advocated withdrawal from Korea. He said that Truman's policy had, among other things, failed to strengthen the Western Hemisphere. This was in tune with isolationist arguments before the Second World War in favor of regional defense of the United States. Thus Kennedy demanded that Truman stop committing resources to what Kennedy called an idle attempt "to hold the line of the Elbe or the line of the Rhine."[2]

The main controversy, however, broke after Truman's appointment a week later of General of the Army Dwight D. Eisenhower as supreme commander of NATO forces. The stage had been set when France finally agreed, under American pressure, to general discussions of future German participation in the defense of Europe without any further delay on a start of deploying NATO units. Europeans were outspoken in urging the selection of Eisenhower, who had led the Allies to victory in Europe in the Second World War. On December 18, 1950, the North Atlantic Council formally asked Truman to designate him; Truman complied.

The White House staff was highly pleased, ironically. "Our view," Charles

Murphy revealed later, "was, good, it will get Ike out of the political picture. It didn't look like he was going to be the Democratic candidate, and we thought the best thing was to get him out of politics."[3] Eben Ayers recalled that Matt Connelly, sometimes considered one of the shrewdest politicians in the White House then, said of Eisenhower, "Let's build him up so that the Republicans will think they are going to make him their nominee and then Eisenhower will pull the rug out from under them and leave them with no one."[4] Admiral Dennison, presidential naval aide, said afterward, "I won't go into all that went on while people were trying to find out whether General Eisenhower was a Republican or a Democrat, or whether he was going to run [in 1952]. . . ."[5] In taking leave from Columbia for his new role, of course, Eisenhower only enhanced his stature, visibility, popularity, and qualifications for the presidency.

On appointing him, Truman said that more American troops would be sent to Europe as soon as possible.[6] The next day Herbert Hoover went on television in New York and delivered a major challenge to administration policy.[7] Truman called the speech isolationist. The former president extolled the concept of a "Gibraltar of Western civilization." He did not advocate simply a "fortress America." Rather he urged that American policy concentrate on preservation of the Western Hemisphere by holding the Atlantic and Pacific Oceans along with the British Isles, Japan, the Philippines, and Formosa. He wanted the United States to shun intervention on the continents of Europe and Asia, saying that it would be "inviting another Korea" to send more troops or money to Europe before the West Europeans had armed themselves to the point of building "a sure dam against the Red flood."

When the new Eighty-second Congress convened in January 1951, Wherry and Representative Frederic R. Coudert, Jr., Republican, of New York, opened what was called at the time "the great debate" by introducing resolutions to put Congress on record against dispatch of American troops abroad without congressional approval.

The next day Truman was asked at his press conference whether he required congressional approval to send additional troops to Europe.

"No, I do not," he replied bluntly.[8]

The day after that Taft made a full-fledged attack in the Senate on Truman's policies, flatly opposing commitment of any American troops to Europe at that time.

"The president," Taft said, "has no power to agree to send American troops to fight in Europe a war between members of the Atlantic pact and the Soviet Union."[9]

Increasingly, he asserted, the administration was resorting to international agreements instead of treaties, thus bypassing the role of the Senate in giving its advice and consent.

In a large sense Taft and the noninterventionists were attacking the growth of foreign entanglements and the domination of the executive branch over national security policy. One of the thirteen senators who had voted against the North Atlantic Treaty, Taft insisted that the pact did not commit the United States to send troops to Europe in existing circumstances. "A new policy is being formulated without consulting Congress or the people," he said.[10] He likened Truman's decision on troops for NATO to the president's commitment of forces to Korea and repeated his charge of the previous July about presidential usurpation of power.[11]

Still, Taft did not favor abandoning Europe nor reneging on NATO commitments. He thought that by enlarging American air and naval power, which he favored, the United States could protect Europe more effectively than by commitment of a few divisions. In his State of the Union message three days later Truman sketched an alarming picture of the Soviet menace and ruled out "appeasement." Under the circumstances military strength was "the only realistic road to peace." "We are" he said, "preparing for a full wartime mobilization, if that should be necessary."[12]

Speaking before the National Press Club the next day, Taft said that he was "quite prepared to sit down with the president of the United States" or any other responsible administration official to discuss foreign policy. If this were an opportunity for collaboration with Taft, then Truman and Acheson coolly let it pass, feeling, probably, that the political and philosophical gap was too great.

In the Senate, Tom Connally, the Democratic chairman of the Foreign Relations Committee, voiced his confidence that the administration would consult Congress on troop commitments. When asked about this at a press conference, Truman stood up for what he considered his rights. As commander in chief, he said, he had the authority to send troops anywhere in the world. "This government," he declared, "will continue to live up to its obligations under the United Nations, and its other treaty obligations, and we will continue to send troops wherever it is necessary to uphold these obligations." He maintained that the administration made no moves without consulting Congress.

Q. In this particular case, with the debate raging in Congress over whether you do or do not have the authority to send troops to Europe—and Mr. Hoover said not another man or another dollar should be sent—the debate has been quite general. Do I understand that you will ask Congress for permission——

A. No.

Q. ——before sending troops——

A. No, you do not want to take that view of the thing. I said that—in case of necessity . . . for the defense of the Atlantic treaty countries—that Congress would be consulted before troops were sent. I don't ask their permission, I just consult them.[13]

Taft supported the Wherry resolution, and debate went on for weeks, highlighted by joint hearings by the Senate Armed Services and Foreign Relations committees. As a prologue Eisenhower, back from a quick tour of NATO capitals, addressed an informal meeting of the Senate and House of Representatives in the Library of Congress. So great were his prestige and popularity that he easily won heavy support for American military commitment to NATO. Western Europe, he said, "is so important to our future, our future is so definitely tied up with them that we cannot afford to do less than our best in making sure that it does not go down the drain."[14]

In his testimony at the hearings Eisenhower said that "we ought to begin to feel . . . really over the hump" if something on the order of forty divisions were to be deployed by NATO by the end of 1952. The anticipated size of the American component was still a secret. Because of questions raised by the controversy, however, Truman authorized Marshall to reveal in his own later testimony that the administration planned to deploy six American divisions in Europe—the two already there on occupation duty and four others. What with air force, navy, and service troops, the new divisions would bring to more than 180,000 the total United States military establishment in Europe.

Marshall testified that the Wherry resolution opposing the assignment of American troops to NATO until Congress had approved such a policy "involves the possibility of, in effect, completely canceling out and neutralizing the North Atlantic Treaty." He maintained that the administration was doing exactly what Congress had insisted upon when it approved the North Atlantic Treaty and the Mutual Defense Assistance Program, namely, executing a plan for the defense of the North Atlantic region.[15]

When the hearings ended Senator Mundt moved to prohibit the dispatch of four more divisions to Europe without approval by joint resolution of Congress. Truman refused to comment in public. He spoke his mind on the subject privately at a meeting with his advisers in Blair House in February or March. "You fellows have to understand something," he said, as one of them later recalled his words. "I have absolutely no intention of sending more than six divisions, but I'll be damned if I am going to permit Congress to limit me, if I can help it, because it may come back and haunt a successor of mine a hundred years from now."[16]

The Mundt amendment was defeated. The split over foreign policy was contained by the enduring consensus, in and out of Congress, that the defense of Europe was of primary concern to American security. Senators who denounced Truman's policy in Asia did not attempt to thwart his policy toward Europe. In the end the great debate simmered down to a sense-of-the-Senate resolution, adopted 69 to 21, having no binding effect on the president. The sense of the Senate, as thus expressed, was that Eisenhower should command NATO forces but that no ground troops in addition to the four new divisions should be sent to Europe without further congressional approval. In a public statement commending the action, Truman ignored the latter point entirely and hailed the Senate's action as "further evidence that the country stands firm in its support of the North Atlantic Treaty."[17]

While the debate was still in progress, the administration made its first comprehensive moves to check rising wages and prices. Wage and price controls having been authorized by Congress, Truman came under increasing pressure to use them. Gradually, the administration put in place a bureaucracy for economic controls similar to that established during the Second World War.

At the top was the policy-making Office of Defense Mobilization. Granting him broad powers, Truman named Charles Wilson, president of General Electric, as its director. In the Second World War Wilson had been vice chairman of the War Production Board. He was respected in Congress, and his background was thought to insure the cooperation of industry in mobilization and stabilization. As an outspoken industrialist, however, he had long aroused considerable hostility among Truman's political allies in labor. Truman was personally attracted to Wilson, who had risen in life from even more obscure origins than the president himself. Wilson had been reared in Hell's Kitchen on the west side of Manhattan Island by an impecunious widowed mother, who supported the two of them by working as a housekeeper and practical nurse. To ease her burdens Wilson quit school for good at the age of twelve and went to work as an office boy in a company that was later absorbed by General Electric. He climbed the ladder from there. In 1946 and 1947 he had handled a major task for Truman in chairing the President's Committee on Civil Rights. Its report, *To Secure These Rights*, was a point of departure for race relations in the United States.

Under the Office of Defense Mobilization was an operating organization, the Economic Stabilization Agency, headed by Dr. Alan Valentine, former president of the University of Rochester. Two main arms of the ESA were the Office of Price Stabilization, headed by Michael V. DiSalle, keen-witted former mayor of Toledo, and the Wage Stabilization Board. The board was composed of three members representing the public, three representing business, and three labor— and it was destined for trouble.

In one respect at least the American people came through the Korean War a great deal better off than was to be the case a generation later with the war in Vietnam. This aspect was inflation. An historic period of inflation, still a plague, began during the Vietnam hostilities. In the opinion of many economists this was due in large measure to the failure of President Johnson either to recommend an increase in taxes before it was too late to check rising prices or to cut Great Society programs.[18] But a legacy of severe inflation was spared the country in the relative economic stability following the Korean War. In the Korean mobilization Truman pursued a quite different course from that later taken by Johnson.

As a former chairman of the Senate Special Committee to Investigate the National Defense Program, Truman had been well versed in the mobilization measures and emergency economic policies as they had evolved during the Second World War. He had some rather strong views about them. He believed, for example, that Roosevelt had relied too heavily on government borrowing in its various forms to finance the war. Borrowing instead of taxing had resulted, as Truman saw it, in a huge, harmful, and unnecessary increase in the national debt. With strong encouragement from Secretary of the Treasury John Snyder and the Council of Economic Advisers, he was determined to avoid that situation in the Korean War. Speaking on television after he had signed the Defense Production Act the previous September, Truman said that there was only one sensible way to pay for the new mobilization. "It is," he said, "the plain, simple, direct way. We should pay . . . as we go out of taxes.[19]

In the months after the North Korean attack he got three large tax bills through Congress, which seem to have contributed to an ultimate leveling-off of prices.

In a special message in February 1951 he declared that taxes in the Second World War had not been high enough. As a result of borrowing, therefore, he noted, inflation struck the country after wartime controls had been removed.

"We could try to escape the financial cost of defense," he said, "by borrowing, but that would only transfer the financial problem to our children and would increase the danger of inflation with its grossly unfair distribution of the burden."[20]

Economic controls got off to a bumpy and controversial start, with Alan Valentine the first casualty. Determined to move slowly toward direct controls, he ran afoul of an impatient Wilson. With Truman backing Wilson, Valentine resigned in mid-January 1951. Truman replaced him with Eric Johnston, president of the Motion Picture Association and former president of the United States Chamber of Commerce. Then wages and prices, except farm prices, were frozen as of January 25.

The initial wage freeze was intended as temporary until a permanent regulation could be adopted. Three weeks later the Wage Stabilization Board decided on a policy of permitting wages to rise 10 percent above the January 15 levels. The vote was 6 to 3—the public and business members in the majority. The three outvoted labor members objected. Labor wanted more. When the vote was recorded, the labor representatives resigned from the WSB on instruction of the United Labor Policy Committee, which represented the AFL, the CIO, the Railway Labor Executives Association, and the International Association of Machinists.

At a cabinet meeting on February 16 Wilson charged that labor was seeking its pound of flesh regardless of the effect on inflation. Secretary of Labor Tobin retorted that if, three weeks earlier, Wilson had agreed to appoint a representative of labor to a policy-making post, he might have counteracted labor's bitterness. Wage controls had caused a great deal of injustice, Tobin said. He complained that 50 percent of labor had had wages frozen at a level that was unfair in light of price increases. Truman was irate at both sides. Matthew Connelly summarized his comment: "There is a conspiracy between labor and management to gouge the country without regard to the public interest. It is a disgraceful situation."[21]

Tobin had correctly captured labor's dissatisfaction with wage controls and its anger at Wilson for not including on his own business-oriented staff a labor representative. Labor leaders complained to Truman personally. He put his special counsel, Charles Murphy, to work on composing differences, but a settlement did not come easily. "The labor people are furious," Richard E. Neustadt, an assistant to Murphy, wrote in a memorandum. "They feel they have no stake in the mobilization program."[22]

On February 28 labor jolted the administration by withdrawing its representatives from all mobilization agencies. The United Labor Policy Committee denounced Wilson for allowing big business to dominate the mobilization program while using labor for "window-dressing."[23] Farm organizations also resented big-business "stewardship."

Assessing labor's attitude, a White House memorandum of March 23 said that labor considered the mobilization program to be "in a state of utter disorder." While prices and rents had not yet been brought under control, "the Administration seeks to impose an inflexible wage formula." Business was favored by tax loopholes and special privileges, according to the memorandum. "I must confess," said the writer, "that there is considerable truth in the foregoing bill of complaints."[24] Truman publicly stated his confidence in Wilson, and labor continued its boycott.[25]

Meanwhile efforts went forward to deal with high prices. The objective was a return to the structure of prices for manufactured goods as it had existed before the Korean War but not to the same level of prices. The new level was to make allowance for direct costs that manufacturers had had to bear since the outbreak of hostilities. Where new prices exceeded these costs, rollbacks were ordered, as in the case of beef and iron and steel scrap.

One regulation that caused Truman a good deal of heat, which he endured, was a price ceiling for raw cotton, since cotton was selling above parity. In a letter to Jonathan Daniels, publisher of the *Raleigh News & Observer* and a former government official, Truman said that every southern Senator "has been to see me or has written me on this subject." He added:

We are having the same difficulty with the woolen industry and now it looks as if labor has made up its mind to get into the same band wagon and get all they can 'while the getting is good.'

It is a very difficult matter to sit here at this desk and understand the attitude of people toward the emergency with which we are faced. Every segment of the economic setup is interested only in its own selfish interests and is making an effort to grab all the traffic will bear. They seem to forget that by taking an attitude of this sort they will wind up with nothing and no country either.[26]

Whether because prices already had crested by January, or taxes had exercised a restraining influence, or controls had taken effect, or high production was stabilizing the economy—or through some combination of these factors—inflation began to break in February 1951. Between then and May the Consumer Price Index rose by less than 1 percent, after having risen about 4.5 percent in the three preceding months and 9.5 percent during the preceding year. Controversies lay ahead, and labor continued to go its own way throughout February, March, and April.

In the fall of 1950 Truman had called the attention of his staff to what the president described, in the words of Eben Ayers, as "a bad feud . . . between Secretary of the Treasury John Snyder and the Federal Reserve Board."[27]

That was an understatement. What had come to a head in the winter of 1950–51 was one of the greatest controversies in the history of the Federal Reserve System. It was a complex dispute, filled with anger and defiance at the pinnacle of American government and American banking. In part a fight over the role of the Treasury, the quarrel tested the powers of the executive branch against those of the Federal Reserve, an independent monetary authority created by Congress in 1913. The skirmish brought into the field not only the secretary of the Treasury, but, among others, Truman, Thomas B. McCabe, chairman of the board of governors of the Federal Reserve, Marriner Eccles, a member of the board who had previously been removed as chairman by Truman, and Allen Sproul, president of the Federal Reserve Bank of New York. Debated in Congress and aired in the press, the controversy lasted for months, and before it was over Truman forced McCabe out as chairman of the board of governors. In the end, however, the fight over Federal Reserve powers was one that Truman could not win, particularly in view of his political weakness by the start of 1951.

Simply stated, the issue was whether the Federal Reserve should support the prices of government securities at predetermined levels. Such an arrangement enabled the Treasury to borrow money cheaply because the interest rate was kept relatively low. The support of government securities had been agreed to by the Federal Reserve during the Second World War. In a sense, therefore, the Federal Reserve had become an agent of the Treasury.[28] At the Treasury's insistence this commitment was continued in the postwar period, although Eccles, one of the most renowned of all Federal Reserve officials, denounced the agreement as an "engine of inflation." His point was that the Federal Reserve's purchase of government securities nullified the efforts of the Federal Reserve to restrain credit expansion. When the Federal Reserve was required to purchase government securities, it pumped large amounts of money into the country's financial system with inflationary effect.

What finally brought the differences between the Federal Reserve and the executive branch to a head was the surge of prices early in the Korean War. Between August 1950 and February 1951, for example, the Federal Reserve was forced to buy $3.5 billion in government securities, as sellers found other more profitable uses for their money. The Federal Reserve Bank of New York, particularly its president, Allen Sproul, took the lead in advocating that interest rates on government securities be allowed to rise so as to restore the ability of the Federal Reserve to restrain monetary expansion.[29] As interest rates rise, the price of bonds falls.

Snyder, a man dedicated to stability, bristled in the manner of a cabinet officer reluctant to see his department shaken out of a comfortable arrangement. A former St. Louis banker, he was convinced that Sproul and New York bankers and brokers were trying to recapture the primacy in fiscal and monetary affairs that had been lost to Washington during the New Deal.[30] Snyder was, or so he recalled later, willing to yield to a gradual rise in interest rates.[31] Such a rise, in fact, had occurred in the case of short-term government securities after the Second World War, as the Federal Reserve began to inch away from its agreement. But in the exigencies of the Korean War Snyder did not wish to see rates go up for fear of the uncertainty it might create among investors. When the original Treasury–Federal Reserve agreement was entered into in 1941, the yield on long-term securities was 2.5 percent, and the Federal Reserve, reluctantly, still supported it at that point in 1950 and early 1951.

Philosophically committed to low interest, Truman backed his old friend John Snyder and convinced himself that the bankers had seized upon a time of emergency to upset the applecart. In a letter to Russell C. Leffingwell, chairman of J. P. Morgan & Co., the president said that financial stability was "entirely wrapped up in the two hundred and fifty-seven billion dollar [national] debt that is now outstanding. There should be no fight between the Federal Reserve and the government. For my part I can't understand why the bankers would want to upset the credit of the nation in the midst of a terrible national emergency. That seems to be what they want to do and if I can prevent it they are not going to do it."[32]

Truman was dead set against the thought of tampering with government bonds, especially because some that he had bought while in the army plunged in value in the depression of 1920–21. It became an article of faith with him that if a person bought a government bond for $100, that person should be able to redeem it for $100. More than that, however, the great expenditures Truman had undertaken in the Marshall Plan, the Korean War, and European rearmament left him concerned that the government be able to finance them in stable conditions. Snyder kept warning him that the Federal Reserve might seriously disturb such stability.

Three weeks after the Korean War began Snyder moved to keep the Federal Reserve in line in preserving a stable market for government securities. He wrote to McCabe, "This involves, first of all, avoiding any course which would give rise to a belief that significant changes in the pattern of rates were under consideration."[33]

This time the Federal Reserve bristled. Ever since the Great Depression the Federal Reserve had fallen into a passive role vis-à-vis the Treasury.[34] Federal Reserve officials were restless for their independence. McCabe and his associates held a rather contentious meeting with Snyder. According to Federal Reserve records, the secretary of the treasury hinted that the administration might ask Congress to intervene on the side of the Treasury if the Federal Reserve balked on supporting government bonds. As the economist Herbert Stein has written, no question existed as to the legal authority of the Federal Reserve to decide what securities it would buy. On the other hand, the Federal Reserve was a creature of Congress, and Congress, perhaps under administration pressure, could always change its authority.[35]

The Federal Reserve's Open Market Committee was defiant. Sproul, vice-chairman of the committee, said that the Federal Reserve should not support "the existing rate structure and should advise the Treasury. . . ." Eccles declared that the time had come when the Federal Reserve, "if it expected to survive as an agency with any independence whatsoever, should exercise some independence."[36] Those officials were speaking against a backdrop of considerable support in Congress for allowing the Federal Reserve discretion in maintaining economic stability, and the Open Market Committee struck out in that direction against Truman's wishes. The president wrote McCabe:

It is of paramount importance that confidence be maintained in the credit of the United States. I have discussed the matter with the Secretary of the Treasury since the Korean outbreak and we are in complete agreement.

I think it is imperative that . . . all operations of the Federal Reserve Board and actions relating to the market for Government securities be so adjusted that outstanding United States Government securities sell at par.[37]

Interest rates on short-term government securities rose during the fall. Bickering continued between Snyder and McCabe, and investors came to realize that the Federal Reserve commitment was increasingly uncertain. In December Truman again wrote to McCabe, calling the situation "very dangerous" and asserting that "the Federal Reserve Board should make it perfectly clear to the Open Market Committee and to the New York bankers that the peg [support for securities] is stabilized." "I hope," he added, "the Board will realize its responsibilities and not allow the bottom to drop from under our securities. If that happens that is exactly what Mr. Stalin wants."[38]

Snyder and McCabe sparred over whether the Federal Reserve was still committed to support long-term securities at 2.5 percent. In a strategem to nail down the commitment Snyder announced in a speech to the New York Board of Trade that the Treasury believed that new long-term issues "will be financed within the pattern of that rate." Federal Reserve officials did not agree and were furious. McCabe protested to Truman that he had not known of Snyder's speech in advance.

With relations unraveling, Truman took the unprecedented step of calling the entire Open Market Committee to a meeting in the White House on January 31, 1951. "The meeting," wrote Stein, "was a masterpiece of deliberate misunderstanding. Neither party said what he really meant, yet each understood what the other meant but preferred to respond as if he didn't and so left the other free to interpret the response as he wished."[39]

The Open Market Committee returned to the Federal Reserve building and secretly voted not to support the bond market at current levels until further notice. Yet the next day the White House formally announced that "the Federal Reserve Board has pledged its support to President Truman to maintain the stability of Government securities as long as the emergency lasts." Then Truman wrote to McCabe personally, thanking the Open Market Committee for its commitment. The White House released the text.

Playing the same game, Eccles then blew the controversy wide open by releasing, without authority, the report on the meeting of January 31, at which the Open Market Committee had voted not to support the bond market.[40]

In bitterness the dispute wound down. Truman already had too many political troubles on his hands without trying to battle against the support for the Federal Reserve in Congress, which was led by a Democrat, Senator Paul Douglas, a man who irked Truman from start to finish.

Snyder and McCabe, former president of the Scott Paper Company, had once been friends. Truman had appointed McCabe chairman of the Federal Reserve on Snyder's recommendation. The dispute between Snyder and McCabe had reached the point, however, where according to Charles Murphy, "they were not on speaking terms with each other."[41] Mistrustful of McCabe's actions, Snyder, while in the hospital for a cataract operation, told Charles Wilson, a visitor, to convey to the president that the secretary of the treasury no longer felt that he could work with the chairman of the board of governors of the Federal Reserve.[42]

It was not an entirely new experience for Truman. Snyder also had had difficulties with Eccles when Eccles had been chairman of the board, and Truman had objected, too, to what he considered Eccles's lack of cooperation. To show Eccles "who's boss" Truman had refused to reappoint him chairman of the board when his term expired in 1948.[43] He named McCabe to succeed him, although Eccles continued as a member of the board. Now Snyder wanted McCabe out, and McCabe was so distressed by the clash with Truman and Snyder, according to Murphy, that he was willing to depart before the end of his term on condition that his successor was someone whom he approved. Finally, all sides agreed on William McChesney Martin, then an assistant secretary of the treasury.

McCabe sent Truman what Murphy described later as a bitter letter of resignation. Murphy took the letter back to McCabe and asked him if he did not wish to word it differently. McCabe did.[44]

In the end the Treasury and the Federal Reserve reached an accord. Temporarily the Federal Reserve supported long-term government securities at 2.5 percent. Thereafter the Treasury issued new bonds at 2.75 percent, and the Federal Reserve was left free to follow a flexible policy. By the time of the Eisenhower administration the Federal Reserve renounced support of the prices of government securities as one of its objectives and was free to raise interest rates.[45]

31. More Scandal, New Bruises

GOSSIP ABOUT DEEP FREEZERS and five percenters had subsided when, in early February 1951, a new scandal hit the administration in the form of a Senate report raising implications of misconduct in the Reconstruction Finance Corporation, a government lending agency.

The tenor of the report, which was a preliminary one, was that RFC policy and loans had been affected by favoritism and by political influence exerted from the White House and the Democratic National Committee.

Truman publicly denounced the report, whereupon the Senate subcommittee that had issued it held public hearings. For days, as a result, newspapers carried stories, citing embarrassing but often inconclusive testimony about alleged influence in the RFC exercised by Democratic National Chairman William Boyle and Donald Dawson, an administrative assistant to Truman.

The hearings disclosed that an $8,540 royal pastel mink coat had been given to a White House stenographer, Lauretta Young, by her husband, E. Merl Young. He was a businessman, a friend of Dawson's, and a political operator on the fringes of the Democratic National Committee and the RFC, where he had once worked as an examiner. After he had left the RFC, the coat had been bought for him by Joseph H. Rosenbaum, an attorney who represented applicants for RFC loans. The implications of the disclosure about the coat were that Rosenbaum had made a gift of it to Merl Young in return for past favors in the RFC.

With the next presidential election barely a year and a half away, the Republicans had striking success in making the mink coat a symbol of Democratic corruption. It was in a play upon this symbol that Nixon in his famous "Checkers" speech of September 23, 1952, defending himself against alleged corruption, sermonized that his wife, Pat, "doesn't have a mink coat. But she does have a respectable Republican cloth coat."[1]

A forerunner of the New Deal, the Reconstruction Finance Corporation was established by President Hoover early in 1932 to combat the depression by lending money at low interest to financial, industrial, and agricultural institutions. With the onset of the Second World War the agency financed construction of defense plants. After the war, when the Truman administration was beset by unfounded fears of a new depression, the scope of RFC lending was rather indiscriminately widened. Thereafter several large loans went into default. To investigate, the Senate Banking and Currency Committee appointed a subcommittee, headed by Senator J. William Fulbright, Democrat, of Arkansas.

At the time the RFC was managed by a five-man board of directors. As the Fulbright subcommittee was in the early stages of its investigation, Truman submitted a plan to reorganize the RFC, an independent agency, by transferring it to the Department of Commerce, where it had once resided. The Senate, however, disapproved the plan. Meanwhile as the Fulbright investigation continued, the senator and his colleagues became suspicious of the conduct of two of the directors: Walter L. Dunham, a nominal Republican, and William E. Willett, a Democrat. Fulbright and Senator Douglas, another member of the subcommittee, called on Truman to discuss their concerns. Whatever may have been said at the meeting, Fulbright and Douglas were shocked when Truman renominated Dunham and Willett upon the expiration of their terms as directors.

Thereafter Fulbright released the preliminary report in February, titled *Study of Reconstruction Finance Corporation: Favoritism and Influence*.[2] It criticized the two directors for favoritism. Dunham, it said, made a practice of discussing RFC affairs freely with representatives of the Democratic National Committee and of paying particular attention to cases in which the committee was interested. Joseph Rosenbaum, the Washington attorney who specialized in handling RFC loan applications for clients, was quoted as having said that he had Dunham and Willett in his hip pocket—an allegation he denied.

Although Dunham was a Republican, his office records indicated that his most frequent visitors were attorneys and others who had been introduced by William Boyle and his assistants. That, of course, suggested that some contributions to the Democratic party had proved to be good investments.

The RFC report incensed Truman. As a politician Fulbright, a former Rhodes Scholar and former president of the University of Arkansas, was not exactly Harry Truman's cup of tea. Then or at some point during the subsequent hearings the president characterized the senator as "an overeducated s.o.b."[3] At a press conference several days after the issuance of the report Truman denounced it as "asinine."[4] In those times the word was rather a strong one for a president to use. Some of his staff were taken aback and so, evidently, was Mrs. Truman. "The madam thinks I shouldn't have any more press conferences," he confided to his staff.[5] Truman was not the kind of incessantly combative president some portraits have depicted. When put on the defensive, however, he was a counterpuncher, and by February of 1951 he had been on the defensive for so long that he often went about with a chip on his shoulder.

At the press conference a reporter asked him if he had found in the Fulbright report "any basis for criticism on your part of the activities of either Mr. Dawson or your RFC directors."

"No, I haven't," Truman said.

He snapped at the Senate Banking and Currency Committee for having, he said, rejected the reorganization plan he had sent up to transfer the RFC to the Department of Commerce.

"The objective of this report," Truman continued, referring to the February document, "seems to have been a reflection on the president himself. And I am sorry for that, because I have never in my life brought pressure on the RFC or any other agency of the government to do anything except in the public interest."

After Truman's taunts Fulbright went at public hearings with a zest, airing testimony about Dawson, Young, Rosenbaum, Boyle, and others in a spectacle that put the administration in an unsavory light. Yet, as denials and explanations offset charges, it was, and is, difficult in many cases to judge the true dimension of guilt. Truman discussed the problem one night at Blair House with some advisers, including Joseph H. Short, his new press secretary. Formerly White House correspondent for the *Baltimore Sun,* he had been chosen by the president to replace the late Charles Ross. At the meeting Truman ventured that the stir over the RFC hearings soon would abate. "Mr. President," Short said, "I don't think this business is going to blow over. I think it is making a deep impression around the country."[6]

Truman was strangely complacent and slow to offer presidential leadership to eliminate unethical conduct and expunge doubts about the probity of government agencies.

Confidence in the correctness of his own conduct doubtless left him somewhat indifferent to the criticism. Apparently, he assumed that criticism voiced about his subordinates was really aimed at himself. Truman's code of dogged loyalty to faithful lieutenants like Vaughan, Dawson, and Boyle affected his reactions. In the old days in Missouri Boyle's mother had been a supporter of Truman's when he needed support. By the time of the RFC hearings Truman had taken years of battering in the White House, which inured him to criticism. He was growing no younger. His decision not to run again perhaps made the political consequences of the Fulbright investigation seem less acute to him than would have been the case otherwise. "Is T so burdened and psychologically worn that he doesn't give much of a damn?" Roger Tubby, by then an assistant White House press secretary, wrote in his journal.[7]

In retrospect, John Steelman, analyzing Truman's attitude toward the ethical problem generally, not just the RFC affair, said that the president resented what he considered exaggerated reports in the press of corruption in his administration. He felt that the press put the worst possible construction on everything, which was sometimes true. Thus, according to Steelman, Truman was less prone to criticize subordinates than he might have been if charges had been reported with less gusto. Steelman said, however, that Truman did not feel that all charges of corruption were completely unjustified.[8]

The line between the discharge of his duties by a public official, like Dawson, and exertion of improper influence is often hard to define, as the senators acknowledged. Fulbright's interim report made no charges against Dawson, Boyle, or, certainly, Truman. Figures like Boyle, Rosenbaum, and Merl Young, the former RFC examiner who gave his wife a mink coat paid for by Rosenbaum, were not federal employees at the time. Mrs. Young, the White House stenographer, had committed no crime in accepting a mink coat from her husband. No incumbent government official was ever indicted in the entire course of the investigation, although Young was later indicted for perjury and sent to jail. Dawson, whose involvement caused some of the most adverse publicity for the administration, was in fact treated by Fulbright and Douglas as a man guilty at worst of something between committing peccadilloes and playing politics with the RFC.

For a number of reasons the spotlight turned on Dawson. A graduate of the University of Missouri, he once had been director of personnel at the RFC. His wife, Ava, was still employed there to supervise records and files. Dawson counted among his friends not only RFC officials, like Dunham and Willett, but also certain borrowers from the RFC. He was also a friend of Merl Young, who operated in a milieu between borrowers and the RFC. Since moving from the RFC to the White House in 1947, Dawson had handled personnel and patronage for Truman and thus was in a position to influence appointments and promotions at the RFC. With Matt Connelly, Dawson also was a principal liaison between the White House and the Democratic National Committee. Furthermore with his smooth appearance, big smile, booming laughter, and well-tailored suits, he looked the part.

There were calls for Dawson's resignation, and some members of the White House staff would have liked to see him go to spare the president further embarrassment. With this new round of charges of corruption following Vaughan's capers, a housecleaning in the administration, even for the sake of a housecleaning, would have taken a burden off the Democrats. Obviously, however, Truman believed that Dawson had committed no offense serious enough to warrant dismissal. On the other hand, without some gesture by the president such as a housecleaning to neutralize the charges, the political harm was bound to continue. Truman never resolved the dilemma. While the public hearings were generating headlines he took a vacation. In scenes such as once were staged in musical comedies to lampoon Tammany Hall, incessant poker games went on in Key West while charges of corruption flew in Washington. Roger Tubby reflected in his journal: "Poker, poker. I wonder why he played so much . . . a feeling of vacuum otherwise, no struggle, excitement? . . . companionship, banter, escape from the pressing problems of state?"[9]

The drift caused dismay and frustration among younger members of the White House staff, which, despite its small size, contained a number of first-rate men. "I read *New Republic* editorial expressing fear lest Truman end up in as bad repute as Harding—though that hardly seems possible . . . the stuff [has] so far been such chicken feed compared to Teapot Dome." So wrote Roger Tubby in his journal while in Key West.[10]

The dismay extended to more than the RFC hearings. In a blatantly political appointment Truman had named Mayor William O'Dwyer, of New York, as ambassador to Mexico. While Fulbright was probing the RFC, Senator Estes Kefauver, Democrat, of Tennessee, was chairing the Senate Special Committee to Investigate Organized Crime in Interstate Commerce, with considerable embarrassment to the Democratic party. In hearings in New York before television audiences huge for their time O'Dwyer admitted to the Kefauver committee that, as mayor, he had appointed to office persons with underworld connections. His name was linked at the hearings with that of crime boss Frank Costello. It was this sort of allegation, echoed in hearings in other states as well, that embarrassed the Democratic party.

There was general agreement among young members of the White House staff, Roger Tubby noted, that it was "too damn bad O'Dwyer was appointed Ambassador. O'D should resign."[11] At another point Tubby also noted: "[T]here was not serious discussion of the issues being developed in the Fulbright and Kefauver committees. In fact both were talked about in a rather disparaging and light-hearted way, by Mr. T and some of the senior members of the staff."[12] Before going to Key West Tubby had felt he should speak up about the need for the president and other Democratic leaders to get out and defend the record of the administration. "Don't say it before Vaughan," George Elsey admonished him. "Vaughan doesn't like anyone who thinks."[13]

One night a Miami newspaper was delivered at Key West with a headline intimating that the Soviets had tested an atomic bomb in Germany. Tubby immediately took the paper to Truman at the poker table. "That sounds bad," the president said over the clatter of the chips and went on with the game. Later he repaired to the living room to play records. "We're in good shape," he assured Tubby, as the latter noted. "I know, can't tell you. But I don't think the Russians have the atom bomb. That explosion of some months back was an accident."[14] In any case, fortunately, the purported Soviet atomic test in Germany turned out to have been a false alarm.

As customary, Truman held a press conference under palm trees while at Key West. A reporter said that Senator Knowland had declared that the president should return to Washington and clean house. "My house is always clean," Truman said.[15]

At his first press conference back in Washington he was asked whether any change was contemplated in the status of Ambassador O'Dwyer. "No," he replied.[16]

The Fulbright hearings dealt with numerous cases, which were rather typical of the scandals exposed during the Truman administration. These did not approach the plunder in the Harding administration. Nor did they involve abuse of legal powers by the highest officers of the government, as in Watergate. At the lower end of the scale they were a smorgasbord of cheap politics and money grubbing by persons of little consequence. In this category were indiscriminate patronage, the use of public office to grant favors of some value to partisans and friends, and acceptance of gifts and favors from businessmen. On a rising scale the corruption included insensitivity to connections between local Democratic leaders and criminals, loose ethics in the Democratic National Committee, bribery, tax-fixing, profiteering by federal officials, cheating on tax returns, conflict of interest, fraud, and laxity by the Department of Justice in prosecuting alleged wrongdoings by influential Democrats. Before it was all over Truman was to find himself in quite deep water, politically, as a result of this corruption.

Merl Young and his wife were from Missouri. She had first gone to work for Truman when he was a senator. Her husband, after having served in the Marine Corps in the Second World War, got a job as an RFC examiner, having given Truman's name as a reference. Some people had the notion that he was distantly related to the president. In 1948 Young did some campaign work for Truman.

Even in the midst of the atrocious publicity over the hearings Young would turn up at the White House in loud sport jackets to pick up his wife. Because of her, he had a White House pass. Once the quick-tempered Short "blew up," according to Roger Tubby, when he saw published news photographs of Mr. and Mrs. Young leaving the building together. Short stormed into Connelly's office demanding that Young's White House pass be recalled. On an occasion when Young was seen arriving, Tubby was so angry that, as he confided to his journal, "for a moment I had an urge to unceremoniously bump into him." And in another entry: ". . . these Goddamned chislers who use T. . . . [H]e should get rid of them as fast as they are forced into the light and can be recognized for what they are."[17] Mrs. Young finally resigned in April.

It was brought out that after Young resigned as an examiner for the RFC he went to work, simultaneously and at good pay, for two companies that were borrowers from the RFC. Established also was the fact that Young was financed in another business venture by an RFC borrower and by Rosenbaum, the Washington attorney specializing in applications for RFC loans. It was in this period, after Young had left the RFC, that the mink coat was purchased.

On one occasion during the Senate hearings into the RFC, as Senator Douglas later recounted, Senator Charles W. Tobey, Republican, of New Hampshire, was summoned from the room to the telephone. Returning, Douglas said in his memoirs, Tobey told the other senators: "That was the President. He told me that the real crooks and influence peddlers were members of this committee, as we might soon find out."[18] According to a more contemporary report in the *New York Times*, Tobey quoted Truman as having said that letters in the RFC files showed that members of Congress had accepted fees for promoting RFC loans. Tobey also said, however, that Truman later recanted.[19] As Douglas recalled, the subcommittee regarded the incident as presidential pressure to curb the investigation.

As a witness at the hearings Dawson generally denied having tried to influence RFC decisions. All appointments of RFC directors, he conceded, were cleared by the Democratic National Committee. His most publicized admission was that on three occasions he had stayed, free of charge, at the pretentious Saxony Hotel in Miami Beach, which had received a $1.5 million RFC loan. Under grilling from the senators he promised not to accept such a favor again.[20]

Fulbright told Dawson at the close of the hearings that the subcommittee had not asserted that "you were out throwing your weight around in seeking and attempting to dominate the RFC. What we are saying is that whether you sought to do it, or attempted to do it, you did influence them." The testimony had made it clear, he added, that the directors, Dunham and Willett, were anxious to do anything to please Dawson. Dawson denied this, and then took advantage of the situation to say that he was pleased that Fulbright thought he had done no wrong. Fulbright backed away from this assertion. "I have not completely made up my mind as to the evaluation of your motive," he said.[21]

Years later Douglas said in his memoirs that Dawson had made a "good showing, and only minor peccadilloes were proved against him."[22] The essence of the criticism in the case was that as a presidential assistant Dawson should have stood completely above reproach.

During the hearings Truman as much as conceded the charges of RFC mismanagement by submitting a reorganization plan, which the Senate approved, providing that the RFC be placed under a single administrator instead of the board of directors. He moved Stuart Symington from the National Security Resources Board to fill the administrator's post.

Finally, the full Senate Banking and Currency Committee issued a report saying that the public hearings had substantiated Fulbright's preliminary report about mismanagement. The former directors, according to the report, had fallen into the habit of discussing the RFC with persons who had no responsibility for it nor valid interest in it.

"It became accepted practice, in many instances," the report added, "for loan applicants to seek introduction to the directors of the RFC or to some of them through officials of the Democratic National Committee."

The report said that directors had responded to outside influence to override recommendations of their own examiners and review boards.

For the Republican minority of the Banking and Currency Committee, Senators Capehart and John W. Bricker, of Ohio, wrote a separate report. They called for the dismissal of Dawson and charged that the RFC had been victimized by the White House staff, "minor employees, political hangers-on and self-proclaimed cronies."[23]

Truman felt aggrieved by the reaction to the charges made that spring. In April he had written to Clark Clifford, then in private law practice: "There have been only two or three Presidents who have been as roundly abused and misrepresented in certain sections of the press as I have. I call your attention to Washington, Jefferson, Jackson, Lincoln and particularly to Grover Cleveland."[24]

Except for the mink coat, it was a case of the administration's being hurt not so much by any single example of political influence alleged in the RFC hearings but by the accumulation of incidents creating an aura of scandal. Nor had Truman seen the end of it by any means. Thus on the heels of the Fulbright inquiry, the investigations subcommittee of the Senate Committee on Expenditures in the Executive Departments held hearings on new revelations about the Democratic national chairman, Bill Boyle.

An old friend and supporter of Truman's, Boyle had risen through the political ranks as an officeholder in Kansas City in the Pendergast days. Early in Truman's second term he became a vice-chairman of the Democratic National Committee and was elected chairman on August 24, 1949. In July 1951, the *St. Louis Post-Dispatch* reported that Boyle had received $8,000 in legal fees in 1949 and 1950 from the American Lithofold Corporation, of St. Louis. Theretofore unsuccessful in its application, the newspaper reported, American Lithofold obtained a large loan from the RFC after retaining Boyle as an attorney. The Senate Permanent Investigations Subcommittee launched an inquiry.

At a White House staff conference the president's correspondence secretary, William Hassett, venerable Vermont newspaperman and New Dealer, made an emotional appeal to Truman. Hassett thought that Boyle should be fired.

"Your friends will destroy you!" he cried.

"It's all right, Bill," the president said, reassuringly. "It's all right."[25]

The Boyle affair was a painful one for Truman because of his friendship with the national chairman. Embarrassments had been numerous. On September 29, 1949, long before the *St. Louis Post-Dispatch* articles on Boyle and American Lithofold, Truman, Vice-President Barkley, and some of the cabinet flew to Kansas City to attend a testimonial dinner for Boyle. "Bill's all right!" Truman told the guests. "Don't let anybody tell you differently."[26] The number of crooks and racketeers at the dinner with a president was a scandal in itself. One of them, Charles Binnagio, was soon to be murdered.[27]

When the Senate investigation of the American Lithofold case began, Truman ordered a confidential investigation by Charles Murphy, a lawyer and government official of the highest repute. Murphy's report to Truman exonerated Boyle.[28] The president thereafter stood by the national chairman at a subsequent press conference.[29] The cigar then blew up in the Republicans' faces when word reached the Senate that Republican National Chairman Guy Gabrielson had intervened with the RFC on behalf of his own firm, Carthage Hydrocol, Inc. The incident spoiled the Republicans' hopes of cashing in on Boyle.

Months later the Senate Permanent Investigations Subcommittee issued its report, which criticized Gabrielson for lack of candor but was sterner on Boyle. His conduct, it said, "was not such that it would dispel the appearance of wrongdoing."

Noting Boyle's public disclaimer that he had ever discussed a loan for American Lithofold with any RFC official, the report emphasized that Boyle had neglected to mention that he had arranged an appointment for American Lithofold officials with Harley Hise, then chairman of the board of the RFC. The subcommittee, recalling the company's previous inability to obtain an RFC loan, drew what it called a reasonable assumption that the loan would not have been made—and in a matter of three days!—"but for the telephone call from Mr. Boyle to Mr. Hise."[30]

Long before the report was issued, however, Boyle had resigned as Democratic national chairman, citing ill health as a reason. Fresh criticism descended on the administration. "I suppose it is necessary to put up with these things," Truman wrote to a friend, "but it hurts sometimes."[31]

32. *MacArthur Crisis: "The Last Straw"*

On the afternoon of April 5, 1951, Roger Tubby was surprised to read a bulletin on the United Press ticker in the White House press office about a letter MacArthur had written to Joseph Martin, the Republican leader of the House of Representatives and a persistent critic of Truman's Far Eastern policies.

In direct conflict with Truman's policies MacArthur's letter to the opposition leader endorsed the proposition, supported by Martin, that Chiang Kai-shek's forces on Formosa should be used to open a second front against the Chinese communists.

The letter struck Tubby, he later wrote, as an act—the "latest" act—of insubordination on the part of General MacArthur. The assistant press secretary took the bulletin to the Oval Office where he found Truman alone. Handing him the copy, Tubby said, "This is more of the MacArthur stuff. It makes me boil."[1]

"Oh, this is more politics," Truman said, calmly. "The UP has put him up to this."

"And *LIFE,* too," Tubby said, pointing to the new issue of that magazine on the president's desk. "They want us to attack China." Echoing Republicans like Knowland and Martin, an editorial in the Henry Luce publication said that the United States should "take full advantage of whatever the Nationalists can do now to help us now in the struggle for Asia," even though that help might assume the form "of a limited beachhead invasion, presumably in South China."[2]

"Well," Truman said, "I think they are maneuvering the general out of a job."

"Good!" Tubby said.

Truman accused MacArthur of a "doublecross."[3]

"This stuff makes me boil, too," he continued. "You know, I can work up to a boil. I can take just so much. I am talking to Marshall on this."[4]

As if on cue, a curtain descended on the White House over the next five days. Doors were closed. Officials were unavailable to reporters. The usual news sources dried up. The press secretaries would not comment on anything pertaining to MacArthur. Limousines came and went through the private gates leading to the north portico. Reporters guessed that meetings were being held that were not listed on Truman's published schedule, though it was impossible to learn what they were about or who attended. As the silence and mystery continued day after day, tension, a feeling of crisis, an expectation of something dramatic enveloped the White House. It seemed obvious that the president was at grips with the MacArthur situation, but what, if anything, might come of it, or when, no one appeared to know. The truth was that Truman had reached one of the great climaxes of his presidency and one of the classic episodes in the history of the presidency.

Ever since November, when MacArthur was denied the right of hot pursuit and American forces were routed by the Chinese, a fundamental conflict had been developing between the commander in chief of the armed forces and a renowned commanding general. The situation contained two main ingredients. One was a flawed personal relationship. The other was a constitutional question as to how far a military officer publicly could carry his opposition to policies adopted by the civilian authorities. The atmosphere in which the problem was now addressed was best described later by the presidential assistant, David Bell, when he recalled, "It was the common view around the White House and I assume—I can't quote the president—but I assume that it was his view also that the relief of MacArthur was long overdue. . . ."[5] Bell's assumption about Truman's attitude was well founded.

For years Truman had been contemptuous of MacArthur's airs and suspicious of his political ambitions. MacArthur, for his part, looked down on Truman, although he acclaimed the president's decision to intervene in Korea. In taking the practically inevitable step of designating MacArthur as United Nations commander, Truman undoubtedly had confidence in MacArthur's competence. MacArthur promptly sent him a message reiterating a pledge "of my complete personal loyalty to you." As in the case of all officers in the armed forces of the United States, the commission MacArthur held directed that he should obey the orders of the president as commander in chief.[6] MacArthur's success at Inchon, when it came, appeared to have been a welcome vindication of Truman's decision to enter the Korean War, and at Wake Island a month later the president overcame his dislike of the general.

Before the Korean War, when MacArthur was proconsul and supreme commander in Japan, the only troublesome difference between him and the Truman administration was over emphasis on the importance of Formosa. MacArthur considered the island so vital to the American position in the Far East that he favored a military defense of it. Under Acheson's influence the administration acknowledged the strategic importance of Formosa but was not ready then to defend it other than by economic and diplomatic means and was reconciled to the prospect of eventual conquest of the island by the Chinese Communists. After Truman supported Acheson's position, MacArthur did not challenge the president. Then, when the war began, Truman and Acheson turned around and adopted MacArthur's position that Formosa should be defended. While the initial purpose of interposing the Seventh Fleet was to confine the fighting to Korea, American policy gravitated toward greater military support for Formosa as the Chinese menace to Korea grew.

MacArthur had rattled the administration by visiting Chiang Kai-shek on Formosa early in the Korean War. Acheson and the allies feared that the general might concoct some new collaboration with Chiang, but no such thing happened. Harriman then went to Tokyo to explain Truman's policy to MacArthur. MacArthur did not challenge it. While he left Harriman with a feeling that the general and the administration did not see eye-to-eye on Chiang, Harriman did not recommend that Truman remove MacArthur. And while MacArthur told Harriman that the United States should fight communists everywhere, the general went on fighting them in Korea only. "General MacArthur and I are in perfect agreement," Truman told the press on August 10, 1950, after the Harriman-MacArthur talks, "and have been ever since he has been in the job he is now. . . . I am satisfied with what he is doing."[7]

The later squabble over MacArthur's message to the Veterans of Foreign Wars was due, chiefly, not to an overstepping of the bounds of the administration's Formosan policy by the general but to the feeling in the administration that MacArthur had usurped the president's voice and disrupted the United Nations. Although Truman said afterward that he had thought of relieving MacArthur over the incident, the notion did not survive the cooling off of the presidential temper. Truman sent MacArthur a conciliatory message, and at Wake MacArthur apologized to him.[8]

While Truman and MacArthur did not have the same view of American interests in Asia, they were able to work together until the calamity of the Chinese intervention in Korea. Nothing that occurred before November or early December caused their relationship to become irreconcilable or to convince Truman that he must relieve the general of his command.

Truman had done all in his power to give MacArthur the forces he wanted in the desperate summer of 1950. The president also supported plans for the Inchon landing.[9] "No commander in the history of war," MacArthur said at the Wake Island conference, "has ever had more complete and adequate support from all agencies in Washington than I have had."[10]

After the first shock of the North Korean invasion the Truman administration saw the war as an opportunity to cross the 38th parallel, unify Korea, and roll back the Soviet orbit. Certainly, there was no disagreement with MacArthur on those aims. MacArthur wished to pursue the North Korean Army across the parallel to destroy it. Truman approved the directive formally authorizing him to do so. The guiding policy paper, NSC 81/1, permitted MacArthur to advance to the Yalu and the Tumen Rivers, barring prior Soviet or Chinese intervention. Although its wisdom was doubted, his plan to separate the Tenth Corps from the Eighth Army was accepted in Washington, as was his decision to use American instead of only South Korean troops in approaching the Soviet and Chinese borders. The president even yielded to his importunities to conduct the great November bombing raid along the Yalu, although MacArthur's conduct set badly with the Joint Chiefs of Staff. Thereafter his superiors in Washington approved his fateful "end-the-war" advance. The only major issue up to that point in the war on which MacArthur had been turned down by higher authority was hot pursuit—and that because of the objection of United Nations allies. In the months after the outbreak of hostilities, Truman had tried to avoid conflict with MacArthur by means of friendly messages, public statements of support, approval of MacArthur's requests, the dispatch of Harriman to Tokyo, and the president's own trip to Wake Island.

During this period, on the other hand, there was no basic issue on which MacArthur, though headstrong and troublesome at times, was insubordinate or defiant, unless the employment of American troops instead of only South Korean units on the approaches to Chinese and Soviet territory is to be considered a matter of fundamental importance. Even in that instance his stretching of a message from the Joint Chiefs of Staff was mitigated by the fact that their directive was somewhat tentative and couched in terms of policy rather than ironclad rule. Furthermore, MacArthur had subsequently received Marshall's ambiguous message, assuring him that he was to feel unhampered, tactically and strategically, in crossing the 38th parallel.

If MacArthur's November offensive had succeeded, he and the administration would have come through the war triumphantly and probably on rather good terms with each other. When the offensive sank into severe reverses, it was a disaster for both and a seedbed of mutual ill feeling and misunderstanding. For the first time also it made MacArthur politically pregnable. While earlier disagreeable episodes like the visit to Chiang Kai-shek and the VFW message had been closed by the president, the memory of them lay near enough to the surface to rise in a new set of differences and to color attitudes. In this sense the latest crisis was a culmination of a long series of trying incidents. Meanwhile the general's heroic aura and influence in the White House and the Pentagon had been deflated by the shattering experience of the Chinese onslaught and by MacArthur's subsequent overly alarming assessments.

The first signs of irreconcilable difficulties with MacArthur appeared early in December when he demanded new political decisions and strategic plans and asserted to General Collins the necessity for unleashing American military power against China. MacArthur told Collins that it would amount to surrender for the United Nations to refrain from attacks against Chinese territory and withhold reinforcements from Korea. Without reinforcements, evacuation soon would be necessary, MacArthur maintained, even as the administration was growing determined to stay in Korea as long as possible without reinforcements.

Then, in criticizing the administration and the European allies in an interview and a message to an editor, MacArthur placed himself in a potentially vulnerable position by causing Truman to prohibit all government officials from issuing public statements dealing with foreign or military policy without clearance from appropriate authorities. "I should have relieved General MacArthur then and there," Truman wrote in his memoirs. "The reason I did not was that I did not wish to have it appear as if he were being relieved because the offensive failed."[11]

The skeins of the final drama came together around the time of the Truman-

Attlee talks. Then for all practical purposes the administration reached the decision to seek a settlement in Korea along a line at or near the 38th parallel rather than widen the war. To MacArthur, one of America's greatest architects of victory, such a policy smacked of grubbing for a substitute for victory.

Throughout December the Joint Chiefs struggled with the dilemma posed by MacArthur's demands: reinforce United Nations troops or alter the rules of engagement, or else evacuate Korea. Specifically, MacArthur had asked for four national guard divisions, which had been called up but had not yet completed training. The day after Christmas, 1950, Truman met in Blair House with Acheson, Marshall, and Bradley to try to resolve the dilemma. Acheson argued that in their present strength United Nations forces should fight on in Korea. Marshall and Bradley believed that these forces could at least hold the line of the Kum River but insisted that MacArthur must not risk the destruction of his forces in Korea since they were the only ones available for the defense of Japan. The JCS then recommended that MacArthur should hold at the Kum until the Chinese began massing for an assault across that river, in which event MacArthur should begin evacuation to Japan.[12]

Perhaps the fairest account of MacArthur's views was stated by one who conferred with him at that time, General Ridgway, who later wrote: "MacArthur, after the success of the Chinese New Year's offensive, agreed that if the JCS decisions stood unchanged—that we were to receive no major reinforcements, that there was to be no blockade of the Chinese coast, nor any air attack upon mainland China, no permission to bomb Manchurian bases, no 'unleashing' of the Chinese Nationalist forces in Formosa—then, in the absence of overriding political considerations, 'the command should be withdrawn from Korea just as rapidly as it is tactically possible to do so.' "[13] What MacArthur evidently ignored was the still latent power of the Eighth Army and the problems posed for the Chinese by their lengthening supply lines and frigid weather.

With Truman's approval, the JCS sent MacArthur a tentative new directive on December 29 to defend Korea in successive positions with his existing forces so long as this could be done without serious losses.[14] To MacArthur the message, as he later wrote, "seemed to indicate a loss of the 'will to win'. . . ."[15] He immediately countered with what has become a famous message, a top-secret one, proposing exploitation of what he considered areas of Chinese vulnerability. Shedding all pretense of limited war and recognizing "the State of War which has been forced upon us by the Chinese authorities," he formally recommended:

1. Blockade of the Chinese coast.

2. Destruction of China's industrial capacity by air and naval bombardment.

3. Use of Chinese Nationalist contingents in Korea.

4. Authorization of the Nationalists to undertake diversionary action against the mainland—the point of his letter to Representative Martin.

MacArthur said that it was a matter of speculation whether or not his proposals would lead the Soviet Union to intervene on behalf of China.[16] It was a speculation filled with foreboding in the administration. Stalin and Mao Tse-tung had entered into a mutual assistance treaty providing that if one of the two powers were attacked by Japan "or a state allied with it," the other power "would immediately render military and other assistance with all the measures at its disposal." The provision haunted decision making in Washington. The main base for American prosecution of the war in Korea was Japan. As Bradley was to testify, the Chinese and Soviets "might very well interpret that as our working with Japan," thus bringing the mutual assistance treaty into operation in the event the United States attacked China.[17]

Other considerations also restrained Truman, Acheson, Marshall, and the Joint Chiefs. In order to be effective, General Collins later testified, a naval blockade would have had to include Dairen, which he described as a *de facto* Soviet port where halting ships "would be a very ticklish thing." An effective blockade, he said, might even have had to include the Soviets' principal eastern port, Vladivostok.[18] "I have no way of estimating the character of the Russian navy," Admiral Sherman, chief of naval operations, said in subsequent testimony, "but if the situation was reversed, I would expect our naval forces involved to go out and fight." He said that a unilateral American blockade "would set us apart from our allies and promote the feeling that the war with China is simply a United States war. The blockade could not be tight without allied cooperation. The fact is that our allies have been unwilling to join us in a naval blockade of China. . . ."[19] As for deployment of Chinese Nationalist contingents in Korea, a contemporary study by the Joint Strategic Survey Committee said that such a strategy could not significantly affect the outcome of the fighting.[20]

A most serious constraint on administration policy was the potential of Communist air power. In the opinion of military leaders in Washington, United Nations forces in Korea benefited every bit as much from what was in effect a privileged sanctuary as the Chinese benefited from their sanctuary in Machuria. While the United Nations shunned hot pursuit of Communist aircraft north of the Yalu, Communist planes refrained from bombing Pusan, the busy seaports in Japan, and allied airfields where planes were often jammed wingtip to wingtip. Washington was loathe to change the unspoken rules of sanctuary. The administration was so fearful of the chaos that would engulf allied ground forces if supplies were choked off by enemy air raids on vulnerable ports and airfields that it avoided anything that threatened to lift the limits of the war.

The Truman administration opposed widening the war because the military authorities were convinced, as General Collins was to testify, that "we are not prepared for a major war, as of now."[21] Neither was Asia the place where the United States wished to become engaged in such a war. Above all, the administration did not want to embroil the United States in a general war with the Soviet Union when both sides had atomic bombs.

The Joint Chiefs did not accept MacArthur's aggressive proposals. Essentially, the chiefs clung to the position that MacArthur should persist as long as possible in Korea, using existing forces to inflict maximum casualties on the enemy, but should withdraw to Japan if the safety of his forces in Korea were threatened.

MacArthur replied without hesitation.[22] He said that his command was not strong enough both to hold in Korea and to defend Japan. He said that the morale of his troops was precarious. He implied that he was not receiving adequate guidance. According to Collins, the JCS sympathized with MacArthur on that point, feeling that the administration had not clearly defined ''what our remaining political objectives were in Korea.''[23] Finally, in language that spread dismay when it reached Washington on January 10, MacArthur said:

As I have before pointed out, under the extraordinary limitations and conditions imposed upon the command in Korea its military position is untenable, but it can hold for any length of time up to its complete destruction if overriding political considerations so dictate.

''We were at our lowest point . . . ,'' Marshall later testified.[24]

''Deeply disturbed,'' as he was to say, Truman called a meeting of the National Security Council for January 12 to deal with the search for answers that had been set off in the highest echelons of the government by MacArthur's message.[25]

In a preliminary meeting with the Joint Chiefs Acheson had agreed that the Eighth Army should not continue to fight beyond the point where its future usefulness in Japan would be impaired. Short of that point, however, he emphasized the importance of gaining as much time as possible in Korea because a new effort to obtain a ceasefire was taking shape in the United Nations. As he saw it, the effort would have a better chance of succeeding if United Nations forces were still in the field.[26]

With Truman presiding, the National Security Council approved another directive to MacArthur.

Based upon all the factors known to us, including particularly those presented in your recent messages [it said], we are forced to the conclusion that it is infeasible under existing conditions, including sustained major effort by Communist China, to hold for a protracted period a position in Korea.

The Truman administration thus accepted the probable necessity of evacuating Korea in the near future, bringing to a shocking and humiliating end more than six months of costly struggle and death. In the new message of January 12, however, MacArthur was still ordered to hold as long as possible to buy time for cease-fire negotiations and only then, when further resistance became too dangerous, to withdraw to Japan.[27]

Two other steps were taken. General Collins was again ordered to Tokyo and Korea to make an independent assessment. Truman sent MacArthur a personal message, dated January 13, to give the United Nations commander guidance and explain the nature of the problem as seen in Washington.

Drafted in the State Department, reviewed by the Joint Chiefs and reworded by Truman, the message was patient and considerate. Its purpose was to explain why the administration believed there were compelling political reasons for holding out in Korea as long as practicable.

Continued resistance would, Truman said, demonstrate the unacceptability of aggression and provide a rallying point "around which the spirits and energies of the free world can be mobilized to meet the world-wide threat which the Soviet Union now poses." Resistance would "deflate the dangerously exaggerated political and military prestige of Communist China. . . ." Resistance would fulfill "our commitments of honor to the South Koreans and . . . demonstrate . . . that the friendship of the United States is of inestimable value in time of adversity." It would facilitate a peace treaty with Japan and enhance Japan's future security. It would lend point "to the rapid build-up of the defenses of the western world." Pending this build-up, "we must act with great prudence in so far as extending the area of hostilities is concerned. Steps which might in themselves be fully justified and which might lend some assistance to the campaign in Korea would not be beneficial if they thereby involved Japan or Western Europe in large-scale hostilities."[28]

The appalling prospect of possibly imminent evacuation had a jarring effect on Truman and the Joint Chiefs. Despite Truman's message and the flurry of directives to MacArthur, a question lingers as to whether the administration was quite as determined as it made out to avoid military action against China. The question goes beyond the talk Attlee had encountered in White House circles in December about a limited war through blockade and presumably covert actions to create internal dissension in China.

Just before Collins departed in mid-January for Tokyo, accompanied by General Vandenberg, the Joint Chiefs of Staff completed an unusual memorandum. Collins took it with him and read it to MacArthur, emphasizing its tentative nature. The document had not received approval from higher authorities, nor had it been accepted by the president and the National Security Council as government policy. Yet it set forth some arresting objectives, tentatively agreed upon by the Joint Chiefs. Among them were the following:

> Prepare now to impose a naval blockade of China and place it into effect as soon as our position in Korea is stabilized, or when we have evacuated Korea, and depending on circumstances then obtaining. . . .
>
> Remove now the restrictions on operations of the Chinese Nationalist forces and give such logistic support to those forces as will contribute to effective operations against the Communists.

Tentatively agreed upon by the JCS also were naval and air attacks on targets in China, but only "at such time as the Chinese Communists attack any of our forces outside of Korea."[29] That was an entirely different contingency, of course, from the situation in Korea about which MacArthur complained. Unquestionably, the United States would have resorted to serious retaliation if American forces had been attacked by the Chinese, say, in Japan.

The memorandum was later cited by MacArthur in his own defense to show that he and the JCS had been in agreement, although Marshall and the Chiefs swore that the memorandum had been prepared only in anticipation of possible evacuation of Korea and was obsolete when the United Nations forces succeeded in staying in Korea. The military leaders, observed the historian John Edward

Wiltz, "seemed to be telling the truth about the genesis and object of the memorandum. Yet, it would appear that on 12 January 1951 they were taking their 'tentative' proposals for expanding the war a good deal more seriously than their testimony . . . the following May indicated."[30]

Truman's message to MacArthur was written at about the same time as the JCS memorandum of the twelfth. In words that have attracted little attention the president assured the general that if the United Nations forces were driven out of Korea, "we shall not accept the result politically or militarily until the aggression has been rectified." In subsequent testimony, which remained censored for many years, Bradley declared, "We just couldn't take" expulsion from Korea "as a final solution." Certainly, the American public would have been in a belligerent mood against China, or, as Bradley said in his long-censored testimony, "if we had been driven back to Pusan beachhead, even if we had been able to hold it or if we had been driven out, I think our people would have demanded something else be done against China."[31] Hence the possibility, as Professor Wiltz, an authority on the Korean War, suggests, that by early January 1951 the Truman administration may have been "on the verge of ordering a dramatic expansion of hostilities in East Asia," if United Nations military operations in Korea collapsed.

Then the picture on which Washington had fixed its troubled gaze changed radically. The prospect of evacaution vanished almost as suddenly as the Chinese troops after their first engagements in Korea. When Collins reached the Far East he discovered that the situation in Korea was not nearly so bad as had been portrayed in MacArthur's messages. In fact, at practically the moment the army chief of staff arrived, the Eighth Army on January 25 launched a limited attack, the first since its ill fated start to the Yalu on November 24. Having fallen back below Seoul, Inchon, and the Han River before the enemy's New Year's offensive, the Eighth Army now struck in a reconnaissance in force against enemy units near Osan, inflicting casualties. This was but the beginning of what is surely a gratifying episode in American military history.

Routed, bled, depleted, disorganized, dispirited, American troops had retreated painfully either on foot, as in the case of the Eighth Army, or partly by sea, as in the case of the Tenth Corps. By mid-January American soldiers were huddled back in the terrain near where Task Force Smith had first gone into action July 5. Another defense perimeter was being prepared around Pusan. In the cruel course of falling back through the snow the Eighth Army had even lost its commander, General Walker, who was killed in a jeep accident two days before Christmas.

The new commander was General Ridgway, previously deputy chief of staff of the army for operations. In the Second World War he had commanded the 82nd Airborne Division in Sicily and Normandy and later the Eighteenth Airborne Corps. Seldom has a commander conducted such a timely rescue of his country from a strategically and politically dangerous predicament as Ridgway did in Korea by restoring, reorganizing, refitting, and reinvigorating the Eighth Army and sending it on its way north again, strengthened by the inclusion of the refurbished Tenth Corps.

On January 17 Collins sent a message to Washington: "Eighth Army in good shape and improving daily under Ridgway's leadership. Morale very satisfactory considering conditions. . . ."[32] The tentative JCS proposals for a naval blockade and landing of Nationalist forces were pigeonholed.

A side effect of the good news from Korea was a further loss of confidence in Washington in MacArthur's judgment. His views, wrote Schnabel and Watson, "no longer commanded the respect that they had once enjoyed."[33]

Late in January, Ridgway ordered a series of strong attacks against Chinese troops, now at the end of a long supply line that was at the mercy of American planes. Such was the success of the offensive that by mid-March Ridgway had recaptured Seoul. With the Chinese in retreat the administration's problem had changed from when to evacuate Korea to whether to cross the 38th parallel again.

To the Truman administration and the allies China's intervention had put United Nations conquest of North Korea out of the question. While there was a willingness to allow Ridgway to cross the parallel for narrow tactical purposes, the hardening war aim of the administration was a cease-fire and settlement that would restore a divided Korea.

Still MacArthur pressed his opinion. This he had a perfect right and duty to do but only within the councils of the government, where his proposals were indeed given careful attention. Once a decision had been made by the president, in this instance against extending the war, MacArthur had no authority to argue his case in public. He continued to do so in disregard not only of custom but of Truman's order of December 5 that statements dealing with diplomatic or military policy must be cleared by higher authority. On February 13 MacArthur issued on his own authority a statement saying that the "concept advanced by some that we should establish a line across Korea and enter into positional warfare is wholly unrealistic and illusory."[34]

Five weeks later he took an astounding step. Its effect was to abort a pending initiative, approved by the president, to obtain a cease-fire. Had the initiative succeeded, it would have ended MacArthur's own hopes for extending the war to China. His action to thwart the initiative brought relations between himself and the president to an intolerable point.

As the Eighth Army approached the 38th parallel it was decided early in March that the president as executive agent for the United Nations should make an open appeal for a halt in the war. The Joint Chiefs and the State Department drafted a declaration, which noted that the "aggressors have been driven back . . . to the general vicinity from which the unlawful attack was first launched last June." The United Nations, the declaration continued, wished to prevent the spread of hostilities, seeking instead a "basis for restoring peace and security in the area. . . ." The United Nations command, therefore, was ready to enter into arrangements to end the fighting and pave the way for a settlement, including withdrawal of foreign troops from Korea. Without mentioning unification of Korea by force, the declaration noted the United Nations position in favor of a unified, independent Korea, whose people were entitled to choose their own form of government. The declaration held out the prospect that a Korean settlement could open the door to broader settlements in the Far East.[35]

The United States moved to obtain clearances of the declaration from other United Nations members having units in Korea. As part of the preparations the JCS on March 20 notified MacArthur: "State planning Presidential announcement shortly that, with clearing of bulk of South Korea of aggression, United Nations now prepared to discuss conditions of settlement. . . . Time will be required to determine diplomatic reactions and permit new negotiations that may develop. . . ."[36]

On March 24 MacArthur stunned the president and the highest authorities in the government and threw the United Nations into anger and suspicion. In a statement brimming with diplomatic and military considerations, yet not cleared by his superiors, MacArthur issued what the press—and later Truman—called an ultimatum to Communist China.[37]

The Eighth Army advance, he said, had revealed that the power of China's ground forces was "exaggerated." Furthermore, the Chinese lacked the industrial capacity and raw materials to create a modern military machine and could not even conquer Korea despite advantages accruing to them through the "inhibitions" placed upon MacArthur.

"These military weaknesses have been clearly and definitely revealed . . ." he said. In words quite contrary to the spirit of the president's pending declaration, he added:

The enemy therefore must by now be painfully aware that a decision of the United Nations to depart from its tolerant effort to contain the war to the area of Korea through expansion of our military operations to his coastal areas and interior bases would doom Red China to the risk of imminent military collapse.

In other words, Communist China could be thoroughly defeated if MacArthur were allowed to take the military measures he had recommended.

Thus "there should be no insuperable difficulty arriving at decisions on the Korean problem if the issues are resolved on their own merits without being burdened by extraneous matters not directly related to Korea, such as Formosa and China's seat in the United Nations." MacArthur, not the president, was excluding Formosa and United Nations membership as possible issues for negotiation.

The general concluded that "I stand ready at any time to confer in the field with the commander in chief of the enemy forces in an earnest effort to find any military means whereby the realization of the political objectives of the United Nations in Korea . . . might be accomplished without further bloodshed."[38]

Word of the statement caused an early-morning meeting of Deputy Secretary of Defense Lovett and the Joint Chiefs of Staff. First they turned to the embarrassment that this dramatic development would inject into negotiations with other United Nations members over the pending presidential statement. Then they took up the problem, once again created by MacArthur, as to whether the general, the president, or the United Nations was to be seen as the negotiating authority. Finally the chiefs brought up the subject of disciplining MacArthur for defiance of Truman's December 5 order.

Lovett telephoned Acheson. The two agreed that if any officer other than MacArthur had committed such a breach, he would have been relieved of his command immediately. While the Joint Chiefs believed that his transgression could not be overlooked, they felt that the consequences of relieving MacArthur would be altogether too startling. Their initial reaction was to reprimand him. Lovett and Acheson decided to go to the White House at noon.[39]

Acheson later described Truman's reaction as a combination of incredulity and controlled fury.[40] Truman was to recall that he considered that MacArthur, "in open defiance of my orders," had issued a statement at cross-purposes with Truman's own proposed declaration and had intimated "that the full preponderance of Allied power might be brought to bear against Red China." This caused the allies themselves to ask whether the United States was changing policy.[41]

The episode, apparently, was the "doublecross" to which Truman referred when Roger Tubby first brought him the news of MacArthur's letter to Joe Martin.

Marshall later testified, "In view of the serious impact of General MacArthur's statement on the negotiations with these nations, it became necessary to abandon the effort, thus losing whatever chance there may have been at that time to negotiate a settlement of the Korean conflict."[42]

In testimony of his own Acheson doubted that the proposed declaration would have found favor with China at that point but said that "it had other important collateral usefulness."[43]

MacArthur insisted that his statement was a routine one in the tradition of field commanders and was not intended to prejudice the president's purposes. In fact, the general described the statement as a psychological warfare device, which had been prepared even before the Joint Chiefs had notified him March 20 that a presidential declaration was imminent.[44]

That did not wash with George Marshall. He testified that MacArthur had violated his own authority in issuing the statement.

"What the issue in this matter is," Marshall said, "is that he himself stepped forward in an approach to a possible settlement with the Communist forces just in advance of the time he knew the president was going to do the same thing and was in communication with our allies to arrange a procedure that would be acceptable to all of them."[45]

MacArthur, his biographer William Manchester was to say, "simply could not bear to end his career in checkmate."[46]

After conferring with Acheson and Lovett on MacArthur's statement the only action Truman took was to order that MacArthur be reminded of the presidential order of December 5. Unbeknown to Truman and his advisers, other events already had been set in train that were destined to dynamite the whole business.

Joe Martin had made a Lincoln Day speech in Brooklyn advocating prompt use of Chiang Kai-shek's forces. "Why not let them open a second front in Asia?" he asked. He condemned what he called a policy "that lets our soldiers die in Korea when, by shipping proper supplies to the generalissimo, a second front could be opened in China without a single GI being forced to place foot on the soil of the Chinese mainland.''

Contemplating further speeches along that line, Martin sent a copy of the text to MacArthur, whom he had known and admired since the 1930s. "I would deem it a great help," Martin wrote, "if I could have your views on this point, either on a confidential basis or otherwise." On March 20 MacArthur replied that Martin's advocacy of the use of Nationalist forces was in conflict neither with logic nor with the American tradition "of meeting force with maximum counter-force." He continued:

It seems strangely difficult for some to realize that here in Asia is where the Communist conspirators have elected to make their play for global conquest, and that we have joined the issue thus raised on the battlefield; that here we fight Europe's war with arms while the diplomats there still fight it with words; that if we lose the war to Communism in Asia the fall of Europe is inevitable, win it and Europe most probably would avoid war and yet preserve freedom. As you point out, we must win. There is no substitute for victory.[47]

The letter, Marshall later testified, "involves foreign policy, involved the reactions of all of our allies in Western Europe and involved our dealings with our allies and the question of what voice spoke from this country in the matter of foreign policy."[48]

Martin knew that publication of such a letter would cause a storm. Yet he noted that MacArthur had not elected to designate his reply as confidential, as Martin had invited him to do, if he wished. Martin secreted the letter, but observed that with each passing day the public seemed to become increasingly confused over the situation in Korea. Finally he rose in the House of Representatives on April 5 and denounced the administration's war policy in a speech in which he read MacArthur's letter. A short time later Roger Tubby saw the story on the news ticker, took it to Truman, and Truman said he would talk with Marshall. "MacArthur's letter to Martin as the leader of the opposition revolted Marshall," Lovett recalled.[49]

On his own calendar Truman jotted:

The situation with regard to the Far Eastern General has become a political one.

MacArthur has made himself a center of controversy, publicly and privately. He has always been a controversial figure.

He has had two wives—one a social light [sic] he married at 42, the other a Tennessee girl he married in his middle fifties after No 1 had divorced him.[50]

The drama in the White House approached a climax.

On April 6 Truman summoned four advisers, whom he was to consult regularly in the next few days on what he described in his diary as the "political bomb" that MacArthur had exploded in the Martin letter.

"This look [sic] like the last straw," Truman jotted.

"Rank insubordination. . . .''

The four advisers were Marshall, Acheson, Harriman, and Bradley. Truman's diary outlined the framework of the proceedings.

"I've come to the conclusion that our Big General in the Far East must be recalled. I don't express any opinion or make known my decision [while the advisers are deliberating]."[51]

The problem, as Acheson was to recall, was not what should be done but how it should be done so that the upheaval could be kept within tolerable limits. The trouble could be surmounted, he had believed, "if the President acted upon the carefully considered advice and unshakable support of all his civilian and military advisers. If he should get ahead of them or appear to take them for granted or be impetuous, the harm could be incalculable."[52]

When Truman asked his advisers what they recommended, therefore, Acheson suggested a deliberate approach toward the removal of MacArthur. Marshall also counseled caution. He was concerned lest an uproar in Congress threaten pending military appropriations. Harriman forthrightly favored relief of MacArthur. Bradley did not immediately recommend such action. He wished to confer with the Joint Chiefs before giving an opinion.[53]

"What worried us most," Truman later told George Elsey and Eben Ayers, "was the situation that had arisen as a result of what MacArthur had done on that United Nations statement [MacArthur's statement of March 24 offering to confer with the enemy]. That was inexcusable. His action on that international document was a terrific thing. It upset the applecart for the U.N. That worried us more than the Joe Martin letter. We also talked about the December [5] directive. MacArthur was acting in flat disobedience of that directive."[54]

Still expressing to them no opinion of his own about action to be taken, Truman asked his four advisers to weigh the problem and return the next day.

On April 7, a Saturday, the four advisers met with Truman again. In his diary he wrote: "It is the unanimous opinion of all that MacArthur be relieved. All four so advise."[55] Truman confided to Charles Murphy that he was going to relieve MacArthur.[56] Memories of the day differed, however. Bradley later testified that on April 7 "we still did not make any specific recommendation except that we recommended he not make any decision until after the weekend."[57] That seems to be correct, because Bradley had not yet consulted the Joint Chiefs. Furthermore, Truman still intended to consult other advisers, including Secretary of the Treasury Snyder. Snyder had been friendly with MacArthur but believed that the general had gone too far for the president to tolerate.[58]

In a private conversation Bradley suggested to Marshall that the problem might be solved if the secretary of defense would write to MacArthur, explaining the difficult position in which he was placing Truman by his statements. Bradley and Marshall drafted such a letter, but nothing more was done about it.[59]

On Sunday, April 8, Bradley assembled the Joint Chiefs of Staff for a two-hour discussion. He then escorted them to Marshall, before whom each of the three chiefs—Collins, Vandenberg, and Sherman—stated his reasons, from a military viewpoint, for believing that MacArthur should be relieved. Bradley, as chairman, expressed no opinion then but testified later that he concurred in the unanimous opinion of the three. As recapitulated by Bradley, the first reason given by the chiefs for their decision was that MacArthur's statements and messages had proved that he was not in sympathy with the official policy to limit the war to Korea. A second reason was that MacArthur had violated the presidential directive requiring that all officials obtain clearance of public statements on military or foreign policy. A third reason was that as a military officer MacArthur had not submitted to civilian control.[60]

Meanwhile in Blair House that Sunday Truman had a long talk with two good friends, Speaker Rayburn and Chief Justice Fred Vinson. While not telling them of his decision, he listened to their advice to be cautious because of the political and constitutional questions involved. He also talked on the telephone to Vice President Barkley, who was in the hospital. After that he leafed through history books for precedents, notably that of Lincoln's relief of General George B. McClellan as commander of the Army of the Potomac in the Civil War because of lack of aggressiveness.[61] It did not escape Truman that McClellan consorted with Lincoln's opposition in Congress and ran against Lincoln for president, unsuccessfully, in 1864.

At a meeting with the Democratic congressional leaders on Monday morning, April 9, Truman confided that he was going to relieve MacArthur.[62] Then he met with his four chief advisers. Bradley reported that the Joint Chiefs of Staff unanimously favored MacArthur's removal. Marshall, Acheson and Harriman declared themselves in favor of removal. The president then stated orally that MacArthur was to be relieved, and directed his advisers to prepare the necessary orders.[63]

Only a small circle of men, including at least Murphy among the White House staff, knew of Truman's decision. The secrecy of recent days remained as tight as ever as Marshall, Acheson and the Joint Chiefs worked on official orders and a public statement of explanation by the president and on a plan for courteous notification of MacArthur. An upset of this plan was to compound all the other troubles that were brewing for Truman.

33. *The Firing of General MacArthur*

ON TUESDAY, APRIL 10, Truman had about come to the end of a, thus far, routine morning staff meeting when he leaned back in his chair and caught most of his staff by surprise.

"So you won't need to read about it in the papers," he said, "I fired MacArthur yesterday from all his jobs."[1]

With relish he added that he would like to make the announcement at his press conference on Thursday and chuckled at the vision of reporters dashing for telephones. But then he said, "I'm afraid it won't hold that long."[2]

The staff erupted with questions and comments, some directed to the importance of a presidential explanation to the people.

"I can show," Truman said, "just how the so-in-so doublecrossed us. I'm sure MacArthur wanted to be fired."[3]

Through his aide, General Whitney, MacArthur later said that he had been stunned by the suddenness of Truman's action.[4]

"He's [MacArthur's] going to be regarded as a worse doublecrosser than McClellan," Truman told his staff. "He did just what McClellan did—got in touch with minority leaders in the Senate. He worked with the minority to undercut the administration when there was a war on."[5]

"Everybody seems to think I don't have courage enough to do it," Truman remarked at another point. "We'll let 'em think so, then we'll announce it."[6]

"It undoubtedly will create a great furor," he wrote to a friend, David M. Noyes, "but under the circumstances I could do nothing else and still be President of the United States. Even the Chiefs of Staff came to the conclusion that civilian control of the military was at stake and I didn't let it stay at stake very long."[7]

In mid-afternoon that same day Truman initialed the order for MacArthur's relief and handed it to Acheson. Acheson was to send it to Pusan for Ambassador Muccio. Muccio was to give it to Secretary of the Army Frank Pace, who, knowing nothing of what had happened in Washington, was on a Korean inspection trip. Pace was to fly to Tokyo and in the most private and considerate manner deliver the notification to MacArthur at the United States embassy, his residence. At such a moment Murphy's Law did not fail. Communications with Pusan broke down. And worse was yet to come.

At around 6 P.M. in Washington that Tuesday White House press secretary Short summoned reporters, who were on edge over all the secrecy, and told them that "the lid was on." This is the traditional signal that the White House has no more news for the day. The reporters went home, and Short joined Bradley, Harriman, Rusk, George Elsey, Matt Connelly, and Roger Tubby, who were in the cabinet room still working on material for release after MacArthur had been notified. The telephone rang. Colonel Chester V. Clifton, aide to the chairman of the Joint Chiefs of Staff, was calling Bradley. Clifton's message was a most unwelcome one. According to Roger Tubby's contemporary account of that evening, Clifton said that Lloyd Norman, the *Chicago Tribune* reporter at the Pentagon, had just put in a query as to whether an important resignation was expected in Tokyo. Bradley was told, furthermore, that the *Tribune* planned to open its Tokyo wire early to handle the resignation story if and when it broke.

The call threw the White House into an acute dilemma and some panic. "Naturally," Tubby noted in his journal, "we were all at once sure that if this were a true report, the resignation would be MacA's. He apparently had gotten wind of T's decision." In the midst of a flurry of suspicion as to who in the government had been party to such a leak, Bradley telephoned Truman at Blair House and reported the *Tribune*'s query.

Truman's first reaction was that the announcement of his decision should be made that night. Then he said he wanted to think it over. He asked Bradley to call in Marshall and Acheson. Marshall had taken his wife to a motion picture. Acheson came, however. He doubted the accuracy of the *Tribune*'s information and opposed making an announcement that night before Pace had notified MacArthur. A debate ensued.

From the first, Roger Tubby argued for immediate announcement. Otherwise, he warned, the risk would have to be run, as his journal noted, that MacArthur could "get jump on President. If he did he would probably say, I am resigning only because I can no longer serve under an Administration which making [sic] such serious blunders in foreign affairs etc etc.' Anything we then said would never catch up with General. The President had to act, better to have Genl lose a little face and have hurt feelings than have President given most serious rebuff."

Gradually, according to the journal, others came round to Tubby's viewpoint. "Rusk holding out last, wanting orderly business and more time for careful preparations." Tubby persisted. "I said, 'Why should we spare the Genl's feelings when he has behaved so outrageously toward President? in unethical, insubordinate, insolent way?' " Harriman, Murphy, and Connelly, three most influential figures in such a situation, sided strongly with Tubby's argument.

At about 10 o'clock Bradley, Harriman, Rusk, Short, and Connelly went across the street to Blair House to confer with Truman, leaving Tubby and Elsey to complete work on the statements.

The telephone in the cabinet room rang around 10:30 P.M. Short, calling from Blair House, instructed Tubby to send to the mimeograph room the statements and the two presidential orders: one relieving MacArthur of his commands, the other naming General Ridgway as MacArthur's successor. In anticipation of a wild night Connelly sent word to all White House telephone operators to report for duty as quickly as possible.

As suspense rose, Tubby found his attention drawn to General Bradley, who worked skillfully under pressure but was "obviously unhappy."

"He thought, it was perfectly clear, that McA should be fired," Tubby noted, "but he was bitter and sad that it should be necessary to do so. Two or three times he said he couldn't understand why Mac should have behaved so. Bradley said he would have been willing to have delivered the order personally to MacA, but glad he didn't have to."

There were times when, Bradley said, according to Tubby, "you have got to tell a man he has to be dropped. I have told a division commander, 'You may be a good man, but your troops have lost confidence in you, and I have lost confidence in you. You have got to go.' "

It was growing late when those who had been to Blair House returned. The mimeograph machines were spewing out pages and the White House staff was checking them. Then word filtered in from somewhere, doubtless through Colonel Clifton, that the Mutual Broadcasting System was setting up for a big story out of Tokyo.

"That was clincher," Tubby wrote.[8] The plans for Pace's call on MacArthur went out the window.

Truman jotted in his diary, "Discussed the situation and I ordered messages sent at once and directly to MacArthur."[9]

On an editor's tip, the source of which was not known to him, Lloyd Norman had indeed made the query reported by Clifton.[10] The origin of the tip that the *Tribune* and possibly the Mutual Broadcasting System had received is a story that has evaporated over the years. MacArthur later testified that he had never considered resigning.[11] The original plan for the courteous notification of the general by Pace probably could have been carried out after all without the news of Truman's decision breaking beforehand.

In the circumstances, however, Joseph Short had the telephone operators call all the reporters and photographers regularly assigned to the White House to tell them he would have an important announcement at 1 A.M., by which time it would be Wednesday, April 11. At a hectic press conference reporters were handed copies of Truman's message to MacArthur, which said:

I deeply regret that it becomes my duty as President and Commander in Chief of the United States military forces to replace you as Supreme Commander, Allied Powers; Commander in Chief, United Nations Command; Commander in Chief, Far East; and Commanding General, U.S. Army, Far East.

You will turn over your commands, effective at once, to Lt. Gen. Matthew B. Ridgway. . . .[12]

In a separate statement Truman acquainted MacArthur with the reasons for his action. He said that MacArthur was "unable to give his wholehearted support to the policies of the United States Government and of the United Nations. . . ." He added:

Full and vigorous debate on matters of national policy is a vital element in the constitutional system of our free democracy. It is fundamental, however, that military commanders must be governed by the policies and directives issued to them in the manner provided by our laws and Constitution. In time of crisis, this consideration is particularly compelling.

General MacArthur's place in history as one of our greatest commanders is fully established. The nation owes him a debt of gratitude for the distinguished and exceptional service which he has rendered to his country in posts of great responsibility. . . .[13]

From the White House the news flash went around the world:

TRUMAN FIRES MACARTHUR

Truman already had retired for a sound night's sleep. He knew well enough that he would awake in a political climate raised to a pitch of hatred and recrimination so severe that it could not fail to stain the remainder of his term in office. Of all the storms he lived through as president, the one about to break was the worst.

In Tokyo on Wednesday, April 11, a military aide heard of Truman's action on a radio. He passed the news to MacArthur's wife, Jean. She told the general.[14] Such an abrupt, haphazard notification not only infuriated his friends but left a bad taste even in the mouths of his critics and engendered public sympathy for him.

In Washington, at 9:30 A.M., a group of Republicans from the Senate, the House, and the national committee met in an angry session in Joe Martin's office. In a blazing speech Taft suggested—but did not pursue the issue—that Truman be impeached.[15]

At the same hour, Truman was holding his usual morning staff meeting, preening himself by deriding "trimmers and faint hearted men." He added, "You have got to decide what is right to do, and then do it, even if it is unpopular."

In otherwise good spirits, he waxed indignant because he believed that Senator Tobey, a New Hampshire Republican, had used a recording device during an earlier telephone conversation with the president about the relief of MacArthur. Truman said that someone had once brought him a recording device but that he had sent it back without using it.*

"I think it's outrageous for anyone to use them," he asserted. "However, I don't care if Tobey releases everything I said to him. I told him I heard he wanted to impeach me. I said, go ahead."

Short reported to the meeting that telegrams were pouring into the White House (Western Union said one hundred and twenty-five thousand arrived in Washington in two days), the overwhelming number of them condemning the president's action.

"They don't bother me a bit," Truman said, according to Roger Tubby.[16]

When Congress convened that day Senator Jenner opened the debate,

*In 1945 Truman removed from the Oval Office a recording device that Roosevelt had used occasionally. Early in the Truman administration someone made between two and three hours audible, though not always intelligible, recordings, including some of Truman's private conversations, apparently in the Oval Office, and one press conference. Many of the recordings contain nothing but background noise and static.

exclaiming: "[T]his country is in the hands of a secret inner coterie which is directed by agents of the Soviet Union. . . . Our only choice is to impeach President Truman. . . ."[17] The galleries applauded. Knowland characterized the president's action as "a Far Eastern Munich."[18] Hearst's *New York Journal-American* suggested in an editorial that Truman may have acted under the influence of "some kind of mental or neural anodyne" administered by a State Department agent.[19] Joe McCarthy chimed in with the suggestion that Truman had made his decision late at night, groggy from "bourbon and Benedictine," if anyone could imagine Truman drinking Benedictine.[20] "The son of a bitch should be impeached," McCarthy also said. The *Chicago Tribune* declared in a front-page editorial: "President Truman must be impeached and convicted. . . . [H]e is unfit, morally and mentally, for his high office."[21]

Now approaching a period of prolonged stalemate, America's first limited war had never seemed so hateful and frustrating. As a leading spokesman of a party that had demanded that Truman draw the line against the Communist advance in Asia, Wherry gave his irate Republican fellows their new line: Korea was "Truman's war." Representative Dirksen intoned that MacArthur's recall was a victory for the State Department and its 10 Downing Street pals, a jibe conveniently abetted by cheering in the House of Commons at the news of Truman's action. Nixon said: "The happiest group in the country will be the communists and their stooges. . . . The president has given them what they have always wanted—MacArthur's scalp."[22]

That Wednesday night, April 11, Truman went on television and told the people that "In simplest terms, what we are doing in Korea is this: we are trying to prevent a third world war." Thus far, he said, "we have prevented aggression from succeeding and bringing on a general war."

"I have thought long and hard about this question of extending the war in Asia. I have discussed it many times with the ablest military advisers in the country. I believe with all my heart that the course we are following is the best course.

"I believe that we must try to limit the war to Korea. . . .

"A number of events have made it evident that General MacArthur did not agree with that policy. . . ."[23]

Probably no major decision that Harry Truman made in nearly eight years in office is more generally upheld by posterity than his relief of MacArthur and for the very reasons stated at the time by Truman, Marshall, and the Joint Chiefs of Staff. By the millions, however, his contemporaries loathed the president for his decision, excoriated him or turned their backs on him for what he had done to a national hero whose objective was the defeat of communism.

"The people, in my section at least," said a southern senator, "are almost hysterical."[24]

From coast to coast the outburst of political passion was on a scale rare in the United States. Frustrated by the war, disgusted over corruption in Washington, worried about alleged subversion in the government, and nearly worshipful of MacArthur, people vented their anger as their mood dictated. They threatened to punch Truman; punched each other; sent nasty telegrams to the 'witling' in the White House; signed petitions; flew the American flag upside down or at half-staff; denounced the president of the United States as a pig, a Judas, a red herring, a little man. They wept; sneered ("This wouldn't have happened if Truman were alive."); cried out from pulpits; and cheered MacArthur. In San Gabriel, California, Truman was hanged in effigy. The Los Angeles City Council adjourned "in sorrowful contemplation of the political assassination" of MacArthur. New York longshoremen left their jobs to demonstrate against Truman. At the opening baseball game in Washington several days later the president was raucously booed to his face in the first such incident in a baseball park since Herbert Hoover's appearance at the World Series of 1931. "The Roosevelt-Truman haters are having a chance to let off their spleen," Harriman wrote to Eisenhower.[25]

Ridgway called on MacArthur in Tokyo on April 12. MacArthur said that he had learned through a physicians' grapevine that Truman "was suffering from malignant hypertension; that this affliction was characterized by bewilderment and confusion . . . and that . . . he wouldn't live six months."[26]

To the anger of Speaker Rayburn, Joe Martin at the meeting with other Republicans had telephoned MacArthur in Tokyo and invited him to address a joint session of Congress without having first discussed the matter with the Democratic leaders who controlled Congress. MacArthur accepted. Truman publicly called the invitation a fitting honor.[27]

Above the storm voices could be heard defending Truman. They were to grow louder. The first to stick his finger in the dike was Senator Robert S. Kerr, a freshman Democrat from Oklahoma, who told the Senate that the Republicans were ducking the real issue.

"If they . . . believe," he said, "that the future security of this nation depends on following the MacArthur policy, let them put up or shut up. Let them submit a resolution . . . expressing it as the sense of the Senate that we should either declare war against Red China or do that which would amount to open warfare against her. . . . If they do not, their support of MacArthur is a mockery."[28]

In West Germany, General Eisenhower commented, "When you put on a uniform there are certain inhibitions you accept."[29]

Some of the middle-of-the road Republicans long identified with "bipartisan foreign policy" defended the president's right to relieve MacArthur. Despite the fire and brimstone of the Hearst, McCormick, and Scripps-Howard newspapers, a number of leading papers soberly supported Truman. Among them were the *New York Herald Tribune*, the *New York Times*, the *Washington Post*, the *Chicago Sun-Times*, the *Christian Science Monitor*, the *Minneapolis Tribune*, the *Denver Post*, the *St. Louis Post-Dispatch*, the *Boston Globe*, and the *Atlanta Journal*.

Truman, of course, grabbed his pen to tell his friends what the trouble was all about.

"I think everyone who stops to think," he wrote to one of them, "will understand that there can't be two policy makers at the head of a Government. I fear very much that our Far Eastern General had decided that he was a big enough 'Proconsul' to tell the Government at home what to do."[30]

To Ambassador Bowers, Truman wrote that MacArthur "understands military procedure and he also knows better than to try to run the policy of the United States Government from the Far East. If he didn't know better before he knows now."[31]

"I was sorry to have to reach a parting of the way with the big man in Asia," he wrote to Eisenhower, "but he asked for it and I had to give it to him."[32]

At a Jefferson-Jackson Day dinner in Washington Truman attacked MacArthur's Republican supporters—"people, I am sorry to say, who are playing petty politics right now with the future of the country and the peace of the world at stake."

"They want us to get out of Korea," he said, "but they urge us to wage an aggressive war against China."[33]

Meanwhile MacArthur was coming home to as great an ovation as the American people have ever given to a man. Returning to continental United States for the first time in fourteen years, he told a roaring crowd in San Francisco, "The only politics I have is contained in the simple phrase known well by all of you: God Bless America." In Washington, Marshall and the Joint Chiefs of Staff were on hand to greet him at National Airport. Truman made his tormentors grate their teeth by sending as a personal emissary the presidential military aide, General Vaughan. Vaughan's name had last been in the newspapers in connection with a letter he had written seeking help for a friend interested in buying materials from the Foreign Liquidation Service.

The drama and emotion of MacArthur's televised appearance before the joint session of Congress on April 19 took on the character of an immortal moment in the life of a nation.[34] In a truly remarkable episode the deposed general eloquently appealed to Congress and the people over the heads of the president and his diplomatic and military advisers. It was defeatism, he said to loud applause, to hold that the United States could not mount as strong a defense for Asia as for Europe.

"You cannot," he said, "appease or otherwise surrender to communism in Asia without simultaneously undermining our efforts to halt its advance in Europe."

Truman's view that Chiang Kai-shek's forces had frittered away American help when they were opposing the Communists on the mainland and thus could be expected to do little to help overturn the Communists while operating from Formosa was scorned by MacArthur.[35]

"On Formosa," the general said, "the government of the Republic of China has had an opportunity to refute by action much of the malicious gossip which so undermined the strength of its leadership on the Chinese mainland."

As for the Korean War, Chinese intervention had called for new decisions

"if our political aim was to defeat this new enemy as we had defeated the old."
To applause, MacArthur added, "Such decisions have not been forthcoming."
He renewed his complaint that he had not been permitted to send planes against
the enemy sanctuary across the Yalu and repeated his proposals for a naval
blockade of China and deployment of Chiang's forces on the Chinese mainland.
He condemned the lack of reinforcements in Korea. Once war is "forced upon
us, there is no alternative than to apply every available means to bring it to a
swift end. War's very objective is victory—not prolonged indecision." There
were, he said, even some—if he did not mean Acheson, others took him to mean
it—who "would appease Red China."

"Why, my soldiers asked of me, surrender military advantages to an enemy
in the field? I could not answer. [Applause]. . . . The magnificence of the courage and fortitude of the Korean people defies description. . . . Their last words
to me were, 'Don't scuttle the Pacific.' "
Then he added:

"Old soldiers never die; they just fade away." And like the old soldier of that ballad,
I now close my military career and just fade away—an old soldier who tried to do his
duty as God gave him the light to see that duty Goodby.

Indubitably, the whole MacArthur drama turned people more than ever
against the frustrating limited war. Indubitably, it divided public opinion on
what should be done in the Far Eastern stalemate. There is little doubt that the
speech strengthened the Republican party and no doubt whatever that it hurt
Truman politically and weakened his leadership in the home stretch. Two things
it did not do.

It did not, despite all the thunder, force a change in the foreign policy of
the Truman administration. Sober second thoughts prevailed.

It did not crush President Truman. A very important reason why it did not
was that throughout, especially in the forthcoming Senate hearings on the relief
of MacArthur, George Marshall, Omar Bradley, Lawton Collins, Forrest Sherman, and Hoyt Vandenberg stood solidly and unshakably behind the president
for all to see. If, on the contrary, the esteemed secretary of defense and the
chairman and members of the Joint Chiefs of Staff had supported General
MacArthur, Truman would have had a staggering task getting through his term.

V

THE END OF 20 YEARS
OF DEMOCRATIC RULE

34. *The Ravages*

TWENTY-ONE MONTHS in office still stretched ahead of Truman after the dismissal of MacArthur. The landscape was strewn with political damage accumulated during the president's six turbulent years in the White House and the Democrats' eighteen consecutive years in power.

The war continued with no expectation of national pride in ultimate victory over the North Korean regime or the Chinese army. American troops were being killed, and were killing, for retention of a Korea divided about as it had been when the war began. It was a galling prospect for the American people after the global triumphs of 1942–45. Actually, the lives of most Americans at home were little affected by the Korean War, except for the early inflation. Times were prosperous. There were no mass protests, no public confrontations, no demonstrations around the White House, no burning of draft cards, no campus disorders. Students in college with good grades were exempt from the draft. The national reaction to hostilities was simply one of dissatisfaction and disillusionment. People were incredulous that the country was in such a war, incredulous that the fighting wore on with no end in sight.

Stories of corruption in Washington had left a sour taste across the country.

In the political crosswinds of war and rising military expenditures the Fair Deal was stranded on the rocks. Korea sidetracked innovative programs like the Housing Act of 1949, the Brannan plan, and Point Four. Civil rights, gilded with hope after Truman's victory in 1948, was completely stalled in Congress. In contrast with the glowing expectations at the start of Truman's second term in 1949, his 1951 State of the Union message was so preoccupied with war, taxes, rearmament, and the perceived Soviet threat that domestic reforms were scarcely mentioned.

The first gratifying victory of the Fair Deal in Congress at the start of the second term—the "21-day rule" curbing the power of the House Rules Committee—was repealed by the conservative Eighty-second Congress, which convened in January 1951. With Republican strength enhanced by the 1950 elections, the House restored the power of the conservative Rules Committee to block liberal legislation.

The war had forced Truman to muffle his differences with southern conservatives. His quest for liberal reforms yielded to his need for the southerners' support of his war policy after the calamity of Chinese intervention and the tumult of MacArthur's dismissal.

Meanwhile the Democratic party was losing ground in the South. The growing wealth of modern southern cities nurtured enthusiasm for conservative Republican principles. In the face of rising demands of blacks for political and social rights, southern states wanted no part of new liberal programs. As it was, the region steamed with resentment against federal interference with its way of life. The race issue already had cracked the erstwhile Solid South, with the national Democratic ticket having lost Alabama, Mississippi, Louisiana, and South Carolina to the Dixiecrats in 1948.

In the large cities of the North, aging Democratic machines were decaying, largely as a result of the shift of political and economic power to Washington that had begun during the New Deal.

The torment of the Communist issue continued with endless hearings, trials, inquiries, and political attacks by McCarthy and others. Weakened by the crisis over General MacArthur, Truman was, if anything, less able than before to counter these attacks effectively. At the same time he was beset by complaints of injustice in the Employee Loyalty Program. That was the program he had established in his first term to neutralize Republican charges that "subversives" were infiltrating his administration.

Regardless of the political pressures that caused him to act in 1947, Truman came off badly on the loyalty issue. His heart was in the right place, and he said all the right things about the necessity of protecting the civil liberties of federal employees. Unfortunately, however, his own best instincts had been betrayed when he allowed the program to be based on wrong principles. By 1951 Washington was honeycombed with loyalty-security boards and loyalty review boards to pass upon federal employees' loyalty to the United States. These boards spread fear, anger, and loss of morale and frequently dispensed justice in a most dubious manner. Some decisions were a pure outrage.

Under the misguided principles, the perceived requirements of national security superseded the traditional rights of the individual. The loyalty boards, which were administrative rather than judicial bodies, were empowered to pass judgment on personal beliefs, associations, and opinions of citizens employed by or seeking employment in the government. The doctrine of guilt by association was introduced in the United States. No provision was made for judicial review of cases.[1] The aspect of the program most criticized by Joseph L. Rauh, Jr., chairman of the executive committee of Americans for Democratic Action, and other liberals was that a person accused of disloyalty had no right to confront his accusers nor to cross-examine witnesses.

Despite the criticism of the program, Truman on April 28, 1951, issued an executive order that, in view of Rauh and others, made things even worse. Hiram Bingham, chairman of the ultimate Loyalty Review Board in the Civil Service Commission, had felt that the wording of the original 1947 program tied the government's hands in seeking to dismiss employees in borderline cases. At his request, therefore, Truman's new order provided for dismissal if "there is a *reasonable doubt* as to the loyalty of the person involved." The original order authorized dismissal only if there were *"reasonable grounds"* for belief in a person's actual disloyalty. Three weeks after the new order Francis Biddle, national chairman of Americans for Democratic Action and attorney geneal under Franklin Roosevelt, sent Truman a memorandum saying, "We believe that this change will be treated in many agencies as an open invitation to start the very 'witch hunt' the President has been so anxious to avoid.''

The sad thing was that while Truman was growing increasingly alarmed over the threat to civil liberties, the whole loyalty apparatus had become such a monster that he could not control it or bring himself forthrightly to make desirable changes. After receiving the Biddle memorandum, Truman sent it to Charles Murphy with a note:

I have been very much disturbed with the action of some of these Boards and I want . . . to put a stop to their un-American activities. I wish you would have one of our staff boys look into this situation very carefully and make a recommendation to me.

Of course, it was the intention to have the Nimitz Commission go into these matters but it looks now as if we are not going to get any Nimitz Commission.[2]

On January 23, 1951, Truman had announced the establishment of the Commission on Internal Security and Individual Rights to be chaired by retired Fleet Admiral Chester Nimitz. Rather than put his own officials to work on the difficulties and correct defects through an executive order, Truman took the expedient course of appointing the commission in the face of the controversy. The nonpartisan group was directed to review the problems of internal security and the best ways to deal with them while still protecting civil liberties. "The Commission," he directed, "will be expected to report on the effectiveness and fairness of the Government's loyalty and security programs."[3]

The expedient fizzled. The whole undertaking was aborted by right-wing senators, fearing, in the words of Alonzo Hamby, "that the commission would take the Communist issue out of politics."[4] Under McCarran's chairmanship, the Senate Judiciary Committee blocked a routine presidential request to grant members of the commission, as part-time government employees, exemption from conflict-of-interest statutes, a common practice in such cases. Members of the commission resigned. Truman then directed the National Security Council to study ways of correcting the loyalty program. The work, however, carried over into his last months in office and resulted in a recommendation for still further study. There matters rested until Eisenhower came to office and made the loyalty program even stricter than it had been under Truman.

Meanwhile the last two years of the Truman administration were marred by especially shocking loyalty cases involving distinguished American diplomats who had once been stationed in China and later became victims of attack by McCarthy and his cohorts.[5]

As far as Truman was concerned, the melancholy story was that a program he had started largely as a political contrivance had become one that he was unable to control or reform, even when he became disturbed by growing signs of injustice. His dismay was captured by Matthew Connelly's typically skeletal summary of a cabinet meeting that took place on August 10, 1951. An outburst of Truman's was summarized: "There is an outrageous condition in connection with loyalty investigations. People are being persecuted without cause. [Truman] urged members to cooperate in correcting these abuses."[6]

Wage and price controls continued, with the usual headaches and dissatisfactions, although Truman did manage to bring labor representatives back into the mobilization agencies. He accomplished that by reconstituting the Wage Stabilization Board with new power to handle labor disputes. Meanwhile the defense production legislation authorizing all controls, including rent control, was due to expire June 30, 1951.

Truman asked Congress to extend the act for two years and strengthen it.[7] In keeping with the way things were going for him, he suffered a blunt rebuff on both counts, largely the handiwork of the old coalition of Republicans and conservative southern Democrats. Reinforcing the opposition was the evidence, underscored by MacArthur's dismissal, that the war would remain limited to the southern half of Korea and would gradually diminish, relieving pressure on the economy.

Truman refused to budge. He said in his special message to Congress that the full impact of the rearmament program still lay ahead and that the United States would not be "over the hump" of inflation for another two years. Meanwhile new orders promulgated by the Office of Price Stabilization and approved by Truman to cut back beef prices led to a battle between the White House and the farm bloc in Congress. It was all reminiscent of the squabbles in 1946 over the price of meat that finally tore apart the controls instituted during the Second World War.

"This is just the same old fight," Truman told a press conference in the spring of 1951. "Whenever you tread on the toes of anybody, he has to scream. . . . If we are going to have controls, we have got to put them into effect as far as we can."[8]

Anti-control sentiment extended well beyond the farm bloc. Truman went on television in mid-June and assailed the National Association of Manufacturers for "giving us the same old song and dance: take off price controls and everything will be just dandy. These people were wrong before, and they are wrong now."[9] An internal White House memorandum declared: "The NAM and the Chamber of Commerce have joined forces with various groups including the livestock industry in a campaign which, if successful, must inescapably lead to the scuttling of all controls and a new wave of uncontrolled inflation. . . ."[10]

In the end the best Truman could get from Congress was extension of substantially weakened controls. The power to roll back prices was restricted. Controls on commercial credits and rents were relaxed. The new bill required that price ceilings reflect increases or decreases in producers' costs through July 26, 1951. Also, retailers were to be allowed their customary margin of profits under price ceilings. Truman itched to veto the measure but dared not because it provided for rent control and other powers that he felt the government needed but would have expired had he withheld approval. The bill was "the worst I ever had to sign," he grumbled to reporters.[11] He besought Congress to enact separate measures restoring some of the former provisions but to no avail. Despite his rhetoric during the fight, the level of prices continued relatively stable.

For weeks after MacArthur's return the controversy reverberated.

Through the initiative of its White House correspondent, Anthony Leviero, and the willingness of Truman or some of his staff to cooperate, the *New York Times* obtained a copy, or at least the substance, of the top-secret report on the Wake Island conference. Thus the same issue of the *Times* that recounted MacArthur's triumphal procession up Broadway also carried a companion story on the front page, reporting that the general had asserted that the Chinese would not enter the war and had declared that victory was so close at hand in October that he soon could release certain divisions for redeployment to Europe.

MacArthur and his friends were outraged by the disclosure. A hullabaloo ensued over the propriety of Miss Anderson's note-taking at Wake, a controversy that still simmers among biographers and historians. In his biography of MacArthur, Manchester maintained that the White House had stooped to "bugging" the general.[12] When Truman had first glimpsed Miss Anderson after the conference ended, he felt, he said later, that she should not have been included in the official party.[13] Theretofore, as he recalled in a personal letter to Senator Edward Martin when the issue erupted in 1951, "I did not know there was a stenographer within ten miles of the place. . . ."[14] Interestingly, on his return from the Pacific trip the White House press secretary himself, Charles Ross, questioned the ethics of Miss Anderson's role.[15] From all that is known, however, she acted innocently and on her own. The issue was really mooted a few hours after the Wake conference when General Bradley, following the usual practice in such cases, required a number of Washington officials who had participated in the conference to compile their own notes and recollections.

Bradley was to testify that "we would have had practically as full notes without hers. . . . Everybody saw us making the notes."[16] The composite document, including Miss Anderson's contributions, had been sent to MacArthur's headquarters without eliciting challenge to its accuracy.

The greatest controversies in the late spring of 1951 swirled around the Senate joint hearings by the Committees on Armed Services and Foreign Relations. Undertaken as an inquiry into the relief of MacArthur, the hearings swelled into weeks of testimony and questioning concerning the administration's Far Eastern policy, the origins of the Korean War, the conduct and strategy of the war, and its future direction. All this led to sharp conflict, along familiar lines, over blame for troubles past and present. The most memorable line was Bradley's in opposing MacArthur's advocacy of attacking China. "Frankly, in the opinion of the Joint Chiefs of Staff," Bradley testified, "this strategy would involve us in the wrong war, at the wrong place, at the wrong time and with the wrong enemy."[17] The last, of course, reflected the administration's view that the ultimate adversary was the Soviet Union.

Skillfully chaired by Senator Russell of the Armed Services Committee, the hearings produced patient exposition of the various viewpoints, having the effect ultimately of calming the MacArthur controversy. The hearings did not make Truman's enemies like him any better than they had before. By his own account he was compelled to pass up his old army unit's reunion in Topeka in June because of an "unusual number of threats" against his life.[18] What the Senate hearings did accomplish in absorbing the shock of MacArthur's dismissal was to bring the administration's position back into the balance and remind the American people of their tradition of civilian control over the military. In the process, as the possible consequences of MacArthur's aggressive aims were aired, the hearings helped to preserve Truman's foreign policy.

Against the backdrop of major new battles in Korea the hearings also etched the outlines of unfolding United States strategy.

Time and again that spring Ridgway's forces repulsed enemy attacks, inflicting what Marshall described as "tremendous" losses on the Chinese. "If they renew the attack and they meet the same result that came from their attack of the last two weeks," he testified early in May, "we will have almost destroyed again, or ruined the fighting power of, some, I think it is, thirty-four new divisions. . . . If we break the morale of their armies but, more particularly, if we destroy their best-trained armies as we have been in the process of doing . . . it seems to me you develop the best probability of reaching a satisfactory negotiatory basis with those Chinese Communist forces. . . ."[19]

Acheson, a subsequent witness, was asked about the possibility of a cease-fire at or near the 38th parallel. He replied that "if you once get the conviction on the part of the Chinese that they cannot—they just haven't got the strength to—do what they want from the military point of view, I think you have a real possibility of working out a stable situation."[20]

Accordingly, Lie, the United Nations Secretary General, declared on June 1 that a cease-fire along, approximately, the 38th parallel would fulfill the principal purposes of the United Nations so long as it was followed by restoration of peace and security in the area. Diplomacy stirred. On June 23 Malik, the Soviet delegate to the United Nations, announced on radio that his government believed the war could be settled. After further diplomacy Ridgway sent a message to the North Korean military commander, offering to appoint a representative to a cease-fire conference. Two days later the North Koreans accepted, and on July 10, 1951, truce talks, destined to be exasperating and interminable, began at Kaesong and were later transferred to Panmunjom.

The fighting went on, since, as Ridgway was to note, "the negotiations were just an extension of the battlefield. Whatever was eventually agreed on would necessarily reflect the military realities, and it was the bitter task of the soldier to impress the enemy with our ability to resist all his efforts to move the battle line farther south."[21]

Truman went through spells of abysmal frustration. In such depths it was characteristic of him to blow off steam with jottings in a style far beyond the realm of his usual sober discourse. One passage in his diary likened the morality of Communist negotiators to that of leaders of a narcotics ring. In the same entry of January 27, 1952, he entertained visions of atomic anihilation of enemy cities and the death of the Soviet Union. He wrote:

> This means all out war. It means that Moscow, St. Petersburg, Mukden, Vladivostock, Pekin [sic], Shanghai, Port Arthur, Dairen, Odessa, Stalingrad and every manufacturing plant in China and the Soviet Union will be eliminated.
>
> This is the final chance for the Soviet Government to decide whether it desires to survive or not.[22]

The next day he calmly sent up a message asking Congress to authorize the St. Lawrence Seaway. And the truce talks droned on. The administration found itself trapped for eighteen months in a situation in which it could neither win the war nor extricate itself from Korea. Men were to be killed and wounded in battle for as long as Truman remained in office. Peace was in the offing somewhere, but the wait was long and sour, causing strain and political damage throughout his last months in the White House.

35. *Showdown: The Attorney General and the President*

A T THE TIME OF the Senate hearings in 1951 that brought down Boyle as Democratic national chairman, David Bell, an administrative assistant to Truman, wrote an internal White House memorandum on some related matters.

Addressed to Charles Murphy as special counsel to the president, Bell's memorandum of October 30 urged that Truman appoint a respected national figure "to head up a complete investigation of possible fraud, corruption and malfeasance" in the Bureau of Internal Revenue. In truth, the bureau, an arm of the Treasury Department, was in scandalous condition. Tips of the iceberg already had appeared. In April 1951 an old friend of Truman's, James P. Finnegan, resigned as collector of internal revenue in St. Louis for having accepted illegal fees. Three months later Truman removed the collector of internal revenue for Massachusetts. Truman just beat the grand jury to the punch, as the man was then indicted on charges of tax fixing and bribery.

Bell said in his memorandum that an investigation of the Bureau of Internal Revenue was necessary "because of very real loss of confidence in the Bureau by ordinary taxpayers."

He then turned his attention to the Department of Justice, headed by Attorney General J. Howard McGrath. "I believe . . . ," Bell wrote, "that many people are convinced (as I am) that the Justice Department has not been as vigorous as it should have been in pressing the prosecution of wrongdoers." The meaning of this was that the Department of Justice was being indulgent and neglectful of crooked dealings by certain Democratic officeholders with political pull. Moreover the department was acquiring a reputation for protecting such persons by withholding cooperation with congressional committees and courts of law. Bell recommended, again, that an outstanding citizen be appointed to investigate the Department of Justice, itself the government's chief investigative agency.[1]

The memorandum was written at a time when the *New Republic* was publishing articles on corruption in Washington and newspapers were demanding an investigation. In fact, Bell's colleague George Elsey wrote a memorandum of his own on December 12, saying that signs of corruption were spreading so fast that the White House staff had not yet been able to document all of them.[2]

In the second half of 1951 a wave of flagrant cases hit the headlines.

Truman fired the collector of internal revenue for Manhattan after Senator John J. Williams, Republican, of Delaware, had accused that official of running an inefficient, politics-ridden office, in which eight deputy tax collectors already had been convicted of crimes involving bribery and favors. The supervisor for New York and Puerto Rico of the old Alcohol Tax Unit, a Treasury agency, resigned under fire. He was accused of having profited by dealings on the side with liquor companies and American Lithofold, the same firm over which Boyle had gotten into trouble. Truman fired the collector of internal revenue in San Francisco, who, along with two assistants, was indicted for conspiring to defraud the government by backdating of tax returns. The internal revenue collector for Long Island was fired. He had cheated on his own tax returns.

The Bureau of Internal Revenue was shaken indeed when its highest official, Commissioner George J. Schoeneman, suddenly resigned on June 27, 1951. Shortly afterward Charles Oliphant, the bureau's chief counsel, resigned while under suspicion. Another startling resignation was that of Daniel A. Bolich, until recently assistant commissioner of internal revenue. Later sentenced to jail for tax fraud, Bolich, like a number of internal revenue officials and former officials, found his name linked in testimony with that of a notorious tax fixer and influence peddler, Henry W. Grunewald, who enriched a number of public officials who dealt with him.

"The fact that a man like Grunewald could enjoy business friendships with most of the highest officials in Federal tax administration is itself an indication of the moral climate in which tax matters were handled," said the report of a House Ways and Means subcommittee.[3]

The Democrats had had a monopoly on public offices for too long. Moreover, the torrent of money generated during and after the Second World War often undermined high standards of conduct. Leeches swarmed around the government, attracted, until V-E Day, by war contracts and then by surplus war supplies and materials needed in the resumption of peacetime construction and manufacturing.

The scandals created a nasty political situation for Truman as an investigation on Capitol Hill raked over allegations of conflict of interest, bribes, favors, shakedowns, negligence, extortion, false statements, and other abuses, all aired in the press for months. One affair, known as the Lasdon case, gave rise to suspicion that a favorable tax ruling had been granted in return for a desperately needed contribution to Truman's 1948 campaign, although Truman himself was not implicated.[4] A startling scandal, which did not come to light until after Truman left office, was the case of his appointments secretary and political lieutenant, Matt Connelly. Connelly was indicted for having accepted, while in the White House, cash, clothing, and a $3,600 oil royalty for his part in a tax-fixing case involving a St. Louis wholesale shoe dealer. He was convicted and sent to jail.

Both Truman and John Snyder insisted that they already had taken steps to reform the Bureau of Internal Revenue by the time reporters and congressional investigators began reaping a bonanza in unsavory cases. In a letter to a friend Truman labeled the criticism political, saying that "The Congress has taken a few isolated instances which were corrected by the Bureau itself and has magnified them so much that it makes it appear the whole Bureau is a crooked organization."[5]

As it was, sixty-six officials and employees of the bureau in 1951 were dismissed or forced to resign. Between the spring of 1951 and December 1952 nine internal revenue collectors had quit or been removed. With news of the scandals mingling with reports of small progress in the Korean truce talks, the Gallup poll indicated toward the end of 1951 that only 23 percent of the people approved Truman's performance.

Early in 1952 he got through Congress a reorganization of the Bureau of Internal Revenue, replacing the sixty-four offices of internal revenue collector with twenty-five district offices. All internal revenue jobs, except commissioner, were placed under civil service, and an independent inspection service was established. Truman maintained that the proposal had originated earlier with the Commission on Organization of the Executive Branch of the Government (Hoover Commission) and was not a step taken in reaction to the scandals.[6]

Without doubt he felt during the commotion over the scandals that he had acted properly, promptly, and fairly in dealing with the cases as unfavorable information reached him. Neither his contemporary critics nor his later ones gave him as high marks as he thought he deserved on the score of acting with dispatch and effectiveness to clean up the whole mess. Some of the men around him at least took comfort from the fact that many of the officials who got into trouble were holdovers from the Roosevelt administration. The fact that such persons had not been appointed by Truman, however, did not satisfy those who held the administration accountable for keeping its house in order, regardless of where officials had come from.

Historically, moreover, Truman had had a hand in staffing the Bureau of Internal Revenue in a manner that was to breed trouble. During the Roosevelt administration, when Truman was a senator from Missouri, he exercised his prerogatives on behalf of the appointment of Robert E. Hannegan, a St. Louis Democratic leader, as head of the bureau. Hannegan, who played a vital role in Truman's reelection to the Senate in 1940, was a wardheeler of low ethical standards and lower qualifications for commissioner of internal revenue. It was he who brought into the bureau a number of unqualified Democratic hacks in his own image. One, who succeeded him as commissioner, was Joseph D. Nunan, Sr., later sentenced to jail. Another, headed in the same direction, was Finnegan.[7]

In Truman's dismal autumn of 1951, however, the nastiest eruption occurred not in the Bureau of Internal Revenue but in the Department of Justice, although the two agencies were mutually involved in the question of prosecution of tax frauds. Early in November the House Ways and Means subcommittee investigating the tax scandals revealed that it was inquiring into the conduct of Assistant Attorney General Theron Lamar Caudle, who was in charge of the Justice

Department's tax division. At issue were not only his own tax returns and other irregularities but his failure to prosecute certain tax fraud cases.

Privately, the subcommittee made available to the White House the facts in its possession. Charles Murphy recommended to the president that Caudle be asked to resign. Truman directed Murphy to instruct Attorney General McGrath to obtain the resignation. Murphy got the word to McGrath through McGrath's deputy. Two or three days passed, and nothing happened. Thereupon, while vacationing at Key West, Truman raised eyebrows around the country by himself asking for Caudle's resignation, which was tendered. In subsequent public testimony McGrath grated on White House nerves by defending the retention of Caudle for so long. Later he was to testify, "I think if firings were going to be the order of the day, there were plenty of places to start besides Lamar Caudle."[8]

Scandal in the Department of Justice is scandal at about its worst. In nearly eight years in office President Truman never really got a grip on the department. Critics were quick to say that his chickens came home to roost because of political considerations that had long entered into his appointments of high Justice officials.

While he was neither the first nor the last president to make political appointments in the Justice Department, Truman's choices had been conspicuous. In the understandable substitution of a cabinet of his own for Roosevelt's cabinet in 1945 he had replaced the elite Attorney General Biddle with Tom Clark of Texas, an assistant attorney general in charge of the criminal division. Clark had supported the nomination of Truman for vice-president in 1944. Clark also enjoyed close relations with Hannegan, then Democratic national chairman, and with two Texas stalwarts in Congress, Speaker Rayburn and Senator Tom Connally. Upon the death of Associate Justice Frank Murphy in 1949, Truman raised Attorney General Clark to the Supreme Court. As in the case of Truman's three other appointments to the court—Chief Justice Fred Vinson and Associate Justices Harold H. Burton and Sherman Minton—the Clark appointment has not been regarded by historians as distinguished.

As Clark's successor at Justice, Truman nominated Senator McGrath of Rhode Island, a former governor of that state and former solicitor general of the United States. In 1948 McGrath had been democratic national chairman, and reward for loyal services during Truman's campaign had much to do with his appointment as attorney general. The Justice Department was rather widely considered as being weak when McGrath took it over. Under him it deteriorated further, its troubles highlighted by the forced resignation of Assistant Attorney General Caudle, who later went to jail for conspiracy in tax frauds.

A dapper, personable man, McGrath was never known to have been tainted with corruption himself. On the other hand, he was lazy, and it was well known in Washington that he drank too much and neglected his responsibilities. He testified that he probably gave more attention to Communists and "subversive activities" than to any other business before him. ". . . I regarded it as the major problem before the department," he said.[9] Under his administration, it was widely believed in legal circles, the department was in fact run by his subordinate,

Deputy Attorney General Peyton Ford, who resigned shortly before the storm broke. McGrath seems not to have been aware of much that was going on around him. Noting Caudle's newly revealed reputation for keeping undesirable companions, for example, Representative Robert W. Kean, Republican, of New Hampshire, asked McGrath at a hearing whether he kept a check on such things. "No, sir, I do not," McGrath replied.[10]

On Truman's return from Key West after Caudle's resignation one of his first callers was Frank E. McKinney, of Indiana, Boyle's successor as Democratic national chairman. Truman and McKinney discussed the scandals. The new chairman then told reporters that Truman was "angry about being sold down the river by disloyal employees." McKinney predicted "drastic action."

In line with suggestions in various editorials Truman called a meeting of McGrath, J. Edgar Hoover, and Robert Ramspeck, chairman of the Civil Service Commission, as a group that the president wanted to assume the task of cleaning up corruption. "There were loud outcries against the suggestion by all three of the gentlemen," Truman noted in a memorandum.[11] At the same time the *Evening Star* appeared in Washington with a column by Doris Fleeson, who had excellent sources in the administration, saying that "it must be concluded that the President has at least grasped the magnitude of his domestic disasters." She quoted an anonymous administration official to the effect that Truman was despondent even though, as Miss Fleeson noted, he "has steadily turned a bold front to his world."[12]

The next day, December 13, he held a press conference and was in no mood for another of Miss Fleeson's efforts. In answer to a question he said that he was not going to take drastic action but was going to *"continue* drastic action," which he had always undertaken when necessary.

"What are you looking at me like that for?" he asked Miss Fleeson. "Do you want to write a sob sister piece about it? I don't need any sob sister pieces!"[13]

Despite his abortive effort with McGrath, Ramspeck, and Hoover to establish an independent commission, Truman made one more attempt to create such a body, asking Judge Thomas F. Murphy to head it. Successful federal prosecutor of Alger Hiss and former New York police commissioner, Murphy had recently been appointed by Truman as a judge of the United States District Court for the Southern District of New York. Judge Murphy accepted the president's offer to take over the investigation of the scandals. The next day he staggered the president by backing out of the commitment, perhaps because he had not been offered power of subpoena.[14]

Balked on a commission, Truman decided to get rid of McGrath and lodge the investigation in the Department of Justice under a new attorney general. He secretly offered the post to Senator Wayne Morse, Republican, of Oregon, former dean of the University of Oregon Law School. After pondering the offer overnight, Morse sent the president a sympathetic letter, declining to give up his Senate seat.

Truman's handwritten reply reflected something of the despondency reported by Doris Fleeson. When Morse's letter had been delivered to him, Truman said, in reply, he had a premonition it contained bad news and deferred opening it until after dinner. "My appetite wouldn't have been good if I had," he added. Lamenting both Morse's declination and the low ethical state of the country, reflected even in recent scandals in sport, the president wrote:

> What is needed is a tough, unbiased approach to a situation which is rampant in the country. Football, basketball—there have been over six hundred bank robberies from the inside in the last year—amounting to hundreds of millions. . . .
> What is needed is an Isaah [sic] or a Martin Luther to put us back into the straight and narrow path. When [Thomas] Murphy failed me I came to the conclusion that another approach with you the spark plug would do the business. Well all I can do is to start again.[15]

He did so by asking Charles Murphy to recommend a new attorney general. Murphy proposed Justin V. Miller, a distinguished Washington authority on criminal law, former dean of Duke University Law School, and former Associate Justice of the United States Court of Appeals for the District of Columbia, who was in 1951 chairman of the board of the National Association of Broadcasters. Truman summoned Miller and asked him if he would accept the post of attorney general. Miller said that he would if the NAB executive board would release him from his contract. The appointment of either Wayne Morse or Miller would have helped Truman materially because of the high repute of both men.

Miller obtained permission from the executive board to resign from the NAB, whereupon, incredibly, Truman withdrew his offer. In the process he almost lost one of his ablest assistants, Charles Murphy, who was on the brink of resigning in exasperation. Murphy's feelings were not in the least assuaged by his suspicion that J. Edgar Hoover had somehow got wind of what was going on, perhaps through his White House friend, Matt Connelly, and had persuaded Truman not to appoint the kind of strong attorney general Miller was likely to have been. The director of the FBI was, and is, a subordinate of the attorney general.

The reason Charles Murphy suspected Hoover's hand was that Miller had recently said in a speech that the FBI as a police organization needed stricter executive control. And the only explanation Truman vouchsafed to Murphy for his change of heart was that he could not appoint an attorney general who had publicly criticized the FBI—an astonishing statement in view of Truman's own periodic unease about the power of Hoover and the FBI.[16]

The price the president was to pay for the Miller decision was very high. Having, it appears, run out of candidates for attorney general, he elected to have the Department of Justice proceed with the investigation under McGrath. The idea of McGrath's department investigating itself did not impress the public. Instead the whole business exploded in an episode that was as preposterous as anything Washington has ever witnessed, taking a fresh toll of Truman's leadership.

Under pressure to entrust the investigation to some esteemed individual in the role of special assistant to the attorney general, McGrath turned to one of the outstanding jurists of the day, Learned Hand, recently retired senior judge of the United States 2nd Court of Appeals in New York. When Hand proved unavailable, McGrath settled on the judge's son-in-law, Newbold Morris, a handsome, charming, aristocratic New York estate lawyer, who had never conducted an official investigation nor had ever been involved with the federal government.

An irregular Republican and politically naïve reformer, Morris had been president of the New York City Council when Fiorello H. LaGuardia was mayor and then had twice run for mayor himself, unsuccessfully. The summons to Washington at the end of January 1952 astonished Morris. On trips to the capital he was assured by McGrath that he could act independently and was approvingly greeted by Truman. Thereupon Morris accepted the job. As he and McGrath were leaving the president's office, reporters asked Morris which agency he would investigate first. When Morris hesitated, McGrath said, "I would be the first to welcome an investigation." "In that case," Morris echoed, innocently lighting the fuse, "I guess we might just as well start with the Department of Justice."

Morris began assembling a staff. On February 11, 1952, he called on Truman and told him, among other things, that he intended to ask all high officials in the government to fill out questionnaires about their sources of income. The president approved enthusiastically. Also, setting the stage for an ultimate showdown between McGrath and Morris, Truman issued an executive order directing all departments and agencies of the government to cooperate with Morris. "I intend to see to it," Truman said, "that Mr. Morris has access to all the information he needs that is in the possession of the executive branch, and the authority to examine and require testimony from all officers and employees of the executive branch."[17] Morris later announced that he would ask Truman to fire anyone who refused to fill out one of his questionnaires.

The House of Representatives already had begun two investigations of the Justice Department, the more current one by a subcommittee of the House Judiciary Committee, chaired by Representative Frank L. Chelf, Democrat, of Kentucky. On the eve of St. Patrick's Day, McGrath addressed a local dinner of the Sons and Daughters of Eire in Rhode Island, and it would not have been uncharacteristic of him if he had been drinking before he spoke. The *Providence Journal* reported on March 17 that in his "cryptic" speech the attorney general had intimated that the investigations sprang from circumstances of "race and religion"—"our faith and our race are at stake," he said, adding, "When the clouds have passed, I will have something to say that will shake this country as it has never been before. . . ." He later declined to elaborate on the words that sounded ominous coming from the attorney general of the United States. He insisted that the remarks were not aimed at the Chelf subcommittee.[18]

On March 26 Morris sent his chief counsel, Samuel Becker, to see the attorney general to inquire, among other things, when Morris's questionnaires would be distributed among Justice Department officials. McGrath said that they would go out before the end of that day. Becker then made a *pro forma* request for McGrath's own correspondence, diaries, appointment books, and records of telephone calls as a first step toward obtaining similar documents from other officials in the Justice Department and elsewhere. McGrath refused, despite the president's previous public assurances to Morris. When Becker challenged McGrath on this, the attorney general said he would discuss the matter with Truman.[19]

The discussion took place on March 28 when McGrath was at the White House for a cabinet meeting. According to his later sworn testimony, partly supported by the cabinet minutes, the attorney general protested to Truman that the questionnaires were a violation of personal rights. "If the president had told me to send out the questionnaires, I would have resigned," McGrath testified. "He agreed with me that they should not be sent out." In another line in his testimony McGrath quoted Truman on the questionnaires, "Don't do anything about it, Howard, until next week, and we will talk about it."[20]

Three days later, on March 31, McGrath appeared before the Chelf subcommittee and publicly testified that he was not sure whether he would fill out a questionnaire or permit his subordinates to do so.[21] At a later hearing he attributed his ambiguity to the president's request that the two of them discuss the question again "next week." At the March 31 hearing McGrath also was asked whether, "in the light of what you know now," he would have appointed Morris. "No, sir," he replied.[22]

The next day, April 1, Charles Murphy gave the president a memorandum saying that the "relationship between the Attorney General and Newbold Morris has become so bad that it will be extremely difficult and probably impossible to continue the present situation." Underscoring the critical predicament in which Truman was caught, Murphy added:

The Attorney General has said publicly that he does not know whether or not he will reply to Newbold Morris' questionnaire. It would appear that under the Executive Order of February 20th, the Attorney General, as well as others in the Executive Branch, is required to furnish Mr. Morris with information such as that requested in the questionnaire. If that be true, the Attorney General has in effect said publicly that he does not know whether or not he will comply with the Executive order of the President. In addition, it should be noted that the President specifically approved in advance Mr. Morris' plan for sending out these questionnaires.[23]

Without coming to a decision, Truman talked with Murphy and White House press secretary Joseph Short about whether he should resolve the showdown by getting rid of McGrath and Morris.[24]

The ground began to shake on April 2. In the morning Truman received McGrath for a tense discussion. After fifteen minutes the attorney general left the White House in obvious wrath but would make no comment.

In the afternoon he and the president were thrown together again at National Airport while awaiting, along with the entire cabinet, the arrival of Queen Juliana of the Netherlands. Out of earshot, reporters could observe Truman and McGrath in what appeared to be an agitated exchange. It grew more intense when Joe Short joined the two. Had reporters been able to hear the words, that day's news would have been a sensation.

A hot-tempered man, Short had previously told both Truman and McGrath that the attorney general should resign for having refused to fill out the questionnaire. Now at the airport Short accused McGrath of thinking only of himself. He practically demanded that McGrath resign to spare the president further difficulty. Presumably Truman could hear the conversation.

"If I go," the attorney general retorted to Short, "I'll really blow the lid off!"

"We can't let him blackmail us," Short later told his assistant, Roger Tubby. On the basis of what Short had recounted to him, Tubby recorded the airport exchanges in his journal.[25]

What explosive exposé McGrath may have had in mind, if any, is a mystery. Reporters would have dug for a clue, if only they had heard the extraordinary threat by an attorney general of the United States to stay the hand of a president from firing him. Doubtless in most administrations the attorney general, if he chose, could embarrass the president, seriously in some cases, merely by revealing the kinds of confidences that pass between a lawyer and his client. Perhaps McGrath was simply engaging in bluster, released by wrath and frustration, uttering a cryptic warning similar to his recent threat in Providence "to shake this country as it has never been before. . . ." He lived until 1966 without lifting the lid on any unknown scandal. Furthermore, congressional hearings went on for months without unearthing the sort of hidden bomb McGrath had seemed to imply at the airport.

In any event, the next morning, April 3, Newbold Morris arrived at his office to find a letter signed by McGrath and dispatched without the president's knowledge. It said:

Sir:

Please be informed that your appointment as Special Assistant to the Attorney General is hereby terminated and your services as an employee of the Department of Justice shall cease at the close of business today.[26]

The news appeared on the White House ticker as Truman's staff was preparing, as usual, to brief him for a press conference scheduled for 4 o'clock. When members of the staff gathered round Truman's desk, Short said that the president's critics were gleeful over the latest fiasco and that McGrath should be fired. Tubby interposed that the feeling among Truman's supporters was that McGrath had betrayed the president.

Truman said, quietly, that he guessed he would have to dismiss McGrath. He did not say when. Short warned him that reporters soon would beseige him with questions. How was he going to reply? Truman observed that he could not say much about McGrath yet. That was too much for Roger Tubby. As he recorded his own words, he said: "Mr. President, if you don't take action on this matter this afternoon or early evening and put it off for some time, you will then be charged with acting only because of pressure. There will be, and already is, an outcry against the Morris firing. You should take action, sir, it seems to me, now—especially if you've already made up your mind."

Truman picked up the telephone and told the operator: ''Get me the attorney general.'' A tense pause ensued while the call was being put through. Then:

''Howard, I've got to ask you to resign. I am going to announce your resignation at my press conference this afternoon.''

McGrath said something that Truman's staff could not hear.

''I am announcing it at the press conference,'' Truman declared and hung up.

''Now what's next on your agenda?'' he asked Short. Amid laughter, the press secretary brought up Korea. Before long, however, Truman again took the phone and asked the operator to call Judge James P. McGranery, of the United States District Court in Philadelphia, an old friend and political supporter, who had once been in the Department of Justice.

''Jim,'' Truman said, ''I've got a job for you and I expect you to take it. I want you to be my attorney general.''

With the Morris investigation wiped out—a bad mark for the Democratic party in the forthcoming presidential election campaign—McGranery assented. Truman hung up and leaned back in his chair.

''I hate to do what I did to Howard,'' he said. ''I hate to do this to anyone. He was crying at the end.''[27]

36. *Constitutional Crisis: Truman Seizes the Steel Industry*

IVE DAYS after firing the attorney general, Truman on April 8, 1952, threw the country into high controversy and precipitated a historic constitutional conflict by seizing the steel industry to avert a strike while the war was still going on. Damaging as it proved to be, this episode was one more curse Korea had in store for Truman. By his act he set the stage for a decision by the Supreme Court affecting the growing concentration of power in the hands of the president.

In executive order No. 10340, directing the takeover of the steel companies, Truman based his authority on "the Constitution and laws of the United States, and as President and Commander in Chief of the armed forces"[1]—the same authority he had claimed in sending troops to Korea and Western Europe without congressional consent.

Through the order Truman pushed to new lengths the legal power of the president at the very time when his own political power was crumbling under the shocks of the Korean War, McCarthyism, and scandals in government. Amid flames of antagonism in the press and in Congress over the steel seizure, fourteen separate resolutions were introduced for the impeachment of the president. The American Association of Newspaper Publishers and the United States Chamber of Commerce censured him. Senator Lyndon Johnson ventured to say that Truman's order showed a trend toward dictatorship.[2] Conservatives charged that it *was* an act of dictatorship.

Not the least remarkable of the ingredients in Truman's bold decision was private encouragement from his close friend, Fred Vinson, chief justice of the United States.

The situation surrounding the impasse between the steel companies and the United Steelworkers of America had several distinctive elements.

The controversy reached its climax in a presidential election year. Truman and the Democratic party had close ties with labor, including the steelworkers and their president, Philip Murray, who also was head of the CIO. The Taft-Hartley Act was anathema to labor. Wage and price controls resulting from the Korean War remained in effect. As a practical matter, therefore, the government was bound to be drawn into a dispute affecting the wages to be paid to workers in a major industry and the price of steel.

A crucial circumstance, too, was that, with truce talks deadlocked, fighting continued in Korea, and steel products were vital to the military. Truman was convinced by the advice of friends and certain high advisers that a strike would imperil the flow of munitions to the battlefields and that the United States, therefore, was confronted by an emergency. In time it became apparent, however, that he exaggerated the danger in light of the existing steel supply.

This worst single domestic predicament in which Truman ever got entangled as president began to develop with the expiration on December 31, 1951, of the labor contracts in the steel industry. The union and management disagreed on new terms. The companies declared that any wage increase would necessitate an equivalent increase in steel prices. The union gave notice of its intent to strike. Truman warned that the dispute "gravely threatens the progress of national defense."[3]

Thus he might have invoked the Taft-Hartley Act, appointed a fact-finding board, as provided, and then, after receipt of its findings, sought an injunction to postpone the strike at least through an eighty-day cooling off period. Invoking Taft-Hartley, as Truman well knew, was no way to conciliate labor. Furthermore, as will be seen, the act had certain deficiencies in the situation at hand. Instead of invoking it, therefore, he certified the dispute to the Wage Stabilization Board and prevailed upon the steelworkers to stay on the job, pending its report.

The decision opened the door to a series of resounding conflicts.

The tripartite WSB became badly divided. Over the dissent of its members representing industry, the board in mid-March recommended that the new contract offer the steelworkers higher wages and fringe benefits and a union shop— a new scale variously estimated at from 18 cents an hour to 30 cents an hour higher than the old scale. The companies rejected the recommendation, maintaining that it would drive up the cost of producing steel by $12 a ton.

Public controversy spread as to whether the WSB proposal was destructive of the anti-inflation program. Even the White House was somewhat startled at first by the WSB report. Upon study, however, the president and his staff accepted the recommendations as fair. In a sense they could not have done otherwise. "If the action of the Board were repudiated by the Administration," said a staff memorandum prepared for Truman, "there can be little doubt that the Board would break up and the stabilization program would be gone."[4]

A conviction took hold of Truman and his staff and of most stabilization agency officials that not only was the WSB report fair but that the companies, because of high profits, could absorb the added cost of the higher wages proposed with at most a modest increase in the price of steel. Those same officials came to see the steel dispute as a critical test of whether the administration could maintain its wage and price policies to prevent further inflation. They viewed the steel companies as waging a strike of their own against the government, holding back from a settlement as a means of "making a deal" for higher steel prices than the government preferred to allow.[5]

The one stabilization official who took a different view was the most powerful of them all. He was Charles Wilson, director of defense mobilization, a formidable figure on the national scene, who had been handpicked for the top job and given sweeping powers by the president. Wilson was shocked by the liberality of the WSB report and believed that the steel companies were entitled to raise prices sufficiently to offset higher wages.

On March 24, 1952, he met with Truman at Key West and apparently came away with the understanding that the president would approve a settlement that would permit a rise of about $4 or $5 a ton.[6] Returning to Washington, Wilson blurted to reporters that the WSB recommendations were "a serious threat to our year-old effort to stabilize the economy."[7] "He might just as well have exploded an A-bomb," Harold L. Enarson, a White House assistant, said in a memorandum.[8] Industry members of the WSB called for abolition of the board. Labor accused Wilson of trying to wreck the stabilization program.

Truman was forced to call a conference of high stabilization officials in the White House March 28, at which Wilson's subordinates argued that a substantial increase in the price of steel would defeat anti-inflation policies. Truman and Wilson suddenly differed as to how much of a price increase the president at their earlier meeting had agreed to allow the steel companies.[9] By his own later account Truman said that he had had to correct Wilson and "put him straight." Wilson afterward maintained that Truman "had changed the plan we had agreed upon" earlier at Key West.[10]

The upshot was that the former president of General Electric returned to his office and wrote a letter of resignation. "He did not stress the substantive disagreement between himself and the President," said one of Wilson's assistants, referring to what Wilson told his staff. "What he stressed to us was that he felt he had been called a liar in front of other people."[11] Truman accepted the resignation. Wilson's departure brought down a torrent of criticism on the White House.

At that rocky time in the stabilization program the steel companies offered the union a new contract well below the terms of the WSB report. Meanwhile the administration let the companies know that prices could be increased by $4.50 a ton.[12] This was not enough to satisfy the companies, and the companies' offer was not enough to satisfy the steelworkers. The union voted to strike at 12:01 A.M. on April 9, landing Truman back where he had started four months earlier. Normally, an administration might at that point have accepted a strike as a fact of life, encouraged collective bargaining as best it could, and ridden out the storm. Truman, however, made up his mind that times were dangerously abnormal because of the war. He resolved to avert at almost any cost a strike that probably would prove to be a long one. In a rather highly charged mood, he prepared to go on television on the eve of the strike.

He was outraged by the attitude of the steel companies.[13] He was determined to preserve his economic stabilization program.

Finally, of course, he was intent on keeping the supply of steel flowing. During frantic White House conferences the day before the strike was to begin Robert Lovett, the new secretary of defense, having succeeded Marshall, who resigned, pointed out, according to Enarson, "the shortage of ammo and said a failure of supply would risk the survival of our troops."[14] The truth of the matter was that the nightmare of dangerous shortages on the battlefield haunted the White House. Why the administration did not see, or allow itself to see, the adequacy of the steel supply for the short run, at least, is inexplicable.

With a strike only hours away Truman had several alternative courses.

As conservatives demanded, he could have invoked the Taft-Hartley Act at last. Continued steel production would not have been assured, however. The union doubtless would have struck while a fact-finding board was being assembled and made its study, which would have taken a week or more. After eighty days of cooling off the union could have resumed the strike. By April 8, the men already had been working for ninety-nine days without higher pay because Truman had asked them to. To him—and this was a guiding consideration throughout the whole affair—it seemed unjust to force the union members to work for another eighty days under injunction, still without more pay while the companies were profiting.

Because Truman had requested the workers to submit to the WSB, it also seemed a breach of faith in the White House to ask them now to endure the Taft-Hartley procedure, particularly since the White House blamed the steel companies for the strike. To have invoked Taft-Hartley in the circumstances surely would have ended labor's cooperation with the stabilization program. While not overlooking the political alliance between labor and the Democrats, there was a case of sorts against using the Taft-Hartley Act. Even if he were not prejudiced, however, Truman incurred the liability of being widely perceived as eschewing the act to win advantage for the Democrats in an election year. Already, at a Jefferson–Jackson Day dinner in Washington on March 29, he had announced his decision, privately committed to paper nearly two years earlier, not to seek reelection himself.[15]

Another alternative was seizure of the steel industry under Section 18 of the Universal Military Training and Service Act (the Selective Service legislation). Under this provision the president could seize plants that failed to deliver defense material they had contracted to supply. Fair compensation would have had to be paid to the companies. Section 18, however, was full of holes in the present instance since it had not been intended to deal with labor disputes. Furthermore the procedure was likely to take so long that the Pentagon opposed this alternative.[16]

Still another course open to the president was to ask Congress for a new law authorizing him to seize the steel industry. Chances of enactment were considered slim. For one thing, in debating the Taft-Hartley bill in 1947, the House had refused to authorize government seizure of property as a method of settling labor disputes. For another, having taken the country to war without congressional approval when intervention in Korea was popular in 1950, Truman stood poorly with Congress in 1952 when the war was despised. Many members of Congress were certain to insist that he use a law already on the books—Taft-Hartley.

Finally, as the strike deadline neared, Truman and his advisers turned to the alternative of seizure under the president's inherent constitutional powers as chief executive and commander in chief of the armed forces. Since seizure was likely to lead to litigation, a crucial question before the White House was whether the Supreme Court would uphold the president on a claim of inherent power.

Two fascinating developments played about Truman as he wrestled with this problem. One was that he and his advisers, according to Charles Murphy, who was in the thick of it all, placed heavy reliance on a memorandum that Associate Justice Tom Clark had submitted on inherent presidential powers while Clark was still attorney general. It had been sent to the White House in February 1949, when Truman was seeking repeal of the Taft-Hartley Act. The substitute bill that Truman wanted Congress to pass did not specify the use of injunctions to halt strikes threatening to cause a national emergency. As Truman said at the time, Attorney General Clark had informed him that he had authority to deal with such a crisis under "implied" constitutional powers. The memorandum supplied by Clark said, "If crises arising from labor disputes in peacetime necessitate unusual steps, such as seizure, to prevent paralysis of the National economy, other inherent powers of the President may be expected to be found equal to the occasion."[17] In the face of just such a dispute three years later the White House relied on the memorandum in charting Truman's course in the steel showdown.

The other and more unusual development was that Fred Vinson, in a most questionable act for a chief justice who might later have to weigh a case in court, privately advised the president to go ahead with seizure, basing the recommendation on legal grounds.

Vinson had a unique standing with Truman. When Truman became president, he found Vinson, a former middle-of-the-road member of Congress from Kentucky, already in the White House as director of War Mobilization and Reconversion. The new president judged Vinson to be, as he said at the time, a "straight shooter . . . a man to trust." Soon Truman appointed him secretary of the treasury and then chief justice. Vinson's ascent to the court did not end his intimate relationship with the president and the president's family. The chief justice frequently cruised on the Potomac with the president on the *Williamsburg* and was one of Truman's fellow poker players.

As the issue in steel came to a head, no one, it appears, argued more intensely with Truman not to seize the companies than Secretary of the Treasury Snyder. Snyder had seen independent studies by economists that convinced him that a strike would not cause steel shortages dangerous to the prosecution of the war. Truman was not persuaded. He replied that the chief justice himself had assured him that the way was clear for the president legally to seize the steel industry. Truman said that Vinson had advised him that such an act would be constitutional.

Soon the public was to hear Vinson's opinion from his own lips on the bench, ". . . the fact that Congress and the courts [he said] have consistently recognized and given their support to such executive action indicates that such a power of seizure has been accepted throughout history."

Four of the nine justices had been appointed by Truman, and all were his personal friends. Five members were Roosevelt's appointees. All this plus the Clark memorandum and Vinson's counsel must have given Truman, one would suppose, some encouragement that a decision by him to seize the steel plants would be sustained by the Supreme Court.

Undoubtedly, of course, numerous pieces of advice from Murphy and other assistants who favored seizure, numerous pressures helped solidify Truman's decision. When he finally announced on April 8 that he would seize the steel mills, the public was startled. In his broadcast Truman accused the companies of "recklessly forcing a shutdown of the steel mills."[18] "My heart was in it. Jesus!" he muttered the next morning.[19] His executive order 10340 directed Secretary of Commerce Charles Sawyer, a wealthy businessman to whom seizure was an abomination, to take possession of the steel plants and operate them. Philip Murray immediately called off the strike, and the union, praising Truman, went to work for the government. Senators Hubert Humphrey and Wayne Morse defended Truman in what was otherwise mostly a wave of antagonism. Newspapers, magazines, steel executives, business organizations, and Republicans excelled their own performances of the Roosevelt years. They attacked Truman as a Caesar, an American Hitler or Mussolini, an author of evil, a bully, a usurper, a lawbreaker, an architect of a labor dictatorship. Four separate congressional investigations were launched. The day after announcing seizure, Truman sent up a special message inviting Congress to act on its own in the situation, if it chose to, preferably passing a new law establishing terms and conditions for government operation of the mills.[20] Congress declined.

For everyone in the White House it had been an exhausting week. "How the President got through at all with his far greater burdens and his advanced years attests to his remarkable stamina," Roger Tubby observed in his journal. "But even he was played out." After the broadcast, Tubby noted, Joe Short "thought the President would collapse on the way to his room." One day when it came time to sign a batch of papers, Truman put the task off until a time "when I'm not so shaky." He acknowledged that he was "terribly tired" and on the previous afternoon had fallen asleep in a chair. His strength and spirits always revived, however. When the critical editorials began coming in, he said, "Tell 'em to read the Constitution. . . . The President has the power to keep the country from going to Hell."

Reflecting the view of the chief justice and others, he added, "There are a number of precedents for this action." He concluded, "I doubt if the courts will issue an injunction to prevent seizure."[21]

The steel companies had moved swiftly in the United States District Court for the District of Columbia for a temporary restraining order to enjoin seizure and for a permanent injunction. From the outset of the several judicial stages lawyers for the companies pressed the constitutional issue, namely, whether the president had inherent power to seize the mills. Before the review by the Supreme Court the main proceeding was before Judge David A. Pine in the district court.

A strict constructionist, he seemed eager to take the case. It quickly developed that his major interest was the constitutional issue, on which he concentrated almost to the exclusion of other aspects of the case, such as the affidavits of the secretary of defense and the chairman of the Atomic Energy Commission on the critical need for steel.[22]

Perhaps as a reflection of the Department of Justice at that period, Assistant Attorney General Holmes Baldridge, who represented the government, was neither well enough prepared nor sufficiently experienced in that type of case to make the best of it. He later acknowledged having delivered a bad argument.[23] Under questioning from the judge, Baldridge made a statement that was widely interpreted as indicating that Truman claimed unlimited powers in an emergency. Dismayed by the headlines, the White House selected one of many letters Truman had received from citizens and released a reply by the president as a contradiction.

The powers of the President [he wrote] are derived from the Constitution, and they are limited, of course, by the provisions of the Constitution, particularly those that protect the rights of individuals. . . . I feel sure that the Constitution does not require me to endanger our national safety by letting all the steel mills shut down in this critical time.[24]

Two days later Pine handed down his opinion: the seizure of the steel industry was "illegal and without authority of law." In enjoining seizure, the judge extinguished Truman's expectation that the precedents of seizures by Woodrow Wilson and Franklin Roosevelt and earlier presidents would justify his own act.

Pine was lionized by the press and extolled by conservatives in Congress. Truman was not only shocked by the breadth of the opinion but was faced with a new crisis. For the first time in the months-long dispute steel workers began walking off the job. Even before the injunction order was signed, the union called a strike. Truman's tortured course to keep steel flowing had come to a dead end in a litter of damage to his leadership.

"I read it, read it and read it," Truman told his staff, referring to the Pine opinion. "I can't understand why he took that position, saying that Jefferson, Lincoln, Wilson, Roosevelt [were] all wrong, therefore, I'm wrong, too. But they weren't wrong, and I'm not."

His mood had turned pessimistic, however, when Roger Tubby inquired how he felt the case might fare in the Supreme Court. Truman complained of what he called the hostility of Associate Justice Robert H. Jackson, commenting that the justice had been against the government "ever since he [had] been on the court." Furthermore, Truman said, Justice Douglas had "really surprised me. He is looking to the future. He is afraid, apparently, that if the President is supported in this case, there would be a serious danger that if the GOP were in power, it could make a lot of seizures against labor unions."[25]

Pending appeal, the government obtained a stay of Pine's order. The mills, therefore, were still under federal seizure. At Truman's urging, Murray ordered the steelworkers back on the job while the Supreme Court weighed the case.

It was a classic confrontation. On the strength of his inherent powers as he understood them upon expert advice, the president had seized the steel plants. With warm support in Congress, in the press, and among a section of the public, the steel companies contested the president's authority for seizure. The Supreme Court pondered whether the president did have the power he claimed. If the court ruled in his favor, it would have enhanced the authority of President Truman and his successors in office. If the court ruled that the president had exceeded his constitutional powers, he either would have to return the properties to the companies with a keen loss of prestige, or else persist in seizure in reassertion of his rights and in defiance of the court, to what end no one knew.

As the hour of decision approached, Truman and Secretary of Commerce Sawyer conferred. As Sawyer later recalled, Truman "confessed he would be terribly shocked, disappointed and disturbed if the Supreme Court went against him." The danger that the crisis might go to an extremity worried Sawyer. He pleaded with Truman "not to defy the Supreme Court." "He assured me that he would not," Sawyer wrote.[26]

On June 2 the justices filed into the marble courtroom. Chief Justice Vinson had an opinion to read in the case of *Youngstown Sheet & Tube Co. v. Sawyer.* It was not the majority opinion, however. Having advised the president that he had the inherent power to seize the steel industry, the chief justice had failed to carry the court with him. Hence he called first, upon Justice Hugo L. Black to read Black's opinion—the majority opinion. By 6 to 3, the high court affirmed Judge Pine's order. Truman's act was unconstitutional.

Siding with Black were Clark, Jackson, Douglas, Felix Frankfurter, and Burton, a Truman appointee. Vinson, Justice Stanley F. Reed, and Minton, another Truman appointee, were in the minority.

Shortly, Truman ordered Sawyer to return control of the mills to the companies.[27]

Those who had accused Truman of acting as a dictator in seizing the plants cheered the loudest over the court's ruling, paying scant attention to the comment in Justice Frankfurter's concurring opinion that it was "absurd to see a dictator in a representative product of the sturdy democratic traditions of the Mississippi Valley."

The Supreme Court decision left the White House in a quagmire. Reacting in full force to the return of the plants to the companies, the United Steelworkers launched a prolonged strike. With political feelings already rising at the approach of the 1952 national political conventions, relations between Congress and the president grew increasingly embittered. He himself described the mood on Capitol Hill as "very much anti-Truman."[28] In the White House advice flew in all directions, much of it in favor of using the Taft-Hartley Act, finally. He refused. New negotiations between the union and management were attempted, only to collapse. A week after the court's decision the president braved the "anti-Truman" sentiment to address a joint session of Congress. Justice Black's opinion had held that there was a total absence of power in the president to seize the steel industry without congressional authorization. Hence Truman said, "The issue is squarely up to you gentlemen of the Congress."[29]

His proposal, though seriously intended, was so wide of the congressional mood as to be bizarre. If the country were going to get steel, he recommended that Congress pass a law authorizing him to seize the plants again until a strike settlement could be reached. Should Congress wish to take another course, he said, it could pass a law directing him to invoke the Taft-Hartley Act, a course he characterized as ineffective and unfair. As in the case of his earlier message after seizure in April, Congress declined to pass any new law. Instead it voted to request—not direct—him to use the Taft-Hartley Act. Despite the urging of some of his own advisers, too, he stubbornly refused. "Don't take the tiger off their back," Truman told his staff. "The Court and the Congress got us into the fix we're now in. Let Congress do something about getting us out of it."[30]

To the general disgust the steel strike dragged on for fifty-three days, and the army was able to go on fighting in Korea. Roger Tubby bespoke what many in and out of the White House and the cabinet were saying when he observed in his journal: "I wonder if it wouldn't have been better to have used Taft-H at the outset. Of course, by doing so President would have alienated much of labor, at least for a time, but he could then have proved act's defects. He is supposed to execute faithfully laws of land. Became more and more difficult to use T-H after negotiations had dragged on and workers had continued working for so long without new contract."[31]

Finally, on the fifty-first day of the strike Secretary of Defense Lovett stated that the stoppage had damaged defense production more than a maximum enemy bombing raid could have done. Truman summoned Murray and Benjamin Fairless, president of the United States Steel Company, and demanded a settlement. On July 24 he got it. The United Steelworkers won a union shop and a rise of 21½ cents an hour in wages and fringe benefits. The steel companies won an increase of $5.20 a ton—the same $4.50 the government had offered in April plus 70 cents to cover increased freight rates. "Some day perhaps," said Roger L. Putnam, the new economic stabilization administrator, "we will know why this strike was dragged out for fifty-three days only to be settled on substantially the same wage *and price* terms which the companies could have had nearly four months ago."[32]

Then and for the rest of his life, evidently, Truman felt a deep anger about the Supreme Court decision. In a letter to Justice Douglas, he somewhat camouflaged his temper by friendly sarcasm. One of the six who had held against the government, Douglas had written to Truman saying that he was leaving on a trip. Truman replied that he was "sorry that I didn't have an opportunity to discuss precedents with you before you came to the conclusion you did on that crazy decision that has tied up the country."

"I don't see how," he said, "a Court made up of so-called 'Liberals' could do what that court did to me. I am going to find out just why before I quit this office."[33]

Following the high court's decision Tubby had noted, "As with Pine's opinion, President has read and re-read Supreme Court majority opinions especially Jackson and Clark who he thinks should have supported him."[34] If they had, the decision would have been tipped to Truman.

In later years scholars gave Clark much credit for his opinion. As in the memorandum he had submitted to the White House when he was attorney general, he declared that the Constitution grants the president extensive authority in times of national emergency. Like Jackson, Frankfurter, and Burton, he was not convinced that the 1952 crisis was grave enough to justify Truman's assertion of inherent power. By the time the case went before the Supreme Court it had become clear that a considerable supply of steel was on hand, offsetting claims of a great emergency. Clark held that rather than seize the plants on his own authority Truman was obliged to use procedures already legislated by Congress, as in the Taft-Hartley Act and the Universal Military Training and Service Act.[35] Thirty years later Truman told the writer Merle Miller:

That damn fool from Texas that I first made Attorney General and then put on the Supreme Court! I don't know what got into me. He was no damn good as Attorney General, and on the Supreme Court—it doesn't seem possible but he's been even worse. He hasn't made one right decision that I can think of. And so when you ask me what my biggest mistake was, that's it. Putting Tom Clark on the Supreme Court of the United States.[36]

37. 1952: Troubles with Eisenhower and Stevenson

AS THE ELECTION YEAR BEGAN—and before Truman made his public announcement on March 29—two questions about politics were uppermost in people's minds.

One was whether Truman would run again. While he had informed his staff in Key West on November 19, 1951, of his decision to retire at the end of his term, he continued to keep the public and the politicians guessing. His secret choice as successor was Chief Justice Vinson. During the stay in Key West Truman saw him and offered to support him for the nomination. By early January the president had not yet received an answer, but he was confident that Vinson would run.[1]

The second question was whether General Eisenhower, who was being importuned by anti-Taft Eastern Republican leaders to enter politics, would be available for the Republican nomination. The new year was but a week old when the supreme commander, Allied Powers, Europe, answered the question himself. In a statement at his headquarters in France he indicated that he would run for president if he received a "clear-cut call to political duty."[2]

The news turned the burner on under emotions in the White House. Slowly, if surely, the kettle began to boil. Douglas MacArthur and Dwight Eisenhower were two of the most renowned military figures not only of their own time but throughout American history. It would not have done at all for Harry Truman to have engaged in a hot feud with only one of them. With General MacArthur at last fading away, as he had said he would, General Eisenhower now sailed across Mr. Truman's bow. Mild at first, the reaction swelled to an angry crescendo, almost resulting in Eisenhower's refusal to ride to the Capitol with Truman for Eisenhower's own swearing in as president.

"At bottom," recalled John Snyder, "the president resented Ike running as a Republican. He thought Ike should have run as a Democrat. They had built him up. Truman had offered him the nomination in 1948. Truman believed more could be done for the country by the Democrats."[3]

This attitude was resented by Eisenhower, according to Sherman Adams, who became head of Eisenhower's campaign staff and later his first assistant in the White House. "Ike," wrote Adams afterward, "had little respect for Truman. . . . The mention of Truman usually irritated Eisenhower with his attitude of 'he did no favor to me.' "[4]

Considerable correspondence had flowed between Truman and Eisenhower since the general had become NATO commander. From the beginning of his presidency Truman had almost always spoken warmly and admiringly of Eisenhower, publicly and privately. "You are doing a grand job," Truman wrote to him, typically, in a "Dear Ike" letter dated September 24, 1951.[5] Eisenhower loathed the new Deal and Fair Deal. His attitude toward Truman was always merely correct. In the face of the growing political speculation Truman wrote to the general in longhand on December 18, 1951, saying, in part:

My own position is in the balance. If I do what I want to do I'll go back to Missouri and *maybe* run for the Senate.* If you decide to finish the European job (and I don't know who else can) I must keep the isolationists [meaning Robert Taft] out of the White House. I wish you would let me know what you intend to do. It will be between us and no one else.

Delivery of the letter was delayed, and Eisenhower did not reply until January 1, 1952. He said:

Part of my answer must almost paraphrase your own language when you say, "If I do what I want to do—". . . . I'd like to live a semi-retired life with my family, given over mainly to the study of, and a bit of writing on, present day trends and problems, with a little dirt farming thrown in on the side. But just as you have decided that circumstances may not permit you to do exactly as you please, so I've found that fervent desire may sometimes have to give way to a conviction of duty. . . .

He did not feel, he continued, that he had a duty to contest for the presidential nomination, despite the pleas of friends. Therefore, he would not "seek" the nomination nor break his silence on the question of a political career. Hence, he told Truman, "you know, far better than I, that the possibility that I will ever be drawn into political activity is so remote as to be negligible. This policy of complete abstention will be meticulously observed by me unless and until extraordinary circumstances would place a mandate upon me that, by common consent, would be deemed a duty of transcendant [sic] importance."[6]

Five days later Senator Lodge, manager of the Eisenhower-for-President campaign, announced in Washington that the popular war hero's name would be entered in the New Hampshire primary. Eisenhower, Lodge revealed, had voted for Dewey against Truman in 1948. In France the next day, January 7, Eisenhower issued his statement. With more of the pieties that he had given Truman about not seeking the nomination, he indicated that he would respond in the right circumstances to his friends' urging. That was all that was needed to galvanize the growing Eisenhower movement across the United States. For whatever it may be worth, Eisenhower in his early months in the White House confided to this writer and Carleton Kent of the *Chicago Sun-Times* that the reason he had run for president was to prevent the Truman administration from continuing in

*Mrs. Truman vetoed this. (Roger Tubby's journal, entry of April 6, 1952)

power. He said he would not have run if he had known that Governor Adlai E. Stevenson of Illinois would be the Democratic nominee.

At the first White House press conference following Eisenhower's statement reporters peppered Truman with questions, to which he replied with praise for the general. Under still more questioning he commented, "I don't want to stand in his way at all, because I think very highly of him, and if he wants to get out and have all the mud and rotten eggs and rotten tomatoes thrown at him, that is his business. . . ."[7]

Truman wrote to a friend in mid-January about Eisenhower, ". . . I fear very much he is going to find himself in a very embarrassing position before he is through with this Republican propaganda move."[8]

Privately, the president grew patronizing and sarcastic toward the general. When his staff showed him a student publication critical of Eisenhower's political views, Truman observed, as Roger Tubby recalled his words. "You know I don't want to hurt him, but he would have a terrible time in politics. He has something of a Messiah complex."[9] As the general's prospects for obtaining the Republican nomination soared, Truman told his staff: "I'm sorry to see these fellows get Ike into this business. There're showing him gates of gold and silver which will turn out copper and tin."[10]

When, at the approach of the Republican convention, Eisenhower resigned his command and came home and began giving talks, Truman grew more acerbic. At a morning staff meeting on June 19 he said, "I don't understand Ike saying that the Russians are no more dangerous than pollywogs." In a speech in Denver, decrying "scary talk" about the Soviets, Eisenhower had declared, "If we are deserving of the heritage of freedom, there is no more reason to fear one hundred and ninety million backward people living on the Russian continent, surrounded by captive and recalcitrant states, than there is to fear pollywogs swimming down a muddy creek." "A year ago he was saying just the opposite," Truman commented, as recorded in Roger Tubby's journal. "That kind of statement makes for complacency. How the politics bug makes people say silly things.!"[11]

Nearly twenty years in power had brought the Democratic party into 1952 in a stale, quarrelsome condition under the leadership of battered, tired, and aging men who had seen great days that were no more. Truman was nearing sixty-eight. Barkley was seventy-four. Vinson was sixty-two and not in good health. The fierce crosscurrents of the postwar period had failed to throw to the surface any new, youthful, commanding Democratic leader who had both national appeal and an appetite for battle. Barkley, Averell Harriman, Senator Kefauver, and Senator Kerr, all potential candidates, had the appetite but not the appeal. Adlai Stevenson had the appeal but not the appetite. He wanted another term as governor of Illinois. He did not want to be president. He did not feel he had the qualifications, temperamentally or otherwise, for the office. He even recognized that a change in the party in power might be a good thing for the country, particularly if Eisenhower were to be the Republican nominee.[12] While the president did not wish to run again either, he very much wanted a winning Democratic candidate who would strive to carry on the Truman policies in the years ahead.

With that in mind he first approached Vinson in 1950.[13] Truman saw in his friend's long service in all three branches of the government an impressive qualification for the White House. His assessment of Vinson's talents was high, rather higher perhaps than would have been offered by some of their contemporaries. After Truman's first approach, however, Vinson was unreceptive to the idea of leaving the court. Then, in November 1951, the president invited him to run but received no immediate answer. "Several weeks later, to the President's complete surprise," wrote Charles Murphy, who was Truman's chief political lieutenant upon the approach of the conventions, "Vinson said 'no.' " It was then found out that the President had no second choice clearly in mind."[14]

Inevitably Stevenson came into the picture. His name had begun cropping up in 1951 as a possible contender in the event Truman bowed out. As an attractive, progressive governor of a large state, Stevenson spoke in liberal enough accents to appeal to northerners, yet was sufficiently conservative to be acceptable to southerners. Clearly, he was a public figure of greater political stature than the other potential or declared candidates, including the early frontrunner from Tennessee, the slightly oafish Senator Estes Kefauver, whom Truman referred to in private as Cowfever.

Truman and Stevenson did not know each other well. The governor, at the president's invitation, called at Blair House for a talk on the evening of January 22, 1952. Beyond the fact that they were two spirited, loyal, and patriotic Democrats, staunch anti-isolationists, and opponents of Soviet imperialism, Truman and Stevenson did not have a great deal in common.

Grandson of Grover Cleveland's vice-president and son of a former secretary of state of Illinois, Stevenson was a graduate of Choate and Princeton, a lawyer, and a former diplomat. A man of good taste, he was intelligent, polished, sophisticated, literate, and at times eloquent. He was also wealthy, divorced, stylish, cosmopolitan—a twentieth century man to the core and, because of, or in spite of it, fragile and self-doubting. In a word, he was almost the opposite of Truman, who was essentially a man of old-fashioned, nineteenth-century virtues. With shorter wing-span than Stevenson perhaps, Truman was a person of tough fiber, plain, warm manners, direct approach, and earthy humor, and he was free of doubts about right and wrong. Nearly seven crushing years in the White House had failed to extinguish his spirits, as he revealed to Stevenson in extolling the presidency and urging him to seek it. Reports of Stevenson's reply vary. Clearly, Truman failed to persuade him to become a presidential candidate. Truman did not give up hope, however.

Shortly, the president had an embarrassing experience. Evidently without any instruction or encouragement from Washington, a lumber dealer in Manchester, New Hampshire, filed petitions entering Truman's name in that state's primary election. The next day the president told a press conference, "All these primaries are just eyewash when the convention meets, as you will find out."[15] The time when primaries would dictate to conventions was some years off. Truman said that he would have his name withdrawn, a statement that brought him a telegram from the publisher of the *Manchester (N.H.) Union Leader,* the ineffable William Loeb. Loeb declared that Truman's decision demonstrated that "in your autumn years your courage is turning distinctly yellow."[16] As a matter of fact, ostensibly in the interest of the Democratic organization, the national chairman, McKinney, persuaded Truman to leave his name in the primary. When the votes were counted, President Truman was roundly beaten by Senator Kefauver.

As weeks went by, Truman talked to Stevenson again, and correspondence passed between the governor and the White House. Stevenson still did not want to run for president and would not agree to, yet there was more to his tactics than met the eye. While he continued to hope that he could run for reelection as governor, it became clear to him that the national convention might draft him, forcing him to run for the presidency. In that case he did not want to run as *Truman's* candidate. For a man of such an independent mind as Stevenson's this probably would have been the case in any election. It was compellingly so in 1952, because Truman's popularity had crumbled and Stevenson did not wish to see his own covered with the rubble. Furthermore on many domestic issues he and Truman did not see eye to eye, Stevenosn being the more conservative of the two. In any case, against the possibility that he might be drafted Stevenson persisted in trying to distance himself from the president. Truman, for his part, initially interpreted Stevenson's conduct as "wishy-washy," as he told Murphy.[17]

In March, Truman still had no candidate of his own and shuddered at the prospect of Kefauver. "For the first time," Murphy recalled, "the president began to give serious thought to running again himself. The question remained open for some time. At one point he had a meeting on the subject with his top White House staff, Chief Justice Vinson and one or two others. The president went around the room and asked whether he should run. Without exception the answer was no." Murphy later recalled: "The administration was going to seed. It needed new blood. We were having trouble getting good people."

The advice of the president's staff and friends, Murphy said, was based entirely on their concerns about Truman's age and health. They all thought, unrealistically, that he or any other Democrat could win.[18]

Murphy said that he was still in doubt about what the president would do until Truman called him in in midday of March 29 and showed him a handwritten paragraph he intended to deliver at the end of his prepared speech that night at the Jefferson-Jackson Day dinner in the National Guard Armory. It read:

> I shall not be a candidate for re-election. I have served my country long and I think efficiently and honestly. I shall not accept a renomination. I do not feel that it is my duty to spend another four years in the White House.[19]

Stevenson was in the audience, as astonished as nearly everyone else by the unexpected timing of the declaration. Still he stuck by his plans to run for governor. With nowhere else to turn, Truman threw his support to Barkley, while giving his blessing to Harriman to run as New York's favorite son. When the convention opened in Chicago in July the labor bosses rejected Barkley, partly because of his age, thereby effectively eliminating him. As governor, Stevenson delivered a great welcoming address to the convention and all but sealed his own fate. The convention went wild. Big states began to climb on the Stevenson bandwagon.

On the second ballot, as on the first, Kefauver led, but Stevenson was closing in. Harriman was a solid fourth with 121 votes. Truman arrived in Chicago. He sent Murphy to ask Harriman to withdraw in favor of Stevenson, and Harriman did.[20] Stevenson was nominated on the third ballot. Truman himself presented the candidate to the convention saying, "I am going to take my coat off and do everything I can to help him win."[21] The morning after the nomination Truman sent a note to Stevenson, "When the noise and shouting are over, I hope you may be able to come to Washington for a discussion of what is before you."[22] From there on the path led Truman downhill to irritation, pain, and disappointment.

Back in the White House after the convention, he told his staff that it was important for them and the Stevenson group to work together. He expressed concern lest Stevenson fail to make use of the experience available in the White House. As Roger Tubby recalled the words, Truman added, "We have got to make contact with Stevenson. We can't have a division between Stevenson, the White House and the Democratic committee." Matt Connelly got Stevenson on the telephone and arranged to have him call on Truman a few days hence.[23]

Before he arrived Stevenson, without notifying the president, replaced Frank McKinney, Truman's man, as Democratic national chairman, with Stevenson's own friend, Stephen A. Mitchell, a Chicago lawyer. Meanwhile the Democratic campaign headquarters was set up in Springfield, capital of Illinois, far from Washington. Trouble was at hand. The editor of the *Oregon Journal* in Portland sent the Democratic nominee a letter asking, "Can Stevenson really clean up the mess in Washington?" Stevenson signed a reply prepared by an assistant, and the *Journal* printed it. "As to whether I can clean up the mess in Washington," Stevenson's letter said, "I would bespeak the careful scrutiny of what I inherited in Illinois and what has been accomplished in three years."[24] To the elation of the Republicans the letter not only did not deny that there was a mess in Washington but used the very term over Stevenson's signature. The phrase became as much associated with the Truman administration as "red herring" and "police action"—and quite as accidentally.

When the Stevenson letter immediately began to blow up into a major campaign issue for the Republicans, Roger Tubby found Truman at his desk, irritated not only at Stevenson but at Stevenson's vice-presidential runningmate, Senator John J. Sparkman of Alabama. Among other things that rankled Truman, Sparkman had said that the administration had "mishandled" the steel strike.

"Trouble is," the president told Tubby, "they are running against me, not against Ike. They can't win that way."[25]

Tubby noticed that Truman had several sheets of pad paper that he had covered with his own handwriting. In all probability these were letters written to Stevenson and to Sparkman, which years later turned up in Truman's papers. While he never mailed them, they paint a rather excrutiating picture of wounded presidential pride and delusions of political power.

The first of the letters to Stevenson said: "I have come to the conclusion that you are embarrassed by having the President of the United States in your corner. . . . Therefore I shall remain silent and stay in Washington until Nov. 4." Also: "I can't stand snub after snub by you. . . ." Truman accused Stevenson of having broken up "the Democratic Committee, which I had spent years in organizing," and of firing "the best chairman of the National Committee in my recollection" in the person of McKinney.[26]

The second letter said that the mess-in-Washington remark "makes the campaign rather ridiculous." "There is no mess in Washington except the sabotage press in the nature of Bertie McCormick's Times-Herald and the anemic Roy Howard's snotty little News." In recalling what he considered his own indispensable contribution to Stevenson's victory in Chicago, Truman added:

> When you say that you are indebted to no one for your nomination, that makes nice reading in the sabotage press, but gets you no votes because it isn't true. . . .
>
> I'm telling you to take your crackpots, your high socialites with their noses in the air, run your campaign and win if you can. Cowfever could not have treated me any more shabbily than you have.[27]

Roger Tubby quoted Truman in his journal as having said later that he was tempted not to campaign for Stevenson after the mess-in-Washington letter.*[28] The president used his press conference of August 21 to let Stevenson and the world know there was no ducking the Truman record. "I am," he said, "the key of the campaign. . . . [T]he Democratic party has to run on the record of the Roosevelt-Truman administrations, and that's all it can run on."[29]

Truman told Sparkman, in the third of the unsent letters, that he had just read the senator's "spasm" on the steel strike. "You are receiving thanks and praise," he continued, "from the great metropolitan dailies for kicking the only friend who can cause your election, just as he caused the nomination of both you and Stevenson. . . . I can enjoy myself in a rocking chair on the famous balcony [the Truman balcony above the south portico of the White House] if thats [sic] what the Democratic Nominees want."[30]

The smell of cordite from the political battlefields yanked Truman from the rocking chair to the whistle stop. His craving for a Democratic victory was whetted by the attacks on his record by Eisenhower and Nixon. "I nearly choked to hear him," Truman said after listening to Eisenhower criticize the foreign policy, of which Eisenhower, in Truman's view, had once been part and parcel.[31]

---

*Tubby became presidential press secretary after the death of Joseph Short on September 18, 1952.

The president wrote to a friend: "It appears to me that the Republicans are going to make a nasty personal smear campaign. . . . You will notice that poor old Ike is trying to use the Democratic Platform for his own welfare and benefit and still wants such good for nothing smear artists as Jenner and McCarthy on the Bandwagon. . . ."[32]

Campaigning by train, à la 1948, to and from Milwaukee, where he gave a Labor Day speech, Truman praised Stevenson and Sparkman and jabbed at "the Republican candidate for president." Truman spoke of "masterminds" in Republican councils teaching the candidate, "how to be a hypocrite in a few easy lessons," such as talking loosely "about liberating the enslaved peoples of Eastern Europe." Obviously, the "master mind" was John Foster Dulles, then Eisenhower's foreign policy adviser. "Surely," Truman said, "the Republican candidate must know the Iron Curtain and the Kremlin walls will not come tumbling down from a few blasts on a campaign trumpet."[33]

Meanwhile Eisenhower was moving almost in triumph through the South calling the situation in Washington "a top-to-bottom mess." On September 17 Truman took the train to Philadelphia for a speech, confiding to Roger Tubby along the way that what he called Eisenhower's "demagoguery" might win the election. Truman worried lest Eisenhower become a dangerous president—"a modern" Oliver Cromwell, to wit, a twentieth-century version of a soldier turned overbearing civilian leader.[34]

Republicans intensified attacks on Truman. Richard Nixon, their vice-presidential candidate, harped on the Hiss case and plugged the Republican theme that the administration's record boiled down to "Korea, communism and corruption." In one attack that Truman never forgave, Nixon accused the president, Acheson, and Stevenson of being "traitors to the high principles in which many of the nation's Democrats believe."[35] The word "traitor" burned itself into Truman's consciousness. Furthermore, the Republicans allowed the Democrats no respite from Mrs. Young's mink coat nor from McCarthy's smears. "No Minks, No Pinks" read placards at Republican rallies. In Iowa, Eisenhower promised to drive out the "crooks and cronies" and substitute an "Honest Deal" for the Fair Deal. The corruption issue was a deadly one for the Democrats.

Truman was ready for a fight, and these attacks were all it took to get his coat off. Turning a scheduled appearance at the dedication of Hungry Horse Dam in Montana into a national whistle-stop tour, he hit Eisenhower harder than the general was accustomed to. In his first speech from the train at Breckenridge, Minnesota, Truman implied that Eisenhower was a "stooge for Wall Street."[36] In Fargo, North Dakota, he said that Eisenhower "has spent all his life in the Army and doesn't know much" about the supposed alliance of Republicans and special interests.[37] In time Eisenhower became so resentful that he complained to their mutual friend, Secretary of the Treasury Snyder. "I tried to convince Ike," Snyder recalled years later, "that it was a politician fighting to win. I reminded Ike of things he had to do to win in Europe. But Ike was not placated."[38]

Early in October, Eisenhower made a wretched mistake, and Truman pilloried him for it. Campaigning in McCarthy's home state of Wisconsin, with McCarthy aboard the train, Eisenhower prepared a speech that included praise of General Marshall, who had recommended him to be supreme allied commander in Europe in the Second World War and for whom Eisenhower had deep respect. McCarthy, on the other hand, had publicly smeared Marshall by linking him to a supposed conspiracy that had brought the Communists to power in China. Walter Kohler, the Republican governor of Wisconsin, pleaded with the candidate's staff on the train that Eisenhower's praise of Marshall would be out of place in the circumstances. Sherman Adams, therefore, recommended to Eisenhower that he delete it. Eisenhower assented, and the news got out.[39]

Truman, with his reverence for Marshall and hatred of McCarthy, had no difficulty overflowing with contempt. In a speech in Utica, New York, he excoriated Eisenhower for having "betrayed his principles" and "deserted his friends." Eisenhower had understood the vileness of McCarthy's attack on Marshall, Truman declared, adding: "General Marshall had been the great friend and benefactor of the Republican candidate. [Eisenhower] knew—and he knows today—that General Marshall's patriotism is above question. . . . Now, in his bid for votes, [Eisenhower] has endorsed Joe McCarthy for re-election—and humbly thanked him for riding on his train. . . . I had never thought the man who is now the Republican candidate would stoop so low."[40]

Assessing Truman's 1952 campaign speeches in general, Charles Murphy later said, "Truman thought Adlai was not hitting hard enough, so he overcompensated."[41] The exhileration of combat raised Truman's hopes. In mid-October he wrote to a friend, "I believe we are going to hang the hide of the Republican Party on the tree to dry on November fifth."[42]

Something that Eisenhower found intolerable was a statement that Truman sent to a Washington conference of the national Jewish Welfare Board on October 17. In it he recalled his veto earlier in the year of the McCarran-Walter immigration bill. His action had been widely applauded because of the feeling that the measure discriminated against European Jews and Catholics wishing to emigrate to the United States. Congress, however, overrode Truman's veto. Nixon and certain Republicans whom Eisenhower endorsed for election in 1952 had been among those voting to override. Truman's statement, therefore, charged that Eisenhower's endorsements and choice of runningmate had revealed "an attack of moral blindness, for today he is willing to accept the . . . practices that identified the so-called 'master race'. . . . We must pick a man for president who understands the sinister forces that are lying in wait for him and for you. Anti-Semitism, anti-Catholicism and antiforeignism grow only in concealment. They have hidden themselves within the Republican party for years."[43]

The remarks were reminiscent of a much-criticized campaign speech which Truman had delivered in Chicago in 1948. By implication it likened Dewey to Hitler and Mussolini in the sense that Dewey was supposedly the front man for fascist elements that might crush American democracy.[44]

In the statement to the Jewish Welfare Board the implied charge was so obvious and unfair that two long-standing critics of Truman—Rabbi Abba Hillel

Silver, former cochairman of the American Zionist Emergency Council, and Bernard Baruch—came to Eisenhower's defense, as did Cardinal Spellman, according to Eisenhower. Campaigning in New England, Eisenhower accused the president, without mentioning him by name, of "terrible" overreaching "lies" and denounced "the campaign of invective that has been launched against me." He said that his Democratic opponents had been adding "a slander a day" to what he called their record of "a scandal a day."[45] Truman had indeed overreached himself. The statement was damaging to Truman, not Eisenhower. At one point at the height of the campaign Eisenhower exclaimed: "I'll never ride down Pennsylvania Avenue with him! I'll meet him at the Capitol steps. Just how low can you get?"[46]

As in 1948, Truman fought to the end by his lights, traversing the country in a special train, speaking to friendly crowds, gossiping with local politicians, and washing his own socks along the way. In 1952, however, he was conducting only a sideshow while Eisenhower and Stevenson performed in the big tent. If the outcome were ever in doubt, Eisenhower ended it dramatically in Detroit on October 24 with a stinging speech heaping blame on the Truman administration for the bitterly stalemated war in Korea—"the burial ground for twenty-thousand American dead." After promising, if elected, to give priority "to the job of ending the Korean War until that job is honorably done," he continued:

That job requires a personal trip to Korea. I shall make that trip. Only in that way could I learn how best to serve the American people in the cause of peace. I shall go to Korea.[47]

In reply Truman nailed Eisenhower on one point. Eisenhower's speech blamed the administration in effect for having invited the North Korean attack by withdrawing American forces from Korea in 1949. In a statement Truman noted that when withdrawal was first proposed by Secretary of War Robert Patterson in 1947, the Joint Chiefs of Staff supported it. And as army chief of staff at the time, Eisenhower participated in their decision.[48]

Such a riposte, of course, could scarcely nick one of the most effective campaign speeches of modern times. At the end of his last campaign trip Truman said to Tubby, "Roger, we may be up against forces we can't control."[49]

In November, twenty years after Herbert Hoover was defeated by Franklin Roosevelt, Dwight D. Eisenhower defeated Adlai Stevenson. However narrowly, the Republicans also captured control of Congress for the first time since 1946. The Roosevelt-Truman era was all but over.

38. Scenes from an Ending

T
HE WHISTLE STOP TOUR on my part didn't work out as well this time as it did before," Truman wrote to Churchill.[1]

Truman's feelings were hurt by some published criticism that his campaigning had damaged the Democrats. While the outcome did not surprise him, he never quite grasped the public's wish to be done with the turbulence and corruption of the Democratic years. Neither did he comprehend the depth of the people's trust in Eisenhower. At a cabinet meeting three days after the election, according to Matthew Connelly's notes, Truman attributed the results to "hero worship" and a combination of McCarthy-Jenner-Nixon poison.[2]

On the morning after the election the president had sent Eisenhower congratulations but ended the telegram with a barb. The presidential plane *Independence,* Truman said, "will be at your disposal if you still desire to go to Korea." To this intimation that Eisenhower's victory had left the victor free to forget about a campaign gimmick the general replied that "any suitable transport plane" would do.[3]

Truman, with Eisenhower's cooperation, then put into effect the first formal transition between administrations that has since become familiar when one party succeeds another in power. The advent of bipartisan foreign policy in the Roosevelt administration and Roosevelt's and Truman's liaison with Dewey, through Dulles, on foreign policy questions in the 1944 and 1948 campaigns had created a germ of the idea. Truman's own unfamiliarity with urgent wartime diplomacy when he suddenly became president had convinced him that presidents-elect needed a complete look at what they faced. Furthermore, in 1948 the prospect of a Dewey victory had prompted some planning in the Truman administration for facilitating a change in power.

Without hesitation, therefore, Truman invited Eisenhower to the White House and offered to work with liaison men whom the president-elect might choose to observe the preparation of the new budget and familiarize themselves with the affairs of the major departments. Accordingly, Eisenhower dispatched two future officials of his administration: Joseph M. Dodge, who would become budget director, and Henry Cabot Lodge, who would be United States permanent representative to the United Nations. Truman also made John Steelman available whenever necessary for consultation with Sherman Adams, chief of the Eisenhower staff being assembled in New York. The president also instructed members of his staff to cooperate with their opposite numbers on the Eisenhower staff. Except for Lodge and Dodge and to some extent Adams, however, the Eisenhower people kept to themselves, inquiring about only the most mundane details. Hence, the first transition arrangement, though an enduring precedent, was nowhere near as elaborate as it was to become.

Eisenhower called at the White House once, on November 18, for a private meeting with Truman and for a briefing in the cabinet room by the president and his senior advisers. At the private meeting between the two of them, Truman later said in his diary, Eisenhower entered with "a chip on his shoulder." Truman volunteered a good deal of information about a president's routine, which Eisenhower doubtless knew. "I think all this went into one ear and out the other," Truman jotted.[4] As a veteran political warhorse, Truman had no difficulty casting aside the acerbities of the campaign. The general's dignity did not heal so easily. In some puzzlement Truman recalled in his memoirs Eisenhower's "frozen grimness throughout."[5]

Eleven days later Eisenhower flew to Korea. Truman wrote to Stevenson: "It seems the Republicans are trying to do the best they know how to 'crawfish' on their attitude toward the Korean situation. Ike's visit resulted exactly as we both had anticipated. The demagoguery used in connection with this tragic situation is almost beneath contempt. I am not going to let them get away with it as long as I am President."[6] As if he had not been stung enough by the success of Eisenhower's promise to go to Korea, Truman may have been freshly agitated also by recent advice from Acheson. It was that Eisenhower's trip might compound the difficulty of getting through the United Nations General Assembly a resolution supporting the American position on a Korean armistice. The trip, Acheson said, threatened to cast doubt on whether the United States delegation now represented the American viewpoint.[7]

When Eisenhower was returning from Korea aboard the cruiser *Helena,* he learned that MacArthur had said in a speech that he had a solution for ending the Korean War and would confide it to Eisenhower, if the president-elect were interested. On December 9 Eisenhower announced that he would see MacArthur.

Truman was returning from his mother-in-law's funeral in Independence when newspapers carrying the story of the impending Eisenhower-MacArthur meeting on the war were put aboard the train in West Virginia. Those two generals! Indignantly, Truman issued a statement demanding that if MacArthur, still technically on active duty by virtue of being a general in the army, had a reasonable plan for ending the war without starting a larger one, he present it to the proper authorities for action.

At a press conference on the eleventh Truman said he doubted that MacArthur had "anything new to offer." Then he let Eisenhower have it. The way this came about was that a reporter called attention to a recent disclosure that Truman had been urged by Democrats during the campaign to announce that *he* would go to Korea and intimate from there that the war would be over by Christmas.

"It was suggested," Truman replied, "and I decided that it wouldn't serve any good purpose—it would just be a piece of demagoguery, and that is what it turned out to be."

When a reporter asked if Truman meant that the current trip to Korea was demagoguery, Truman castigated Eisenhower.

"Yes," he said, "The announcement of that trip was a piece of demagoguery, and then, of course, he had to take it after he had made the statement."[8]

Resentful of the remark, Eisenhower called on MacArthur in New York. MacArthur's "solution" was that, after taking office, Eisenhower hand Stalin an ultimatum: the Soviet Union must, among other things, agree to the unification of Germany and Korea, or Eisenhower would order atomic bombs dropped on North Korea and China's industrial centers.[9] The recommendation had about the same appeal to Eisenhower that it would have had to Truman.

The NATO council in mid-December adopted a resolution declaring that French resistence to Communist forces in French Indochina conformed with the aims of the alliance and deserved the members' support. In his last days, therefore, Truman made a substantial increase in the American commitment to the French cause. Having recognized the Bao Dai regime in Vietnam and given it initial military assistance in 1950 and having decided to increase the assistance when the Korean War broke out, Truman now, in response to the NATO council's action, approved $30.5 million more in defense funds for Vietnam, Laos, and Cambodia. The escalation in the American involvement in Vietnam thus continued. By the end of the Truman administration, Acheson reported, the United States already was bearing between one-third and one-half of France's burden in the Indochinese War.[10]

One of Truman's last decisions pointedly reflected the extent to which for nearly eight years his policies at home as well as abroad had been influenced by the Cold War.

Long an opponent of monopoly and trade restrictions, the president in June of 1952 had ordered the Department of Justice to begin a grand jury investigation of an alleged international oil cartel.[11] This raised the possibility of criminal indictments against Standard Oil of New Jersey (Exxon), Socony Mobil (Mobil), Standard Oil of California (Socal), Texaco, and Gulf Oil along with two alleged co-conspirators, Royal Dutch Shell and Anglo-Iranian Oil (now British Petroleum, or BP).

The "majors," as they were called, dominated oil production, refining, and distribution in the Middle East and throughout the world. Truman's order for an investigation was prompted by a Federal Trade Commission report indicating that these giant multinationals violated American antitrust laws prohibiting combinations in restraint of trade.

Truman's move against the oil companies was a reversal of years of policy in Washington, even under Roosevelt, in which a close working relationship existed between the government and the companies. The government in fact had long used the oil majors for furthering American aims abroad. Truman's decision in favor of grand jury action drew strong opposition from the national security agencies of the government. They argued that it was against the national security interests to threaten the companies with possible criminal prosecution. Their argument was strengthened by chaos in the Iranian oil fields following Iran's nationalization of British Petroleum under Prime Minister Mohammed Mosadeq. The Korean War was on. Rearmament was going forward in Europe. The prospect of Europe's supply of imported oil being in jeopardy alarmed American policymakers. Truman was forced to recognize, as was Eisenhower when he became president, that the major oil companies were the only ones in the 1950s with established facilities for refining and distributing Middle Eastern oil.

On January 9, 1953, the National Security Council met to review the question. The Justice Department submitted a brief urging continuance of the grand jury investigation. The department held that the cartel was in effect a private treaty "negotiated by private companies to whom the profit incentive [was] paramount." The Departments of State, Defense, and Interior argued for an end to the investigation.

On January 12, eight days before the close of his term, Truman, foe of monopoly and trade restrictions, wrote to Attorney General McGranery terminating the grand jury investigation. He directed a switch from criminal proceedings to civil litigation, which never amounted to much, as things turned out. Later he told Leonard Emmerglick of the Justice Department that he had acted not on the advice of either the NSC or his cabinet but on the assurance of General Bradley, chairman of the Joint Chiefs of Staff, that the national security required such a decision.

To the end, a resolution of the Korean truce talks eluded the administration. For Truman this meant that he had to leave office without being able to terminate a war to which he had committed American forces. The obstacle was a mountain of time-consuming complexities over the repatriation of prisoners of war. Even a summary of the intracicies would be voluminous.

After the Second World War, many Soviet citizens who had defected to the German army were understandably terrified at the thought of being returned to the Soviet Union. Notwithstanding, the United States and Great Britain sent them back. Truman regretted this. In 1949, the Geneva convention on prisoners of war was adopted. The United States signed it but did not ratify it. It provided that prisoners shall promptly be released and repatriated after cessation of hostilities. When the truce negotiations began in Korea, a situation developed similar to the one that Truman had regretted in Europe. North Korea had captured thousands of South Koreans along with Chinese loyal to the Nationalists. The North Koreans pressed these captives into military service. Many of them surrendered to United Nations forces. In the truce talks, Kim Il-sung's representatives demanded that these people be sent back to North Korea with the rest of the prisoners.

American military authorities warned that the captured South Koreans and Chinese would be severely punished or killed, if returned to the Communist government. Instead of such repatriation, it was suggested, the South Koreans in question should be released to the Rhee government and the Chinese sent to Formosa. Inducing enemy soldiers to surrender during hostilities is a prime aim of psychological warfare. If the prisoners being held by the United Nations were to be returned to slavery or death, military officials said, the future of American psychological warfare would be impaired.

From these considerations emerged in Washington a doctrine of voluntary repatriation. Only prisoners who volunteered to go back to North Korea would be sent back. The idea commended itself both for humanitarian and political reasons. As the historian Barton J. Bernstein noted, Truman and Acheson presently "defined voluntary repatriation as an irrevocable moral principle."[12] Another major consideration also permeated the administration's thinking. Giving prisoners a choice could mean that Communist troops taken prisoner in any future wars with the West could decide against being returned, whether to North Korea or China or even to the Soviet Union for that matter. Establishment of such a precedent could open the door to wholesale defection by Communist soldiers. Awareness of the danger might even deter future Communist aggression.

The implications were not lost on Communist negotiators in the Korean truce talks. They insisted on repatriation by force, if necessary. Truman, however, declared, "We will not buy an armistice by turning over human beings for slaughter or slavery."[13] His position was supported in Congress and in the country, at least until the consequence of the further impasse sank in. The prolongation of the war yielded new criticism and trouble for him.

With neither side yielding on the issue, the negotiations provided a backdrop for Communist propaganda, including charges that the United States had resorted to germ warfare. The armistice talks passed the one-year mark in July 1952. As the political campaign began in the fall, the stalemate was obviously a handicap for the Democrats. At a meeting with his highest military advisers on September 15, however, Truman said he saw "no real prospect of getting an armistice" except by continuing on the existing course and intensifying military pressure on the enemy.[14] At another conference of military and diplomatic advisers nine days later he said that he was not willing to obtain an armistice "just for the sake of an armistice," particularly if it would leave Communist China in a position to resume heavy fighting. Not for that, he said, had he worked for seven years to avoid a third world war. He declared that he did not wish to see the United States lose the gains it has made since intervening in Korea.[15]

Truman's refusal to agree to deliver unwilling prisoners forcibly to the Communists brought the Korean truce talks to an indefinite halt on October 8, 1952. Heavy fighting resumed. News of casualties hurt the Democrats in the election. On inauguration day the war was to become Eisenhower's responsibility—another story. Six weeks after Eisenhower took office Stalin died. International tensions eased. Furthermore, Eisenhower, unlike Truman, threatened through diplomatic channels to use nuclear weapons if a settlement were not reached.[16] The war ended on July 26, 1953. Total American casualties: 32,629 killed in action; 20,617 died of other causes; 103,284 were wounded in action. Twenty-nine years later American troops are still stationed in South Korea.

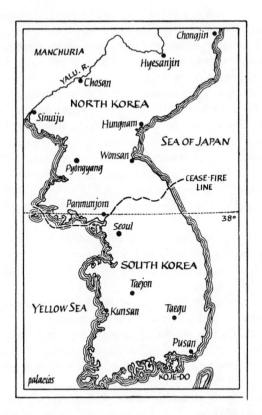

The deepest, most lasting troubles that had beset Truman were those in the Far East: Korea, China, Vietnam, Formosa. The turbulence of the events themselves, together with Cold War attitudes in Washington and the relentless attacks of Republican extremists, confined the making of Far Eastern policy in Washington to a whirlpool. As the Truman administration drew to a close, the situation in Asia was highly unsatisfactory to American interests. The regime that ruled China was hostile to the United States. A war was still being fought by American forces in Korea. The seeds of a longer one were germinating in Vietnam. The future of Formosa was uncertain. If there were a better course the United States could have followed in the face of the historic upheaval in Asia, the Truman administration never found it.

On the evening of January 15, 1953 Truman delivered a televised farewell address—a simple, neighborly account of his stewardship—which he had drafted.

"I suppose," he said, presciently, "that history will remember my term in office as the years when the 'cold war' began to overshadow our lives. I have hardly had a day in office that has not been dominated by this all-embracing struggle. . . . And always in the background there has been the atomic bomb."

"Starting an atomic war," he declared, "is totally unthinkable for rational men."

Far into the future, Truman probably will be most remembered for the first use of the atomic bomb. The more Hiroshima recedes into the past, the easier it will be to forget the great momentum that had developed behind the bomb as a weapon to be used even before Truman had become president. The easier it will be, too, to lose the sense of the mighty pressure on him to avert the slaughter predicted in the planned Allied invasion of the Japanese home islands. It is a pity that after the Second World War Truman did not have a vision of how, through a different policy toward the Soviet Union, the subsequent nuclear arms race could have been averted. It is a wish that has elements of asking a human being to solve what was in the circumstances a nearly superhuman problem.

Truman said in his speech that his most important decision in the White House had been the one to halt the Communist attack in Korea. He speculated that ultimate change in the Soviet system might come through trouble in the satellite countries.

He was right in perceiving an awakening of the American conscience on civil rights, but far too optimistic in his vision of future social conditions in America and throughout the world. As for his presidency, "I have tried to give it everything that was in me."[17]

It was too late to talk about new programs. Partly because of the spent force of the New Deal and the Fair Deal and partly because of the Korean War in particular and the Cold War in general, many of the domestic measures Truman had proposed failed to pass during his administration. He was to live long enough—until December 26, 1972, nearly twenty years after leaving office—to see some of them become law in one form or another.

These included the St. Lawrence Seaway, statehood for Hawaii and Alaska, part of the Brannan farm plan, Medicare, higher Social Security benefits, expanded public housing, home rule for the District of Columbia, establishment of a permanent commission on civil rights, abolition of poll taxes, fair employment practices legislation, and protection of voting rights for blacks.

Truman also sent up a final budget message, one aspect of which has been remarked upon subsequently. Although the Soviet Union was only four and a half years away from launching Sputnik I, the Truman administration, preoccupied with Korea and rearmament, never initiated a space program.

Truman, however, left other monuments. Notable among them were the reconstruction of postwar Western Europe and the forging of the Atlantic community through the Marshall Plan and NATO. By means of the airlift, Truman thwarted a Soviet attempt to dominate all of Germany, if not Europe, by land blockade of Berlin. Under Truman, the former enemy states of Japan and Germany (West Germany at least) were brought into friendly and constructive relationships with the United States. Although Roosevelt had marked the way, it was during Truman's presidency, too, that the United States became a member of the United Nations. Truman initiated the special relationship with Israel. If Communist China was not recognized, neither were its cities bombed into rubble, as MacArthur and his supporters desired.

At home, Truman kept control of atomic weapons in civilian hands. If he failed to get many of his major social programs enacted, at least he thwarted efforts to abandon basic reforms of the New Deal. His success in pushing three tax bills through Congress during the Korean War probably had a more beneficial effect on the economy than some celebrated pieces of legislation that might come to mind. The Council of Economic Advisers, the Central Intelligence Agency, and the National Security Council, all were created under Truman. Furthermore, the organization of the military was placed on a modern footing by the establishment of the Department of the Air Force and a single Department of Defense. Finally, the report of Truman's Commission on Civil Rights in 1947 was the starting point in the modern era of improved race relations in the United States.

True to form, Truman's last important decision was a controversial one. Four days before the end, he issued an executive order setting aside the oil-rich submerged lands of the continental shelf as a naval petroleum reserve. In a statement hailed by most liberals he said that the oil and gas deposits rightly belonged to all the people of the United States and not just to states like California, Texas, and Louisiana. After Truman left office, the conservative Republican-controlled Eighty-third Congress passed legislation conferring ownership of the deposits on the states. Eisenhower signed it.

Dwight Eisenhower and Harry Truman were to meet seldom after President Truman left office, most notably in a call Eisenhower paid to the Truman Library in 1961 and a visit the two men seemed thoroughly to enjoy in Blair House after the funeral mass for President Kennedy in 1963.[18]

If memory serves, Truman had a reconciliation of one sort or another with practically everyone, including Nixon, with whom he had feuded in the White House. A striking exception was MacArthur.

Following the inaugural ceremonies for Eisenhower, Acheson gave a luncheon in honor of his old boss before the Trumans took the train home to Independence. When John Snyder arrived, he saw the former president standing alone glancing out a window. "You're looking very pensive," Snyder said. "Come and have a drink." Truman looked at him. "Two hours ago," he mused, "I could have said five words and been quoted in fifteen minutes in every capital of the world. Now I could talk for two hours and nobody would give a damn."[19]

Probably more than he realized, Truman cast a long shadow across the history of the second half of the twentieth century. That history is not always written in a way that Mr. Truman would have approved. In the tormented epoch that began in 1914 no president has emerged from the office as a saint or a hero. Surely, for many reasons good and bad, for his serious mistakes as well as for his wise decisions, not to mention his vintage American character, Truman's was a most extraordinary presidency.

BIBLIOGRAPHICAL NOTE
REFERENCES
INDEX

Bibliographical Note

———

The following abbreviations are used in the References.

FR   *Foreign Relations of the United States,* cited by year and volume. Publications of the Department of State, these volumes contain diplomatic correspondence, cables, memorandums, reports of conversation, National Security Council papers, and the like. The volumes are published not less than twenty-five years after the events to which they pertain. They are published by the U.S. Government Printing Office in Washington, D.C.

HSTL   Harry S Truman Library, Independence, Missouri.

OF   Official File, Truman Papers. Harry S Truman Library.

OH   Oral History Transcript, Harry S Truman Library. The transcripts are of interviews conducted under the auspices of the Library with former officials of the Truman administration, journalists, friends of the president, and others who had a special reason to know him and to have seen the operations of his administration.

PP   *Public Papers of the Presidents of the United States: Harry S Truman,* cited by year. Under the direction of the National Archives and Records Service, Office of the Federal Register, a volume under this title is issued for each year a president is in office. Each volume contains such papers for that year as presidential messages, addresses, certain correspondence, transcripts of presidential press conferences, and statements of one kind or another. The volumes are issued by the U.S. Government Printing Office.

PSF   President's Secretary's File. Harry S Truman Library.

ROK   Republic of Korea.

The References contain numerous citations from two other sources.

Eben A. Ayers's Diary. Ayers was Assistant White House Press Secretary from 1945 to late 1950. The diary is in the Harry S Truman Library.

Roger W. Tubby's Journal. A former State Department press officer, Tubby transferred to the White House in late 1950 as an assistant press secretary and in 1952 became the White House Press Secretary. His journal is deposited at the Yale University Library but is closed. The author of this book was given complete access to the parts of it pertaining to the Truman years.

References

1. VINDICATION

1. The scene at Excelsior Springs was related to the author by Henry J. Nicholson, one of the Secret Service agents present.
2. *PP*, 1948, p. 941.
3. Letter, Harry S Truman to John B. Clark, December 18, 1948. PSF: Political File, Wyoming Folder. Box 61.
4. Unfinished, unmailed letter, Truman to Elmo Roper, December 30, 1948. Eben Ayers Papers. Personal—Truman Notes. Letter Folder. Box 24. HSTL.
5. Letter, Truman to Claude G. Bowers, December 1, 1948. PSF: Personal File. Letters—election victory, 1949 Folder. Box 315.
6. Letter, Truman to Maury Maverick, November 25, 1948. Texas Folder. Box 61. PSF.
7. Memorandum for Bill Bray from the president, December 3, 1948. Political File. Voting Statistics Folder. Box 61. PSF.

Also, *U.S. News & World Report*, December 10, 1948, p. 14.
8. Alfred Steinberg, *Sam Rayburn. A Biography* (New York, 1975), p. 250.
9. Interview with Oscar R. Ewing, October 1, 1973.
10. Interview with Major General Harry H. Vaughan (ret.), May 2, 1972.
11. Eben Ayers Diary, entry of November 6, 1948.
12. OH, John R. Steelman.
13. *PP*, 1950, pp. 257–58.
14. Eric F. Goldman, *The Crucial Decade. America, 1945–1955* (New York, 1956), p. 92.
15. Margaret Truman (with Margaret Cousins), *Souvenir: Margaret Truman's Own Story* (New York, 1956), p. 255.

2. A DISTURBING BEGINNING

1. Quoted in Alonzo L. Hamby, *Beyond the New Deal: Harry S. Truman and American Liberalism* (New York, 1973), p. 311.
2. Charles E. Wilson to Truman, December 1, 1948. Truman to Wilson, December 18, 1948. PSF: General File. "W" Folder.
3. Clark M. Clifford Papers. State of the Union, 1949: Drafts. Box 23. HSTL.
4. OH, George M. Elsey, vol. 1, pp. 102–3.
5. Text of the State of the Union message, *PP*, 1949, p. 1 ff.
6. *PP*, 1948, p. 121 ff.
7. Telephone interview with Charles S. Murphy, January 6, 1982.
8. Letter, Truman to George I. Hall, February 2, 1949. PSF: Subject File. Foreign Affairs—Alaska Folder. Box 170.
9. Ed. Francis H. Heller, *The Truman White House. The Administration of the Presidency 1945–1953* (Lawrence, Kansas, 1980), p. 28.
10. *PP*, 1950, p. 269.
11. Text of Vandenberg Resolution in *FR* 1948, vol. 3, pp. 135–36.
12. NSC 20/4, *FR*, 1948, vol. 1, pt. 2, pp. 662–69.
13. Memorandum, Benjamin H. Hardy to Jonathan Daniels, November 19, 1950. Hardy Papers. Point IV Folder #2. Box 1. HSTL.
14. *PP*, 1949, pp. 114–15.
15. Robert A. Pastor, *Congress and the Politics of U.S. Foreign Economic Policy, 1929–1976.* (Berkeley, 1980), p. 269.

16. Robert A. Taft. Lincoln Day speech. Text in *Congressional Record*, vol. 94, pt. 9, pp. A994–96.
17. Nancy Bernkopf Tucker, "Nationalist China's Decline and Its Impact on Sino-American Relations, 1949–1950" in Eds. Dorothy Borg and Waldo Heinrichs, *Uncertain Years. Chinese-American Relations, 1947–1950* (New York, 1980), pp. 167–68.
18. Ross Y. Koen, *The China Lobby in American Politics* (New York, 1974), p. 238, n. 9.
19. Ibid., p. 94.
20. *Life*, December 20, 1948, p. 24.
21. *New York Times*, June 26, 1948, p. 1.
22. The Ambassador in China (Stuart) to Secretary Marshall, August 23, 1948. *United States Relations With China. With Special Reference to the Period 1944–1949.* Based on files of the Department of State. U.S. Government Printing Office, Washington, D.C., 1949.
23. PP, 1948, p. 432.
24. Allen Weinstein, *Perjury. The Hiss Chambers Case* (New York, 1978), pp. 186–87, 188–89.
25. *PP*, 1948, p. 959.
26. Ayers Papers, November 8, 1952. Dairy—Talks with President Truman Folder. Box 17, HSTL.
27. Richard M. Nixon, *Six Crises* (Garden City, N.Y., 1962), p. 62.

3. ACHESON AND THE APPROACHING STORM

1. Dean Acheson, *Present at the Creation. My Years in the State Department* (New York, 1969), p. 338.
2. Ibid., p. 104.
3. Marx Leva oral history. Office of the Secretary of Defense.
4. Interview with Charles E. Bohlen, January 25, 1973.
5. Interview with Philip C. Jessup, January 15, 1980.
6. Harold L. Ickes Diary, entry of February 3, 1946. Manuscript Division, Library of Congress.
7. Dean Acheson, *Morning and Noon* (Boston, 1965), p. 165.
8. Interview with James E. Webb, March 6, 1978.
9. Quoted in *Hearings Before the Committee on Foreign Relations. United States Senate. Eighty-first Congress, First Session. On the Nomination of Dean Acheson to be Secretary of State.* January 13, 1949, p. 6. U.S. Government Printing Office.
10. Ibid., p. 9.

11. Ibid., pp. 7, 8.
12. *Executive Sessions of the Senate Foreign Relations Committee (Historical Series). Vol. 2. Eighty-first Congress. First and Second Sessions, 1949–1950.* pp. 12, 13.
13. Ibid., pp. 4–37.
14. Interview with Kingsbury Smith, July 5, 1948.
15. *FR*, 1949, vol. 3, p. 666.
16. Paper Prepared by the Division of Research for Europe, May 17, 1949, Ibid., p. 909–13.
17. Alfred Grosser, *Germany in Our Time. A Political History of the Postwar Years* (New York, 1971), p. 71.
18. Harry S Truman, *Years of Trial and Hope* (Garden City, N.Y., 1956), p. 130.
19. Official account of Jessup-Malik talks in *FR*, 1949, vol. 3, p. 994 ff.
20. Official account of foreign ministers meeting, ibid., p. 856 ff.

21. The Secretary of State to the Embassy in the United Kingdom, May 11, 1949, pp. 872–74.
22. Paper Prepared by the Policy Planning Staff, November 12, 1948. *FR*, 1948, vol. 2, p. 1325 ff.
23. The Secretary of State to the Embassy in France, May 18, 1949. *FR*, 1949, vol. 3, pp. 884–85.
24. Proposal of the United States, United Kingdom and French Delegations to the Council of Foreign Ministers, May 28, 1949. Ibid., pp. 1041–43.
25. *PP*, 1949, p. 325.

4. THE NORTH ATLANTIC TREATY

1. *PP*, 1949, p. 198.
2. Ibid., pp. 196–98
3. Robert E. Osgood, *Alliances and American Foreign Policy* (Baltimore, 1971), chapter 3.
4. Ed. Walter Millis (with the collaboration of E. S. Duffield), *The Forrestal Diaries*, p. 341.
5. Memorandum of a Conversation, by the Chief of Protocol (Woodward), April 7, 1949. *FR*, 1949, vol 3, pp. 173–75.
6. For documents on origins of the Atlantic alliance see, *FR*, 1948, vol. 3, pp. 1–16.
7. The Ambassador in France (Caffery) to the Secretary of State, March 2, 1948. Ibid., pp. 34–5.
8. The Secretary of State to the Embassy in Italy, March 11, 1948. Ibid., pp 45–6.
9. Ibid., pp. 46–8.
10. Ibid., p. 48.
11. Ibid., p. 50.
12. *PP*. 1948, p. 184.
13. NSC 7, March 30, 1948. Collection of National Security Council documents. Modern Military Branch, National Archives, Washington, D.C.
14. Text in *The Vandenberg Resolution and the North Atlantic Treaty. Hearings Held in Executive Session Before the Committee on Foreign Relations. Eightieth Congress. Second Session. On S. Res 239 . . . and Eighty-first Congress. On Executive L, the North Atlantic Treaty. Historical Series*, pp. 345–51. U.S. Government Printing Office.
15. Ibid., pp. 110–15.
16. Ibid., p. 134.
17. Ibid., p. 138.
18. Ibid., p. 213.
19. Ibid., p. 276.
20. Memorandums of conversation by Acheson, February 28 and March 1 and 2, 1949. *FR*, 1949, vol. 4, pp. 125, 135–36, and 141–42.
21. *North Atlantic Treaty. Hearings Before the Committee on Foreign Relations. United States Senate. 1949. Pt. 1, pp. 12, 13*. U.S. Government Printing Office.
22. Ibid., p. 16.
23. Ayers Diary, entry of July 25, 1949.
24. Memorandum by the Secretary of State to the President, April 8, 1949, *FR*, 1949, vol. 3, pp. 175–76.
25. Excerpts in *New York Times*, February 26, 1947, p. 15. Truman's *Years of Trial and Hope* (cited in chapter 3, n. 18) p. 154.
26. Ayers Diary, entries of January 13 and 22, 1949.
27. Memorandum of Conversation, by the Chief of Protocol (Woodward), op. cit.
28. *New York Times*, September 29, 1949, p. 1.
29. *Reviews of the World Situation: 1949–1950. Hearings Held in Executive Session Before the Committee on Foreign Relations. United States Senate, First and Second Sessions . . . Historical Series*. U.S. Government Printing Office, pp. 42–3.
30. Ayers Diary, entry of August 24, 1949.
31. Ibid., entry of February 12, 1949.
32. Ed. Arther H. Vandenberg, Jr., with the collaboration of Joe Alex Morris, *The Private Papers of Senator Vandenberg* (Boston, 1952), p. 503–4.
33. Acheson's *Present at the Creation* (cited in chapter 3, n. 1) p. 310.

5. FORRESTAL, LOUIS JOHNSON, AND UPHEAVAL OVER NATIONAL SECURITY

1. *The Forrestal Diaries* (cited in chapter 4, n. 4), p. 462–65.
2. Interview with W. Stuart Symington, October 16, 1973.
3. Arthur W. Radford (Ed. Stephen Jurika, Jr.), *From Pearl Harbor to Vietnam. The Memoirs of Arthur W. Radford* (Stanford, California, 1980), p. 107.
4. Steven L. Rearden, *History of the Office of the Secretary of Defense. Vol. 1. The Formative Years, 1947–1950*. Office of the Secretary of Defense. Historical Office, Washington, D.C., chapter 1. (I read this volume while it was still in manuscript, without final page numbers.)
5. Kenneth W. Condit, *The History of the Joint Chiefs of Staff. The Joint Chiefs of Staff and National Policy. Vol. 2, 1947–1949*. Historical Division. Joint Secretariat. Joint Chiefs of Staff, Washington, D.C., p. 153.
6. *PP*, 1948, p. 182 ff.
7. Interview with David E. Bell, administrative assistant to President Truman, January 10, 1979.
8. *The Forrestal Diaries*, op. cit., pp. 431–32.
9. Cited in Gregg Herkin, *The Winning Weapon: The Atomic Bomb in the Cold War 1945–1950* (New York, 1980), p. 254.
10. Statement by the President to the Secretary of Defense, the Secretaries of the Three Departments, and the Three Chiefs of Staff, May 13, 1948. PSF: Subject File. Military—President's Program Folder. Box 146.
11. Condit, op. cit., p. 206.
12. Statement by the president to the secretary of Defense, etc., op. cit.
13. Letter, Truman to Edwin G. Nourse, March 24, 1948. Nourse Papers, HSTL.
14. Letter, Truman to Frank I. Kent, April 14, 1949. PSF: General File. Kent, Frank I., No. 1 Folder. Box 125.
15. Interview with Charles S. Murphy, April 27, 1978.
16. George C. Marshall to James V. Forrestal, November 8, 1948. *FR*, 1948, vol. 1, pt. 2, p. 655.
17. Memorandum, Truman to James E. Webb. Supplied the author by Webb.
18. *The Forrestal Diaries*, op. cit., pp. 536–37.
19. *PP*, 1948, p. 953.
20. *The Forrestal Diaries*, op. cit., p. 544.
21. *Time*, January 24, 1949, p. 16.
22. Interview with Donald S. Dawson, July 13, 1977.
23. Arnold R. Rogow, *James Forrestal. A Study of Personality, Politics and Policy* (New York, 1963), pp. 277–78. In an interview July 12, 1977, John H. Ohly, an assistant to Forrestal, said that the secretary had contributed to Truman's campaign, but Ohly did not know the amount. For a contrary version, see OH, Brigadier General Louis H. Renfrow, p. 74. A close friend of Louis Johnson's, Renfrow said Forrestal had told Johnson in 1948 that he would not contribute a dime to the campaign.
24. Arthur Krock, Memoirs. *Sixty Years on the Firing Line* (New York, 1968), p. 253.
25. *The Journals of David E. Lilienthal, vol. 2. The Atomic Energy Years 1945–1950* (New York, 1964), p. 385–86.
26. Interview with John W. Snyder, July 26, 1977.
27. Interview with Snyder, February 2, 1978.
28. Carl W. Borklund, *Men of the Pentagon from Forrestal to McNamara* (New York, 1966), p. 68.
29. Interview with William J. Bray, formerly of the Democratic National Committee, August 27, 1977.
30. Marx Leva oral history. Office of the Secretary of Defense.
31. Ayers Diary, entry of August 15, 1949.
32. Truman memorandum concerning Louis Johnson, September 12, 1950. PSF: Personal File, ''J'' Folder. Box 314.
33. Rearden, op. cit., chapter 7.
34. OH, Robert L. Dennison, pp. 107–8. Sullivan's letter to Johnson, dated April 26, 1949, is in OF 1285 C, HSTL.
35. The statements of the members of the Joint Chiefs of Staff are in PSF: General File, U Folder. Box 139.
36. OH, Sullivan, p. 62.
37. Interviews with John Snyder, July 26, 1977, and with Admiral Robert L. Dennison, July 15, 1977.
38. Ayers Diary, entry of April 26, 1949.
39. Ibid., entries of April 27 and 28, 1949.

6. THE CHINA TIME BOMB

1. Michael Schaller, *The U.S. Crusade in China, 1938–1945* (New York, 1979), p. ix.
2. Ibid., p. 61.
3. Ibid., p. 187.
4. Ibid., chapter 11.
5. Letter, Truman to Will Durant, November 7, 1951. PSF: General File, D Folder.
6. George M. Elsey Papers. China Folder, HSTL.

7. Schaller, op. cit., p. 216.
8. Memorandum, Truman to Major General Harry H. Vaughan, August 12, 1950. PSF: General File, Ba–Bh Folder. Box 113.
9. James F. Schnabel, *The History of the Joint Chiefs of Staff. The Joint Chiefs of Staff and National Policy. Vol. 1. 1945–1947. Historical Division. Joint Secretariat. Joint Chiefs of Staff.* pp. 401–2.
10. Ibid., pp. 407–78.
11. Ibid., p. 405.
12. Ibid., pp. 410–11. Truman's statement to T. V. Soong is in *United States Relations with China* (cited in chapter 2, n. 22), p. 939.
13. Schnabel, op. cit., pp. 420–21.
14. Henry A. Wallace (Ed. John Morton Blum), *The Price of Vision. The Diary of Henry A. Wallace* (Boston, 1973), pp. 519–22.
15. Schnabel, op. cit., pp. 420–21.
16. *United States Relations with China,* op. cit., pp. 581–84.
17. Russell D. Buhite, *Patrick J. Hurley and American Foreign Policy* (Ithaca, N.Y., 1973), chapter 11.
18. George C. Marshall, memorandum of conversation with President Truman, Secretary of State Byrnes and Admiral Leahy, December 11, 1945. *FR,* 1945, vol. 7, pp. 767–69.
19. Marshall memorandum of conversation with the president

and Dean Acheson, December 14, 1945. Ibid., p. 770.
20. *PP,* 1945, pp. 534–35.
21. Memorandum by the Secretary of State to the Under Secretary of State (Lovett), November 26, 1948. *FR,* 1948, vol. 8, p. 220.
22. *Economic Assistance to China and Korea: 1949–50. Hearings Held in Executive Session Before the Committee on Foreign Relations. United States Senate. Eighty-first Congress. First and Second Sessions. . . . Historical Series,* U.S. Government Printing Office, p. 9.
23. Memorandum of Conversation, by the Secretary of State, December 3, 1948. *FR,* 1948, vol. 8, pp. 299–302. Telegram, The Acting Secretary of State to the Ambassador in China (Stuart), December 13, 1948. Ibid., p. 302.
24. Wallace, op. cit., p. 587.
25. *Committee on International Relations. Selected Executive Session Hearings of the Committee, 1945–1950. Vol. 7. United States Policy in the Far East, pt. 1. Historical Series. U.S. House of Representatives,* U.S. Government Printing Office, p. 9.
26. The Ambassador in China (Stuart) to the Secretary of State, January 13, 1949. *FR,* 1949, vol. 8, pp. 45–6.
27. Memorandum by the Joint Chiefs of Staff to the Secretary of Defense (Forrestal), November 24, 1948. *FR,* 1949, vol. 9, pp. 261–62.

7. DEBACLE: "THE LOSS OF CHINA"

1. Memorandum by the Policy Planning Staff, September 7, 1948. *FR,* 1948, vol. 8, pp. 146–55.
2. Notes on cabinet meetings, 1945–'53 (Post-presidential File. These notes were made by Matthew J. Connelly, Truman's appointments secretary. Entry of January 19, 1949.
3. *Committee on International Relations. . . . United States Policy in the Far East, pt. 1* (cited in chapter 6, n. 25), pp. 179–81.
4. *Congressional Record,* vol. 95, pt. 1, p. 422.
5. Special Message to the Congress on Greece and Turkey: The Truman Doctrine, March 12, 1947. *PP,* 1947, p. 176 ff.
6. Text in *Congressional Record,* vol. 95, pt. 2, pp. 1950–51.
7. For Marshall's views see *United States Relations with China* (cited in chapter 2, n. 22), p. 280.
8. Lewis McCarroll Purifoy, *Harry Truman's China Policy. McCarthyism and the Diplomacy of Hysteria 1947–1951* (New York, 1976), p. 102.
9. *Congressional Record,* vol. 95, pt. 2, p. 1950 ff.
10. Ibid., vol. 95, pt. 5, pp. 6307–9.
11. Ibid., vol. 95, pt. 1, p. 464.
12. Ibid., vol. 95, pt. 12, pp. A1344–46.
13. For Hurley, see Ibid., vol. 95, pt. 12, p. A1344; For Knowland, Ibid., vol. 95, pt. 4, pp. 4862–63.
14. Ibid., vol. 95, pt. 1, p. 1350.
15. NSC 13/3, May 6, 1949. *FR,* 1949, vol. 7, pt. 2, pp. 730–36.
16. *Time,* May 9, 1949, p. 32.
17. *New York Times,* April 24, 1949, p. 10 E, Section 4.
18. *Congressional Record,* vol. 95, pt. 6, p. 8293.
19. Truman, handwritten note, June 7, 1949. June 7, 1949 Folder. Box 7. Clark M. Clifford Papers. HSTL.
20. Memorandum of Conversation, by Mr. Jacob D. Bean, April 4, 1949. *FR,* 1949, vol. 7, pt. 2, pp. 1138–41. (Although the memorandum is by Beam, the State Department historical office says the first-person discourse referred to was by Acheson.)
21. Quoted by Warren I. Cohen, "Acheson, His Advisers, and China, 1949–1950" in *Uncertain Years* (cited in chapter 2, n. 17), p. 33.
22. The Secretary of State to the Ambassador in China (Stuart), April 6, 1949. *FR,* 1949, vol. 8, pp. 230–31.
23. The Ambassador in China (Stuart) to the Secretary of State, May 14, 1949. Ibid., pp. 754–57.
24. Statement by the Central Committee of the Chinese Communist Party, February 1, 1947. *United States Relations with China,* op. cit., pp. 719–20.
25. The Secretary of State to the Consul General in Peiping (Clubb), February 3, 1949. *FR,* 1949, vol. 9, p. 11.
26. The Ambassador in China (Stuart) to the Secretary of State, May 3, 1949. Ibid., pp. 14, 15.
27. Michael H. Hunt, "Mao Tse-tung and the Issue of Accommodation with the United States, 1948–1950" in *Uncertain Years,* op. cit., pp. 203–4.
28. The Consul General at Peiping (Clubb) to the Secretary of State, June 1, 1949. *FR,* 1949, vol. 8, pp. 357–60.
29. Steven M. Goldstein, "Chinese Communist Policy Toward the United States: Opportunities and Constraints, 1944–1950" in *Uncertain Years,* op. cit., 274–75.
30. The Acting Secretary of State to the Consul General at Peiping, June 14, 1949. *FR,* 1949, vol. 8, pp. 384–85. Memorandum by the Acting Secretary of State of a Conversation with the President, June 16, 1949. Ibid., p. 388.

31. The Ambassador to China to the Secretary of State, June 8, 1949. Ibid., pp. 752–53.
32. The Ambassador to China to the Secretary of State, June 30, 1949. Ibid., pp. 766–67.
33. Memorandum by Mr. John P. Davies of the Policy Planning Staff to the Director of the Staff (Kennan), June 30, 1949. Ibid., pp. 768–69.
34. Ayers Diary, entry of June 27, 1949.
35. The Secretary of State to the Ambassador in China, July 1, 1949. *FR,* 1949, vol. 8, p. 769. For the fact of Truman's call to Acheson see Robert M. Blum, *Drawing the Line: The Origin of the American Containment Policy in East Asia* (New York, 1982), chapter 4.
36. William Whitney Stueck, Jr., *The Road to Confrontation. American Policy toward China and Korea, 1947–1950* (Chapel Hill, N.C., 1981), p. 124.
37. John K. Fairbank's introduction to Gary May, *China Scapegoat. The Diplomatic Ordeal of John Carter Vincent* (Washington, D.C., 1979), p. 15.
38. *United States Relations with China* (cited in chapter 2, n. 22).
39. Ayers Diary, entry of May 17, 1949.
40. The Secretary of Defense (Johnson) to the Secretary of State, July 27, 1949. *FR,* 1949, vol. 9, p. 1387. The Secretary of State to the Secretary of Defense, August 3, 1949. Ibid., p. 1391–92.
41. *New York Times,* August 6, 1949, p. 1.
42. Ibid., August 7, 1949, p. 1.
43. Ibid., August 6, 1949, p. 16.
44. *Congressional Record,* vol. 95, pt. 9, p. 11677.
45. Ibid., vol. 95, pt. 10, p. 13264.
46. Memorandum on the White Paper on *United States Relations with China,* Ibid., vol. 95, pt. 15, pp. A5451–54.
47. The Consul General at Peiping (Clubb) to the Secretary of State, October 2, 1949. *FR,* 1949, vol. 9, pp. 93, 94.
48. *PP,* 1949, p. 520.
49. Memorandum of Conversation, by the Acting Secretary of State, October 1, 1949. *FR,* 1949, vol. 9, p. 1141.
50. Memorandum by the Acting Secretary of State, October 31, 1949. Ibid., p. 1355.
51. Memorandum by the Under Secretary of State (Webb), November 14, 1949. *FR,* 1949, vol. 8, p. 1008. Memorandum by the Chairman of the Joint Chiefs of Staff (Bradley) to the Secretary of Defense (Johnson), November 18, 1949. Ibid., pp. 1011–13.
52. *Military Situation in the Far East. Hearings Before the Committee on Armed Services and the Committee on Foreign Relations. United States Senate. Eighty-second Congress. To Conduct an Inquiry into the Military Situation in the Far East and the Facts Surrounding the Relief of General MacArthur. . . .* Pt. 3, p. 1672. U.S. Government Printing Office. Note: Various passages in the testimony were censored at the time of the 1951 hearings. Two decades later the complete hearings were declassified and are on microfilm in the National Archives. Hereafter, references to previously censored material will be cited as appearing in *Declassified Hearing Transcripts, Military Situation in the Far East.*
53. Memorandum by the Joint Chiefs of Staff to the Secretary of Defense (Johnson), August 17, 1949. *FR,* 1949, vol. 9, pp. 376–78.
54. *Military Situation,* op. cit., p. 1672.
55. Rearden's *History of the Office of the Secretary of Defense,*

vol. 1, (cited in chapter 5, n. 4), chapter 5. Also Cohen's "Acheson, His Advisers, and China" op. cit., p. 32.
56. Waldo Heinrichs, "American China Policy and the Cold War in Asia" in *Uncertain Years* (cited in chapter 2, n. 17), pp. 286–87.
57. Notes of a Conversation with Mr. Paul Griffith, June 3, 1950. Also Notes of a Conversation with Mr. Louis Johnson, June 30, 1950. V. K. Wellington Koo Papers, Butler Library, Columbia University.
58. Rearden op. cit., chapter 5.
59. Memorandum of Conversation, by the Chief of the Division

of Northeast Asian Affairs (Bishop), February 16, 1949. *FR, 1949*, vol. 7, pp. 655–58.
60. *PP, 1950*, pp. 11, 12.
61. Acheson's *Present at the Creation* (cited in chapter 4, n. 1), p. 352.
62. Personal Message from Mr. Bevin to Mr. Acheson, December 16, 1949. *FR, 1949*, vol. 9, pp. 225–26.
63. Editorial Note. *FR, 1950*, vol. 6, p. 278.
64. NSC 48/2, December 30, 1949. Collection of National Security Council Documents. Modern Military Branch, National Archives.

8. KOREA: A MALIGNANCY. AMERICAN OCCUPATION TROOPS WITHDRAW

1. Korea: Occupation and Military Government: Composition of Forces, March 29, 1944. *FR, 1944*, vol. 5, pp. 1224–28.
2. *FR, 1945*, vol. 6, p. 1039.
3. R-G 332 (U.S. Theaters of War, World War II). USAFIK. "XXIV Corps Journal". Box 22, 1945-December 1948. Washington National Records Center, Suitland, Maryland.
4. PSF: Subject File, Foreign Affairs: Korea Folder. Box 182.
5. James F. Schnabel, *United States Army in the Korean War. Policy and Direction: The First Year*. Office of the Chief of Military History. United States Army, Washington, 1972, pp. 14–21.
6. Truman to Edwin W. Pauley, June 23, 1946. *FR, 1946*, vol. 8, pp. 713–14.
7. Report to the President on China-Korea, September, 1947. Submitted by Lieutenant General A. C. Wedemeyer. *FR, 1947*, vol. 6, pp. 796–807.
8. Memorandum by the Secretary of Defense to the Secretary of State, September 29, 1947. Ibid., pp. 817–17.
9. James F. Schnabel and Robert J. Watson, *The History of the*

Joint Chiefs of Staff. The Joint Chiefs of Staff and National Policy. Vol. 3. The Korean War. Pt. 1. Historical Division. Joint Secretariat. Joint Chiefs of Staff., pp. 13, 14.
10. NSC-8. *FR, 1948*, vol. 6, pp. 1164–70.
11. Schnabel's *United States Army in the Korean War*, op. cit., p. 29.
12. The Special Representative in Korea (Muccio) to the Secretary of State, January 27, 1949. *FR, 1949*, vol. 7, pp. 947–52.
13. Memorandum of Conversation, by the Secretary of the Army (Royall), February 8, 1949. Ibid., pp. 956–58.
14. Schnabel and Watson, op. cit., p. 23.
15. Ibid., pp. 25–27.
16. NSC 8/2. *FR, 1949*, vol. 7, pt. 2, pp. 969–78.
17. Memorandum for the Chief of Staff, U.S. Army. Ibid., pp. 1056–57.
18. The President of the Republic of Korea (Rhee) to President Truman, August 20, 1949. Ibid., pp. 1075–76.

9. STUNNING NEWS FROM SIBERIA: THE SOVIET ATOMIC BOMB

1. Detection of the First Soviet Nuclear Test, a declassified report furnished the author by Richard G. Hewlett of the Department of Energy, who is also the historian of the former Atomic Energy Commission.
2. Telephone interview with Clark M. Clifford, February 23, 1978.
3. *The Private Papers of Senator Vandenberg* (cited in chapter 4, n. 32), p. 518.
4. *The Forrestal Diaries* (cited in chapter 4, n. 4), pp. 461–62, p. 487.
5. Ibid., p. 502.
6. *The Journals of David E. Lilienthal*, vol. 2 (cited in chapter 5, n. 25), p. 464.
7. Condit's *The History of the Joint Chiefs of Staff*, vol. 2 (cited in chapter 5, n. 5), pp. 283–300.
8. President Truman to the Executive Secretary of the National Security Council (Souers), July 26, 1949. *FR, 1949*, vol. 1, pp. 501–3.
9. Frank Pace, Jr., to Truman, April 5, 1949. Atomic Energy Budget Folder AF-PSF.
10. Statement by the President at a Meeting at Blair House, July 14, 1949. *FR, 1949*, vol. 1, pp. 481–82.
11. The Chairman of the Joint Congressional Committee on Atomic Energy (McMahon) to the Secretary of Defense (Johnson), July 14, 1949. *FR, 1949*, vol. 1, pp. 482–84.

12. Quoted in Rearden's *History of the Office of the Secretary of Defense*, vol. 1 (cited in chapter 5, n. 5), chap. 12.
13. *PP, 1949*, p. 485.
14. Lilienthal Journals, op. cit., pp. 570–2.
15. Interview with Clifford, op. cit.
16. *PP, 1945*, pp. 381–82.
17. Lewis L. Strauss, *Men and Decisions* (Garden City, N.Y., 1962), p. 216.
18. Condit, op. cit., p. 524.
19. *Committee on International Relations. Selected Executive Session Hearings of the Committee, 1943–1950. Military Assistance Programs, Pt. 1. Mutual Defense Assistance Act of 1949. Historical Series. U.S. House of Representatives*. U.S. Government Printing Office, pp. 438–39.
20. Report to the President by the Special Committee of the National Security Council on the Proposed Acceleration of the Atomic Energy Programs, October 10, 1949. Ibid., pp. 559–64.
21. Truman to Louis Johnson, October 19, 1949. Confidential File. Box 4. Atomic Bomb and Energy Folder, HSTL.
22. Condit, op. cit., p. 536.
23. Strauss's *Men and Decisions*, op. cit., p. 517.
24. Richard G. Hewlett and Francis Duncan, *Atomic Shield 1947/1952 vol. 2. A History of the United States Atomic Energy Commission* (University Park, Pa.), p. 368.

10. THE REVOLT OF THE ADMIRALS

1. *New York Times*, September 1, 1949, p. 1.
2. Ibid., September 13, 1949, p. 1.
3. Ibid., September 14, 1949, p. 18.
4. Paul Y. Hammond, "Super Carriers and the B-36 Bombers: Appropriations, Strategy and Politics" in Harold Stein, ed., *American Civil-Military Decisions. A Book of Case Studies*. A Twentieth Century Fund Study (Birmingham, Alabama, 1963), p. 538.
5. *New York Times*, September 16, 1949, p. 1.
6. *PP, 1949*, p. 480.
7. *New York Times*, October 6, 1949, p. 1.
8. Ibid., October 4, 1949. Texts of the three letters, p. 3.
9. Radford's *From Pearl Harbor to Vietnam* (cited, chap. 5, n. 3), p. 113.
10. *The National Defense Program—Unification and Strategy. Hearings Before the Committee on Armed Services. House of Representatives. Eighty First Congress. First Session*. U.S. Government Printing Office, 1949, p. 127.
11. OH, Robert L. Dennison, p. 15.
12. *The National Defense Program—Unification and Strategy*, op. cit., p. 2 ff.
13. Ibid., pp. 45, 51.

14. Ibid., p. 41.
15. Condit's *The History of the Joint Chiefs of Staff*, vol. 2 (cited, chap. 5, n. 5), p. 330.
16. *The National Defense Program—Unification and Strategy*, op. cit., pp. 46–9; 58.
17. Ibid., p. 43.
18. *Investigation of the B-36 Bomber Program. Hearings Before the Committee on Armed Services. House of Representatives. Eighty-first Congress. First Session. On H. Res 234*. U.S. Government Printing Office, p. 216.
19. *The National Defense Program—Unification and Strategy*, op. cit., p. 50, 51, 55, 56.
20. David Alan Rosenberg, "American Atomic Strategy and the Hydrogen Bomb Decision" in *The Journal of American History*, June 1979, pp. 76–8.
21. *The National Defense Program—Unification and Strategy*, op. cit., pp. 49, 50, 67.
22. Ibid., pp. 62, 65, 75, 81, 88, 93, 96.
23. Ibid., pp. 241, 265.
24. *Time*, October 24, 1949, p. 27.
25. *The National Defense Program—Unification and Strategy*, op. cit., 350–62.

26. Condit, op. cit., p. 343.
27. *The National Defense Program—Unification and Strategy*, op. cit., p. 408.
28. Meeting with the President, October 20, 1949. Dean Acheson Papers. October-November, 1949, Folder. Box 64, HSTL.
29. *The National Defense Program—Unification and Strategy*, op. cit., pp. 534–36.
30. *PP*, 1949, p. 531.
31. *New York Times*, October 28, 1949, p. 1.
32. Ibid., October 29, 1949, p. 1.
33. Letter, Francis P. Matthews to Truman, October 27, 1949.

PSF: Personal File, Matthews, F. P. Folder. Box 318.
34. Letter, Truman to Harold L. Ickes, November 1, 1949. PSF: General File, ''I'' Folder. Box 123.
35. *New York Times*, March 2, 1950, p. 1.
36. On August 25, 1950, Matthews said in a speech in Boston that the United States might have to consider a preventive war. With White House backing, the State Department disavowed the secretary of the navy's words. Matthews telephoned to Truman and offered to resign. Truman told him to forget it. In 1951, however, he resigned and was appointed Ambassador to Ireland.

11. AN AURA OF SCANDAL: "FIVE PERCENTERS" AND "DEEP FREEZERS"

1. Harold L. Ickes Diaries, entry of October 13, 1945. Manuscript Division, Library of Congress, Washington, D.C.
2. Interview with Paul D. Grindle, October 4, 1973.
3. Ibid.
4. *New York Herald Tribune*, June 20, 1949, p. 1.
5. OH, John R. Steelman.
6. Ayers Diary, entry of April 19, 1947.
7. Interview with Harry H. Vaughan, March 3, 1973.
8. *U.S. Congress. Senate. Committee on Expenditures in the Executive Departments. Influence in Government Procurement. Hearings Before the Investigations Subcommittee of the Senate Committee on Expenditures in the Executive Departments. . . . Eighty-first Congress, First Session.* U.S. Government Printing Office, p. 231. (Hereafter "Hearings").
9. Interview with Henry J. Nicholson, September 11, 1972.
10. Hearings, op. cit., pp. 420–22.
11. Text in Jules Abels, *The Truman Scandals* (Chicago, 1956), p. 43.
12. Hearings, op. cit., pp. 497, 583.
13. *U.S. Congress. Senate. Committee on Expenditures in the Executive Departments. Subcommittee on Investigations. The 5-Percenter Investigation. S. Report 1232, Eighty-first Congress. Second Session.* Senate Miscellaneous Reports, vol. 1, p. 15. (Hereafter "Report").
14. Hearings, op. cit., pp. 311–15, 498.
15. Nicholson interview, op. cit.
16. Report, op. cit., p. 14.
17. *PP*, 1949, p. 420.
18. Quoted in Hamby's *Beyond the New Deal* (cited in chapter 2, n. 1), p. 312.
19. This passage draws on Donald R. McCoy and Richard T. Ruetten, *Quest and Response. Minority Rights and the Truman Administration* (Lawrence, Kansas, 1973), chapter 9; and William C. Berman, *The Politics of Civil Rights* (Columbus, Ohio, 1970), chapter 4).
20. Ayers Diary, entry of February 28, 1949.
21. *PP*, 1949, pp. 146–47.
22. R. Alton Lee "Harry S. Truman and the Taft-Hartley Act." Ph. D. dissertation, University of Oklahoma, 1962, p. 185.
23. Ibid., p. 179.
24. Ibid., p. 195.
25. *PP*, 1949, p. 4.

26. For Tom Clark's advice see the Department of Justice memorandum, "Inherent Executive Power to Deal with Emergencies Resulting from Labor Disputes in Vital Industries Affecting the Health, Safety, and Welfare of the Entire Nation," February 7, 1949. Holmes Baldridge Papers. Box 1. Inherent Executive Power . . . Folder. HSTL.
27. *PP*, 1949, p. 126.
28. Gerald Pomper, "Labor and Congress: The Repeal of the Taft-Hartley Act" in *Labor History*, fall, 1961, p. 343.
29. Ayers Diary, entries of May 3 and 4, 1949.
30. *PP*, 1949, p. 243.
31. Ibid., p. 340.
32. Barton J. Bernstein and Allen J. Matusow, eds., *The Truman Administration. A Documentary History* (New York, 1966), pp. 135–36.
33. Zbigniew Brzezinski and Samuel P. Huntington, *Political Power: USA / USSR*, p. 324.
34. Hamby, op. cit., p. 305 ff.
35. Allen J. Matusow, *Farm Policies and Politics in the Truman Administration* (Cambridge, 1967), p. 196.
36. Edwin L. Dale Jr., "Brannan Crop Plan Now Reality," *New York Times*, August 11, 1973, p. 1.
37. *PP*, 1949, p. 5.
38. Ibid.
39. Ibid., p. 25.
40. Joseph P. Lash, *Eleanor: The Years Alone* (New York, 1972), chapter 7.
41. Ayers Diary, entry of August 3, 1949.
42. *PP*, 1949, p. 5.
43. Ibid., pp. 66, 67.
44. Letter, Truman to Ben Turoff, April 12, 1949. PSF: Personal File, "T" Folder. Box 324.
45. Ayers Diary, entries of January 11 and May 23, 1949.
46. Richard H. Rovere, "Letter From Washington," in *The New Yorker*, March 17, 1949.
47. Truman, diary entries of October 22 and November 1, 1949. Ayers Papers. Personal-Truman Notes-Letters Folder. Box 24. HSTL.
48. Richard O. Davis, *Housing Reform During the Truman Administration* (Columbia, Missouri, 1966), pp. 110, 135.
49. *PP,** 1949, p. 381.
50. Davis, op. cit., p. 136.

12. 1950: A SAVAGE YEAR BEGINS

1. *Khrushchev Remembers, With an Introduction, Commentary and Notes by Edward Crankshaw* (Boston, 1970), pp. 367–68.
2. *PP*, 1950, p. 2 ff.
3. *New York Times*, January 5, 1950, p. 1.
4. Condit's *The History of the Joint Chiefs of Staff*, vol. 2 (cited in chapter 5, n. 5), p. 280.
5. Memorandum by the Deputy Chief of the Division of Estimates, Bureau of the Budget (Schaub), to the Executive Secretary of the National Security Council (Lay), May 8, 1955. *FR*, 1950, vol. 1, p. 299.
6. Records of Actions by the National Security Council, January 5, 1950. National Security Council Documents. Records of Actions. National Security Council Actions 219–449 Folder. Modern Military Branch. National Archives.
7. Interview with Henry J. Nicholson, October 6, 1978.

8. Weinstein's *Perjury. The Hiss-Chambers Case* (cited in chapter 2, n. 24), p. 10.
9. Ibid., p. 194.
10. Interview with James E. Webb, October 20, 1978.
11. Interview with Carlisle H. Hummelsine, March 20, 1978.
12. Acheson's *Present at the Creation* (cited in chapter 3, n. 1), p. 360.
13. *Congressional Record*, vol. 96, pt. 1, p. 889 ff.
14. Acheson, op. cit.
15. Text in *American Foreign Policy. Basic Documents, 1950–1955*. Department of State. U.S. Government Printing Office.
16. Memorandum of Conversation, by Mr. John Z. Williams of the Office of Northeast Asian Affairs, January 20, 1950. *FR*, 1950, vol. 7, pp. 11–14.
17. *PP*, 1950, p. 109.

13. VIETNAM: THE FIRST GRAVE STEP

1. Walter LaFeber, "Roosevelt, Churchill and Indochina: 1942–1945", *American Historical Review*, December, 1975, p. 1277 ff.
2. Dean Acheson to Charles S. Reed (for Abbott Low Moffat), December 8, 1946. *FR*, 1946, vol. 8, pp. 66–69.
3. James F. Byrnes to Jefferson Caffery, December 24, 1946. Ibid., pp. 77, 78.

4. The Acting Secretary of State to the Embassy in France, January 17, 1949, vol. 7, pt. 1, pp. 4, 5.
5. Louis A. Johnson to Sidney Souers, June 10, 1949. Collection of National Security Council Documents. Modern Military Branch, National Archives.
6. Philip C. Jessup, *The Birth of Nations* (New York, 1974), pp. 29, 30.

7. NSC 48 / 2 (cited in chapter 7, n. 64).
8. Problem Paper Prepared by a Working group in the Department of State, February 1, 1950. *FR*, 1950, vol. 6, pp. 711–15.
9. The Ambassador in France to the Secretary of State, March 6, 1949. *FR*, 1949, vol. 7, pt. 1, pp. 9, 10.
10. The Ambassador in France to the Secretary of State, March 16, 1949. Ibid., pp. 12–14.
11. The Secretary of State to the Consulate General at Saigon, May 10, 1949, Ibid., pp. 23–25.
12. The Consul General at Saigon (Abbott) to the Secretary of State, June 14, 1949. Ibid., pp. 47–49.
13. The Chief of State of Vietnam (His Majesty Bao Dai) to President Truman, August 31, 1949. Ibid., p. 74.
14. The Secretary of State to the Embassy in France, December 1, 1949. Ibid., pp. 101–2.
15. The Ambassador in France (Bruce) to the Secretary of State, December 11, 1949. Ibid., pp. 105–110.
16. The Consul General at Saigon (Abbott) to the Secretary of State, December 27, 1949. Ibid., p. 114.
17. The Ambassador in India (Henderson) to the Secretary of State, January 7, 1950. *FR*, 1950, vol. 6, pp. 692–93.
18. Memorandum of Conversation, October 12, 1949. PSF: Subject File, Foreign Affairs, India-Nehru Folder. Box 180.
19. The Secretary of State to the Embassy in Thailand, January 17, 1950. *FR*, 1950, p. 697.
20. The Secretary of State to the Consulate at Saigon. January

20, 1950. Ibid., pp. 698–700. The Secretary of State to the Embassy in the United Kingdom, January 30, 1950, pp. 703–4.
21. Memorandum by the Secretary of State to the President, February 2, 1950. Ibid., pp. 716–17.
22. Memorandum of Conversation, by the Secretary of State, February 3, 1950. Ibid. 719. Cabinet Meeting February 3, 1950. Notes on Cabinet Meetings: January 6-December 29, 1950 Folder. Matthew J. Connelly Papers. Box 1. HSTL.
23. The Ambassador in France (Bruce) to the Secretary of State, February 7, 1950. *FR*, 1950, vol. 6, pp. 722–23.
24. The Consul General at Saigon (Abbott) to the Secretary of State, February 9, 1950. Ibid., pp. 725–26.
25. The Consul General At Saigon to the Secretary of State, February 11, 1950. Ibid., pp. 726–27.
26. Memorandum of Conversation, by the Secretary of State, February 16, 1950. Ibid. pp. 730–33.
27. NSC 64, February 27, 1950. Ibid., 744–47.
28. Notes on the President's Meeting with Under Secretary of State James Webb March 26, 1950. . . . Webb Folder. Box 6. Personal Files. HSTL.
29. Editorial Note. *FR*, 1950, vol. 6, p. 812.
30. *The Pentagon Papers. The Secret History of the Vietnam War. The Complete and Unabridged Series as Published by the New York Times* (New York, 1971), pp. 9, 10.
31. *PP*, 1951, p. 506.

14. THE HYDROGEN BOMB DECISION

1. Hewlett's and Duncan's *Atomic Shield* (cited in chapter 9, n. 24), pp. 373–34.
2. Ibid., pp. 375–77.
3. *The Journals of David E. Lilienthal, vol. 2* (cited in chapter 5, n. 25), p. 577.
4. Stanley A. Blumberg and Gwinn Owens, *Energy and Conflict. The Life and Times of Edward Teller* (New York, 1976), p. 223.
5. Strauss's *Men and Decisions* (cited in chapter 9, n. 17), p. 212.
6. *In the Matter of J. Robert Oppenheimer. Transcript of Hearing before Personal Security Board and Texts of Principal Documents and Letters.* United States Atomic Energy Commission. (MIT Press, Cambridge, 1971), pp. 242, 243.
7. Condit's *The History of the Joint Chiefs of Staff, vol. 2* (cited in chapter 5, n. 5), p. 544.
8. Statement Appended to the Report of the General Advisory Committee, October 30, 1949. *FR*, 1949, vol. 1, pp. 570–71.
9. An Opinion on the Development of the "Super", October 30, 1949. Ibid., pp. 572, 573.
10. *In the Matter of J. Robert Oppenheimer*, op. cit., p. 80.
11. Henry L. Stimson and McGeorge Bundy, *On Active Service in Peace and War* (New York, 1948), p. 617.
12. Bernstein's and Matusow's *The Truman Administration: A Documentary History* (cited in chapter 11, n. 32), p. 15.
13. Memorandum, Truman to Acheson, May 7, 1946. PSF: Subject File, Atomic Tests Folder. Box 201.
14. Interview with James Webb, March 6, 1978. Also *Atomic Shield*, op. cit., p. 388.
15. Strauss, op. cit., p. 219.
16. Blumberg and Owens, op. cit., pp. 220–21.
17. R. Gordon Arneson, "The H-Bomb Decision". This article appeared in two parts in the *Foreign Service Journal* of May and June, 1969. This particular reference is in Pt. 1.
18. Condit, op. cit., pp. 547–49.
19. The Chairman of the United States Atomic Energy Commission (Lilienthal) to President Truman, November 9, 1949. *FR*, 1949, vol. 1, pp. 576–85.
20. Hewlett and Duncan, op. cit., p. 398.

21. The Chairman of the Joint Committee on Atomic Energy (McMahon) to President Truman, November 21, 1949. *FR*, 1949, vol. 1, pp. 588–95.
22. Strauss, op. cit., pp. 219–20.
23. *In the Matter of J. Robert Oppenheimer*, op. cit., p. 81.
24. Blumberg and Owens, op. cit., p. 216.
25. President Truman to the Executive Secretary of the National Security Council (Souers), November 19, 1949, *FR*, 1949, vol. 1, pp. 587–88.
26. Lilienthal Journals, op. cit., p. 617, n.
27. Memorandum by the Joint Chiefs of Staff to the Secretary of Defense (Johnson), January 13, 1950. *FR*, 1950, vol. 1, pp. 503–11.
28. Memorandum of Telephone Conversation, by the Secretary of State, January 19, 1950. Ibid., pp. 511–12.
29. Lilienthal Journals, op. cit., pp. 613–14.
30. Ayers Diary, entry of June 29, 1949.
31. Arneson, pt. 1, op. cit.
32. Ayers Diary, entry of January 21, 1950.
33. Lilienthal Journals, op. cit., p. 630.
34. Report of the Special Committee of the National Security Council to the President, January 31, 1950. *FR*, 1950, vol. 1, pp. 513–23.
35. Lilienthal Journals, op. cit., pp. 632–33.
36. Samuel F. Wells, Jr., "Domestic Pressures Against Taking Risks for Peace." Paper Read at the annual meeting of the Organization of American Historians, Atlanta, Ga., April 7, 1977.
37. Arneson, op. cit., pt. 1, p. 27.
38. *PP*, 1950, p. 138.
39. *Washington Post*, February 1, 1950, p. 10.
40. The Secretary of Defense to the President, February 24, 1950. *FR*, 1950, pp. 538–39.
41. David Holloway, "Research Note. Soviet Thermonuclear Development." *International Security*, winter, 1979 / 80, pp. 192–97.
42. Report of the Special Committee of the National Security Council to the President, March 9, 1950. *FR*, 1950, p. 542, n. 1.

15. NSC 68

1. Arneson's "The H-Bomb Decision", pt. 1 (cited in chapter 14, n. 17).
2. Paul H. Nitze later conceded the point. See Fred M. Kaplan, "Our Cold War Policy, Circa '50" in *New York Times Magazine*, May 18, 1980, p. 91.
3. Record of the Eighth Meeting (1950) of the Policy Planning Staff of the Department of State, February 2, 1950. *FR*, 1950, vol. 1, pp. 142–43.
4. Interview with John Snyder, July 26, 1977.
5. *The Journals of David E. Lilienthal, vol. 2* (cited in chapter 5, n. 25), p. 565.
6. Interview with James Webb, March 6, 1978.

7. Interview with Lucius D. Battle, May 3, 1975.
8. Memorandum of Conversation at the State Department, March 22, 1950. *FR*, 1950, vol. 1, pp. 203–6.
9. Acheson's *Present at the Creation* (cited in chapter 3, n. 1), p. 373. In his account Acheson said he had been convinced that Johnson was mentally ill. Johnson did later undergo surgery for a brain tumor. Persons who saw him subsequently and throughout his final years, however, found him perfectly rational.
10. Ibid., pp. 373–74.
11. Ibid., p. 374.
12. Text in *FR*, 1950, vol. 1, p. 234 ff.

16. THE McCARTHY ONSLAUGHT

1. Telegram, Joseph R. McCarthy to Truman, February 11, 1950. Draft of letter, Truman to McCarthy, undated. PSF: General File. McCarthy, Joseph Folder. Box 128.
2. Text in *PP*, 1948, pp. 181–82.
3. *PP*, 1950, p. 163.
4. Ibid., p. 164 ff.
5. Richard M. Fried, *Men Against McCarthy* (New York, 1976), p. 42.
6. *Congressional Record*, vol. 96, pt. 2, p. 1952 ff.
7. William S. White, *The Taft Story* (New York, 1954), p. 85.
8. Michael Paul Rogin, *The Intellectuals and McCarthy: the Radical Specter* (Cambridge, 1967), p. 216.
9. Richard H. Rovere, "Letter from Washington" in *The New Yorker*, April 22, 1950.
10. Interview with John R. Steelman, August 23, 1974.
11. Memorandum, Truman to David D. Lloyd, March 3, 1950. PSF: Personal File, "L" Folder. Box 315.
12. Ed. Francis H. Heller, *The Truman White House*, (cited in chapter 2, n. 9), p. 150.
13. Letter, Truman to Harold Ickes, September 8, 1950. PSF: General File, Ickes, Harold L. Folder. Box 123.
14. Letter, Truman to Brian McMahon, May 31, 1950. PSF: General File, Mc-general Folder. Box 128.
15. Letter, Truman to Julius Ochs Adler, August 17, 1950. PSF: Personal File, "A" Folder. Box 305.
16. Letter, Truman to Chester Bowles, June 23, 1950. PSF: Political File, Connecticut Folder. Box 55.
17. Letter, Truman to Acheson, March 31, 1950. PSF: Subject File, State, Secretary of—Dean Acheson Folder. Box 160.
18. Letter, Truman to Arthur H. Vandenberg, March 27, 1950. PSF: General File, "V" Folder. Box 140.
19. Notes on the President's Meeting with Under Secretary of State James Webb, March 26, 1950. Charles G. Ross Papers. Webb Folder. Box 6. HSTL.
20. Townsend Hoopes, *The Devil and John Foster Dulles* (Boston, 1973), pp. 85–8.
21. Notes on the President's Meeting with . . . Webb. op. cit.
22. Letter, President Truman to Ralph Truman, March 26, 1950. PSF: Family Correspondence File, Truman, Mr. and Mrs. Ralph Folder. Box 331.
23. Letter, Vandenberg to Acheson, March 31, 1950. Memorandum of Conversation. Acheson Papers. 1950 March Folder. Box 65. HSTL.
24. Memorandum of Conversation with the President, April 4, 1950. Acheson Papers. April, 1950, Folder. Box 65. HSTL.
25. Memorandum of Acheson-Dulles telephone conversation, April 6, 1950. Ibid.
26. Memorandum, J. F. Dulles to Acheson, May 2, 1950. Acheson Papers. Box 65. Memos of Conversation Folder. HSTL.
27. Letter, Millard E. Tydings to Truman, March 22, 1950. George M. Elsey Papers. McCarthy Charges #2 Folder. Box 69. HSTL.
28. *PP*, 1950, pp. 229–31.
29. Ibid., pp. 240–41.
30. David Caute, *The Great Fear. The Anti-Communist Purge Under Truman and Eisenhower* (New York, 1978), p. 319.
31. Letter, Truman to Mrs. Eleanor Lattimore Andrews, April 17, 1950. PSF: Personal File, "A" Folder. Box 305.
32. *PP*, 1950, pp. 234–36.
33. Ibid., p. 252.

17. INTERLUDE: A QUIET DECISION

1. Truman, handwritten note, April 16, 1950. PSF: "Longhand Notes" File. Longhand personal memos, 1950 Folder. Box 333.
2. Interview with George M. Elsey, August 6, 1974.
3. *Congressional Record*, vol. 96, pt. 2, p. 1953.
4. Quoted in Thomas I. Emerson and David M. Helfeld, "Loyalty Among Government Employees" in *The Yale Law Journal*, December, 1948, pp. 10, 11.
5. OH, David E. Bell, p. 192.
6. Letter, Clair Wilcox to Roger W. Tubby, April 1, 1950. Roger W. Tubby's Journal, entry of April 6, 1950.
7. Ibid., entry of March 15, 1950.
8. Ibid., entries of May 6 and May 21, 1950.
9. *PP*, 1950, p. 267 ff.
10. *New York Times*, May 5, 1951, p. 1.
11. Memorandum, Charles Murphy to Donald Dawson, May 8, 1950. Robert L. Dennison Papers. White House Message Traffic. 1950 Folder. Box 3. HSTL.
12. Ayers Diary, entry of February 28, 1950.
13. Letter, Vandenberg to Truman, March 29, 1950. PSF: General File, "V" Folder. Box 140.
14. Memorandum, Truman to Charles Sawyer, April 20, 1950. PSF: Subject File, Commerce, Secretary of—Charles Sawyer Folder. Box 156.

18. THE GATHERING CLOUDS ABROAD

1. *Reviews of the World Situation* (cited in chapter 4, n. 29), p. 292.
2. Lawrence S. Kaplan, *A Community of Interests: NATO and the Military Assistance Program, 1948–1950*. Office of the Secretary of Defense. Historical Office. U.S. Government Printing Office, pp. 71–78.
3. Report to the National Security Council by the Secretary of Defense, June 8, 1950. *FR*, 1950, vol. 4, pp. 686–87.
4. Memorandum by the Chairman of the Joint Chiefs of Staff (Bradley) to the Secretary of Defense (Johnson), May 3, 1950. *FR*, 1950, vol. 3, pp. 1560–62.
5. Memorandum by the President to the Secretary of State, June 16, 1950. *FR*, 1950, vol. 4, p. 688.
6. Meeting with the President, May 9, 1949. May-June 1949 Folder. Box 64. Acheson Papers. HSTL.
7. Memorandum for the Secretary of State from the President, August 2, 1951. PSF: Subject File, Foreign Affairs: Spain Folder. Box 188.
8. Memorandum by the President to the Secretary of State, June 16, 1950. *FR*, 1950, vol. 4, pp. 688–89.
9. *To Amend the Mutual Defense Assistance Act of 1949. Hearings before the Committee on Foreign Affairs. House of Representatives. Eighty-first Congress. Second Session.* U.S. Government Printing Office, p. 8.
10. Text of treaty in *Military Situation in the Far East* (cited in chapter 4, n. 52). p. 3172 ff.
11. Rearden's *History of the Office of the Secretary of Defense, vol. 1* (cited in chapter 5, n. 4), chap. 6.
12. The Ambassador in Korea (Muccio) to the Secretary of State, January 18, 1950. *FR*, 1950, vol. 7, pp. 8–11.
13. Schnabel and Watson, *The History of the Joint Chiefs of Staff, vol. 3, pt. 1* (cited in chapter 8, n. 9), pp. 42–43.
14. Ibid., p. 41.
15. Memorandum of Conversation, by the Officer in Charge of Korean Affairs (Bond), May 10, 1950. *FR*, 1950, vol. 7, pp. 78–81.
16. This passage is based on Schnabel's *United States Army in the Korean War* (cited in chapter 6, n. 9), pp. 61–65.
17. Roy E. Appleman, *United States Army in the Korean War. South to the Naktong, North to the Yalu (June-November 1950)*. Office of the Chief of Military History. Department of the Army, 1961. U.S. Government Printing Office, p. 19.
18. The Ambassador in Korea (Muccio) to the Secretary of State, June 14, 1950. *FR*, 1950, vol. 7, p. 105.
19. *To Amend the Mutual Defense Assistance Act of 1949*, op. cit., pp. 138–39.
20. Schnabel, *United States Army in the Korean War*, op. cit., p. 64.
21. *Military Situation*, op. cit., p. 1991.
22. Memorandum by the Central Intelligence Agency, June 19, 1950. *FR*, 1950, vol. 7, pp. 109–21.
23. *PP*, 1950, p. 285.
24. *Committee on International Relations. Selected Executive Session Hearings . . . 1943–50. vol. 8. United States Policy in the Far East. Pt. 2. . . . Historical Series. House of Representatives.* U.S. Government Printing Office, p. 464.
25. Roberta Wohlstetter, *Pearl Harbor. Warning and Decision* (Stanford, 1962), pp. 392, 399.
26. Schnabel, *United States Army in the Korean War*, op. cit., p. 52.
27. *New York Times*, March 30, 1950, p. 1.

19. A SUMMER DAY IN INDEPENDENCE, MISSOURI

1. Merle Miller, *Plain Speaking. An Oral Biography of Harry S. Truman* (New York, 1973), p. 32.
2. *St. Louis Post-Dispatch*, June 25, 1950, p. 1.
3. *PP*, 1950, pp. 489–91.

4. Ayers Diary, entry of June 25, 1950.
5. Appleman, *United States Army in the Korean War* (cited in chapter 18, n. 17), p. 22.
6. The Ambassador in Korea (Muccio) to the Secretary of State,

June 25, 1950. *FR*, 1950, vol. 7, pp. 125–26.
7. Truman, *Years of Trial and Hope* (cited in chapter 3, n. 18), p. 332.

20. SUNDAY NIGHT AT BLAIR HOUSE

1. Editorial Note. *FR*, 1950, vol. 7, p. 128.
2. The Ambassador in Korea (Muccio) to the Secretary of State, June 25, 1950. Ibid., p. 129.
3. Schnabel and Watsons, *The History of the Joint Chiefs of Staff, vol. 3, pt. 1* (cited in chapter 8, n. 9), p. 65.
4. The Ambassador in Korea to the Secretary of State, June 25, 1950. *FR*, 1950, vol. 7, pp. 132–33.
5. Memorandum of Teletype Conference, June 25, 1950. Ibid., pp. 134–38.
6. The Ambassador in the Soviet Union to the Secretary of State, June 25, 1950. Ibid., pp. 139, 140.
7. The Acting Political Adviser in Japan to the Secretary of State, June 25, 1950. Ibid., p. 140.
8. Schnabel and Watson, op. cit., pp. 66–67.
9. Editorial Note. *FR*, 1950, vol. 7, p. 143–44.
10. Schnabel and Watson, op. cit., pp. 72–73.
11. Teleconference, July 25, 1950. George M. Elsey Papers. Korea—June 25, 1950 Folder. Box 71. HSTL.
12. Memorandum, undated. Ibid.
13. Truman, *Years of Trial and Hope* (cited in chapter 3, n. 18), p. 332.
14. Margaret Truman, *Souvenir* (cited in chapter 1, n. 15), p. 275.
15. The quote appears in the *New York Times*, July 2, 1950, Section E, p. 1, but does not cite the source. Edwin W. Darby later told the author the source was General Graham.
16. *New York Times*, June 26, 1950, p. 7.
17. Interview with Henry Nicholson, October 6, 1978.
18. Text in *FR*, 1950, vol. 7, pp. 155–56.

19. Intelligence Estimate Prepared by the Estimates Group, Office of Intelligence Research, Department of State, June 25, 1950. Ibid., pp. 148–54.
20. *Chicago Tribune*, June 26, 1950, p. 1.
21. Interview with James Webb, March 14, 1979.
22. Jessup, *The Birth of Nations* (cited in chapter 13, n. 6), p. 10.
23. Memorandum on Formosa, by General of the Army Douglas MacArthur . . . June 14, 1950. *FR*, 1950, vol. 7, pp. 161–65.
24. Ensuing passage is based almost entirely on Memorandum of Conversation by the Ambassador at Large (Jessup), June 25, 1950. Ibid., pp. 157–61.
25. Schnabel and Watson, op. cit., p. 80.
26. Ibid., pp. 81–82.
27. Matthew B. Ridgway, *SOLDIER: The Memoirs of Matthew B. Ridgway* (New York, 1956), p. 192.
28. *Military Situation in the Far East*, (cited in chapter 7, n. 52), p. 948.
29. OH, John D. Hickerson.
30. Acheson, *Present at the Creation* (cited in chapter 3, n. 1), p. 415.
31. Roger Tubby Journal, entry of June 27, 1950.
32. *PP*, 1950, p. 529.
33. Excerpts from the telegram in George F. Kennan, *Memoirs, 1925–1950* (Boston, 1967), p. 547 ff.
34. *United States Relations with China* (cited in chapter 2, n. 22), pp. 607–9.
35. *New York Herald Tribune*, June 29, 1950, p. 29.

21. THE COMMITMENT OF U.S. AIR AND NAVAL FORCES

1. The Ambassador in Korea to the Secretary of State, June 26, 1950. *FR*, 1950, vol. 7, p. 170.
2. *PP*, 1950, pp. 491–92.
3. Report of NSC Meeting in the Summer of 1950. PSF: General File, NSC Meetings—Memos for President. Meeting Discussions (1950) Folder. Box 220.
4. President Truman's Conversation with George M. Elsey, July 26, 1950. Korea-June, 26, 1950, Folder. Box 71. Elsey Papers. HSTL.
5. *New York Times*, June 26, 1950, p. 26.
6. *Congressional Record*, vol. 96, pt. 7, pp. 9154, 9157 ff, 9180, 9184.
7. Schnabel and Watson, *The History of the Joint Chiefs of Staff, vol. 3, pt. 1* (cited in chapter 8, n. 9), p. 84.
8. Ensuing passage is based on Memorandum of Conversation, by the Ambassador at Large (Jessup), June 26, 1950. *FR*, 1950, vol. 7, pp. 178–83.
9. *PP*, 1950, p. 492.
10. Thomas Terry Connally, as told to Alfred Steinberg, *My Name Is Tom Connally* (New York, 1954), p. 346.
11. Ensuing passage is based on George M. Elsey's notes. Korea-Congressional Leaders Folder, July 27, 1950. Box 71. Elsey Papers. HSTL. And on Memorandum of Conversation by the Ambassador at Large (Jessup), June 27, 1950. *FR*, 1950, vol. 7, pp. 200–2.
12. *PP*, 1950, p. 492.
13. *Congressional Record*, vol. 96, pt. 7, p. 9229.
14. *PP*, 1950, p. 496.
15. Dwight D. Eisenhower, *The White House Years. Mandate for a Change, 1953–1956* (Garden City, L.I., 1963), p. 82.
16. Text in *FR*, 1950, vol. 7, p. 211.

17. Joseph O'Mahoney to Truman, June 27, 1950. Truman to O'Mahoney, June 28, 1950. PSF: Korean War File, Korean War Data—General Folder. Box 243.
18. Appleman, *United States Army in the Korean War* (cited in chapter 18, n. 17), p. 44.
19. Memorandum of Conversation (by Ambassador Jessup), June 28, 1950. State Department Central Files. 795.00/6-2850. National Archives.
20. Memorandum of Conversation. NSC Meeting, June 28, 1950. Ibid.
21. Schnabel and Watson, op. cit., pp. 100–101.
22. Courtney Whitney, *MacArthur. His Rendezvous With Destiny* (New York, 1956), p. 326.
23. Schnabel and Watson, op. cit., pp. 103–4.
24. Ensuing account is based on Memorandum of Conversation [by Ambassador Jessup], June 29, 1950. State Department Central Files 795.00/6-2950. Also on Elsey notes, Korea-White House-State-Defense Meeting 5 P.M.—June 29, 1950 Folder Box 71. Elsey Papers. HSTL.
25. Text in *FR*, 1950, vol. 7, pp. 229–30.
26. *New York Times*, June 29, 1950, p. 4.
27. The Joint Chiefs of Staff to the Commander in Chief, Far East (MacArthur), June 29, 1950. *FR*, 1950, vol. 7, pp. 240–41.
28. Memorandum of Conversation, by the Acting Deputy Director of the Office of Chinese Affairs (Freeman), June 30, 1950. Ibid., pp. 262–63.
29. Truman, *Years of Trial and Hope* (cited in chapter 3, n. 18), p. 342.
30. Schnabel and Watson, op. cit., p. 127.

22. TRUMAN'S FATEFUL DECISION: GROUND FORCES IN ASIA

1. The Commander in Chief, Far East (MacArthur) to the Secretary of State, June 30, 1950. *FR*, 1950, vol. 7, pp. 248–50.
2. J. Lawton Collins, *War in Peacetime. The History and Lessons of Korea* (Boston, 1969), p. 21.
3. Memorandum of Teletype Conference, Prepared in the Department of the Army, June 30, 1950. *FR*, 1950, vol. 7, pp. 250–53.
4. Truman's *Years of Trial and Hope* (cited in chapter 3, n. 18), p. 343.
5. Memorandum of Teletype Conference, op. cit., pp. 252–53.
6. Acheson, *Present at the Creation* (cited in chapter 3, n. 1), p. 412.

7. *Military Situation in the Far East* (cited in chapter 7, n. 52), p. 1651.
8. Truman, op. cit., p. 343.
9. Note, June 30, 1950. Subject: President's call to Pace and Call from Louis Johnson. Elsey Papers. Korea-June 30, 1950 Folder. Box 71. HSTL.
10. Truman, op. cit., p. 343.
11. *Military Situation*, op. cit., p. 280.
12. Schnabel and Watson, *The History of the Joint Chiefs of Staff, vol. 3, pt. 1* (cited in chapter 8, n. 9), pp. 117–18.
13. *PP*, 1950, p. 513.
14. Korea-Congressional leaders. 11 A.M.—6/30/50 Folder. Elsey Papers. Box. 71. HSTL.

15. Glenn D. Paige, *The Korean Decision (June 24–30, 1950)* (New York, 1968), p. 264.
16. *Military Situation*, op. cit., p. 1112.
17. *Washington Post*, July 1, 1950, p. 6. *New York Times* July 1, 1950, p. 14.

18. The Joint Chiefs of Staff to the Commander in Chief, Far East, June 30, 1950. *FR*, 1950, vol. 7, p. 263.
19. Appleman, *United States Army in the Korean War* (cited in chapter 18, n. 17), p. 60.

23. A COSTLY MISTAKE: WAR WITHOUT CONGRESSIONAL APPROVAL

1. *Congressional Record*, vol. 96, pt. 7, p. 9228 ff.
2. Ibid., pp. 9319–23.
3. The Secretary of State to the United States Mission at the United Nations, July 3, 1950. *FR*, 1950, vol. 7, pp. 295–97.
4. Connally's *My Name Is Tom Connally* (cited in chapter 21, n. 10), p. 346.
5. OH, Frank C. Pace, Jr., p. 79.
6. Korea-Congressional leaders. 11 A.M.—6 / 30 / 50 Folder. Elsey Papers. Box 71. HSTL.
7. Truman's *Years of Trial and Hope* (cited in chapter 3, n. 18), p. 340.
8. *PP*, 1950, pp. 502–6.
9. Elsey memorandum to Beverly Smith (of the *Saturday Evening Post*). Subject: Congressional Resolution, July 16, 1951.

10. Elsey Papers. Korea-July, 1950, Folder. Box 71. HSTL.
11. Ibid.
12. Draft, July 3, 1950. Elsey Papers. Korea-July, 1950, Folder. Box 71. HSTL.
13. Ensuing account is based on Memorandum of Conversation, by the Ambassador at Large (Jessup), July 3, 1950. *FR*, 1950, vol. 7, pp. 286–91. Also, Memorandum of Telephone Conversation, by Miss Barbara Evans, Personal Assistant to the Secretary of State, July 3, 1950. Ibid. pp. 282–83. Also, Acheson's *Present at the Creation* (cited in chapter 3, n. 1), p. 414.
14. Ayers Diary, entry of July 11, 1950.
15. See Elsey's memorandums on preparation of Truman's July 19th message. Elsey Papers. Box 71. HSTL.

24. KOREA: SPRINGBOARD FOR A U.S. GLOBAL BUILD-UP

1. Memorandum of Conversation, by Mr. Frederick E. Nolting, Special Assistant to the Deputy Under Secretary of State (Matthews), June 30, 1950. *FR*, 1950, vol. 7, pp. 258–59.
2. Memorandum by Mr. Charles E. Bohlen, July 13, 1950. *FR*, 1950, vol. 1, pp. 342–44.
3. Memorandum of Conversation, by the Secretary of State, July 14, 1950. *FR*, 1950, vol. 1, pp. 344–46.
4. See two undated memorandums in the Elsey Papers. Korea-Message to Congress on Korea situation, 7 / 19 / 50 Folder. Box 71. HSTL.
5. Text in *PP*, 1950, p. 527 ff.
6. Note, undated. Korea-Message to Congress on Korean Situation—7 / 19 / 50 Folder. Elsey Papers. Box 71. HSTL.
7. Memorandum by the Executive Secretary of the National Security Council (Lay) to the Ad Hoc Committee on NSC 68, July 28, 1950. *FR*, 1950, vol. 1, pp. 351–52.
8. *PP*, 1950, p. 609 ff.
9. Policy Guide Statement Prepared in the Department of State, September 22, 1950. *FR*, 1950, vol. 1, pp. 398–99.
10. Samuel F. Wells, Jr., "The Origins of Massive Retaliation" in *Political Science Quarterly*, Spring, 1981, pp. 50–2. Walter S. Poole, *The History of the Joint Chiefs of Staff. The Joint Chiefs of Staff and National Policy, vol. 4. 1950–1952*. Historical Division. Joint Secretariat. Joint Chiefs of Staff. pp. 100–101.
11. Hans W. Gatzke, *Germany and the United States. A Special Relationship?* (Cambridge, 1980), p. 182.

12. The Chargé in the United Kingdom (Holmes) to the Secretary of State, September 1, 1949. *FR*, 1949, vol. 3, pp. 269–71. Also, Memorandum by the Assistant Secretary of State for European Affairs (Perkins) to the Secretary of State, October 11, 1949. Ibid., pp. 285–86.
13. Memorandum by the Secretary of State on a Meeting With the President, July 31, 1950. *FR*, 1950, vol. 3, pp. 167–68.
14. The Ambassador in the United Kingdom (Douglas) to the Secretary of State, July 12, 1950. Ibid., pp. 130–32.
15. Acheson, *Present at the Creation* (cited in chapter 3, n. 1), p. 438.
16. Kaplan, *A Community of Interests* (cited in chapter 18, n. 2), pp. 112–13.
17. The President to the Secretary of State, August 26, 1950. *FR*, 1950, vol. 3, pp. 250–51. The Secretary of State and the Secretary of Defense to the President, September 8, 1950. Ibid., pp. 273–78.
18. *PP*, 1950, p. 626.
19. United States Minutes, Private Meeting of the Foreign Ministers, New York, September 12, 1950. *FR*, 1950, vol. 3, pp. 1198–1201.
20. Report to the National Security Council by the Executive Secretary (Lay), September 30, 1950. *FR*, 1950, vol. 1, p. 400.

25. BITTER SUMMER: FIRST TROUBLES WITH MACARTHUR, LAST WITH JOHNSON

1. Combat scenes draw on Appleman's *United States Army in the Korean War* (cited in chapter 18, n. 17) and William F. Dean, as told to William L. Worden, *General Dean's Story* (New York, 1954).
2. The Commander in Chief, Far East, to the Joint Chiefs of Staff, July 9, 1950. *FR*, 1950, vol. 7, p. 336.
3. Schnabel's *United States Army in the Korean War* (cited in chapter 8, n. 5), p. 105.
4. Appleman, op. cit., pp. 207–8.
5. Ibid., chap. 13.
6. Ibid., p. 250.
7. Ayers Diary, entry of August 14, 1950.
8. Schnabel and Watson, *The History of the Joint Chiefs of Staff, vol. 3, pt. 1* (cited in chapter 8, n. 9), p. 177.
9. Matthew B. Ridgway, *The Korean War* (Garden City, N.Y. 1967), p. 88.
10. *Military Situation in the Far East* (cited in chapter 7, n. 52), p. 1379.
11. Schnabel and Watson, op. cit., pp. 44–47.
12. *Time*, November 27, 1950.
13. Schnabel and Watson, op. cit., pp. 178–99.
14. PSF: Political File. Transcript of Truman's handwritten memorandum. September 1, 1950—Radio-TV Report to the Nation on the Korean War Folder. Box 49.
15. Schnabel and Watson, op. cit., p. 174.
16. Diaries of Harold L. Ickes, Manuscript Division, Library of Congress.
17. Ed. Robert H. Ferrell, *Off the Record. The Private Papers of Harry S. Truman* (New York, 1980), pp. 46–47.
18. Harry S. Truman, *Year of Decisions* (Garden City, N.Y., 1955), pp. 520–21.

19. Margaret Truman, *Harry S. Truman* (New York, 1973), p. 293. Ayers Diary, entry of July 1, 1950.
20. John M. Allison, *Ambassador from the Prairie or Allison in Wonderland* (Boston, 1973), p. 129.
21. Ayers Diary, entry of July 1, 1950.
22. Schnabel and Watson, op. cit., pp. 507–8.
23. Meeting with the President. Item 5. Formosa, August 3, 1950. Acheson Papers. August 1950 Folder. Box 65. HSTL.
24. Acheson, *Present at the Creation* (cited in chapter 3, n. 1), p. 422.
25. *New York Times*, July 31, 1950, p. 1.
26. Ibid., August 2, 1950, p. 6.
27. Douglas MacArthur, *Reminiscences* (New York, 1964), p. 340.
28. Meeting with the President, op. cit.
29. Interview with W. Averell Harriman, February 24, 1974.
30. *Time*, August 14, 1950, p. 8.
31. Memorandum of Conversations—General MacArthur and W. A. Harriman. Complete text in Harriman's private papers in Washington. Excerpts in Truman's *Years of Trial and Hope* (cited in chapter 3, n. 19), pp. 349–53.
32. Interview with General Harry H. Vaughan, April 23, 1979.
33. Letter, Truman to Major General Frank E. Lowe, August 11, 1950. PSF: Frank E. Lowe File, Correspondence, 1947–1952 Folder #2. Box 245.
34. Excerpts of letter in *Military Situation*, op. cit., pp. 1999–2000. Truman's statement that the United States had no designs on Formosa was contained in his aforementioned message to Congress July 19, 1950, *PP*, 1950, p. 531.
35. Text in *Military Situation*, op. cit., pp. 3187–89.
36. Ibid., pp. 1217, 1590–91.

37. Memorandum by Mr. Lucius D. Battle, Special Assistant to the Secretary of State, for the Record of Events of August 26, 1950. [and Annex]. *FR*, 1950, vol. 6, pp. 453–60.
38. MacArthur, op. cit., p. 341.
39. *New York Times*, August 29, 1950, p. 1.
40. Ayers Diary, entry of August 26, 1950.
41. Truman, *Years of Trial and Hope*, op. cit., pp. 355.
42. Ayers Diary, entry of August 26, 1950.
43. Ibid., entry of March 27, 1950.
44. Interview with Harriman, op. cit.
45. One such person was Theodore Tannenwald, Jr., an assistant to Harriman. Tannenwald told the author in an interview July 28, 1975, that although he and Johnson had never before met, Johnson poured out his anger about Acheson to him in a chance automobile ride in mid-August, 1950.
46. Telephone interview with Ernest B. Vaccaro, August 20, 1979.

47. Interview with Wilfred J. McNeil . . . by Alfred Goldberg and Harry B. Yoshpe, May 31, 1974. Office of the Historian of the Department of Defense, Washington.
48. Truman memorandum, September 12, 1950. PSF: Personal File, ''J'' Folder. Box 314.
49. Truman's handwritten note, September 11, 1950. PSF: Longhand Notes File, Longhand Personal Memos 1950 Folder. Box 33.
50. Ayers Diary, entry of September 18, 1950.
51. Memorandum of Conversation by the Chief of the Division of Northeast Asian Affairs (Bishop), February 16, 1949. *FR*, 1949, vol. 7, pt. 2., pp. 655–58.
52. *Congressional Record*, vol. 96, pt. 11, pp. 14913–18.
53. Letter, Truman to Lyndon B. Johnson, September 22, 1950. PSF: General File, Johnson, Lyndon Folder. Box 124.

26. PRELUDE TO DISASTER: THE DECISION TO CROSS THE PARALLEL

1. Memorandum by the Director of the Office of Northeast Asian Affairs (Allison) to the Assistant Secretary of State for Far Eastern Affairs (Rusk), July 1, 1950. *FR*, 1950, vol. 7, p. 272.
2. The President of the Republic of Korea (Rhee) to President Truman, July 19, 1950. Ibid., pp. 428–30.
3. The Secretary of State to the Embassy in Korea, July 14, 1950. Ibid., p. 387.
4. Memorandum by Mr. John Foster Dulles, Consultant to the Secretary of State, to the Director of the Policy Planning Staff (Nitze), July 14, 1950. Ibid., pp. 386–87.
5. Memorandum by the Director of the Office of Northeast Asian Affairs to the Assistant Secretary of State for Far Eastern Affairs, July 15, 1950. Ibid., pp. 393–95.
6. Draft Memorandum Prepared by the Policy Planning Staff, July 22, 1950. Ibid., pp. 449–54.
7. Memorandum by the Director of the Office of Northeast Asian Affairs to the Director of the Policy Planning Staff, July 24, 1950. Ibid., pp. 458–60.
8. Draft Memorandum Prepared by the Policy Planning Staff, July 25, 1950. Ibid., pp. 469–70.
9. Collins's *War in Peacetime* (cited in chapter 22, n. 2), p. 144.
10. Draft Memorandum Prepared in the Department of Defense, July 31, 1950. Ibid., pp. 502–10.
11. Acheson's *Present at the Creation* (cited in chapter 3, n. 1), p. 445. For Rusk's influence see Warren I. Cohen, *Dean Rusk;* Ed. Robert H. Ferrell, *The American Secretaries of State and Their Diplomacy* (Totawa, N.J.), p. 55.
12. The Secretary of State to the Ambassador in Korea (Muccio) August 10, 1950. *FR*, 1950, vol. 7, pp. 553–54.
13. See, for example, Memorandum by the Counselor (Kennan) to the Secretary of State, August 21, 1950, vol. 7, p. 623 ff.
14. Memorandum Prepared by the Central Intelligence Agency, August 18, 1950. Ibid., pp. 600–603.
15. Interview with Averell Harriman, June 26, 1974.
16. Draft Memorandum by Messrs. John M. Allison and John K. Emmerson of the Office of Northeast Asian Affairs, August 21, 1950. *FR*, 1950, pp. 617–23.
17. *New York Times*, July 21, 1950, p. 4.
18. Truman to Vic H. Householder, August 8, 1950. PSF: Personal File, Householder, Vic H. Folder. Box 313.
19. Draft Memorandum Prepared in the Department of State for National Security Council Staff Consideration Only, August 30, 1950. *FR*, 1950, vol. 7, pp. 660–66.
20. Memorandum Prepared in the Preliminary Tripartite Conversations for the Consideration of the Foreign Ministers, September 1, 1950. Ibid., pp. 682–83.
21. Report by the National Security Council to the President, September 9, 1950. Ibid., pp. 712–21.
22. Michael Langley, *Inchon Landing. MacArthur's Last Triumph* (New York, 1979), pp. ix, 5. David Rees, *Korea: The Limited War* (New York, 1964), p. 96.
23. Memorandums of Conversation, by the Director of the Office of United Nations Political and Security Affairs (Bancroft), September 23, 1950. *FR*, 1950, vol. 7, pp. 759–62.
24. The Secretary of State (Marshall) to the President, September 27, 1950. Ibid., pp. 792–93.
25. Schnabel's and Watson's *The History of the Joint Chiefs of Staff, vol. 3, pt. 1* (cited in chapter 8, n. 9), p. 230.

26. Ibid., pp. 233–38.
27. Cabinet Meeting, September 29, 1950. Notes on Cabinet Meetings—January 6-December 29, 1950, Folder. Matthew J. Connelly Papers. Box 1. HSTL.
28. Schnabel and Watson, op. cit., p. 241. Trygvie Lie, *In the Cause of Peace. Seven Years with the United Nations* (New York, 1954), pp. 344–45.
29. The Secretary of Defense to the Commander in Chief, Far East, September 29, 1950. *FR*, 1950, vol. 7, p. 826. Appleman's *United States Army in the Korean War* (cited in chapter 18, n. 17), p. 608.
30. *Military Situation in the Far East* (cited in chapter 7, n. 52), p. 245.
31. Schnabel and Watson, op. cit., p. 243.
32. Letter, Joseph O'Mahoney to Truman, September 30, 1950. PSF: General File. ''O'' Folder. Box 132.
33. *Congressional Record*, vol. 96, pt. 11, p. 15412.
34. *New York Herald Tribune*, September 27, 1950, p. 8.
35. Memorandum for the President, September 8, 1950. PSF: Subject File. NSC Meetings—Memos for President. Meeting Discussions (1950) Folder. Box 222.
36. Acheson testimony, *Military Situation*, op. cit., p. 2258.
37. The Ambassador in India (Henderson) to the Secretary of State, September 27, 1950. *FR*, 1950, vol. 7, pp. 790–92.
38. Schnabel's *United States Army in the Korean War* (cited in chapter 8, n. 5), p. 197.
39. Memorandum of Conversation, by the Deputy Assistant Secretary of State for Far Eastern Affairs (Merchant), September 27, 1950. *FR*, 1950, vol. 7, pp. 793–94.
40. Memorandum by the Director of the Office of Chinese Affairs (Clubb) to the Assistant Secretary of State for Far Eastern Affairs (Rusk), September 27, 1950. Ibid., pp. 795–96.
41. The Ambassador in India to the Secretary of State, September 28, 1950. Ibid., pp. 808–10.
42. Memorandum of Conversation, by the Special Assistant to the Secretary of State (Battle), September 28, 1950. Ibid., pp. 811–12.
43. The Acting Secretary of State to the Embassy in India, September 28, 1950, Ibid., pp. 819–21.
44. The Ambassador in the Soviet Union (Kirk) to the Secretary of State, September 29, 1950. Ibid., pp. 21–22.
45. The Ambassador in India to the Secretary of State, September 29, 1950. Ibid., pp. 823–24.
46. Schnabel's *United States Army in the Korean War*, op. cit., p. 197.
47. Ibid., p. 195.
48. The Chargé in the United Kingdom (Holmes) to the Secretary of State, October 3, 1950. *FR*, 1950, vol. 7, p. 839.
49. Memorandum by the Deputy Assistant Secretary of State for Far Eastern Affairs to the Assistant Secretary of State for Far Eastern Affairs, October 3, 1950. Ibid., p. 848.
50. Acheson, *Present at the Creation*, op. cit., p. 452.
51. Truman, *Years of Trial and Hope* (cited in chapter 3, n. 18), p. 362.
52. Harriman interview, op. cit.
53. *Military Situation*, op. cit., p. 2101.
54. Text in *FR*, 1950, vol. 7, pp. 904–6.
55. Schnabel and Watson, op. cit., p. 249.
56. Quoted in Allen S. Whiting, *China Crosses the Yalu. The Decision to Enter the Korean War* (Stanford, 1960), p. 115.

27. THE WAKE ISLAND CONFERENCE

1. Letter, Truman to Nellie Noland, October 13, 1950. Ed. Ferrell, *Off The Record* (cited in chapter 25, n. 17). pp. 195–96.
2. Interview with Henry Nicholson, October 6, 1978.

3. Samuel I. Rosenman, quoted in D. Clayton James, *The Years of MacArthur. Vol. 2, 1941–1945* (Boston, 1975), pp. 527–28.
4. The author was one of the reporters.

5. Dictated by Truman April 4, 1951. Korea-Hawaii-Wake-San Francisco. Elsey Papers. October, 1950, Folder. Box 72. HSTL.
6. Elsey Note, undated. Ibid.
7. Interview with Charles S. Murphy, April 27, 1978.
8. Ambassador John J. Muccio, who accompanied MacArthur from Japan to Wake Island, described the general's attitude to the historian John Edward Wiltz. See Wiltz's "Truman and MacArthur: The Wake Island Meeting" in *Military Affairs*, December 1978, p. 171.
9. Nicholson interview, op. cit.
10. *PP*, 1950, p. 613.
11. Schnabel and Watson, *The History of the Joint Chiefs of Staff* (cited in chapter 8, n. 9), p. 262.
12. Meeting with the President, October 9, 1950. Acheson Papers, October, 1950, Folder. Box 65. HSTL.
13. Ayers Diary, entry of October 19, 1950.
14. Interview with Vernice Anderson, January 9, 1979.
15. Letter of Transmittal, Omar N. Bradley to Senator Richard B. Russell, May 2, 1951, printed in *Substance of Statements Made at Wake Island Conference, October 15, 1950. Com-* piled by General of the Army Omar N. Bradley, chairman of the Joint Chiefs of Staff. From Notes Kept by the Conferees from Washington. Prepared for the use of the Committee on Armed Services and the Committee on Foreign Relations, United States Senate. U.S. Government Printing Office.
16. This account is based on *Substance of Statements Made at Wake Island Conference*, op. cit. Also on Venice Anderson's shorthand record in RG 218, Office of the Joint Chiefs of Staff. Chairman's File (Bradley). CJCS Folder. Wake Island (1950). Modern Military Branch, National Archives.
17. MacArthur, *Reminiscences* (cited in chapter 25, n. 27), p. 362. Radford's *From Pearl Harbor to Vietnam* (cited in chapter 5, n. 3), p. 244.
18. Memorandum by the Assistant Secretary of State for Far Eastern Affairs, October 16, 1950. *FR*, 1950, vol. 7, pp. 961–62.
19. Courtney Whitney, *MacArthur: His Rendezvous With History*, (cited in chapter 21, n. 22), pp. 389–90.
20. Interview with Vernice Anderson, op. cit.
21. Schnabel and Watson, op. cit., p. 269.

28. THE DEPTHS

1. Interview with Charles S. Murphy, April 27, 1978.
2. *PP*, 1950, p. 674.
3. Ibid., p. 679.
4. Ayers Diary, entry of October 19, 1950.
5. Appleman, *United States Army in the Korean War* (cited in chapter 18, n. 17), p. 669.
6. *New York Times*, October 29, 1950, Section 4, p. 8-E.
7. Appleman, op. cit., p. 673. Schnabel's and Watson's *The History of the Joint Chiefs of Staff, vol. 3, pt. 1* (cited in chapter 8, n. 9), p. 279.
8. The Chargé in Korea (Drumright) to the Secretary of State, October 29, 1950. *FR*, 1950, vol. 7, pp. 1013–14.
9. Schnabel and Watson, op. cit., pp. 281–82.
10. The Chargé in Korea to the Secretary of State, October 30, 1950. *FR*, 1950, vol. 7, p. 1014.
11. This account is based on Robert J. Donovan, *The Assassins* (New York, 1955), chap. 8. Originally an article in *The New Yorker*, that chapter drew on Federal court records, the Secret Service file in the case and interviews with Mrs. Oscar Collazo, Secret Service agents, White House assistants and attorneys for Oscar Collazo.
12. *PP*, 1948, p. 154.
13. Letter, Rudolph Friml to the author, 1952.
14. Memorandum by the Director of the Central Intelligence Agency (Smith) to the President, November 1, 1950. *FR* 1950, vol. 7, pp. 1025–26.
15. Schnabel and Watson, op. cit., p. 287.
16. *New York Times*, November 6, 1950, p. 1.
17. Ibid., August 13, 1950, p. 3.
18. James T. Patterson, *Mr. Republican. A Biography of Robert A. Taft* (Boston, 1972), p. 465.
19. *PP*, 1950, p. 588.
20. Ibid., p. 571 ff.
21. Ibid., p. 645 ff.
22. Quoted in Fawn M. Brodie, *Richard Nixon. The Shaping of His Character* (New York, 1981), p. 242.
23. David Halberstam, *The Powers That Be* (New York, 1979), p. 263.
24. *Newsweek*, November 6, 1950, p. 23.
25. *Congressional Record*. vol. 96, pt. 18, p. A6901.
26. *PP*, 1950, p. 702.
27. Quoted in John Edward Wiltz, "The Korean War and American Society" in Ed. Francis H. Heller, *The Korean War. A 25 Year Perspective* (Lawrence, Kansas, 1977), p. 127.
28. Ayers Diary, September 15, 1950.
29. Ibid.
30. Letter, Truman to Cliff Langsdale, November 29, 1950. PSF: Political File, Missouri Folder. Box 58.
31. George M. Elsey, speech before the Smithsonian Resident Associate Program, Washington, D.C., November 17, 1977.
32. *Military Situation in the Far East* (cited in chapter 7, n. 52), p. 19.
33. Acheson, *Present at the Creation* (cited in chapter 3, n. 1), p. 455.
34. Schnabel and Watson, op. cit., pp. 247–48.
35. Truman, *Years of Trial and Hope* (cited in chapter 3, n. 18), p. 362.
36. Schnabel and Watson, op. cit., p. 230.
37. Ibid., 291.
38. Memorandum of Conversation, by the Secretary of State, November 6, 1950. *FR*, 1950, vol. 7, pp. 1055–56. Memorandum by the Secretary of State, November 6, 1950. Ibid., p. 1057.
39. The Joint Chiefs of Staff to the Commander in Chief, Far East, November 6, 1950. Ibid., pp. 1057–58.
40. Text in Truman, op. cit., p. 375.
41. Schnabel and Watson, op. cit., p. 520.
42. The Joint Chiefs of Staff to the Commander in Chief, Far East, November 6, 1950. *FR*, 1950, vol. 7, pp. 1075–76.
43. Schnabel and Watson, op. cit., p. 299.
44. *Military Situation*, op. cit., p. 1912.
45. Memorandum by the Acting Special Assistant to the Secretary of State for Intelligence (Howe) to the Ambassador at Large (Jessup), November 18, 1950. *FR*, 1950, vol. 7, pp. 1188–90.
46. *PP*, 1950, p. 711 ff.
47. *New York Times*, November 18, 1950, p. 3.
48. *Time*, November 27, 1950, p. 15.
49. Schnabel and Watson, op. cit., p. 301.
50. Ibid., pp. 301–302. For MacArthur's estimate of Chinese strength in Korea see Memorandum of Conversation, by the Ambassador in Korea, November 17, 1950. *FR*, 1950, vol. 7, pp. 1175–76.
51. Memorandum of Conversation, by the Ambassador at Large (Jessup), November 21, 1950. Ibid., pp. 1204–89. The Secretary of State to the Embassy in the United Kingdom, November 24, 1950. Ibid., pp. I2280–89.
52. Schnabel, *United States Army in the Korean War* (cited in chapter 8, n. 5), p. 251. The Commander in Chief, United Nations Command to the Joint Chiefs of Staff, November 25, 1950. *FR*, 1950, vol. 7, pp. 1231–33.
53. *Military Situation*, op. cit., p. 974.
54. Schnabel and Watson, op. cit., pp. 305, 341.
55. Ibid., p. 345.
56. Memorandum for the President, November 10, 1950. PSF: Subject File. NSC Meetings—Memos for the President. Meeting Discussions (1950) Folder. Box 220.
57. Memorandum by the Joint Chiefs of Staff to the Secretary of Defense, November 9, 1950. *FR*, 1950, vol. 7, pp. 1117–21.
58. Schnabel and Watson, op. cit., p. 331.
59. Ibid., p. 301. Commander in Chief, Far East, to the Joint Chiefs of Staff, November 7, 1950. *FR*, 1950, vol. 7, pp. 1076–77.
60. Text in *Military Situation*, op. cit., pp. 3491–92.
61. Truman, op. cit., p. 381. Memorandum by the Central Intelligence Agency, November 24, 1950. *FR*, 1950, vol. 7, pp. 1220–22.
62. William Manchester, *American Caesar. Douglas MacArthur 1880–1964* (Boston, 1978), p. 606.
63. Schnabel and Watson, op. cit., p. 334.
64. The Commander in Chief, Far East, to the Joint Chiefs of Staff, November 28, 1950. *FR*, 1950, vol. 7, pp. 1237–38.
65. "Tuesday, November 25, 1950. W. A. Harriman." A memorandum by Harriman. Harriman's personal papers, Washington, D.C. Also Ayers Diary, entry of November 28, 1950.
66. John Hersey, "Profiles" in *The New Yorker*, April 14, 1951.
67. *Reviews of the World Situation* (cited in chapter 4, n. 29), pp. 370, 372, 374.
68. This account draws on Schnabel and Watson, op. cit., pp. 339–42.
69. "Tuesday, November 25, 1950. W. A. Harriman", op. cit.
70. Cabinet Meeting, November 28, 1950. Notes on Cabinet Meetings—January 61-December 29, 1950, Folder. Matthew Connelly Papers. Box 1. HSTL.
71. *New York Times*, November 30, 1950, p. 1. Memorandum

of Conversation, by the Ambassador at Large (Jessup), December 1, 1950. *FR*, 1950, vol. 7, pp. 1276–81.
72. Schnabel and Watson, op. cit., pp. 343–44.
73. The Commander in Chief, Far East, to the Joint Chiefs of Staff, November 30, 1950. *FR*, 1950, vol. 7, p. 1260.
74. *PP*, 1950, p. 724 ff.
75. Ibid., p. 562.
76. Memorandum by the Director of the Policy Planning Staff (Nitze), *FR*, 1950, vol. 7, pp. 1041–42.
77. Schnabel and Watson, op. cit., pp. 372–73.
78. *PP*, 1950, p. 727, n. 3.
79. Memorandum of Conversation, by Mrs. Franklin D. Roosevelt, December 1, 1950. *FR*, 1950, vol. 1, p. 116.

80. John Hersey, "The Wayward Press Conference in Room 474" in *The New Yorker*, December 16, 1950, p. 78 ff.
81. *New York Herald Tribune*, December 6, 1950, p. 1.
82. Margaret Truman, *Harry S. Truman* (cited in chapter 25, n. 19), p. 499.
83. The story of how the letter was mailed was related to the author by Henry Nicholson of the Secret Service.
84. Truman had heard the expression from Stephen T. Early. See letter, Truman to Isador Lubin, July 18, 1949. PSF: Personal File, "L" Folder. Box 315.
85. The author obtained a photocopy of the letter from a colleague on the *Washington Post*.

29. NATIONAL EMERGENCY

1. Schnabel and Watson, *The History of the Joint Chiefs of Staff, vol. 3, pt. 1* (cited in chapter 8, n. 9), pp. 365–66.
2. This was confided to the author at the time by White House Press Secretary Charles G. Ross.
3. Memorandum by Mr. Lucius D. Battle, Special Assistant to the Secretary of State, of a Meeting Held on December 2, 1950, December 3, 1950, (and Annex), *FR*, 1950, vol. 7, pp. 1310–13.
4. Truman, handwritten note, December 2, 1950. PSF: "Longhand Notes" File, Longhand Personal Memos, 1950, Folder. Box 333.
5. Memorandum of Conversation, by the Ambassador at Large, December 1, 1950. *FR*, 1950, vol. 7, pp. 1276–81.
6. The Commander in Chief, United Nations Command, to the Joint Chiefs of Staff December 3, 1950. Ibid., pp. 1320–22.
7. Ibid., p. 1333, n. 5.
8. General Marshall's statement to congressional leaders at the White House, December 13, 1950. See memorandum on subject in PSF: Subject File, Meeting of President and Congressional Leaders—December, 19, 1950 Folder, p. 5. Box 164.
9. Memorandum of Conversation, by the Ambassador at Large, December 3, 1950. *FR*, 1950, vol. 7, pp. 1323–34.
10. Memorandum by Mr. Lucius D. Battle, Special Assistant to the Secretary of State, December 4, 1950. Ibid., pp. 1345–47.
11. Acheson, *Present at the Creation* (cited in chapter 3, n. 1), pp. 476–77.
12. Truman, *Years of Trial and Hope* (cited in chapter 3, n. 18), pp. 382–84.
13. Text of interview and statement in *Military Situation in the Far East* (cited in chapter 7, n. 52), pp. 3532–34.
14. Text, Ibid., p. 3536.
15. *FR*, 1950, vol. 7, p. 1364.
16. Ibid., p. 1368.
17. Ibid., p. 1395.
18. Schnabel and Watson, op. cit., p. 433.

19. *FR*, 1950, vol. 7, p. 1432.
20. The Secretary of State to the Embassy in the United Kingdom, July 10, 1950. Ibid., pp. 347–51.
21. Ibid., pp. 1451, 1458.
22. Ibid., p. 1399.
23. The Secretary of State to the Embassy in the United Kingdom, op. cit.
24. *FR*, 1950, vol. 7, p. 1402.
25. Ibid., pp. 1405–6.
26. Ibid., p. 1456, 1458.
27. Position Paper Prepared for the Truman—Attlee Talks, Ibid., pp. 1464–65. Acheson, op. cit., p. 484.
28. Memorandum for the Record by the Ambassador at Large, December 7, 1950. *FR*, 1950, vol. 7, p. 1462.
29. Communique, Ibid., pp. 1476–79. For Attlee's view see Records Office, London. Cabinet 85 (50) Conclusions of a Meeting of the Cabinet held at 10 Downing Street on 12th December, 1950, pp. 224–25.
30. *FR*, 1950, vol. 7, p. 1371.
31. The Acting Secretary of State to the United Nations Mission at the United Nations, December 20, 1950. *FR*, 1950, vol. 7, pp. 1583–84.
32. *PP*, 1950, p. 741 ff.
33. Memorandum by the Assistant Secretary of State for Public Affairs (Barrett) to the Secretary of State and the Under Secretary of State, December 5, 1950. *FR*, 1950, vol. 1, pp. 423–25.
34. Meeting of the President with Congressional Leaders, December 13, 1950. PSF: Subject File, Meeting of the President with Congressional Leaders—December 13, 1950, Folder. Box 164.
35. Quoted in Craufurd D. Goodwin and R. Stanley Herren in "The Truman Administration: Problems and Policies Unfold" in Ed. Goodwin, *Exhortation and Controls. The Search for a Wage-Price Policy 1945–1971* (Washington, D.C. 1975), p. 74.

30. 1951: A YEAR OF WAR, MOBILIZATION, AND THE "GREAT DEBATE"

1. Special Estimate. International Implications of Maintaining a Beachhead in South Korea. Central Intelligence Agency, January 11, 1951. PSF: Intelligence File. Central Intelligence Reports. S.E. (Special Estimate). No. 1–9 Folder. Box 258.
2. *New York Times*, December 13, 1950, p. 8.
3. Interview with Charles S. Murphy, October 23, 1975.
4. Ayers Diary, entry of October 25, 1950.
5. OH, Robert L. Dennison, p. 157.
6. *PP*, 1950, p. 753.
7. Text in *New York Times*, December 21, 1950. p. 22. Truman's comments in *PP*, 1950, p. 761.
8. *PP*, 1951, p. 4.
9. *Congressional Record*, vol. 97, pt. 1, p. 59.
10. Ibid., p. 55.
11. Ibid., p. 57.
12. *PP*, 1951, p. 10.
13. Ibid., p. 17 ff.
14. *Assignment of Ground Forces of the United States to Duty in the European Theater. Hearings Before the Committee on Foreign Relations and the Committee on Armed Services. United States Senate. 1951.* U.S. Government Printing Office, p. 5.
15. Ibid., pp. 20, 40, 52, 39.
16. Interview with Theodore Tannenwald, Jr., July 28, 1975.
17. *PP*, 1951, pp. 217.
18. See, for example, Adam Smith, *Paper Money* (New York, 1981), pp. 20–1.
19. *PP*, 1950, p. 628.
20. *PP*, 1951, p. 135.
21. Cabinet Meeting, February 16, 1950. Notes on Cabinet

Meetings—January 2-December 31, 1951, Folder. Box 1. Matthew Connelly Papers. HSTL.
22. Memorandum, Richard E. Neustadt, February 16, 1951. Lucas Committee Amendment Folder. Harold Enarson Papers, HSTL.
23. *New York Times*, March 1, 1951, p. 1.
24. Labor's Controversy With the Administration on the Defense Program, March 23, 1951. Wage and Stabilization Board Policies Folder. Enarson Papers. HSTL.
25. *PP*, 1950, p. 175.
26. Letter, Truman to Jonathan Daniels, February 20, 1951. PSF: Personal File, Daniels, Jonathan Folder. Box 309.
27. Ayers Diary, entry of September 14, 1950.
28. Milton Friedman, Anna Jacobson Schwartz, *A Monetary History of the United States* (Princeton, N.J., 1963), p. 12.
29. Herbert Stein, *The Fiscal Revolution in America* (Chicago, 1969), p. 245.
30. Interview with John Snyder, February 3, 1975.
31. OH, John Snyder, vol. 3, p. 559.
32. Truman to R. C. Leffingwell, February 10, 1951. PSF: General File, "L" Folder. Box 125.
33. John Snyder to Thomas B. McCabe, July 17, 1950. PSF: Subject File. Treasury, Secretary of—John Snyder Folder #2. Box 160.
34. Friedman and Schwartz, op. cit., p. 12.
35. Stein, op. cit., p. 250.
36. Ibid., p. 264.
37. Truman to McCabe, August 25, 1950. PSF: Subject File, Federal Reserve Board Folder. Box 144.
38. Quoted in Stein, op. cit., p. 269.
39. Ibid., p. 272.

40. Ibid., pp. 273–74.
41. OH, Charles S. Murphy, p. 105–6.
42. Interview with John Snyder, op. cit.

43. Ayers Diary, entry of May 6, 1948.
44. OH, Charles Murphy, op. cit.
45. Friedman and Schwartz, op. cit., p. 625.

31. MORE SCANDAL, NEW BRUISES

1. Text of Nixon's speech in *New York Times*, September 24, 1952, p. 1.
2. U.S. Congress. Senate. Committee on Banking and Currency. *Study of Reconstruction Finance Corporation: Favoritism and Influence. S. Report 76, Eighty-second Congress, First Session, 1951. Senate Miscellaneous Reports, vol. 1.*
3. Paul H. Douglas, *In the Fulness of Time: The Memoirs of Paul H. Douglas* (New York, 1971), p. 222.
4. *PP*, 1950, p. 143 ff.
5. Roger Tubby Journal, entry of February 15, 1951.
6. Ibid., entry of March 4, 1951.
7. Ibid., entry of March 8, 1951.
8. OH, John R. Steelman.
9. Roger Tubby Journal, entry of April 2, 1951.
10. Ibid. (Tubby's reference was to an editorial, titled "Truman Is To Blame" in the *New Republic*, March 26, 1950, p. 5, 6.)
11. Ibid.
12. Ibid.
13. Ibid., entry of March 12, 1951.
14. Ibid., entry of April 2, 1951.
15. *PP*, 1950, p. 191.
16. Ibid., p. 203.
17. Roger Tubby Journal, entries of April 2, March 4 and March 12, 1951.
18. Douglas, op. cit., p. 223.

19. *New York Times*, August 21, 1951, p. 1.
20. U.S. Congress. Senate. Subcommittee on Banking and Currency. Subcommittee on Reconstruction Finance Corporation. *Study of Reconstruction Finance Corporation: Lending Policy, pts. II and III. Hearings Before . . . Subcommittee . . . Pursuant to S. Res. 219, Eighty-second Congress, First Session, 1951*, pp. 1710–6, 1717–33, 1759–76.
21. Ibid., pp. 1811–27.
22. Douglas, op. cit., p. 224.
23. *New York Times*, op. cit.
24. Truman to Clark M. Clifford, April 27, 1951. PSF: General File, Clifford Folder.
25. Roger Tubby Journal, entry of July 26, 1951.
26. *PP*, 1950, p. 492.
27. Stanley High, The Missouri Gang" in *Reader's Digest*, June, 1952, p. 43 ff.
28. Memorandum, Murphy to Truman, August 9, 1951. PSF: Political File. Boyle, William Folder. Box 54.
29. *PP*, 1951, p. 531.
30. U.S. Congress. Senate. Committee on Expenditures in the Executive Departments. Permanent Subcommittee on Investigations. *American Lithofold Corporation, William M. Boyle, Guy George Gabrielson. House Report 1142, Eighty-second Congress, Second Session, 1952*, pp. 22–5.
31. Letter, Truman to John L. Sullivan, October 15, 1951. PSF: Personal File, "S" No. 1 Folder. Box 322.

32. MACARTHUR CRISIS: "THE LAST STRAW"

1. Episode is related in Roger Tubby's Journal, entry of April 5, 1951.
2. *Life*, April 9, 1951, p. 36.
3. Roger Tubby Journal, entry of May 21, 1951.
4. Encountering Tubby in the press office several days later, Charles Murphy remarked, "Here's the man who got MacArthur fired." Roger Tubby Journal, entry of April 5, 1951.
5. OH, David E. Bell.
6. Ridgway, *The Korean War* (cited in chapter 25, n. 9), pp. 233–34.
7. *PP*, 1950, p. 580.
8. Schnabel and Watson, *The History of the Joint Chiefs of Staff, vol. 3, pt. 1* (cited in chapter 8, n. 9), p. 518.
9. Ed. Heller, *The Korean War* (cited in chapter 28, n. 27), p. 26.
10. *FR*, 1950, vol. 7, p. 952.
11. Truman's *Years of Trial and Hope* (cited in chapter 3, n. 18), p. 384.
12. Schnabel's and Watson's op. cit., pp. 395–96.
13. Ridgway, op. cit., p. 91.
14. Schnabel and Watson, op. cit., pp. 397–99.
15. MacArthur, *Reminiscences* (cited in chapter 25, n. 27), 378.
16. Schnabel and Watson, op. cit., pp. 399–401.
17. *Military Situation in the Far East* (cited in chapter 7, n. 52), p. 993.
18. Ibid., pp. 1188–89.
19. Ibid., pp. 1538, 1914.
20. Schnabel and Watson, op. cit., p. 405.
21. *Military Situation*, op. cit., p. 1188.
22. Schnabel and Watson, op. cit., pp. 410–11.
23. Collins's *War in Peacetime* (cited in chapter 22, n. 2), p. 248.
24. *Military Situation*, op. cit., p. 329.
25. Truman, op. cit., p. 434.
26. Schnabel and Watson, op. cit., p. 413.
27. Ibid., pp. 415–16.
28. Truman, op. cit., pp. 435–36.
29. Schnabel and Watson, op. cit., pp. 417–19.
30. John Edward Wiltz, "The MacArthur Hearings of 1951: The Secret Testimony" in *Military Affairs*, December, 1975, p. 170.
31. *Declassified Hearing Transcripts, Military Situation in the*

Far East (cited, chap. 7, n. 52), pp. 2625–26.
32. Schnabel and Watson, op. cit., pp. 437–38.
33. Ibid., p. 340.
34. *Military Situation*, op. cit., p. 3539.
35. Truman, op. cit., pp. 439, 440.
36. *Military Situation*, op. cit., p. 3541.
37. President's Conference with ADA leaders—May 21, 1951. White House Miscellaneous Folder. David Lloyd Papers. Box 11. HSTL.
38. *Military Situation*, op. cit., pp. 3541–42.
39. A Memorandum of a Telephone Conversation, March 24, 1951. Acheson Papers. March 1951 Folder. Box 66. HSTL.
40. Acheson's *Present at the Creation* (cited in chapter 3, n. 1), p. 519.
41. Truman, op. cit., p. 442.
42. *Military Situation*, op. cit., pp. 346–47.
43. Ibid., p. 1916.
44. Ibid., pp. 69, 71, 72.
45. Ibid., pp. 428, 445.
46. Manchester's *American Caesar* (cited in chapter 28, n. 62), p. 617.
47. Joseph W. Martin, Jr., as told to Robert J. Donovan, *My First Fifty Years in Politics* (New York, 1960), pp. 203–5.
48. *Military Situation*, op. cit., p. 412.
49. Interview with Robert A. Lovett, November 8, 1978.
50. Truman, handwritten diary entry, April 5, 1951. PSF: Diaries, Diary 1951 Folder Box 278.
51. Ibid.
52. Acheson, op. cit., p. 521.
53. Truman, op. cit., p. 447. Schnabel and Watson, op. cit., p. 537.
54. MACARTHUR (From George M. Elsey's Notes). Eben Ayers Papers. Korea-MacArthur-Wake Folder. Box 7. HSTL.
55. Truman, handwritten diary entry, April 7, 1951, op. cit.
56. MACARTHUR, op. cit.
57. *Military Situation*, op. cit., p. 1047.
58. Interview with John Snyder, March 30, 1978.
59. Schnabel and Watson, op. cit., p. 539.
60. *Military Situation*, op. cit., 878–79.
61. MACARTHUR, op. cit.
62. Ibid.
63. *Military Situation*, op. cit., p. 519.

33. THE FIRING OF GENERAL MACARTHUR

1. Roger Tubby Journal, entry undated.
2. MACARTHUR (cited in chapter 32, n. 54).
3. Roger Tubby Journal, op. cit.
4. *New York Times*, April 24, 1951, p. 1.

5. MACARTHUR, op. cit.
6. Roger Tubby Journal, op. cit.
7. Letter, Truman to David M. Noyes, April 10, 1951. PSF: General File, "N" Folder. Box 131.

8. Roger Tubby Journal, op. cit.
9. Truman's handwritten notes, April 9, 1951. PSF: Diaries, Diary-1950 Folder. Box 278.
10. Interview with Lloyd Norman, July 5, 1980.
11. *Military Situation in the Far East* (cited in chapter 7, n. 52), p. 286.
12. Ibid., p. 3546.
13. Ibid., p. 3547.
14. Ibid., p. 26.
15. Martin's *My First Fifty Years in Politics* (cited in chapter 32, n. 47, p. 208.
16. Roger Tubby Journal, op. cit.
17. *Congressional Record*, vol. 97, pt. 3, pp. 3618–19.
18. Ibid., p. 3623.
19. *New York Journal-American*, April 18, 1951, p. 34.
20. Manchester's *American Caesar* (cited in chapter 28, n. 62), pp. 650–51.
21. *Chicago Tribune*, April 12, 1951.
22. Manchester's *American Caesar*, op. cit.
23. *PP*, 1951, p. 223 ff.
24. *New York Times*, April 12, 1951, p. 11.
25. Letter, W. Averell Harriman to Dwight D. Eisenhower, April

26, 1951. Harriman's Private Papers.
26. M. B. Ridgway, memorandum for diary 12 April 1951 (paraphrase of MacArthur), box 20, Ridgway MSS. Also see Ridgway oral history, 81, American Military History Institute, Carlisle, Pa. Quoted in Barton J. Bernstein, "New Light on the Korean War" in *The International History Review*, April 1981, p. 268.
27. *PP*, 1951, p. 227.
28. *Congressional Record*, vol. 97, pt. 3, p. 3649.
29. *New York Times*, April 12, 1951, p. 1.
30. Letter, Truman to Roy W. Harper, April 17, 1951. PSF: Personal File, Harper, Roy Folder. Box 312.
31. Letter, Truman to Claude G. Bowers, April 25, 1951. PSF: Subject File, Foreign Affairs: Chile #2 Folder. Box 172.
32. Letter, Truman to Eisenhower, April 13, 1951. PSF: General File, NAT Folder #1. Box 132.
33. *PP*, 1951, 227 ff.
34. Text in *Military Situation*, op. cit., p. 3533 ff.
35. For Truman's attitude see Letter, Truman to Burnet R. Maybank, December 14, 1950. PSF: Subject File, Military Training Folder. Box 146.

34. THE RAVAGES

1. John Lord O'Brian, *National Security and Individual Freedom* (Cambridge, 1955), p. 22.
2. Letter, Truman to Charles Murphy, May 24, 1951. PSF: General File, Murphy, Charles Folder. Box 131. Biddle correspondence is in PSF: General File, Bo Folder. Box 113.
3. *PP*, 1951, pp. 119–20.
4. Hamby's *Beyond the New Deal* (cited in chapter 2, n. 1), p. 468.
5. This refers to the celebrated cases of John Stuart Service, John Carter Vinson, John Patton Davies and O. Edmund Clubb.
6. Cabinet Meeting, August 10, 1951. Notes on Cabinet Meetings—January 2-December 31, 1951. Matthew Connally Papers. Box 1. HSTL.
7. *PP*, 1951, p. 244 ff.
8. Ibid., p. 276.
9. Ibid., p. 335.
10. Memorandum for John Carroll, July, 1951. Harold Enarson Papers, HSTL.

11. *New York Times*, August 1, 1951, p. 1.
12. Manchester's *American Caesar* (cited in chapter 28, n. 62), p. 592.
13. Ayers Diary, entry of October 18, 1950.
14. Letter, Truman to Edward Martin, July 27, 1951. PSF: General File, MacArthur, Douglas Folder. Box 129.
15. Ayers Diary, entry of October 25, 1950.
16. *Military Situation in the Far East* (cited in chapter 7, n. 52), p. 928.
17. Ibid., p. 732.
18. *Off the Record* (cited in chapter 25, n. 17), p. 212.
19. *Military Situation*, op. cit., pp. 352, 365.
20. Ibid., 1782–83.
21. Ridgway's *The Korean War* (cited in chapter 25, n. 9), p. 197.
22. PSF: "Longhand Notes File," Longhand Personal Memos, 1952, Folder #1. Box 333.

35. SHOWDOWN: THE ATTORNEY GENERAL AND THE PRESIDENT

1. David E. Bell, Memorandum for Mr. Murphy. Scandals in the Bureau of Internal Revenue, October 30, 1951. Bell Folder. George Elsey Papers. Box 101. HSTL.
2. George Elsey, Memo for C.M.C. [Clark M. Clifford], December 12, 1951. Memoranda, 1951–52 Folder. Clark Clifford Papers. Box 22. HSTL.
3. *Internal Revenue Investigation. Report to the Committee on Ways and Means, House of Representative, by the Subcommittee on Administration of the Internal Revenue Laws*. U.S. Government Printing Office. 1953, p. 17.
4. Ibid., pp. 10–12. Also Abels's *The Truman Scandals* (cited in chapter 11, n. 11), pp. 124–29.
5. Truman to McKinley W. Kriegh, October 26, 1951. PSF: General File, "K" Folder. Box 124.
6. *PP*, 1952–53, p. 6.
7. Abels, *The Truman Scandals*, op. cit., pp. 53–4.
8. *Investigation of the Department of Justice. Hearings Before the Special Subcommittee to Investigate the Department of Justice. Committee on the Judiciary. House of Representatives. Eighty-first Congress, Second Session, pt. 2*. U.S. Government Printing Office, 1952, pp. 1132–33.
9. Ibid., pt. 1, p. 60.
10. Washington *Evening Star*, December 11, 1951, p. 1.
11. Memorandum, December 26, 1950. *Off the Record* (cited in chapter 25, n. 17), pp. 220–22.
12. *Evening Star*, December 12, 1951, p. A-17.
13. *PP*, 1951, p. 641 ff.

14. Interview with Charles Murphy, January 29, 1951. Also, Memorandum, December 26, 1951, Off the Record, op. cit.
15. Wayne Morse to Truman, December 22, 1951. Truman to Morse, December 23, 1951. PSF: Personal File, "M" Folder. Box 316.
16. Murphy Interview, op. cit.
17. *PP*, 1952–53, pp. 152–53.
18. *Investigation of the Department of Justice*, op. cit., pt. 1, p. 71 ff.
19. Richard H. Rovere, *The American Establishment and Other Reports, Opinions and Speculations* (New York, 1962), pp. 87, 89, 91, 108–10.
20. *Investigation of the Department of Justice*, op. cit., pt. 2, p. 1933. Also Cabinet Meeting, March 28, 1952. Notes on Cabinet Meetings, January 4, 1952-January 16, 1953, Folder. Matthew Connally Papers. Box 1, HSTL.
21. *Investigation of the Department of Justice*, op. cit., pt. 1, p. 54.
22. Ibid., p. 55.
23. Memorandum, Charles Murphy to Truman, April 1, 1952. PSF: Subject File, Attorney General—J. Howard McGrath. Box 155.
24. Roger Tubby Journal, entry of April 3, 1952.
25. Ibid.
26. *New York Times*, April 4, 1952, p. 1.
27. Roger Tubby Journal.

36. CONSTITUTIONAL CRISIS: TRUMAN SEIZES THE STEEL INDUSTRY

1. Maeva Marcus, *Truman and the Steel Seizure Case. The Limits of Presidential Power* (New York, 1977), p. 84. This chapter draws extensively on that book.
2. William H. Harbaugh, "The Steel Case Reconsidered" in *The Yale Law Journal*, May, 1978, p. 1274.
3. *PP*, 1951, pp. 651–52.
4. The Steel Case, an undated memorandum attached to a Note to Files by Harold L. Enarson, April, 1952. Enarson Papers. HSTL.

5. Memorandum to John Steelman from Harold L. Enarson on Next Steps in the Steel Dispute, January 9, 1952. Ibid.
6. Harold L. Enarson, Memo to Files, March 25, 1952. Ibid.
7. *New York Times*, March 25, 1952, p. 1.
8. Enarson's Memo to Files, op. cit.
9. See Charles E. Wilson's letter of resignation. Text in *New York Times*, March 31, 1952, p. 30.
10. Truman's *Years of Trial and Hope* (cited in chapter 3, n. 18), p. 469. Wilson's letter of resignation, op. cit.

11. OH, James L. Sundquist, p. 37.
12. Harold L. Enarson, handwritten Memo to File, April 7, 1952. Enarson Papers. HSTL.
13. Roger Tubby Journal, entry of April 13, 1952.
14. Harold L. Enarson, handwritten memorandum for the files. Subject: Events Preceding the President's Speech on April 8 and Resort to Seizure. Undated. Enarson Papers. HSTL.
15. *PP*, 1952–53, p. 225.
16. Memorandum, Milton P. Kayle to David Stowe, April 3, 1952. Enarson Papers. HSTL.
17. *PP*, 1949, p. 126. For Justice Department memorandum see Inherent Executive Power to Deal With Emergencies, etc. (cited in chapter 11, n. 26), p. 15.
18. *PP*, 1952–53, p. 249.
19. Roger Tubby Journal, op. cit.
20. *PP*, 1952–53, pp. 250–51.
21. Roger Tubby Journal, op. cit.
22. Harbaugh, op. cit., pp. 1278–79.

23. Maeva Marcus, op. cit., p. 310, n. 107.
24. *PP*, 1952–53, p. 301.
25. Roger Tubby Journal, entry of May 3, 1952.
26. Charles Sawyer, *Concerns of a Conservative Democrat* (Southern Illinois University Press, 1968), pp. 267–68.
27. Ibid., p. 269.
28. Ibid., p. 270.
29. *PP*, 1952–53, p. 410 ff.
30. Roger Tubby Journal, entry of June 12, 1952.
31. Ibid.
32. Maeva Marcus's, op. cit., p. 253.
33. Letter, Truman to William O. Douglas, July 9, 1952. PSF: General File, Douglas, William O. Folder. Box 118.
34. Roger Tubby Journal, entry of June 12, 1952.
35. Maeva Marcus, op. cit., pp. 209–10. Harbaugh, op. cit., pp. 1276–77.
36. Miller, *Plain Speaking* (cited in chapter 19, n. 1), p. 242.

37. 1952: TROUBLES WITH EISENHOWER AND STEVENSON

1. Letter, Charles Murphy to Robert Dennison, August 18, 1972. Dennison Papers. President Truman's Decision Not to Run in 1952 Folder. Box 1. HSTL.
2. Text in *New York Times*, January 8, 1952, p. 15.
3. Interview with John Snyder, February 14, 1978.
4. Letter, Sherman Adams to the author, January 12, 1973.
5. Truman to Eisenhower, September 24, 1951. PSF: General File, Eisenhower, Dwight D.—NATO Folder. Box 118.
6. Truman to Eisenhower, December 18, 1950. Eisenhower to Truman, January 1, 1952. PSF: General File, Eisenhower, Dwight D #2 Folder. Box 118.
7. *PP*, 1952–53, pp. 21–2.
8. Letter, Truman to Frank Hodges, January 15, 1952. PSF: Political File, Eisenhower, D.D. Folder. Box 56.
9. Roger Tubby Journal, entry of January 27, 1952.
10. Ibid., entry of April 13, 1952.
11. Ibid., entry of June 23, 1952. Report on Eisenhower's Denver speech in *New York Times*, June 17, 1952, p. 20.
12. John Bartlow Martin, *Adlai Stevenson of Illinois* (Garden City, N.Y., 1976), p. 524.
13. Truman, *Years of Trial and Hope* (cited in chapter 3, n. 18), p. 490.
14. Murphy to Admiral Dennison, op. cit.
15. *PP*, 1952–53, p. 132.
16. *Manchester (N.H.) Union Leader*, February 2, 1952, p. 1.
17. Interview with Charles Murphy, June 11, 1976.
18. Ibid.
19. *PP*, 1952–53, p. 225.
20. Interview with W. Averell Harriman, February 24, 1974.
21. *PP*, 1952–53, p. 504.
22. Truman to Adlai Stevenson, Chicago, July 26, 1952. PSF: Personal File, Stevenson, Adlai E. Folder. Box 324.
23. Roger Tubby Journal, entry of August 6, 1952.

24. Martin, op. cit., p. 644.
25. Roger Tubby Journal, entry of August 21, 1952.
26. *Off the Record*, (cited in chapter 25, n. 17), pp. 266–67.
27. Ibid., pp. 268–69.
28. Roger Tubby Journal, entry of September 25, 1952.
29. *PP*, 1952–53, p. 530.
30. Letter, Truman to John Sparkman, undated (unsent). *PSF: "Longhand Notes" File, Longhand Personal Memos, 1952, Folder #1. Box 333.*
31. *Roger Tubby Journal, entry of September 14, 1952.*
32. *Letter, Truman to Harry H. Woodring, September 15, 1952. PSF: Personal File, Woodring, Harry H. Folder. Box 328.*
33. *PP*, 1952–53, pp. 550–52.
34. Roger Tubby's Journal, entry of September 17, 1952.
35. *New York Times*, October 28, 1952, p. 14.
36. *PP*, 1952–53, p. 597.
37. Ibid., p. 600.
38. Interview with John Snyder, February 14, 1978.
39. William Bragg Ewald, Jr., *Eisenhower the President. Crucial Days, 1951–1960* (Englewood Cliffs, N.J., 1981), pp. 58–63.
40. *PP*, 1952–53, pp. 784–85.
41. Interview with Charles Murphy, op. cit.
42. Letter, Truman to Justice Sherman Minton, October 15, 1952. PSF: Personal File, Minton, Sherman Folder. Box 319.
43. *PP*, 1952–53, p. 863.
44. *PP*, 1948, p. 848 ff.
45. *New York Herald Tribune*, October 21, 1952, p. 1.
46. Ewald, op. cit., p. 32.
47. *New York Herald Tribune*, October 25, 1952, p. 1. Text, p. 8.
48. *PP*, 1952–53, p. 945 ff.
49. Information supplied the author by Roger Tubby.

38. SCENES FROM AN ENDING

1. Letter, Truman to Winston S. Churchill, November 12, 1952. PSF: General File, Churchill, Winston 1951–53 Folder. Box 115.
2. Cabinet Meeting, November 7, 1952. Notes on Cabinet Meetings—January 4, 1952-January 16, 1953. Matthew Connelly Papers. Box 1. HSTL.
3. Texts in Truman, *Years of Trial and Hope* (cited in chapter 3, n. 18), p. 505.
4. Truman, personal memorandum, November 20, 1952. PSF: General File, Eisenhower, Dwight D—President-elect Folder. Box 118.
5. Truman's *Years of Trial and Hope*, op. cit., p. 521.
6. Letter, Truman to Stevenson, December 11, 1952. PSF: Personal File, Stevenson, Adlai E. Folder, Box 324.
7. Meeting with the President. Subject: Korean Resolution in UN. November 5, 1952. Acheson Papers. November, 1952, Folder. Box 67. HSTL.
8. *PP*, 1952–53, pp. 1073 ff.
9. Manchester's *American Caesar* (cited in chapter 28, n. 62), pp. 688–89.

10. Truman, *Years of Trial and Hope*, op. cit., p. 519.
11. This passage is largely based on Burton I. Kaufman, *The Oil Cartel Case. A Documentary Study of Antitrust Activity in the Cold War Era* (Westport, Conn., 1978), chapters 1–3.
12. Barton J. Bernstein, "The Struggle Over the Korean Armistice: Prisoners of Repatriation?" Paper presented at the East Asian seminar, Stanford University, October 1979, p. 17.
13. *PP*. 1952–53, p. 321.
14. James F. Schnabel and Robert J. Watson. *The History of the Joint Chiefs of Staff. The Joint Chiefs of Staff and National Policy, vol. 3. The Korean War, Pt. 2. Historical Division. Joint Secretariat. Joint Chiefs of Staff*, p. 893.
15. Ibid., p. 901.
16. Eisenhower's, *The White House Years* (cited in chapter 21, n. 15), p. 181.
17. *PP*, 1952–53, p. 1197 ff.
18. OH, Robert Dennison, pp. 208–11.
19. Interview with John Snyder, February 17, 1977.

Index